DISCARDS

D1071667

SHORT STORIES
for Students

Advisors

Jayne M. Burton is a teacher of English, a member of the Delta Kappa Gamma International Society for Key Women Educators, and currently a master's degree candidate in the Interdisciplinary Study of Curriculum and Instruction and English at Angelo State University.

Mary Beth Maggio teaches seventh grade language arts in Schaumburg, Illinois.

Tom Shilts is the youth librarian at the Okemos branch of Capital Area District Library in Okemos, Michigan. He holds an MSLS degree from Clarion University of Pennsylvania and an MA in U.S. History from the University of North Dakota.

Amy Spade Silverman has taught at independent schools in California, Texas, Michigan, and New York. She holds a bachelor of arts degree from the University of Michigan and a master of fine arts degree from the University of Houston. She is a member of the National Council of Teachers of English and Teachers and Writers. She is an exam reader for Advanced Placement Literature and Composition. She is also a poet, published in *North American Review*, *Nimrod*, and *Michigan Quarterly Review*, among others.

Mary Turner holds a BS in Secondary Education from East Texas State University and a Master of Education from Western Kentucky University. She teaches English 7 and AP English 12 literature and composition at SBEC in Southaven, Mississippi.

Brian Woerner teaches English at Troy High School in Troy, Ohio. He is also a Program Associate of the Ohio Writing Project at Miami University.

SHORT STORIES
for Students

**Presenting Analysis, Context, and Criticism
on Commonly Studied Short Stories**

VOLUME 37

Matthew Derda, Project Editor

Foreword by Thomas E. Barden

GALE
CENGAGE Learning

Detroit • New York • San Francisco • New Haven, Conn • Waterville, Maine • London

Short Stories for Students, Volume 37

Project Editor: Matthew Derda

Rights Acquisition and Management:
Christine Myaskovsky, Robin Young

Composition: Evi Abou-El-Seoud

Manufacturing: Rhonda A. Dover

Imaging: John Watkins

Product Design: Pamela A. E. Galbreath,
Jennifer Wahi

Digital Content Production: Allie Semperger

Product Manager: Meggin Condino

For product information and technology assistance, contact us at
Gale Customer Support, 1-800-877-4253.
For permission to use material from this text or product,
submit all requests online at **www.cengage.com/permissions**.
Further permissions questions can be emailed to
permissionrequest@cengage.com

While every effort has been made to ensure the reliability of the information presented in this publication, Gale, a part of Cengage Learning, does not guarantee the accuracy of the data contained herein. Gale accepts no payment for listing; and inclusion in the publication of any organization, agency, institution, publication, service, or individual does not imply endorsement of the editors or publisher. Errors brought to the attention of the publisher and verified to the satisfaction of the publisher will be corrected in future editions.

Gale
27500 Drake Rd.
Farmington Hills, MI, 48331-3535

ISBN-13: 978-1-4144-8742-7
ISBN-10: 1-4144-8742-8

ISSN 1092-7735

This title is also available as an e-book.
ISBN-13: 978-1-4144-8759-5
ISBN-10: 1-4144-8759-2
Contact your Gale, a part of Cengage Learning sales representative for ordering information.

Printed in Mexico
1 2 3 4 5 6 7 17 16 15 14 13

Table of Contents

Why Study Literature At All?

Short Stories for Students is designed to provide readers with information and discussion about a wide range of important contemporary and historical works of short fiction, and it does that job very well. However, I want to use this guest foreword to address a question that it does *not* take up. It is a fundamental question that is often ignored in high school and college English classes as well as research texts, and one that causes frustration among students at all levels, namely why study literature at all? Isn't it enough to read a story, enjoy it, and go about one's business? My answer (to be expected from a literary professional, I suppose) is no. It is not enough. It is a start; but it is not enough. Here's why.

First, literature is the only part of the educational curriculum that deals directly with the actual world of lived experience. The philosopher Edmund Husserl used the apt German term *die Lebenswelt*, "the living world," to denote this realm. All the other content areas of the modern American educational system avoid the subjective, present reality of everyday life. Science (both the natural and the social varieties) objectifies, the fine arts create and/or perform, history reconstructs. Only literary study persists in posing those questions we all asked before our schooling taught us to give up on them. Only literature gives credibility to personal perceptions, feelings, dreams, and the "stream of consciousness" that is our inner voice. Literature wonders about infinity, wonders why God permits evil, wonders what will happen to us after we die. Literature admits that we get our hearts broken, that people sometimes cheat and get away with it, that the world is a strange and probably incomprehensible place. Literature, in other words, takes on all the big and small issues of what it means to be human. So my first answer is that of the humanist we should read literature and study it and take it seriously because it enriches us as human beings. We develop our moral imagination, our capacity to sympathize with other people, and our ability to understand our existence through the experience of fiction.

My second answer is more practical. By studying literature we can learn how to explore and analyze texts. Fiction may be about *die Lebenswelt*, but it is a construct of words put together in a certain order by an artist using the medium of language. By examining and studying those constructions, we can learn about language as a medium. We can become more sophisticated about word associations and connotations, about the manipulation of symbols, and about style and atmosphere. We can grasp how ambiguous language is and how important context and texture is to meaning. In our first encounter with a work of literature, of course, we are not supposed to catch all of these things. We are spellbound, just as the writer wanted us to be. It is as serious students of the writer's art that we begin to see how the tricks are done.

Seeing the tricks, which is another way of saying "developing analytical and close reading skills," is important above and beyond its intrinsic literary educational value. These skills transfer to other fields and enhance critical thinking of any kind. Understanding how language is used to construct texts is powerful knowledge. It makes engineers better problem solvers, lawyers better advocates and courtroom practitioners, politicians better rhetoricians, marketing and advertising agents better sellers, and citizens more aware consumers as well as better participants in democracy. This last point is especially important, because rhetorical skill works both ways when we learn how language is manipulated in the making of texts the result is that we become less susceptible when language is used to manipulate us.

My third reason is related to the second. When we begin to see literature as created artifacts of language, we become more sensitive to good writing in general. We get a stronger sense of the importance of individual words, even the sounds of words and word combinations. We begin to understand Mark Twain's delicious proverb "The difference between the right word and the almost right word is the difference between lightning and a lightning bug." Getting beyond the "enjoyment only" stage of literature gets us closer to becoming makers of word art ourselves. I am not saying that studying fiction will turn every student into a Faulkner or a Shakespeare. But it will make us more adaptable and effective writers, even if our art form ends up being the office memo or the corporate annual report.

Studying short stories, then, can help students become better readers, better writers, and even better human beings. But I want to close with a warning. If your study and exploration of the craft, history, context, symbolism, or anything else about a story starts to rob it of the magic you felt when you first read it, it is time to stop. Take a break, study another subject, shoot some hoops, or go for a run. Love of reading is too important to be ruined by school. The early twentieth century writer Willa Cather, in her novel *My Antonia*, has her narrator Jack Burden tell a story that he and Antonia heard from two old Russian immigrants when they were teenagers. These immigrants, Pavel and Peter, told about an incident from their youth back in Russia that the narrator could recall in vivid detail thirty years later. It was a harrowing story of a wedding party starting home in sleds and being chased by starving wolves. Hundreds of wolves attacked the group's sleds one by one as they sped across the snow trying to reach their village. In a horrible revelation, the old Russians revealed that the groom eventually threw his own bride to the wolves to save himself. There was even a hint that one of the old immigrants might have been the groom mentioned in the story. Cather has her narrator conclude with his feelings about the story. "We did not tell Pavel's secret to anyone, but guarded it jealously as if the wolves of the Ukraine had gathered that night long ago, and the wedding party had been sacrificed, just to give us a painful and peculiar pleasure." That feeling, that painful and peculiar pleasure, is the most important thing about literature. Study and research should enhance that feeling and never be allowed to overwhelm it.

Thomas E. Barden
Professor of English and Director
of Graduate English Studies,
The University of Toledo

Introduction

Purpose of the Book

The purpose of *Short Stories for Students* (*SSfS*) is to provide readers with a guide to understanding, enjoying, and studying short stories by giving them easy access to information about the work. Part of Gale's "For Students" Literature line, *SSfS* is specifically designed to meet the curricular needs of high school and undergraduate college students and their teachers, as well as the interests of general readers and researchers considering specific short fiction. While each volume contains entries on "classic" stories frequently studied in classrooms, there are also entries containing hard-to-find information on contemporary stories, including works by multicultural, international, and women writers.

The information covered in each entry includes an introduction to the story and the story's author; a plot summary, to help readers unravel and understand the events in the work; descriptions of important characters, including explanation of a given character's role in the narrative as well as discussion about that character's relationship to other characters in the story; analysis of important themes in the story; and an explanation of important literary techniques and movements as they are demonstrated in the work.

In addition to this material, which helps the readers analyze the story itself, students are also provided with important information on the literary and historical background informing each work. This includes a historical context essay, a box comparing the time or place the story was written to modern Western culture, a critical overview essay, and excerpts from critical essays on the story or author. A unique feature of *SSfS* is a specially commissioned critical essay on each story, targeted toward the student reader.

To further help today's student in studying and enjoying each story, information on audiobooks and other media adaptations is provided (if available), as well as reading suggestions for works of fiction and nonfiction on similar themes and topics. Classroom aids include ideas for research papers and lists of critical and reference sources that provide additional material on the work.

Selection Criteria

The titles for each volume of *SSfS* were selected by surveying numerous sources on teaching literature and analyzing course curricula for various school districts. Some of the sources surveyed include: literature anthologies, *Reading Lists for College-Bound Students: The Books Most Recommended by America's Top Colleges*; *Teaching the Short Story: A Guide to Using Stories from around the World*, by the National Council of Teachers of English (NCTE); and "A Study of High School Literature Anthologies," conducted by Arthur Applebee at the Center for the Learning and Teaching of Literature and sponsored by the National Endowment for the

Arts and the Office of Educational Research and Improvement.

Input was also solicited from our advisory board, as well as educators from various areas. From these discussions, it was determined that each volume should have a mix of "classic" stories (those works commonly taught in literature classes) and contemporary stories for which information is often hard to find. Because of the interest in expanding the canon of literature, an emphasis was also placed on including works by international, multicultural, and women authors. Our advisory board members—educational professionals— helped pare down the list for each volume. Works not selected for the present volume were noted as possibilities for future volumes. As always, the editor welcomes suggestions for titles to be included in future volumes.

How Each Entry Is Organized

Each entry, or chapter, in *SSfS* focuses on one story. Each entry heading lists the title of the story, the author's name, and the date of the story's publication. The following elements are contained in each entry:

Introduction: a brief overview of the story which provides information about its first appearance, its literary standing, any controversies surrounding the work, and major conflicts or themes within the work.

Author Biography: this section includes basic facts about the author's life, and focuses on events and times in the author's life that may have inspired the story in question.

Plot Summary: a description of the events in the story. Lengthy summaries are broken down with subheads.

Characters: an alphabetical listing of the characters who appear in the story. Each character name is followed by a brief to an extensive description of the character's role in the story, as well as discussion of the character's actions, relationships, and possible motivation.

Characters are listed alphabetically by last name. If a character is unnamed—for instance, the narrator in "The Eatonville Anthology"—the character is listed as "The Narrator" and alphabetized as "Narrator." If a character's first name is the only one given, the name will appear alphabetically by that name.

Themes: a thorough overview of how the topics, themes, and issues are addressed within the story. Each theme discussed appears in a separate subhead.

Style: this section addresses important style elements of the story, such as setting, point of view, and narration; important literary devices used, such as imagery, foreshadowing, symbolism; and, if applicable, genres to which the work might have belonged, such as Gothicism or Romanticism. Literary terms are explained within the entry, but can also be found in the Glossary.

Historical Context: this section outlines the social, political, and cultural climate in which the author lived and the work was created. This section may include descriptions of related historical events, pertinent aspects of daily life in the culture, and the artistic and literary sensibilities of the time in which the work was written. If the story is historical in nature, information regarding the time in which the story is set is also included. Long sections are broken down with helpful subheads.

Critical Overview: this section provides background on the critical reputation of the author and the story, including bannings or any other public controversies surrounding the work. For older works, this section may include a history of how the story was first received and how perceptions of it may have changed over the years; for more recent works, direct quotes from early reviews may also be included.

Criticism: an essay commissioned by *SSfS* which specifically deals with the story and is written specifically for the student audience, as well as excerpts from previously published criticism on the work (if available).

Sources: an alphabetical list of critical material used in compiling the entry, with bibliographical information.

Further Reading: an alphabetical list of other critical sources which may prove useful for the student. Includes full bibliographical information and a brief annotation.

Suggested Search Terms: a list of search terms and phrases to jumpstart students' further information seeking. Terms include not just titles and author names but also terms and topics related to the historical and literary context of the works.

In addition, each entry contains the following highlighted sections, set apart from the main text as sidebars:

Media Adaptations: if available, a list of audiobooks and important film and television adaptations of the story, including source information. The list also includes stage adaptations, musical adaptations, etc.

Topics for Further Study: a list of potential study questions or research topics dealing with the story. This section includes questions related to other disciplines the student may be studying, such as American history, world history, science, math, government, business, geography, economics, psychology, etc.

Compare and Contrast: an "at-a-glance" comparison of the cultural and historical differences between the author's time and culture and late twentieth century or early twenty-first century Western culture. This box includes pertinent parallels between the major scientific, political, and cultural movements of the time or place the story was written, the time or place the story was set (if a historical work), and modern Western culture. Works written after 1990 may not have this box.

What Do I Read Next?: a list of works that might give a reader points of entry into a classic work (e.g., YA or multicultural titles) and/or complement the featured story or serve as a contrast to it. This includes works by the same author and others, works from various genres, YA works, and works from various cultures and eras.

Other Features

SSfS includes "Why Study Literature At All?," a foreword by Thomas E. Barden, Professor of English and Director of Graduate English Studies at the University of Toledo. This essay provides a number of very fundamental reasons for studying literature and, therefore, reasons why a book such as *SSfS*, designed to facilitate the study of literature, is useful.

A Cumulative Author/Title Index lists the authors and titles covered in each volume of the *SSfS* series.

A Cumulative Nationality/Ethnicity Index breaks down the authors and titles covered in each volume of the *SSfS* series by nationality and ethnicity.

A Subject/Theme Index, specific to each volume, provides easy reference for users who may be studying a particular subject or theme rather than a single work. Significant subjects from events to broad themes are included.

Each entry may include illustrations, including photo of the author, stills from film adaptations (if available), maps, and/or photos of key historical events.

Citing Short Stories for Students

When writing papers, students who quote directly from any volume of *SSfS* may use the following general forms to document their source. These examples are based on MLA style; teachers may request that students adhere to a different style, thus, the following examples may be adapted as needed.

When citing text from *SSfS* that is not attributed to a particular author (for example, the Themes, Style, Historical Context sections, etc.), the following format may be used:

> "How I Met My Husband." *Short Stories for Students.* Ed. Sara Constantakis. Vol. 36. Detroit: Gale, Cengage Learning, 2013. 73–95. Print.

When quoting the specially commissioned essay from *SSfS* (usually the first essay under the Criticism subhead), the following format may be used:

> Dominic, Catherine. Critical Essay on "How I Met My Husband." *Short Stories for Students.* Ed. Sara Constantakis. Vol. 36. Detroit: Gale, Cengage Learning, 2013. 84–87. Print.

When quoting a journal or newspaper essay that is reprinted in a volume of *SSfS*, the following form may be used:

> Ditsky, John. "The Figure in the Linoleum: The Fictions of Alice Munro." *Hollins Critic* 22.3 (1985): 1–10. Rpt. in *Short Stories for Students.* Vol. 36. Ed. Sara Constantakis. Detroit: Gale, Cengage Learning, 2013. 92–94. Print.

When quoting material from a book that is reprinted in a volume of *SSfS,* the following form may be used:

> Cooke, John. "Alice Munro." *The Influence of Painting on Five Canadian Writers.* Lewiston, NY: Edwin Mellen Press, 1996. 69–85. Rpt. in

Short Stories for Students. Vol. 36. Ed. Sara Constantakis. Detroit: Gale, Cengage Learning, 2013. 89–92. Print.

We Welcome Your Suggestions

The editorial staff of *Short Stories for Students* welcomes your comments and ideas. Readers who wish to suggest short stories to appear in future volumes, or who have other suggestions, are cordially invited to contact the editor. You may contact the editor via E-mail at: **ForStudentsEditors@cengage.com.** Or write to the editor at:

Editor, *Short Stories for Students*
Gale
27500 Drake Road
Farmington Hills, MI 48331-3535

Literary Chronology

1828: Leo Tolstoy is born on September 9 in Tula Province, Russia.

1872: Leo Tolstoy's "The Long Exile" is published as "Bog pravdu vidit, da ne skoro skazhet" in *Beseda*.

1876: Sherwood Anderson is born on September 13 in Camden, Ohio.

1878: Horacio Quiroga is born in Salto, Uruguay, on December 31.

1894: James Thurber is born on December 8 in Columbus, Ohio.

1899: Yasunari Kawabata is born on June 14 in Osaka, Japan.

1907: Quiroga's "The Feather Pillow" is written.

1910: Leo Tolstoy dies of pneumonia on November 20 in Astapovo, Russia.

1916: Shirley Jackson is born on December 14 in San Francisco, California.

1920: Sherwood Anderson's "The Egg" is published in the March issue of *Dial* magazine.

1920: Ray Bradbury is born on August 22 in Waukegan, Illinois.

1927: Gabriel García Márquez is born on March 6 in Aracataca, Colombia.

1930: Chinua Achebe is born in Ogidi, Nigeria, on November 16.

1932: John Updike is born on March 18 in Reading, Pennsylvania.

1937: Quiroga commits suicide in Buenos Aires, Argentina, on February 19.

1941: Sherwood Anderson dies of peritonitis on March 8 in Panama.

1945: James Thurber's "The Princess and the Tin Box" is published in the *New Yorker*.

1949: Yasunari Kawabata's "The Jay" is published in Japanese as "Kakesu." It is published in English in 1988 in *Palm-of-the-Hand Stories*.

1953: Chinua Achebe's "Dead Men's Path" is published in the *University Herald* of University College, Ibadan, with no title. It is published in 1962 in *The Sacrificial Egg and Other Short Stories* and in 1972 in *Girls at War and Other Stories*.

1953: Andrea Lee is born in Philadelphia, Pennsylvania.

1954: (Karen) Louise Erdrich is born on June 7 (some sources say July 6) in Little Falls, Minnesota.

1960: Ray Bradbury's "The Drummer Boy of Shiloh" is published in the *Saturday Evening Post*.

1961: James Thurber dies of pneumonia on November 2 in New York, New York.

1962: Gabriel García Márquez' "Tuesday Siesta" is published.

1965: Shirley Jackson dies of heart failure on August 8 in North Bennington, Vermont.

1965: Shirley Jackson's "The Possibility of Evil" is published.

1967: Jhumpa Lahiri is born on July 11 in South Kingston, Rhode Island.

1968: Yasunari Kawabata is awarded the Nobel Prize in Literature.

1969: Edwidge Danticat is born on January 19 in Port-au-Prince, Haiti.

1972: Yasunari Kawabata dies of suicide on April 16 in Hayama, Japan.

1982: John Updike is awarded the Pulitzer Prize for Fiction for *Rabbit Is Rich*.

1982: Gabriel García Márquez is awarded the Nobel Prize for Literature.

1983: Andrea Lee's "New African" is published in the *New Yorker*. It is published in 1984 in *Sarah Phillips*.

1991: John Updike is awarded the Pulitzer Prize for Fiction for *Rabbit at Rest*.

1998: John Updike's "Oliver's Evolution" is published in *Esquire* magazine in April.

1999: Jhumpa Lahiri's "Interpreter of Maladies" is published in *Interpreter of Maladies*.

2000: Jhumpa Lahiri is awarded the Pulitzer Prize for Fiction.

2001: Louise Erdrich's The Shawl is published.

2004: Edwidge Danticat's "Night Talkers" is published.

2009: John Updike dies of lung cancer on January 27 in Danvers, Massachusetts.

2012: Ray Bradbury dies after a lengthy illness on June 5 in Los Angeles, California.

2013: Chinua Achebe died on March 21, after a brief illness.

Acknowledgements

The editors wish to thank the copyright holders of the excerpted criticism included in this volume and the permissions managers of many book and magazine publishing companies for assisting us in securing reproduction rights. We are also grateful to the staffs of the Detroit Public Library, the Library of Congress, the University of Detroit Mercy Library, Wayne State University Purdy/ Kresge Library Complex, and the University of Michigan Libraries for making their resources available to us. Following is a list of the copyright holders who have granted us permission to reproduce material in this volume of *SSfS*. Every effort has been made to trace copyright, but if omissions have been made, please let us know.

COPYRIGHTED EXCERPTS IN *SSfS*, VOLUME 37, WERE REPRODUCED FROM THE FOLLOWING SOURCES:

Ogede, Ode. From *Achebe and the Politics of Representation: Form Against Itself, from Colonial Conquest and Occupation to Post-Independence Disillusionment*. Africa World Press, Inc., 2001. Copyright © Africa World Press, Inc., 2001. Reproduced by permission of the publisher.—*African American Review*, 29.1, Spring 1995. Copyright © 1995 by *African American Review*. Reproduced by permission of the publisher.—*American Book Review*, 10.6, January/February 1989. Copyright © 1989 by *American Book Review*. Reproduced by permission of the publisher.—*American Quarterly*, 20.4, 1968. Copyright © 1968 by Johns Hopkins University Press. Reproduced by permission of the publisher.—*Antioch Review*, 62.4, Fall 2004. Copyright © 2004 by *Antioch Review*. Reproduced by permission of the publisher.— Tsanoff, Radoslav A. From *Autobiographies of Ten Religious Leaders: Alternatives in Christian Experience*. Trinity University Press, 1968. Copyright © 1968, Trinity University Press. Reproduced by permission of the publisher.— *Booklist*, 93.3, October 1, 1996. Copyright © 1996 by *Booklist*. Reproduced by permission of the publisher.—*Booklist*, 105.6, November 15, 2008. Copyright © 2008 by *Booklist*. Reproduced by permission of the publisher.— Carroll, David. From *Chinua Achebe: Novelist, Poet, Critic*. Macmillan, 1990. Copyright © Macmillan, 1990. Reproduced by permission of the publisher.—*Christian Science Monitor*, 93.5, 2000. Copyright © 2000 by *Christian Science Monitor*. Reproduced by permission of the publisher.—*Christian Science Monitor*, 101.42, January 27, 2009, for "A Louise Erdrich Sampler" by Yvonne Zipp. Copyright © *Christian Science Monitor* 2009. Reproduced by permission of the author.—*Commonweal*, 104, April 1977. Copyright © 1977 by *Commonweal*. Reproduced by permission of the publisher.— *Conversations with Ray Bradbury*, 2004, for "Future Tense Sci—Fi Legend Bradbury Going Strong" by Jim Cherry. Copyright © 2004. Reproduced by permission of the author.—

Schade, George D. From introduction to *The Decapitated Chicken and Other Stories by Horacio Quiroga*. Edited by Margaret Sayers Peden. University of Texas Press, 1976. Copyright © 1976, University of Texas Press. Reproduced by permission of the publisher.—Pelayo, Rubén. From *Gabriel García Marquez: A Critical Companion*. Greenwood Press, 2001. Copyright © Greenwood Press, 2001. Reproduced by permission of the publisher.—Brushwood, John S. From *The Latin American Short Story: A Critical History*. Edited by Margaret Sayers Peden. Twayne Publishers, 1983. Copyright © 1983, Twayne Publishers. Reproduced by permission of the publisher.—*Library Journal*, 134.2, February 1, 2009. Copyright © 2009 by *Library Journal*. Reproduced by permission of the publisher.—*MELUS*, 19.4, Winter 1994. Copyright © 1994 by *MELUS*. Reproduced by permission of the publisher.—*MELUS*, 29.3-4, Fall/Winter 2004. Copyright © 2004 by *MELUS*. Reproduced by permission of the publisher.—*Moderna Språk*, 80.1, 1986. Copyright © 1986 by *Moderna Sprak*. Reproduced by permission of the publisher.—*My Literary Passions*, for "Tolstoy". Harper & Brothers, 1895.—*New Republic*, 191.21, November 19, 1984. Copyright © 1984 by *New Republic*. Reproduced by permission of the publisher.—*New Republic*, 192.5, Febuary 4, 1985. Copyright © 1985 by *New Republic*. Reproduced by permission of the publisher.—*New Republic*, 77.993, December 13, 1933. Copyright © 1933 by *New Republic*. Reproduced by permission of the publisher.—*Publishers Weekly*, 243.42, October 14, 1996. Copyright © 1996 by *Publishers Weekly*. Reproduced by permission of the publisher.—*Spectator*, 286.9008, March 31, 2001. Copyright © 2001 by *Spectator*. Reproduced by permission of the publisher. —*Spectator*, 308.9398, October 11, 2008. Copyright © 2008 by *Spectator*. Reproduced by permission of the publisher.—*Studies in Short Fiction*, 15.3, Summer 1978. Copyright © 1978 by *Studies in Short Fiction*. Reproduced by permission of the publisher.—*Studies in Short Fiction*, 17.2, Spring 1980. Copyright © 1980 by *Studies in Short Fiction*. Reproduced by permission of the publisher.—*Studies in Short Fiction*, 18.4, Fall 1981. Copyright © 1981 by *Studies in Short Fiction*. Reproduced by permission of the publisher.—*Virginia Quarterly Review*, 67.4, Autumn 1991. Copyright © 1991 by *Virginia Quarterly Review*. Reproduced by permission of the publisher.—McNally, Willis E. From *Voices for the Future: Essays on Major Science Fiction Writers, Volume 1*. Edited by Thomas D. Clareson. Bowling Green University Popular Press, 1976. Copyright © Bowling Green University Popular Press, 1976. Reproduced by permission of the publisher.—Stupple, A. James. From *Voices for the Future: Essays on Major Science Fiction Writers, Volume 1*. Edited by Thomas D. Clareson. Bowling Green University Popular Press, 1976. Copyright © Bowling Green University Popular Press, 1976. Reproduced by permission of the publisher.—*Women's Review of Books*, 21.8, May 2004. Copyright © 2004 by *Women's Review of Books*. Reproduced by permission of the publisher. —*World Literature Today*, 63.2, Spring 1989. Copyright © 1989 by *World Literature Today*. Reproduced by permission of the publisher.—*World Literature Today*, 64.1, Winter 1990. Copyright © 1990 by *World Literature Today*. Reproduced by permission of the publisher.—*World Literature Today*, 74.2, Spring 2000. Copyright © 2000 by *World Literature Today*. Reproduced by permission of the publisher.—*World Literature Today*, 76.1, Winter 2002. Copyright © 2002 by *World Literature Today*. Reproduced by permission of the publisher.—*World Literature Today*, 79.1, January-April, 2005. Copyright © 2005 by *World Literature Today*. Reproduced by permission of the publisher.

Contributors

Bryan Aubrey: Aubrey holds a PhD in English. Entry on "Interpreter of Maladies." Original essay on "Interpreter of Maladies."

Jennifer Bussey: Bussey is a freelance writer specializing in literature. Entry on "The Shawl." Original essay on "The Shawl."

Catherine Dominic: Dominic is a novelist and a freelance writer and editor. Entries on "The Long Exile" and "The Princess and the Tin Box." Original essays on "The Long Exile" and "The Princess and the Tin Box."

Kristen Sarlin Greenberg: Greenberg is a freelance writer and editor with a background in literature and philosophy. Entry on "Night Talkers." Original essay on "Night Talkers."

Michael Allen Holmes: Holmes is a writer with existential interests. Entries on "Dead Men's Path" and "New African." Original essays on "Dead Men's Path" and "New African."

Sheri Karmiol: Karmiol teaches literature and drama at the University of New Mexico, where she is an adjunct professor in the University Honors Program. Entry on

"The Feather Pillow." Original essay on "The Feather Pillow."

David Kelly: Kelly is an instructor of literature and creative writing. Entry on "The Egg." Original essay on "The Egg."

Amy Lynn Miller: Miller is a graduate of the University of Cincinnati and now resides in New Orleans, Louisiana. Entry on "The Jay." Original essay on "The Jay."

Michael J. O'Neal: O'Neal holds a PhD in English. Entries on "The Drummer Boy of Shiloh" and "Oliver's Evolution." Original essays on "The Drummer Boy of Shiloh" and "Oliver's Evolution."

Rachel Porter: Porter is a freelance writer and editor who holds a bachelor of arts in English literature. Entry on "The Possibility of Evil." Original essay on "The Possibility of Evil."

Laura B. Pryor: Pryor has a master's degree in English and over twenty-five years experience as a professional writer. Entry on "Tuesday Siesta." Original essay on "Tuesday Siesta."

Dead Men's Path

CHINUA ACHEBE
1953

"Dead Men's Path" is one of the earliest short stories by Nigerian author Chinua Achebe, who is widely viewed as the forefather of the entire tradition of African literature in the English language. Raised in a Christian family in the 1930s and 1940s and educated through the university level in missionary and colonial schools, Achebe gained broad exposure to the Western literary canon. However, members of his extended family, part of the Igbo (or Ibo) ethnic group, continued to follow native religious traditions, which fascinated him, and he was quick to realize the racist views of African peoples presented in such literature as Joseph Conrad's *Heart of Darkness* and the adventure novels of Rider Haggard. He thus grew determined to write fiction that would reveal the truths about African life that only an African could know and present to the world.

In accord with Achebe's foremost thematic intents, "Dead Men's Path" revolves around cultural conflict. It begins as the fortuitous story of Michael Obi, who has recently been appointed headmaster of an underperforming village school. Modern and traditional ways collide when Obi discovers that the villagers persist in using an ancestral path that crosses the school compound. The earliest version of "Dead Men's Path" appeared without a title in the *University Herald* of Nigeria's University College, Ibadan, in 1953, Achebe's last year as a student there. He included the tale, with the added title "Dead

Chinua Achebe (©*AP Images*)

Men's Path," in his five-story collection *The Sacrificial Egg and Other Short Stories*, published in 1962 by a small press in Onitsha, Nigeria. That version of the story was revised slightly from the original, but Achebe made more extensive revisions, especially to the dialogue, for the final version included in his internationally published collection *Girls at War and Other Stories* in 1972.

AUTHOR BIOGRAPHY

Albert Chinụalụmọgụ Achebe was born as the fifth of six surviving children on November 16, 1930, in Ogidi, Nigeria, near the southern market town of Onitsha. In those days his father, a converted Protestant and catechist for the Church Missionary Society, was serving as a preacher in a town twelve miles away. The name *Chinụalụmọgụ* means "May *chi* fight for me"—where the Igbo term *chi* refers to an individual's personal divinity—while *Achebe*, a shortened version of *Anichebe*, means "May Ani (the earth goddess) protect"; Achebe was

christened Albert in honor of Queen Victoria's husband.

Just as his name reflects a confluence of Igbo and Western culture, Achebe gained balanced exposure to both traditions through his family: in his parents' Christian home they sang hymns and read the Bible daily, whereas in his uncle's home, they still followed Igbo religious practices, such as offering food to wooden representations of gods. Attending church schools, Achebe was first taught in Igbo but began learning English by age eight. After two years of transitional schooling, English was used for all instruction. Meanwhile, he enjoyed listening to traditional stories told by village elders and his mother. With the village roughly split between Christians and "heathens," he overheard many lively cultural discussions at home.

An accomplished student, Achebe gained entrance to a prestigious secondary boarding school about a hundred miles from Ogidi, the Government College in Umuahia, which offered a curriculum roughly equivalent to that found in England. After graduating in 1948, he went on to attend University College, Ibadan, which was established that year in southwest Nigeria, on a scholarship to study medicine. After a year he switched from the sciences to the arts, to focus on English literature, religion, and history; he lost his scholarship, but his brother's generous support allowed him to continue. Achebe soon began submitting contributions to student magazines, including the society-oriented *Bug* and the more literary *University Herald*. He often made liberal use of wit and parodies of scientific logic to make his points. In his third year, Achebe became editor of the *University Herald*, in which he would publish his first two short stories, "The Old Order in Conflict with the New" in 1952 and an untitled story—later called "Dead Men's Path"—in 1953, the year he graduated.

In the back of Achebe's mind through university was the goal of writing a novel. He was especially motivated by Joyce Cary's *Mr. Johnson*, a highly regarded work that presented a portrait of Nigerians that Achebe found patently absurd. He was fairly angered by this outsider's view passed off as an insightful look at Nigerian life and culture. He finished the manuscript for his breakthrough novel *Things Fall Apart* by 1956. That year, having gained work as a radio broadcaster with the Nigerian Broadcasting

Company, he was sent to London for eight months of training with the BBC, and he was able to make contacts and get his novel published in 1958. It was very well received, enabling Achebe to publish three more acclaimed novels within the next decade: *No Longer at Ease* (1960), *Arrow of God* (1964), and *A Man of the People* (1966). Achebe married Christie Okoli in 1961, and they would have two sons and two daughters.

Following Nigerian independence in 1960, political strife led to the secession of the eastern region, including the Igbo lands, in 1967, sparking the Nigerian Civil War. Achebe, like other writers, became a spokesman for the cause of Biafra, his region, but Biafra lost the war. Achebe would spend most of the rest of his career as an academic, publishing poetry and nonfiction more often than fiction. In 1967, he became a research fellow at the University of Nigeria, Nsukka, and he founded *Okike: A Nigerian Journal of New Writing* in 1971. After serving as a visiting professor in the United States from 1972 to 1976, he returned to Nsukka to become a full professor. He became politically active in the 1980s.

In 1990, Achebe was involved in a tragic car accident that left him paralyzed from the waist down; he has been confined to a wheelchair ever since. Through the 1990s he served as a professor at Bard College, in New York, and in 2009 he joined the faculty of Brown University. Although he was slighted for the Nobel Prize, which was instead awarded to his countryman Wole Soyinka in 1986 (perhaps because Achebe, citing echoes of colonialism, had declined an invitation to a summit in Sweden that year), Achebe is recognized as the most widely read and admired African author in history. Achebe died on March 21, 2013, after a brief illness.

PLOT SUMMARY

As "Dead Men's Path" opens in January 1949, Michael Obi has just been appointed Ndume Central School's headmaster, a post he had been hoping to attain. The school is run by a mission—a religious ministry of foreign origin, understood to be Christian—which favored Obi's energetic character in hopes of making the school more progressive. Obi had succeeded in his secondary schooling and has made evident his low opinion of the narrow mind-set of many long-serving (and often less educated) teachers.

In conversation with his wife, Nancy, Obi expresses confidence that they shall do an admirable job shaping up the school. His wife is a devoted ally; she, too, favors "modern methods" over the traditional teaching style—considered by Obi no more dignified than the crass hawking of market traders—and believes that they can make a difference through their work. She especially looks forward to planting attractive gardens and being the school's most important woman. She envisions other teachers' wives looking up to her, but then frets that there may not be any other wives—a possibility Obi confirms as true. He believes it is a good thing that the other teachers are unmarried, because this means they will not be distracted by family. Nancy is disappointed at first but soon shrugs this off, remaining happily supportive of her husband's exciting new position. Watching him sit pensively, she asks what he is thinking about; he is dwelling on the golden opportunity that has been presented to them to show the local staff how such a school ought to be managed.

Ndume School is indeed found to be operating in a "backward" way—using outdated old methods rather than approved modern ones. Devoting his life to his new position, as his wife does hers, Obi focuses on two aims: maintaining the highest possible quality of teaching and making the school compound beautiful. When the rains come, Nancy's gardens blossom, as bordered by hedges of hibiscus and allamanda.

One day, Obi is astounded and offended when an old woman meanders through the compound along a seldom-used path, cutting straight through the hedges and a bed of marigolds. He expresses his indignation to a teacher, who relates that the path connects two sites of ritual importance to the village: a shrine and a cemetery. The teacher is unsure why the people should be allowed to continue to use the path despite the existence of the school, but he does know that a quarrel developed when they tried to close the path once. Knowing that a government education officer will be visiting the following week, Obi takes a stand as headmaster: he asserts that the path will now be definitively closed, and he bars the openings through the hedges with strong branches and barbed wire.

Three days later, Obi is visited by the old village priest beholden to Ani; the highest Igbo goddess, Ani has dominion over the earth and fertility, is the judge of human morality, and consorts with departed spirits whose bodies have been interred. Supporting his points by tapping his walking stick, the priest asserts that the path predates not only the school but also the life spans of Obi and even Obi's father. He stresses its importance as a byway for the travels of both departing and incoming spirits—those of the recently deceased and of the not-yet born.

With a patronizing attitude, Obi replies that such traditional spiritual beliefs are nonsense; dead people have no need of footpaths. The duty of the school, as Obi sees it, is to lead people away from such fantastic notions. The priest acknowledges that factual truth may be on Obi's side, but tradition is on the priest's and the people's side. He cites a proverb suggesting that competing cultures, like predator birds of similar stature, should let each other be and refrain from trying to usurp each other's position. The headmaster softens his tone but continues to insist that, because of regulations, the school grounds cannot be used as a public byway. He offers to get his students to help build a new path, which the spirits surely would not mind using instead, but the priest is already out the door and finished with the conversation.

After a couple days, a woman in the village dies while giving birth. A diviner is consulted, and he proposes that sacrifices must be made to appease the aggrieved ancestors. In the morning, Obi finds that the school grounds have been decimated. The hedges have been torn down, the flowers trampled upon, and a school building has also been destroyed. When the white supervisor visits that very day, he is led to conclude that a state of tribal war is arising because of the errant ambitiousness of the headmaster.

CHARACTERS

Diviner

When a village woman dies in childbirth after the permanent closure of the ancestral path, the diviner determines that sacrifices must be made to appease the ancestors.

Michael Obi

The new headmaster of Ndume Central School is the sort of person who has the best of intentions but whose understanding of the world is grounded more in theory than in practical experience. Therefore his ideas sometimes fail to bring about the ideals he seeks. Obi fully subscribes to the modern notions propagated in the course of his own (Western-model) schooling about the best teaching and school-management methods. His modern, Western understanding of the world evidently encompasses spirituality, because he dismisses the priest's objection to the closure of the ancestral path as grounded in pagan nonsense. Given his status as an administrator in a mission school, Obi is presumably Christian. However, it is the word of law—in terms of property and educational regulations—that leaves him feeling justified in barring public access to the ancestral path. Nonetheless, the law cannot predict the people's response, and Obi is made to look bad when the mission supervisor arrives because of the damage to the school grounds.

Nancy Obi

Obi's wife is fully devoted to her husband's concerns. She is able to forget her own interests—like the desire for a convivial (and subordinated) community of teachers' wives—knowing that her husband's attainment of a headmaster position offers him the perfect career opportunity. Her primary concern, upon learning the news of his appointment, is evidently the state of the gardens, a domain of the school that she would be able to control. Nancy learns things like English conversational idioms, such as the phrase "a penny for your thoughts," from a woman's magazine.

Old Woman

An old woman leaves the headmaster dumbfounded when she strolls across the grounds during the school day.

Priest

The old priest is an exacting foil to Obi: they oppose each other in terms of age (old versus young), career status (long-standing versus newly appointed), social position (religious versus secular), and cultural perspective (traditional versus modern). When the priest fails to persuade the headmaster that it would be best to leave the ancestral path open, he turns away from any purported compromise.

Supervisor

A white government education officer visits the school after the gardens are destroyed, and he draws the conclusion that the headmaster has caused a state of tribal war to develop between the school and the village.

Teacher

The teacher with whom Obi speaks about the footpath through the school compound is not certain about why it remains open. He (based on the era, the teacher can be presumed a man) only knows that it holds religious significance and that a quarrel developed when the school once tried to close it.

THEMES

Education

In the early part of the narrative, Achebe's story nominally revolves around philosophy of education. Newly appointed Ndume Central School's headmaster, Michael Obi is an enthusiastic follower of "modern methods," which the mission authorities believe will effectively turn this "unprogressive" school around. Achebe is quite spare with his language in this story, and so the reader is left to fill in the blanks with regard to what these terms imply.

Without trying to guess specifics where none are given, the reader can imagine that the so-called unprogressive approach to schooling may involve mostly basic, hands-off efforts on the teacher's part. Class might consist primarily of lecturing by the teacher and/or rote copying by the students, who might be expected to sit in silent obedience without any chance to ask questions. Such teaching would allow ambitious, self-motivated, and naturally intelligent students to succeed, but the progress of other students could be thwarted by small points of confusion or simply lack of language ability. (Generally beyond the first few years, schooling in colonial Nigeria was conducted in English.) The modern methods, on the other hand, perhaps entailed more student-teacher interaction, diversified student activities, and greater numbers of assignments—which loosely governed teachers might decline to give in order to conserve their own time and energy. In this era, most villagers, including paid teachers, would have had their own farmland to tend to and family members to support.

The fact that Achebe declines to elaborate within the story on the implications behind words like *modern* and *unprogressive* suggests that educational theory is not a primary focus here. Indeed, the reader may have little notion as to what these terms suggest but can still grasp the story's thematic import, given that the "modern" methods have evidently been learned within the Nigerian educational system—modeled on the British one—whereas the teachers practicing "unprogressive" methods are understood to have limited schooling themselves. Thus, the conflict between modern and dated educational methods may be seen to signify a conflict between adopted Western and applied African ideologies. As a practical matter, in large families with limited resources and energy for child care, African children are sometimes left to fend for themselves more than Western children are. Such an approach to child rearing, well suited to the particular circumstances of many, would naturally correspond to a less involved approach to schooling.

Religion

It is not long before Obi comes into conflict with local religious tradition. Both he and his wife place a high priority on beautifying the school compound, and accordingly, they plant flowering bushes and hedges. To the Western reader, this priority may seem misplaced, as focusing on appearance rather than substance. However, one should keep in mind that a recently founded or underfunded school in mid-twentieth-century (or even present-day) Africa might have had little more than the bricks and roofs constituting the buildings; the rooms might not even have had glass in the windows. Thus, beautifying a compound could have served to symbolically raise the students' conception of the place from that of, say, a village project to that of an official institution, and students' motivation and efforts could thus have been dramatically enhanced.

When Obi realizes they have incidentally blocked a village path that has religious significance, the notion of deferring to the villagers never crosses his mind. His sense of propriety is so fully oriented toward rules and regulations that he immediately dismisses the notion that the ancestral path might be allowed to remain. In this matter, of course, he is beholden to his superiors, including not only the mission that hired him but also government officials, such as the supervisor who later visits. After his decisive

TOPICS FOR FURTHER STUDY

- Write a story that depicts a conflict between two parties. In your narration, try to present the circumstances objectively, leaving unclear whether the actions of either party are approved or condemned. Conclude the story by introducing a third party whose comments or actions bear subtle relation to the conflict in question, clarifying or muddying the matter as you see fit.

- Read "The Rain Came," a short story by Kenyan author Grace Ogot, found in her collection *Land without Thunder* (1968). Appropriate for young adults, the story revolves around the difficult decision a chief must make when a rainmaker calls for the sacrifice of his only daughter to end a drought. Write a paper comparing the role of traditional religion in this story and in "Dead Men's Path." For each story, consider the demands that the religion makes of its people, the impact these demands have on the community, the justness of the actions taken at the behest of the community's religious figures, and above all, how these traditions do or do not conform with laws and expectations in modern society and what this suggests regarding the survival of the traditions.

- Visit the Igbo Language Center on the Igbo-Net website (http://ilc.igbonet.com/). Proceed at least through Lesson 2, which is fairly challenging, and then prepare a brief bilingual oral report to demonstrate how much success one can have in learning an African language through an online resource.

- Research the various aspects of traditional Igbo religion, including the pantheon of gods and goddesses, modes of worship, moral precepts, roles of community religious figures, and so forth. Prepare a written paper on what you learn.

comment to the teacher that the path "will not be used now," Obi's very next thought—readily understood as voiced to justify his decision—is about what the government officer would think to find the path still in use. The religious undertones in the matter arise in Obi's following (overblown) concern, that the pagan villagers might very well conduct a ritual in a school building during the upcoming inspection.

Obi's line of thinking here makes clear his disdain for the traditional religious beliefs that he has clearly rejected, or perhaps never knew. Although the teacher has informed him that the closure of the path caused a quarrel before, Obi does not hesitate to repeat that closure. While he neglects to communicate with any local authority— such as the priest of Ani—before taking action, he partly justifies his decision by declaring that the pagans' unpredictability could prove to be a problem. But he has no grounds for making such a statement, because he has not consulted anyone who knows precisely what role the ancestral path plays. Even when the priest pays a visit, Obi does not truly listen to him but receives him from a place of condescending supremacy, a fact signified by his "satisfied smile" at the priest's argument. Believing in the supreme authority of the law and being dismissive of the claims of traditional African religion—regardless of how many people adhere to such traditions—Obi takes for granted that people will simply accept the authority with which he has been endowed as headmaster.

The suppression of religious practice is one of history's most common motivations for communal acts of emigration, secession, or rebellion. If a people's religious tradition puts them in conflict with the law, then they will naturally not disavow their religion but seek a way to thwart or live outside the law; and the lawmaker seeking to maintain broader unity would be wise to accommodate religious practices. In the United States, such accommodation is seen in, for example, the permission granted American Indian groups whose religious traditions involve the consumption of peyote, which is otherwise an illegal drug. (In the past, to the contrary, US law at times forbade any practice of Native religion, such as at Indian boarding schools.) In "Dead Men's

In "Dead Men's Path," Michael is a young, modern-facing teacher in Nigeria. *(© lenetstan | ShutterStock.com)*

Path," Obi makes no exceptions; but the people's religion proves stronger than the law he has laid down, and his school suffers the consequences.

Colonialism

Although the conflict depicted in this story centers around two African personages, ultimately that conflict can be traced back to Nigeria's colonial situation, and so the story can be seen as a critique of the colonialist perspective. Achebe has made clear his disdain for the colonialist approach to Africa, such as in a 1969 speech at the University of Texas, Austin, where he noted that effectively "Europe came to Africa and said, 'You have no culture, you have no civilization, you have no religion, you have no history.'" In actuality, Europeans simply did not comprehend the flourishing cultures, civilizations, and religions they happened upon, and African history was transmitted orally, not written down.

Nonetheless, implicit in the entire colonial project was the assumption that to bring Western civilization and Christianity to Africans would be to "save" them from ignorance and irrelevance. In the imposition of Western models of religious practice, schooling, and government, African traditions were almost entirely disregarded. Michael Obi, influenced by the Western values of his education, is emblematic of precisely such colonial disregard. Favoring rule of law—white-imposed colonial law—and scientific rationality over tradition and religious tolerance, Obi concedes no ground in the dispute with the village priest. But as Achebe affirmed in a post-speech interview at the University of Texas,

> It is not possible for one culture to come to another and say, "I am the way, the truth, and the life; there is nothing else but me." If you say this, you are guilty of irreverence or arrogance. You are also stupid. And this is really my concern.

In his character Michael Obi, Achebe appears to have intently combined these three unfortunate traits, in such a way that Obi's identity as a black African makes the contrast between his own colonial mind-set and the traditionalist mind-set of the priest all the more apparent.

STYLE

Proverb

Achebe has been noted for his distinguished use of proverbs in his fiction, where a *proverb* is a concise statement, often metaphorical, that encapsulates a value or a rule of conduct. An example from Western usage is "The early bird catches the worm," meaning that one who sets out to accomplish something before one's fellows will have a distinct advantage in accomplishing the goal; the value of self-motivation is expressed. The reader can see from this example how such a value can actually be better communicated with the brief proverb than with the rational explanation of the idea; that is, a metaphorical picture can be worth a thousand words.

In an essay highlighting the significance of proverbs in Achebe's fiction, Bernth Lindfors cites a well-known remark of the author's: "Among the Igbo the art of conversation is regarded very highly, and proverbs are the palm-oil with which words are eaten." This remark reveals the loyalty to oral tradition that the author demonstrates through his extensive use of proverbs. In Achebe's four major novels, *Things Fall Apart*, *No Longer at Ease*, *Arrow of God*, and *A Man of the People*, Lindfors tallies some 234 appearances of proverbs, with some reiterated in more than one work. One effect of this steadily employed stylistic factor is a continual emphasis on societal morality as well as the individual characters' moral perspectives. Achebe has made clear his opinion that the honest writer's work must be shaped by a moral obligation to his people, to both illuminate society as it is and identify the critical values being followed, or not, by the people. As Achebe stated in his University of Texas interview, "I think a good story immediately carries a huge message. Any good story."

The proverb that stands out in "Dead Men's Path" is the one uttered by the priest as he concludes his argument with the headmaster: "What I always say is: let the hawk perch and let the eagle perch." This saying expresses the notion that where two creatures (or communities) with significant power are involved, each would be wise to let the other one be. If the eagle and hawk attack each other, they might very well bring about not victory for either but their mutual destruction, whereas if they leave each other be, they should find more than enough prey in the world to go around. As applied to the circumstances in the story, the proverb suggests that the village's religious community and the institution of the school need not try to overrun each other's sphere of influence; they should be able to coexist without conflict.

The headmaster appears to pay little heed to this comment—he at once only remarks, "I am sorry," signaling that, as far as he is concerned, the matter is already closed. The priest evidently recognizes the extent of the headmaster's close-mindedness, because he does not even try to negotiate a compromise and is already out the door by the time the headmaster finishes making his offer to help build a new path. Although from the secular, functional perspective of a school, a path is just a path, from the perspective of a religion, the hallowed ground of an ancestral path may not be negotiable.

In the West, such a conflict is decided by simple reference to property law—whoever owns the land may decide how it is used. However, the villagers never had any need for property law with regard to such matters, because everyone in the village adequately respected their own community to ensure that an ancestral path would not be overrun by any other building or concern. The headmaster, being an outsider, has no concern for the ancestral path, and being versed in Western practices, he gladly considers property law the deciding factor in this dispute. Because the land, according to the property laws laid down by the British colonial government, now belongs to the school, it falls under school regulations, and the headmaster is entitled to decide its use. In other words, the headmaster is the hawk who will not tolerate an eagle nesting within the bounds of the circle of land it claims to possess—even if the eagle was there first. Of course, the eagle cannot just flee and abandon its nest (and perhaps its young); it must fight for its life. So does the religion fight for its survival and its traditions in prescribing, through the person of the diviner, the destruction of the hedges and gardens that obstruct the ancestral path.

The reader is left to imagine what becomes of this conflict from here, but Achebe's point lies not in the ultimate conclusion of the affair but in the mutual destruction (however temporary) brought about by the headmaster's obstinacy. The priest tried to preach open-mindedness and tolerance to the Westernized headmaster—but to no avail. The reader, cued by the proverb, undoubtedly concludes that Mr. Obi unwisely courted the fate that befell his school.

African Literature

Without fail, Achebe's name is mentioned in any discussion of the origins of modern African literature. Because African cultures generally did not have written traditions, their verbal skill and accomplishments were historically demonstrated through oral traditions: the poems, songs, and tales passed down by bards (known as *griots* in French West Africa). Thus, the era of written literature began once the various African languages developed their own orthographies—systems of representation of sounds through letters—and subsequent written traditions.

The first novels in Nigerian languages appeared in the early twentieth century. The 1930s witnessed the first literature in the Hausa language of northern Nigeria, where the culture bore Islamic influences (and where writings in Arabic by such authors as Uthman dan Fodio had been appearing since the early nineteenth century). Also conceived that decade in southern Nigeria were the earliest works by Yoruba and Igbo authors in their respective languages. Pita Nwana's *Omenuko* (1933) is seen as the first major Igbo work. The African literary tradition in English got underway by the 1950s, and among British colonies, Nigeria was at the forefront of this tradition. Cyprian Ekwensi wrote *The Leopard's Claw* (1950) and *People of the City* (1954), and it was in this era that Achebe first started writing. The earliest version of "Dead Men's Path" appeared in the *University Herald* of University College, Ibadan, in 1953. T. M. Aluko's *One Man One Wife* appeared in 1958, but it was the publication that year of Achebe's novel *Things Fall Apart* that would prove to be the foundation of the tradition of African literature in English to come.

Achebe has expressed that his foremost intention as an author was to demonstrate that African culture did not begin with the introduction of Western-style culture in the colonial era.

As he stated in his University of Texas interview, "We started off—and this was necessary—showing that there was something here—a civilization, a religion, a history." As one of his two earliest works of fiction, "Dead Men's Path" aptly reflects this formulation of his earliest concerns. The conflict portrayed is ultimately one between the traditional culture, embodied in the person of the priest of Ani, and the imposed Western culture, embodied in Mr. Obi. The fact that Achebe chose to embody Western culture in an African character can be seen to reflect his intuitive inclination not to use his writings to simply vilify Westerners and modern culture (an approach that might have complicated his later publication through Western publishing houses). Rather, he wished both to focus on his own people and to yet show how life in Nigeria was being affected by the colonial presence.

HISTORICAL CONTEXT

Education and Religion in Colonial Nigeria

As a west-central African nation with coastline along the Atlantic, Nigeria was one of the regions prized by Europeans as a source of slaves as early as the fifteenth century. Islam, spreading from North Africa, gained a foothold in northern Nigeria by 1804, when the Sokoto caliphate was established, while Christianity became a serious presence in the south by 1842. The British established a consulate in Lagos in 1861; the Royal Niger Company was chartered to conduct trade and sign treaties beginning in 1886; and by 1900 the bulk of what was now called "Nigeria" was a British protectorate. The conquering of the eastern lands in 1902–1903 was not accomplished without violence; when deemed necessary, entire villages were razed, resisters were imprisoned, and village elders were executed. All in all, a colonial infrastructure, however skeletal, was well established throughout Nigeria by the time of Achebe's youth in the 1930s.

As for Christianity, missionaries reached Achebe's hometown of Ogidi in 1892, and the Igbo eventually welcomed them, if not for their creeds then at least for the societal advancements they brought, especially the schools and education that were expected to lead the Igbo toward attaining the same wealth and material comfort that white people enjoyed. Meanwhile, the

COMPARE & CONTRAST

- **Mid-twentieth century:** While still a colony and protectorate ruled by a British-appointed governor, Nigeria passes a provisional constitution in 1946 and adopts a final federal constitution in 1951, significant steps on the way to gaining independence in 1960.

  Today: Beginning in 2010, the Federation of Nigeria is led by President Goodluck Jonathan, formerly a state governor and then the vice president, who upon assuming office emphasized his administration's commitment to electoral reform, positive governance, and fighting corruption.

- **Mid-twentieth century:** The Yaba College of Technology, a polytechnic school founded in 1947, and University College, Ibadan (now called the University of Ibadan), founded in 1948, become Nigeria's first institutions of higher education.

  Today: Nigeria is home to some ninety accredited universities, including federal, state, and private institutions, as well as some thirty-six unaccredited universities.

- **Mid-twentieth century:** As of 1953, the total population of Nigeria is around 36 million, including some 267,000 in Lagos and 459,000 in Ibadan, where Achebe is finishing school. With population density in Igboland high, Igbos generally seek as much education as possible and gravitate toward cities and the white-collar employment to be found there.

  Today: As of 2010, the estimated population of Nigeria is over 164 million, with the coastal city of Lagos the largest, home to 1.5 million in the city proper and around 8 million in the greater metropolitan area, while Ibadan's population is about 1.35 million. The Igbo account for just under one-fifth of the population.

---

missionaries saw fit to equate an existing Igbo god seen as the highest, Chukwu, with the Christian God, which facilitated the eventual persuasion of many Igbo to forsake traditional devotion to many gods—framed as heathenish and sinful—to worship only the one God. By the time Achebe was being raised in Ogidi, the town was roughly split between converts and those who adhered to traditional Igbo religion. Given this circumstance, it can be said that religion was the most significant aspect of the Western presence at the time in rural Nigerian towns, even if cities were seeing more dramatic alterations in urbanized ways of life.

The Igbo people did not witness the increasing deviation from their own traditions without concern. As the authors of *Chinua Achebe: Teacher of Light* relate,

> Many Igbo believed that the aim of British colonialism was to penetrate the minds of the Igbo people and thus to alienate them from their own values. In their view, Christianity came hand in hand with colonialism to pacify the spirit and the resistance of the Igbo, so that colonialism could conquer their bodies.

Those who valued foremost the spiritual integrity of the Igbo people could not dispute the material advantages offered by alliance with Christianity. Aside from the evidence of British success in the world—their clothing, medicines, books—the Igbo people recognized that the British favored those who converted, and the British, largely because of their firearms, were in control. That is, in wielding guns the British benefited from a terrible power imbalance in relation to the native people. As many Igbo saw it, the only sure way to rectify this imbalance was to assimilate into British culture and religion; and the Igbo had not only the British but also the Yoruba, the other most dominant cultural presence in the south, with whom to compare themselves and compete.

Michael wants to bring modern ideas to Nigerian schoolchildren. *(© Hector Conesa / ShutterStock.com)*

Thus the Yoruba people's ready adoption of Christianity—a process begun decades earlier than in Igboland—fueled the Igbo people's adoption of the same.

Life quality and other material concerns among the Igbo were so strong, in fact, that one indignant Church Missionary Society official, quoted by E. A. Ayandele in his essay "The Collapse of 'Pagandom' in Igboland," remarked, "The African desire for education, Europeanization, though good in itself—is so strong *commercially*, that in the majority of cases it completely obliterates the desire for Christianity." Nevertheless, Christianity was adopted as deemed fit, and Ayandele concludes that "by far the real *coup de grâce* to pagandom in Igboland was the Western-style education which the population patronized beyond the limits the CMS missionaries . . . considered safe for the propagation of Christianity." This is to say that while missionaries sought only to advance Igbo education far enough to allow them to read their newfound Bibles, the Igbo themselves were already seeing beyond the religion to the societal advantages that lay behind it. Achebe's story "Dead Men's Path" illustrates just how the interests of education, as advanced by such Westernized Nigerians as Michael Obi, were both capable of and intent on steamrolling the interests of traditional Igbo religion.

CRITICAL OVERVIEW

Achebe is known primarily for his novels, and in fact *Girls at War and Other Stories* (which includes all the stories from his earlier volume *The Sacrificial Egg and Other Short Stories*) is the only full story collection he has published. In his preface to the later volume, he acknowledges that "a dozen pieces in twenty years must be accounted a pretty lean harvest by any reckoning." He also expresses the hope that his slight revisions to two of the "student pieces (I dare not call them stories)" have not destroyed their "primal ingenuousness."

Notwithstanding Achebe's modesty, the stories have been the subject of substantial critical commentary. In *A Reader's Companion to the Short Story in English*, Charles Dameron affirms that Achebe's contributions to the short story as a form align with his contributions as a novelist, encompassing "stylistic innovations, such as his frequent use of traditional proverbs and his precise handling of pidgin English and school English, and thematic insights into traditional culture, the clash of cultures"—all aspects evident in "Dead Men's Path." Dameron considers this story "the best of Achebe's undergraduate stories," and he highlights Achebe's evident objectivity as a narrator, because the situation devolves into "a standoff that could have been avoided with some compromising on both sides. Neither position, Achebe implies, is blameless."

G. D. Killam echoes this assessment of the story in *The Writings of Chinua Achebe*, stating, "Achebe is impartial here: neither side is supported." Killam thus concludes that "the force of the story lies in its suggestiveness rather than any explicit statement it makes." On the collection *Girls at War and Other Stories*, Killam remarks, "In the best stories the conflict between the traditional and the modern has its base in the general beliefs which underlie the former."

In *Chinua Achebe: Novelist, Poet, Critic*, David Carroll suggests that while Achebe as narrator may be objective in "Dead Men's Path," the story itself reveals that Achebe favors the perspective of the priest. Considering the story in the context of the author's broader oeuvre, Carroll notes, "Again and again in the fiction a simplified, dogmatic assertion of values achieves the opposite of what it intends by refusing to acknowledge any rival claims"—this being the headmaster's approach to the conflict; "the village priest, in contrast, suggests that there is room for different views . . . and in this story his voice is that of reasonableness."

Similarly, in his essay "Artistic and Pedagogical Experimentations: Chinua Achebe's Short Stories and Novels," Iniobong I. Uko notes that "Dead Men's Path" demonstrates "the need for flexibility in life," as through the character of Mr. Obi, "Achebe clearly condemns obstinacy. The futility of all of Mr. Obi's efforts stresses that Mr. Obi should have considered the validity of other people's opinion and values." Uko concludes that the fact that Mr. Obi is

> consequently crushed in and by the system he cherishes . . . emphasizes Achebe's thesis that the individual is only an aspect of the society and has to be subject to the community that enlivens and empowers him.

> **THE READER MAY INDEED CONCLUDE THAT THE 'TRIBAL-WAR' REFERENCE IS A BIT OF A JOKE— THE WHITE SUPERVISOR IS MANIFESTLY IGNORANT— BUT ACHEBE DOES NOT SIMPLY MEAN THIS JOKE TO BE FUNNY."**

In *Chinua Achebe*, C. L. Innes highlights the story's nuanced narration, which is seen as "flexible and accomplished, suggesting the language and cultural experiences which have formed the consciousness of the characters described, while retaining the slight detachment which encourages the reader not to take that consciousness for granted." Innes admires how the story gives "force and substance to the Igbo traditional world."

CRITICISM

Michael Allen Holmes

Holmes is a writer with existential interests. In the following essay, he considers how the closing line of "Dead Men's Path" redoubles the story's thematic implications.

Chinua Achebe employs a fairly unique literary strategy of his at the close of "Dead Men's Path." Introducing a new character in the very last line of the story—something few authors risk doing—Achebe allows the white supervisor to dictate the final words of a story in which he plays only a tangential role. The actual dispute here is between the headmaster and the villagers, as represented by the priest of Ani, and a reader may imagine that it could have been more fitting for one of these two main characters, or perhaps the objective narrator, to get the last word.

This aspect of the story—the introduction of an outside perspective, and an uninformed one at that, at the very end—may be what has led some commentators to judge that the story as a whole declines to take sides in the dispute. Mr. Obi's treasured gardens and hedges are destroyed, while there is no indication that the villagers will regain access to their path as a result of their actions. It seems that nobody wins, and the stray final line seems to confirm this.

WHAT DO I READ NEXT?

- The name Obi, which means "The mind at last is at rest," is one Achebe has frequently given to his characters. In this respect "Dead Men's Path" can be linked with his novel *No Longer at Ease* (1960), which likewise portrays a man named Obi who assimilates himself into the British culture that educates and employs him, with ultimately unfortunate results.

- Nobel Prize–winner Wole Soyinka was a fellow undergraduate of Achebe's at University College, Ibadan. One of the Yoruba author's best-known plays is *The Lion and the Jewel* (1959), in which the character Lakunle seeks to modernize his community's social traditions, despite a lack of support, as an exercise of power.

- Soyinka has written several memoirs, including a 1994 volume that covers his undergraduate period, *Ibadan: The Penkelemes Years; A Memoir, 1946–1965*.

- One of Nigeria's best-known female authors is Buchi Emecheta, whose novel *The Joys of Motherhood* (1979) includes a lead male character, Nnaife, who adopts Christianity and favors Western-style notions of identity but who continues to practice polygamy and only flounders at the margins of society in urban Lagos. The education of his and central protagonist Nnu Ego's (male) children is an overarching concern.

- Nnedi Okorafor-Mbachu's young-adult novel *Zahrah, the Windseeker* (2005) is a fantasy tale that envisions a society with wondrously intertwined aspects of traditional Nigerian (particularly Igbo) and Western civilization.

- The anthology *Literature across Cultures* (1994), edited by Sheena Gillespie, Terezhinha Fonseca, and Carol Sanger, presents a wide range of stories, including Achebe's "Dead Men's Path," that explore ethnic identity and cultural differences.

- Many authors from India offer an alternate perspective on how a nation has been affected by its status as a British colony. India's only Nobel Prize winner has been Rabindranath Tagore (in 1913), sixteen of whose stories, set during the nation's colonial era, are collected in *Short Stories from Rabindranath Tagore* (1999).

In *Telling Stories: Postcolonial Short Fiction in English*, Alain Séverac goes so far as to dismissively declare that the story "merely brushes over the subject of the irreconcilable opposition between occult and positivist [i.e., religious and scientific] rationality, never choosing between them, concluding with a joke as the white supervisor blames the conflict on the zeal of" Mr. Obi. The reader, of course, is not necessarily expected to agree with the white supervisor in this story by a Nigerian about Nigerians, but a closer look at the supervisor's comment suggests that, far from being no more than a "joke," the final line adds an entire additional layer of meaning to the story.

As the narrator of "Dead Men's Path" relates, the white supervisor's assessment of Ndume School can be broken down into two parts. First, he quite understandably writes "a nasty report on the state of the premises," which can be taken by the reader as no more than an objective description of the destruction evident on the school grounds. That is, this element of his assessment does not ring with any ethical shortcoming such as religious discrimination or racism. Achebe confirms such a reading with the wording that follows; the supervisor wrote this objective report, "but more seriously" also wrote an amateur cultural analysis of what has taken place: he judges the destruction to be evidence of "the 'tribal-war situation developing between the school and the village, arising in part from the misguided zeal of the new headmaster.'"

There is without doubt irony and humor here, as the reader may be amused to find the white supervisor, who is by necessity invested in the project of British colonialism—is a colonialist—seems to be taking sides *against* his own subordinate African agent of colonialism and *for* the inadequately colonized villagers. In reflecting on the villagers' belief that their deceased ancestors need the footpath, Obi himself reports that

> the whole purpose of our school...is to eradicate just such beliefs as that.... The whole idea is just fantastic. Our duty is to teach your children to laugh at such ideas.

The reader easily imagines that Obi has imbibed this perspective as poured out by the white educators who directed him along the course he has taken, giving him the prized designation of "pivotal teacher" to "set him apart from the other headmasters in the mission field." Whether or not the white supervisor in this story is as disdainful of traditional religion as Mr. Obi is, that supervisor is the sole representative of the colonial culture that has inculcated Mr. Obi with Westernized values and condescension toward the native culture. Thus, regardless of the room Achebe leaves for the white supervisor to be imagined by the reader as anything from a colonial racist to a color-blind philanthropist, the negative qualities exemplified by Mr. Obi will be traced back by the reader (subconsciously at least) to this one white character.

From such an angle, what stands out most in the supervisor's words is not the (fair) judgment of the headmaster's role in the incident but the (evidently uninformed) judgment of the situation as one of tribal war. Achebe gives little indication of ethnic group in the course of this story. It is not clear whether Ndume Central School is meant to refer to an actual place or school in Nigeria. However, Mr. Obi's casual comparison of old-fashioned teachers to "traders in the Onitsha market" does refer to a real place, the market town of Onitsha, only seven miles from Achebe's hometown of Ogidi, in the heart of Igboland. That he would make such a comparison suggests that the headmaster, at least, is Igbo. In turn, the priest who visits is specifically "the village priest of *Ani*," a deity

described by Tijan M. Sallah and Ngozi Okonjo-Iweala in *Chinua Achebe: Teacher of Light* as "the earth-goddess and great mother, the supporter of Igbo life who increases the fertility of the people and their land." This is an Igbo goddess. Thus, the reader can reasonably conclude that the headmaster and the villagers alike are Igbo; there is no real possibility for a "tribal-war situation" between them.

Considering this, the reader may indeed conclude that the "tribal-war" reference is a bit of a joke—the white supervisor is manifestly ignorant—but Achebe does not simply mean this joke to be funny. Rather, it is an incisive comment on the way white society has unfortunately conceived and portrayed African societies in the twentieth century. Achebe zeroed in on this conception in a 1969 speech he gave at the University of Texas, Austin, published in *Early Achebe* as "The Writer and the African Revolution." He lamented in the speech that recently, he had received a letter from Norwegian students inviting him to deliver an address, on a topic that had been chosen for him: "Tribalism, the Black Man's Burden." (This alludes to a famous Rudyard Kipling poem that praises the benevolence of white colonizers, titled "The White Man's Burden.") Achebe's sympathetic audience, understanding the discriminatory attitude reflected in the phrasing of this assigned topic, laughed. Achebe responded,

> Well, I didn't find it funny at all. I was in fact in despair.... It seemed to me that in that letter Europe had framed yet another charge against Africa, and I was being called to come forward and begin my defense all over again.

Achebe explained that he was using the collective first person there, representing through his own self how Africans as a race "have argued endlessly in the past"—telling slave traders that they were humans, not commodities; telling missionaries that their existing culture was perfectly adequate to their needs and desires; and pointing out that colonialists' that their truest intention was evidently not to bring civilization but to extract wealth through government-sanctioned looting of natural and human resources.

In considering the Norwegian students' letter, what Achebe felt forced to argue over was the implicit accusation that Africans are afflicted with a hopeless tribalism that debilitates politics and society. He noted that the then-ongoing Nigerian Civil War (1967–1970), also called the Biafran War, likely inspired this question, because that war could have easily been perceived by outsiders as a fracture along tribal lines. Essentially, in that war the Igbo people, having been the victims of recent political exclusion and violence, seceded from Nigeria to form the republic of Biafra. They declared themselves a nation, but opposing interests saw fit to dismiss them as no more than a *tribe*, a word that Achebe suggested carries connotations not of a collective will but of constant and ungovernable hostility. He relayed, "In Africa—this is the mind of Europe I'm reporting—there are no nations, only tribes. In Africa there is no logic or reason, only that irrational passion."

The conception of African ethnic groups as *tribes* rather than *nations* suggests that there are no boundaries or rules of conduct that need to be respected with regard to the tribe; the tribe's presumed hostility justifies any hostility toward it on the part of others. Achebe pointed out that the invasion of a body conceived as a nation by another nation inspires an indignant international response; he used the contemporary example of the invasion of Czechoslovakia by Russia, but a more recent corollary would be the 1990 invasion of Kuwait by Iraq; the Western world rose to Kuwait's defense. In the Biafra situation, however, where Nigeria was assisted by the Russians and British, those nations' implicit defense of their action was that they did so "to prevent Africa from relapsing back into tribalism—you know, that fatal disease which it is the mission of Europe to cure in Africa."

Achebe went on to assert that the tendency to see Africa only in terms of hostile tribes "is the greatest block to an understanding of Africa by the white world. It makes it impossible for the white world to know and understand what is going on in Africa." Having been confronted once in Holland by the contention that Africans have always chased after each other with spears, Achebe affirmed that this myth

> was invented by Europeans to distinguish between themselves and their African victims of colonial exploitation. It was necessary, it was absolutely necessary to invent it, because if you didn't, you would have to concede that Africans were people, and were nations. Then you would face a crisis of conscience.

Recognizing that a workable definition is needed, Achebe offered, "A nation is a people with common cultural consciousness. Where this consciousness exists, you have a nation. . . . Where it doesn't exist, you may have a formal state but you haven't got a nation." Such a common consciousness allows the people to govern themselves as they wish to be governed, to interact with other nations as they choose to interact, and to follow internally acknowledged laws and societal precepts that ensure the peaceable continuation of the culture.

Traditional Igbo communities, for example, were not governed by individual chiefs with any primary overarching power or influence; rather, councils of male elders in each village made decisions that reflected the collective will of the people, with certain decisions deferred instead to women's councils. Village meetings were held in markets and open to participation by any and all. Such broad-based local governance, of course, did not lend itself to central control by the British colonial regime, and so district commissioners and local warrant chiefs were appointed, regardless of whether they had actually earned any respect or authority in their given areas.

Such a system, placing power in the control of individuals who are directly responsible not to the people themselves but rather to their superiors in the government hierarchy, is precisely the sort of system that leads to what the white world has labeled "tribalism"—individuals with power acting for the benefit of their own ethnic group and at the expense of others. The various African tribes—that is, the various original African nations—had previously governed themselves in ways that avoided this very dilemma; even in those nations with supreme chiefs, those chiefs ruled only the people whose respect they had earned. Not the original African nations but the system of colonial governance imposed on them by European powers, that of expansive states with arbitrarily drawn borders encompassing arbitrary collections of ethnic groups—this system was what instigated what became pejoratively known as "tribalism."

Achebe concluded his talk on more positive notes. He assured his listeners that the situation in African politics was not hopeless, although the resolution of ethnic antagonism would require positive commitments among the peoples who find themselves in the various modern African states. He remarked,

> Today, some of these states are striving, are struggling to become nations. Some of them will succeed when they have created a common cultural and spiritual consciousness through the will of their people, the revolutionary will of their people, to be a nation.

Michael puts up a fence to block the "dead men's path." *(© Andrr | ShutterStock.com)*

In Achebe's story "Dead Men's Path," the notion of tribalism or tribal war is not even on the table for the bulk of the story. The conflict has obvious roots in the headmaster's condescending Westernized attitude—clearly learned somewhere along the way from white society—and the villagers' insistence on doing whatever their traditional ways dictate. Even to characterize the villagers' motivations thus is to slight them: they are not simply stubborn traditionalists but are acting based on their most sincere spiritual beliefs. Deceased ancestors are understood to still wield influence over their lives, a circumstance that is seen to be demonstrated by the untimely death of the village woman in childbirth. When the diviner concludes that they must tear down the obstructions to the ancestral path or risk greater misfortune befalling the community, they have no choice but to act on this belief.

Mr. Obi, however, a scientific, Westernized man who cannot give any credence to the idea that dead people need paths, can only follow the white people's ways he has learned and, instead of working out community conflicts on a case-by-case basis, refer back to the rules and regulations that make further human interaction unnecessary. By the end of the story, the reader must be well aware of the role played by white culture as the source of Mr. Obi's perspective. Then in the final line, the white supervisor's comments not only fail to identify the problematic aspects of Mr. Obi's perspective, namely, the Western aspects—instead laying the blame on Mr. Obi's own "misguided zeal"—but also blindly suggest that tribal antagonism must be at the heart of the matter. Thus, from the bulk of the story the reader understands that white culture has caused this story's conflict, whereas from the last line the reader also understands that white culture cannot and does not recognize this fact, falling back as it does on the false conviction that tribalism, indeed, is the black man's burden. With the stroke of a single ingenious sentence, Achebe effectively redoubles the power of the story.

Source: Michael Allen Holmes, Critical Essay on "Dead Men's Path," in *Short Stories for Students*, Gale, Cengage Learning, 2013.

Ode Ogede

In the following excerpt, Ogede discusses how Achebe's story collection fits into the larger socio-political context of modern Nigeria.

Like many other creative writers from Africa, Achebe made his writing debut with the short story form, a convention that unquestionably has proven to be Africa's most effective counter to the imported narratives. However, the reason he did not consolidate his efforts within the short story goes hand in hand with the general disdain with which the short story is held by critics of modern African writing. Wilfried Feuser puts the case in perspective when he laments in his *Jazz and Palmwine* that critics of African writing have "paid scant attention to the short story and have treated it as a footnote to the novel" although "it is bursting with life." The short story has proven itself the form upon which an alternative tradition could be built, but Africans have neglected—if not abandoned—it entirely, undoubtedly because the prize for fiction has traditionally gone to the novelist, whom Feuser suitably terms "the long-distance runner" while the short story writer or "the sprinter" is consigned to obscurity.

Numerically Achebe's showing as a short story writer may not quite place him at a par with that of other world-class writers. Edgar Allan Poe, Nawal El Saadawi, Alex La Guma, Herman Melville, Nurudin Farah, Nathaniel Hawthorne, Buchi Emecheta, Anton Chekhov, Bessie Head, Henry James, Najib Mahfuz, James Joyce, Nadine Gordimer, Salman Rushdie, Albert Camus, Ama Ata Aidoo, William Faulkner, Gabriel Marquez, F. Scott Fitzgerald, V. S. Naipaul, Richard Wright, Dambudzo Marechera, Margaret Artwood, Jamaica Kincaid, Ngugi wa Thiong'o, and Ernest Hemingway all not only distinguished themselves as master novelists but were equally at home in the terrain of short fiction. However, Achebe's effort is quite commendable. Despite its scantiness, Achebe should take solace in the very high quality of his output. Achebe's stories merit attention not only because of the thematic links they bear with his longer narratives, but also because of the range of stylistic experimentation they put on display. In this chapter, I analyze Achebe's only book of short stories *Girls at War and Other Stories* (1972) to argue that all of his narrative experimentation in his short fiction can best be appreciated in the context of a debt to the oral tradition. Even the casual reader of Achebe's stories soon becomes aware of the reciprocal relationships that he strikes between his shorter and longer narratives. Though all his stories appear to move away from the direct communal concerns of the longer narratives, this is not really the case. In most of his stories, Achebe uses the experiences of individuals to explore the problems of the larger society. And so, ultimately, the stories constitute precious documents which portray socio-political, cultural, and economic changes of the community.

While growing up in the village of Ogidi in Eastern Nigeria during the 1930s, Achebe heard tales told both in the home by the fireside and in the wider community, for traditional storytelling flourished in the home as well as in the schools. As noted by Isidore Okpewho in his important book *African Oral Literature*, though different storytellers have different performance styles, there are certain resources which all performers have in their repertoire. Among these are repetition, tonal variation, parallelism, piling and association, the direct address, ideophones, digression, imagery, hyperbole, allusion, and symbolism. In addition, traditional tales tend to end with a moral appended to them often to confirm the norms of the society in which they are performed. Of these, the direct address (which ensures interaction with the audience), digression, exaggeration and didacticism are the features most prominently deployed by Achebe in his short stories. Though traditional storytelling influenced Achebe's short stories as much as—if not more than—it did his novels, this fact has surprisingly escaped the notice of his critics. Even more astonishing is the fact that some critics have made an effort to deny Achebe's oral heritage entirely. Among them is his long-time associate Ossie Enekwe, who claims that Achebe "developed as a writer in an environment where the short story form is not taken seriously, where there was no flourishing tradition of short fiction." By arguing that Achebe "developed as a short story writer through dint of hard work and perseverance," Enekwe seems to excuse the presumed lack of short fiction in Achebe's oeuvre by blaming the unfavorable background in which Achebe grew up. Nonetheless, Enekwe's allegation that Achebe "made mistakes," that "these were steadily and systematically eliminated as he perfected his skill" is unwarranted; such special pleading sweeps aside not only the fact that the Igbos generally hold storytelling in high regard, but also the fact that the art of storytelling can legitimately be taken as Achebe's greatest literary influence.

. . . All of Achebe's short stories stress the importance of ancient cultural traditions and habits in the survival and organizing of indigenous societies. This is evident even in early and amateurish pieces such as "Akueke" (in which the experience of a proud girl who refuses all suitors in the neighborhood serves to accentuate not only the primacy of marriage as a traditional institution but also the importance of family and of values like compassion and love) and "Marriage Is a Private Affair" (which questions the custom of arranged marriage by exposing the prejudice against inter-tribal marriage and calls for tolerance and understanding in order to protect the institution of marriage which forms the bedrock of society). It is also evident in "Dead Men's Path" (a story employing the overzealousness of a young headmaster to teach basic lessons in moderation) and the stories "The Voter," "Vengeful Creditor," and "Girls at War," which focus on contemporary society, where corruption is pervasive, and in which the author attributes the malaise to the repudiation of traditional values that once cushioned people from moral depravity and the crisis it inevitably inflicts. . . .

Source: Ode Ogede, "The Politics of Storytelling," in *Achebe and the Politics of Representation: Form against Itself, from Colonial Conquest and Occupation to Post-Independence Disillusionment*, Africa World Press, 2001, pp. 101–14.

David Carroll

In the following excerpt, Carroll categorizes the stories in Girls at War and Other Stories *into three natural groupings.*

GIRLS AT WAR AND OTHER STORIES

Achebe has been publishing short stories since his student days and his most comprehensive collection, *Girls at War and Other Stories* (1972), brings together thirteen stories written over a period of twenty years. As he says in the Preface this is 'a pretty lean harvest.' Yet the stories which range from the 'primal ingenuousness' of the student pieces to the bitter assessments of the Civil War succinctly reveal aspects of the writer not apparent in the novels.

> AGAIN AND AGAIN IN THE FICTION A SIMPLIFIED, DOGMATIC ASSERTION OF VALUES ACHIEVES THE OPPOSITE OF WHAT IT INTENDS BY REFUSING TO ACKNOWLEDGE ANY RIVAL CLAIMS."

The stories fall naturally into three groups. The four student pieces develop from humorous squibs to the preliminary treatment of some of Achebe's major themes. The wit of 'Polar Undergraduate' (1950) and 'In a Village Church' (1950) is based on the application of a bizarre logic, first to the classification of students and secondly to the understanding of a church service. They are slight undergraduate sketches but the second hints at later developments in Achebe's writing. Here, the recognised rituals of the local church service are shown to be in disarray with the singing discordant, the sermon irrelevant, the bibles disintegrating, and the congregation asleep. But the philosophical narrator ironically insists on finding meaning and order. If, for example, the convention of singing verses in unison is not observed then the 'advantage of this system was that at any given time . . . there was always a voice to be heard.' This also furthers the real purpose of the service for the 'custom was that any group that finished before the others went in to help them in true Christian fellowship.' By looking at the other unorthodox aspects of the service in this way the narrator uncovers the congregation's own peculiar 'system' which expresses their habits and peccadilloes. This wry account of the assimilation of alien conventions is to become a familiar feature in the novels.

The other two student pieces are more serious attempts to deal with social conflicts which cannot be resolved by whimsical irony. In 'Marriage Is a Private Affair' (1952) the marriage in metropolitan Lagos of Nnaemeka and Nene offends against the customs of the bridegroom's village by cutting across religious, tribal and family beliefs. Everything is against Nene: she comes from Lagos, she is not an Igbo and she is a school-teacher. Such an event has never happened before in the history of the village and the opposition is summed up in Nnaemeka's father who is implacably against the marriage and who, after the event, rejects any kind of reconciliation. The villagers suggest various solutions, even a good herbalist is mentioned, but he rejects them all: 'Nnaemeka's father was known to be obstinately ahead of his more superstitious neighbours in these matters.' But this detail tactfully suggests that what at first seems an added reluctance to influence his son is in fact a sign of what father and son have in common—a refusal to be controlled by ancient custom—which will eventually lead to a reconciliation. But after eight years there has been no change in the father. 'By a tremendous effort of will he had succeeded in pushing his son to the back of his mind.' But when a letter from his daughter-in-law arrives telling him about his unknown grandsons, his rigid opposition begins to weaken. Achebe presents this as a victory of the natural forces of kind and affection over custom. As the father seeks to reaffirm his opposition a storm is blowing up bringing the first rain of the year, in contrast to the parching December weather in which the conflict started. 'It was one of those rare occasions when even Nature takes a hand in a human fight.' He tries to hum a hymn tune to stiffen his resolve but the rain prevents him, first by loudly pattering on the roof and then by calling up an image of his grandsons. Upon this the story ends: 'By a curious mental process he imagined them standing, sad and forsaken, under the harsh angry weather—shut out from his house.' The open conflict of the first and second generations is resolved naturally, it seems, through the innocent third generation.

In 'Dead Men's Path' (1953) no such reconciliation between old and new is possible. The new headmaster of the mission school with his modern values, modern methods and modern wife is not prepared to tolerate the ancient path which crosses his compound from the village shrine to the traditional place of burial, even though the village priest tells him the whole life of the village depends on it. 'Our dead relatives depart by it and our ancestors visit us by it. But most important, it is the path of children coming in to be born . . .' But this only confirms the ambitious and dogmatic teacher in his opposition: 'Our duty is to teach your children to laugh at such ideas.' Nemesis comes when a woman in the village dies in childbirth and the ancestors insulted by the obstruction of their path have to

be propitiated. The teacher next day finds his beautiful compound destroyed and, more seriously, a growing opposition to his school in the village. He is severely criticised in the inspector's next report. This is a slighter story than the previous one but it sketches a recurrent theme in Achebe's writing. Again and again in the fiction a simplified, dogmatic assertion of values achieves the opposite of what it intends by refusing to acknowledge any rival claims. The village priest, in contrast, suggests there is room for different views—'Let the hawk perch and let the eagle perch'—and in the story his voice is that of reasonableness. Accommodation is later shown to contain its own dangers.

One expression of Achebe's mistrust of absolutism of any kind, it was suggested in the Introduction, is his fascination with Onitsha. Sitting as it does at the crossroads of the world the town distrusts singlemindedness. It is 'the occult no man's land between river-spirits and mundane humans,' and as a result it 'can be opposite things at once.' Achebe places two of his next group of stories, 'The Sacrificial Egg' (1959) and 'Uncle Ben's Choice' (1966), in a thinly disguised Onitsha, here called Umuru, to explore this 'zone of occult instability' where different kinds of reality meet in bewildering permutations. The first is the more ambitious story dealing with both a private and a public crisis in the town. The great market on the Niger is presented as the meeting place first of the forest people and the strange riverain folk, and secondly of human beings and the beautiful spirits, the 'mammy-wota who have their town in the depths of the river.' Here too old meets new; the deity who has presided over the market since antiquity still casts her spell on the original market day, but with the coming of the trading companies Umuru has turned into 'a busy, sprawling, crowded and dirty river port, a no-man's land where strangers outnumbered by far the sons of the soil.' The balance has been upset—'there is good growth and there is bad growth'—so that traditional duties and rituals are neglected in favour of money-making and revelry. This is the public crisis, and nemesis comes in the shape of the evil deity, Kitikpa, demanding 'the sacrifice the inhabitants owed the gods of the soil' and decorating his chosen victims with smallpox of which he is the incarnate power.

These events are brought into focus through the memory of Julius Obi, a clerk with the

European trading company which controls the palm-kernel trade on the river. Looking over the now deserted market place he recalls despondently his last meeting with his fiancée, Janet, a few days ago when her mother insisted that they stop meeting at present for Kitikpa forbade it, pointing out in justification the houses whose doorways were barred with yellow palm-fronds, the sign of the smallpox. But the additional cause for his concern is the disturbing episode which followed this parting. Walking along the river bank late at night he had heard the approach of the dangerous night-mask in revelry and turning quickly for home he stepped on something which burst with a 'slightly liquid explosion.' It was an egg offered in sacrifice. 'Someone oppressed by misfortune had brought the offering to the cross-roads in the dusk. And he had stepped on it. There were the usual young palm-fronds around it. But Julius saw it differently as a house where the terrible artist was at work.' His private worries are being entangled in the larger crisis as his mind jumps from the palm-fronds on the ground to the sign of Kitikpa's visitation. And then, as the fleet-footed mask bore down on him, he hid in fear beside the road where 'the rattling staff of the spirit and the thundering stream of esoteric speech' enter his mind, compounding his alarm and fear. It is an apocalyptic moment—'the commotion in the air and on the earth—the thunder and torrential rain, the earthquake and the flood'—during which the destruction of the egg becomes associated in his mind with the actions of the night-mask whose revelries have further provoked Kitikpa. As he relives the terror of the incident he looks back across the gulf of time separating him from Janet and her mother. The story ends on this note of fear and pathos: 'This emptiness deepened with every passing day. On this side of it stood Julius, and on the other Ma and Janet whom the dread artist decorated.' The state of mind in which he looks over the deserted market poignantly epitomises and heightens the wider conflict and crisis. And Julius himself embodies some of the main forces in conflict: he comes from a bush village but has passed his Standard Six and now works for the European company; he is fully aware of the power of the night-mask but he sings in the choir of the C.M.S. church. The central incident in the story seems to have undermined his mental equilibrium. The terror of the broken egg and the mask involve him personally in Kitikpa's punishment for which he now holds himself in some way responsible.

By contrast, 'Uncle Ben's Choice' (1966) is a comic account of life among the uncertainties of Umuru. The central character is again a clerk in the Niger Company and he recalls over a gap of many years a crucial episode in his life in the year 1919. However, instead of the brooding retrospect of Julius, this story is in the form of a lively and idiomatic dramatic monologue which captures brilliantly Ben's character and the world he inhabited as a man-about-town. His problem was that the predatory women of Umuru were attracted to his financial success, and so he has to take precautions. 'I had a Raleigh bicycle, brand new, and everyone called me Jolly Ben. I was selling like hot bread. But there is one thing about me—we can laugh and joke and drink and do otherwise but I must always keep my sense with me.' So to protect his interests he never shows the sharp women of the town where he lives and he is careful to avoid any love-medicines. But one New Year's Eve, after a night drinking White Horse and smoking Guinea Gold, he returns to his room, falls like a log into his big iron bed only to find there a woman. 'She was hundred per cent naked.' At first he thinks it is Margaret who has designs on him; then he notices her hair is soft as a European's; then she speaks to him in Igbo; her voice seems familiar and then strange. But he resists her seductions and after striking a match despite her prohibition—it is an Onitsha version of Cupid and Psyche—he flees in a panic with his head swelling 'like a barrel' to his friend Matthew where he collapses. From Matthew he discovers he has been visited by Mami Wota, the lady of the River Niger, who bequeathes untold riches on her lovers in return for their complete obedience. In other words, she offers in her person a resolution of Ben's conflicting desires, but at a price. And this is how the monologue returns to the situation in which it is being delivered: 'Today whenever my wives make me vex I tell them: "I don't blame you. If I had been wise I would have taken Mami Wota." They laugh and ask me why did I not take her.' But in his old age, despite his quarrelsome wives and lack of wealth, Ben knows that the young clerk's decision was the right one. It is a fine story in which the natural and occult explanation of events are held in suspension in Ben's racy garrulousness without contradicting each other.

In both of these Umuru stories Achebe seeks to embody the natural and supernatural within one reality through the mind of his central character. In 'Akueke' (1962) the same purpose is achieved through the rituals and beliefs of the clan. The story opens with Akueke close to death with the swelling disease, waiting bitterly for her brothers to carry her to the bad bush as an abomination to the land. As she waits she recalls her childhood, her happy visits to her grandfather, her role as village beauty; but then came the time she rejected all her suitors and her brothers warned her against the sin of pride. 'And Akueke did not listen. And now her protective spirit despairing of her had taken a hand in the matter and she was stricken with this disease.' None of the medicine men can cure her and so eventually she has to be taken to the bad bush; the following morning she has disappeared, eaten it is assumed by wild animals. This is where the first half of the story ends.

On the public level the explanation is that she has offended against the *mores* of the clan by rejecting her brothers' advice and so annoying her protective spirit. But Achebe suggests a more personal explanation by means of her memories of childhood. Through those early visits she has come to love her maternal grandfather, and he to love her, for a special reason:

> He was very fond of his granddaughter who, they said, was the image of his own mother. He rarely called Akueke by her name: it was always *Mother*. She was in fact the older woman returned in the cycle of life. During the visits to Ezi, Akueke knew she could get away with anything, her grandfather forbade anyone to rebuke her.

This suggests where her stubborn pride which caused the impasse and abomination was fostered; it also prepares the way for a resolution of the dilemma. Akueke is not dead; she has been taken to her grandfather's home at Ezi where the old man confronts the brothers with what they see as the ghost of their sister and asks why they did not bring her to him to be cured. In effect, he says, she had died and returned in the cycle of life as his daughter, to be known in future as Matefi. 'She was no longer a daughter of Umuofia but of Ezi.' The public explanation of events seen through the eyes of the brothers who have innocently carried out their family and clan duties is questioned and rejected by the irate grandfather—'How could she die and then be here?'—who brings her back to life by means of the special relationship which caused her death in the first place. Again there is no encouragement for the reader to adopt simply one frame of reference; Akueke's stubbornness, her illness, her disappearance and rebirth are the elements out of which the pattern of events is constructed. A fourth story, 'The Madman' (1971), is of a similar kind.

This is a succinct story with a fable-like structure which explores the uneasy relationship between the occult and the socially respectable. At first, everything seems to be in favour of the confident, complacent Nwibe, a man of standing in the clan who is about to apply for membership of the powerful *ozo* society and who rules his family with an iron hand, dismissing any opposition to his commands as evidence of his wives' madness. But he is tricked by his opposite, the outcast madman, who wanders naked from market to market abused by the people who project upon him their fears and anger. 'He was drawn to markets and straight roads' and moves along the highway, passing from the 'occult territory' of one market to that of another and back again. When he comes upon Nwibe bathing in the stream he sees an opportunity of getting his own back on this world which abuses him. He picks up Nwibe's cloth and puts it on. Here, at the centre of the story, the roles are reversed: the madman is respectably clothed while the naked Nwibe loses control of himself. '"I will kill you," screamed Nwibe as he splashed towards the bank, maddened by anger. "I will whip that madness out of you today!"' But now the madness is transferred as Nwibe pursues the madman frenziedly along the highway until, as the villagers see it, he comes irrevocably within the occult powers of the market. Then it is too late: 'No man can touch him thereafter. He is free and yet no power can break his bondage. He is free of men but bonded to a god.' He recovers from his bout of madness but is never the same again, having become in this incident everything he despises: '. . . a fine, hefty man in his prime, stark naked, tearing through the crowds to answer the call of the market-place.' He is never invited to join the *ozo* society. This is reminiscent of Okonkwo and the way in which his unyielding, dogmatic assertion of clan customs indicated a loss of equilibrium which led eventually to his overthrow in a final act of sacrilege. Reality is dialectical; outraged respectability quickly turns into madness. 'Two people,' as the Igbo say, 'cannot be mad at the same time.' And Achebe dramatises this with a deft touch as the angry, self-important Nwibe is led by the ironical laughter of the madman along the highway into the occult zone of freedom and madness.

There are some striking similarities in the stories discussed so far. Most of them centre on a conflict of values, either between the clan and the modern world, or between the social and the occult, or within the clan between the community and the individual. These themes find more complex treatment in the novels, but here they are sketched quickly and sharply. The way in which Achebe achieves this is to focus the action at some point in the mind of one character, either by retrospective narration or by ending a story with a glimpse of a mind in conflict. He is clearly most interested in the human mind either when it is brooding over its inability to reconcile discordant values or seeking to recover its equilibrium after a familiar reality has been overturned. These moments, Achebe implies, are an essential part of life; we all inhabit our own Onitshas with their exciting but dangerous zones of instability where the belief in simple certitude is the height of folly. . . .

Source: David Carroll, "Short Stories and Poetry," in *Chinua Achebe: Novelist, Poet, Critic*, Macmillan, 1990, pp. 146–66.

SOURCES

Achebe, Chinua, Preface and "Dead Men's Path," in *Girls at War and Other Stories*, Doubleday, 1973, pp. ix–x, 73–78.

————, "The Writer and the African Revolution" and "A Group Interview with Achebe in 1969," in *Early Achebe*, by Bernth Lindfors, Africa World Press, 2009, pp. 231–57.

Ayandele, E. A., "The Collapse of 'Pagandom' in Igboland," in *Nigerian Historical Studies*, Frank Cass, 1979, pp. 167–91.

Bockting, Margaret, "Traffic with Others," in *CLA Journal*, Vol. 46, No. 3, March 2003, pp. 337–48.

Carroll, David, "Short Stories and Poetry," in *Chinua Achebe: Novelist, Poet, Critic*, Macmillan, 1990, pp. 146–66.

Dameron, Charles, "Chinua Achebe," in *A Reader's Companion to the Short Story in English*, edited by Erin Fallon, et al., Greenwood Press, 2001, pp. 1–11.

Falola, Toyin, *Culture and Customs of Nigeria*, Greenwood Press, 2001, pp. 29–53.

Innes, C. L., *Chinua Achebe*, Cambridge University Press, 1990, pp. 4–20, 102–20.

Killam, G. D., *The Writings of Chinua Achebe*, rev. ed., Heinemann, 1977, pp. 99–104.

Lindfors, Bernth, *Early Achebe*, Africa World Press, 2009, pp. 5–36, 51–56.

"Nigeria," Population Statistics, February 29, 2004, http://www.populstat.info/Africa/nigeriag.htm (accessed August 29, 2012).

"Nigeria Swears in New President," Al Jazeera website, May 8, 2010, http://www.aljazeera.com/news/africa/2010/05/20105681641917266.html (accessed August 29, 2012).

Omiegbe, Odirin, "Chinua Achebe and Igbo (African) Traditional Religion," in *Emerging Perspectives on Chinua Achebe*, Vol. 2, *Isinka, the Artistic Purpose: Chinua Achebe and the Theory of African Literature*, edited by Ernest N. Emenyonu and Iniobong I. Uko, Africa World Press, 2004, pp. 187–208.

Ottenberg, Simon, "Ibo Receptivity to Change," in *Igbo Religion, Social Life, and Other Essays*, edited by Toyin Falola, Africa World Press, 2006, pp. 179–94; originally published in *Continuity and Change in African Cultures*, edited by William R. Bascom and Melville J. Herskovits, University of Chicago Press, 1959, pp. 129–43.

Sallah, Tijan M., and Ngozi Okonjo-Iweala, *Chinua Achebe: Teacher of Light; A Biography*, Africa World Press, 2003, pp. 1–65, 123–40.

Séverac, Alain, "Achebe's Short Stories: Their Intertextual Relationship to His Novels," in *Telling Stories: Postcolonial Short Fiction in English*, edited by Jacqueline Bardolph, Rodopi, 2001, pp. 241–54.

Uko, Iniobong I., "Artistic and Pedagogical Experimentations: Chinua Achebe's Short Stories and Novels," in *Emerging Perspectives on Chinua Achebe*, Vol. 2, *Isinka, the Artistic Purpose: Chinua Achebe and the Theory of African Literature*, edited by Ernest N. Emenyonu and Iniobong I. Uko, Africa World Press, 2004, pp. 57–70.

UniversitiesOfNigeria.com, http://universitiesofnigeria.com/ (accessed August 29, 2012).

FURTHER READING

Achebe, Chinua, *The Education of a British-Protected Child: Essays*, Alfred A. Knopf, 2009.

Although Achebe has not written an autobiography, a number of his essays in this volume reflect on how he was shaped by his upbringing and education, while others touch on identity, politics, and literature in Nigeria and greater Africa.

Davidson, Basil, *The Black Man's Burden: Africa and the Curse of the Nation-State*, James Currey, 1992.

This book is a more expansive treatment of what Achebe communicated in his address at the University of Texas, Austin, in 1969: that "tribalism" is not an inherent African characteristic but was inflicted on Africa by the Western imposition of systems of colonial governance that were then simply transferred to newly created states with disregard for traditional ruling structures.

Eboh, Simeon Onyewueke, *African Concept of Law and Order: A Case Study of Igbo Traditional Society*, Transaction Publishers, 2003.

This volume directly addresses the issue of primary concern in "Dead Men's Path": how traditional Igbo culture formulates notions of law and order.

Umeh, John Anenechukwu, *After God Is Dibia: Igbo Cosmology, Divination & Sacred Science in Nigeria*, Karnak House, 1997.

A comprehensive exploration of the theological perspective and religious practices of the Igbo people is provided in Umeh's book.

SUGGESTED SEARCH TERMS

Chinua Achebe AND Dead Men's Path

Achebe AND Girls at War and Other Stories

Achebe AND African literature

Achebe AND Nigerian literature

Nigeria AND British colony

Nigeria AND Christianity

Nigeria AND Igbo

Igbo AND religion OR education

Chinua Achebe AND Wole Soyinka

Achebe AND interview

Achebe AND Igbo tradition

The Drummer Boy of Shiloh

RAY BRADBURY

1960

"The Drummer Boy of Shiloh" is a short story by Ray Bradbury first published on April 30, 1960, in the *Saturday Evening Post*, where it was illustrated by Ken Davies, a prominent realist painter. It first appeared in a book collection in Bradbury's *The Machineries of Joy*, published in 1964 and reissued in numerous editions since then. Bradbury is best known today for his future-set dystopian novel *Fahrenheit 451*. For "The Drummer Boy of Shiloh," however, the author turned to American history, specifically the Civil War's Battle of Shiloh (also called the Battle of Pittsburg Landing), which took place in Hardin County in southwestern Tennessee on April 6–7, 1862. The story reveals the thoughts and emotions of a young drummer boy on the eve of the battle, considered one of the major engagements of the Civil War. Interestingly, the story never specifies whether the boy is attached to the Union (Northern) or Confederate (Southern) army. "The Drummer Boy of Shiloh" is included in *Bradbury Stories: 100 of His Most Celebrated Tales*, published in 2003.

AUTHOR BIOGRAPHY

Raymond Douglas Bradbury was born on August 22, 1920, in Waukegan, Illinois, the third son of Leonard Spaulding Bradbury and Esther Moberg Bradbury. Waukegan, an idyllic

Ray Bradbury *(The Library of Congress)*

small town north of Chicago where Bradbury spent much of his youth, is essentially the setting of many of his stories under the name "Green Town." In his youth, a much-beloved aunt gave him books of fairy tales and took him to see such movies as *The Phantom of the Opera* and *The Hunchback of Notre Dame*, and these, along with the Buck Rogers movies and such tales as Frank Baum's *The Wonderful Wizard of Oz*, stimulated his imaginative life.

In search of work, Bradbury's father twice moved the family between Illinois and Arizona from 1926 to 1933. Bradbury began writing fiction in about 1931, recording his first stories on butcher's paper. In 1934, his family moved permanently to Los Angeles, where Bradbury graduated from high school in 1938 and lived the remainder of his life. He joined the Los Angeles Science Fiction League in 1937 and, in 1938, published his first short story, "Hollerbochen's Dilemma," in the magazine *Imagination!* During World War II, he was exempted from service because of poor eyesight. Through the 1940s, he wrote stories for such pulp magazines as *Weird Tales* and *Amazing Stories* and was

already showing signs of being a prolific author. In 1941, after three of his stories were published, he decided to abandon his job as a newspaper salesman for a career as a writer. In 1944, he sold an astonishing forty stories, earning $800. In 1947, he published his first collection, *Dark Carnival*. That year, too, he married Marguerite McClure and in time became the father of four daughters.

The first of his major works was *The Martian Chronicles*, published in 1950. The book comprises a collection of loosely related stories about the colonization of Mars, using the stories to comment on technology, nuclear war, racism, and censorship. Censorship is also a theme of his other key work, *Fahrenheit 451* (1953), which was inspired by the issue of freedom of thought surrounding the era of McCarthyism. At the core of the novel are government censorship and book burning in a world where books are illegal; 451 degrees Fahrenheit is the temperature at which paper ignites. Other major works include *The Illustrated Man* (1951), a collection of eighteen short stories later turned into a 1969 film; *Something Wicked This Way Comes* (1962), a horror novel about boys in a traveling carnival; and *I Sing the Body Electric!* (1969), a collection of short stories whose title is taken from a poem by the American poet Walt Whitman. Although he has often been called a science-fiction writer, Bradbury insisted that the term as applied to him was inaccurate. In his view, he was a fantasy writer because he wrote about things that *could not* happen; science fiction, in contrast, was about things that *could* happen. In his opinion, *Fahrenheit 451* was his only work of science fiction.

Many of Bradbury's stories were turned into episodes on such television shows as *The Twilight Zone*, *Alfred Hitchcock Presents*, and the *Ray Bradbury Theater*. He wrote the treatment for the first 3-D science-fiction film, *It Came from Outer Space* (1953), and the film adaptation of *Moby Dick* (1956). He was the recipient of numerous prizes, among them the O. Henry Award (1947 and 1948), the World Fantasy Award for Life Achievement (1977), the PEN Body of Work Award (1985), and the Damon Knight Memorial Grand Master Award from the Science Fiction and Fantasy Writers of America (1989). In 1988, he received three Horror Writers' Association Bram Stoker Awards: one for a short story ("The Thing at the Top of the Stairs"), one for a fiction collection (*The Toynbee Convector*), and one for Lifetime Achievement. He also received an Emmy (1994) for his teleplay *The Halloween Tree* and was nominated for an Academy Award for his animated film *Icarus Montgolfier Wright* (1962). He was a recipient of the National Book Foundation's 2000 Medal for Distinguished Contribution to American Letters, and in 2004 President George W. Bush presented him with a National Medal of Arts.

In his later years, Bradbury became a popular public speaker. He stayed close to home, living in the same Los Angeles house for fifty years. In 1999 he suffered a stroke that required him to use a wheelchair, but he continued to write until his death on June 5, 2012, from a lengthy illness.

PLOT SUMMARY

The story is set on an April night. Blossoms fall from a peach tree, causing light taps on a drum. A peach pit that managed to hang on to the tree breaks loose and strikes the drum, startling a boy, who bolts upright and listens to the sound of his beating heart. Fourteen-year-old Joby, the drummer boy of the title, turns the drum on its side so that he does not have to hear it. He reflects on the solemnity of the time, for he is part of an army camped in a peach-tree field near Owl Creek and a church called Shiloh. He tries to count the nearby shadows, but he stops because of the darkness. Mention is then made of the forty thousand exhausted and nervous men in the surrounding army, all trying to sleep but unable to do so because of their dreams of battle. A mile away is another army. The boy hears wind, but in reality the wind is the sound of whispering men. Joby thinks that the men are whispering about how they will survive the coming battle; he is discouraged because the only thing he has is a drum, which will not provide him with the protection that gunpowder and bullets would and is therefore worse than a toy. Joby turns onto his side as a peach blossom brushes his face as a moth would. He reflects that perhaps when the new day dawns, the soldiers will go away, taking the war with them, and they will not notice him.

A man appears and stands over Joby. The man has heard the boy crying and says that crying now is good, for there will not be time to cry during the coming battle. The man is about to move on when Joby accidentally brushes the drum, alerting the man to the fact that he is talking to the army's drummer boy. Joby then recognizes the man as the general, whose name is never given; tipping him off is the man's row of brass buttons. Joby starts to rise to his feet, but the general tells him to remain as he is. He asks the boy his name, how long the boy has been with the army (three weeks), and whether the boy has enlisted legitimately. Joby's silence after the last question tells the general that Joby has run away from home to join the army. The general reflects on how young and raw his troops are. He asks Joby whether he is ready for battle, then confesses to the boy that he cried the previous night because of the mistaken belief on both sides that the war would end quickly. The general takes out a cigar and continues to talk. He notes that there are about a hundred thousand men poised for battle and that few of them know much about fighting. He wishes that he had four more months to train his soldiers. He further reflects that the two armies think they are driven by bloodlust and that the battle is likely to be a massacre on both sides. He calls Joby's attention to the innocence and boyish enthusiasm of the troops and maintains that it will be these qualities that will get many of them killed.

The general pauses in his reflections. He makes a little pile of leaves and twigs, as though he intends to start a fire that will allow him to see his way through the coming days. Joby starts to speak, but he hesitates. The general resumes his monologue by answering the question he thinks Joby was about to ask: Why is the general telling him these things? The general's response to this unspoken question is that the troops under his command are like a bunch of untrained, wild horses. Each soldier is his own army. The general's job is to turn them into a single army. To do that, he needs the drummer boy. Joby is astonished by this statement, but the general goes on to say that the drummer boy is the heart of the army. If, during the coming battle, Joby beats his drum lazily, the men will move slowly, lagging by the wayside. But if Joby beats his drum more briskly, the men will mount a well-ordered charge. The sound of the drum will get them to move their knees, stiffen their spines, flare their nostrils, and tighten their hands. The sound will be like steel armor. Men who are shot will feel less pain because their blood has been stirred by the drum. The general then asks Joby whether he is up to the task, pointing out that in his own way, he, Joby, is the general of the army.

Joby tries to reassure the general that he will perform his duty well. The general tells him that in the future, when Joby is older than the general is now, people will ask him what he did at the battle; the general is uncertain whether it will be called the Battle of Owl Creek, the Tennessee River, or Shiloh. The boy will be able to respond that he was the drummer boy at Shiloh. The general then gets up and bids good night to Joby, who is unable to see where the general goes as he disappears into the dark. Joby swallows, wipes his eyes, clears his throat, and turns his drum so that it faces upward, toward the sky. He spends the rest of the night lying next to his drum, feeling its muted thunder as the peach blossoms fall on it.

CHARACTERS

General

The general is unnamed, but presumably he is the commanding general of the army to which Joby is attached. During the night, as Joby thinks of the next day's battle, the general appears and speaks in a kindly fashion to the boy, asking him his name, how long he has been with the army, and whether he has joined up legitimately or has run away from home. He has heard Joby crying and confesses to the boy that he, too, cried the previous night, knowing that the men on both sides are unprepared for the carnage they are about to face. In particular, he recognizes that many of the men are barely out of their boyhood. His principal role, however, is to infuse Joby with courage and a sense of high purpose. He points out to Joby that a drummer boy is the heart of an army, for the steadiness and speed of his drum rolls can inspire the men to fight courageously.

Joby

Joby is the drummer boy of the story's title. When the story opens, Joby is fearful about the battle he knows is coming. He is not sure about his role, and when peach blossoms and a peach pit fall onto the head of his drum, he turns the drum on its side so that he does not have to listen to the portentous sound it makes. As the story progresses, he thinks about the two armies,

which are camped for the night just a mile or so from each other. He hears the whispering of the men, like a wind, as they murmur to themselves and to each other about their fate the following day. Joby is discouraged, for the other men have guns and bayonets to fight with, but he has only his drum, which he regards as being too much like a toy. The drum will not protect him as would gunpowder, a ramrod, and minié balls (that is, conical-headed bullets used in muzzle-loading rifles). Joby hopes that the two armies will simply vanish.

Joby then engages in conversation with the general, who appears before him. He listens to the general, who speaks about the youth of the soldiers, their lack of training, and his own sorrow based on his knowledge that the soldiers mistakenly believe that the war will end soon. He senses that Joby, a mere boy, is fearful and perhaps fails to understand his importance in the coming battle. The general explains to him that his role in communicating with the troops through his drum is vitally important. Joby then, slowly but firmly, turns his drum so that it faces upward toward the sky—a symbolic action that indicates his acceptance of his role and its importance in the battle that will take place the next day.

THEMES

Warrior-Heroes

The American Civil War began in 1861 with a high sense of optimism and pride on both sides. The Confederates, believing that they were fighting to protect a culture and a way of life, thought that they would whip the Yankees of the North and send them back home with their tails between their legs. For their part, Northerners thought that the war would last for no more than weeks, perhaps months, and that the Union would be preserved. On both sides, men enthusiastically joined military units, hoping to win glory on the field of battle. Bradbury hints at this attitude in "The Drummer Boy of Shiloh." He refers to the soldiers' "romantic dreams of battles yet unfought." Joby imagines the soldiers thinking that they will live through the battle: "I'll go home. The band will play. And I'll be there to hear it." He refers to the soldiers' "firm and fiery family devotion, flag-blown patriotism and cocksure immortality." The general goes on

TOPICS FOR FURTHER STUDY

- Conduct research on drummer boys during the nation's early wars, including the Civil War and also the Revolutionary War. What was their purpose? How important were they? Who typically would be made a drummer boy? Present the results of your findings in an oral report for your classmates. If you have any talent for playing the drums, supplement your presentation by playing Civil War drum rolls. (See Sounddogs.com at http://www.sounddogs.com/results.asp?Type=1&CategoryID=1040&SubcategoryID=10.)

- Using "The Drummer Boy of Shiloh" as a source of inspiration, write a poem about the experiences of young men during the Civil War (or any war) on the eve of battle. Post your poem on a blog and invite your classmates to comment on it.

- Locate the words and music for "The Drummer Boy of Shiloh," an 1863 song by William S. Hays written for the magazine *Harper's Weekly*, on the Mudcat Café website at http://www.mudcat.org/@displaysong.cfm?SongID=6191. If you have musical ability, perform the song for your classmates, perhaps enlisting another musician so that one of you plays the tune while the other sings.

- Conduct research into the legend of John Lincoln Clem, who retired from the US Army as a general but who, during the Civil War, served as the drummer boy for the Twenty-Second Regiment Michigan Volunteer Infantry. (At the time of the Civil War, his name was written as "Klem.") To what extent do you believe Bradbury might have based his story on the legend surrounding Clem? Share your findings and thoughts in an oral report.

- The Battle of Shiloh was one of the major early engagements of the Civil War. Conduct online research and locate images of the battle, along with maps; a place to start for maps is the website of the Civil War Trust at http://www.civilwar.org/battlefields/shiloh/maps/shilohmap.html and Stephen G. Hyslop and Neil Kagan's *Atlas of the Civil War: A Complete Guide to the Tactics and Terrain of Battle* (2009). Prepare a PowerPoint presentation for your classmates, walking them through the days before and during the battle.

- Joyce Hansen's *Which Way Freedom* (1992) is a young-adult novel about Obi, a young slave who longs to escape and sees the Civil War as an opportunity to do so. Using this novel as a starting point, write a brief report about the reactions of African Americans, both slaves and freemen, to the advent of the Civil War.

- Joseph Bruchac is an Abenaki Indian who has written fiction for young adults about his tribe. His novel *March toward the Thunder* (2008) tells the story of a fifteen-year-old Abenaki Indian from Canada who fights in the Civil War as part of an Irish brigade. Using this novel to get started, conduct research about the effects of the Civil War on North American Indians. Share your findings with your classmates in an oral report.

- A person who wants to serve in the military simply enlists in one of the branches, the US Army or the US Navy, for example. But during the Civil War, men (and sometimes women in disguise) enlisted in regiments with names like the Third Wisconsin Infantry Regiment or the Twentieth Regiment Massachusetts Volunteer Infantry. Why was the military structured in this way at the time? Conduct research on a Civil War military unit from your state, a state where your family has roots, or one you would like to visit. Locate photos of the unit and share them with your classmates using Flikr or a similar tool.

The Civil War battlefield at Shiloh, Tennessee (© Sherry Yates / ShutterStock.com)

to tell Joby that "more innocents will get shot out of pure Cherokee enthusiasm than ever got shot before." Thus, a key part of Joby's reflections on the eve of battle is the widespread belief that warfare is an arena for heroism and winning the adulation of the community back home.

Adolescence

Joby is just fourteen years old. Many of the soldiers in the army that surrounds him are probably not much older; it has been estimated that up to one hundred thousand Union soldiers (of a total of about two million) were younger than fifteen years of age, even though the official minimum age for enlistment was eighteen; the figure on the Confederate side was likely higher. "The Drummer Boy of Shiloh" emphasizes the youth of the soldiers. Joby reflects on what the men of the other army will do when the battle begins: "a yell, a blind plunge their strategy, raw youth their protection and benediction." Each of the soldiers is referred to as a "man-boy." Later, the general tells Joby, "Owl Creek was full of boys splashing around in the noonday sun just a few hours ago. I fear it will be full of

boys again, just floating, at sundown tomorrow." The youth of many of the soldiers stands in ironic juxtaposition to the enormity of the task ahead of them: to march into battle, to offer themselves as targets for the enemy, and perhaps to die for a cause that many of them may not even fully understand.

Courage and Fear

It is clear that Joby is fearful about the battle that he suspects is to take place the following day. One way in which that fear is exposed is through his behavior with the drum. As he tries to sleep, peach blossoms fall on the drumhead, and Joby panics when he hears the sound of a stray peach pit hitting the drum. In response, he turns the drum on its side, a suggestion that he is fearful and does not want to have anything to do with the drum. Later, Joby reflects that he is without a weapon or a shield: "Me, thought the boy, I got only a drum, two sticks to beat it, and no shield." He thinks of his drum as "worse than a toy in the game to be played tomorrow." When the general appears, it is apparent that Joby has been crying, yet the general himself confesses that he was crying the previous night because he, too, is fearful about impending events. The men in the army surrounding Joby are "exhausted by nervous expectation." Thus, "The Drummer Boy of Shiloh" captures the fear that nearly every soldier must feel on the eve of battle. However, Joby finds his courage, largely through the empathy shown him by the general. After the general leaves, Joby gathers his courage: "He swallowed. He wiped his eyes. He cleared his throat. He settled himself." Then, in a symbolic gesture, "very slowly and firmly, he turned the drum so that it faced up toward the sky." The suggestion is that he now accepts his role and its importance in the coming battle, allowing him to overcome his fear.

STYLE

Irony

"The Drummer Boy of Shiloh" is set in a peach orchard near Owl Creek and the Tennessee River in Tennessee. In the story's first sentence, mention is made of peach blossoms falling from the tree, and that image is repeated in the final sentence of the story. This emphasis on the peach blossoms and peach trees in the spring is reinforced when the general refers to the fuzz of a peach as being like Joby's boyish facial hair. These details are ironic. The following day will witness the horrible carnage of battle. But on the eve of battle, all is peaceful, and the peach blossoms lend an air of almost feminine beauty and serenity to the otherwise masculine scene. That irony is reinforced by the historical fact that *Shiloh* comes from a Hebrew word that means "place of peace."

Metaphor

In "The Drummer Boy of Shiloh," Bradbury makes frequent use of metaphor—a comparison that creates an equivalency between two otherwise differing things. He compares the soldiers' rifles to skeletons in the phrase "similarly strewn steel bones of their rifles." The shape and color of Joby's drum skin is compared to the moon's "great lunar face." The enemy is described as "turning slow, basting themselves with the thought of what they would do when the time came"; the enemy, turning over and over in restless sleep, is compared to something cooking over a fire and being turned on a spit. The soldiers are said to "put on their bravery with their caps." This type of wordplay is technically called

a *syllepsis*, a figure of speech in which a single word or phrase—in this case, "put on"—that governs or modifies two or more other words or phrases—in this case, "bravery" and "caps"— must be understood differently with respect to each of those words. A similar figure of speech is used when the general refers to "taking our sulphur with cannons instead of with molasses"; the reference is to a home remedy compounded of sulphur and molasses that was thought to cleanse the blood.

The fuzzy facial hair of youth is compared to peach fuzz in the line "There's your cheek, fell right off the tree overhead." The soldiers are compared to wild, untrained horses in the phrase "bunch of wild horses on a loose rein." A key line of dialogue in the story is the general's statement "You are the heart of the army," a metaphor that compares Joby and the beat of his drum to a beating heart. The sound of Joby's drum is referred to metaphorically as "muted thunder." Joby listens to his own heart "ruffle away," comparing the beating of his heart to a drum roll (*ruffle*). Another type of metaphor Bradbury uses is *metonymy*, a figure of speech that functions through association. With metonymy, a thing or concept is called not by its own name but by the name of something closely associated with it. Joby identifies the general by his sensory perceptions of him: "And, tobacco, brass, boot polish, salt sweat and leather, the man moved away through the grass."

Simile

Bradbury also uses simile to good effect. While metaphors are implied comparisons, similes are explicit comparisons, usually signaled by such words as *like*, *as*, or *similar to*. Thus, the soldiers' bayonets are said to be "fixed *like* eternal lightning," comparing the shiny metallic bayonets to lightning shining in the moonlight. Joby's imagination converts the sound of a peach pit hitting his drum to that of panic when he thinks the pit "struck once, *like* panic." The whispering of soldiers is compared to the sound of an approaching wind when it is said to be "*like* a natural element." Joby's drum is seen as an ineffective weapon, for it is "worse *than* a toy," and Joby, too, is "no more *than* a toy himself." The marching of the soldiers is explicitly compared to a wave: "their knees would come up in a long line down over that hill, one knee after the other, *like* a wave on the ocean shore." Bradbury reverses the figure when he writes about "waves rolling in *like* a well-ordered cavalry charge to the sand." As a final example, the adrenaline rush of battle is compared to donning armor: "put steel armor all over the men, for blood moving fast in them does indeed make men feel *as if* they'd put on steel."

Personification

At one point the narration reads that "the careless bones of the young men" were "harvested by night and bindled around campfires." In this line, the night is personified—that is, given human characteristics—as a farmer that has gathered the men up like stalks of corn and placed them around the fires; typically, *bindle* is a noun referring to a bundle or sack on a stick such as hobos stereotypically carry, but Bradbury uses it as a verb to suggest objects being bundled together and carried. Another example of personification is contained in the expression that the "sun might not show its face because of what was happening here," suggesting that the sun can feel the human emotion of shame. A third example is the personification of Joby's drum when its face is said to have "peered" at him.

HISTORICAL CONTEXT

"The Drummer Boy of Shiloh" takes place on the eve of the Civil War's Battle of Shiloh, which was fought on April 6 and 7, 1862. The battle is so named because it was fought in the vicinity of a church named Shiloh Meeting House in southwestern Tennessee, just over the border from Corinth, Mississippi. While the battle might not be as famous as some of the Civil War's other great battles—Vicksburg, Antietam, Gettysburg—it is no exaggeration to say that the battle in many respects altered the course of the war.

The Civil War had broken out almost exactly a year earlier, on April 12, 1861, when the Confederacy bombarded Fort Sumter on the South Carolina coast. The first major engagement of the war took place on July 21, 1861, at Manassas Junction, Virginia; because the site of the battlefield was along a branch of the Potomac River called Bull Run, the battle is often called the Battle of Bull Run. (In a historical footnote, the Union tended to name battles after the nearest creek or river; the Confederacy tended to name them after the nearest town or city.) The outcome was a chaotic defeat for the

North, prompting President Abraham Lincoln to call for more deliberate and thorough preparations for war. Money was appropriated, troops were enlisted, and command of the Union's Army of the Potomac (and later of all US land forces) was turned over to the talented and charismatic General George B. McClellan. In the months that followed Bull Run, McClellan imposed firm discipline on his army, rigorously trained the troops under his command, and ensured that the army had more than sufficient logistical support. Only then would he strike at the Confederate capital, Richmond, Virginia. In the end, McClellan was regarded as too hesitant and as being much better at mobilizing, training, and equipping an army than actually fighting with one.

In the meantime, the Union army in the West was under the command of General Henry W. Halleck. (At the time, the American West was the region that encompassed such states as Illinois, Missouri, Arkansas, Kentucky, and Tennessee.) One of Halleck's commanders was General Ulysses S. Grant. From a base in Cairo, Illinois, Grant invaded Tennessee and became an almost overnight hero by capturing Fort Henry and Fort Donelson, Confederate strongholds on the Tennessee and Cumberland Rivers. In the process he took fourteen thousand prisoners of war. He then marched on Corinth, an important railroad junction; the goal of the Union's western armies was to cut off lines of communication and supply along the Mississippi River and its tributaries and to disrupt Confederate railroad transport.

The Confederates, though, were not sitting on their hands. A Confederate force of about forty thousand men under the command of General Albert Sidney Johnston moved west from Decatur, Alabama, to check Grant's advance. (In "The Drummer Boy of Shiloh," Bradbury never specifies which army Joby is with, but the story mentions that he is part of an army of forty thousand, suggesting that he is a Confederate.) While Grant engaged in cautious preparations for an attack on Corinth, Johnston's forces launched a surprise attack on Grant's position on the morning of April 6, 1862 (again suggesting that Joby is to be thought of as a Confederate, for he appears to know or suspect that the attack would begin the next morning). The Union troops were caught totally unprepared; many lost their lives while half-dressed, eating

COMPARE & CONTRAST

- **1862:** The United States of America and the Confederate States of America are engaged in a bloody civil war, fought largely over the issue of slavery.

  1960: The Civil Rights Act of 1960, passed in response to policies that disenfranchised African Americans, is designed to prevent interference with the right to vote.

  Today: Debate over voting rights continues. Several states enforce laws requiring voters to present picture identification; some people contend that these laws interfere with voting rights, particularly the rights of minorities.

- **1862:** Just a week after the Battle of Shiloh, the Confederacy begins drafting men into military service; the Union begins drafting men in 1863.

  1960: The United States drafts men into the military under the provisions of the Selective Training and Service Act, a peacetime draft law passed in 1940.

  Today: The US military is strictly an all-volunteer force, although most men between the ages of eighteen and twenty-six are required to register for the Selective Service System.

- **1862:** Battlefield commanders often communicate with troops through snare drums played by drummer boys; a particular drum roll tells troops to advance or retreat, for example.

  1960: On October 4, the United States launches Project Courier, a tactical military communications satellite.

  Today: The United States and other developed nations rely on advanced communications technologies, including computer systems, to deploy and manage troops and logistics in the field in real time.

---

breakfast, tending to their equipment, or even still sleeping, and military historians continue to wonder how Grant could have been surprised by tens of thousands of men and why he did not post scouting patrols. After a day of furious fighting, the Confederates held a distinct advantage. Fighting resumed the following day, but Grant's forces were fortified with fresh troops that arrived overnight under the command of General Don Carlos Buell. The tide turned, and the exhausted and demoralized Confederates fell back to Corinth. By the time the smoke cleared, thirteen thousand out of sixty-six thousand Union troops had been killed, and the Confederates had lost more than ten thousand. As a point of comparison, about eight thousand Americans died on the battlefield during the *entire* Revolutionary War.

Grant failed to press his advantage, allowing the Confederacy to maintain control of Vicksburg, Mississippi, and the Mississippi River. It was felt in the North that an opportunity had been lost, and as a consequence Grant was relieved of his command (though he would replace McClellan as general of the army in 1864 and later serve as president from 1869 to 1877). Thus, even though Shiloh was a Union victory, Union losses were heavy, and the Confederate army in the West was still standing.

The outcome of the battle had a number of consequences. One was that generals on both sides began to pay far more attention to defensive tactics and fortifications, with the result that future engagements were more likely to be lengthy pitched battles. A second was that the division between North and South was deepened; the bitter animosity that had led to war turned into a kind of ferocious hatred as Americans north and south nursed their wounds and contemplated the loss of their sons and brothers. A primary consequence was recognition on both sides that the war would not end soon. When the

A drummer boy on the battlefield *(© egd | ShutterStock.com)*

war broke out, troops on both sides, as well as their families back home, believed that it would be over in weeks, months at most—a view expressed by the general in "The Drummer Boy of Shiloh." Morale was high, and optimism swelled. The Battle of Shiloh altered those perceptions. If Americans were horrified by the loss of five thousand men at Bull Run, the loss of twenty-three thousand at Shiloh seemed unthinkable. Both sides hunkered down, expecting a lengthy, bloody conflict. Both sides were correct.

CRITICAL OVERVIEW

Bradbury has occupied a unique place in modern American letters. As George Edgar Slusser wrote in the *Dictionary of Literary Biography*, "In a sense he has been the victim of a genre. To consider his work as 'science fiction' or 'fantasy'— no matter how good—is to damn it, for invariably these modes are dismissed as secondary." On the other hand, Willis E. McNelly, in "Two Views: Ray Bradbury—Past, Present, and Future," notes that Bradbury has been "hailed

as a stylist and a visionary" by such writers as Christopher Isherwood and Aldous Huxley and that he "remained for years the darling, almost the house pet, of a literary establishment other wise unwilling to admit any quality in the technological and scientific projections known as science fiction." McNelly goes on to praise Bradbury's writings in glowing terms: "Bradbury's major themes transform the past, present, and future into a constantly shifting kaleidoscope whose brilliance shades into pastels or transforms language into coruscant vibrations through his verbal magic."

Critics have long been drawn to Bradbury's short stories. In a review of his collection *We'll Always Have Paris* in *Library Journal*, Neil Hollands notes approvingly the "humor, empathy, and quirky approach that have been the hallmarks of his career." Roger A. Berger, in a *Library Journal* review of *Bradbury Stories: 100 of His Most Celebrated Tales* (in which "The Drummer Boy of Shiloh" appears), objects that Bradbury's writing can sometimes be "stiff with affectation," but he also grants that the stories are "gently mesmerizing." In a *Booklist* review of the same collection, Ray Olson asserts that

Bradbury has "a raconteur's magnetic style" and calls the collection "storytelling genius for virtually all ages." Finally, a *Kirkus Reviews* contributor, again reviewing *Bradbury Stories*, refers to their "wonder-bearing pages" in which "the fantastic weaves through the banality of everyday life."

Numerous critics have said that although Bradbury wrote novels, poems, and plays, his strong suit was the short story. As Slusser puts it,

> His real mode . . . is short fiction. His plays . . . are all adaptations of stories. More important, his longer prose works too (in some way or another) are derivatives of the tale.

Slusser further explains, "The short novel *Fahrenheit 451* (1953) expands upon an earlier story, 'The Fireman.' Both *The Martian Chronicles* (1950) and *Dandelion Wine* (1957) are frame collections, cycles of sketches and tales given thematic coherence."

"The Drummer Boy of Shiloh," though, is a departure for Bradbury. Rather than employing the mode of science fiction or fantasy set in a dystopian future, he wrote a realistic story set in the historical past. It is impossible to know his motive for writing a story so markedly different from those he typically wrote. But as Rodney M. White notes in "Teaching History Using the Short Story," "through the thoughts of Joby . . . readers experience the impending battle much more meaningfully than by reading textbook accounts that typically present generals' names, dates, places, and results of the battle in a matter-of-fact way." White continues:

> In this story, readers are vividly projected into the camp setting near the little creek on that April night in Tennessee. Through Joby's thoughts and conversations with other soldiers, readers share the loneliness and fear of the night before the battle. They feel the tense atmosphere and dread of what will happen the next day. . . . What becomes clear are the realities of war—that issues and causes blur in the midst of death.

CRITICISM

Michael J. O'Neal

O'Neal holds a PhD in English. In the following essay, he examines the use of figurative language in "The Drummer Boy of Shiloh."

> AT THE END OF THE STORY, BRADBURY, THE READER, AND JOBY COME FULL CIRCLE. JOBY HAS ABSORBED THE WISDOM OF THE GENERAL. HE NOW KNOWS THAT HE WILL PLAY A CRUCIAL ROLE IN THE BATTLE TO COME."

"The Drummer Boy of Shiloh" is rife with figurative language and symbolic action, almost to the extent that the story becomes less a narrative and more an evocative prose poem. That Bradbury would rely on figurative language and symbolism in this story is understandable, for little actually happens: a drummer boy in a Civil War encampment is startled and turns his drum away; he reflects on the soldiers around him and worries about the coming battle; he has a conversation with a general, and as a result, he feels better.

The story succeeds not on the level of plot, for it contains no suspense, no plot twists that startle the reader, no red herrings or misdirection. Nor does it offer an in-depth portrait of a character, for readers learn little of Joby's background, his motivations, his thoughts about the war, or his goals for the future. He says little to the general, giving only a few brief responses to the general's questions and observations, so the reader gains little sense of Joby's voice. Readers' only understanding of Joby comes from their exposure to him in a snippet of time.

Thus, in writing "The Drummer Boy of Shiloh," Bradbury set himself a difficult task. He wanted to create for readers a picture of a boy on the eve of battle and a sense of the boy's initial fear, which is then converted to pride and resolve through his conversation with the general. He also wanted to convey the pathos of the boy's situation: Joby is only fourteen years old, yet the next day he will be expected to leave his gentle peach orchard and march into battle, with soldiers on the other side of the lines firing real bullets and the men on the field shedding real blood. Ultimately, the story prompts readers to reflect not only on the terror that young men the world over must feel when battle looms and the possibility of death draws nigh but also on how sound and empathetic leadership can serve as an effective motivator.

WHAT DO I READ NEXT?

- Bradbury's short story "Downwind from Gettysburg" (1969), from *Bradbury Stories: 100 of His Most Celebrated Tales* (2003), tells the tale of a man who creates a mechanical computerized robot of Abraham Lincoln (who was assassinated just after the end of the Civil War) that is wrecked by a publicity hound named Booth (the name of Lincoln's real-life assassin).

- One participant in the Battle of Shiloh was the author Ambrose Bierce, widely known for his frequently anthologized short story "An Occurrence at Owl Creek Bridge," about a Confederate sympathizer who is to be hanged from the bridge at Owl Creek. Bierce wrote a firsthand account of his experience as a soldier at the Battle of Shiloh, published as "What I Saw of Shiloh" (1881).

- Based on first-person accounts from diaries, memoirs, and journals and written for young adults, Jim Murphy's *The Boys' War: Confederate and Union Soldiers Talk about the Civil War* (1993) provides readers with glimpses of the role boys played in the Civil War.

- Joseph A. Altsheler's *The Guns of Shiloh: A Story of the Great Western Campaign* (1914) is an old-fashioned adventure yarn about the Battle of Shiloh written for young adults.

- Perhaps the definitive novel about the Civil War and its effects on young men is Stephen Crane's classic *The Red Badge of Courage* (1895). The novel takes a hard look at cowardice and heroism in the face of the horrors of war.

- Ann Rinaldi's young-adult novel *Girl in Blue* (2001) provides the perspective of a young girl in the Civil War. Sarah escapes her abusive father in Michigan, dresses as a boy, and enlists in the Union army, serving both as a spy and as a battlefield soldier in Virginia.

- For the nonfiction account of a woman who fought in disguise at the Battle of Shiloh, read Loreta Janeta Velázquez's *The Woman in Battle: A Narrative of the Exploits, Adventures and Travels of Madame Loreta Janeta Velázquez, Otherwise Known as Lieutenant Harry J. Buford, Confederate States Army* (1876). Velázquez, a Cuban by birth, enlisted, fought at Bull Run, was dismissed, and reenlisted in time to fight at Shiloh.

- Among the novels about the Battle of Shiloh is Shelby Foote's *Shiloh* (1991), which is written from the perspective of individual soldiers on both the Union and Confederate sides.

- Readers interested in military history and the political situation in Tennessee before the Civil War might find Thomas L. Connelly's *Civil War Tennessee: Battles and Leaders* (1979) informative.

- William Sumner Dodge is the author of *Robert Henry Hendershot; or, The Brave Drummer Boy of the Rappahannock* (1867), a narrative about a drummer boy who took part in Civil War battles in 1862.

The problem for Bradbury is that his protagonist is only a boy. He has little to say. He can only react to his situation. He forms what is often referred to in fiction as a "primitive consciousness," a term that refers to a literary point of view structured around a character who cannot articulate his or her own responses to events so that the reader, to gain an understanding of the narrative, has to rely on a broader narrative voice. Bradbury could have told readers, in the fully formed thoughts of adults, what Joby was thinking and feeling, but such an approach would have ruined the story's artistry: He might just as well have written a dull, academic-sounding essay with a title like "How Boys Feel When They're Going into Battle and How They Feel Better When

Their General Is Nice to Them." So the artistic problem became how the workings of Joby's mind could be unfolded to the reader without explaining them in a way that is plodding and inartistic.

The story's extensive use of figurative language accomplishes this goal, for figurative language replaces rational exposition with perceptions and reactions. Take, for example, the opening paragraphs. The narration places the action firmly on an April night. The location is a peach orchard, and peach trees are blossoming. The attentive reader knows, then, that the action is taking place in a more southerly location; the peach trees in Minnesota are likely not blooming quite yet. The blossoms fall and strike the drumskin. So, too, does a lingering peach pit. The sound startles the boy, but notice that the narration does not say that "the sound startled the boy, who panicked and jerked upright." Rather, the peach pit "struck once, like panic, which jerked the boy upright." In the silence, then, the boy hears "his own heart ruffle away," the word *ruffle* referring to a low, vibrating drumbeat. What follows is a symbolic action combined with personification: The boy turns the drum on its side so that "its great lunar face peered at him whenever he opened his eyes." At no point in these opening paragraphs does Bradbury tell the reader what to think, nor does he tell the reader what Joby is thinking or feeling. Rather, the emotions of the scene are captured in images, metaphors, and symbolic action that create for the reader a response, a picture. They elicit emotion without explanation.

Bradbury wants his readers to understand the situation of the armies, which are encamped just a mile from each other. Again, he could directly tell his readers, who might have then quickly turned the page of the *Saturday Evening Post* to look at an advertisement for a newfangled television set. But again he relies on figures of speech. The soldiers in the opposing army are "basting" themselves as they toss and turn, trying to sleep. The army is "strewn helter-skelter," like a handful of pick-up sticks. The soldiers' bones are "harvested by night and bindled around campfires." Joby can also see the "strewn steel bones of their rifles, with bayonets fixed like eternal lightning lost in the orchard grass." The narration then turns to Joby, who, without weapons,

> felt his family move yet farther off away in the dark, as if one of those great prairie-burning

trains had chanted them away never to return, leaving him with this drum which was worse than a toy.

Joby's sense of isolation and loneliness is conveyed here entirely by figurative language. The other soldiers are his family. The trains are said to burn the prairies as they pull away. They "chant" the family away, inviting the reader to imagine the chuffing of a train as it disappears into the distance. The drum is compared to a toy; on a literal level, a drum to many youngsters would, in fact, be a toy, but the comparison here takes on poignancy because it is Joby's way of feeling his defenselessness on the field of battle.

This emphasis on figurative language continues after the general appears like an apparition in the night, almost like a ghost come to fortify the young and frightened boy. It is dark, so Joby cannot really see the general, and thus the reader gets no description of him. Once again, Bradbury relies on other sensory perceptions: "He smelled as all fathers should smell, of salt sweat, ginger tobacco, horse and boot leather, and the earth he walked upon." Joby's perceptions continue: "He had many eyes. No, not eyes, brass buttons that watched the boy." Again, all of this relieves Bradbury of the need to offer a set-piece description of the general. The general emits a distinctive masculine smell that tells Joby and the reader all they need to know, and he watches the boy with his personified brass buttons that tell Joby all he needs to know. The reader gains an immediate sensory picture of the two, of man and boy comforting each other in the dark of the night.

Still, the reader would like to have a sense of the general as a fully formed character. The alternative is to allow the general to remain a stick figure who delivers a monologue that is of little artistic interest to the reader. So Bradbury puts a figure of speech into his mouth: referring to the coming battle, he says, "It's wrong, boy, it's wrong as a head put on hind side front and a man marching backward through life." He goes on to say that the battle will be a massacre "if one of their itchy generals decides to picnic his lads on our grass." The ironic contrast between picnicking on a field of grass and fighting a battle on a blood-soaked field adds to the dramatic impact of the scene. These colorful figures of speech create a sense of character in a way that Joby would not have been able to.

Joby, the drummer boy, plays dead during the battle. (© *Jeff Kinsey* | *ShutterStock.com*)

At the end of the story, Bradbury, the reader, and Joby come full circle. Joby has absorbed the wisdom of the general. He now knows that he will play a crucial role in the battle to come. In a symbolic action, he reverses the position of the drum, turning it so that it faces upward, toward the sky. Now, he can "lay next to it, his arm around it, feeling the tremor, the touch, the muted thunder as . . . the peach blossoms fell on the drum." The figure is complete. The reader knows that Joby's frame of mind has been transformed. With the hindsight of history, the reader knows that on an "April night in the year 1862, near the Tennessee River, not far from the Owl Creek, very close to a church named Shiloh," one boy has taken an important step toward becoming a man. And Bradbury never had to say so.

Source: Michael J. O'Neal, Critical Essay on "The Drummer Boy of Shiloh," in *Short Stories for Students*, Gale, Cengage Learning, 2013.

Jim Cherry

In the following interview, Bradbury answers questions regarding spirituality, genre, and the life of a writer.

[Cherry:] You lived in Arizona as a boy?

[Bradbury:] I lived there when I was six in 1926, and for a year when I was twelve. I was a curious kid. When I was six and lived in Tucson, I was on the university grounds all the time, especially the natural science building, which was full of snakes and tarantulas and Gila monsters. They used to throw me off campus, and I'd creep back and hide. Tucson's a very special place to me.

Do you think your peripatetic childhood had an impact on your becoming a writer?

I think that I was born to be a writer—it was genetic. You can't teach that; what you can teach is good habits. When you read my books you can't imagine anyone else writing them.

There seems to be a spiritual quality that runs through your work. Do you subscribe to the Eastern idea of an impersonal God or the Western idea of a personal one?

I have a delicatessen religious outlook—"I'll take some a' deez, some a' doze and some a' deez." I believe in American Indian ideas, ideas of the Far East; they're all fascinating and nothing is proved.

Do you "write drunk and revise sober" or compose everything carefully in your mind before setting it down?

It's got to be an explosion. I get an idea and then, bang! I'm at the typewriter, and two hours later it's done. All of my short stories have taken two or three hours.

You don't consider yourself a science-fiction writer. Instead, you're a fantasy writer, is that correct?

Correct.

There's a timelessness to your work.

It's mythological—I write Greek myths, Roman myths, Egyptian myths. It's metaphorical, but there's no science in them. The only book I've written that's science fiction is *Fahrenheit 451*. That's political and psychological science fiction.

In that way, your book is like A Clockwork Orange.

Oh, don't say that! That's a sick book! I hate *A Clockwork Orange*. It's so vulgar. The characters don't lift you up in any way.

Do you have any idea how many copies of Martian Chronicles *you've sold?*

Oh, I don't know, it's never been a bestseller. It only sold five thousand copies its first year. But, it's been a cumulative bestseller. You sell fifty thousand to one hundred thousand paperbacks a year for fifty years and you have quite a few million. None of my books sell worth a damn when they first come out.

How many movies have been made from your books?

Oh, four or five. *Illustrated Man*, which is no good; *Something Wicked This Way Comes*, which was very good. *Fahrenheit 451*, which had things missing but was still a good job. *Martian Chronicles* on TV was a bore, but we're going to do it over next year as a theatrical movie.

Do you hand the book over to the movie studio and let them do their thing?

No, I have to be in there, or I won't let them do it.

Did you see computers and the Internet coming?

I could see them coming, but nobody could predict some of the problems that would be connected to that.

Such as?

Well, all this business with Napster, and stealing all that music—thieving millions of dollars of music away from people without paying for it. That's ridiculous. They should be destroyed. They're behaving like the Russians and Chinese, who've been stealing my books for forty years.

What do you think of alien visitors and UFOs?

No such, no way. It's ridiculous; there's absolutely no proof anywhere, at any time.

You've never driven a car?

I never learned. I was too poor. Writers can't afford things like that. My wife and I didn't have enough money to buy a car till we were thirty-seven and thirty-eight—then she learned to drive. Becoming a writer is a very slow process and there's not much money in it for a long time.

Your musical Dandelion Wine *is set to play in L.A.*

I did it first at Lincoln Center thirty years ago; now we're bringing it back, at the Colony Theater in Burbank.

What are you working on now?

I have a new book of essays called *A Chapbook for Burnt-Out Priests, Rabbis and Ministers*, a book of philosophic essays, a new book called *One More for the Road*, a novel *From the Dust Returned*, and a book of poetry. That's more than enough, don't you think?

Source: Jim Cherry, "Future Tense Sci-Fi Legend Bradbury Going Strong," in *Conversations with Ray Bradbury*, edited by Steven L. Aggelis, University of Mississippi Press, 2004, pp. 191–93.

A. James Stupple

In the following excerpt, Stupple explores the relationship between the past and the future in Bradbury's short stories.

Anyone who has ever watched those classic "Flash Gordon" serials must have been puzzled by the incongruous meeting of the past and the future which runs through them. Planet Mongo is filled with marvelous technological advancements. Yet, at the same time, it is a world which is hopelessly feudal, filled with endless sword play and courtly intrigues. It is as if we travel

> CHANGE AND PROGRESS CALL FOR A
> REJECTION AND A SLOUGHING OFF. THIS PLACES A
> GREAT STRESS UPON THE SCIENCE FICTION WRITER,
> FOR PERHAPS MORE THAN ANY OTHER LITERARY
> GENRE, SCIENCE FICTION IS DEPENDENT UPON
> TRADITIONS—ITS OWN CONVENTIONS OF
> CHARACTER, PLOT, SETTING, 'SPECIAL EFFECTS,'
> EVEN IDEAS."

deep within the future only to meet instead the remote and archaic past. This is not, however, a special effect peculiar to adolescent space operas. On the contrary, this overlapping of past and future is one of the most common features of science fiction. It is found, for example, in such highly acclaimed works as Frank Herbert's *Dune* and Ursula LeGuin's *The Left Hand of Darkness*, futuristic novels whose settings are decidedly "medieval." A similar effect is also created in such philosophical science fiction novels as Isaac Asimov's *Foundation* trilogy, Walter Miller's *A Canticle for Leibowitz*, and Anthony Burgess' *The Wanting Seed*. In each of these works a future setting allows the novelist an opportunity to engage in an historiographical analysis; in each the future provides the distance needed for a study of the patterns of the past. But of all the writers of science fiction who have dealt with this meeting of the past and the future, it is Ray Bradbury whose treatment has been the deepest and most sophisticated. What has made Bradbury's handling of this theme distinctive is that his attitudes and interpretations have changed as he came to discover the complexities and the ambiguities inherent in it.

Bradbury began to concentrate upon this subject early in his career in *The Martian Chronicles* (1951). In a broad sense, the past in this work is represented by the Earth—a planet doomed by nuclear warfare, a "natural" outgrowth of man's history. To flee from this past, Earthmen begin to look to a future life on Mars, a place where the course of man's development has not been irrevocably determined. But getting

a foothold on Mars was no easy matter, as the deaths of the members of the first two expeditions show. To Captain Black's Third Expedition, however, Mars seems anything but an alien, inhospitable planet, for as their rocket lands in April of the year 2000, the Earthmen see what looks exactly like an early twentieth century village. Around them they see the cupolas of old Victorian mansions, neat, whitewashed bungalows, elm trees, maples and chestnuts. Initially Black is skeptical. The future cannot so closely resemble the past. Sensing that something is wrong, he refuses to leave the ship. Finally one of his crewmen argues that the similarity between this Martian scene and those of his American boyhood may indicate that there is some order to the universe after all—that perhaps there is a supreme being who actually does guide and protect mankind.

Black agrees to investigate. Setting foot on Martian soil, the Captain enters a peaceful, delightful world. It is "a beautiful spring day" filled with the scent of blossoming flowers and the songs of birds. After the flux of space travel it must have appeared to have been a timeless, unchanging world—a static piece of the past. But Black is certain that this is Mars and persists in his attempt to find a rational explanation. His logical mind, however, makes it impossible for him to accept any facile solutions. Eventually, though, despite his intellectual rigor, the Captain begins to succumb to the charms of stasis:

> In spite of himself, Captain John Black felt a great peace come over him. It had been thirty years since he had been in a small town, and the buzzing of spring bees on the air lulled and quieted him, and the fresh look of things was a balm to his soul.

As soon as he begins to weaken, he learns, from a lemonade-sipping matron, that this is the year 1926 and that the village is Green Town, Illinois, Black's own home town. The Captain now *wants* to believe in what he sees and begins to delude himself by theorizing that an unknown early twentieth century expedition came to Mars and that the colonizers, desperately homesick, created such a successful image of an Earth-like reality that they had actually begun to believe that this illusion was reality. Ironically, this is precisely what is done by Black and his crew. And it kills them.

Since by this time the Earthmen had become completely vulnerable to the seductiveness of this world of security and stasis, they now unreservedly accept "Grandma Lustig's" claim that "all we know is here we are, alive again, and no questions asked. A second chance." At this point the action moves rapidly. The remainder of the crew abandons ship and joins in a "homecoming" celebration. At first Black is furious at this breach of discipline, but soon loses his last trace of skepticism when he meets Edward, his long-dead "brother." Quickly, he is taken back to his childhood home, "the old house on Oak Knoll Avenue," where he is greeted by an archetypal set of midwestern parents: "In the doorway, Mom, pink, plump, and bright. Behind her, pepper-gray, Dad, his pipe in his hand." Joyfully the Captain runs "like a child" to meet them. But later, in the apparent security of the pennant-draped bedroom of his youth, Black's doubts arise anew. He begins to realize that all of this could be an elaborate reconstruction, culled from his psyche by some sophisticated Martian telepathy, created for the sole purpose of isolating the sixteen members of the Third Expedition. Recognizing the truth too late, the Captain is killed by his Martian brother as he leaves his boyhood "home" to return to the safety of the rocket ship.

Bradbury's point here is clear: Black and his men met their deaths because of their inability to forget, or at least resist, the past. Thus, the story of this Third Expedition acts as a metaphor for the book as a whole. Again and again the Earthmen make the fatal mistake of trying to recreate an Earth-like past rather than accept the fact that this is Mars—a different, unique new land in which they must be ready to make personal adjustments. Hauling Oregon lumber through space, then, merely to provide houses for nostalgic colonists exceeds folly; it is only one manifestation of a psychosis which leads to the destruction not only of Earth, but, with the exception of a few families, of Mars as well.

As a genre, science fiction ... must deal with the future and with technological progress. This is its lifeblood and what gives it its distinctiveness. In order to enter the future, however, if only in a theoretical, purely speculative sense, one is forced to come to grips with the past. Change and progress call for a rejection and a sloughing off. This places a great stress upon the science fiction writer, for perhaps more than any other literary genre, science fiction is dependent upon traditions—its own conventions of character, plot, setting, "special effects," even ideas. It is

as stylized an art form as one can find today in America. It is therefore ironic that such a conventionalized genre should be called upon to be concerned with the unconventional—with the unpredictability of change and process. In other words, this stasis-change conflict, besides being a function of Bradbury's own history and personality, also seems to be built into the art form itself. What distinguishes Bradbury and gives his works their depth is that he seems to be aware that a denial of the past demands a denial of that part of the self which is the past. As an examination of *I Sing the Body Electric*, his latest collection of short stories, will show, he has not been able to come to any lasting conclusion. Instead, he has come to recognize the ambiguity, the complexity, and the irony within this theme.

Of the stories in *I Sing the Body Electric* which develop the idea that the past is destructive and must be rejected before peace can be achieved, the most intense and suggestive is "Night Call Collect." In this grim little tale, eighty-year-old Emil Barton has been living for the past sixty years as the last man on Mars when he is shocked to receive a telephone call from, of all people, himself. In the depths of his loneliness Barton had tinkered with the possibilities of creating a disembodied voice which might autonomously carry on conversations. Now suddenly in the year 2097, long after he had forgotten about this youthful diversion, his past, in the form of his younger self, contacts him. Finding himself in a world peopled only by the permutations of his own self, the "elder" Barton tries desperately to break out of this electronic solipsism. He fails, however, and begins to feel "the past drowning him." Soon his younger self even becomes bold enough to warn him, "'All right, old man, its war! Between us. Between me.'" Bradbury has obviously added a new twist to his theme. Instead of the future denying the past, it is reversed. Now the past, in order to maintain its existence, must kill off the present. Young Barton now tells his "future" self that he "'had to eliminate you some way, so I could live, if you call a transcription living.'" As the old man dies, it is obvious that Bradbury has restated his belief that the past, if held on to too tightly, can destroy. But there is an added dimension here. At the end of the story it is no longer clear which is the past, which is the present, and which is the future. Is the past the transcribed voice of the "younger" twenty-four-year-old, or is it the *old* man living at a later date in time? Or perhaps they are but two manifestations of the same temporal reality, both the "present" and the "future" being forgotten?

Of the stories in this collection one contradicts "Night Call Collect" by developing the idea that the past can be a positive, creative force. "I Sing the Body Electric" opens with the death of a mother. But, as in so many of Bradbury's writings, there is a possibility of a second chance. "Fantocinni, Ltd." offers "the first humanoid-genre minicircuited, rechargeable AC-DC Mark V Electrical Grandmother." This time the second chance succeeds: the electric grandmother is the realization of a child's fantasy. She can gratify all desires and pay everyone in the family all the attention he or she wants. Appropriately, the grandmother arrives at the house packed in a "sarcophagus," as if it were a mummy. Despite the pun, the machine is indeed a mummy, as the narrator makes clear:

> We knew that all our days were stored in her, and that any time we felt we might want to know what we said at x hour at x second at x afternoon, we just named that x and with amiable promptitude . . . she should deliver forth x incident.

The sarcophagus in which this relic was packed was covered with "hieroglyphics of the future." At first this seems to be only another of those gratuitous "special effects" for which science fiction writers are so notorious. After further consideration, however, those arcane markings can be seen a symbol for the kind of ultra-sophisticated technology of which the grandmother is an example. Thus, both the future and the past are incarnated within the body of this machine. The relationship between the two is important, for what the story seems to suggest is that what the future (here seen as technological progress) will bring is the static, familiar, secure world of the past.

There is one other story in this collection which is important because in it is found one of Bradbury's most sophisticated expositions of the subtle complexities of this theme. "Downwind from Gettysburg" is, once again, a tale about a second chance. Using the well-known Disneyland machine as his model, Bradbury's story concerns a mechanical reproduction of Abraham Lincoln. In itself, this Lincoln-robot is a good thing. The past has been successfully captured and the beloved President lives again, if only in facsimile. Within this limited framework, then, the "past" is a positive force. But there are

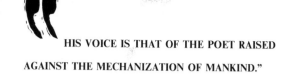

HIS VOICE IS THAT OF THE POET RAISED AGAINST THE MECHANIZATION OF MANKIND."

complications, for just as Lincoln gets a second chance, so does his murderer. Just as John Wilkes Booth assassinated a Lincoln, so does Norman Llewellyn Booth. Thus, as Bradbury had discovered through his years of working with this theme, the past is not one-dimensional. It is at once creative and destructive. It can give comfort, and it can unsettle and threaten. Clearly, then, this story is an important one within Bradbury's canon, for it is just this set of realizations which he had been steadily coming to during two decades of writing.

Source: A. James Stupple, "Two Views: The Past, the Future, and Ray Bradbury," in *Voices for the Future: Essays on Major Science Fiction Writers*, Bowling Green University Popular Press, 1976, pp. 175–84.

Willis E. McNelly

In the following excerpt, McNelly purports that Bradbury's short fiction is thematically tied to mainstream American tradition.

Ray Bradbury, hailed as a stylist and a visionary by critics such as Gilbert Higher and authors such as Aldous Huxley and Christopher Isherwood, remained for years the darling, almost the house pet, of a literary establishment other wise unwilling to admit any quality in the technological and scientific projections known as science fiction. Within the field of science fiction itself, Bradbury's star zoomed like the *Leviathan '99* comet he later celebrated in a significant but ill-fated dramatic adaptation of the *Moby-Dick* myth. Fans pointed to Bradbury with ill-concealed pride, as if to prove that, at least with him, science fiction had come of age and deserved major critical attention.

Certainly America's best-known science fiction writer, Bradbury has been anthologized in over 300 different collections. His own individual works number in the dozens and have been translated into even more languages. After some ten million words—his own estimate—he feels almost physically ill unless he can spend four hours a day at the typewriter. His aim is to work successfully in virtually every written medium before he changes his last typewriter ribbon. His plays have been successfully produced both in Los Angeles and off Broadway. He is currently researching the history of Halloween for a TV special, and he still collects his share of rejection slips for short stories, novellas, or movie scripts, with a larger share of acceptances.

Bradbury's major themes transform the past, present, and future into a constantly shifting kaleidoscope whose brilliance shades into pastels or transforms language into coruscant vibrations through his verbal magic. Contemporary literature to reflect its age, he believes, must depict man existing in an increasingly technological era, and the ability to fantasize thus becomes the ability to survive. He himself is a living evocation of his own theory—a sport, a throwback to an earlier age when life was simpler. Resident of a city, Los Angeles, where the automobile is god and the freeway its prophet, Bradbury steadfastly refuses to drive a car. He has no simplistic anti-machine phobia; rather his reliance on taxicabs or buses springs from the hegira his family made from Waukegan, Illinois, to Los Angeles during the depths of the Depression when he was 14. The roads, he recalls, were strewn with the hulks of broken cars. Since that time his continual concern has been the life of man, not the death of machines. Man must be the master of the machine, not its slave or robot. Bradbury's art, in other words, like that of W. B. Yeats, whom he greatly admires, is deeply dependent upon life. Like Yeats in "The Circus Animals' Desertion," Bradbury must ". . . lie down where all the ladders start, / in the foul rag-and-bone shop of the heart."

If Bradbury's ladders lead to Mars, whose chronicler he has become, or to the apocalyptic future of *Fahrenheit 451*, the change is simply one of direction, not of intensity. He is a visionary who writes not of the impediments of science, but of its effects upon man. *Fahrenheit 451*, after all, is not a novel about the technology of the future, and is only secondarily concerned with censorship or bookburning. In actuality it is the story of Bradbury, disguised as Montag, and his lifelong love affair with books. If the love of a man and a woman is worth notarizing in conventional fiction, so also is the love of a man and an idea. A man may have a wife or a mistress or two in his lifetime, and the situation may become the valuable seedstuff of literature.

However, that same man may in the same lifetime have an endless series of affairs with books, and the offspring can become great literature. For that reason, Bradbury feels that Truffaut was quite successful in translating the spirit of the novel, and the viewer who expects futuristic hardware or science fiction gimmickry will be disappointed in the motion picture. "Look at it through the eyes of the French impressionists," Bradbury suggests. "See the poetic romantic vision of Pissaro, Monet, Renoir, Seurat, or Manet that Truffaut evokes in the film, and then remember that this method was his metaphor to capture the metaphor in my novel."

"Metaphor" is an important word to Bradbury. He uses it generically to describe a method of comprehending one reality and then expressing that same reality so that the reader will see it with the intensity of the writer. His use of the term, in fact, strongly resembles T. S. Eliot's view of the objective correlative. Bradbury's metaphor in *Fahrenheit 451* is the burning of books; in *The Illustrated Man*, a moving tattoo; and pervading all of his work, the metaphor becomes a generalized nostalgia that can best be described as a nostalgia for the future.

Another overwhelming metaphor in his writing is one derived from Jules Verne and Herman Melville—the cylindrical shape of the submarine, the whale, or the space ship. It becomes a mandala, a graphic symbol of Bradbury's view of the universe, a space-phallus. Bradbury achieved his first "mainstream" fame with his adaptation of Melville's novel for the screen, after Verne had aroused his interest in science fiction. *Moby-Dick* may forever remain uncapturable in another medium, but Bradbury's screenplay was generally accepted as being the best thing about an otherwise ordinary motion picture. John Huston's vision was perhaps more confining than Ray Bradbury's.

Essentially a romantic, Bradbury belongs to the great frontier tradition. He is an exemplar of the Turner thesis, and the blunt opposition between a tradition-bound Eastern establishment and Western vitality finds itself mirrored in his writing. The metaphors may change, but the conflict in Bradbury is ultimately between human vitality and the machine, between the expanding individual and the confining group, between the capacity for wonder and the stultification of conformity. These tensions are a continual source for him, whether the collection is named *The Golden Apples of the Sun, Dandelion Wine,* or *The Martian Chronicles.* Thus, to use his own terminology, nostalgia for either the past or future is a basic metaphor utilized to express these tensions. Science fiction is the vehicle.

Ironic detachment combined with emotional involvement—these are the recurring tones in Bradbury's work, and they find their expression in the metaphor of "wilderness." To Bradbury, America is a wilderness country and hers a wilderness people. There was first the wilderness of the sea, he maintains. Man conquered that when he discovered this country and is still conquering it today. Then came the wilderness of the land. He quotes, with obvious approval, Fitzgerald's evocation at the end of *The Great Gatsby*: ". . . the fresh, green breast of the new world . . . for a transitory enchanted moment man must have held his breath in the presence of this continent . . . face to face for the last time in history with something commensurate to his capacity for wonder."

For Bradbury the final, inexhaustible wilderness is the wilderness of space. In that wilderness, man will find himself, renew himself. There, in space, as atoms of God, mankind will live forever. Ultimately, then, the conquest of space becomes a religious quest. The religious theme in his writing is sounded directly only on occasion, in such stories as "The Fire Balloons," where two priests try to decide if some blue fireballs on Mars have souls, or "The Man," where Christ leaves a far planet the day before an Earth rocket lands. Ultimately the religious theme is the end product of Bradbury's vision of man; the theme is implicit in man's nature.

Bradbury's own view of his writing shows a critical self-awareness. He describes himself essentially as a short story writer, not a novelist, whose stories seize him, shake him, and emerge after a two or three hour tussle. It is an emotional experience, not an intellectual one; the intellectualization comes later when he edits. To be sure, Bradbury does not lack the artistic vision for large conception or creation. The novel form is simply not his normal medium. Rather he aims to objectify or universalize the particular. He pivots upon an individual, a specific object, or particular act, and then shows it from a different perspective or a new viewpoint. The result can become a striking insight into the ordinary, sometimes an ironic comment on our limited vision.

An early short story, "The Highway," illustrates this awareness of irony. A Mexican peasant wonders at the frantic, hurtling stream of traffic flowing north. He is told by an American who stops for water that the end of the world has come with the out-break of the atom war. Untouched in his demi-Eden, Hernando calls out to his burro as he plows the rain-fresh land below the green jungle, above the deep river. "What do they mean 'the world?'" he asks himself, and continues plowing.

Debate over whether or not Bradbury is, in the end, a science fiction writer, is fruitless when one considers this story or dozens like it. The only "science" in the story is the "atom war" somewhere far to the north, away from the ribbon of concrete. All other artifacts of man in the story—the automobile, a hubcap, a tire—provide successive ironies to the notion that while civilization may corrupt, it does not do so absolutely. A blownout tire may have brought death to the driver of a car, but it now provides Hernando with sandals; a shattered hubcap becomes a cooking pan. Hernando and his wife and child live in a prelapsarian world utilizing the gifts of the machine in primitive simplicity. These people recall the Noble Savage myth; they form a primary group possessing the idyllic oneness of true community. The strength of Hernando, then, is derived from the myth of the frontier; the quality and vigor of life derive from, indeed are dependent upon, the existence of the frontier.

Yet irony piles on irony: the highway—any highway—leads in two directions. The Americans in this fable form a seemingly endless flowing stream of men and vehicles. They ride northward toward cold destruction, leaving the tropical warmth of the new Eden behind them. Can we recreate the past, as Gatsby wondered? Perhaps, suggests Bradbury, if we re-incarnate the dreams of our youth and reaffirm the social ethic of passionate involvement. And nowhere does he make this moral quite as clear as in *Fahrenheit 451.*

Originally cast as a short story, "The Fireman," *Fahrenheit 451* underwent a number of transmutations before finding its final form. From the short story it became an unpublished novella, "Fire, Fire, Burn Books!" and was again transformed by twenty days of high speed writing into the novel. An examination of a photocopy of the original first draft of "The Fireman," reveals how carefully Bradbury works. His certainty with words makes for extremely clean copy: three or four revisions on the first page; none on the second. He adds an adverb, "silently"; cuts an unnecessary sentence; sharpens the verb "spoke" to "whispered"; eliminates another sentence; anglicizes a noun. Nothing more. Yet the artistry is there, the clean-limbed expressive prose, the immediacy of the situation heightened by the terseness of the dialogue, the compounded adjectives, the brevity and condensation everywhere evident.

Inspection of his rewrite of the same page shows some further small but significant changes, changes that give Bradbury's prose its evocative poetic quality. Note the modifications in the following sentences: "Mr. Montag sat among the other Fire Men in the Fire House, and he heard the voice tell the time of morning, the hour, the day, the year, and he shivered." This becomes sharper, more intense: "Mr. Montag sat stiffly among the other Fire Men in the Fire House, heard the voice-clock mourn out the cold hour and the cold year, and shivered." The voice now "mourns," not "tells," and the appeal to the senses is clarified, the general made specific as "some night jet-planes... flying" becomes "five hundred jet-planes screamed." These changes may be minor, to be sure, but they indicate the method of the writer at work. Titles which Bradbury provided to successive drafts indicate something of the way his mind moves: "The Fireman," "The Hearth and the Salamander," "The Son of Icarus," "Burning Bright," "Find Me in Fire," "Fire, Fire, Burn Books!" These metamorphosed into *Fahrenheit 451*, as anguished a plea for the freedom to read as the mid-twentieth century has produced.

Yet even *Fahrenheit 451* illustrates his major themes: the freedom of the mind; the evocation of the past; the desire for Eden; the integrity of the individual; the allurements and traps of the future. At the end of the novel, Montag's mind has been purified, refined by fire, and phoenix-like, Montag—hence mankind—rises from the ashes of the destructive, self-destroying civilization. "'Never liked cities,' said the man who was Plato," as Bradbury hammers home his message at the end of the novel. "'Always felt that cities owned men, that was all, and used men to keep themselves going, to keep the machines oiled and dusted'" ("The Fireman").

The leader of the book-memorizers at the end of the novel is significantly named Granger, a farmer, a shepherd guiding his flock of books along the road to a new future, a new Eden. "Our way is simpler," Granger says, "and better and the thing we wish to do is keep the knowledge intact and safe and not to anger or excite anyone, for then if we are destroyed the knowledge is most certainly dead.... So we wait quietly for the day when the machines are dented junk and then we hope to walk by and say, here we are, to those who survive this war, and we'll say Have you come to your senses now? Perhaps a few books will do you some good."

This vision of the future which Bradbury provides at the end of *Fahrenheit 451* shows his essentially optimistic character. In fact, Bradbury seized upon the hatreds abroad in 1953 when the book was written, and shows that hatred, war, desecration of the individual are all self-destructive. Bradbury's 1953 vision of hatred becomes extrapolated to a fire which consumes minds, spirits, men, ideas, books. Out of the ashes and rubble revealed by this projected vision, Bradbury reveals one final elegiac redemptive clash of past, present, and future:

> Montag looked at the mens' faces, old all of them, in the firelight, and certainly tired. Perhaps he was looking for a brightness, a resolve, a triumph over tomorrow that wasn't really there, perhaps he expected these men to be proud with the knowledge they carried, to glow with the wisdom as lanterns glow with the fire they contain. But all the light came from the campfire here, and these men seemed no different than any other man who has run a long run, searched a long search, seen precious things destroyed, seen old friends die, and now, very late in time, were gathered together to watch the machines die, or hope they might die, even while cherishing a last paradoxical love for those very machines which could spin out a material with happiness in the warp and terror in the woof, so interblended that a man might go insane trying to tell the design to himself and his place in it. They weren't at all certain that what they carried in their heads might make every future dawn brighter, they were sure of nothing save that the books were on file behind their solemn eyes and that if man put his mind to them properly something of dignity and happiness might be regained.

What has been Ray Bradbury's contribution to science fiction? The question might well be rephrased: What has been Ray Bradbury's contribution to mid-twentieth century American literature? Neither question is easy to answer without risking the dangers of over-generalization. From the viewpoint of science fiction, Bradbury has proved that quality writing is possible in that much-maligned genre. Bradbury is obviously a careful craftsman, an ardent wordsmith whose attention to the niceties of language and its poetic cadences would have marked him as significant even if he had never written a word about Mars.

His themes, however, place him squarely in the middle of the mainstream of American life and tradition. His eyes are set firmly on the horizon-Frontier where dream fathers mission and action mirrors illusion. And if Bradbury's eyes lift from the horizon to the stars, the act is merely an extension of the vision all Americans share. His voice is that of the poet raised against the mechanization of mankind. Perhaps, in the end, he can provide his own best summary:

> The machines themselves are empty gloves. And the hand that fills them is always the hand of man. This hand can be good or evil. Today we stand on the rim of Space, and man, in his immense tidal motion is about to flow out toward far new worlds, but man must conquer the seed of his own self-destruction. Man is half-idealist, half-destroyer, and the real and terrible thing is that he can still destroy himself before reaching the stars. I see man's self-destructive half, the blind spider fiddling in the venomous dark, dreaming mushroom-cloud whispers, shaking a handful of atoms like a necklace of dark beads. We are now in the greatest age of history, capable of leaving our home planet behind us, of going off into space on a tremendous voyage of survival. Nothing must be allowed to stop this voyage, our last great wilderness trek.
>
> [William F. Nolan, "Bradbury: Prose Poet in an Age of Space," *F&SF*, May 1963]

Source: Willis E. McNelly, "Two Views: Ray Bradbury—Past, Present, and Future," in *Voices for the Future: Essays on Major Science Fiction Writers*, Bowling Green University Popular Press, 1976 pp. 167–75.

SOURCES

Aggelis, Steven L., ed., Introduction to *Conversations with Ray Bradbury*, University Press of Mississippi, 2004, pp. xi–xxv.

"American Civil War Soldier Web*Quest*," Civil War Voices: Soldier Studies, http://www.soldierstudies.org/index.php?action=webquest_1 (accessed June 28, 2012).

"Army Tactical Communication Network Organization Reflects on Its Rich History," DefenceTalk, April 24, 2012, http://www.defencetalk.com/army-tactical-communication-network-organization-reflects-on-its-rich-history-41910/ (accessed June 26, 2012).

Berger, Roger A., Review of *Bradbury Stories: 100 of His Most Celebrated Tales*, in *Library Journal*, August 2003, Vol. 128, No. 13, p. 138.

Bradbury, Ray, "The Drummer Boy of Shiloh," in *Bradbury Stories: 100 of His Most Celebrated Tales*, William Morrow, 2003, pp. 54–59.

Fischer, Hannah, "American War and Military Operations Casualties: Lists and Statistics," U.S. Navy Department Library website, July 13, 2005, http://www.history.navy.mil/library/online/american%20war%20casualty.htm (accessed June 26, 2012).

Garraty, John A., *The American Nation*, 2nd ed., Harper and Row, 1971, pp. 477–78, 483–84.

George, Lynell, "Ray Bradbury Dies at 91; Author Lifted Fantasy to Literary Heights," KWCH.com (Wichita, Kansas), June 6, 2012, http://www.kwch.com/news/national/sns-la-me-ray-bradbury-20120607,0,4258779.story?page=1 (accessed June 24, 2012).

Hollands, Neil, Review of *We'll Always Have Paris: Stories*, in *Library Journal*, Vol. 134, No. 1, January 1, 2009, p. 86.

McNelly, Willis E., "Two Views: Ray Bradbury—Past, Present, and Future," in *Voices for the Future: Essays on Major Science Fiction Writers*, Bowling Green University Popular Press, 1976, pp. 167–75.

Muchowski, Keith, "Conscription (Civil War)," in *The Encyclopedia of Arkansas History and Culture* website, http://www.encyclopediaofarkansas.net/encyclopedia/entry-detail.aspx?search=1&entryID=6400 (accessed June 26, 2012).

Nilsson, Jeff, "The *Post* Mourns Ray Bradbury," in *Saturday Evening Post*, June 6, 2010, http://www.saturdayeveningpost.com/2012/06/06/art-entertainment/post-mourns-ray-bradbury.html (accessed June 23, 2012).

Olson, Ray, Review of *Bradbury Stories: 100 of His Most Celebrated Tales*, in *Booklist*, Vol. 99, No. 21, July 2003, p. 1844.

Review of *Bradbury Stories: 100 of His Most Celebrated Tales*, in *Kirkus Reviews*, Vol. 71, No. 12, June 15, 2003, p. 834.

"Selective Service Records," National Archives website, http://www.archives.gov/st-louis/archival-programs/other-records/selective-service.html (accessed June 26, 2012).

"Shiloh," Civil War Trust website, http://www.civilwar.org/battlefields/shiloh.html (accessed June 23, 2012).

Slusser, George Edgar, "Ray Bradbury," in *Dictionary of Literary Biography*, Vol. 2, *American Novelists since World War II, First Series*, edited by Jeffrey Helterman and Richard Layman, Gale Research, 1978, pp. 60–65.

"Teaching with Primary Sources across Tennessee: Women and the Civil War," Middle Tennessee State University Library website, http://library.mtsu.edu/tps/Women_and_the_Civil_War.pdf (accessed June 27, 2012).

White, Rodney M., "Teaching History Using the Short Story," in *Clearing House*, Vol. 66, No. 5, May–June 1993, pp. 305–306.

Winters, Kelly, "Ray Bradbury," in *Scribner Encyclopedia of American Lives*, edited by Arnold Markoe and Kenneth T. Jackson, Charles Scribner's Sons, 2003.

FURTHER READING

Cottrell, Steve, *Civil War in Tennessee*, Pelican, 2001.
This book, illustrated by Andy Thomas, examines the major Civil War battles fought in Tennessee. Among them were the battles of Lookout Mountain, Chickamauga, and Stones River, as well as the Battle of Shiloh.

Foote, Shelby, *The Civil War: A Narrative*, 3 vols., Vintage, 1986.
This three-volume set is perhaps the definitive history of the Civil War for the nonspecialist reader. Volume 1 is *Fort Sumter to Perryville*, volume 2 is *Fredericksburg to Meridian*, and volume 3 is *Red River to Appomattox*.

Mogen, David, *Ray Bradbury*, Twayne, 1986.
This volume is part of the Twayne United States Authors Series. It provides a critical overview of Bradbury's work, written with younger readers in mind.

Reid, Robin Anne, *Ray Bradbury: A Critical Companion*, Greenwood, 2000.
As the title suggests, this volume is a critical guide to Bradbury's major works. It includes discussion of plot, character development, themes, setting, and an "alternative perspective" on the work being discussed. The book is suitable for young-adult readers.

Weller, Sam, *The Bradbury Chronicles: The Life of Ray Bradbury*, Harper Perennial, 2006.
This volume is an authorized biography of the author by a journalist, who interviewed Bradbury himself as well as members of his family, his friends, and his editors. Weller was also given access to archival material, including letters, photographs, and other documents.

SUGGESTED SEARCH TERMS

Ray Bradbury

Bradbury AND The Drummer Boy of Shiloh

Battle of Shiloh

Civil War

Civil War AND western theater

Ulysses S. Grant

Albert Sidney Johnston

drummer boys AND Civil War

Fahrenheit 451 AND Bradbury

Martian Chronicles AND Bradbury

Machineries of Joy AND Bradbury

The Egg

SHERWOOD ANDERSON

1920

Sherwood Anderson, the author of "The Egg," is widely considered to be one of the masters of American fiction and, in particular, one of the great visionaries who first saw what could be done in the short story format. Among his admirers were such literary heavyweights as William Faulkner and Ernest Hemingway, both of whom studied Anderson's style and sought his advice about writing. The stories that show off Anderson's revolutionary style include the ones that make up his classic 1919 collection *Winesburg, Ohio* and a few others, including "The Egg," which was published in 1920, when he was at the height of his talent.

This tragicomic story involves a young man growing up in rural Ohio at the end of the nineteenth century. As his mother focuses on what it will take to make him a success in the world, his father struggles to make the family financially stable. They run a chicken farm, and the narrator explains in detail how being isolated on a farm with the chickens drives him to despise the stupid, frail creatures. When the family buys a diner near town, to give the boy a chance to attend school, the father convinces himself that he can bring in customers by being witty and entertaining. These are two traits that nothing in his life has prepared him for. He tries and fails at magic tricks, and his collection of deformed chickens, born with extra limbs or conjoined to other chicks and preserved in jars of alcohol, fail to provide the kind of dining experience he wants

Sherwood Anderson (The Library of Congress)

to be remembered for. Through it all, readers are left to wonder about the effect this odd man and his stubborn ways have had on his son.

"The Egg" was first published in the *Dial* magazine in 1920 before being included in Anderson's collection *The Triumph of the Egg and Other Stories* in 1921. It is a testament to Anderson's continuing reputation that that book is still in print nearly a hundred years later. The story is also available in *The Portable Sherwood Anderson* (1949) and online at http://www.eldritchpress.org/tales/egg.html.

AUTHOR BIOGRAPHY

Anderson was born in Camden, Ohio, on September 13, 1876. His mother, Emma, came from a poor family and spent most of her teens as a hired housekeeper in the home of a farm family. She married Anderson's father at the age of twenty, which was somewhat old for the time. His father, Irwin, had been quite successful as a harness maker earlier in his life. When Sherwood was young, however, Irwin's trade succumbed to mechanical processes that could make harnesses

more quickly and cheaply. Throughout Anderson's childhood, his family moved from town to town while his father sought work, establishing a pattern of motion that would come to define Anderson's life.

While his father worked occasionally, when he found it convenient, Anderson was ambitious from the start. As a teenager he earned the nickname "Jobby" for his willingness to take on any job that came his way. When he was nineteen, he enlisted in the Ohio National Guard, and he soon after left Ohio for his first trip to Chicago, working in a warehouse there. He was in the army from 1899 until 1900, serving in the Spanish-American War, and then attended school at Wittenburg Academy in Springfield, Ohio.

With his military service and education behind him, Anderson's adult life began. He moved to Chicago and worked in advertising for a few years, and then in 1906 he returned to Ohio as the president of United Factories Company in Cleveland, a mail-order business that was troubled from the start. In 1907, he moved to nearby Elyria and started a paint distribution business, Anderson Manufacturing Company, which was successful beyond all expectations. He married the first of his four wives, Cornelia Lane, in 1904 and started a family in Elyria.

In November 1912 he walked away from his business, moving to Chicago in early 1913 to pursue the life of a writer. He took a job in advertising and struggled to survive. His first story, "The Rabbit Pen," was published in *Harper's* in 1914, and in the following years several other stories came out. He divorced Cornelia in 1915; in 1916, he married his second wife, Tennessee Mitchell, and published his first novel, *Windy McPherson's Son*. Other publications followed until Anderson's biggest success, *Winesburg, Ohio*, a collection of interrelated stories, came out in 1919. That book, which stands to this day as his most notable achievement, gave him international prominence and the success that he had sought as a writer.

In 1921, his next story collection, *The Triumph of the Egg*, was published, including the short story "The Egg." Anderson won the prestigious *Dial* magazine prize that year. With his reputation established, he was finally able to support himself with writing and with speaking fees. He bought and published two newspapers in Virginia. Several more novels and short-story collections followed, as well as a stage adaptation of *Winesburg, Ohio.* He divorced and remarried in 1924 and again in 1933. His writings of the 1930s were not as well received as his earlier works, and his career was severely hampered by his support for the American Communist Party. Anderson died of peritonitis in Panama, while on a cruise, on March 8, 1941.

PLOT SUMMARY

"The Egg" begins with the first-person narrator speculating about the life his father led as a bachelor, before the narrator was born. He surmises that the father was a kind man, a cheerful man, which invites an implicit contrast to the kind of man he was when the narrator knew him. As a younger man, the father worked on a farm outside of town. He owned a horse and would ride into town on Saturdays to spend a few hours at a bar with other local workers, with no ambition for anything better.

That changed when he met the narrator's mother, a schoolteacher, and married her. She urged him to become ambitious and to start making money. The narrator speculates that it was her background in education that was the cause, as she most likely had read about great figures from history and wanted greatness for her son. So, with her encouragement, they rented a farm of their own, for raising chickens.

The narrator's childhood was spent in isolation, living among chickens and not among other children, a fact that he relates with some resentment. He lists the many terrible things that he knew to occur among farm chickens: diseases, birth abnormalities, and a simple lack of intelligence. As an adult, he says, he looked into the ways that chicken farming is promoted through advertisements as a way that one can start an independent, profitable small business, but he directly warns readers to beware of falling for such foolishness. In his experience, chicken farming was difficult, disgusting, and unprofitable.

After the digression about chicken farming generally, the narrator returns to the subject of his father and mother. They tried farming chickens for ten years and never made a profit from it, so they bought a restaurant in town. His father, by then forty-five, was balding and fatter and no longer the young man he had been when he had married the narrator's mother. He had worked hard, hiring himself out as a laborer part-time at

surrounding farms while trying to make his own farm work, and he had little to show for it. One thing that he did take with him from his farming days, which the narrator characterizes as his "greatest treasure," is a box containing jars of chickens that were malformed at birth, with extra pairs of legs or wings, perhaps, or an extra head. Such abnormalities could not survive long after hatching, but it was the father's fantasy that he could raise one and have a full-grown mutated hen or rooster, which he could display at fairs.

The restaurant that the narrator's family starts is outside of the main town of Bidwell, Ohio, in a place called Pickleville. It is near enough to Bidwell to get the narrator into a school in town, aiding his rise in the world, and it is across from the railroad station. The parents hope that travelers going to and from the train station will stop there and eat, making the restaurant profitable. As they prepare the restaurant, the father builds a shelf for his jars of deformed chicken, to display them to the customers. The narrator, as a ten-year-old boy, is happiest when he goes off to school and is away from the somber mood of the restaurant.

To keep the restaurant open day and night, the narrator's parents have to work split shifts, with his father sleeping days while his mother tends the restaurant and then staying at the counter overnight, when some freight trains stop at Pickleville to reorganize.

Working the lonesome overnight shifts makes the father realize that he needs to attract customers to the restaurant by offering them a cheerful place to go at night. He imagines that groups of people who have nowhere to go after hours would head out to his restaurant because it is a fun place to be. This presents a problem because he is not an innately cheerful person. He tries to make himself more fun. He smiles more, and as a result his wife and child smile more too. Neither of them, though, puts much faith in the father's new mania for making the restaurant a happy place where the town's young people will want to go.

One night, the narrator and his mother are awakened by the father's loud, angry voice downstairs, followed by the slamming of the front door. In a few minutes, the father comes upstairs with an egg in his hand. He stands there in a rage for a few moments, then breaks down crying, consoled in his sorrow by his wife. The narrator, speaking from a later vantage point in his life, does not remember exactly what the father told them about the events of that evening, but he can nonetheless relate what happened as if he had witnessed everything.

That evening a wealthy young man from town, Joe Kane, comes into the diner, waiting for the train that is bringing his father home from a business trip. Joe is the kind of socially connected young man whom the father wants to spend time at the restaurant, and so he is anxious to make sure that Joe will be impressed. He lingers around, staring at him, trying to determine how he could amuse him, but Joe interprets his attention more as anger than as kindness. Joe considers waiting outside, but a sudden rain stops him from leaving. What Joe interprets as anger and suspicion is actually the father's own awkwardness and, as the narrator puts it, "an attack of stage fright."

Eventually, to amuse his customer, the father begins a monologue that he has rehearsed for just such an occasion, setting up a trick he has learned. To introduce his trick about balancing an egg on its end, he starts a talk about Christopher Columbus. Columbus, according to this story, had promised to make an egg stand on its end, but he achieved his goal only by cheating and cracking the egg, while the father was about to demonstrate how such a feat could really be done. To Joe, the narrator assumes, this talk about Christopher Columbus and eggs comes from out of nowhere, and the man delivering the talk is awkward, nervous, and mumbling.

To do the trick, the narrator's father rolls the egg between his hands, continuing his nervous patter. But when he puts it down on the counter, it falls over on its side. He tries again and again for a half hour, failing continuously.

Embarrassed, the father decides that he can amuse Joe by showing him his malformed chickens preserved in alcohol. The deformed little bodies are a sickening sight to Joe, but his host tries to act like the cheerful men he had observed long ago, when he used to go to the bar on Saturday nights. He grabs the departing Joe by the arm, and is finally able to keep his customer by offering him a free cup of coffee and a cigar.

For Joe's entertainment, the narrator's father tries one last trick: he claims that he will put an egg, complete in its shell, into a narrow-necked bottle. To soften the egg's shell, he soaks it in a pan of heated vinegar: as the vinegar is heating, Joe's attention drifts back to his newspaper, and his lack of interest frustrates the father. The softened egg is not going into the bottle, and Joe's train has arrived; Joe stands up and walks out the door. The father makes one last attempt to force the egg into the bottle, and it shatters in his hand. In the act of leaving, Joe looks back through the open doorway, sees the bald, irate man with the smashed egg dripping from his fingers, and laughs. The father flies into a rage, grabs a fresh egg from the basket on the counter, and throws it at his customer, ensuring that his dream—a diner where Joe Kane and the town's other rich young people would gather—will never be realized.

When the father comes upstairs, still in a rage, he holds a new, fresh egg in his hand. His wife quickly calms him down. He puts the egg down and closes the diner for the night, returning to go to bed early. During the night, the narrator looks at the egg on the table and wonders what the idea of a delicate egg means to him, the son of a man like his father.

CHARACTERS

Thomas Butterworth
Thomas Butterworth is mentioned but does not actually appear in the story. He is the man who owns the farm where the narrator's father worked in his bachelor days.

Father

The narrator's father is the focus of most of this story. He began as a farmhand and was presumably a cheerful and kindly man when he met the narrator's mother. When he started a family he went into business for himself, working hard for ten years trying to make a living with a chicken farm that never paid for itself, and also hiring himself out to nearby farms when he had some free time after his son was born.

After ten years of trying to raise chickens, he and his wife rent out a small diner outside of town, near a train station. It is not a success either, because the business from train customers and workers is not as brisk as it should be and the diner is too far away from downtown to attract customers. Still, he works hard at the business, staying up nights to work the counter while his wife works the day shift.

The father has never been a very socially adept person. He makes a conscious decision to be more outgoing in order to attract customers. When he has a chance to try out his new outgoing personality on one of the young men from town, he embarrasses himself: he is too pushy, too insistent, following the young man around and joking with him uncomfortably, awkwardly grabbing his arm the way that he has seen friendly men grab the arms of other men. Straining to be entertaining, he tries to show tricks that he can do with eggs, but they fail. In his frustration, he shouts at the young man and throws an egg at him, ensuring that the business will never prosper in the way he hoped.

The father has a macabre, inexplicable interest in the chickens that hatch deformed and die young. He preserves their bodies in alcohol in jars. To him they are interesting, though others find them disturbing.

Albert Griggs

Albert Griggs is the person who lends the narrator's family a wagon to move their belongings from the chicken farm to the diner. He is mentioned in the story but does not appear. The route they travel to the diner is identified as "Griggs's Road."

Joe Kane

Joe Kane is exactly the sort of customer the narrator's father wants to bring into the restaurant. He is from a wealthy family, he is young, and he is popular. If he were to like the diner and

tell his friends about it, the diner would have the kind of clientele that the father dreams of.

When Joe is stuck at the diner waiting for his father's train, it offers a perfect opportunity for the restaurateur to show off what a fun place the diner can be. The narrator's father does whatever he can to entertain Joe, but he is not a naturally outgoing person: his attempts at jokes fall flat, and his attempts to make physical contact are awkward and unsettling. When the father shows off his prized collection of deformed chickens, Joe is disgusted rather than amused. His attempts to politely turn his attention away are met with the father's aggressive insistence that he watch the magic tricks he can do with eggs. The tricks fail so miserably that Joe has to laugh, enraging his host.

Mother

The narrator's mother is the driving force of the family, socially. While his father is portrayed as being somewhat sedate in his ways, the mother is very ambitious, pushing her husband to start his own farm. As their son grows older, she devises the plan to open the restaurant so that they can move closer to town and send him to school, hoping that this will give him the opportunity to advance in the world.

The mother's ambition seems to be a destructive force: her husband is pushed beyond his limits, working day and night to create the kind of life for his family that she aspires to, and her son shows no particular fondness for her. In the end, however, when her husband suffers the humiliating defeat upon failing to transform himself into a cheerful innkeeper, her mere presence calms him, indicating that the two of them have a deeper relationship than the narrator could ever understand.

Narrator

This story is told by a grown man. At the start of the story, he is remembering the days of his childhood and speculating on what his parents were like before he was born. He describes his early childhood on the chicken farm outside of Bidwell as a lonely existence, lamenting that the days that should have been the most joyous of his life were instead spent among chickens, with their many ailments, chronic stupidity, and grotesque deformities. He says he was ten years old when his parents gave the farm up and moved to the diner, and he speaks well of the eight-mile walk behind the wagon full of their belongings, which gave him a chance to "see the wonders of the world."

When the family moves to Pickleville, the boy is able to attend school in the nearby town of Bidwell, but he is still isolated and somber. He recalls one incident when, walking home alone, he tried hopping and singing, because he had seen some girls do that, but soon he became self-conscious about being so cheerful, which he thinks is a result of having been raised around so much constant death at the chicken farm.

One of the story's key points is the son's relationship with his father. This is characterized by two impressions he has of the man while he is asleep. The first, soon after the move to town, is of looking at his bald father asleep in a chair on Sunday afternoons and imagining his head to be a broad road that could take one to great unknown worlds. Later, however, he looks at the egg that his father has brought upstairs from the diner after having failed to impress Joe Kane, and he makes a mental connection between his father's head and the egg.

THEMES

Wealth

This story operates on a clear distinction between wealth and poverty. The narrator's family is poor, and so they have to work long hours for little money. Life on the chicken farm is difficult, with any profits fed back into medicines that are supposed to keep the chickens healthy. The father has to work on other farms in his spare time for extra cash. They are still in poverty when they leave the chicken farm, traveling in a borrowed wagon to a rented diner. To run the diner, the husband and wife have to work separate shifts, one sleeping while the other is working.

The mother's dream for rising out of this poverty is for her son to gain a good education. The father's hope for rising and being a success is to bring in young, wealthy clients. If they find the diner an interesting place, he reasons, they will attract other wealthy customers.

When Joe Kane arrives, the father has his opportunity to impress the sort of wealthy, socially connected patron who can spread the word to other wealthy patrons. He does not know how to amuse such a man, though. When

his attempts to spark Joe's interest fail, he first tries to keep him there by giving him free coffee and a free cigar, spending money that he probably cannot afford. In the end, Joe looks at this older, poorer man as a bungling fool: he is much more sophisticated and worldly than a chicken farmer/fry cook can ever imagine.

Ambition

The narrator of this story makes much of the fact that his mother was ambitious. She is the one who has dreams of greatness and success for her son, dreams that are presumably the result of her studies of US presidents who rose from poverty to the heights of power. The story notes that she has no ambition for herself, but she is filled with ambition for her husband and son.

It is at the mother's insistence that the narrator's father quits being a farmhand on another man's farm and tries his hand at chicken farming. It is not a profession that suits him, though, and the family struggles for ten years, barely making a living. The mother's ambitions for the son remain. Their next move is also undertaken to feed her ambitions. They give up the farm and open the diner in order to be closer to the town of Bidwell, so that the son can enroll in a town school for a better education.

To some extent, readers can see that the ambitions that the narrator's mother had for him have paid off. There is no explanation about what the son went on to be when he grew up, but his use of language and his imaginative way of filling in the unknown parts of his parents' background indicate that he has a level of intelligence and sophistication far beyond what he would have had if he had spent his life on a chicken farm.

Rural Life

The distinction between country life and city life is crucial to the family presented in "The Egg." When talking about the father's bachelor life, spent working on a farm owned by a man named Thomas Butterworth, the story gives no information about his responsibilities but instead covers what it would be like for him to go to town on Saturday evenings, giving readers a picture of a country man overwhelmed by life in a city tavern.

Life in the country is very clearly covered in the part of the story dealing with the chicken farm. It is shown to be a cruel life, as Anderson catalogs the diseases that can befall chickens,

TOPICS FOR FURTHER STUDY

- Lucy Maude Montgomery's young-adult novel *Anne of Green Gables* and its sequels have been favorites of young adults since the first book's publication in 1908. The story concerns a young orphan girl who is brought to a secluded farm on Prince Edward Island in Canada in the early 1900s. Read *Anne of Green Gables* and make a list of the ways that her experiences are different from and similar to the experiences of the narrator of this story. Then, use those similarities and differences to support an essay about why their outlooks on life are so different.

- The parents of this story's narrator believe that they can make their diner succeed because they are across from the train station, on Turner's Pike. Interview two people responsible for starting new businesses in your community in the past year, and then write a report on their experiences. In particular, how important do you think location is in the success of a business?

- This story mentions some of the many difficulties facing a person running a small chicken farm in the early 1900s. Research what the poultry farming business was like at that time, before electricity or telephones were in common use, and prepare a report with graphics that show your classmates just what had to be done.

- The kinds of tricks that the father does in this story—balancing an egg, and putting an egg in a bottle—use the materials that he has at hand in the diner. Research some similar tricks that can be done using materials in your classroom, and perform them for your classmates in a way that keeps the physics of how they are done a mystery until you reveal them.

- China is now by far the world's largest chicken producer, with an output of more than twice as many chickens per year as the second-place United States. Using the Internet, research both Chinese and American methods of chicken farming. Produce a chart using the computer program of your choice that shows how techniques differ in the two cultures.

- Anderson had a considerable influence on the generation of writers who followed him. Find quotes from four or five writers who talk about how Anderson influenced them, and then use examples from "The Egg" to illustrate the aspects of his writing that those writers found influential. Present your findings in an oral or written report.

---

their physical and mental weaknesses, and the fact that the people running such a farm have to work excessively hard and can expect little gain. As the story's narrator points out, this is where he spent the years when a boy should be happy and carefree.

As a result of growing up surrounded by the constant deaths and partial births of the chickens, he grows into a grim and morose boy, just as his father was a quiet and verbally awkward farmhand. When the family moves close to town, the boy is able to observe the happiness of other children, but he still lives too far away to play with them after school: he walks home along Turner's Pike by himself. Rural life is, in this story, the cause of isolation, making people more familiar with illness and death than with the company of other people.

Self-Image

Although he has few social skills, the father in this story, trying to make his business thrive, wills himself to believe that he can be entertaining. He forces himself to smile, which his wife and son imitate, as if happiness can be created. He tries to act like other cheerful men he has

"The Egg" is set in a rural Ohio town, a familiar setting for Anderson's work. *(© Cynthia Kidwell / ShutterStock.com)*

observed in his life, thinking that he might have the ability to be as likable as them. He memorizes clever things to say, believing that he can deliver tricks that will amuse and captivate the kinds of customers he wants.

The father's greatest delusion regards his collection of deformed baby birds, such as a five-legged hen or a two-headed rooster. To him, they represent the tragedy of life, and he sees that tragedy as being so poignant that he is sure that everyone must, like him, be fascinated by their preserved corpses. He imagines that his collection can be his ticket to popularity and even to wealth. To everyone else, however, the dead chickens are too horrible to think about. What the father dreams will make him a famous entertainer, other people find grotesque.

STYLE

First-Person Narration

Telling a story in the first person, as Anderson does with "The Egg," offers a writer particular benefits and difficulties. Since the speaker of the story refers to himself or herself as "I," readers feel close to the story, as if they are hearing it from someone who was really there. Beginning readers often confuse a first-person narrator with the author, especially in cases where the circumstances of the character's life are close to the biographical facts known about the author.

Using a first-person narrator allows Anderson to imply facts about the narrator without coming out and saying them. For instance, readers can see that he is bitter about his parents' relationship with each other and is somewhat resentful about having grown up among chickens, which he speaks of angrily.

The traditional problem with using first-person narration, however, is that it limits the narrator's access to information. Logically, first-person narrators cannot know about things that happened when they were not there, unless they were told about them. Anderson brushes this limitation aside by declaring, "For some unexplainable reason I know the story as well as though I had been a witness to my father's discomfiture." While this does not explain how the narrator can recall what happened, it does at least acknowledge that his knowing it so well is hard to explain.

Unnamed Characters

The narrator and his parents live in obscurity, with their names withheld from the reader. To some extent, this is a natural result of the story's use of the first-person narrator. The narrator is talking about a time when he was a child, and a child would not refer to his parents by name, nor would a person talking about himself find it necessary to use his own name. Many authors do, however, find ways of giving characters names, even when writing in the first person. The parents might be quoted talking to each other, for instance, or the father might have introduced himself to Joe Kane, the only present character with a name, while he was trying to befriend him. By leaving the characters unnamed, Anderson makes their desperate lives even more desperate, making their doomed business even more irrelevant to society.

Controlling Metaphor

In the story "The Egg," eggs mean several things. Their significance cannot be narrowed down to one symbolic meaning or another. The father's bald head is pictured as an egg, and the thousands of chicken eggs on the poultry farm have to be nurtured and cared for. The eggs sometimes produce deformed chickens that die quickly, but they can also be a source of amazement if the tricks they are used for work. The father smashes an egg just when he realizes that his hopes for a prosperous future are smashed, but he also throws an egg in anger at the man he was trying to entertain.

There is no single narrow meaning about what eggs mean in this story, but it is undeniable that eggs are central to "The Egg." As such, eggs can be considered a controlling metaphor: a metaphor that dominates the piece to such an extent that the story is shaped around it.

HISTORICAL CONTEXT

Modernism in American Literature

"The Egg" was published just as the literary movement called modernism was on the rise. As with most literary movements, modernism is open to interpretation and can mean different things to different people. Most critics agree, however, that it arose from the artistic world's reaction to the devastation of World War I, which caused destruction across Europe on a scale that had never been experienced before. The war realigned the old view of culture, starting in England, where it brought the stodginess and prudish, conservative assumptions of the Victorian era, which dominated most of the previous century, into the fast-paced, competitive twentieth century. As the Literature Network website explains it, "the War demonstrated that no guiding spirit rules the events of the world, and that absolute destruction was kept in check by only the tiniest of margins."

Following that drive toward progress, literary modernism sought to leave behind the traditions of the past and struggled to create new forms that writers could use to express themselves. Poets such as Ezra Pound and T. S. Eliot broke poetry down to its basic elements, throwing away the forms that had once been assumed to be the mark of what was good in writing. English-language novelists such as Ernest Hemingway, Virginia Woolf, and James Joyce tried to shift readers' focus away from the way their stories were told to reveal the core consciousness of their characters.

Although the war is seen as the event that brought modernism into the foreground of art in the 1920s, there were already characteristics of it in art and literature when the war began. Imagism, for example, is an artistic movement that began to flourish around 1914; it focused on conveying the writer's message in precise imagery rather than dealing with ideas. In literature, the most well-known imagist is Ezra Pound, who bridged the imagist movement and the later, larger modernist movement. Modernism became more widespread and better recognized, however, and critics consider it the prevailing artistic movement well into the 1950s.

The Chicago Renaissance

In 1913, Anderson left Elyria, Ohio, where he had struggled to make a living as president of Anderson Manufacturing Company, and moved to Chicago, Illinois, to pursue a career as a writer. He arrived in Chicago during a period of literary activity that received international attention, referred to by critics and historians as Chicago's literary renaissance.

COMPARE
&
CONTRAST

- **1920:** Chickens are most frequently raised on farms owned and operated by families.

  Today: Since the 1960s, industrial farms have taken over poultry farming, raising chickens in controlled environments that limit their mobility, their food intake, and their exposure to the outdoors. Antibiotics are used freely to limit their diseases.

- **1920:** About 55 percent of the people in the United States live in rural environments, and 45 percent live in urban environments.

  Today: About 80 percent of the US population live in urban areas, and only about 20 percent live in rural areas.

- **1920:** Restaurants that try to capture the attention of travelers are often located near train stations, since that is the main mode of transportation.

  Today: Restaurants can lease space in airports, but many choose to build on locations near highways, taking advantage of the US interstate highway system that was developed after World War II.

- **1920:** A small business owner might try to draw young, affluent customers to a shop by practicing an entertaining routine, even if the owner is not a naturally entertaining person.

  Today: A small business owner might try to use social media to make the business appealing to young, affluent customers.

- **1920:** Farmers looking to protect their stock might read trade papers, as the people in this story do when they find Wilmer's White Wonder Cholera Cure or Professor Bidlow's Egg Producer in the "poultry papers."

  Today: Professions are united by the Internet, giving small farmers access to information through trade associations and professional publications. Some smaller websites, though, might resemble the trade papers of earlier days in printing ads that promise more than they can deliver.

- **1920:** A small restaurant owner might keep bottles of deformed young chickens for the amusement of customers.

  Today: Even if customers would find grotesque oddities such as deformed chickens amusing, there are more laws and zoning codes that prohibit having them in close proximity to food preparation or service.

According to the online *Encyclopedia of Chicago*, the city has actually had three eras of literary significance, spread out across the twentieth century. The first took place just as the century was beginning, when the city was a financial dynamo, the country's greatest center of manufacturing and transportation, using Industrial Revolution technology to bring the grain and livestock of the fertile Midwest to the growing urban areas of the world. That time produced writers such as Hamlin Garland and Theodore Dreiser, whose works are known to this day as sterling examples of American realism. The third great wave of Chicago literature was said to be the one that reached its peak in the 1940s, when writers such as Richard Wright, James T. Farrell, Nelson Algren, and Saul Bellow drew attention to the city's ethnically diverse neighborhoods, writing stories of little people struggling to survive.

The Chicago renaissance that Anderson entered came between these two. Between 1910 and the mid-1920s, Chicago was a magnet for literary talent. During that time, the poets Carl Sandburg and Vachel Lindsay lived in Chicago. Edgar Lee Masters lived there when he wrote his poetry collection *Spoon River Anthology*, and its publication made him an overnight success. There the poet Harriet Monroe started the influential magazine *Poetry*, which was an important place for the greatest poets to publish their

The narrator's father tries to run a chicken farm. (© Catalin Petolea / ShutterStock.com)

works then and is still just as important a hundred years later. Other influential literary publications of the time, such as the *Dial* (which originally published "The Egg" in March 1920) and *Friday Literary Review*, were also published in Chicago. Noted novelists in Chicago at the time were Anderson, Dreiser (who had been a part of the first movement and remained around), and Floyd Dell. As H. L. Mencken, one of the most celebrated journalists of the age, put it, Chicago was "the Literary Capital of the United States" at that time, the place where small-town aspirations met the cold reality of urban life.

CRITICAL OVERVIEW

Since the publication of his groundbreaking story collection *Winesburg, Ohio* in 1919, and up to the present day, Sherwood Anderson has been hailed as one of the great writers of American literature. However, although most of the literary world understood and appreciated what he was trying to achieve, Anderson's artistic ambitions sometimes made it difficult for non-literary readers to see why he was considered a sensation. For instance, when *America* magazine reviewed *The Triumph of the Egg*, the collection containing the story "The Egg," upon its publication in 1921, the reviewer characterized the book as "a series of studies...in mental deficiency" and deemed Anderson's handling of this subject "very unsatisfactory." This anonymous writer ends the review by faulting the book for lacking enough data to be of scientific value. Still, as John Bassett pointed out in 2006, "*The Triumph of the Egg* was widely praised when it appeared in the fall of 1921 by, among others, H. L. Mencken, Rebecca West, Padraic Colum, and John Peale Bishop." Anderson might not have been a popular success, but he certainly was respected by the critics.

By 1927, though, Anderson's literary significance was widely recognized. He even warranted a book-length examination of his writing career, which at that time was barely a decade old: *The Phenomenon of Sherwood Anderson*, by N. Bryllion Fagin. Fagin acknowledges the author's complexity as he notes, "The fact that Anderson baffles most of his contemporaries and public does not change his significance. He is a phenomenon none the less."

Over the years, "The Egg" has come to stand out as one of Anderson's most accomplished stories, a pillar of Anderson's reputation, along with *Winesburg, Ohio* and a few other significant short stories. As Irving Howe, frequently recognized as one of the great literary critics of the twentieth century, put it in his book-length study of Anderson's career in 1951, the fable that is at the heart of "The Egg" "is so appalling that...it needs to be cooled by a prose which is dry and unimpassioned." This appreciation of Anderson's technique leads Howe to the conclusion that "of all Anderson's short fictions 'The Egg' most deserves to be placed among the greatest stories of the world."

New analyses of Anderson's career, and of this story, continue to this day. On a regular basis, scholarly essays are prepared about "The Egg," as critics come up with ever-new interpretations and different ways of reading the story and its style.

CRITICISM

David Kelly

Kelly is an instructor of literature and creative writing. In the following essay, he looks at the central relationship of "The Egg" and how the different things that eggs can symbolize all help make that relationship clear.

After finishing Sherwood Anderson's story "The Egg," readers are left with a number of unanswered questions hanging in the air. Two, though, stand out as the crucial for making the story make sense. The first one is a literary question: what is the significance of the title? There are several eggs in the story, but do they all mean the same thing, or different things? The second big question is a matter of storytelling. The egg might be symbolic of something, but symbolism is useless unless it is attached to a central, coherent story. This particular story holds together only if the main relationship it examines, that of the narrator and his father, has meaning. These two characters seldom interact, leaving readers to look for clues to Anderson's message.

First comes the question of what the story means. It is an accepted truism that when a story

> IN THIS CASE, THE STORY IS ABOUT A MAN WHOSE DRIVE TO SUCCEED SOCIALLY IS NOWHERE NEAR HIS ABILITY TO BE A SOCIAL BEING, AND ANDERSON USES THE FATHER'S TOUCHING AFFINITY FOR THE DEFORMED, HOPELESS YOUNG CHICKENS TO SHOW HOW FAR HIS MIND IS FROM MAINSTREAM SOCIETY."

is told by a first-person narrator, that narrator will be the main character of the story, the one who is most affected by the events. In "The Egg," though, little is known about the narrator. Many critics and readers try to fix this lack of information by understanding the narrator to be Sherwood Anderson himself. This is easy to do. The details given in the story match those of Anderson's biography well enough, with a father unprepared for family life, moving from job to job, trying to fit into the world as he feels a grown man should. That may be true, and there may even be evidence that Anderson himself thought that he was writing about his own life in "The Egg." Also, reading it this way offers critics the comfort of thinking they know the unstated outcome of story: they believe the sad, lonesome boy grows up to be a hardworking businessman and then a successful writer, as Anderson did.

The problem with this kind of interpretation is that taking a first-person narrator to be the story's author robs the story of its autonomy. It makes the story an incomplete part of a larger work. This is not fair, nor is it reasonable. The story is an independent unit. It has a title, a designated beginning, and an end. It has its own terms, and readers should accept it as such, instead of treating it as just a sliver of something else.

Leaving Anderson's life out of it makes the narrator, who is supposed to be the center of the story, an enigma. He says little about himself, either as a child or as the adult speaking to the reader. He focuses instead on the behavior of the parents, especially his father. What little readers know about the narrator's adult life they infer

WHAT DO I READ NEXT?

- This short story was adapted by Raymond O'Neil as a play called "The Triumph of the Egg" (the story's original title, as well as the title of the collection in which it was originally published). It appears as a part of Anderson's collection *Plays: Winesburg and Others*, published in 1937.

- *Sherwood Anderson Remembered*, edited by Welford Dunaway Taylor and published in 2009, contains dozens of anecdotes about the author from writers and others who knew him well, including such literary greats as Gertrude Stein (who, like Anderson, was an early mentor to Hemingway and was also later betrayed by Hemingway in print), Floyd Dell, and Henry Miller.

- Anderson's stories in *Winesburg, Ohio* are usually all considered together as parts of one continuous story. When considering individual stories, critics usually look at "The Egg" and "Death in the Woods," from his 1933 story collection *Death in the Woods and Other Stories*.

- Modern author Rick Moody wrote an homage to this story—one he refers to as a "cover version"—with his short story "The Double Zero," originally published in *McSweeney's*

in 2000 and then included in Moody's 2002 collection *Demonology: Stories*.

- The narrator's experience of moving from the farm to the city, where he is a stranger to the customs, is familiar to immigrant people across the world and has been written about frequently. One of the best books on this subject is Kashmira Sheth's young-adult novel *Blue Jasmine* (2004), about a girl whose family takes her from a rural town in India to Iowa City.

- Anderson was known for his many friendships within the literary community. One of his longest friendships was with literary critic Van Wyck Brooks. Anderson's "Letters to Van Wyck Brooks," published in *Homage to Sherwood Anderson, 1876–1941*, offer a particularly good insight into the type of man Anderson was. The book, edited by Paul P. Appel, was published in 1970 and includes the views of many famous authors about Anderson.

- For direct insight into Anderson's thinking, consult the massive *Sherwood Anderson's Memoirs*, edited by Ray Lewis White. Originally published in 1942, it was revised with new material in 1969.

---

from the tone he takes. When he assumes that his father's life was happy as a bachelor or says that he knows "for some unexplainable reason" what happened when he was not present, he is showing how strong the bond between himself and his father was, without talking about it. The narrator sees the world as his father did. He does not tell readers what he has become since childhood, but they can see that person because the story gives such a clear portrait of the father.

Though the story takes place during the narrator's childhood, little is revealed about his ideas about the world at that time. He talks about the loneliness of growing up on a chicken

farm during his formative years, and readers can understand what it would be like to be thrown into the social order of a town school at age ten. The boy only becomes clear in one scene, during which Anderson captures him on his own. Walking home, alone of course, he remembers how the children he has seen had played, and he awkwardly emulates them, hopping down the dirt road, singing "shrilly" and looking "doubtfully about." The grown narrator knows how pathetic it was for a boy to mimic others so; the language he uses in relating the scene tells readers that. What the narrator does not do, though, is spell out a direct connection between the boy's cluelessness about what makes human enjoyment and the father's same confusion.

The father has two levels of focus in this story, public and private. For the public sphere, he tries to pull from within himself the sorts of things he thinks people will like, such as smiling, funny patter, and magic tricks. He is terrible at these for the same reason his son is terrible at amusing himself by hopping down the road and singing a nonsense song: he does not feel the entertainment when he does these things, so his antics are not entertaining. The narrator knows that spending his first ten years on a chicken farm made him too aware of death to hop and sing ("It must have seemed to me that I was doing a thing that should not have been done," he says, with sorrowful discomfort). The father feels that his parlor tricks should be done, but he does not feel that he wants to do them. He is willing to study how to be entertaining in a calculated move to help his struggling business advance. Though the story does not say so, his frustration and anger when his egg tricks fail are an unspoken acknowledgment that he has no business thinking that he can amuse others.

If he were not saddled with trying to expand his business, the father would focus on his actual interest: the deformed, just-hatched chickens that he has collected over the years. He is so fascinated by them that he has preserved them in jars. They are oddities, grotesques, each too unusual to survive, just as he and perhaps his son are not suited to thrive in the commercial atmosphere of town. These oddities fascinate the father for the same reasons that they would repel any average person—in fact, as they repel Joe Kane, the influential young man whom the father is trying to impress in the story. After a decade on the chicken farm, watching thousands of eggs fail or succeed or hatch to leave infant chicks vulnerable to disease or accident, the father's mind is accustomed to the ways things can go wrong in a way that diners at his restaurant cannot imagine. The chickens that interest him most are the ones who stand out, while chickens that have no outstanding traits are the ones the general public gets to know.

As a grown man, the narrator implies that this kind of interest is a part of his own worldview as well. He mentions in passing how his familiarity with death on a farm that had so many young chicken lives coming and going probably blinded him to the aspects of death

In "The Egg," the narrator's mother is a rural schoolteacher. (© ChipPix / ShutterStock.com)

that others would find gruesome. Anderson labeled his stories "grotesques" because they frequently focused on one overstated characteristic of a person. In this case, the story is about a man whose drive to succeed socially is nowhere near his ability to be a social being, and Anderson uses the father's touching affinity for the deformed, hopeless young chickens to show how far his mind is from mainstream society.

Eggs have numerous symbolic implications, and they all apply to this story. They bring to mind fragility, with their shells protecting young, forming lives that are not yet ready for the world—embryos that are developing, just as the young boy, raised in isolation on a farm, is not ready for the social world of Bidwell, Ohio. They bring up questions of the cycle of life, the eternal question of "Which came first, the chicken or the egg?" This story, which ends with both father and son reduced to tears about their own hopeless futility, certainly blurs the regular line of generational progress. Above all, eggs represent the hope of a new beginning, seen all over Anderson's story: in the story's long dissertation about how egg farming is sold to the hopeless as a way out of poverty, in the boy who views his father's egg-like bald head as a road that Caesar might use to lead his legions out into the unknown world, and in the basic hope that any one egg, out of the millions laid and hatched, might be the one to yield something truly magnificent.

"The Egg" is a story of ambition and deformity. These are characteristics shared by the father and son in the story, and, to some extent, by all eggs. Anderson does not directly tell readers how much these traits have carried on into the narrator of the story as he has grown up, but he gives enough evidence for readers to draw conclusions that cannot stray too far from what he must have intended.

Source: David Kelly, Critical Essay on "The Egg," in *Short Stories for Students*, Gale, Cengage Learning, 2013.

Mark Savin

In the following essay, Savin focuses on the confusion in the surface text of the story "The Egg."

So easy is it to see Sherwood Anderson's "The Egg" as a tale of parental ambition gone berserk that one may not see that the narrator's story is as much a repetition of his father's acts as it is a remembrance of them. The narrator's most obvious accomplishment—describing this father's wretched attempt to "get up" in the world—is not the same as his most important one—reconstructing in words, in a story, the experience of his father. The conventional assumption about "The Egg" that "although the experiences of his parents have had a lasting effect on the narrator, he can take a detached view of them," confuses the surface text of the story—the sometimes maddening desire of parents to provide a better life for their children—with its subtext—the awkward and troubling recognition of a son's deep similarity to his father. The story centers on attachment even as it assumes a pose of detachment. Anderson gives us a tale which, if we observe how it is told, proves to be as much about what is implied as what is made explicit, as much about the act of storytelling as the story told.

"The Egg"'s unnamed narrator begins his story with an awkwardly qualified sentence calculated by the author to call attention to the

> THE POWER OF 'THE EGG' RESIDES NOT IN IMPERSONAL MEMORY, NOT IN THAT OUTER SHELL, BUT IN THE REVELATION OF THE SOFTER WORLDS OF THE IMAGINATION."

process of the narrator's telling: "My father was, I am sure, intended by nature to be a cheerful, kindly man." Though the reader is not explicitly told that the narrator's father has ended a gloomy and broken man, one has little doubt that such is implied. Characteristic of this narrator is that even his most straightforward biographical statements tend to be conspicuously oblique or ambiguous, often needing to be read against their apparent or public meaning. While such statements may be regarded as merely humorous, to do so wrongly denies the possibility of serious meaning embedded in comic language; and in a story whose latent subject is the suppressed attachment and identification of son to father it makes sense that the narrator's joking means more than it says. Describing his own birth he adopts a distant and understated voice which skips over what he does not wish to consider explicitly:

> It was in the spring of his thirty-fifth year that my father married my mother, then a country school-teacher and in the following spring I came wriggling and crying into the world. Something happened to the two people. They became ambitious.

"Something happened," he tells us with a Heller-like indirection that neatly yokes together two very different events. What happened, of course, refers not merely to what we are told in the succeeding sentences—that his parents became ambitious, rented a farm, later moved to Bidwell (more properly Pickleville), opened a wayside cafe—but to what is referred to in the previous sentence—that he was born. The ambiguity of "something happened" to describe the fact of his own birth from a narrator who elsewhere latches on to the fine points of chicken physiology, small town geography or whatever else passes into view, suggests not only how uncomfortable he is at the role his own birth has played in the miserable affairs of his parents, but also how difficult it is for him to bring this subject into words. What matters most in Anderson's text, as distinct from the story told by the narrator, is that attention be drawn to how the narrator uses words, for that is where Anderson's story, again as distinct from the narrator's story, lies.

In part, of course, the narrator's self-conscious narration may be explained by the guilt he assumes over this thing that "happened," his birth. But to read "The Egg" only as a story of repressed guilt, important as that notion is, fails to account for curious turns and deeper feelings present in the text. When in the story's penultimate sentence the narrator suddenly declares, "I am the son of my father," the reader is likely caught off guard. How does the narrator come to make this affecting statement when the apparent effect of much of what he has told the reader before has been to distinguish and thereby separate the apparently knowing son from the manic father. Whatever role the son's birth may have played in the father's antic ventures, whatever guilt may have been generated by the happening of his birth, it is not simply guilt that binds them. As throughout the story humor serves to mask guilt, so guilt serves to mask the son's fear of how much he resembles his father. It is easier for the unnamed narrator to accept the self-declared culpability of his birth (something for which the reader knows that he cannot really be held responsible) than to accept his essential likeness to his father.

No scene more powerfully suggests the awkward and intense nature of their relationship than the unexplained but twice repeated incident of father and son weeping together in the dim light of the upstairs bedroom:

> Late one night I was awakened by a roar of anger coming from father's throat. Both mother and I sat upright in our beds. With trembling hands she lighted a lamp that stood on the table by her head. Downstairs the front door of our restaurant went shut with a bang and in a few minutes father tramped up the stairs. He held an egg in his hand and his hand trembled as though he were having a chill. There was a half-insane light in his eyes. As he stood there glaring at us I was sure he intended throwing the egg at either mother or me. Then he laid it gently on the table beside the lamp and dropped on his knees beside mother's bed. He began to cry like a boy, and I, carried away by his grief, cried with him. The two of us filled the little room with our wailing voices.

The scene is a turning point in the story: not only does it recall the traumatic moment when his father collapses under the burden of a failed public self, but also it marks the first time the narrator seriously places himself in the action of the story, ties his own actions to those of his father. "For some unexplainable reason," the narrator tells us as he responds to the memory of their crying and seeks to explain the genesis of the event, "I know the story as well as though I had been a witness to my father's discomfiture. One in time gets to know many unexplainable things." Only as one can explain his knowledge of this "unexplainable" story of what happened downstairs does the otherwise obscure relationship between father and son come into focus. The elaborately detailed recollection of how his father attempted to entertain the indifferent traveller, Joe Kane, with tricks and comic patter comes not from anything the narrator witnessed or was told, but from what he knows—consciously or not—of himself. "My own imagination has filled in the blanks," he says, but the discrepancy between what the father may have actually said and what his son has written so exceeds the sort of petty amplification implied by the phrase "fill in the blanks" that one should recognize that the son is reconstructing and not merely rephrasing his father's history. The elaborate posturing and histrionic appeal to authority described in the public performances of the father are enacted as well in the narrative performances of the son. The obsessive desire to amuse and entertain which so marks the narrator's writing repeats the desire to entertain that characterizes the father's behavior. In telling these anecdotes the narrator attempts to distract himself from his own unhappiness just as his father had done before him. Both are terribly lonely men, desperately eager to please a world which seems to disregard them except as they frantically contend for its attention. The difficulty for both is that the act of entertainment, whether jokes or writing, can succeed only if understood to mean more than it says, yet to admit to such special meaning seems impossible except in cryptic declarations or wordless weeping.

If the narrator's relationship to the world around him is understood as essentially similar to that of his father, then the apparently meandering collection of anecdotes and digressions that compose the narrator's tale may be seen as the metamorphosis of his father's collection of grotesque chickens into words. (Like Sherwood Anderson himself, this teller forms his grotes-ques from words.) The narrator's peculiarly enthusiastic denunciation of the duplicitous nature of chicken raising echoes the enthusiasm with which his father denounces the duplicity of Columbus's egg trick. The narrator's attempt to hold the reader's attention by telling us when he has exaggerated or digressed recalls his father's attempt to ingratiate bored Joe Kane by telling him the secret of the egg in the bottle. By playing both comic and historian, by hyperbole and anecdote, the narrator hopes to catch our attention just as his father once hoped to catch the notice of any stranger whose attentive glance might break the loneliness of his own despair. The narrator's search for a voice which will be accepted by his readers is as compelling as his father's quest for objects or tricks which will entertain; both hope that imaginative invention will displace the despair of feeling unwanted while at the same time not making that despair explicit. "People," said the father in a lesson well heeded by his son, "like to look at strange and wonderful things."

To the numerous images of the egg which critics have noted in this story perhaps one more should be added. The narrative structure is itself egg-like: within the shell of history lies a second and more vulnerable sphere, the fictions one creates about oneself and one's genesis. The power of "The Egg" resides not in impersonal memory, not in that outer shell, but in the reve-lation of the softer worlds of the imagination. Anderson, the architect of this doubled scheme, knows that the narrator's story is in some ways unspeakable; its very importance prevents him from speaking of it directly. The story works by lodging the significant and implicit so neatly within the trivial and explicit that each accom-modates and protects the other, a fertile center contained within a protective shell.

Source: Mark Savin, "Coming Full Circle: Sherwood Anderson's 'The Egg,'" in *Studies in Short Fiction*, Vol. 18, No. 4, Fall 1981, pp. 454–57.

David R. Mesher

In the following essay, Mesher discusses the important elements in the short stories "Death in the Woods" and "The Egg," including the impact of clumsiness of perspective and the associations with ambition.

> INDEED, THE NARRATOR HAS RESISTED ATTEMPTS TO FORCE HIM INTO THE AMERICAN PURSUIT OF SUCCESS JUST AS THE EGG—HIS SYMBOL—RESISTS THE FATHER'S ATTEMPTS TO GET IT INSIDE A BOTTLE, THE SECOND TRICK; AND LIKE THAT EGG, THE NARRATOR HAS BEEN BROKEN."

Sherwood Anderson's two best stories, "Death in the Woods" and "The Egg," share an odd but central detail: the narrator's open admission that he has fabricated the most impor-tant elements of the story he is telling. Irving Howe, discussing "Death in the Woods," terms this the story's "one significant flaw: a clumsi-ness of perspective which forces the narrator to offer a weak explanation of how he could have known the precise circumstances of the old woman's death." Jon S. Lawry, however, sees in Howe's flaw the point of the story. The nar-rator need not explain his knowledge of the old woman's life and death—indeed, need not even have such "knowledge"—because the movement of the story, for Lawry, is the "narrator's prog-ress from recorder to creator." The narrator recreates the details of the woman's death as an expression of the self he has discovered through the sympathy he feels for her; the story is there-fore about him, not her, and concern for the source of his information is superficial.

Nevertheless, in "Death in the Woods," the narrator does attempt a realistic explanation of his knowledge. He had seen the woman's body in the snow, he says, and had heard "the whispered com-ments of the men" at the scene, and "later, in town . . . must have heard other fragments of the old woman's story." The narrator of "The Egg" is much more straightforward about the story of his father and Joe Kane. "For some unexplainable reason," he claims, "I know the story as well as though I had been a witness to my father's dis-comfiture." Yet as astute a reader as Irving Howe, who faults "Death in the Woods" for a lesser imposition on his willing suspension of disbelief, ignores this inexplicability and says only that "the narrator, deliberately avoiding a direct dramatic line, then tells what happened in the store below."

"The Egg" has usually been treated, by Howe and others, as an autobiographical expression of Anderson's relationship with his father and, on a larger scale, "as a parable of human defeat"—meaning, of course, the defeat of the narrator's father. But, if the parallel with "Death in the Woods" holds, "The Egg" is a story about not the father but the son who, as narrator-turned-creator, projects the reality of his own psychology onto the history of his subject.

In "Death in the Woods," Anderson prepares his reader for the coming departure from narrative conventions at the beginning of the story. Though the details of the woman's background are not such as would require a great deal of personal knowledge, the narrator makes a point of recalling them, or in Lawry's term "recovering" them, with the justification that "all country and small-town people have seen such old women"; at the same time, however, the narrator also undercuts the most common details of his tale by continuing, "but no one knows much about them." Obviously, the narrator knows a lot about one—as it turns out, in practical terms, too much. A different technique is employed in "The Egg" to achieve the same undercutting effect. The story begins with a romanticized portrait of the father's bachelor-hood as a farm hand. At this early point, assertions like "he had then a horse of his own and on Saturday evenings drove into town to spend a few hours in social intercourse with other farm hands" seem unremarkable. But as the narrator turns from father to mother, he passes from assertion to assumption, even though the specifics to be assumed about the mother are far more probable than the details presented as facts about the father. "At ten o'clock," we are told indicatively, "father drove home along a lonely country road, made his horse comfortable for the night and himself went to bed, quite happy in his position in life." But in discussing his mother and how, after marriage, "the American passion for getting up in the world took possession" of his parents, the narrator inundates us with subjunctives and conditionals:

> It may have been that mother was responsible. Being a school teacher she had no doubt read books and magazines. She had, I presume, read of how Garfield, Lincoln, and other Americans rose from poverty to fame and greatness and as I lay beside her—in the days of her lying-in—she may have dreamed that I would some day rule men and cities.

The narrator's definite knowledge of the precise and orderly actions of a drunken farm hand, as opposed to his assumption that a school teacher has read books and magazines, has two effects. First, it immediately identifies the son with his father; second, it distances him from his mother, who has introduced ambition into her husband's previously idyllic existence.

Ambition, for the narrator, is always associated with the egg. The couple's first, ill-fated venture is a chicken ranch, and this early exposure to eggs and chickens, according to the narrator, is responsible for his adult fatalism:

> I grew to boyhood on the place and got my first impressions of life there. From the beginning they were impressions of disaster and if, in my turn, I am a gloomy man inclined to see the darker side of life, I attribute it to the fact that what should have been for me the happy joyous days of childhood were spent on a chicken farm.

The narrator then launches into the marvellous "digression" on "the many and tragic things that can happen to a chicken," which forms the crux of the story's symbolism. The various fates awaiting the egg, it turns out, are not only dismal but very much like those awaiting the human baby. "Small chickens, just setting out on the journey of life, look so bright and alert and they are in fact so dreadfully stupid. They are so much like people they mix one up in one's judgment of life." The identification of chickens with people readily marks the hen as a symbol for the mother, and the egg as a symbol for the son and narrator. "My tale does not primarily concern itself with the hen," the narrator proclaims, though the mother's ambitions are the initial cause of trouble. "If correctly told it will center on the egg," that is, on the narrator himself. That the story's "I" is linked with the egg is perhaps a pun on the narrative "ego."

And yet, one might argue, the story centers on neither mother nor son, but on the father, who carries the malformed chickens, "preserved in alcohol and put each in its own glass bottle" from the chicken ranch to the restaurant, the family's next venture. "The grotesques were, he declared, valuable. People, he said, like to look at strange and wonderful things." Human grotesques are similarly valuable to Anderson, who uses them to depict alienation from modern society. But the father's attempts to exhibit his grotesques, especially later for Joe Kane, are futile. Instead, we have the narrator exhibiting his father as a grotesque, a human failure shaped by naive belief in the American dream—and Anderson depicting his own grotesque, the narrator himself. Thus, even when the narrator is discussing his father, the story is still focused on the son.

This is clearest in the crucial scene of the story—the father's disastrous attempt to entertain Joe Kane, which must be read primarily for its content about the son, not the father, because it is also the scene about which the narrator admits he can have no reasonable knowledge. He is only sure of the scene's aftermath, which he witnesses and therefore reports before the recreated scene itself:

> Late one night I was awakened by a roar of anger coming from my father's throat. Both mother and I sat upright in our beds. With trembling hands she lighted a lamp that stood on a table by her head. Downstairs the front door of our restaurant went shut with a bang and in a few minutes father tramped up the stairs. He held an egg in his hand and his hand trembled as though he were having a chill. There was a half-insane light in his eyes. As he stood glaring at us I was sure he intended throwing the egg at either mother or me. Then he laid it gently on the table beside the lamp and dropped on his knees beside mother's bed. He began to cry like a boy and I, carried away by his grief, cried with him.

The narrator has thus constructed his version of the events out of that roar of anger, the bang of the door, his father's emotional state, the egg his father was carrying, his father's plan "to try and entertain the people who came to eat at our restaurant," and, of course, his own *unrelated* memories of the chicken ranch, associations of eggs with failure, and sense of personal inadequacy.

The incidents that the narrator invents to explain his father's breakdown in the bedroom both involve eggs. The first is a parable of his father's grotesqueness, the second of his own. According to the narrator, the father begins with an attack on the legend of Christopher Columbus and the egg. "That Christopher Columbus was a cheat," the father says, because he broke an egg to make it stand on its end. The father then attempts to do in fact what Columbus did only by trickery. "When after a half hour's effort he did succeed in making the egg stand for a moment he looked up to find that his visitor was no longer watching." The American dream is not achieved by those innocent and

sincere enough to follow the rules. Columbus, with whom that dream began, knew this; the father does not.

But the father's defeat is not that of the narrator, who knows of the treachery contained in "the American passion for getting up in the world," and had already warned the reader not to believe in the literature written about that segment of the American dream he has encountered. Indeed, the narrator has resisted attempts to force him into the American pursuit of success just as the egg—his symbol—resists the father's attempts to get it inside a bottle, the second trick; and like that egg, the narrator has been broken.

The key to the narrator's personality is given in the last line of the story, where he describes "the complete and final triumph of the egg—at least as far as my family is concerned." He says "family" to include himself, even though the events of the story occur while he is a boy; in no direct way do we have a defeat of the narrator. The line only makes literal sense when we understand the events as reconstructions of a defeated mind seeking to place the seeds of his defeat—and the blame for it—as far from himself as possible. If the problem originates with his parents, then the solution would be an imaginative negation of their marriage—a wish that finds expression in the idealized bachelorhood of his father as described in the beginning of the story.

On another level, however, where the egg is the narrator's symbol, the triumph at the end is his as well. And the "defeat"—not "of" but only "concerning" his family—is ambiguous enough to allow for this. Not his parents but the system is the ultimate villain for the narrator, and his triumph against it consists simply of recognizing its dangers and refusing to become involved in it. Willed abstention may take a form no more consequential than an interruption in the cycle of the chicken and the egg; but in it, the narrator finds exoneration of his father and himself. According to Lawry, Anderson believed that "men must get rid of self, but at the same time the whole task of art is to gain knowledge of self." In "The Egg," the negative attributes of self are characterized by the ambition the narrator forgoes; and through the telling of his largely invented story, the narrator has come not only to knowledge and acceptance of himself, but of others as well.

> IN 'THE EGG' AS IN NO OTHER STORY OF ANDERSON'S, THE LANGUAGE, IMAGES, DETAILS AND THEMES COALESCE AND ENRICH ONE ANOTHER IN EXTREMELY SUBTLE RELATIONSHIPS, THE COMPLEXITY OF WHICH VERGES ON POETRY AND DEFIES LOGICAL EXPOSITION."

Source: David R. Mesher, "A Triumph of the Ego in Anderson's 'The Egg,'" in *Studies in Short Fiction*, Vol. 17, No. 2, Spring 1980, pp. 180–83.

Michael D. West

In the following excerpt, West reviews the early reviews and analyzes the uniqueness of the literary devices used in "The Egg."

. . . Anderson's affection for the story led him to give its original title to his collection of short stories of 1921. Then worrying lest that seem "a book printed for the sake of one story," he had Huebsch shorten the title of the story to "The Egg."

Early reviewers often singled out the story for praise and all modern interpretive biographies recognize its surpassing merit. James Schevill terms it "one of Anderson's greatest stories and one of the outstanding tales in American literature," and Irving Howe states flatly that "of all Anderson's short fictions 'The Egg' most deserves to be placed among the great stories of the world." Yet, hampered by space, critics of the story have dealt only haphazardly with the reasons for its greatness. Even Howe's admirable discussion relies heavily on plot synopsis and cites but one detail to demonstrate that the story is "complex and ironic." Assuming familiarity with the plot as a point of departure, I hope to substantiate the more acute perceptions embodied in the scanty critical literature on the story.

Anderson's greatest fault as a prose stylist is his saturation in the facile, vaguely evocative phrases of advertising. It saps his command of colloquial expression. But in "The Egg" this facility becomes a virtue. Only an adman could have created the pathetic touch of the father's naively simple, straightforward and honest sign,

EAT HERE, "the command that was so seldom obeyed." Anderson knew that it takes a come-on to bring in the customers; on top of his paint factory in Elyria was the sign, ROOF-FIX: SEND FOR FREE CATALOG. Or take the words with which the father introduces his attempt to bottle the egg: "People will want to know how you got the egg in the bottle. Don't tell them. Keep them guessing. That is the way to have fun with this trick." The short, choppy sentences and the awkward and unidiomatic failure to contract *that is* perfectly mimic the prose of the cheap pamphlets promising to teach you One Hundred and One Easy Tricks, which is also the prose of the cheap mail-order catalogues that vend them. How moving the tyro entertainer's parrot-like repetition of his patter! A curious coincidence enables us to see exactly how in this story Anderson's mail-order prose (his specialty as a copywriter) is transmuted. Alyse Gregory quite properly stigmatized the effusively meaningless language in which Anderson's ideals are often couched, such as the vague phrase "a kind of white wonder of life." Pure Anderson, admittedly, and pure tin—but note how the same combination of words appears in "The Egg": "Wilmer's White Wonder Cholera Cure...advertised in the poultry papers." Clearly, Anderson's often shoddy lyricism derives from his advertising background; but, just as clearly, in this story the lyric impulse is mastered and directed ironically against that background. Consider in this light the paired adjectives in each of the following sentences:

> If, in my turn, I am a gloomy man inclined to see the darker side of life, I attribute it to the fact that what should have been for me the happy joyous days of childhood were spent on a chicken farm.

> I...dreamed I was a tiny thing going along the road into a far beautiful place where there were no chicken farms.

> It is a hopeful literature and declares that much may be done by simple ambitious people who own a few hens.

> In the evening bright happy groups would come singing down Turner's Pike.

In *Mid-American Chants* Anderson tries to make serious statements in language of such falsified simplicity. Here, the phrases are used, without exception, ironically.

Another strand woven into the irony of "The Egg" is the frequent Biblical phraseology. Anderson publicized his indebtedness to the

Bible by tearing pages out of the copies placed in hotel rooms. But when he attempts to use it as a conscious framework, it constricts rather than inspires his imagination, as in the story of Jesse Bentley, the most unsatisfactory section of *Winesburg*. In "The Egg," however, Scriptural echoes, beautifully diffused, expand the significance of the characters and their actions. At times the language is not strictly Biblical but merely has an archaic flavor: "in the days of her lying-in." Sometimes the echo is more specific; the chicken "born out of an egg" that "lives for a few weeks as a tiny fluffy thing...gets diseases...stands looking with stupid eyes at the sun, becomes sick and dies" does so to the cadences of Job's *Man that is born of a woman*. "One might write a book concerning our flight from the chicken-farm into town" suggests, as well as the flight of an army and that of chickens, the Flight into Egypt. Significantly, the first chapters of Genesis bulk largest in Anderson's consciousness. Literature on chicken farms should "be read by the gods who have just eaten of the tree of the knowledge of good and evil." Repeated references to the sweat on the father's brow enhance the meaning of his small life: *In the sweat of thy face shalt thou eat bread*. And the crucial incident of the story is given a weird resonance by the slaying of Abel. After the father has offered the *firstlings of his flock*, Kane's amused rejection of him, though understandable, is also a re-enactment of Cain's murder. This is, of course, in no sense the "meaning" of the scene; the great effectiveness of the Scriptural echoes in this story lies in the fact that they occur with evocative rather than informative value, and with a touch of irony. The father is, after all, the personification of the un-Abel, and there is a twist in having the man whom we know as the "innkeeper" and "restaurant keeper" aspiring to be his *brother's keeper*.

Another skein of language and imagery in this story is spun from Anderson's interest in contemporary psychology. It was undoubtedly this aspect of the story that made Anderson particularly desire the psychiatrist Burrow (with whom in 1916 he had disputed the validity of psychoanalysis) to read the story. In his *Memoirs* Anderson records of the years 1916–17:

> Freud had been discovered at the time and all the young intellectuals were busy analyzing each other and everyone they met. Floyd Dell was hot at it. We had gathered in the evening in somebody's rooms. Well, I hadn't read Freud (in fact, I never did read him) and was rather ashamed of my ignorance. Floyd walked up and down before us...and now he had begun psyching us. Not Floyd alone but others in the group did it. They psyched me. They psyched men passing in the street. It was a time when it was well for a man to be somewhat guarded in the remarks he made, what he did with his hands.

Whether Anderson read Freud or not, his friends certainly made him aware of the basic concepts of psychoanalysis. But while Anderson could recognize the justice of many tenets of Freudian theory and apply them to his work, his distrust of the intellect and intellectuals made him at the same time leery of anything that might be called a science of the mind, anything that seemed to jeopardize what has been aptly termed his corn-fed mysticism. Thus, while the working out of the father-son relationship in "The Egg" bears the unmistakable imprint of Freud, as I shall show in due course, Anderson also uses the story to launch a gleeful attack on certain metaphysical and ethical implications drawn from psychological data. In particular, Anderson takes aim at current misconceptions of the Freudian wish expounded by such books as Edwin B. Holt's *The Freudian Wish and its Place in Ethics* (New York, 1915). The age was able to find warrant in Freud for its own simple-minded brand of optimistic voluntarism, the attitude perhaps most successfully exploited by Emile Coué, who asserted the power of mind over matter to the extent of effecting organic changes in nature, as in supposed cases of prenatal influence. The father in "The Egg" becomes the living denial of the efficacy of positive thinking; and the concept of the grotesque is played against the idea of prenatal influence. Ironic references throughout the story glance at this theme, from the first words:

> My father was, I am sure, intended by nature to be a cheerful, kindly man.

> As I lay beside her—in the days of her lying-in—she may have dreamed that I would some day rule men and cities.

> He decided that he had in the past been an unsuccessful man because he had not been cheerful enough and that in the future he would adopt a cheerful outlook on life.

> There was something pre-natal about the way eggs kept themselves connected with the development of his idea.

Anderson might have been disturbed by the ease with which Coué's famous phrase lent itself to a commercial ethic of growing richer every day in every way. The story treats "the American passion for getting up in the world" as a disease, as the kind of truth which makes grotesques of its devotees. The mother is "incurably ambitious," the father becomes "feverish in his anxiety to please," and the child, "catching the infection," smiles at the cat. This sickness is linked with the diseases plaguing the unfortunate chickens. Thus, facile voluntaristic psychology serves as a perfect bull's-eye at which Anderson can aim his distrust of his intellectual friends, his brooding conviction that life is not ameliorated by scientific certainty. The outer rings of the target include scientific quackery in general—the nostrums "advertised in the poultry papers," the father's mumbo-jumbo about "the electricity that comes out of the human body."

In "The Egg" as in no other story of Anderson's, the language, images, details and themes coalesce and enrich one another in extremely subtle relationships, the complexity of which verges on poetry and defies logical exposition. Random examples must, then, suffice. For instance, though the common idioms *bald as an egg, hen-pecked* and *rooster's egg* do not appear in the story, they are squeezed for all they are worth; the language makes them feed into the story's content. Notice that details such as Pickleville's defunct cider mill and pickle factory, while in no sense symbolic, yet harmonize oddly with "the tree of the knowledge of good and evil" and the father's effort to pickle an egg by boiling it in vinegar. Or listen to the changes rung on the theme of wonder:

> . . . Wilmer's White Wonder Cholera Cure . . .
> . . . the wonders of an unknown world . . .
> . . . see the wonders of the world . . .
> He dreamed of taking the wonder about to country fairs.
> People, he said, liked to look at strange and wonderful things.

And notice especially how this beautifully resonant repetition of an image reinforces the sense of a child's terror at a disturbance affecting his parents:

> They [i.e., deformed chickens] go quickly back to the hand of their maker that has for a moment trembled.

> With trembling hands she lighted a lamp that stood on a table by her head . . . and in a few minutes father tramped up the stairs. He held an egg in his hand and his hand trembled as though he were having a chill.

As much as anything in the story, this image shows us that what the narrator is trying to reduce to the dimensions of an anecdote, seemed to him as a child—and was—nothing less than tumult in heaven, the violation of his parents' Olympian superiority to life. . . .

Source: Michael D. West, "Sherwood Anderson's Triumph: 'The Egg,'" in *American Quarterly*, Vol. 20, No. 4, Winter 1968, pp. 675–93.

SOURCES

Anderson, David D., *Sherwood Anderson: An Introduction and Interpretation*, Barnes & Noble, 1967, pp. ix–x, 4–18.

Anderson, Sherwood, "The Egg," in *The Portable Sherwood Anderson*, edited by Horace Gregory, Viking Press, 1949, pp. 448–62.

Bassett, John E., *Sherwood Anderson: An American Career*, Susquehanna University Press, 2006, p. 66.

"Books and Authors," in *America*, Vol. 26, No. 10, December 24, 1921, p. 236.

"Census 2000 Population Statistics: U.S. Population Living in Urban vs. Rural Areas," U.S. Department of Transportation, Federal Highway Administration website, http://www.fhwa.dot.gov/planning/census_issues/archives/metropolitan_planning/cps2k.cfm (accessed August 13, 2012).

"Chicago Literary Renaissance," in *Encyclopedia of Chicago*, Chicago Historical Society, 2005, http://www.encyclopedia.chicagohistory.org/pages/257.html (accessed August 11, 2012).

Fagin, N. Bryllion, *The Phenomenon of Sherwood Anderson: A Study in American Life and Letters*, Russell and Russell, 1973, p. 19.

Howe, Irving, *Sherwood Anderson*, Stanford University Press, 1951, p. 168.

"Modernism," Literature Network, 2011, http://www.online-literature.com/periods/modernism.php (accessed August 14, 2012).

Rideout, Walter B., *Sherwood Anderson: A Writer in America*, Vol. 1, University of Wisconsin Press, 2006, p. 15.

"Urban and Rural Population for the U.S. and All States: 1900–2000," State Library of Iowa, State Data Center website, http://data.iowadatacenter.org/datatables/UnitedStates/urusstpop19002000.pdf (accessed August 13, 2012).

"U.S. Chicken Industry History," National Chicken Council website, 2012, http://www.nationalchickencouncil.org/about-the-industry/history/ (accessed August 13, 2012).

FURTHER READING

Bassett, Patrick, and Barbara Bassett, "Anderson's 'The Egg,'" in *Explicator*, Vol. 40, No. 1, 1981, pp. 53–54.

This summary of the story covers the major details that a casual reader might not have seen as important on first reading, as well as important ideas explored in the story.

Kazan, Alfred, "The New Realism: Sherwood Anderson," in *Sherwood Anderson's "Winesburg, Ohio": Text and Criticism*, edited by John H. Ferres, Viking Press, 1966, pp. 321–30.

This essay, originally in Kazan's 1942 book *On Native Grounds: An Interpretation of Modern American Prose Literature*, gives readers a solid, traditional interpretation of Anderson's significance in the national literary tradition, written by one of the most respected critics of his time.

Mesher, David R., "A Triumph of the Ego in Anderson's 'The Egg,'" in *Studies in Short Fiction*, Vol. 17, No. 2, 1980, pp. 180–83.

The author looks at this story beside "Death in the Woods," another famous short story by Anderson, using that story to understand the narrator of "The Egg" in depth.

Savin, Mark, "Coming Full Circle: Sherwood Anderson's 'The Egg,'" in *Studies in Short Fiction*, Vol. 18, No. 4, 1981, pp. 454–57.

This essay looks at ways that the narrator is, and ways that he is not, repeating the mistakes of his father.

Williams, Kenny J., *A Storyteller and a City: Sherwood Anderson's Chicago*, Northern Illinois University Press, 1988.

This book takes an in-depth look at Anderson's life during his most productive period of writing, when he had freed himself of the business world and let himself blossom as an artist.

SUGGESTED SEARCH TERMS

Sherwood Anderson AND The Egg

Sherwood Anderson AND Winesburg, Ohio

The Triumph of the Egg

The Egg AND grotesque

Sherwood Anderson AND poultry farm

Sherwood Anderson AND rural life

Chicago renaissance

Sherwood Anderson AND father

The Feather Pillow

HORACIO QUIROGA

1907

The Uruguayan author Horacio Quiroga's short story "The Feather Pillow" was first published in Spanish (as "El almohadón de pluma") in an Argentinian magazine, *Caras y caretas* (Faces and masks), in 1907. This brief story uses foreshadowing and horror to create a tale filled with tension. The heroine, Alicia, is a new bride who has wed expecting a fairy-tale kind of marriage. Her husband, Jordan, is pragmatic and cold, but he does love his new bride. Quiroga was an admirer of Edgar Allan Poe, and "The Feather Pillow" includes the familiar blend of gothic horror, foreshadowing, and mysterious death that readers would expect to find in Poe's short stories.

There are two important themes in "The Feather Pillow": the effect that fairy tales have on marriage and the symbolic meaning of illness and death. In addition, Quiroga teases his readers with clever word associations. For instance, when the sick heroine begins having hallucinations, she imagines an anthropoid—a humanlike creature—crouching on the carpet near her bed. One of the more common parasites to inhabit bird feathers is the arthropod. It is a subtle difference in words, but the effect is to force the reader to rethink the story. An English translation of "The Feather Pillow" can be found in *The Decapitated Chicken, and Other Stories*, published in 1976. The story is also available online at several sites, including Project Gutenberg: http://gutenberg. net.au/ebooks06/0606301h.html.

Horacio Quiroga

AUTHOR BIOGRAPHY

Horacio Silvestre Quiroga was born in Salto, Uruguay, on December 31, 1878. When he was only a few months old, his father, who had been an Argentinian consular official, died in a shotgun accident. When he was a child, Quiroga's mother and stepfather moved several times. He lived in Salto, Córdoba, and finally Montevideo, where he studied at the University of Montevideo. When Quiroga was eighteen years old, his stepfather committed suicide.

By the time he was nineteen, Quiroga had begun publishing his first essays in magazines and newspapers, using the pseudonym Guillermo Eynhardt, a character from an obscure nineteenth-century French novel. Several months in Paris during the spring and summer of 1900 increased Quiroga's interest in poetry and fiction. The following year, Quiroga's first book of poetry, *Los arrecifes de coral* (The coral reefs) was published. In 1902, he accidentally shot and killed a friend. After he was exonerated, Quiroga moved to Buenos Aires, Argentina. In 1904, he published his first collection of short stories, *El crimen del otro* (The crime of another).

To support himself while writing, Quiroga held a succession of teaching positions. "The Feather Pillow" was written in 1907 and published

in an Argentinian magazine, *Caras y caretas* (Faces and masks). Quiroga's first novel, *Historia de un amorturbio* (Story of a troubled love), was published in 1908. The following year, Quiroga married Ana María Cires. The newly wedded couple then moved to Misiones, Argentina, where they lived an isolated life in the jungle. Their daughter was born in 1911 and a son in 1912. In 1914, Quiroga's young wife committed suicide by taking poison. In 1916, Quiroga returned to Buenos Aires with his children but kept his property in Misiones and continued to visit it.

Quiroga's fourth book, *Cuentos de amor, de locura y de muerte* (Tales of love, of madness and of death), a collection of short stories, was published in 1917. Two more collections of short stories, *Cuentos de la selva para los niños* (1918, translated as *South American Jungle Tales*) and *El salvaje y otros cuentos* (The savages and other stories, 1920), soon followed. In 1920, Quiroga published his only play, *Las sacrificadas* (The sacrificed women). This play was followed by more short stories, including "Anaconda" in 1921 and "El desierto" ("The Wilderness") in 1924. One of his most famous short-story collections, *La gallina degollada, y otros cuentos* (The Decapitated Chicken, and Other Stories) was published in 1925. The following year, another collection of Quiroga's short stories, *Los desterrados: Tipos de ambiente* (The Exiles and Other Stories), was published. Very few of Quiroga's writings have been translated into English. These later collections, translated in 1976 and 1987, respectively, along with his jungle tales for children, are the only ones available in English.

In 1927 Quiroga married for a second time. María Elena Bravo was nearly thirty years his junior. The following year, she gave birth to Quiroga's third child and second daughter. But his wife was unable to tolerate the isolated life in the jungles of Misiones that Quiroga enjoyed and soon left her husband. Quiroga's second novel, *Pasado amor* (Past love), came out in 1929. His last collection of short stories, *Más allá* (Farther on), was published in 1935. The following year, Quiroga, who was in poor health, returned to Buenos Aires, where he learned that he had cancer. He committed suicide by swallowing cyanide on February 19, 1937.

MEDIA ADAPTATIONS

- A nine-minute film adaptation of "The Feather Pillow" (with the same title as the story), directed by Gregorio Rabuñal and Terrance Azzuolo, is available for online viewing at http://www.youtube.com/watch?v=S7p3HzrS_Yw. *The Feather Pillow* was produced by GT Productions in 2007.

- The play *The Feather Pillow: A Story of Horacio Quiroga*, written in 2012 by Jonathan Lamb, was performed in South America in March of that year by the UK London Touring Theatre Company. The play, a murder mystery with a focus on horror, is one hour long and includes music. It has not been recorded, nor has it been printed for sale.

PLOT SUMMARY

"The Feather Pillow" opens with the memory of a honeymoon. For the young bride, whose name the reader soon learns is Alicia, the honeymoon was both exciting and fearful. The bride is young and innocent. Her dreams of the perfect marriage and of a husband who is gentle and kind are not the reality she experiences after her honeymoon. After they are married, the bride discovers that her husband, Jordan, is rough and distant. She is slightly afraid of him and even shudders with apprehension when, after the honeymoon ends, the newly married couple approach their home for the first time. The narrator reassures readers that the groom loves his new bride very much but is determined not to show his love.

The first three months of the marriage pass quickly, and although the bride remains unsure of herself and a bit afraid of her new husband, she is not unhappy. The narrator describes the house in which the couple lives as cold and white and empty enough that footsteps echo in the vacant spaces. Alicia is determined, though, to make her best effort to be a good wife. She tries to put aside her dreams of an idyllic marriage and home and largely sleepwalks through the days spent in the empty house. The narrator characterizes the house as hostile to Alicia; it seems to have taken on a malicious personality, even though it is an inanimate entity.

Alicia loses weight and suffers from a mild attack of influenza that lingers for an indeterminate time. She is never completely well again. One day she is able to walk in the garden with Jordan's help. When he caresses her hair, she collapses in his arms and begins to cry. She tells him of all her fears and longings during the past three months, and as he continues to comfort her, she sobs even more loudly. This is the last time that Alicia is well enough to leave her room.

Jordan calls the doctor to visit his wife, but the doctor cannot find the cause of Alicia's illness. She is weak, but there is no known physical cause. The doctor tells Jordan to call him the next day if she is still unwell. The following day, Alicia is sicker than on the previous day. Although she no longer faints, she is severely anemic and grows progressively worse each day.

Every day, Alicia's room is kept illuminated and silent. Jordan maintains a vigil nearby in the drawing room, which is the parlor of the house. Jordan paces as he worries about his young wife. After several days of lying in bed sleeping, Alicia begins to have hallucinations. At first she thinks that she sees an indistinct shape in the air, but later she thinks that she sees something vaguely humanlike hovering on its fingertips on the carpet. Quiroga refers to the vague shape as an anthropoid, which is a term used to describe the ape genus in biology. When Alicia screams, Jordan runs into the room, and she mistakes him for the monster on the carpet. When she finally recognizes her husband, Alicia is calm. The hallucination of an anthropoid crouching on the carpet is the most common hallucination that she endures throughout her illness.

The doctors continue to visit Alicia but admit they have no idea what is wrong. It is obvious to everyone that she will soon die. Her husband is in despair at the doctors' inability to help his wife. The narrator explains that Alicia's illness always worsens at night but that during the day she improves somewhat. The improvement allows her to leave her bed briefly to sit in her room. Soon her condition worsens again; each morning when she awakens, Alicia feels as if a gigantic weight is sitting upon her. This worsened state lasts for three days, and eventually Alicia is unable to move even her head. She insists that her bedcovers not be touched.

Alicia's hallucinations continue, and she imagines monsters climbing on her bed. The narrator describes these hallucinations as "crepuscular terrors," referring to animals that are active in the twilight. Alicia cries out in her delirium. These are the only sounds she makes during the final two days of her life. The house has begun to resemble a funeral parlor, with the quiet and the low illumination that now permeates the house. Soon, Alicia dies.

When the servant changes the bedding, she discovers blood on the pillowcase. The spots look like punctures. The servant calls Jordan, and he asks her to hold the pillow toward the light so that he can see more clearly. The servant quickly drops the pillow, though, because it seems very heavy. Her fear is palpable and causes a sudden fear in Jordan as well.

Jordan takes the pillow to the dining room and rips it open. Both Jordan and the servant see a ball of swollen animal, engorged with so much blood that its mouth is difficult to visualize completely. Every night, the monster in the pillow attached itself to Alicia's temples and consumed her blood. She was momentarily better during the day, after the servant plumped the pillow and Alicia had a few moments of respite from the animal's incessant sucking. During the final five days of her life, when she was unable to leave the bed, the monster in the pillow drank her blood without impediment.

Quiroga finishes "The Feather Pillow" with a few comments about the nature of the monster in the pillow. He observes that these parasites, which typically hide in the feathers of birds, are usually quite small but, when given access to blood, can grow quite large. They especially enjoy human blood. Moreover, the presence of these blood-feasting parasites is not at all rare in feather pillows.

CHARACTERS

Alicia

Alicia is blond, angelic, and timid. Although her age is never mentioned by Quiroga, she is described as young and girlish. Her dreams of marriage are childish, but she is much loved by her husband, Jordan. Alicia is slightly afraid of her husband, although it is not suggested that he has mistreated her in any way. His distant and cold persona does not reassure her; indeed, his somewhat cold manner frightens her. Alicia is afraid of the new changes in her life. When she anticipated marriage, she had the fairy-tale expectation of a gentle and sweet husband who would be a match for her own naive lack of experience.

Alicia is not without inner strength. Although Jordan does not live up to her expectations of an ideal husband, rather than demand that he change or that he at least attempt to meet her expectations, Alicia simply buries her desires and her wish for a gentle and loving husband. When her health begins to falter, Jordan's gentle caressing of her hair causes Alicia to dissolve into sobs. This is when Alicia is finally able to tell Jordan about all of her longings and fears. Quiroga describes the period before this emotional collapse as Alicia's determination to "live like a sleeping beauty." This reference to the fairy tale once again reminds readers that Alicia sees herself as some sort of fairy-tale heroine waiting for a prince to rescue her.

Quiroga makes clear that a significant part of the fear that causes Alicia's shudders and the chills that she experiences are caused by the atmosphere of the house. The house inhabits Alicia's psyche in a way that is never fully explained. The house is cold and empty, devoid of warmth, and Alicia is especially vulnerable to this atmosphere. Her spirit is gentle and easily influenced. She lacks the emotional strength to withstand the house's possession of her.

Doctors

There are a series of doctors in "The Feather Pillow," but none is given a name or a distinguishing description. They are all vague entities who visit Alicia and report to her husband that they have no idea what is wrong. They clearly recognize that she is losing blood and is anemic but have no idea why. They also do not know how to treat a disease they cannot diagnose.

What is obvious to the doctors is that they are helpless to stop the worsening of Alicia's mysterious illness and helpless to stop her steady progression toward death.

Jordan

Jordan is Alicia's husband. There is little description of him, except that he loves his wife very much but does not allow anyone to witness the depth of his love. He does not even permit his wife to see his love for her. This suggests the perceived necessity of a macho image, which is what the husband wishes others to see. Jordan's distant love for his wife and his seemingly rough demeanor counter what the narrator tells readers about his deep love for his wife. The impression is that Jordan thinks his love for Alicia will make him appear weak, rather than strong.

For most of the story, Jordan is little more than a shadowy figure. What readers know of him is mediated by Alicia, who is searching for a romantic prince and instead finds herself with a human man, who lacks perfection. Jordan does not know that he is supposed to be a gentle prince, and it is only after Alicia's sobbing collapse in his arms that he realizes that she was expecting something very different from marriage. Jordan's age is not given, but he is likely much older than Alicia. He is no longer naive and innocent. He is a man, whereas she is still a girl.

Jordan is quick to call the doctors at the first sign of Alicia's illness. When she becomes ill, he remains at home in the house with her. He no longer goes to work, and he stays up all night, pacing back and forth across the drawing-room carpet. The extent of Jordan's worry and concern for his young wife is made clear in the "tireless persistence" with which he paces day and night. Although readers know of Jordan's devotion and love, Alicia does not. In her hallucination, she mistakes him for a monster that threatens her. Jordan must gently reassure his wife that he is her loving husband and that he seeks only to help her. He is not some imagined monster.

Servant

The role of the servant is very brief. She does not even have a name and is largely invisible. The servant has been in the house all along, but her presence does not allay Alicia's fears about the house. Readers hear about the servant only after Alicia has died. It is the servant who discovers the blood on the pillowcase. She is also present when Jordan cuts open the pillow to discover the parasitic monster that has been consuming Alicia's lifeblood.

THEMES

Fairy Tales

The fairy-tale motif is an important theme in "The Feather Pillow." While the fairy tale itself is in no way represented in Quiroga's short story, Alicia identifies with the fairy-tale heroine's happy ending as somehow representative of the kind of life she expects to have when she marries. Alicia envisions a romantic marriage based on fairy-tale stereotypes. She has always thought of herself as the princess and her husband-to-be as the gentle and handsome prince. The reality is far different. "The Feather Pillow" begins by telling readers that Alicia "had dreamed about being a bride." Dreaming about being a bride is not uncommon for many young women, but Quiroga continues in "The Feather Pillow" to explain that Alicia decides to force herself to put aside her dreams. Instead she will "live like a sleeping beauty" every day until her husband returns home in the evening. The reference to the fairy-tale "The Sleeping Beauty" suggests that Alicia needs her husband to come home each day and awaken her to life and marriage. When he is gone, she is like the heroine of a fairy tale, asleep until her Prince Charming appears and rescues her.

The reason that Alicia must put aside her dreams is that her new husband is not at all like the husband of her dreams. He is rough and cold and distant in his dealings with her. Jordan's presence chills his new wife, who expected a warmer husband—one who could tell her of his love and who would treat her with kindness. Instead, Jordan is a husband who loves his wife very much but who is determined not to show his love. He is not tender with her, and Alicia wishes that he could be "more expansive" in his affection toward her. She is unable to tell Jordan of her needs because he seems cold and distant and not approachable. He can let hours pass without speaking to her. Quiroga does not provide any background to either of their lives, except to tell readers that Alicia is very young and girlish. She is timid and childish and completely unprepared for the reality of such a marriage.

TOPICS FOR FURTHER STUDY

- Edgar Allan Poe wrote American short stories about death, including about death connected to or caused by animals. Choose either "The Black Cat" or "The Murders in the Rue Morgue" and prepare an oral presentation in which you use a chart to show the similarities and differences between the Poe short story and "The Feather Pillow."

- Watch the short video of "The Feather Pillow" on YouTube (http://www.youtube.com/watch?v=S7p3HzrS_Yw) and then prepare a multimedia presentation in which you incorporate brief scenes from the video in a discussion of the director's interpretation of this short story. Focus on how the characters and the events are depicted on screen. Do not neglect any aspect of the director's choices, from the actors selected to costuming, set, music, lighting, and so on. Draw comparisons between the film and Quiroga's story and discuss both the similarities and the differences in the two formats.

- Choose a short story by Gabriel García Márquez, whose stories are part of a literary tradition called *magic realism*, which is often associated with Latin American literature. Research magic realism and the literary elements that most closely define this style of writing. After reading Márquez's short story, write an essay in which you compare the elements of magic realism in his story with those found in "The Feather Pillow."

- Artists are often inspired by writers to create the most beautiful art imaginable. For instance, the poetry of John Milton spurred William Blake to create illustrations of the poet's finest work. Look through art at online sites and select five pictures that you feel best illustrate "The Feather Pillow." Use a PowerPoint presentation to show your choices to your classmates and ask them to choose the image they think best exemplifies Quiroga's story. Ask them to explain their choices and to note the similarities and differences between artwork and prose.

- *Like Water for Chocolate* (1992), based on the 1989 novel by Laura Esquivel, is a film with Latin American characters and magic realism at its core. Watch this film and then prepare an oral presentation that compares the kinds of messages that Quiroga and *Like Water for Chocolate* director Alfonso Arau relate to their respective audiences. Engage your classmates in a discussion of which format delivers the message most clearly and why that particular format is more successful than the other. This film is rated R and contains a brief scene of nudity.

- Rudyard Kipling's short story "They," first published in 1904, was written only three years before Quiroga wrote "The Feather Pillow." Kipling's ghost story for teenage readers focuses on nature. Read "They," which is readily available online (http://www.readbookonline.net/readOnLine/8677/), and write an essay in which you compare Quiroga's short story with Kipling's. The focus in your essay should be the way in which each author uses language and sentence structure to create mystery and fear in the reader.

The setting for "The Feather Pillow" adds to the fairy-tale theme of the story. The house, like its master, is distant and cold. Despite its chill atmosphere and "glacial brilliance," it does fulfill the fairy-tale requirement that it be a palace fit for a princess. It is, indeed, described as an "enchanted palace," but the enchantment is not friendly to Alicia. Like the princess's surroundings in "The Sleeping Beauty," the palace in "The Feather Pillow" appears abandoned and empty, devoid of life and warmth. Sounds echo through the emptiness and create both tension and a

Alicia was already frail when she and Jordan were married. (© vefora | ShutterStock.com)

this impression largely through the depiction of the house, which is cold and threatening, even "hostile," and the description of Alicia's hallucinations, in which she thinks her husband is a monster threatening her life. It is only in the final paragraph that the author divulges that Alicia has died from the ill effects of a pest commonly found in nature.

"The Feather Pillow" is not so much about death as it is the experience of death as a result of parasitism. Although Alicia dies at the conclusion of the story, most of the story is about the process of her dying and the fear that grips her as she dies. Alicia's fear is of the unknown, but in the final paragraph the author explains that while the tale appears to be a horror story, the cause of Alicia's death is quite straightforwardly attributable to a creature found in nature. The feathers in her pillow are infested by an unidentified bird parasite common in the natural world and in bird feathers. In this case, a new bride has died from the effects of a bird parasite, which Quiroga assures readers is found in many feather pillows. A woman is defeated by nature.

STYLE

Foreshadowing

Foreshadowing is a technique that allows the writer to create a darker mood by suggesting an ominous change in events in the future. In a detective story, a writer might use foreshadowing to provide clues to help a reader solve the crime. In "The Feather Pillow," Quiroga describes the house as hostile and frightening to Alicia. Right away, readers are apprehensive for her safety. Then she falls ill, and doctors cannot diagnose the illness. All of these events produce an atmosphere of foreboding. Readers know that the heroine's life is at risk. It is not clear exactly what is happening, but the danger is very real. The sense of foreboding not only creates mystery but also adds to the tension within the story and keeps readers interested in the unfolding developments.

Gothic Fiction

Gothic stories are defined as mysterious tales with horror and an atmosphere of foreboding. The young, innocent, and naive heroine is a common character in gothic fiction, as is the older, more experienced, but coldly remote

sense of foreboding. Alicia and Jordan's married life does not bear out the happy fairy-tale ending of marriage between a princess and a prince. The story moves toward its inevitable end, with the princess dead. No prince is able to save her.

Death

Throughout most of "The Feather Pillow," the story appears to be one of a mysterious, unexplained illness that results in death. The heroine's death seems inevitable when her doctors declare themselves both unable to diagnose her illness and unable to save her life. It is only at the end of the story that a small bloodsucking monster is found in her pillow. Even at this point in the story, the events that have unfolded do not seem to have occurred as a result of natural causes. Nature, with its cycle of birth, life, and death, is not blamed. Alicia's death has such an air of mystery about it that it seems as though supernatural events are at work. Quiroga creates male protagonist. Even the house in gothic fiction has a tale to tell. It often appears to pose a danger to the heroine. A feeling of terror—danger from an unknown source—is a common element, as in "The Feather Pillow," when Alicia senses something wrong in the house but is unsure exactly what the danger might be. Romance and realism are also hallmarks of the genre. Alicia loves her husband, but he represents an unknown risk to the young, inexperienced bride. The horror in the tale is represented by Alicia's unexplained illness and her descent toward death. The final horror is revealed when the parasitic monster that fed on Alicia is found at the end of the story.

Magic Realism

Magic realism is the mixing of realism with contrasting elements of fantasy, dreams, visions, and the supernatural. There are often two seemingly conflicting messages in magic realism, with the rational being paired with the supernatural. In magic realism the real world may blend with some aspect of a supernatural world that is not obviously magical but also not quite real. In "The Feather Pillow," Alicia thinks that the house is "hostile" to her, as if the house were a living entity that threatens her. After she falls ill, she has hallucinations in which she imagines a monster crawling up on the bed with her or in which her husband is a monster. It is only after her death that the hallucinations are explained. The author's final comments about the risk of using feather pillows is also designed to describe a frightening conclusion as being within the realm of possibility.

Symbolism

Symbolism is the use of one object to stand in for another—employing a concrete object to represent an idea. Symbolism flourished during the nineteenth century and has continued to be an important force in literature into the twenty-first century. The *symbol* is an object or image that implies a reality beyond its original meaning. This is different from a metaphor, which summons forth an object in order to describe an idea or a quality. There are a couple of examples of symbolism in "The Feather Pillow." The narrator describes the house in which Alicia and Jordan live as white inside and outside and quiet, except for the echoes of footsteps whenever anyone walks through the empty space. The house is not warm and welcoming, and its coldness is

frightening to Alicia. It symbolizes the emptiness and coldness of her marriage to Jordan, who also frightens Alicia. He is quiet, and his emotional distance is empty of warmth in much the same way as the house. After she becomes ill, Alicia suffers hallucinations of a monster stalking her. These hallucinations are symbolic of her fear of her new husband, who is cold and distant but also fearsome and strange.

Alicia and Jordan marry in the early fall, a time during which nature begins to prepare for winter. This is a period of decline following the abundance of the harvest. Trees lose their leaves, and animals fatten up in preparation for the long months of winter. Alicia's initial illness takes place during the three months of fall. She is only slightly ill but begins to lose weight; like nature her body is in decline. It is winter when she dies, a period characterized by death in nature before the great rebirth of spring. The symbolism of the seasons is emphasized by the narrator in telling the story of Alicia's decline in health and her lingering death.

HISTORICAL CONTEXT

Women's Lives in Argentina

Although Quiroga was born in Uruguay, he spent most of his adult life in Argentina, where the history and culture figured in his short stories. Alicia's life in "The Feather Pillow" is one spent waiting for her husband to return home. For many women living in Argentina and other Latin American cities in 1907, a brief life spent at home (such as Alicia's) would not have been abnormal. At the end of the nineteenth century most women were not employed outside the home, although many woman were involved with issues of social reform in Argentina. There was a strong feminist movement, and many women wanted to be equal to men, but political reform was slow to include women in any significant way. Women in Argentina were talking about political and social equality, but the reality was far different. Although they were not permitted to vote or hold office, women in Argentina were heavily influenced by the new female émigrés who were arriving from Europe in the first decades of the twentieth century. They were also influenced by feminist activities under way in North America. Women were not all limited to occupying only the space of their

COMPARE
&
CONTRAST

- **1907:** At the beginning of the twentieth century, Argentina is considered the richest country in South America, with a population of nearly four million people, many of them wealthy emigrants from Europe.

  Today: The economy in Argentina suffers from a near recession, and austerity measures cause many young people to leave the country looking for work elsewhere.

- **1907:** Argentinian beef is so highly regarded in Europe that large quantities are loaded onto newly developed refrigerated ships for transport to Europe. The export of beef and wool from sheep makes ranching one of the most important industries in Argentina.

  Today: Taxes on exports have been raised to such a degree that the once-flourishing export business of beef and wool is seriously threatened.

- **1907:** Only the landed oligarchy are allowed to vote. As a result, only the wealthiest men

have any input in government decisions. Women are not allowed to vote at all.

  Today: Argentina is currently governed by a woman president, Cristina Fernández de Kirchner. This is only the second time in Argentina's history that a woman has held the highest office in the country. Like Eva Perón before her, Kirchner is the widow of the previous president.

- **1907:** In general, health care in Argentina is superior to that in many other areas of Latin America, largely because British doctors have assumed control of medical care.

  Today: Health care in Argentina is generally regarded as very good. Nearly 10 percent of Argentina's gross national product is spent on health care, which is comparable to that in western European countries. Hospitals are modern, and doctors are well trained, with the best level of care available in such larger communities as Buenos Aires.

---

homes, as Alicia was. Many women expressed themselves through public writing, especially journalism, even while in literature written by men they continued to be limited to the family home and domestic sphere of the past. Women also worked as schoolteachers, which was one of the more acceptable employment opportunities for them. They also demanded equal access to education and wanted equality in divorce and issues related to family law and equal pay in the few fields in which women competed with men. In their demands for equality, they were not completely successful in achieving their desires.

Women living in Argentina were interested in child care, nutrition, and women's health, but the influx of so many new European immigrants in the late nineteenth and early twentieth centuries created conflict in the traditional view of women's lives, as dictated by the Catholic Church, which had heavily influenced the

domestic sphere in Latin America for many decades. In 1880, Pope Leo XIII felt a need to reaffirm the role of women in marriage and society. He issued two papal bulls: *Rerum novarum* addressed the condition and duties of the working classes and *Arcanum divinae sapientiae* covered the sacrament of marriage. With respect to women, these bulls were intended to reestablish limits on their lives, especially their role in marriage. Women were reminded that husbands were the head of the family and that they were to be obeyed, although men were cautioned that a wife's status was that of a companion and not a servant. Most important, women were to remain in the home, while their husbands supported them. Pope Leo XIII instructed women that they were naturally best suited for housework and for raising children. If it was necessary for women to work outside the home, they were to remember that they were subservient to men and

After Alicia died, the maid discovered the secret in the feather pillow. *(© Artbox / ShutterStock.com)*

should remain pious and modest in their behavior. Women were discouraged from working in factories and offices. They could be educated, but their education should include a significant emphasis on moral behavior. The pope reminded women that the family was the most important unit in Argentinian society, as had been the tradition in the past. It is easy to see how a woman like Alicia in "The Feather Pillow" would be determined to accept her unhappy isolation and remain in a home that frightened her, where she would find her only happiness in waiting for her husband to return home after work each day.

CRITICAL OVERVIEW

As is often the case with poems, individual short stories are not usually reviewed by critics. Quiroga's short story "The Feather Pillow" is included in the collection *The Decapitated Chicken, and Other Stories*, selected and translated for publication by Margaret Sayers Peden in 1976. This collection was reviewed by several different publications, including the *New Yorker*. In the *New Yorker* article, the anonymous reviewer fills much of the space by recounting all of the tragedies in Quiroga's life, which are put forward to account for a collection of tales that are "in some way marked by violence and tragedy." The reviewer does note that most of the stories are "lucid and written with

great economy." This reviewer makes a brief comparison to Poe, writing that Quiroga's stories are "full of psychological shocks and eerie effects, and are bracingly, if ruthlessly, realistic."

In a review of *The Decapitated Chicken, and Other Stories* that appeared in *Latin American Literary Review*, Robert Brody begins by mentioning how fortunate readers are to finally have access to an English translation of these twelve Quiroga stories. Brody tells readers that before the publication of *The Decapitated Chicken, and Other Stories*, "it has been difficult for readers of English to fully appreciate Quiroga's preeminent role in the development of the short narrative in Latin America." One of the major strengths of this collection is the translator's choice of stories. As a result, readers "are able to appreciate the full range of talents of this extraordinary writer." Brody points out that "obsession with violent death . . . forms a principal thematic nucleus" in Quiroga's work and specifically cites "The Feather Pillow" in this respect, which he says "calls to mind the Gothic horror tale." In his *Books Abroad* essay "The Present State of Fiction in Latin America," the Argentinian novelist and short-story writer Julio Cortázar agrees, saying that "for Quiroga the fantastic appears in a climate of which Edgar Allan Poe would have approved" and citing as his example "one of his best stories," "The Feather Pillow," with its "monstrous and entomological ending."

The review of *The Decapitated Chicken, and Other Stories* that appeared in *Commonweal* was even more celebratory. Critic Ronald de Feo compares Quiroga to Poe and claims that "Quiroga has the ability to thrust the reader into the heart of a story and hold him there." De Feo is especially complimentary of Quiroga's mastery of the short-story genre, which is well suited to his "superb craftsmanship and lively powers of invention." Many of de Feo's comments focus on Quiroga's subject matter and his ability to turn ordinary details into extraordinary events. According to de Feo, in Quiroga's hands, "commonplace reality takes on a mysterious and a mythic quality." Although de Feo never mentions translator Peden by name or "The Feather Pillow" by title, he does claim that *The Decapitated Chicken, and Other Stories* includes some of Quiroga's "very finest work in a superbly designed volume." From these reviews it becomes clear that the arrival of an English translation of Quiroga's short stories was a long-awaited event applauded by those who admire Latin American literature.

CRITICISM

Sheri Karmiol

Karmiol teaches literature and drama at the University of New Mexico, where she is an adjunct professor in the University Honors Program. In the following essay, she discusses how well "The Feather Pillow" fits Quiroga's often-quoted decalogues for writing a short story.

Eighteen years after he wrote "The Feather Pillow," Quiroga published an essay in which he provides a decalogue for writing the perfect short story. Three years later, in 1928, he published an additional two essays, once again listing the requirements for the successful short story. In a fourth essay, published in 1931, Quiroga focuses on the short story as the genre by which his own literary talents would be judged. These four essays suggest that Quiroga felt the need to justify his talent as a writer of short stories, which he worried would be judged to be less significant than the work of novel writers. As a result, Quiroga wanted to separate the short-story genre from that of the novel. In these essays, he seeks to define the parameters of the short story as a complex and worthy endeavor for writers. What becomes clear after reading these four essays is that throughout his career as a short-story writer, Quiroga had been

> ALTHOUGH IT WAS WRITTEN MUCH EARLIER IN HIS CAREER, 'THE FEATHER PILLOW' ABLY DEMONSTRATES QUIROGA'S ADHERENCE TO THE DECALOGUES THAT HE WOULD NOT FORMALLY PUBLISH UNTIL ALMOST TWO DECADES LATER."

compiling a set of formal guidelines for perfecting the short-story genre. Although it was written much earlier in his career, "The Feather Pillow" ably demonstrates Quiroga's adherence to the decalogues that he would not formally publish until almost two decades later.

As a writer of more than two hundred short stories, Quiroga carefully crafted the genre throughout nearly thirty years of writing. As he neared the end of his literary life, Quiroga set forth the guidelines that he had developed over his long career. What is astonishing is that he published these decalogues three separate times. Then, in a fourth essay, "Before the Tribunal," Quiroga defends his choice to focus his career on short-story writing. The first essay, "A Manual for the Perfect Short Story Writer," is translated and reprinted in an article by William Peden, "Some Notes on Quiroga's Stories." Margaret Sayers Peden has edited and translated both of Quiroga's 1928 essays on the rules of short-story writing, "The Crisis of the National Short Story" and "The Rhetoric of the Short Story," as part of "Horacio Quiroga on the Short Story." She also includes "Before the Tribunal," in which Quiroga imagines he has to defend the short-story genre in court. All four of these essays articulate the talent needed to write an effective and entertaining short story.

Quiroga's first rule for writing short stories is to look to the masters of the genre. These are the men whose reputations were established through their talents for writing short stories. Quiroga cites Edgar Allan Poe, Rudyard Kipling, and Guy de Maupassant among the masters of the genre. Quiroga did not think it necessary to discuss these men's contributions to the genre separately. Instead, he writes in "The Rhetoric of the Short Story" that they are "all one and the same thing in their 'storyness.'" Their nationalities do

WHAT DO I READ NEXT?

- Quiroga's collection *The Decapitated Chicken, and Other Stories*, translated into English and published in 1976, contains twelve short stories that span his career (dating from 1907 to 1935), including the title story, "The Decapitated Chicken," which is considered a masterpiece of short fiction.

- Another of Quiroga's collections, *The Exiles and Other Stories*, translated into English and published in 1987, contains thirteen tales and a chronology of Quiroga's life.

- *The Eye of the Heart: Short Stories from Latin America* (1973), edited by Barbara Howes, features more than forty short stories from such authors as Jorge Luis Borges, Pablo Neruda, Octavio Paz, and Gabriel García Márquez. Howes includes a Quiroga short story, "The Alligator War," which was originally published in 1918.

- Quiroga is often compared to Edgar Allan Poe. *The Complete Short Stories of Edgar Allan Poe* (2012) is a two-volume set of all of Poe's short stories.

- *The Oxford Book of Latin American Poetry* (2009) is a bilingual anthology of poetry written by Latin American poets over a span of five hundred years. The poetry in this anthology offers a contrast to Latin American short stories and highlights the wealth of literature created by Latin American writers.

- *Gothic! Ten Original Dark Tales* (2004), edited by Deborah Noyes, is a collection of gothic-themed short stories for teenage readers written by young-adult authors M. T. Anderson, Caitlín R. Kiernan, Garth Nix, and others.

- *Japanese Gothic Tales* (1996), by Izumi Kyoka, is a collection of Japanese ghost stories. Kyoka has been called the Japanese Poe. These four short stories also serve to teach readers lessons about Japanese cultural life and values.

- *A Walk in My World: International Short Stories about Youth* (2000) is a collection of short stories about young adults intended for young-adult readers. The stories take place in many different countries, including Chile, Ghana, Russia, Egypt, and India.

- *Edgar Allan Poe in Hispanic Literature* (1934), by John Eugene Englekirk, is a very early examination of the influence of Poe's writings on Latin American authors. One chapter focuses on how Poe influenced Quiroga's writing.

- *A Hammock beneath the Mangoes: Stories from Latin America* (1992) is a collection of short stories from Central and South America and the Caribbean. There are stories by many of the leading Latin American writers, including Quiroga's "The Dead Man," Jorge Luis Borges's "The Circular Ruins," and Isabel Allende's "Toad's Mouth."

---

not matter, nor does the era in which they wrote. Rather, says Quiroga, it is "the concept, the courage in the telling, the intensity, the brevity," which are the same for all writers. In writing "The Feather Pillow," Quiroga looked to the paradigm established by earlier writers, most clearly Poe, whose gothic horror is much in evidence in the mysterious illness and death of Alicia. In a chapter devoted to Poe's influence on Quiroga, John

Eugene Englekirk writes in *Edgar Allan Poe in Hispanic Literature* that Quiroga, more than any other Hispanic writer, found inspiration in Poe. Englekirk claims that "in manner and in style, in the exotic and extraordinary temper of his themes, and in the wedding of psychological acumen to states of horror," Quiroga is one of the "most successful adherents to the Poesque genre of the short story." Quiroga's use of psychological terror in "The Feather Pillow" is revealed through Alicia's unease in her new home, which she senses is "hostile" to her. Then, as her psychological terror grows, Alicia imagines that her husband is a monster. Finally, at the end of the story, Quiroga reveals the monster in her pillow and then terrifies his reader by explaining that "human blood seems particularly favorable to them [these parasitic creatures], and it is not rare to encounter them in feather pillows." Since many of Quiroga's readers might be sleeping on feather pillows, this final line of the story is designed to leave the reader perched on a precipice of horror and in the midst of his or her own psychological terror.

Quiroga believed that the short story should be concisely written and that it was not necessary for it to have the clearly plotted beginning, middle, and end that are so important in a novel. Quiroga claims in his essay "The Crisis of the National Short Story" that "the short story writer has the capacity to suggest more than he says." This is an idea that Quiroga put to use in "The Feather Pillow," where, in the opening lines, he uses only a few words to tell readers all that they need to know about Alicia, who is "blond, angelic, and timid" and "chilled by her husband's rough character." From these few words, readers know that Alicia is innocent, naive, immature, and unsure of herself. She is also a bit frightened by her husband, who is a grown man, while she is still just a girl. Quiroga did not believe in using flowery language and admonished short-story writers not to pad their stories with unnecessary "descriptions, dialogues and circumstances," which constitute a novel. In its brevity, a short story, according to Quiroga, "should never exceed one page," although later in his essay he writes that "1256 words" is "better still." At 1,320 words, "The Feather Pillow" exceeds by only 5 percent Quiroga's suggested word length.

Quiroga also felt that it is necessary for the short-story writer to have the ability to convey power in his prose as well as the capacity to infuse his words with a power that would hold the readers' attention. In "The Crisis of the National Short Story," Quiroga describes this as the "triple capacity for feeling with intensity, for attracting attention, and for communicating sentiments with energy." These three elements create an intensity of expression that is important in the short story, where the necessary brevity limits the writer's words. The first line in "The

Feather Pillow" incorporates all three of these ideas in one succinct sentence: "Her entire honeymoon gave her hot and cold shivers." The first line is a grabber that pulls the reader into the story. There are no wasted words. This simple sentence is intense and filled with meaning. There is passion associated with the honeymoon, but there is also fear. It is not yet clear whether the fear is associated with her husband's strength or his demands or whether it is the wife's own childishness and innocence that are responsible for such conflicting emotions.

Quiroga states in "The Crisis of the National Short Story" that the qualities of a short-story writer are sufficiently different that it is not possible to cross the line between different genres. In his view, none of the great novelists—among them, Leo Tolstoy, Fyodor Dostoyevsky, Émile Zola, and Joseph Conrad—have been able to master the short story. The converse is true of the great short-story writers—Bret Harte, Guy de Maupassant, Anton Chekhov, and Rudyard Kipling, for example—whose novels were never as good as their short stories. This is so because, suggests Quiroga, "the novelist, to achieve an equal effect, requires much more space." According to Quiroga, each genre requires a different talent. Quiroga is best known for his short stories and not for his poems, play, or two novels (a fact he himself acknowledged in his lifetime); nearly three decades of writing established him as a talented short-story writer and not as a novelist, and thus he knew that the talents for each are uniquely different.

In "A Manual for the Perfect Short Story Writer," Quiroga admonishes his readers not to write for friends or for an unknown audience. Instead, writers should write the short story as if the characters have come to life under the writer's pen. Writers should write for the characters. It is the characters' story, and it is also the writer's story; thus, suggests Quiroga, a writer should write as if the author is a character in the story. "Only in this way," says Quiroga, "is the life of the story obtained." This instruction is tenth in this essay's decalogue, but it fits well with Quiroga's fourth admonition to "love your art as your sweetheart, giving it all your heart." Both of these instructions are useful in creating a compelling short story such as "The Feather Pillow," in which a character like Alicia dominates. Her transformation from an uneasy young bride in the first lines of the story to a

What was the role of the giant leech? *(© Denis Barbulat | ShutterStock.com)*

woman seized by an unknown psychological terror in the conclusion pulls the reader into the story to share Alicia's fear and perhaps her fate.

Finally, it is the fifth in Quiroga's list of commandments for writing the perfect short story that demands the perfect synthesis of character, action, and plot. Quiroga states that "the first three lines have almost the same importance as the last three" in writing "an accomplished story." In the first three lines of "The Feather Pillow," readers are told everything they need to know about the bride—her unease with her new husband, her youth and inexperience, her fairy-tale-like dreams about her wedding, and the fact that none of her dreams has quite worked out as she thought they would. At the end, the young bride dies, after "the monster had drained Alicia's life away." Because the first lines establish a sense of unease about the husband, readers expect her husband to be responsible for his bride's death. Quiroga throws in a surprise ending, but perhaps readers should have been prepared for the twist at the end. The monster in the pillow has simply been feeding off the young, naive, neglected, and unhappy wife, whose life was so clearly defined in the first lines of "The Feather Pillow." There are no wasted words in a Quiroga short story. Every word has meaning, but some provide clues that are especially important not to ignore.

In the brief space of this essay it is not possible to discuss each of Quiroga's decalogues separately or in depth. Their influence in "The Feather Pillow," though, is obvious, especially the author's reliance on a model established by Poe. Although Quiroga initially admonishes his readers in "A Manual for the Perfect Short Story Writer" to "resist imitation," he also tells them to "imitate if the influence is too strong," as it evidently is with Poe's model. The brevity of "The Feather Pillow" is in keeping with Quiroga's admonition to make sure the story is "stripped of padding" and to eliminate the use of flowery language or unnecessary adjectives. In addition, the imagination and vividness of Quiroga's prose transform "The Feather Pillow" into a short story that is difficult to stop reading. In "Before the Tribunal," Quiroga imagines that he is testifying in court. He explains why he fought so hard to perfect the short story and to define its parameters: "This is what I dedicated myself to demonstrate, to give the short story what belonged to the short story, and to verse, its own essential virtues." Quiroga ends this essay wondering how time will judge his life's work. If "The Feather Pillow" is any indication, he will be judged most favorably.

Source: Sheri Karmiol, Critical Essay on "The Feather Pillow," in *Short Stories for Students*, Gale, Cengage Learning, 2013.

John S. Brushwood

In the following excerpt, Brushwood discusses Quiroga's "statement of principles" regarding short story writing, examines the manifestation of these principles in Quiroga's works, and studies them in relation to two stories by other Latin American writers.

QUIROGA AND THE BASIS OF THE TWENTIETH-CENTURY SHORT STORY

If asked for the name of an outstanding Spanish American *cuentista* ("short-story writer"), a specialist in the literature would very likely think of Horacio Quiroga (Uruguay, 1878–1937) or Jorge Luis Borges (Argentina, 1899–). A second probability is corollary—that two decades ago, the answer would have been Quiroga; more recently, Borges would come to mind first. The latter's substantial influence goes back farther than two decades to the mid-1940s, however, some years passed before his name became virtually a household word internationally. This [essay] does not undertake an analysis of the complete Borges phenomenon, but considers some of his early stories. From Quiroga's first important collection, *Cuentos de amor, de locura y de muerte* (*Stories of Love, Madness and Death*) in 1917 to Borges's *Ficciones* in 1944, the trajectory of short fiction shows a

> **VIOLENCE IS FREQUENT IN QUIROGA'S WORK, BUT ITS SIGNIFICANCE VARIES IN IMPORTANT WAYS.**

gradual but clear change in subject matter and in narrative technique.

Quiroga was the first Spanish American writer to pay close attention to how a story is made, and at the same time, dedicate himself almost exclusively to writing short fiction. In a statement of principles for the *cuentista*, he sets forth several ideas that are especially interesting because of his importance as *magister*. Although Quiroga did not consistently assume such a role for himself and was quite aware that some younger writers were not entirely sympathetic to his work, his decalogue for the perfect *cuentista* states his case in no uncertain terms. He first exhorts the writer to have limitless faith in his literary master, and specifically mentions Poe, Maupassant, Kipling, and Chekov. The first two are quite clearly present in Quiroga's work; Kipling is apparent in the stories about anthropomorphized jungle beasts; Chekov's presence is not as easy to specify, but there is certainly no reason to doubt its existence. Beyond this oath of allegiance, Quiroga says that the writer should know before beginning the narration how the story is going to develop. It seems unlikely that he would have much patience with the writer whose characters take charge of the work. He warns against excessive use of adjectives, claiming that if the writer controls language well enough to choose the best substantive, modifiers need be used only sparingly. Writing under the impulse of emotion should be avoided, Quiroga says; once the emotion has cooled, however, the writer does well to re-create it in the experience of his work. Interesting an audience should not be a concern; rather, the *cuentista* should feel certain that what he writes is of interest to the characters about whom he is writing.

In general, these principles suggest a rather comfortable fit into the realist-naturalist tradition. That is indeed where Quiroga is based in literary history, but with modifications caused by the Spanish American literary milieu. He began writing in the early years of the twentieth century, toward the end of *modernismo* and at a time when realism and naturalism were generally recognized, but not always understood. One of his early stories, "Cuento sin razó, pero cansado" (1901; "Story Without Cause, But Weary"), may be safely thought of as *modernista* because one of its qualities is the sense of ennui associated with the French decadents. There is also in it some of naturalism's inevitability, and this characteristic becomes dominant in many stories, including the well-known "La gallina degollada" (1909; "The Decapitated Chicken").

In this story, four idiot brothers commit an act of violence that is suggested to them by their having witnessed an ordinary act that seems analogous—to them—and quite acceptable. Quiroga introduces the brothers in an initial scene, then provides some background followed by emphasis on the parents' marital problems. The conflict that is developed in much of the story is based on the attitude of the parents toward their offspring. When this conflict reaches a climax, it points the reader in a direction different from that actually taken by the story. The narrator—always completely in control of the characters and recounting their actions without detailed characterization—removes the brothers from their regular routine, relates how they witnessed the stimulus action, and returns them to the place in which he first described them. Their subsequent action, wordless and in common accord, is an inevitable result of their mental condition.

The action of "La gallina degollada" takes place in the environs of Buenos Aires, but the story is in no way regionalistic. Quiroga often placed his stories in settings that were familiar to him, but his themes are universal. In "Juan Darién" (1920), the jungle is a factor, but not in terms of the man-against-nature theme found in many works located in unsettled areas. Rather, "Juan Darién" is a story of human injustice in the most general sense, not in terms of an attack on a specific or localized social problem. An animal is transformed into a human being and when his identity is discovered, he suffers the fate of those who threaten society because they are different.

The general structure of "Juan Darién" is what one would expect in a realist story: introduction, exposition of conflict, development, climax, and denouement. It is not a realistic story; it is a fantasy, and Quiroga never leaves any

room for doubt about what kind of tale we are reading. At the beginning, the narrator states the fact of the animal's marvelous transformation. There is no time to wonder whether or not there may be some natural explanation for this phenomenon. We are dealing with a kind of fairy tale, and the language so indicates when the narrator uses expressions that are similar to English, "Once there was . . ." or "Well of course . . . ," as introductions to paragraphs. The conflict in "Juan Darién" is between animal violence and human violence. Humans are always unjust; their only redeeming trait appears to be in the maternal role—the mother alone knows "the sacred rights of life."

Violence is frequent in Quiroga's work, but its significance varies in important ways. In "La gallina degollada," it creates horror; in "Juan Darién," it is related to justice and injustice. In "El hombre muerto" (1920; "The Dead Man"), the protagonist comes to a violent end by accident, and one thinks less about the violence itself than about the man's awareness, or lack of awareness, of his condition. The general ambience of "El hombre muerto" tends to make the story appear more regionalistic than is actually the case. The setting is tropical and rural. The man falls on his machete in the course of his work and dies in a period of thirty minutes that are accounted for in the narration. There is no surprise ending, nothing that need be withheld in a discussion of how it works out. It is impossible to summarize the story without duplicating it, however, because the experience of this narrative is the man's growing awareness of his condition. The basic conflict is quite simply between life and death; its development is what the man thinks of his total situation (his immediate condition and its implications). Quiroga uses repetition with good effect as his protagonist becomes increasingly aware of what is happening to him and what it means in terms of the world in which he has lived. The narrator speaks mainly in free, indirect style, so we see what the man sees even though we are being informed by the third-person voice; an occasional comment from this point of view does not alter the basic narration in any significant way. Probably the outstanding device used by Quiroga in this story is a shift of focus in the last paragraph so that we are no longer seeing as the man sees but as he is seen. This change justifies the title; before this conclusion, the man is dying, but has not reached the end. The fact that "El hombre muerto" cannot be synopsized satisfactorily characterizes it as a more modern story than the other two by Quiroga. It would be difficult, and pointless, to say that one manner is more typical of the author than the other.

The perspective in which we see Quiroga in the early twentieth century as a kind of pillar of the Spanish American short story may be illuminated by reference to two stories by authors of the same generation. One of these, "En provincia" (1914; "In the Provinces") is by Augusto D'Halmar [Augusto Geomine Thompson] (Chile, 1882–1950), who is considered a naturalist writer; the other is "El hombre que parecía un caballo" (1915; "The Man Who Resembled a Horse"), by Rafael Arévalo Martínez (Guatemala, 1884–), who may be called either modernist or postmodernist. Neither of these stories is *typical* of either naturalism or modernism; each, however, has sufficient characteristics of the heritage that was Quiroga's, that their publication, so contemporaneous to Quiroga's own stories, emphasizes the sense of change that one experiences in reading the latter's work.

The small-town atmosphere of D'Halmar's story is faithful to the title, but identification with a specific geographical area is extremely difficult. The protagonist, an unimportant employee of a commercial firm, is a confirmed bachelor whose only social contact is made through playing a musical instrument. The humdrum quality of his life and, indeed, the generally slow pace of the town are readily appreciable; however, the effect of the story is not to elicit sympathy for a lonely person—he is quite content with his life. The conflict is triggered by a woman who involves him in an adulterous affair, using him for her own benefit. "En provincia" will not do as a textbook example of naturalism, because the case of adultery is so extreme as to seem used as satire and because the situation is not treated as though it were a clinical study. It is narrative procedure that gives the story its special personality.

The protagonist is the first-person narrator. He introduces himself, describes his situation and the way he lives, and gives a few words about his background. Then he comments on his ambivalence concerning whether or not to tell his story, and concludes that although he will write it, no one will ever see it. Now the reader enters into a fascinating relationship with the narrator—the secret is out, or is going to be. It is worth noting that D'Halmar does not

use the familiar device of the "found" manuscript. Of course, if we are to believe the narrator, someone must have found what he wrote, and he did not intend to have it discovered. The important effect is that the narrator's attitude toward the telling is really a part of the story we read, and the first conflict we are aware of has to do with that attitude. Then the protagonist moves into an account of the most important event in his life. This second conflict develops on the basis of his natural rights as an individual against the exigencies of social organization. Repeated episodes of sustained emotional intensity bring this conflict to a climax. The man's acceptance of his role, at this point, completes his characterization of himself and brings the reader to the starting point of the story of the adultery.

Arévalo Martínez's "El hombre que parecía un caballo" is more character sketch than traditionally plotted story. The narrative does move in time, enough to indicate change taking place in a friendship, but even this process of change is essentially a means of characterizing Aretal, the principal figure. A metaphor is established in terms of the equine analogy, which begins with reference to physical appearance and then becomes relevant to the more subtle manifestations of Aretal's personality. Arévalo Martínez also uses many metaphors that are very *modernista*, such as references to jewels, and the word azure to indicate the soul or the finer side of human personality. The story has its amusing side, created especially by Aretal's exterior similarity to a horse. He holds his head to one side, trots around the salon, sidles up to ladies, and whinnies. The revelation of his character is far more profound than these examples might indicate, however, and since we see him entirely from the narrator's point of view, the story is actually an evaluation of Aretal's personality.

Arévalo Martínez's affinity for *modernismo* is apparent enough in "El hombre que parecía un caballo," but he avoids the lush estheticism that characterized some *modernista* work and provoked a movement by some writers toward portrayal of the commonplace, the familiar. This is the phenomenon frequently called *criollismo*. In the early years of the century, there was a complex of "isms" that were different from each other in some respects but not in others, and were also concurrent to a degree. One of the functions of *modernismo* was as a reaction against the ugliness of realism and naturalism, and

criollismo was a reaction against the hyperesthe-
ticism of the *modernistas*, but these movements
and countermovements did not cancel the characteristics of any of the forces involved. No
movement comes to a standstill when a reaction
makes itself felt. That is why "En provincia" and
"El hombre que parecía un caballo" show characteristics of two different movements without
being perfect examples. Change is taking place;
at the same time, some stories continue to hew
close to the line of one "ism" or another.

Alfonso Hernández Catá's (Cuba, 1885–
1940) "Noventa días" ("Ninety Days") is a naturalist story about a deteriorating infatuation told
as if it were a case history. Its development follows a very orthodox pattern in which the narrator establishes the setting, introduces the
principal character, and then initiates the action,
which in turn follows a standard pattern. Spring,
an important factor in the atmosphere, becomes
even more important in the action as the narrator
personifies the season and shows how it inspires
an infatuation that is doomed never to blossom
into real love. The conflict is represented in the
personalities of the two principals, who are
entirely different from each other and little
inclined to make concessions once the magic of
spring is lost; it is developed through a series of
similar incidents until the story ends in tragedy.
Hernández Catá's story, on the trajectory of literary history, could fit comfortably before or
after *modernismo*.

These early stories use a wide variety of anecdotal material, the nature of which says a great
deal about what the authors were doing in ways
that went beyond classification by literary movement. Of the three Quiroga stories, "La gallina
degollada" may seem at first to be terrifyingly
real. It is certainly terrifying, but on second
thought it seems less a representation of reality
than "El hombre muerto," because in the first
story Quiroga's material is a psychological principle rather than a normally observed happening.
"Juan Darién" is a fantasy that may have been
born of observed reality, but its incident comes no
closer to experienced reality than allegory does.
On the basis of "La gallina degollada" and "Juan
Darién," one would hardly call Quiroga a *criollista*, since these stories are not reproductions of
everyday, familiar Spanish American reality. "El
hombre muerto" is a different matter. Its theme is
universal, but the actual happening takes place in
the tropics where a man has a banana grove and

works with a machete. These facts provide some
of the quality of our-own-Spanish-American-
reality sought by the *criollistas*.

In fact, the themes of all the stories mentioned so far are universal, although some of
the material may be slightly less so. "El hombre
muerto" uses the most clearly regionalistic material. The setting of "En provincia" is provincial,
but not identified with a region in that the action
itself is not influenced by regional characteristics; "Noventa días" belongs anyplace where
spring suggests romance. In both stories, the
authors are relating ordinary human situations,
but it is doubtful that there is a sense of close-
ness, of personal relationship, between them and
the material. Interestingly, the story that may
seem most fanciful, "El hombre que parecía un
caballo," is probably closest to real life, a fanta-
sized account of something that really happened.

Narrative technique has a great deal to do
with how the reader understands the story. Arévalo Martínez might have told of his friendship
with Señor Aretal in countless different ways. His
decision to use the horse analogy in combination
with words suggesting great refinement creates a
contrast that is both amusing and perceptive. If
he had narrated a typically realist story, the
actions of the two people with respect to each
other would be the same, but the effect would be
different. The story could be more psychological,
for example, but the suggestive contrast would
not be emphasized. In the case of "La gallina
degollada," Quiroga decided to characterize the
parents more than the idiot sons. This creates a
more complex understanding of the parents while
presenting the four boys with clinical objectivity;
as their role becomes preeminent, attention
focuses on the psychological principle. The
same story told any other way might change
emphasis, but not the relationship of persons to
actions. Quiroga might even have chosen to stress
the ambience of a particular area, in which case
the story would have seemed more *criollista*, as
does "Juan Darién."

Source: John S. Brushwood, "The Spanish American
Short Story from Quiroga to Borges," in *The Latin Amer-
ican Short Story: A Critical History*, edited by Margaret
Sayers Peden, Twayne Publishers, 1983, pp. 71–96.

Ronald de Feo

*In the following review, de Feo discusses the ele-
ment of "strangeness" found in Latin American
writing, as evident in this collection.*

If there is one virtue, aside from sheer technical skill, that is shared by many of the best contemporary Latin American writers it is an ability to bring to their narratives an element of strangeness, to handle even prosaic material in such a way that the ordinary is transformed into the extraordinary, that commonplace reality takes on a mysterious and a mythic quality. Even the work of such socially and politically conscious writers as Mario Vargas Llosa and Carlos Fuentes seems to transcend its realistic foundations. Horacio Quiroga, a short story writer who was born in Salto, Uruguay in 1878 and died in Buenos Aires in 1937, was one of those authors who pointed the way to today's Latin American fiction. His tales are perhaps not as sophisticated or as complex as many of the tales we read now, but their strangeness is just as prominent. And while it may be difficult to directly link Quiroga's work with that of any of today's writers (though we find a similar bluntness and compression in the stories of Dalton Trevisan and Juan Rulfo), his peculiar spirit is much in evidence.

Quiroga was, to say the least, a restless and troubled man, and his life, filed with deaths of various sorts, was as odd and tragic as were many of his tales. In fact, suicides and fatal accidents seemed to have haunted him throughout his life. His father, the Argentine consul to Uruguay, was fatally wounded as a result of a shotgun accident at a family gathering. Later, his seriously ill step-father shot himself to death. In 1902, Quiroga accidentally killed a best friend with a pistol. Years later, one of the frequent quarrels between Quiroga and his first wife about the upbringing of their two children prompted the young woman to take a fatal dose of poison. And in 1937, when the already severely depressed Quiroga learned that he was suffering from terminal cancer, he brought his suffering and his life to an abrupt, perhaps merciful, end by swallowing poison.

Quiroga spent most of his time in Argentina, living in Buenos Aires and making trips to San Ignacio (in the northern jungle province of Misiones) near which he had purchased some land. This primitive and exotic tropical region, with its strange animal and plant life, its struggling laborers and ruthless exploiters, its wide variety of human outcasts and misfits, obviously appealed to him greatly for he would repeatedly abandon urban existence and security to return for a time to the crude jungle cottage he had built with his own hands. Many of his stories, from those focusing on various animals and their struggle for survival to those centering on man against nature and on man against man, are set in this untamed region he knew so well. The harshness and brutality of jungle life, and the torment he experienced in his personal life are clearly reflected in his fiction. Even in *South American Jungle Tales* (now out of print in English), a collection of Kipling-like animal stories supposedly designed for children, there are graphic depictions of violence.

Many of the tales in *The Decapitated Chicken*, which presents some of his very finest work in a superbly designed volume, concentrate on various acts of revenge, struggles with nature, savage quirks of fate. Quiroga's style is perfectly suited to his subject matter. The crisp, unadorned language, the almost breathless pace of the narrative, match the tenseness of events. In part, the strangeness of the tales can be attributed to both this laconic quality and a narrow, intense focus. All extraneous matter is eliminated. Thoughts flash by. Sensations, emotions and conflicts are heightened. "The Dead Man" begins with the protagonist accidentally falling on the machete he has been using to cut bananas in a grove. The rest of this brief, unsettling tale relates the thoughts going through the man's mind as he dies. Here, by concentrating on those few remaining minutes before the inescapable end, Quiroga makes them as important for us as they are for the victim. The man is unable to believe what has happened, unable to accept such a tragedy occurring on his land, on a peaceful, ordinary day. Death is simply an absurd intruder. In "Drifting," Quiroga again records the thoughts of a dying man. This time the protagonist is the victim of an attack by a poisonous snake. Unable to accept his fate, he climbs into a canoe and drifts down the Paraná River, all the while trying to convince himself that he will survive the fatal bite. Here the time scheme is more extended than that of "The Dead Man," but the intensity and terror are just as strong.

Most of the stories in this volume end in death. Sometimes the deaths are described at length, as those in the two tales mentioned and in "Sunstroke," another story about an absurd tragedy. At other times, they are related briefly or merely hinted at, but are no less frightening or haunting because of the comparatively abrupt treatment. In the symbolic horror story, "The Yellow Pillow," we only discover the cause of the young bride's mysterious illness and death at the very end of the tale: a monstrous, parasitic animal, lodged in her pillow, has been draining her blood.... In "The Decapitated Chicken," one of Quiroga's most brutal tales of revenge, the author cuts away from a murder before it is completed, but a father's cry upon discovering the body of his daughter is enough to convey the horror and savagery of the act.

Quiroga has often been compared with Poe and did, in fact, acknowledge him as one of his masters. Yet Poe, though certainly no less obsessed and morbid than Quiroga, is a more ornate, introspective and cerebral writer. By comparison, Quiroga sometimes seems simple and blunt and too anecdotal. But like Poe, Quiroga has the ability to thrust the reader into the heart of a story and hold him there. His superb craftsmanship and lively powers of invention are especially in evidence in "Anaconda," in which he effortlessly and convincingly tells the story of a snake community and human intruders from the snakes' point of view. Like the best of Quiroga's tales it seems as unusual, imaginative and alive as the work being produced by fellow Latin Americans today.

Source: Ronald de Feo, Review of *The Decapitated Chicken, and Other Stories*, in *Commonweal*, Vol. 104, April 1977, pp. 285–86.

George D. Schade

In the following introduction to The Decapitated Chicken, and Other Stories, *Schade offers biographical details on Quiroga's life that are apparent in his narratives, and surveys several of the stories contained in the collection.*

A new edition of Horacio Quiroga stories— in this case, the first selective translation into English ranging over his complete work— reminds us of a superb writer and offers a pretext for talking about him. Of course, the round dozen stories which make up this volume can speak for themselves, and many translations appear unescorted by an introduction; nonetheless, readers who are not acquainted with Quiroga may wish to learn something further about this author, generally regarded by the critics as a classic and one of the finest short-story writers Latin America has produced. Surveying his work afresh, we find that this favorable verdict still holds true and that his achievement

> IN THE BEST STORIES, MANY OF WHICH APPEAR IN THIS COLLECTION, ACTION IS PERFECTLY ILLUSTRATIVE: THE STORIES HAVE NOT ONLY MOVEMENT BUT ALSO DEPTH."

continues to be admirable. Quiroga stands apart from the bulk of his contemporaries in Spanish American literature and head and shoulders above most of them.

Certain thematic designs run through Quiroga's life and also through his stories. He was born the last day of the year 1878 in El Salto, Uruguay, and died by his own hand in February, 1937, in Buenos Aires, Argentina. The fifty-eight-year span of his lifetime was crammed with adventure, hazardous enterprise, and recurrent tragedy and violence, particularly suicide. When he was a babe in arms, his father was accidentally killed when a shotgun went off on a family outing. Later his stepfather, desperately ill and of whom Horacio was fond, shot himself, and the young Quiroga, seventeen at the time, was the first to come upon the grisly scene. In 1902 Quiroga accidentally shot and killed, with a pistol, one of his best friends and literary companions. In 1915 his first wife, unable to endure the hardships of life in the jungle of Misiones where Quiroga insisted on living, committed suicide by taking a fatal dose of poison, leaving the widower with two small children to raise. Finally, Quiroga himself took cyanide to end his own life when he realized he was suffering from an incurable cancer.

His love affairs and marriages were also turbulent. He married twice, both times very young women; his second wife, a friend of his daughter, was nearly thirty years his junior. The first marriage ended with his wife's suicide; the second, in separation. This singular amount of violence marring the writer's personal life cannot be overly stressed, for it explains a great deal about his obsession with death, which is so marked in his work.

Quiroga's zest for adventure and the magnetic attraction the jungle hinterland of northern Argentina held for him are also biographical details that have great impact on his work. His first trip to the province of Misiones occurred in 1903, when he accompanied his friend and fellow writer Leopoldo Lugones as photographer on an expedition to study the Jesuit ruins there. Next came a trip to the Chaco to plant cotton, where he built his own hut and had his first pioneering experience. In 1906 he bought some land in San Ignacio, Misiones, and from that date on divided his time between the hinterland and Buenos Aires. He tried various experiments in Misiones, such as the making of charcoal and the distillation of an orange liqueur. These endeavors ended in failure but provided him with good material for his stories, as did his myriad other activities there, like constructing his bungalow, furniture, and boats and hunting and studying the wildlife of the region.

In his teens Quiroga began writing under the aegis of the Modernist movement, which dominated the Spanish American literary scene at the turn of the century. Soon, however, he reacted against the decadent and highly artificial mode of his first book, *Los arrecifes de coral* (Coral reefs, published 1901), which contained Modernist poems, prose pieces, and stories, and turned to writing tales firmly rooted in reality, though they often emphasized the bizarre or the monstrous.

Commentators have tended to discount the significance or merit of some of Quiroga's early works, such as the longish story "The Pursued." Recently this tale has received more favorable critical attention. Our translator, who has made an excellent selection of Quiroga's stories that few would quarrel with, maintains that "The Pursued" is the most modern piece he wrote because of what it anticipates. It is undeniably one of Quiroga's more ambiguous and inscrutable stories, lending itself to various interpretations as it elaborates on the theme of madness.

Another early story, "The Feather Pillow," first published in 1907, is a magnificent example of his successful handling of the Gothic tale, reminiscent of Poe, whom he revered as master. The effects of horror, something mysterious and perverse pervading the atmosphere, are all there from the beginning of the story, and Quiroga skillfully, gradually readies the terrain, so that we are somewhat prepared for, though we do not anticipate, the sensational revelation at the end. But this story takes on much more meaning and subtlety when we realize that the anecdote can be interpreted on a symbolical level: the ailing Alicia suffers from hallucinations brought on by her husband's hostility and coldness, for he is the real monster.

For three decades Quiroga continued writing and publishing stories in great quantity—his total output runs over two hundred—many of them also of impressive quality. Certain collections should be singled out as high points: *Los desterrados* (The exiled, published 1926) and *Cuentos de amor, de locura, y de muerte* (Stories of love, madness, and death, published 1917). The splendid title of *Cuentos* sets forth his major themes and could properly be the heading for his entire work. Quiroga also achieved great popularity with his *Cuentos de la selva* (published 1918), translated into English as *Jungle Tales*, a volume for children of all ages, permeated with tenderness and humor and filled with whimsy. These delightful stories are peopled by talking animals and are cast in a fable mold, usually with an underlying moral.

"Anaconda," which describes a world of snakes and vipers and how they battle men and also one another, is one of Quiroga's most celebrated stories. It moves at a more leisurely pace than the typical Quiroga tale, with spun-out plot, lingering over realistic details. The characters in this ophidian world are more compelling than believable, and the animal characterization is not perhaps as striking as that of some shorter narratives like "Sunstroke." But Quiroga, the fluent inventor at work, can almost always make something interesting happen. "Anaconda" lies on the ill-defined frontier between the long story and the novella and will gainsay those who think Quiroga sacrifices everything to rapid narrative. Consequently, it loses something of the dramatic intensity of other stories, despite its original title of "A Drama in the Jungle: The Vipers' Empire." The tight-knit, tense structure we can perceive in "Drifting," "The Dead Man," and many other Quiroga stories is considerably slackened here. On the other hand, Quiroga compensates for this by offering us a story of exuberant imagination, rich in irony, with abundant satirical implications about man and his behavior. Like the *Jungle Tales*, "Anaconda" will have a special appeal for children, but, unlike the former, it is essentially directed to a mature audience.

If we examine Quiroga's stories attentively, we will find moments full of vision concerning mankind, often illuminating a whole character or situation in a flash. Quiroga has an astute awareness of the problems besetting man on every side, not only the pitfalls of savage Nature but also those pertaining to human relationships. Man is moved by greed and overweening ambition, hampered by fate, and often bound by circumstances beyond his control. Quiroga penetrates the frontiers of profound dissatisfaction and despair felt by man. His vision is clear and ruthless, and his comments on human illusions can be withering. Yet it is man's diversity that emerges in these stories, his abjectness and his heroism. Though Quiroga never palliates man's faults and weaknesses, the heroic virtues of courage, generosity, and compassion stand out in many of his stories.

All this rich and multifarious human material is shaped and patterned into story form by a master craftsman. Quiroga was very conscious of the problems involved in the technique and art of the short story, and, like Edgar Allan Poe and other masters of the genre, he wrote about them. His most famous document on technique is what he dubbed a "Manual of the Perfect Short Story Writer," a succinct decalogue filled with cogent and compelling advice. The usual warnings stressing economy of expression are here: for instance, "Don't use unnecessary adjectives"; and also those concerned with careful advance planning: "Don't start to write without knowing from the first word where you are going. In a story that comes off well, the first three lines are as important as the last three." It is easy to find apt examples of the latter dictum in Quiroga's work: "Drifting," "The Dead Man," "The Decapitated Chicken," "The Feather Pillow," and so on, to cite only from the stories translated in this collection.

The last commandment in Quiroga's decalogue to the person desiring to write perfect short stories is probably the most suggestive: "Don't think about your friends when you write or the impression your story will make. Tell the tale as if the story's only interest lay in the small surroundings of your characters, of which you might have been one. In no other way is *life* achieved in the short story." Quite rightly Quiroga emphasizes the word *life*, for it is this elusive and vital quality which lies at the core of his stories. The idea that the author or his narrator might be one of the characters is also significant, for he often was one of the characters, at least in some aspect, or felt that he was one of them.

Certainly in his best stories Quiroga practiced the economy he talks about in his manual and which is characteristic of good short-story writers. Almost every page will bear testimony to this laconic quality. It is a brevity which excludes everything redundant but nothing which is really significant. Wonderful feats of condensation are common, as in "The Dead Man," where he shows his powers in dramatic focus on a single scene, or in "Drifting," a stark story in which everything seems reduced to the essential, the indispensable. The brief opening scene of "Drifting," where a man is bitten by a venomous snake, contains the germs of all that comes afterward. The language is terse and pointed, the situation of tremendous intensity, the action straightforward and lineal. Everything moves in an unbroken line from beginning to end, like an arrow to its target, to use Quiroga's phrase referring to technique in the short story. The title, too, is particularly appropriate: while the dying protagonist literally drifts in his canoe downriver seeking aid, we see him helplessly adrift on the river of life, unable to control his fatal destiny from the moment the snake sinks its fangs into his foot.

In "Drifting," "The Son," "The Dead Man," and other stories, Quiroga plays on a life/death vibration, juxtaposing the two. While the throes of death slowly diminish the protagonist of "The Dead Man," Nature and the landscape surrounding him pulsate with life—the ordinary domestic quality of daily life he is so accustomed to—so that he cannot accept the fact of his dying. Our curiosity is kept unfalteringly alive by Quiroga's dramatic technique. At his finest moments Quiroga reaches and maintains a high degree of emotional intensity, as in the three stories cited above, which have in common their magnificent treatment of death. Quiroga flinches from none of the difficulties perhaps implicit in this theme. In his dealing with death he is natural and matter-of-fact; we find no mawkish romantic sentimentality, no glossing over of realistic attributes, and no gloating over ugly clinical details characteristic of naturalistic writers.

There is also much suggestion and implication, rather than outright telling, in Quiroga's best work. "The Dead Man" is probably the most skillful instance of this technique, but interesting examples abound throughout Quiroga's narratives. A case in point is the heartfelt story "The Son," where the protagonist father, suffering from hallucinations, imagines that his young son, who went hunting in the forest, has had a fatal accident. The father stumbles along in a frenzy, cutting his way through the thick and treacherous jungle, seeking a sign of the boy. Suddenly he stifles a cry, for he has seen something in the sky. The suggestion, confirmed later by the boy's death at the end of the story, is that the father saw a buzzard.

Dialogue does not play a heavy role in Quiroga's work. Occasionally we listen to scraps of talk, but, in the main, his stories do not move by dialogue; they are thrust along by overt action. Exceptions to this rule are "Anaconda" and some other animal tales. A stunning example of Quiroga's handling of dialogue occurs in "A Slap in the Face" toward the end of the story where the peon wreaks his terrible revenge on Korner, beating the boss into a bloody, inert pulp with his riding whip. Here Quiroga contrasts most effectively Korner's silence, symbolical of his beaten condition, with the peon's crackling commands *Levántate* ("Get up") and *Caminá* ("Get going"), the only words uttered in the latter part of this violent, sadistic scene. The word *caminá*, repeated four times at slight intervals, suggests an onomatopoeic fusion with the sound of the cracking whip, another instance of Quiroga's technical genius—language functioning to blend auditory effects with content.

Narrative interest seems to prevail over other elements which often dominate in the short story, such as the poetical, symbolical, or philosophical. And Quiroga does not have a social ax to grind. But some of the most trenchant social commentary in Spanish American fiction can be perceived in his stories, particularly those concerned with the exploitation of Misiones lumberjacks, like "Los mensú" ("The Monthly Wage Earners") and "A Slap in the Face." In these tales no preaching is involved. Quiroga is clearly on the side of the oppressed but does not express their point of view exclusively. Consequently, the reader draws his own conclusions, and the social impact is more deeply felt.

Setting, as well as narrative technique, is vitally important to Quiroga, because it is inseparable from the real, the ordinary, domestic, day-to-day experience of human existence. Quiroga's feelings are bound up in place, in his adopted corner of Argentina, Misiones province, rather than the urban centers of Buenos Aires or Montevideo, where he also lived. He is vastly attracted to the rugged jungle landscape, where the majority of his best stories take place (nine of the twelve translated here). And he makes us feel the significance of his setting, too—the symbolic strength of the rivers, especially the Paraná, and the power and hypnotic force of its snake-infested jungles. So does this dot on the map that is Misiones come throbbingly alive for us. It is not just a framework in which to set his stories but an integral part of them, of Quiroga himself, brimming over with drama and life.

In the best stories, many of which appear in this collection, action is perfectly illustrative: the stories have not only movement but also depth. The apparent spareness allows for a greater complexity and suggestion. A fine short story should have implications which will continue to play in the reader's mind when the story is done and over, as we can attest in "The Feather Pillow," "The Dead Man," and almost all the stories included here. We are struck at the end of "A Slap in the Face" by the dual function of the river, which provides the final solution. The peon thrusts the almost lifeless, despicable Korner onto a raft where he will drift inevitably to his death, while the peon takes off in a boat in the opposite direction toward haven on the Brazilian shore. Thus the river assumes the role of justice, meting out death to the guilty and life to the accused. "Juan Darién" is probably one of the most subtle and interesting stories Quiroga ever penned. Rich in suggestions, it opens up to us a world of fantastic reality in which the protagonist is a tiger/boy. At one point in the story Quiroga has the inspector say that truth can be much stranger than fiction. Interpretations of this story will vary, but the most rewarding one may well be that of Juan Darién as a Christ-like figure.

Swift recognition for his mastery of the short story came to Quiroga fairly early in his career, and he continued to enjoy fame throughout his lifetime. In the Spanish-speaking world he is still popular today and almost universally admired, though the type of story he excelled at, in which man is pitted against Nature and rarely if ever wins out, is no longer so commonly composed in Latin America. The contemporary Argentine Julio Cortázar, a writer very unlike Quiroga but also topflight in the short-story genre, has pointed out perspicaciously Quiroga's best and most lasting qualities: he knew his trade in and out; he was universal in dimension; he subjected his themes to dramatic form, transmitting to his readers all their virtues, all their ferment, all their projection in depth; he wrote tautly and described with intensity so that the story would make its mark on the reader, nailing itself in his memory.

Quiroga's is an art that speaks to us clearly and passionately, charged with the emotion of his jungle setting. The action is usually of heroic simplicity. Quiroga does not transcribe life; he dramatizes it. His vision is fresh, intense, dramatic. He seems caught up in it, and so are we.

Source: George D. Schade, Introduction to *The Decapitated Chicken, and Other Stories*, edited and translated by Margaret Sayers Peden, University of Texas Press, 1976, pp. ix–xviii.

SOURCES

Bergmann, Emilie L., *Women, Culture, and Politics in Latin America*, University of California Press, 1990, pp. 1–26.

Brody, Robert, Review of *The Decapitated Chicken, and Other Stories*, in *Latin American Literary Review*, Vol. 6, No. 11, Fall–Winter 1977, pp. 107–109.

Carrio, Elisa María, "Argentina: A New Look at the Challenges of Women's Participation in the Legislature," in *Women in Parliament: Beyond Numbers*, http://www.idea.int/publications/wip2/upload/Argentina.pdf (accessed July 10, 2012).

Cortázar, Julio, "The Present State of Fiction in Latin America," translated by Margery A. Safir, in *Books Abroad*, Vol. 50, No. 3, Summer 1976, pp. 522–32.

Danielson, J. David, ed. and trans., "A Quiroga Chronology," in *The Exiles and Other Stories*, University of Texas Press, 1987, pp. 154–56.

De Feo, Ronald, Review of *The Decapitated Chicken, and Other Stories*, in *Commonweal*, Vol. 104, April 1977, pp. 285–86.

Deutsch, Sandra McGee, "The Catholic Church, Work, and Womanhood in Argentina, 1890–1930," in *Confronting Change, Challenging Tradition: Women in Latin American History*, edited by Gertrude Matyoka Yeager, Scholarly Resources, 1994, pp. 127–51.

Englekirk, John Eugene, "Horacio Quiroga," in *Edgar Allan Poe in Hispanic Literature*, Instituto de las Españas en los Estados Unidos, 1934, pp. 340–69.

Harmon, William, and Hugh Holman, *A Handbook to Literature*, 11th ed., Pearson Prentice Hall, 2009, pp. 51, 222, 235–36, 253–54, 329, 361, 511–12, 540–41.

Lavrin, Asunción, "Women's Politics and Suffrage in Argentina," in *Women, Feminism, and Social Change in Argentina, Chile, and Uruguay, 1890–1940*, University of Nebraska Press, 1998, pp. 257–85.

Mabry, Donald J., "Argentina, 1912–30," Historical Text Archive, http://historicaltextarchive.com/sections.php?action = read&artid = 765 (accessed July 10, 2012).

Pallot, Peter, "Expat Guide to Argentina: Health Care," in *Telegraph* (London, England), March 14, 2012, http://www.telegraph.co.uk/health/expathealth/9133655/Expat-guide-to-Argentina-health-care.html (accessed July 10, 2012).

Peden, William, "Some Notes on Quiroga's Stories," in *Review: Literature and Arts of the Americas*, Vol. 10, No. 19, 1976, pp. 41–43.

Quiroga, Horacio, "Horacio Quiroga on the Short Story," edited and translated by Margaret Sayers Peden, in *Denver Quarterly*, Vol. 12, No. 3, Fall 1977, pp. 41–43, 45–53.

———, "The Feather Pillow," in *The Decapitated Chicken, and Other Stories*, edited and translated by Margaret Sayers Peden, University of Texas Press, 1976, pp. 5–9.

Review of *The Decapitated Chicken, and Other Stories*, in *New Yorker*, August 9, 1976, pp. 76–77.

Rock, David, "Machine Politics in Buenos Aires and the Argentine Radical Party, 1912–1930," in *Journal of Latin American Studies*, Vol. 4, No. 2, November 1972, pp. 233–56.

Schade, George, Introduction to *The Decapitated Chicken, and Other Stories*, edited and translated by Margaret Sayers Peden, University of Texas Press, 1976, pp. ix–xviii.

"Twentieth Century," Argentina Autentica, http://www.argentinaautentica.com/twentiethcentury.php (accessed July 10, 2012).

"21st Century," Argentina Autentica, http://www.argentinaautentica.com/twentyfirstcentury.php (accessed July 10, 2012).

FURTHER READING

Brandariz, Gustavo, *Argentina*, El Ateneo, 2001.
This book is filled with photographs from all areas of Argentina, including views of the rivers and fields, of the countryside and villages, and of the people and towns. One of the strengths of the text is that it is in English and Spanish, which allows readers to learn both the Spanish and English names for a region.

Bueno, Eva Paulino, and María Claudia André, eds., *The Women in Latin American and Spanish Literature: Essays on Iconic Characters*, McFarland, 2012.
In their introduction, the editors suggest that readers can learn a great deal about the culture of Latin America by examining the different

ways in which Latin American authors portray women in their writings. This volume has essays that focus on a wide selection of literature, including that of the early twentieth century, when Quiroga was writing.

Burdick, Michael, *For God and Fatherland: Religion and Politics in Argentina*, State University of New York Press, 1996.

This text is an academic study of one hundred years of religious and political history in Argentina, beginning in the late nineteenth century. It is accessible to ordinary readers who are interested in the intersection of politics, government, and religion in Argentinian life.

Frank, Patrick, *Los Artistas del Pueblo: Prints and Workers' Culture in Buenos Aires, 1917–1935*, University of New Mexico Press, 2006.

This book focuses on what has been called the "golden age" of Argentina, which was also the time when Quiroga was living and writing in that country. It examines the work of four Argentinian artists whose work portrayed the reality of life for workers, immigrants, and the poor.

McEwan, Colin, Luis Alberto Borrero, and Alfredo Prieto, eds., *Patagonia: Natural History, Prehistory, and Ethnography at the Uttermost End of the Earth*, Princeton University Press, 1998.

This book features stunning photographs and a narrative history of the peopling of Patagonia, the southern region at the tip of Argentina that was previously covered by a glacier. This collection of essays constitutes an interdisciplinary examination of a part of the world that is not well known to many people.

Nouzeilles, Gabriela, and Graciela Montaldo, eds., *The Argentina Reader: History, Culture, Politics*, Duke University Press, 2002.

Although Quiroga was born in Uruguay, he spent much of his life in Argentina. This book provides a mix of history and culture of the country, using essays, poetry, and speeches to create a picture of life in Argentina.

Rivera-Barnes, Beatriz, and Jerry Hoeg, *Reading and Writing the Latin American Landscape*, Palgrave Macmillan, 2009.

This text is an interdisciplinary examination of Latin American literature that also considers the influence of ecology and environment. Much of Quiroga's fiction derives from his personal experience of living in the jungle in Misiones, Argentina.

SUGGESTED SEARCH TERMS

Horacio Quiroga AND short stories

Horacio Quiroga AND The Feather Pillow

Horacio Quiroga AND The Decapitated Chicken

Horacio Quiroga AND Latin American literature

Horacio Quiroga AND Edgar Allan Poe

Horacio Quiroga AND magic realism

Horacio Quiroga AND gothic stories

Horacio Quiroga AND Argentina

literature AND Argentina

Latin American short stories

Interpreter of Maladies

JHUMPA LAHIRI

1999

"Interpreter of Maladies" is a short story by Jhumpa Lahiri, an American writer of Indian descent. It was first published in 1998 in *Agni Review* and then reprinted in 1999 as the title story in the author's first short-story collection, which was awarded the Pulitzer Prize. "Interpreter of Maladies" received the O. Henry Award and was included in the 1999 edition of *Best American Short Stories*. The story is about the Das family, an American family of Indian descent who are on a trip to India to visit relatives. They hire an Indian tour guide who takes them by car to visit places of interest to tourists. The guide, Mr. Kapasi, also works as an interpreter for a doctor, some of whose patients speak a language the doctor does not understand. During the trip, Mrs. Das, who is unhappily married, confesses to Mr. Kapasi a secret from her past that is tormenting her, hoping that he will be able to offer a cure for her malady.

Lahiri explained in an interview for the Houghton Mifflin Harcourt website that she first had the idea for the story in 1991, when she was a graduate student at Boston University. An acquaintance of hers was working as an interpreter for a doctor who had Russian patients who did not speak English. Lahiri decided that one day she would write a story titled "interpreter of maladies." It was not until five years later, however, that the basic outline of the story came to her. When she was putting together her first short-story collection, she knew that "Interpreter

Jhumpa Lahiri (© *Aurora Photos | Alamy*)

of Maladies" had to be the title story of the collection "because it best expresses, thematically, the predicament at the heart of the book—the dilemma, the difficulty, and often the impossibility of communicating emotional pain and affliction to others, as well as expressing it to ourselves."

AUTHOR BIOGRAPHY

Nilanjana Sudeshna Lahiri was born to Indian parents in London, England, on July 11, 1967. When she was three, the family immigrated to the United States, and Lahiri was raised in South Kingston, Rhode Island. Her father was a librarian at the University of Rhode Island, and her mother was a schoolteacher.

Although they lived in the United States, Lahiri's parents considered themselves Indian, and every few years they made trips to Calcutta, accompanied by their two daughters. Lahiri would stay in India for periods lasting up to six months, although she did not feel at home there. Nor did she feel quite at home in Rhode Island, where she was conscious of her different ethnic background and often felt like an outsider.

Lahiri became an avid reader when she was a child, and she also began to write stories. At the age of seven, she would coauthor with her classmates stories of up to ten pages in length. The first name by which she became known, Jhumpa, was a nickname bestowed on her by a teacher in elementary school.

She attended South Kingstown High School and then Barnard College, from which she received a bachelor of arts degree in English literature in 1989. Continuing her studies, she received three master of arts degrees from Boston University, in English, creative writing, and comparative literature and the arts. She also obtained a doctoral degree in Renaissance studies from the same university. While still a graduate student, Lahiri had already begun writing short stories and had won the Henfield Prize from *Transatlantic Review* in 1993 and the *Louisville Review* fiction prize in 1997.

Lahiri taught creative writing at Boston University and the Rhode Island School of Design, but her goal was to write fiction. Her breakthrough occurred when the *New Yorker* published three of her stories and named her one of the twenty best young writers in the United States. Her collection of nine short stories, *Interpreter of Maladies*, which includes the story of the same name, was published in 1999. It won the Pulitzer Prize for Fiction in 2000. The title story was awarded the O. Henry Award in 1999.

In 2003, Lahiri's first novel, *The Namesake* was published. The novel is about a family that moves from Calcutta to New York. One of the main characters is a second-generation Indian American named Gogol, who struggles to find his place in the world. The novel was nominated for the 2003 *Los Angeles Times* book award for fiction. It was made into a movie directed by Mira Nair. Lahiri's second short-story collection, *Unaccustomed Earth*, appeared in 2008. It won the Frank O'Connor International Short Story Award in 2008 and an Asian American Literary Award in 2009.

Lahiri married Alberto Vourvoulias, an American-born journalist, in 2001. They have two children, Octavio (b. 2002) and Noor (b. 2005). As of 2012, they live in Brooklyn, New York.

PLOT SUMMARY

As "Interpreter of Maladies" begins, Mr. and Mrs. Das are visiting India to see their parents.

The couple are of Indian descent, but they were born in the United States and live in New Brunswick, New Jersey. They dress and talk like Americans. They are accompanied by their three young children, Tina, Robby, and Bobby. On the day the story takes place, the family is on a sightseeing trip, and they have hired a tour guide, the middle-aged Mr. Kapasi, who is driving them to see the Sun Temple at Konarak. It is a two-and-a-half hour journey by car. The children are excited by the monkeys they see in the trees that line the road. They have never seen monkeys outside of a zoo before. Mr. Das asks the guide to stop the car so he can take a photograph. Shortly afterward, they stop again so Mr. Das can take a picture of an emaciated man sitting on top of a cart of grain sacks.

As the American couple converses with Mr. Kapasi, he tells them some details about his life. He works as an interpreter for a doctor. Mr. Kapasi speaks Gujarati, a language that the doctor does not understand but that is spoken by many of his patients. Mrs. Das shows some interest in this and gets him to talk more about it. Mr. Kapasi gives an example of a patient who had a pain in his throat. After Mr. Kapasi translated the man's description of his symptoms, the doctor was able to prescribe the correct medicine. Mr. and Mrs. Das agree that the interpreter has a big responsibility in these situations. The patients depend on his translations being accurate. For his part, however, Mr. Kapasi does not like his job. In his youth he had wanted to become an interpreter for diplomats and world leaders, helping to settle disputes between nations. But his dreams were never realized. He had taught English in a grammar school, but then his son had contracted a fatal illness, and he had taken the job with the doctor because it was better paid, and he needed money to pay all the medical bills.

Mr. Kapasi is flattered by the interest Mrs. Das shows in him, which contrasts with the indifference he experiences from his wife. He tells her about more of the patients whose symptoms he has translated to the doctor. She listens attentively.

They stop at a restaurant for lunch, and Mrs. Das asks Mr. Kapasi for his address, so they can send him copies of the photographs Mr. Das has been taking. Mr. Kapasi writes his address down on a piece of paper and gives it to her. He allows himself to hope they will correspond with each other, confide in each other, and become good friends.

In the afternoon, they reach the Sun Temple, which was built in the thirteenth century. As they examine it, Mr. Das reads aloud details from a guidebook. The whole family enjoys seeing the temple, which pleases Mr. Kapasi. He is especially pleased that Mrs. Das seems interested in the temple. He likes her because she has taken an interest in him. He wants to be alone with her so they can continue their conversation. She inquires about one of the bronze sculptures of Surya, the sun god, and he is able to answer her. He looks forward to the correspondence he anticipates that they will have, in which they will explain things about their respective countries to each other. This will, he thinks, in a way fulfill his dream of being an interpreter between nations.

After two hours, Mr. Kapasi starts to drive the family back to their hotel. But he is reluctant to see them go, so he suggests visiting another tourist destination, where monastic dwellings were carved out of the hillsides.

When they arrive there, Mrs. Das says she is tired and will remain in the car. Mr. Das takes the children up to the hills, while Mrs. Das talks to Mr. Kapasi. He is surprised to hear her confess that one of her sons, Bobby, is not her husband's son. Her husband does not know this, however, since Mrs. Das has kept it secret from him for eight years. Mr. Kapasi is the first person she has told.

Mrs. Das goes on to tell Mr. Kapasi the story of her marriage. She had known Raj Das since they were children, and they married young. She got lonely staying at home raising their children while her husband worked as a schoolteacher. When a friend of Raj Das's came to stay with them for a week because he had job interviews in the area, Mina Das allowed herself to be seduced by him. The friend later married, and the two couples stay in touch, but Mrs. Das never informed the man that he was Bobby's father. She tells Mr. Kapasi that she feels terrible about this, and she hopes he can offer her some advice. She wants him to say something that will make her feel better.

Unfortunately, Mr. Kapasi feels depressed by her story. He even feels insulted that she should seek his assistance. Nonetheless, he decides it is his duty to help her. He thinks he may advise her to confess the truth to her husband. Then perhaps he, Mr. Kapasi, could act as a mediator. He begins by asking her whether what she feels is really pain, or is it guilt? She appears displeased by the question and declines to answer it. Without uttering a word, she gets out of the car and begins to walk up the path. She eats some puffed rice, but it keeps falling through her fingers, and soon there are half a dozen monkeys following her, eating the rice that falls. Mr. Kapasi gets out of the car and follows her, trying to scare the monkeys away.

Mrs. Das joins her family, where Mr. Das is preparing to take a family photo. Then they realize that Bobby is missing. They search for him, to find him crying and terrified, surrounded by about a dozen monkeys who are pulling at his tee shirt. Puffed rice is on the ground, and one monkey has been beating him about the legs with a stick. Mrs. Das appeals to Mr. Kapasi for help. Mr. Kapasi manages to drive the monkeys away with a fallen tree branch. He picks Bobby up and carries him to his parents. Bobby has not suffered any serious harm. They all agree that they should return immediately to the hotel. Mrs. Das reaches into her bag for a hairbrush, and as she pulls it out, the piece of paper on which Mr. Kapasi wrote his address comes out too, and it flutters away in the breeze, eventually coming to rest in the trees with the monkeys. No one but Mr. Kapasi notices.

CHARACTERS

Bobby

Bobby is close in age to Ronny and is being raised as the son of Mr. and Mrs. Das. In fact, Mr. Das is not his father. His father is a friend of Mr. Das's who stayed for a week at their house in New Brunswick, New Jersey, while he was interviewing for jobs in the area. Bobby does not know this and thinks Mr. Das is his father. In the story, Bobby gets separated from the family as they visit the hills and is attacked by a group of monkeys. He is not seriously injured.

Mrs. Mina Das

Mrs. Das is twenty-eight years old, the mother of three small children. Like her husband, she is of Indian heritage but was born in the United States and has lived there all her life. On the car journey to the Sun Temple, she gives the impression of being bored, and she does not interact in any meaningful way with her young daughter, even though the girl seeks her mother's attention. Nor does Mrs. Das communicate much with her husband, other than to complain that

he failed to rent an air-conditioned car just because he wanted to save a small amount of money. Mrs. Das does, however, take an interest in Mr. Kapasi, asking him questions about his job and complimenting him about it. Later, she talks to Mr. Kapasi in a surprisingly personal way, telling him the history of her marriage. She had married while still in college and quickly gave birth to a son. But she had been overwhelmed by the responsibility of raising a child. She did not have a wide social circle, and her friends gradually fell away, leaving her feeling isolated as she stayed at home all day looking after the child. She was always tired.

Mrs. Das even tells Mr. Kapasi a secret that she has kept from her husband: Mr. Das is not the father of her son Bobby. The boy was fathered by a friend of her husband's during the time he was staying at their house in New Jersey. Mrs. Das is distressed by having to carry this secret. She has told no one of it, and Bobby is now eight years old. She turns to Mr. Kapasi, hoping that he can say something that will ease her pain, but she is disappointed in his response. For his part, her revelation dampens his interest in her, and he is unable to console her.

Mr. Raj Das

Mr. Das was born in America to Indian parents. Raised in America, he teaches science at a middle school in New Brunswick, New Jersey. Now in his late twenties, he is returning to India with his wife to visit their retired parents. Everything about Mr. Das, from his firm handshake to the way he speaks and dresses, marks him as an American. Despite his heritage, he knows little of India.

He and Mrs. Das are not especially happy together and bicker a lot. They have been married for more than eight years and were both still in college when they married. Mr. Das is not very perceptive in his emotional life. He does not realize that over the years his wife has ceased to be able to talk to him about anything important. Mrs. Das tells Mr. Kapasi that her husband thinks she is still in love with him.

Mr. Das has a relaxed parenting style, not imposing much discipline on his children. During the car trip, he seems more interested in his guidebook than in his family. One of his hobbies appears to be photography, since he has an expensive camera and takes a lot of photographs of the family and the places they visit. He wants to take a photo including all the family that he can use on their Christmas cards. It appears that he likes to maintain the image of a happy family and is ignorant of the fissures within it, including his wife's estrangement and the fact that the younger son, Bobby, is not in fact his biological son.

Mr. Kapasi

Mr. Kapasi is a neatly dressed Indian man in his midforties. He has two occupations. His main job is working as an interpreter for a doctor who does not speak the language that many of his patients speak. Mr. Kapasi translates their descriptions of their symptoms so that the doctor can prescribe the correct treatment. Two days a week, Mr. Kapasi works as a tour guide, driving tourists to local places of interest. When he was young, Mr. Kapasi had a more ambitious dream of how his life would turn out. He wanted to be a high-level interpreter, working for governments, helping to solve problems between nations. He is a self-taught man who learned several languages. However, opportunity did not come his way. Instead, when he was younger he worked as an English teacher in a grammar school. Then his seven-year-old son contracted a fatal illness and he took the job as interpreter, which paid twice as much as the teaching position, so he could pay the medical bills. In spite of the adequate salary, however, it is not a job he likes or feels proud of. For him, it is a sign of his failure.

Mr. Kapasi, who has several children other than the boy who died, is unhappily married. He and his wife have nothing in common other than their children. She does not support his career and refers to him not as an interpreter but as a "doctor's assistant," a term he finds demeaning. He thinks that his occupation merely reminds his wife of the son they lost.

Given his own dissatisfaction with his life, it is perhaps not surprising that Mr. Kapasi is flattered by the interest Mrs. Das takes in his occupation. She seems to respect him for it, commenting that he has a big responsibility. She even calls his work "romantic." Mr. Kapasi finds himself thinking about her in a mildly erotic way, and he also allows himself to entertain a daydream about becoming friends with her through the exchange of letters. But when she makes her confession to him about her act of adultery, he does not receive it well, feeling

insulted that she should expect him to give her advice on such a matter.

Ronny

Ronny is the older son of Mr. and Mrs. Das. He is about nine years old.

Tina

Tina is the young daughter of Mr. and Mrs. Das. She is on her first trip to India. Her mother does not pay much attention to her needs.

THEMES

Communication

The theme of communication is conveyed in several ways in Lahiri's story. Mr. Kapasi's job as a translator for a doctor involves communication. He acts as an intermediary between two people, doctor and patient, who would otherwise be unable to communicate at all because of language differences. His work as a translator demands accuracy, and the communication he facilitates allows the doctor to heal his patients. This smooth form of communication that Mr. Kapasi helps to facilitate in his occupation stands in contrast to the breakdown in communication between people that characterizes much of the story. This applies especially to the two central characters, Mr. Kapasi and Mrs. Das, both of whom suffer from emotional isolation. During the course of the story they both try to break out of their isolation in ways that are ill-thought out and that do not produce the results they had hoped for.

What Mr. Kapasi and Mrs. Das have in common is an unhappy marriage. Mr. Kapasi and his wife do not communicate much, and she has no respect for his job of interpreter. He regards himself and his wife as a "bad match." They are two people formally joined together by marriage but with little in common. When he observes "the bickering, the indifference, the protracted silences" between Mr. and Mrs. Das, he recognizes it as similar to what he experiences in his own marriage.

Because of their unhappy marriages, both Mr. Kapasi and Mrs. Das feel somewhat isolated. Mr. Kapasi has a deep desire to connect with someone more closely. It is because of this that he gets carried away when Mrs. Das shows some polite interest in his work and asks for his address

TOPICS FOR FURTHER STUDY

- Read another story by Lahiri in the collection *Interpreter of Maladies* and write an essay in which you compare and contrast it with "Interpreter of Maladies." What themes are common to both stories?

- Using the Internet, research the topic of second-generation South Asian Americans. Do they tend to identify entirely with the American culture, or do they also try to preserve their South Asian heritage? How does their experience in the United States resemble or differ from that of other immigrant groups? Make a class presentation in which you discuss your research.

- Consult *Talk: Teen Art of Communication* (2006), by Dale Carlson and Kishore Khairnar, a book for teens that offers practical advice about how to communicate effectively with the different people they know. Take some of the examples in the book and practice with a partner the art of communication. One suggestion: Read pages 60–62, about the need to listen without judging or interpreting. Find a partner. One person then talks for a couple of minutes about some emotional issue he or she is dealing with. The other person listens without interrupting and then takes a minute to speak back to the first person what he or she has just said, without judging, commenting, or interpreting.

- Imagine that "Interpreter of Maladies" is being made into a movie. Go to Glogster. com and create an interactive poster to advertise the movie version. Link it to your Facebook or Twitter page so all your friends can see and comment on it.

so she can send him a copy of the photograph her husband took of them sitting together. Mr. Kapasi imagines corresponding with Mrs. Das, building up a friendship, sharing details of their lives in a way that neither is able to do in their respective marriages. He even compares the feeling he gets from imagining this to the pleasure he used to experience when he was learning to translate from French or Italian. Communication, crossing the differences between languages and between people, seems to be something that Mr. Kapasi values very deeply. He has a momentary desire to embrace Mrs. Das, "to freeze with her, even for an instant," but of course this is an act of intimacy that can never occur. The impossibility of it is shown symbolically at the end, when the piece of paper on which Mr. Kapasi has written his address escapes from Mrs. Das's bag, blows away, and nestles high in the trees.

Similarly, Mrs. Das makes an attempt at communicating with Mr. Kapasi, not for the sake of establishing a friendship with him, but simply to unburden herself of a dark secret that she has been carrying around for eight years. She confesses to Mr. Kapasi that her son Bobby was fathered not by her husband but by her husband's friend, and she goes on to tell the surprised tour guide the story of her unhappy marriage. It is ironic that she is able to confide in a stranger but not in her own husband. Her demand that Mr. Kapasi produce some balm for her malady is unrealistic. Trapped in her emotional isolation, she has no sensible plan for how to break out of it since the lack of communication between herself and her husband has become almost absolute. The story thus shows how difficult it is to escape from the prison of isolation. Both of these characters seize on what they think is an opportunity to do so, but neither ends up any better off than when they started.

Responsibility

Mr. and Mrs. Das, as seen through the eyes of Mr. Kapasi, are presented as not being very mature or responsible. When he first sees them, Mr. Kapasi is struck by how young they look. The narrator comments that Mr. Das's voice, "somehow tentative and a little shrill, sounded as though it had not yet settled into maturity." Mr. Das observes that the couple does not act like parents. They do not supervise their children very closely. When Tina plays with the lock in the car, for example, Mrs. Das does nothing to stop her. The parents' joint failure to supervise Bobby leads to the attack on him by the monkeys. Nor do the parents discipline the children. When Bobby shows no inclination to obey an instruction from his father, Mr. Das does nothing about it. Mr. Kapasi thinks they are

Ronny and Bobby are the sons of American tourists visiting India. (© *Arvind Balaraman /* *ShutterStock.com*)

not responsible parents. He observes that Mr. and Mrs. Das "behaved like an older brother and sister, not parents. It seemed that they were in charge of the children only for the day; it was hard to believe they were regularly responsible for anything other than themselves." The lack of responsibility is also shown in Mrs. Das's act of marital infidelity and the secret she keeps from both father and son. It appears that she has been so overwhelmed by her responsibilities as mother and wife that she has developed a habit of ignoring them that she cannot now break. "She was lost behind her sunglasses," Mr. Kapasi observes, and she walks past her children "as if they were strangers."

STYLE

Point of View

The story is told by a limited third-person narrator from the point of view of Mr. Kapasi. This means that the narrator has insight only into the thoughts and feelings of Mr. Kapasi. The other characters are seen through his eyes. In other words, the reader gets to know Mr. and Mrs. Das by means of the impressions they make on Mr. Kapasi and the ideas he forms of them, in addition to their actions and the things they say directly.

Imagery and Symbolism

Mr. Das is not as central to the story as his wife and Mr. Kapasi, but he is neatly characterized by the author with the help of a recurring image, that of the camera. Mr. and Mrs. Das, it must be remembered, do not have a happy marriage, but Mrs. Das tells Mr. Kapasi that she thinks her husband still believes that she loves him. Mr. Das is therefore ignorant of his wife's true feelings as well as being completely unaware that one of the boys he has raised as his son is not his biological son. Mr. Das is seen often with his expensive high-tech camera, snapping photographs of the local sites and of his family. He knows how to look at things from the outside, but he seems oblivious to the inner condition of his marriage. Shortly after Mrs. Das has explained her unhappiness to Mr. Kapasi, Mr. Das is shown wanting to get yet another shot of the entire family. He wants to use it for their Christmas cards that year. His photos may appear to show a happy, intact family, but the reality is rather different, and the reader gets a keen sense of the irony of the situation.

Mrs. Das is presented as being careless and irresponsible, and this is symbolized by the trail of puffed rice that she spills as she walks to rejoin her family after making her confession to Mr. Kapasi. She is unaware that as she eats the rice, chunks of it fall to the ground. It is this trail of puffed rice that causes the crisis in which the monkeys attack Bobby. Mrs. Das's untidiness, her failure to exert self-control, is symbolic of her conduct in her marriage.

Another image is that of the wild, unruly monkeys. They might perhaps be seen as symbolic of the turbulent emotions that are felt by the two central characters but are not expressed—or at least, in Mrs. Das's case, not expressed to the right person. Both these characters keep up a surface appearance that is not related to their inner dissatisfaction.

COMPARE & CONTRAST

- **1990s:** According to the 2000 Census, the Indian American community in the United States numbers 1,678,765. It is the third-largest Asian community after Chinese Americans and Filipino Americans. The numbers are growing rapidly, with an increase of 106 percent from 1990 to 2000.

  Today: According to the 2010 Census, there are 2,846,914 Indian Americans living in the United States. The average annual growth rate for the Indian American community is 10.5 percent.

- **1990s:** The Indian American community shows high levels of educational attainment. Some 58 percent of Indian Americans have received a bachelor's degree or higher, compared with only 20 percent of the US population as a whole. Indian Americans are also successful in their careers. Nearly 44 percent of those in the workforce are in managerial or specialist positions. Over 5,000 Indian Americans teach in US colleges; 30,000 Indian American doctors practice in the United States.

  Today: Indian Americans are among the most successful and prosperous of immigrant groups in the United States. Nearly 67 percent hold bachelor's or higher degrees. About 77 percent hold a professional position. Median income for Indian American families is $69,470, as compared to $38,885 for all American families. There are 200,000 Indian American millionaires.

- **1990s:** According to the 2000 Census, the largest Indian American populations are in California (314,819), New York (251,724), New Jersey (169,180), Texas (129,365), Illinois (124,723), and Florida (70,740).

  Today: According to the 2010 Census, the largest Indian American populations are in California (528,176), New York (313,620), New Jersey (292,256), Texas (245,981), Illinois (188,328), and Florida (128,735).

HISTORICAL CONTEXT

Indian Immigration and Cultural Assimilation

"Interpreter of Maladies" illustrates the interaction of two cultures, American and Indian. Although both Mr. and Mrs. Das have Indian parents, they were born and raised in the United States and dress and behave as Americans. They do not speak Indian languages, and in India they act like tourists rather than Indian people returning home. This aspect of the story illustrates the theme of immigration and cultural assimilation. Mr. and Mrs. Das are second-generation immigrants. Usually, people in that category either experience some conflict about their cultural identity or identify with the only country they have known. First-generation immigrants tend to identify more with the culture of their homeland. This appears to have been the case with the parents of Mr. and Mrs. Das, who have returned to India rather than continue to live in the United States.

The interaction of these two cultures, Indian and American, is a theme in many of Lahiri's stories. Lahiri was raised in the United States by Indian immigrant parents who still identified with their country of origin. She therefore understood the experience of the Indian immigrant in America. The Indian American community grew considerably during the latter years of the twentieth century, following the 1965 Immigration and Naturalization Act. This act removed the national origins quota system in favor of criteria that emphasized possession of desirable skills. In the story it was probably around this time that the parents of Mr. and Mrs. Das came to the United States, and Mina Das and Raj Das would have been born around the early 1970s.

The story takes place as the Indian tour guide Mr. Kapasi takes American couple Mr. and Mrs. Das and their children to the Sun Temple at Konarak. (© *Dr. Ajay Kumar Singh* | *ShutterStock.com)*

During the 1970s, large Indian American communities developed in the United States, mainly in four states, California, New York, New Jersey (where Mr. and Mrs. Das are from), and Texas. Indian immigrants on the whole adjusted quickly to life in the United States, and they became one of the most prosperous of immigrant groups. Many became highly paid professionals such as doctors. During the 1980s, the Indian American community became more diverse, as those who were already in the United States sponsored their relatives to join them. In the 1990s, Indian immigrants made significant contributions to the booming information technology industry. Many Indian entrepreneurs settled in California's Silicon Valley and established their own successful high-tech companies there.

Indian Literature in English
Coinciding with the increase of Indian immigration to the United States has been the growth of literature written by Indians in English. In addition to Lahiri, Indian writers who have settled in the United States, such as Bharati Mukherjee, have taken as their subject matter the collective experience of Indian immigrants in North America. With *Interpreter of Maladies*, then, Lahiri was contributing to a growing body of work by Indians or those of Indian heritage living in the West.

During the 1990s, when Lahiri was writing the stories in *Interpreter of Maladies*, several other new writers of Indian origin made their mark. Vikram Seth is known for his novel *A Suitable Boy* (1993). Kiran Desai, a permanent resident of the United States who was born in India, published her well-received first novel, *Hullabaloo in the Guava Orchard*, in 1998. She is the daughter of Anita Desai, also a noted Indian author. Vikram Chandra, also born in India, received widespread recognition when he published his first novel, *Red Earth and Pouring Rain: A Novel*, in 1995 and the five stories that make up his collection *Love and Longing in Bombay* (1997). Pankaj Mishra's novel *The Romantics* (1999), set in India, deals with the clash between Eastern and Western culture. The novel won the Los Angeles Times Art Seidenbaum Award for First Fiction.

CRITICAL OVERVIEW

As the title story in a Pulitzer Prize–winning collection, "Interpreter of Maladies" attracted the attention of literary critics. In his essay "Jhumpa Lahiri: *Interpreter of Maladies* (2000)," Paul Brians states that the story is "of two people crossing at an angle through each other's lives, neither satisfied with the response of the other." He notes also that "Lahiri skillfully builds the tension as we gradually realize how much Mr. Kapasi desires Mrs. Das, and how much he has let his fantasies carry him away in dreams of a romantic future." Noelle Brada-Williams, in "Reading Jhumpa Lahiri's *Interpreter of Maladies* as a Short Story Cycle," notes the contrast between the characterization of Mrs. Das and that of Mr. Kapasi. The latter takes care with everything, from his appearance to his manners and his occupation, and he takes his responsibilities seriously. Mrs. Das, however, does not. This contrast between the two, according to Brada-Williams,

> makes their final disconnect inevitable. While they both can be seen longing for communication with others, Mrs. Das is a woman with a life of relative comfort and ease who yearns to be freed of the responsibilities of marriage and children, and Mr. Kapasi is a man who has given up his dreams to support his family and who only yearns for some recognition and interest in his life.

Not every critic has seen the story in entirely positive terms. In the *Dictionary of Literary Biography*, Rezaul Karim remarks that the style is "marked by occasional overwriting, excessive symbolism, unnatural dialogue, an ironic tone, and some editorializing." According to Karim, the story reveals the Das family's "attitude to India as one of snobbish distance and their interest in India as tourists' interest." For Purvi Shah, reviewing the story in *Amerasia Journal*, the story is "well-crafted, like all of Lahiri's stories. But the writing, as in other pieces in the collection, feels like material produced for a writing workshop—too belabored and mechanical."

CRITICISM

Bryan Aubrey

Aubrey holds a PhD in English. In the following essay, he discusses "Interpreter of Maladies" in

> THIS IS A STORY ABOUT A CERTAIN KIND OF LONELINESS. IT IS ABOUT EMOTIONAL DISAPPOINTMENT AND FRUSTRATION, THE BARREN OR TORMENTING PRIVATE WORLDS IN WHICH PEOPLE LIVE AND THEIR IMPULSIVE URGE TO BREAK OUT OF THOSE WORLDS TO ACHIEVE SOME PEACE OF MIND OR HAPPINESS."

terms of the frustration involved in communicating authentically with another person about emotional truth.

Jhumpa Lahiri's "Interpreter of Maladies" is a story about the emotional distances between people who should be close to each other, and the frustrations they experience in trying to fill the void in their lives or simply to communicate truthfully with another person. It is not an optimistic story. Neither of the two main characters, Mrs. Das or Mr. Kapasi, finds a way to ease their pain and isolation, the reality of which they feel more keenly than ever as a result of their failure. They both have maladies they are unable to cure. Each seeks in the other an interpreter, someone who would be able to heal their pain and allow them to live in a more authentic, emotionally satisfying manner. But in both cases, their attempt is so inept, so inappropriate, and so unlikely to succeed that it smacks of desperation. The reader is not encouraged to feel that either character has the qualities of character that would be needed to heal their respective maladies.

Like many of Lahiri's stories, "Interpreter of Maladies" also shines a light on cross-cultural interactions and the experiences of Indian immigrants to the United States. Raj and Mina Das are second-generation immigrants, and a wide gulf separates them from their parents. Lahiri provides few details of these parents except to point out that they lived for an unspecified time in the United States, where they gave birth to Raj and Mina, before deciding to return to their native India. It would appear that like many first-generation immigrants, the parents continued to identify with their country of origin rather than the country in which they lived. When the

WHAT DO I READ NEXT?

- *Unaccustomed Earth* (2008) is Lahiri's second collection of short stories. These eight stories, like those in *Interpreter of Maladies*, deal with families of Indian heritage and show how they are adjusting across generations to the experience of immigration to the United States. Lahiri examines with an acute eye for telling detail the forces that shape and challenge such families and marriages.

- Like her short stories, Lahiri's first novel, *The Namesake* (2003), deals with the experience of the second-generation Indian immigrant in the United States. Gogol Ganguli was born in the United States to Indian parents who had immigrated from Calcutta and settled in Cambridge, Massachusetts. But as he matures Gogol feels like an outsider, belonging neither to Indian nor American culture. The novel traces his painful attempts to discover his self-identity until he finally learns to accept both the American and the Indian aspects of his heritage.

- *The Middleman and Other Stories* (1988) is a collection of eleven stories by Indian-born American writer Bharati Mukherjee. She explores the immigrant experience in the United States, including that of not only Indians but also Italians, Filipinos, West Indians, and others. In the title story, an Iraqi Jew who is a recently naturalized American citizen finds himself working for a corrupt American rancher in a Central American country that is in the throes of a guerrilla insurgency. Mukherjee's stories document how immigration has changed the ethnic composition of the United States. They also examine the challenges faced by those who have recently arrived in an unfamiliar culture in which they are not always welcome.

- *Scent of Apples: A Collection of Stories*, by Filipino American writer Bienvenido Santos, was first published in 1979. Santos (1911–1996) wrote frequently about the experiences of Filipino immigrants to the United States. A typical story is "Immigration Blues," which examines the loneliness and sense of exile suffered by an old Filipino American widower who lives alone. He has been a US citizen since the end of World War II. Another story, "The Day the Dancers Came," shows how Filipino immigrants were often confined to low-status, low-wage jobs. *Scent of Apples* is available in a fifth edition published in 1997.

- *Immigration: The Ultimate Teen Guide* (2011), by Tatyana Kleyn, is a treasure trove of information and different perspectives regarding immigration in the United States. In twelve chapters, Kleyn, an immigrant herself, covers issues such as history and relevant terminology; statistical and demographic information; why people immigrate to the United States; undocumented immigration; refugees and those who have sought asylum; homesickness; language and cultural differences; discrimination; and laws and policies relating to immigration. Kleyn also discusses some of the myths regarding immigration and argues strongly against anti-immigrant sentiment. There are also many real-life stories of teens and young adults.

- In *Becoming American, Being Indian: An Immigrant Community in New York City* (2002), Madhulika S. Khandelwal describes the Indian immigrant community in New York City and how it has developed since it began in the 1960s. Drawing on interviews, Khandelwal examines how immigrants have preserved their own culture but have also been changed by their American experience.

- For those readers intrigued by the description of the Sun Temple at Konarak in "Interpreter of Maladies," *The Hindu Temple: An Introduction to Its Meaning and Forms*, by George Michell (1988), will be a fascinating book. Michell discusses the Konarak temple as well as numerous other examples of Hindu temples. The author explains the cultural, religious, and architectural significance of the temple, and the book includes numerous photographs.

time came to retire, after presumably achieving some level of material prosperity in the United States, it was natural for them to return to India.

For Mr. and Mrs. Das, however, it is different. Having been born in the United States, they know nothing of India, and Mrs. Das tells Mr. Kapasi that she has not been close to her parents. For these two second-generation immigrants, the United States is their home, and for all intents and purposes they are Americans. They visit India as tourists, knowing nothing of the country and its ways. They get their information from travel books and from Mr. Kapasi, the tour guide. They are outsiders exploring a new country rather than expatriates joyfully returning home. As he observes them, Mr. Kapasi is aware of how Westernized they are, with customs that are very different from those he is familiar with. When he first sees them, he observes that "the family looked Indian but dressed as foreigners did." When they first meet, Mr. Kapasi puts his hands together in a traditional Indian greeting, but Mr. Das reaches out and shakes his hand vigorously, American-style. Mr. and Mrs. Das talk with an American accent, the kind that Mr. Kapasi is familiar with only from American television programs. Mr. Kapasi is also struck by the couple's slack parenting style, their reluctance to discipline their children. The reader must assume that this is intended to reflect an American rather than an Indian approach to child rearing. Mr. Kapasi's noting of the fact that Mr. Das refers to his wife by her first name when talking to their daughter suggests something similar. Mr. and Mrs. Das might be considered examples of second-generation immigrants who have been happy to identify with the land of their birth rather than experiencing conflict or divided feelings because of the different national origins of their parents.

Be that as it may, the assimilation of second-generation immigrants such as Mr. and Mrs. Das into American culture is not the main point of the story. This is a story about a certain kind of loneliness. It is about emotional disappointment and frustration, the barren or tormenting private worlds in which people live and their impulsive urge to break out of those worlds to achieve some peace of mind or happiness. Right from the beginning, Mrs. Das is presented as living in a world of her own. She is self-absorbed. She doesn't interact much with her children or with her husband. "Leave me

alone" she says to her young daughter when the girl wants some attention. Mrs. Das prefers to polish her nails undisturbed by the needs of a little one. But then, for some reason, she shows an interest in Mr. Kapasi and his work, and this is the catalyst for Mr. Kapasi to suddenly feel a romantic, even erotic interest in her and daydream about an unlikely friendship blossoming between them through the exchange of letters after her return to America.

It is here that Mr. Kapasi reveals his own disappointments, although unlike with Mrs. Das's confession to him later, he does not communicate them directly to the American woman. Mr. Kapasi is a disappointed man both professionally and personally. When he was younger, he hoped to become a high-level interpreter, helping to resolve all kinds of conflicts between people and nations. This turned out to be the unrealistic dream of a self-educated man of modest talents, and his present occupation as an interpreter for a doctor is far less glamorous. He feels as if he has failed in life. And in that respect, his wife is no help to him. This is the source of his emotional pain. He has no one with whom he can share his inner life. He gets no respect from his wife for what he does to earn the money. She never asks him about his work or compliments him about it. Also, at one point in the story, as he looks with admiration at Mrs. Das's bare legs, he remembers that he has never seen his wife completely naked. Even when they make love, she remains partially covered. This is a telling observation of the lack of intimacy in their marriage, which applies at more than the physical level. They simply do not find much to say to each other.

Given the emptiness he experiences where intimacy ought to be, it is not at all surprising that Mr. Kapasi should suddenly be awash with a fantasy about the close friendship he and Mrs. Das will attain through the correspondence that he imagines will take place between them. ("In time she would reveal the disappointment of her marriage, and he his.") It is a hopeless if understandable dream—so much extrapolated on the basis of so little—and it does not even survive the few minutes they spend alone together, in which Mrs. Das's confession that her husband is not the father of one of her sons leaves Mr. Kapasi feeling insulted and depressed. Once he has gotten over the pain arising from the demise of this brief infatuation with a foreign married woman—

An open air market in India, where the tea stall is located (© *Pawel Pietraszewski | ShutterStock.com*)

which made him feel his own unhappiness even more acutely—he is going to have to find some other way of alleviating his feelings of emptiness and loneliness.

As for Mrs. Das, she is in an even more difficult situation than Mr. Kapasi, from which there appears to be no escape that does not involve great emotional pain, not only for herself but also for her husband, and perhaps for her son Bobby, too. She is caught in a trap of her own making. Living with a guilty secret imposes a great burden on her, as it would on anyone, and confessing the secret requires some courage. Unfortunately for her, she does not possess such courage and is only able to confess the truth to a virtual stranger. She makes the mistake of assuming that because Mr. Kapasi plays a role in curing people's physical maladies, he will have an equal ability to address psychic maladies. Of course, he does not. However, Mrs. Das's confession to him reflects a strange truth of human social interaction: people will sometimes say things to strangers that they would never say to

their friends or family. In meeting a stranger, with whom one shares no personal history, the constraints on self-disclosure that people develop during the stresses and strains of a long-term relationship may simply not be present. Those who unburden themselves in this way may believe that since the stranger has no relationship with them, he or she may not judge them harshly and may indeed prove to be a sympathetic listener. The sudden, startling confession thus seems to offer the potential for some kind of emotional release that is unobtainable elsewhere. Of course, the resulting personal disclosures or confessions might still be seen as wildly inappropriate and may backfire, as in the case of Mrs. Das, who gains nothing at all from her disclosure and loses the respect of Mr. Kapasi. She has revealed her pain but gained no release from it, which must make her predicament even worse than before.

In "Interpreter of Maladies," then, what begins as a pleasant interaction between tourist and tour guide eventually turns into a disappointment for both. Lahiri's sharp eye for the torments that lie beneath placid surfaces makes for an engaging and sad short story. Two people, each in their own way, and each with their own emotional needs, reach out for each other in very different ways in the expectation of receiving something that will act as a balm for their maladies. But the communication and healing of psychic wounds, Lahiri suggests, is no easy matter. It is fraught with danger and may well fail.

Source: Bryan Aubrey, Critical Essay on "Interpreter of Maladies," in *Short Stories for Students*, Gale, Cengage Learning, 2013.

Noelle Brada-Williams

In the following excerpt, Brada-Williams discusses some of the interconnecting motifs and themes in Interpreter of Maladies, *including in the title story.*

It may at first seem strange to describe Jhumpa Lahiri's *Interpreter of Maladies* as a short story cycle rather than simply as a collection of separate and independent stories. After all, from Sherwood Anderson's *Winesburg, Ohio* to Sandra Cisneros' *House on Mango Street*, readers of the modern short story cycle are often cued to the unity of a collection by a single location and/or a small ensemble of recurring characters that serve to unite the various components into a whole, while Lahiri's Pulitzer Prize-winning work features diverse and unrelated characters, a variety of narrative styles, and no common locale. Indeed, the text even transcends national boundaries, being set in both India and the United States. However, a deeper look reveals the intricate use of pattern and motif to bind the stories together, including the recurring themes of the barriers to and opportunities for human communication; community, including marital, extra-marital, and parent-child relationships; and the dichotomy of care and neglect.

The short story cycle is a notoriously difficult genre to define. Forrest L. Ingram points out this difficulty by describing the cycle's method of making meaning:

> Like the moving parts of a mobile, the interconnected parts of some short story cycles seem to shift their positions with relation to the other parts, as the cycle moves forward in its typical pattern of recurrent development. Shifting internal relationships, of course, continually alter the originally perceived pattern of the whole cycle. A cycle's form is elusive. (13)

> MR. AND MRS. DAS'S LACK OF CAREFULNESS IN RAISING THEIR CHILDREN EXTENDS TO THEIR CARELESSNESS IN MAINTAINING THEIR MARRIAGE VOWS, AT LEAST ON MRS. DAS'S PART."

Susan Garland Mann asserts that the essential characteristic of the short story cycle is the "simultaneous self-sufficiency and interdependence" of the stories which make up the whole (17). Mann comments on Ingram's conception of the tension which short story cycles create between the individuality of its components and the unity of the whole by noting that the "tension is revealed in the way people read cycles" (18).

An analogous tension can be found in the way people read ethnic literature. The unique vision of an individual artist and the unique representation he or she provides of a community are often challenged by readers from both within and outside the community being represented as various readers lobby for the value of one representation over another. Such claims on writers include the demand for more sanitized, more stereotype-affirming, or simply more diverse, representations. Examples range from controversies over the use of dialect in early twentieth-century African American literature to the depictions of sexuality and gender roles in virtually all ethnic American literatures up to the present time, including, most recently, Lois-Ann Yamanaka's depiction of a Filipino American sexual predator in *Blu's Hanging*. Although most rational readers are aware of the diversity and individuality of any given ethnic group (especially the vast population Lahiri engages of South Asia and its diaspora), the logic of representation implies, especially with regards to groups under-represented within a national literature, that a work depicting a part of a community "represents" the whole.

We see the logic of representation at work in the naïve reader who naturally bases his or her understanding of a particular demographic unit on the few representations he or she has come across, as well as the experienced literature professor who attempts to create a syllabus that is "representative" of diverse populations through what can be read in a single term. Readers both new to ethnic literature and those who are experts in the field thus face the common dilemma of obscuring part and whole due to the inevitably finite nature of both available representations and one's own reading. Not only does this problem of obscuring part and whole work to the advantage of the short story cycle as a genre but the genre can, as we see in *Interpreter of Maladies*, work towards solving the problem of representing an entire community within the necessarily limited confines of a single work by balancing a variety of representations rather than offering the single representation provided by the novel or the individual short story.

The popularity and critical success of Lahiri's *Interpreter of Maladies* in both the United States and India could in part be due to the delicate balancing of representations she provides through the cycle as a whole. For example, the cheating husbands of "Sexy" are balanced by the depiction of the unfaithful Mrs. Das of "Interpreter of Maladies." The relative ease with which Lilia of "When Mr. Pirzada Came to Dine" participates in an American childhood is contrasted with the separation and stigmatization that the Dixit children experience in the story "Sexy." Mrs. Sen's severe homesickness and separation from US culture is contrasted with the adaptability of Lilia's mother and Mala in "The Third and Final Continent." The balancing of the generally negative depiction of an Indian community in "A Real Durwan" with the generally positive portrayal in "The Treatment of Bibi Haldar" is yet another example not only of the resulting balanced representations that the genre affords Lahiri but is itself one of many ways through which Lahiri constructs a conversation among her pieces.

. . . "Interpreter of Maladies" similarly focuses on a young couple with severe marital problems, but their carelessness is most often evoked in their treatment of their three children. "Interpreter of Maladies" is a third-person narrative filtered through the point of view of Mr. Kapasi, the family's driver while sight-seeing in India. The story opens with the parents bickering over who will take their daughter to the restroom. Mr. Kapasi will later think that the family is "all like siblings . . . it was hard to believe [Mr. and Mrs. Das] were regularly responsible for anything other than themselves." The first paragraph of the story notes that the mother "did not hold the little girl's hand as they walked to the restroom." As in "A

Temporary Matter," small signs of negligence add up to reveal deeper emotional difficulties and detachments. This otherwise unremarkable scene acts as foreshadowing for what may be called the twin climaxes of the story: the attack on one of the boys by monkeys and the revelation of his illegitimate birth. Notably it is the popcorn that his mother has carelessly dropped that draws the monkeys to her son as well as the fact that he is left unsupervised that leads to the attack.

Mr. and Mrs. Das's lack of carefulness in raising their children extends to their carelessness in maintaining their marriage vows, at least on Mrs. Das's part. Although their driver, Mr. Kapasi, recognizes similarities between the Das's marriage and his own, he himself functions as a stark contrast to Mr. and Mrs. Das's lack of care. Not unlike Mr. Pirzada, Mr. Kapasi is characterized by his carefully tailored clothing and meticulous manners. Simon Lewis has read this story as a rewriting and updating of the trip to the Marabar Caves in E. M. Forster's *A Passage to India*, this time from the perspective of an Indian national, Mr. Kapasi in the role formerly held by Dr. Aziz (219). Lewis's argument can be supported by Mr. Kapasi's dream "of serving as an interpreter between nations" (Lahiri) which he fantasizes fulfilling through a future correspondence with Mrs. Das. The way in which Mr. Kapasi gives Mrs. Das his contact information is illustrative of their essential differences as characters: she hands "him a scrap of paper which she had hastily ripped from a page of her film magazine" upon which he writes "his address in clear, careful letters." She then tosses "it into the jumble of her bag." The clear differences in these two characters in their relationship to care or lack of care, specifically in relation to responsibility, make their final disconnect inevitable. While they both can be seen longing for communication with others, Mrs. Das is a woman with a life of relative comfort and ease who yearns to be freed of the responsibilities of marriage and children, and Mr. Karpasi is a man who has given up his dreams to support his family and who only yearns for some recognition and interest in his life. By the time his address falls out of Mrs. Das's bag and is borne off by the wind, Mr. Kapasi has already let go of his fantasy of communicating across continents and between individuals. . . .

Source: Noelle Brada-Williams, "Reading Jhumpa Lahiri's *Interpreter of Maladies* as a Short Story Cycle," in *MELUS*, Vol. 29, Nos. 3–4, Fall–Winter 2004, pp. 451–64.

Ronny Noor

In the following review, Noor praises Interpreter of Maladies *not only for exploring the experience of immigrants but also for considering larger human issues.*

Born in England of Indian parents and raised in America, Jhumpa Lahiri has evidently benefited from all three cultures. Their aroma drifts from the pages of her first collection of short fiction, titled *Interpreter of Maladies*, where she has woven their idiosyncrasies into well-crafted stories with a keen eye for observation and an admirable gift for details. Eight of the nine stories have been previously published, in slightly different form, in various literary and nonliterary journals across the nation. They not only study the experiences of immigrants but also deal with perennial universal issues.

The title story, "Interpreter of Maladies," is about a young couple named Mr. and Mrs. Das, by birth American, who go to India with their three children to visit the land of their ancestors. While viewing monastic dwellings on the hills of Udayagiri, Mrs. Das confides in the car driver, a translator for a doctor, that her husband has not sired their eight-year-old boy. He is the product of an encounter with a guest in the house. This is the secret, the malady if you will, which she hides from her husband, just the way Dev hides his extramarital affair from his wife in "Sexy." Shoba is not so lucky in "A Temporary Matter." She thinks that her husband did not see the stillborn baby she had delivered while he was away at a conference. But when Shukumar tells her that he returned early from the conference to hold his son in his arms before the boy was cremated, the secret is out, adding more pain to their already miserable marriage.

Lahiri's stories are not just about this malady of secrets between spouses, but also concern broader social issues. In "A Real Durwan" the residents of a Calcutta tenement unjustly cast out an old sweeper because of a theft in the building while she was away in town. They show no sympathy for the innocent victim despite her pleading. Such lack of understanding forces Bibi to lead a desolate life in "The Treatment of Bibi Haldar," and pushes a professor's wife into an embarrassing car accident in "Mrs. Sen's." Compassion, on the other hand, goes a long way toward resolving differences in "This Blessed House," "When Mr. Pirzada Came to Dine," and "The Third and Final Continent." The last story, hitherto unpublished, is a first-person narrative of a man who has journeyed from India to America via England in search of a livelihood. He marries a traditional Indian woman who seems to be steeped in her native customs, which he, as a modern man, finds hard to accept. But when they visit his former landlady, an ancient who once found happiness in his sympathy, the old woman thinks his wife is "a perfect lady," a compliment that makes the couple smile at each other, lessening the distance between them. Thus, with sympathy, understanding, and a smile, one can narrow the gap not only between spouses but also between continents. E. M. Forster expressed it best with his "only connect" precept.

The value of these stories—although some of them are loosely constructed—lies in the fact they transcend the confined borders of immigrant experience to embrace larger human issues, age-old issues that are, in the words of Ralph Waldo Emerson, "cast into the mould of these new times" redefining America. So it is not surprising that the title story of Jhumpa Lahiri's laudable collection has been selected for both *The Best American Short Stories* and the year 1999's O. Henry Award.

Source: Ronny Noor, Review of *Interpreter of Maladies,* in *World Literature Today,* Vol. 74, No. 2, Spring 2000, pp. 365–66.

SOURCES

Brada-Williams, Noelle, "Reading Jhumpa Lahiri's *Interpreter of Maladies* as a Short Story Cycle," in *MELUS,* Vol. 29, Nos. 3–4, Fall–Winter 2004, pp. 451–64.

Brians, Paul, "Jhumpa Lahiri: *Interpreter of Maladies* (2000)," in *Modern South Asian Literature in English,* Greenwood Press, 2003, p. 198.

"A Conversation with Jhumpa Lahiri," Houghton Mifflin Harcourt website, http://www.houghtonmifflinbooks.com/readers_guides/interpreter_maladies.shtml (accessed July 31, 2012).

"The Indian American Community in the United States of America," Out of India, http://www.outofindia.net/abroad/WashingtonDC/indian_american_community.htm (accessed August 7, 2012).

"Indian-Americans: Demographic Information Updates," US India Political Action Committee (USINPAC) website, 2011, http://www.usinpac.com/indian-americans/demographic-info.html (accessed August 7, 2012).

Karim, Rezaul, "Jhumpa Lahiri," in *Dictionary of Literary Biography,* Vol. 323, *South Asian Writers in English,* edited by Fakrul Alam, Thomson Gale, 2006, pp. 205–10.

Lahiri, Jhumpa, "Interpreter of Maladies," in *Interpreter of Maladies: Stories,* Houghton Mifflin, 1999, pp. 43–69.

Shah, Purvi, Review of *Interpreter of Maladies*, in *Amerasia Journal*, Vol. 27, No. 2, 2001, pp. 183–86.

"Trading Stories: Notes from an Apprenticeship," in *New Yorker*, June 13, 2011, http://www.newyorker.com/reporting/2011/06/13/110613fa_fact_lahiri (accessed July 31, 2012).

FURTHER READING

Bala, Suman, ed., *Jhumpa Lahiri, the Master Storyteller: A Critical Response to "Interpreter of Maladies,"* Khosla Publishing House, 2002.

> This collection of essays offers a wide range of critical responses to Lahiri's stories.

Das, Nigamananda, ed., *Dynamics of Culture and Diaspora in Jhumpa Lahiri*, Adhyayan Publishers, 2010.

> This is a collection of eighteen essays by Indian scholars on all aspects of Lahiri's work. Of particular interest is the essay by Dipendu Das titled "Interpreting Maladies of the Exile: 'Interpreter of Maladies.'" Das explores the story in terms of the theme of exile.

Dhingra, Lavina, and Floyd Cheung, eds., *Naming Jhumpa Lahiri: Canons and Controversies*, Lexington Books, 2012.

> This is a collection of ten scholarly essays on Lahiri's work. In "Intimate Awakening: Jhumpa Lahiri, Diasporic Loss, and the Responsibility of the Interpreter," Rani Neutill employs psychoanalytic theory to analyze the story in terms of how the characters deal with loss.

Srikanth, Rajini, *The World Next Door: South Asian American Literature and the Idea of America*, Temple University Press, 2004.

> This is a scholarly study of the contribution to American literature made by South Asian American writers from countries including Bangladesh, Pakistan, India, Sri Lanka, and Burma. Srikanth also offers a reading of Lahiri's "Interpreter of Maladies" (pp. 248–52).

SUGGESTED SEARCH TERMS

Jhumpa Lahiri

Interpreter of Maladies

Konarak

Sun Temple

Surya

second-generation immigrants

immigration AND United States

Indian literature in English

South Asian American literature

The Jay

YASUNARI KAWABATA

1949

Yasunari Kawabata was a renowned Japanese author of short stories and novels, but his favorite form of storytelling was one of his own invention. He called this form of writing "palm-of-the-hand" storytelling. Like poetry, his palm-of-the-hand stories are brief and dense in imagery. Stylistically, they resemble a prose version of Japanese haiku, an ancient form of poetry revered for its simplicity and beauty. Kawabata's very short fiction relies on succinct, subtle writing that often tells a story much larger than appears on the page. "The Jay," originally published in 1949, is an excellent example of this type of story, describing the teenage girl Yoshiko's life at home as she worries about a jay in her garden who has lost her chick. As the jay sings, frantically searching for her chick, Yoshiko prepares to meet the mother of her fiancé—a marriage her father has arranged. "The Jay" appears in Kawabata's *Palm-of-the Hand Stories* (1988), translated by Lane Dunlop and J. Martin Holman.

AUTHOR BIOGRAPHY

Kawabata was born in Osaka, Japan, on June 14, 1899, to a prominent Buddhist family. He experienced terrible loss as a child, as his father, mother, grandmother, only sister (named Yoshiko), and, finally, his beloved blind grandfather

Yasunari Kawabata (© *AF Archive | Alamy*)

disconcerting habit, Kawabata was well loved by his contemporaries. He edited many magazines throughout his life, always supportive of the work of upcoming writers. As early as the 1920s, Kawabata began to develop his signature stories. Lane Dunlop and J. Martin Holman quote Kawabata: "Many writers, in their youth, write poetry: I, instead of poetry, wrote the palm-of-the-hand stories." *Bungei Jidai* (The Artistic Age), a short-lived magazine of great artistic influence, served as the vehicle for publishing these tales, which he wrote from the 1920s through the 1960s.

When World War II broke out, Kawabata turned his attention to children's reading and writing programs in an attempt to distance himself from the volatile political atmosphere. After the war, Kawabata's reputation grew with the publication in 1947 of his novel *Snow Country*, a work that he had published in bits and pieces since 1935 and which is considered by many to be his masterpiece. He was made president of Japan's PEN club in 1948, using the position to promote Japanese writing both inside and outside the country. "The Jay" was published in 1949 as "Kakesu," part of a group of postwar palm-of-the-hand stories concerned with modernity and tradition in Japan.

Awards and accolades rolled in through the years. Kawabata accepted membership in the Japan Art Academy in 1953, the position of vice president of International PEN in 1958, the German Goethe Medal in 1959, and the Medal of Culture from Japan in 1961. But no award could compare with the Nobel Prize in Literature, which Kawabata received in 1968, becoming the first Japanese writer to win the award. After receiving the Nobel Prize, Kawabata became an internationally celebrated author, touring the world on a mission to introduce Japanese literature to new audiences and most particularly to the English-speaking world.

In later years, Kawabata's health began to decline. On April 16, 1972, Kawabata committed suicide by gas inhalation—astonishing his friends and fans alike. Some, including his widow, were left believing it had been an accident. In response to his death, an outburst of mourning throughout Japan included touring exhibits and the installation of monuments celebrating the life and work of a man who had, as Van C. Gessel writes, "contributed more than perhaps any other individual to the legitimization of contemporary Japanese fiction in the international world."

died—leaving him orphaned before he turned fifteen. He attended First High School in Tokyo, living in the dormitories and founding a literary club. His early compositions drew the admiration of his teachers and classmates. In 1920, he enrolled at Tokyo Imperial University, where he began to publish in literary magazines, the cornerstone of the Japanese literary scene. In 1924, he graduated with a degree in Japanese literature, and in 1925, he met his future wife, Matsubayashi Hideko—just as his writing career took off. The publication of his short story "The Izu Dancer" in 1926 was his first major success. This story of a quiet schoolboy who joins a group of traveling performers is much beloved in Japan and has been adapted into film regularly since its publication.

Thoroughly shaped by the tragic deaths in his family, Kawabata was nicknamed "Master of Funerals" for his solemn demeanor. He had an intimidating habit of staring into people's faces intensely, which he had picked up from living with his blind grandfather as a teen. Despite this

PLOT SUMMARY

"The Jay" opens on a family at breakfast as a jay sings outside their home in the garden behind the house. The brother is annoyed—the jay has been singing urgently since dawn—but the grandmother and daughter, Yoshiko, praise the jay. The grandmother explains that the jay is a mother bird looking tirelessly for her lost child. Yoshiko admires her grandmother for her perceptiveness despite the fact that she is nearly blind from cataracts and needs assistance in even basic tasks around the house. The grandmother sometimes goes to the glass door and, spreading her fingers against the sun, attempts to look out at the world. These moments alarm Yoshiko, who hides, frightened because her grandmother "was concentrating all the life that was left to her into that many-angled gaze."

Yoshiko clears the table after breakfast as the jay continues to sing from a neighbor's roof. A very gentle rain falls, visible against the dark leaves of the trees. Yoshiko watches the bird flit from branch to branch and fly low to the ground, still searching and singing to the lost chick. Yoshiko realizes the mother bird will not leave the area because the chick is nearby. She goes to her room, but the jay is on her mind. She applies makeup in preparation for a visit from her father, her mother, and the mother of her fiancé. Noticing the white stars under her nails, she remembers an old saying that stars under one's nails are "a sign that you would receive something." But Yoshiko once read "in the newspaper that it meant a deficiency of Vitamin C or something." Her makeup and kimono are easy to put on, making her look perfect. She considered having her mother help with her kimono but then decided to dress on her own.

Yoshiko's father lives separately with his second wife, whom Yoshiko calls her second mother or, simply, mother. Her father divorced Yoshiko's own mother when she was four and her brother was two. Yoshiko was told they divorced because her mother was a flashy dresser and spent too much money, but she doubts this was the real reason. She believes "that the real cause lay deeper down."

The story flashes back in time. When Yoshiko's brother was much younger, he found a picture of their mother and presented it to their father. Wordlessly, the father tore it up with an expression of absolute anger on his face. When

their father remarried, Yoshiko accepted his wife as a new mother and member of the family. They got along very well. Yoshiko assumes her father had stayed single for ten years out of respect for her feelings. The new family enjoyed peace and harmony until Yoshiko's younger brother—then living in his school's dormitory—returned one day, ecstatic about meeting their birth mother and acting strangely cold toward their stepmother. He told Yoshiko that their birth mother was beautiful, had remarried, and had welcomed the sight of her son. Yoshiko was stunned into silence at this news and trembled. Their stepmother entered the room, saying that it was natural and good that he had met her, that she had expected this to happen. But Yoshiko noticed that she looked extremely weak. Their stepmother had to sit down before speaking. Despite their stepmother's understanding tone, Yoshiko's brother left the room haughtily. Yoshiko, angry, wanted to hit him, but her stepmother told her to stay silent—speaking about the matter might make her younger brother turn for the worse. Yoshiko started to cry.

After the incident, their father brought her brother home from the dormitory to live with the grandmother and Yoshiko and then moved out of the house with their stepmother. This disturbed Yoshiko greatly: "It was as if she had been crushed by the power of masculine indignation and resentment." She saw the same power in her brother in the way he walked out of the room so suddenly the day of his revelation, and she came to believe that her brother and father shared this trait. At the same time, however, Yoshiko gained a new understanding of her father's emotional battle over the ten years he was alone. She felt sympathy for him.

Yoshiko's father returned into her life with the prospect of an arranged marriage, surprising Yoshiko. He explained to Yoshiko that he had told the boy's mother of her situation at home—that Yoshiko's future mother-in-law should treat her as a child rather than a bride. He blamed himself for her troubles. Yoshiko wept after this conversation. Because Yoshiko was the only one capable of caring for her brother and grandmother, the families of Yoshiko and her future husband were to live together after the wedding. Although Yoshiko did not want to be married because of her father's guilt, once arrangements began, she was not so upset by the idea.

Time returns to the present. After her preparations, Yoshiko enters her grandmother's room. She asks whether her grandmother can see the red in her kimono. Her grandmother can barely make it out and must hold the fabric close. She says, "I've already forgotten your face, Yoshiko. I wish I could see what you look like now." Yoshiko wants to giggle but instead lays her hand affectionately on her grandmother's head. Anxious and tired of waiting on her visitors, Yoshiko goes out to the garden to search for the jay's chick. She finds it, weak and unmoving, in the tall grass by a bamboo thicket. She takes it into her hand but cannot find its mother nearby. She brings the bird inside to show her grandmother, who calmly tells her to give it a drink of water. Yoshiko pours water into a rice bowl, and the chick drinks eagerly, recovering enough strength to sing. The mother, hearing its song, returns—perching on a telephone wire. The mother and child sing to each other.

Yoshiko's grandmother tells her to quickly return the chick to its mother. The grandmother is pleased with how swiftly the mother bird has answered her chick's call. Going outside, Yoshiko raises her hand to show the chick to its mother and then gently lowers the chick to the ground. She returns inside, watching the birds' reunion in the garden. The mother, wary at first, approaches her child slowly as the chick continues to sing. The mother lands on a low branch of a tree. When the chick tries to fly to her, it stumbles but keeps singing. Finally, the mother flies straight to the chick. The baby bird is overcome with happiness, spreading its wings. The two birds reunite, and the mother gives the chick something to eat. The story ends as Yoshiko watches them through the glass door: "Yoshiko wished that her father and stepmother would come soon. She would like to show them this, she thought."

CHARACTERS

Chick

The jay's chick is lost in the family's back garden. When Yoshiko finds the baby bird, it does not resist being picked up. After drinking water, the chick begins to sing. The mother bird returns, and the two sing to each other, but the chick falls over when it tries to fly. The mother bird brings the chick something to eat. The mother and child reunite in the garden as Yoshiko watches from the glass door.

Father

Yoshiko's father does not live with Yoshiko, her brother, and grandmother. He moved away with his second wife after his son had tracked down and met his first wife, whom he had divorced when the children were very young. He was single for ten years after the divorce, which Yoshiko believes was for her sake. The father also brought his son home from living at his school dormitory just after the incident, before abruptly moving out. He finds Yoshiko a husband to ameliorate his feelings of guilt, but he told the boy's mother that Yoshiko should be treated like a child and not a bride.

Fiancé's Mother

The mother of Yoshiko's fiancé does not appear in the story. Yoshiko is getting ready for her arrival at the house. After her marriage to the son, the households will combine, and Yoshiko and the fiancé's mother will live together with the rest of the family.

Grandmother

Yoshiko's grandmother is very elderly and going blind from cataracts. She is a kind woman, encouraging Yoshiko to help the chick. She is also very perceptive, though she can barely see the red in Yoshiko's kimono and has forgotten what Yoshiko looks like. Without seeing the jay, she knows the bird has lost her child. Without seeing the chick, she knows it is thirsty. Yoshiko helps her grandmother around the house. The two have a loving relationship.

Jay

The jay has lost her chick in the family's garden and will not leave the area. She sings all morning, flying from perch to perch in the yard, searching for her child. Both the mother and grandmother feel sorry for the bird. The brother is annoyed by her unending song. When she finally finds her chick, she approaches slowly but eventually flies straight to its side with something for her baby to eat.

Mother

The biological mother of Yoshiko and her younger brother is no longer in contact with her children. She and their father divorced when Yoshiko was four and her brother was two, because (the children are told) the mother dressed in flashy clothes and spent money too freely. Yoshiko thinks this is not the full extent of the reason for their divorce. The father ripped up a picture his son found of her after the divorce. When her son finally tracked her down, he learned that she had remarried and was very beautiful. She had been very pleased to see him. This visit caused enormous trouble at home.

Stepmother

After ten years of single life, the father married the stepmother. Yoshiko is very fond of her, calling her a second mother. The family lived together without tension after the stepmother joined the house, until the younger brother came home after meeting his biological mother and treated the stepmother coldly. The stepmother, a small woman, looked especially frail and hurt after this incident, although she claimed that everything was fine. She told Yoshiko not to confront her younger brother about his behavior. After that, the father and stepmother moved out of the house.

Yoshiko

Yoshiko is the elder teenage daughter of a broken family. She lives with her younger brother and grandmother, caring for them both. Her biological mother is remarried and lives elsewhere. Her father and stepmother moved away after an incident involving her younger brother. Yoshiko feels sympathy for her father, but when he arranges a marriage for her, she weeps to learn he told the boy's mother that Yoshiko should be treated as a child and not a wife. She gets used to the idea of marriage, however, and as she waits for the visit of her father and future mother-in-law, she applies makeup and puts on a kimono in preparation to meet her fiancé's mother. The jay in the yard looking for its child stays on her mind, and she goes outside to find the bird, helping to revive it and returning it to its mother. As she watches the birds reunite, she wishes she could show the scene to her father and stepmother. Yoshiko is closest to her grandmother, who also sympathizes with the mother bird and lost chick. Because Yoshiko must care for her brother and grandmother, it has been decided by her father that after her wedding her fiancé's family will join with Yoshiko's household, lessening the burden on Yoshiko around the house.

Younger Brother

Yoshiko's brother is younger by two years. In the story, he is a teenager. He complains about the jay at breakfast. When he was young, he found a picture of his mother, which his father furiously ripped to shreds. While living on his own in his school's dormitory (a common practice for Japanese students), he tracked down his biological mother and arranged to meet her. He came back to his family's home joyfully encouraging Yoshiko to do the same, because his mother was beautiful and had treated him with love. However, he acted coldly toward his stepmother, whom he once loved very much. When she tried to underplay her reaction to his news, he left the room without a word. After that, his father brought him from the dormitory to live at home and then moved out with the stepmother.

THEMES

Family

"The Jay" is essentially a story about family. Kawabata blurs the line when the time comes to define the family unit. Are Yoshiko and her younger brother's birth mother still family? Her younger brother thinks so, causing a rift to form: his father and stepmother on one side, and Yoshiko, her brother, and grandmother on the other. Are the siblings' father and stepmother still family? The day the story takes place, they are coming to visit for the first time in quite a while. They will bring with them a proposition to create a new family: Yoshiko and her husband and mother-in-law will join households. The convolutions of Yoshiko's family "circumstances," as her father calls it, have hurt her younger brother immensely. No longer at his school's dormitory as a result of the feuding, he is bothered by something as harmless as a bird's song. Yoshiko, however, seems to understand her role in the ever-changing arrangement of families. Still, it is telling that Yoshiko wants more than anything to show her father and stepmother the mother bird and chick in the garden. She envies so simple a relationship as the chick spreading its wings in happiness at the nearness of its mother.

Marriage

Three marriages are described in the story. There is Yoshiko's upcoming marriage, arranged so that the two households can combine, shifting

TOPICS FOR FURTHER STUDY

- What happens next? Does Yoshiko get a chance to show her father and stepmother the jays? Does she make a good impression on her fiancé's mother? Do her father and brother make amends? Take the story into your own hands: Write the next chapter in Yoshiko's life. Mimic Kawabata's writing style as you compose a palm-of-the-hand story of your own, using the characters from "The Jay."

- Using your online search skills, find and print a picture of your best guess on what species of jay is singing in the family's garden, using context clues from the text. If you can, find a recording of that species' birdsong to play for the class. Create a PowerPoint presentation for your class of images and descriptions from the story.

- Choose another palm-of-the-hand story by Kawabata to read. Write an essay in which you summarize the story and offer your thoughts about its content and writing style. What do you notice about the palm-of-the-hand form? What goes unsaid in the story that you might find implied through the setting, dialogue, or characters' actions? Address what you think is important in the short story. Attach a copy of the story to your essay when you turn it in.

- Read Curtis Sittenfeld's *Prep* (2005), a young-adult novel about the life of an American teenager, Lee, at an East Coast prep school. Considering the two works, what do you feel are common threads uniting the teens portrayed in "The Jay" and Sittenfeld's characters in *Prep*? Are some trials of young adulthood universal? Try to find three unifying characteristics of being a teenager portrayed in the works. Then examine the differences in family culture and how they affect the characters of Yoshiko and Lee. Finally, how would you compare the writing styles of this contemporary American author with Kawabata, writing in the twentieth century? Write a comparative essay using quotes from both works to support your arguments. Upload your essay to your blog and allow your classmates to comment.

caregiving duties away from Yoshiko and allowing her to be a child again. Then there is the father's marriage to his second wife: a joyful one until the son tracks down his birth mother and the family divides into separate households. Finally, there is the father's original marriage to the mother of his children. The breakup of this marriage causes all the difficulties that follow in the story. Marriage, like sympathy, unites the diverse characters of the story as family. However, marriage also divides. Yoshiko, a dutiful daughter, is willing to marry without love (or even the acquaintance of her husband-to-be) in order to mend the rifts that have formed as a result of her father's broken first marriage. Whether this will be the true solution or bring its own set of problems, Kawabata does not say.

Motherhood

Yoshiko is surrounded by mother figures in "The Jay." Yoshiko has not seen her birth mother since she was four years old, while her grandmother can no longer see Yoshiko as a result of her near blindness. The jay's mother cannot see her chick in the tall grass, while Yoshiko's stepmother has not arrived in time to see the two birds reunite. Yoshiko prepares to meet her fiancé's mother, yet she still has not seen her by the story's conclusion. These mothers—birth mother, stepmother, fiancé's mother, grandmother, and jay—represent motherhood in many forms and attitudes, but a unifying characteristic is the peculiar distance Kawabata grants each of them. Yoshiko is a good daughter to all of these mothers, but even so these relationships are characterized by separation—through blindness, obstacles, or emotional

Yoshiko is about to enter an arranged marriage. *(© BirDiGoL | ShutterStock.com)*

and physical distance. This is true even of the mother bird. Yoshiko helps find her chick, but she must watch their happy reunion alone through the glass door.

Sympathy

All of the action of "The Jay" is driven by sympathy. For example, Yoshiko and her grandmother both feel an overwhelming compassion for the mother bird and her lost child. They are driven to help resolve the situation—the main action of the short story. The father, for better or worse, has chosen to arrange a marriage for Yoshiko in part out of the guilt he feels about leaving her alone in the house to take care of her grandmother and younger brother. His statement to Yoshiko that "rather than treating you like a bride, she should try to bring back the happy days of your childhood" is not meant to be insulting; rather he believes that her childhood has been taken from her by her situation. Out of sympathy for her feelings, Yoshiko believes, the father remained alone for ten years after his divorce. The stepmother, hearing that the younger brother had met his birth mother, tried to be understanding and sympathetic to the boy, who never knew his real mother. It is important that both the men of the house have trouble with sympathizing, after all: "It seemed to her that her brother . . . had inherited the frightening male intransigence of his father." The younger brother does not sympathize with his father, his stepmother, the jay, or Yoshiko. The only feelings of compassion he has are for his birth mother. The father leaves his children behind quite coldly and then attempts to fix the situation in a complex way (arranging a marriage), instead of simply forgiving his son and returning home. Yoshiko's most admirable quality in the story is her ability to feel for others: her grandmother, her father, her stepmother, even the two birds. Sympathy links each member of the scattered family, and Yoshiko is at the heart, the center, of these connections.

STYLE

Flashback

Much of "The Jay," an already very short story, is told through flashback as Yoshiko's mind wanders while waiting for her visitors to arrive. A flashback takes a narrative back in time to elaborate on the history of the present situation. Without the flashback, Yoshiko would hear the bird, clean up after breakfast, get ready in her room, and then find the chick in the garden. With the flashback, Yoshiko's story is very different. The history of her family's dysfunction is over a decade long. For her father the last decade was one of loneliness, quiet rage, and regrets. For Yoshiko the years should have been her happy childhood, and it is her father's goal to return those lost years by arranging a marriage in which Yoshiko will be treated as a child. For Yoshiko's younger brother, only two when his mother left, the years have been spent dreaming of a mother he barely remembers. Without this knowledge, provided through flashback, the story has no tension.

Imagery

Imagery—the writer's vivid descriptions of persons, places, and things—is used to enhance or contradict other elements in a work of literature. Kawabata's image of the worried mother jay and the quietly traumatized chick runs throughout "The Jay" as a unifying narrative. Aural imagery, or sound imagery, is used from start to finish in the jay's singing. The singing affects each character in the house. To the younger brother, the song is intolerable. The grandmother can read the jay's song for meaning without even seeing the jay nervously scanning the garden. For Yoshiko, the song is urgent—she cannot stop thinking of the jay as she goes about her routine. The youngest member of the family is tone-deaf to the jay's suffering. Yoshiko, caught between these two perspectives just as she is caught between tradition and modernity, joins the jay's search—joins the natural world—just long enough to return the jay to its mother. Then she must watch from inside her world, the house, as the birds come together.

Another characteristic aspect of Kawabata's use of imagery, related to his succinctness, is his ability to create images of mystery and ambiguous meaning. In "The Month of Cherry Blossom," Jason Cowley writes, "Kawabata challenges you to interpret and imagine, to color in and shade the empty spaces of his stories." The spaces between the grandmother's fingers, as she feels the sunlight and looks out into the garden, terrify Yoshiko. She at once wants to hold her grandmother and to run from her. Yet

the grandmother does not notice Yoshiko's fright as she gazes out the window to nature with all the strength she has left. An overall positive force in "The Jay," the grandmother recharges at the glass window—gathers her strength from the outside sun and garden. This same spot at the glass door is where Yoshiko stands at the story's conclusion; the door is a physical divider between those in the household "circumstances" and those in the natural world, where mothers search tirelessly for a lost child. The chick—alone, afraid, powerless, but earnest—is a double of Yoshiko. But the chick (like the younger brother) finds its mother, while Yoshiko is left at the end still waiting for the arrival of a stranger.

HISTORICAL CONTEXT

Literary Magazines

The backbone of the literary community in Japan was, in Kawabata's time (and to some extent still today), the small group and small journal. Michael Brownstein explains in *Masterworks of Asian Literature*:

> Such groups were a characteristic feature of the literary landscape; . . . they made up the *bundan* or "literary circles." They typically published their own literary magazines in which they would present their critical manifestos and publish their fiction or poetry.

Kawabata was an editor or contributor to countless of these little magazines: the *Bungei Jidai*, the *Bungakukai*, and the *Bungeishunju* were the most notable of his career. The magazines were never guaranteed to last beyond the next issue, but this impermanence allowed for variety and reinvention among Japanese writers as they switched from one school of writing to the next.

Palm-of-the-hand stories suit small literary magazines perfectly: they are short, powerful vignettes that can be brought together to form a larger whole (as Kawabata did with his novel *Snow Country*, originally published as various palm-of-the-hand stories) or simply left by themselves (for example, "The Jay"). Part of Kawabata's great success is his invention of the form—stories so small that they can figuratively fit in the palm of a hand lend themselves to publication in low-budget magazines whose editors wish to include as many authors as they can. As an editor of these magazines,

COMPARE
&
CONTRAST

- **1949:** Following the end of World War II, which devastated Japan, the country sustains the process of rebuilding and redefining itself as a country.

  Today: Modern Japan is a world power, praised for its technological achievements, business practices, and contributions to the arts. Japanese people still honor the traditional and cultural heritage of their ancestors.

- **1949:** Japanese literature, though thriving inside the country, is not read throughout the world. The Japanese have many works in translation available from other countries, but Japanese literature itself is rarely translated into other languages.

  Today: Translations of Japanese works from all centuries are available to readers across the globe, and current Japanese fiction is translated as it is published.

- **1949:** Arranged marriages, though no longer as common as they were before the war, are still practiced by Japanese families as a way of ensuring their children's future prosperity.

  Today: Arranged marriages are no longer acceptable in modern Japan, and those of marrying age may choose to marry whom they please.

Kawabata helped support the work of young and obscure writers. As a contributor, he gained recognition among established writers and a fan base of loyal readers.

Tradition and Modernity

After World War II ended with the Japanese surrender in 1945, Japanese traditionalists were stunned. Japan, no longer an isolated island culture, had changed, and prewar ideas no longer held meaning. Modernity in the form of Western influence began to creep across the country while traditions such as arranged marriages began to fade. "The Jay" references these changes with Kawabata's subtle touch:

> It was said that, when stars came out under your nails, it was a sign that you would receive something, but Yoshiko remembered having read in the newspaper that it meant a deficiency in vitamin C or something.

Yoshiko is caught between the shifts in culture that occurred after World War II—tradition and modernity both occupy her thoughts. She is the child of a divorce, yet she is subject to an arranged marriage.

Artists continued to experiment with new styles after the war, redefining themselves and their country, but some mourned the great loss of traditional ways. Beauty and sadness—two words interconnected in the Japanese tradition—became important themes in the work of those artists, like Kawabata, who felt longing for a time past, a time before the war had shattered the country. As Yoshiko stands at the window in her kimono, watching the birds wistfully, the scene is at once sad and beautiful. In the time after World War II, the Japanese people navigated the changing cultural tides as Western influence swept in and certain traditions faded away.

CRITICAL OVERVIEW

Kawabata wrote 146 palm-of-the-hand stories during his career. Van C. Gessel states of them in *Three Modern Novelists*, "They are often regarded by critics as keys to understanding Kawabata's literature." "The Jay," published in 1949 as Kawabata's fame was growing, was not translated into English until 1988. Lane Dunlop, in his translator's notes to *Palm-of-the-Hand Stories*, admires "the microscopic concision, capable of being magnified with no loss of proportion, of Kawabata's method." Dunlop refers to the brevity of Kawabata's palm-

Yoshiko's grandmother is very perceptive in spite of her blindness. (© Harris Shiffman / ShutterStock.com)

of-the-hand stories: though the story is short, "The Jay" could easily be expanded. This unique duality of conciseness and potential for expansion in the palm-of-the-hand stories has caught the attention of many critics. Cowley notes how Kawabata was strongly "influenced by the formal austerity and sparse, fragile lyricism of haiku" and says that "he is a miniaturist: he compresses where others seek to inflate and enlarge."

Gessel, who called the palm-of-the-hand stories the "keys" to interpreting Kawabata's enigmatic longer works, explains, "The essentially fluid nature of Kawabata's fiction made it possible for him to say that many of his works could end at any point, and that specific chapters could easily be deleted." The palm-of-the-hand stories show Kawabata actively working out the "fluid nature" of his prose writing. In "The Jay," the fluidity of time as Yoshiko prepares for her visitors, as well as the conclusion, leaving the protagonist wishing for her stepmother and father to arrive, are examples of trends in Kawabata's longer works: open endings and nebulous

time frames. On the topic of protagonists, Gessel writes that they seem "to exist in the void, too uncomfortable to make a place for themselves in the present day, but too conscious of the fact that there is no longer a past to return to." Although Gessel refers to Kawabata's male protagonists (female main characters being rare in his writing), the trait of empty confusion describes Yoshiko's gentle obedience to her parents at the cost of her memories of the past and place in her household. (In her upcoming marriage, she is to be treated as a child, even though she currently acts as a responsible caregiver.) Yoshiko must ready herself physically to meet her fiancé's mother by putting on makeup and a kimono, yet emotionally she gets ready by remembering what led her to this turning point.

Gwenn Boardman Petersen remarks in *The Moon in the Water*, "Kawabata can also convey the loneliness of marriage. . . . He shows the loneliness of parents intensely aware of a distance from their children that they cannot bridge." Yoshiko's father best fits this characterization. His relationship with his son has eroded completely, and he can only think to offer his daughter the prospect of an arranged marriage (which she at first abhors) to mitigate his responsibility for her present home life.

On Kawabata's writing style, Varley notes in *Japanese Aesthetics and Culture* that despite his early experimental phase, "Kawabata is probably more Japanese in what is generally understood as the traditional sense than any other modern novelist." More than exemplifying tradition, he shows the erosion of traditional values by modern progress (as with the old saying Yoshiko remembers about stars beneath fingernails set against the article she read about vitamin C deficiency). J. Martin Holman, another of Kawabata's translators for *Palm-of-the-Hand Stories*, sums up the grand effect and overall positive reception of Kawabata's very short stories: "His juxtapositions of images scintillate with a unique and succinct perception, and the plots, though diminutive, are intriguing and memorable."

CRITICISM

Amy Lynn Miller
Miller is a graduate of the University of Cincinnati and now resides in New Orleans, Louisiana. In the following essay, she discusses the method of Kawabata's subtle prose style as it applies to "The Jay."

WHAT DO I READ NEXT?

- Kawabata's *Snow Country* (1947) is considered a masterpiece. The novel is set in a rural hot springs town in the coldest region of Japan, where the wealthy but emotionally detached Shimamura meets Komako, a lively geisha. With characteristic reticence and attention to beautiful details, Kawabata tells the sad love story of two people who cannot come together. Edward Seidensticker's translation best communicates the snowbound loneliness of Kawabata's world.

- Kawabata's protégé Yukio Mishima rose to enormous celebrity in Japan for his writing, modeling, directing, and acting. In his 1954 novel *The Sound of Waves*, a boy from a small fishing village falls in love with a beautiful pearl diver. Like "The Jay," Mishima's *The Sound of Waves* portrays family life in Japanese culture with a focus on the unique pressures placed on teens by parents eager to raise honorable members of society.

- Giles Murray's *Exploring Japanese Literature* (2007) is an ideal resource for Japanese literature in translation. By providing side-by-side original Japanese text with English translations and explanations of language, Murray allows readers to experience the work of Japanese greats Kawabata, Mishima, and Junichiro Tanizaki in their purest form.

- Otsu-ichi's *Calling You* (2007) is a collection of three short stories for young adults that combine magic realism with urban Japanese settings. Heartfelt and sometimes heart-breaking, the three stories in *Calling You* are imaginative and original.

- *The Makioka Sisters* by Junichiro Tanizaki (1943–1948) tells the story of four sisters who wish to preserve traditions and class in the years before World War II. This is an epic family drama set in the wider context of Japan's entrance into war. The sisters face a social battle as they try to find a husband for sister Yukiko while fighting off changes to their comfortable lives and good name in high society. Tanizaki is a legendary author in Japan, and *The Makioka Sisters* is considered one of the best Japanese novels.

- *Jasmine* (1989), by Bharati Mukherjee, tells the story of a girl the same age as Yoshiko who is raised in a small village in India. To fulfill her duties to her family, she (like Yoshiko) weds in an arranged marriage. When her husband dies, leaving her a widow at age seventeen, she undergoes a transformation that leads her to an unexpected new life in the United States.

- *Modern Japan: A Very Short Introduction* (2009), by Christopher Goto-Jones, explores and explains the island country's enormous impact on the world as a cultural, business, and technology center in the modern world. Briefly summarizing the history of Japan up to its post–World War II modernization, *Modern Japan* focuses on the shifts in culture that changed Japan from an isolated nation to a world power.

Yasunari Kawabata's prose in "The Jay" is accessible, clear, and even simplistic. Yet the density of information contained in the brief story stretches over a decade in the lives of the characters. Consider how much is known of Yoshiko's father despite the fact that he never appears in the present scenes of the story. Translators Lane Dunlop and J. Martin Holman, in their editorial note to *Palm-of-the-Hand Stories*, introduce this paradox: "Just as a *haiku* may contain a richness rivaling that of a longer poem, so these stories . . . rival longer prose fictions." Although Kawabata's prose is light, it can be unpacked almost infinitely for meaning. Kawabata accomplishes this feat through his mastery of subtle language and ambiguity.

ALTHOUGH KAWABATA'S PROSE IS LIGHT, IT CAN BE UNPACKED ALMOST INFINITELY FOR MEANING. KAWABATA ACCOMPLISHES THIS FEAT THROUGH HIS MASTERY OF SUBTLE LANGUAGE AND AMBIGUITY."

Gwenn Boardman Petersen, in *The Moon in the Water*, writes, "Misty qualities . . . always suggest much more than they reveal at first glance." This is an excellent observation, for throughout "The Jay" a mist is falling: "She held out her hand . . . but the rain was so fine that it didn't wet the palm." Kawabata's careful pen, too, works so delicately as to not be noticed.

Before looking closer at "The Jay," it must be remembered that the palm-of-the-hand stories are works in translation. When approaching a work through the aid of a translator, readers must try their best to trust the text, just as the translator tried his or her best to recreate the original. Literature is boundless, but languages are not. While the original Japanese would be the ideal medium for reading Kawabata, much has been done to preserve his voice in English. To read only works written in one's native language is to miss opportunities to learn about an unfamiliar culture and miss as well some of the best literature ever written. Petersen, the most concerned of Kawabata's critics with the consequences of his translation to English, affirms, "Even in translation Kawabata is clearly a poet, steeped in tradition, yet viewing contemporary life with an extraordinarily perceptive eye."

The Japanese haiku is a three-line poem with a set number of syllables (five, seven, five) that traditionally features two images in contrast. Kawabata, who is compared to haiku masters almost universally among critics, was indeed a master of adapting this poetic form to fiction. In "The Jay," the birds outside the house contrast to the family inside the house. Yoshiko takes the baby bird inside for a moment, and then she spends a moment outside. Balance, like this brief inside/outside movement of the chick and Yoshiko, is contrasted by imbalance: the mother bird comes to the chick's rescue, but Yoshiko is left still waiting for her trio of visitors to arrive.

That only the baby bird and Yoshiko are capable of moving between the natural outside world and family "circumstances" inside the house links them together, just as the father and son are linked together through "the power of masculine indignation and resentment."

A product of Kawabata's postwar focus on sadness, "The Jay" features human characters who simply cannot connect. Susan J. Napier writes in *The Fantastic in Modern Japanese Literature*, "The gulf between human beings, especially between male and female, is usually treated as ultimately unbridgeable." Perhaps the only moment of successful human connection in the entire story occurs after the grandmother admits that she cannot see Yoshiko anymore: "Yoshiko stifled a desire to giggle. She rested her hand lightly on her grandmother's head." Yoshiko and her grandmother are a positive pair, the closest in spirit to the mother bird and chick. As for the other characters, discord is the standard. The father represents one of those "unbridgeable" gulfs, as Napier puts it, typical of Kawabata's male characters. The brother follows closely behind in his coldness, in love with a mother he has never known, despite the proliferation of mother figures surrounding him (Yoshiko included, as she has been a caregiver to her brother and grandmother).

The contrast to these human complications is nature's simplicity. The mother bird has lost her chick and will not rest until she finds it. A simple, animal, motherly panic has set in, causing her to sing day in and day out for her chick. Like with the grandmother's "many-angled gaze," the mother bird uses all her energy, moving from branch to branch and to a neighbor's roof and back again, seeking every perspective. Any comparison of the jay to Yoshiko's birth mother falls flat. Her stepmother as well drops out of the picture after moving away. Yoshiko's many mother figures are not like the mother bird, so it is in vain that Yoshiko wants her stepmother and father to see the birds celebrating their reunion. Only the grandmother understands the jay's panic, with a knowledge that comes from years and not from sight.

Kawabata accomplishes all of this storytelling without many words. Jason Cowley, in "The Month of Cherry Blossom," writes, "His is a fiction of extreme economy, even of emptiness." The emptiness, the result of his brevity and light touch, allows readers to fill in what Kawabata does not say. The mystery of the images works to make reading his work seem easy, yet gives way to myriad interpretations. For example, perhaps the baby chick is most like Yoshiko's younger brother. Weak and alone, it has no strength. Reunited with its mother, it wants to take flight. Yoshiko's brother must have wanted to meet their mother for years. He is the one to find the picture of her as a child that their father so terribly rips to shreds. When he does meet her, she consumes his entire identity. No longer does he love his stepmother, with whom he had formerly gotten along. Yoshiko does not share these feelings, and so it is fitting that in the end she must watch mother and chick reunite while she is trapped within the house, within her traditional roles as a caregiver and bride of an arranged marriage. Yoshiko is a female prisoner watching as her more independent brother—off at the school dormitories—attempts to break free (though, like the chick, he stumbles clumsily and is grounded). In this way, a second interpretation emerges from the misty rain, so light as to be seen only "against the dense foliage" of the garden.

To allow many complex interpretations in such a short piece is part of Kawabata's talent. H. Paul Varley in *Japanese Aesthetics and Culture* writes, "Often called a writer of *haiku*-like prose, he uses the spare, aesthetically polished language of poetry to sketch his settings and evoke his moods." Varley's use of "sketch" is an apt description of Kawabata's writing style in his palm-of-the-hand stories. Like Varley, many critics focus on the expandability of these pieces. "The Jay" is just ambiguous enough to be beautiful: there is no right way to read the story, but any reader will come away with the same impression of beautiful melancholy, of a girl surrounded by mother figures who are incapable of seeing her—through divorce, family feuds, arranged marriages, or physical blindness. Petersen writes, "For Kawabata, 'contemporary problems' are those of the individual, especially his loneliness." Comparing the loneliness of the jay and her lost chick when they are accidentally separated to the self-inflicted loneliness of the father and brother, it is clear that Kawabata feels a modernist's sorrow at the difficulty of navigating contemporary life. The emptiness of the narrative and disconnection of the characters are not a result of any issues of translation, but as Gessel writes, it is "rather from the fortuitous blending of a classical consciousness with a modernist technician that such features are born."

A blue jay (© Chas | ShutterStock.com)

Writers after Kawabata were naturally more subject to modernity as outside influence came to Japan in the years after World War II. But Kawabata's career, as well as his sensibilities, balanced and blended the two worlds into his own reality of past and present.

Despite, or possibly because of, Yoshiko's tradition-based obedience to her ever-changing parental figures, she is lost to the will of the adults around her. Her younger brother, headstrong and disobedient, is forced back home by that same will. In a clever inversion of the jays never directly acknowledged in the story, it is the parents—not the children—who fly away from the nest. Her father's prospect of an arranged marriage seeks to replace his presence as an adult in the house. Rather than come home, he will send another surrogate: the fiancé's mother. But in the natural world there are no surrogates. The jay is devastated: "It was flying around until late in the evening. Doesn't she know where it is? But what a good mother. This morning she came right back to look." If Yoshiko's parents are as worried about her, their concern is obliquely expressed through the arranged marriage. Yoshiko desires and acts out of love. What she gets in life are separations.

Kawabata's feather-light touch only implies, never states. But what Kawabata implies is the sad exchange of tradition and modernity in a contemporary household. Some members of the family follow old rules while others subvert them, and some voices are heard while others whisper; connections between them fail again and again. Her grandmother cannot see Yoshiko dressed up prettily to make a good impression on her future mother-in-law. She stands alone in her red kimono at the sliding glass door, looking out on a scene that can never be hers, as the two birds meet again.

Source: Amy Lynn Miller, Critical Essay on "The Jay," in *Short Stories for Students*, Gale, Cengage Learning, 2013.

Martin Lebowitz

In the following review, Lebowitz discusses the prevalent themes in Kawabata's Palm-of-the-Hand Stories *and analyzes how their compactness "reflects elements at once of primitivism and sophistication."*

If, as historians have noted, giantism is an aspect of decadence, miniaturization—emblematic of love, tenacity, and control—expresses the mystique or teleology of a humane society. These stories [in *Palm-of-the-Hand Stories*] are rarely more than four pages in length. The particularity and concreteness of the Japanese mentality reflect a sort of primitive vitalism or vitality. Still, it is correct to say of all liberal, humane, and progressive societies that they embody, along with pristine elements of energy, formal prototypes that are civilizing in their implications and effect. So far as miniaturization partakes of the primeval energy of things, it reflects elements at once of primitivism and sophistication. One is tempted to say that the combination of these two factors defines civilization, as opposed, for one thing, to decadence.

In one of these stories, a character remarks that the girl he loves is remembered well, but only by his finger (!). Human association—"love"—particularly in our time, contains something so casual that it is nothing as much as physical or material contact. It is not simply violence or sex that accounts for such events but the random character of modern experience in which the immanence and imminence of disorder impart a physical ascendancy to romanticism itself. Romantic materialism as an aspect of modernity is a notable subject, quite relevant here.

In the same story, snow is symbolic of repression. The woman in this story has "cold hair," and the hero is psychologically cold. This "coldness" reflects something essential to an advanced or cultivated association—the creative

dialectic of passion and repression—plus that formal principle essential to functional progress. The elusive question is what here to define as primitive.

Kawabata died in April 1972, a suicide. A Nobel laureate (1968), his controlling themes are loneliness, love, time as something concrete both for the mystic and the rationalist, and perhaps above all death. Death for the Japanese mentality, as mystical as it is rationalistic, becomes a sort of obsession for Kawabata, in respect to the tone of his writings and its pervasive overtones. Its overtones becomes a subject matter, and death is a controlling theme.

The publisher prints one of the stories on the dust jacket, called "Love Suicides." The protagonist takes a dislike to his wife and deserts her. Two years later, a letter comes from a distant land, saying, "Don't let the child bounce a rubber ball. It strikes at my heart." The wife complies. More and more letters come making similar requests. The wife continues to comply. Finally a letter from a different land insists, "don't make any sound at all, the two of you, not even the ticking of a clock!" Thus they cease eternally to make even the faintest sound. The husband lies down, curiously, beside them and dies, too.

On a prosaic level the theme is that husband and wife never parted, overcome rather by a fatal disenchantment or spell. The true theme is that the incongruity or ambivalence of so-called interpersonal relations is itself a type of suicide.

An old lady planning to sell her daughter to a strange man, possibly brutal and oppressive, confronts the bus driver who is to take them to their destination. The bus driver is the incarnation of courtesy and graciousness, and the lady remarks, "So it's your turn today... If she has you to take her there, Mr. Thankyou, she is likely to meet with good fortune. It's a sign that something good will happen." Is the view expressed here based on psychology, metaphysics, superstition, or mysticism? Or is it based on naturalism? Naturalism, too, is an effort to integrate moral and existential considerations. It is the philosophy of the Orient, particularly Japan and China, that suggests that the cultivated personality has it all over intellectualism as such.

The culture of the Orient, based on formalism, repression, and teleology, is highly cultivated but not lacking in primitive overtones. This is a combination of attributes that may define the quality of humanistic society in any age. Yet again, it is not easy to define what, if anything, in this context is truly primitive.

Primitivism is a static relation to the past, an incarceration in the past. Primitivism may be defined as the opposite of moral development, which may be synonymous with development itself. Thus the question whether the culture of Japan is primitive or not—or in what degree—is not that easy. One might note that the alterations introduced by science are existential rather than moral, although they sometimes have more effects.

No doubt the cultures of Japan and China defy the conventional categories of primitive or retrograde as against progressive and enlightened. The essence of Japanese culture is sufficiently "advanced" without being decidedly humane to be better than much in the West. Without being truly liberal or "forward-looking," some cultures may be superior to others that are.

Source: Martin Lebowitz, "The Mysterious East," in *Virginia Quarterly Review*, Vol. 67, No. 4, Fall 1991, pp. 778–79.

Sidney DeVere Brown

In the following review, Brown praises the spare style of Kawabata's Palm-of-the-Hand Stories.

Kawabata's masterpiece, the novel *Snow Country*, is written in a spare, elliptical style. It seems as abbreviated as a work of literature can possibly be—until one reads the author's "palm-of-the-hand stories," which often tell a story or evoke an image in less than a page. "Gleanings from Snow Country," indeed, presents the highlights of the novel in a series of haiku-like images in five pages. That is much longer than the usual story, however.

Most of the selections juxtapose two images in less than a page and reveal a story by indirection. If Japanese literature requires much of its readers because it relies on suggestion rather than graphic detail and because resolution of the plot is incomplete, then the palm-of-the-hand stories require an incredible effort, but an enjoyable one. The orphaned girl of "A Sunny Place" stares at her blind grandfather as he turns toward the sun; at the same time she remembers being at a sunny place on the beach with him earlier. In "Hair" an exhausted hairdresser who is called upon to do the hair of all the village girls because soldiers are billeted in town passes word to her hairdresser friend in the next village that

she would do well if she followed soldiers around; the second woman's husband, a miner, is not amused and slaps her around just as a trumpet sounds. "Hometown" centers on a village festival to which everyone is invited back to partake of dumplings in bean soup. Men are few in wartime, and the sister-in-law who has a letter from the front has grown plump.

What do the stories mean? Each reader will craft his own plot from the fragmentary evidence, which often is even less revealing than in the three examples cited above. Kawabata wrote palm-of-the-hand stories throughout his career, from 1923 to 1972, and they evidently had a market value in the periodicals of his time. Certain themes recur. Kawabata was a cultural traditionalist who wrote of hot springs, girls in the bath at an inn, or beautiful black hair in several contexts; but he also wrote of a taxi dancer in Asakusa (1932), of the water shortage in wartime Manchuria (1944), and of a woman who fled to London to recover from a failed marriage (1962). Prewar pride in culture, wartime privation, and postwar affluence and cosmopolitan life-style all come through in the works of this most Japanese of modern writers. The translators have performed the exacting task of transferring the obscure thoughts and misty images of his palm-of-the-hand stories into English successfully.

Source: Sidney DeVere Brown, Review of *Palm-of-the-Hand Stories*, in *World Literature Today*, Vol. 64, No. 1, Winter 1990, p. 197.

James T. Araki

In the following essay, Araki traces Kawabata's changing style and notes "a steady progression in the refinement of his technical mastery and a development of the ability to enter deeply into his characters."

Although Yasunari Kawabata has for years been considered the most distinguished member of the Japanese world of letters, the news of the selection of the sixty-nine-year-old author as the recipient of the 1968 Nobel Prize in Literature—a surprise to readers throughout much of the world—was initially received with a sense of disbelief by his countrymen. The insight revealed in the citation by the Nobel Committee, which praised the author for "his narrative mastership, which with great sensibility expressed the essence of the Japanese mind," seemed to mystify all but

> **THE READER MIGHT BE FOREWARNED, HOWEVER, OF ONE PECULIARITY OF KAWABATA'S STORIES THAT IS DISTINCTLY JAPANESE. ALMOST ALL OF HIS STORIES REPRESENT A NON-DRAMATIC MODE OF FICTION AND REMAIN UNRESOLVED."**

the most sensitive readers and critics, to whom the judgment seemed incredibly astute.

The typical Japanese reader tends, like readers elsewhere, to favor a well-paced narrative designed to quicken his interest in the story. He has been content to accept the high evaluation of Kawabata by professional critics and, rather than read his stories, has been inclined to enjoy them through the modified medium of the cinema. Indeed, Japanese moviemakers since the early fifties have produced some twenty film versions of his novels. The general reader in Japan has probably regarded Kawabata as a modernist rather than a traditionalist, for his stories are often difficult to apprehend fully, owing to the rich, allusive imagery, a suggestive quality that requires a matured sensibility of the reader, an elliptical sentence style, and a mode of story progression that often relies on linking through imagery rather than through contextual or sentence logic—a technique of the traditional *renga* or "linked verse." Many native readers are now avidly reading Kawabata novels to discover for themselves the traditional Japanese qualities that foreign readers were able to perceive through the reading of translations.

Snow Country (*Yukiguni*), *Thousand Cranes* (*Semazuru*) and *The Old Capital* (*Koto*) are the novels by which the Nobel Committee judged Kawabata's worth as a writer of fiction. These are novels in which the author's bent for the traditional is particularly evident, in depiction of outward forms of traditional culture (the tea ceremony, folk art, Shinto festivals, Buddhist temples) and the use of nature imagery for their cumulative, traditional lyrical implications, yet they do not fully represent the vast range of the author's creative capacity.... Translations of several of Kawabata's short stories have appeared in anthologies or magazines—among them, "The Izu Dancer" ("Izu no odoriko"), "The Mole" ("Hokuro no tegami") "Reencounter" ("Saikai"), and "Moon on the Water" ("Suigetsu").

In Japan, in the twentieth century, new literary trends were frequently set by coteries of writers who cooperated in the publication of literary journals. A particularly memorable year was 1924, when, in June, "Literary Battle Line" (*Bungei Sensen*) was founded as a monthly for Marxist writers and, in October, the publication of "Literary Era" (*Bungei Jidai*) was inaugurated by a group of young authors who were concerned primarily with the esthetics of literature. Yokomitsu Toshikazu (1898–1947) and Kawabata were the prime movers of the latter group, who were promptly labeled the "neoperceptionists" by the critic Kameo Chiba. In an essay, "The Birth of the Neoperceptionists" (in *Seiki*, November 1924), Chiba stated, "There is no doubt whatever that these writers, whom we might call the 'Literary Era' coterie, are sensually alert to diction, lyricism, and rhythm that are far fresher than anything ever before expressed by any of our sensitive artists." The expressive style of the neoperceptionists, literary historians tell us, was influenced considerably by the many startling examples of figurative language those young writers discovered in Paul Morand's *Ouvert la nuit*, which had appeared in Japanese translation that year.

Kawabata, by his own admission, has probably participated in the setting of more new trends than any other living writer. More important, however, has been his ability to experiment with new approaches and techniques and to adopt them into a larger embodiment which can be identified as a style uniquely his own; and his many years of experience, starting in his twenties, as a practicing critic have without doubt contributed much to the development of his own literary sensibility.

Although imprints of literary expressionism and psychological realism are rather clearly evident in Kawabata's stories, traditional Japanese themes have been more subtly infused into his writings. We may note coursing through all his major novels a sense of sorrow and loneliness, a recognition of an emotional and spiritual vacuity in man, and the recurring theme of the evanescence and meaninglessness of passion, even of temporal existence. The general tenor of the author's outlook has much in common with that of the *Tale of Genji* and diaries of the Late Classical Era (10th–12th century), with much of the prose of the Medieval Era (12th–16th century), and with traditional poetry. Because Kawabata avoids the explicit, his stories often seem veiled by vagueness, a quality that the native reader finds attractive. Because his writings contain so many diverse elements, they are at once subtle and complex, and they can be enjoyed for their sheer tonal and textural beauty.

Reading Kawabata's major works in chronological sequence, one may note a steady progression in the refinement of his technical mastery and a development of the ability to enter deeply into his characters. "The Izu Dancer," best known among his earliest writings, is a lyric description of a journey made by a high-school student, from the vicinity of Mount Fuji to the lower tip of Izu Peninsula, in the company of a troupe of traveling entertainers. Narrated in the first person and in a confessional vein, the short tale depicts a love that stirs the heart of the youth, whose eyes filter out the unsightly and create an idealized image of a lovely dancer who is about to blossom into womanhood. The inevitable parting and the lonely aftertaste remind him of the sorrow of having grown up an orphan, yet the memory of the fleeting encounter becomes a pleasurable one even while he continues to shed tears of regret. In composing this attractive tale, the author employed none of the techniques that were to characterize his later writings.

Kawabata's first full-length novel, *The Crimson Gang of Asakusa* (*Asakusa kurenaidan*), published in 1930, is considered the only noteworthy product of a short-lived movement for modernity and artistry that was launched by a loosely organized group of writers intent on stemming the tide of proletarian literature. This novel is in many respects antithetical to "The Izu Dancer." The Crimson Gang is a band of delinquents whose members are caught in a web of sex and violence. The setting is Asakusa, the colorful, raucous and sinful center of urban entertainment for the middle and lower classes of Tokyo. The author presents a panorama which unfolds in a series of rapidly changing scenes sketching various aspects of life in Asakusa. The ugly and evil are depicted along with the innocent and beautiful. Descriptions of the activities of the gang are woven into the panorama so that some semblance of unity is achieved. The author is a keenly sensitive observer, uninvolved in the story.

Snow Country, which was written sporadically between 1934 and 1937 and expanded into its present form after the war, is the first novel in which we find all the artistic elements, both modern and traditional, that have since characterized the distinctive style of Kawabata. Rich in imagery and symbolism, suggestive by association, the novel can be reexplored through repeated readings to new discoveries of meaning. The opening passage is arresting: "When the train came out of the long tunnel separating the provinces, it was in the snow country. The bottomless depth of the night was imbued with whiteness." Typical of the author's style is the delicacy of expression that verbalizes the profundity of a common winter scene, the subtle contrast between black sky and night-darkened snow.

The hero, Shimamura, studies the face of a girl reflected in the train window. The mirror filters out the ugly and the unpleasant; what remains for Shimamura to observe is only the beautiful, detached from those associations of sadness and pain that are evident in the totality of the image. As Shimamura concentrates on the reflected face, his time track shifts from the external to the "concrete" or internal psychological time; we are presented with a flashback, and then a flashback within a flashback, as the image evokes one recollection and then another in his mind.

Even though the point of view of *Snow Country* is essentially that of Shimamura, the author does not enter deeply into him. The novel can hardly be considered autobiographical. Shimamura is the observer of two women—the innocent Yoko, whose reflected image has fascinated him, and the sensual geisha Komako. Through his characterization of these two, the author describes the eternal sorrow of the Japanese woman as well as his admiration for her quality of forlornness and passivity. The vacuity in Shimamura's heart, however, may well be the vacuity in the heart of the author, or of an archetype of the modern Japanese male. The concluding paragraph presents the reader with an example of the author's elliptical sentence style: "The voice that shouted the half-crazed Komako Shimamura tried to get nearer to. . . ." This English approximates the syntactic and idiomatic level of the original. A Japanese would reread and ponder it before he could grasp the intended meaning: "The voice that shouted was Komako's; Shimamura recognized it and tried to get nearer to the half-crazed Komako. . . ." The concluding sentence, "The River of Heaven (the Milky Way) seemed to flow down with a roar into Shimamura," seems to be an expressionistic attempt to objectify an inexpressibly complex state of mind.

Thousand Cranes is a novel that exhibits many of the qualities of *Snow Country*, but we note a bolder approach to the topic of eroticism. The mode of fiction is that of imaginative storytelling, the author being nowhere evident. The relationship depicted is at best an unhealthy one—that between a young man and the women who had been mistresses to his late father. The motif is similar to that in Maupassant's "Hautot and His Son," but the eroticism in *Thousand Cranes* is more explicit, and is pervaded by a sense of sin and guilt which is absent from the French story. Kawabata adds to the complexity of incestuous relationship by involving the young hero in carnal association with the daughter of his father's former mistress. Here, as in *Snow Country*, we are afforded glimpses of traditional esthetic forms—graphic patterns, the tea ceremony, ceramics—often invested with symbolic suggestion. The instant transitions and fantastic leaps in time are techniques that anticipated those used many years later in films—recently in *The Graduate*, for instance.

Kawabata's finest novel in his unique modernist-traditionalist mode of fiction is *Sound of the Mountain* (*Yama no oto*), published in 1954. Because the novel sheds much light on the immemorial Japanese household—an extended family—and on the often fast-and-loose world of Japanese business, we may say that it resembles the "novel of manners," which Japanese literary critics tend to regard with disdain. *Sound of the Mountain*, however, is essentially a psychological novel in which the process and effects of aging are drawn with remarkable sensitivity.

The narrative point of view is that of the sixty-year-old Ogata, who might be a fictional extension of the youthful "I" of "The Izu Dancer" and Shimamura of *Snow Country*. Like the shadowy hero of *Snow Country*, the gentle, aging Ogata is constantly observing and listening, absorbing all that happens about him, but, unlike Shimamura, he is keenly aware of his own reactions and gropes to identify the motives for his own thoughts and actions. His married son is involved in a sordid extramarital liaison with a war widow. Kikuko, the son's neglected wife, has a beauty that symbolizes purity and innocence—womanly qualities attractive to Ogata—and a mutual bond of sympathy and understanding draws the two close together. Kikuko shares Ogata's sensibilities, which his wife does not. The Western reader might be amused to note the corresponding levels of perceptivity assigned to Ogata, his daughter-in-law, and Mrs. Ogata, and to Mr. Bennet, Elizabeth, and Mrs. Bennet in *Pride and Prejudice*. The fading but persistent yearning for youthful femininity in Ogata's unconscious is revealed to him occasionally in erotic dreams. In a moment of stupefying realization, Ogata identifies the faceless woman he has often embraced in dreams with his own daughter-in-law. The eroticism, however, is presented subtly, and the texture of *Sound of the Mountain* is softened considerably by frequent references to traditional esthetics.

Although, having completed *Sound of the Mountain*, Kawabata could have rested on his laurels, he was busily at work in 1954 writing *The Lake* (*Mizuumi*), a novel of stark psychological realism, infused with a dark lyricism which places it a fictional world apart from *Sound of the Mountain* and marks the beginning of yet another phase in the author's creative career. It is remarkable for its absence of references to traditional beauty. Instead, its emphasis is on symbolism, the bold use of interior monologue, the constantly shifting time track, and particularly the characterization of the hero: Gimpei's overpowering desire for beautiful women will never be fulfilled because of the ugliness of his feet—feet which he himself can regard only with morbid fascination, if not with abhorrence.

Another novel in a similar vein, *House of the Sleeping Beauties* (*Nemureru bijo*), depicting the behavioral and psychological manifestations of eroticism in the aging male, was published in 1961 and was immediately acclaimed as Kawabata's major work by a number of critics and authors. The novelist Yukio Mishima, among others, expressed regret that the Nobel Committee could not have read *Sleeping Beauties* to learn how the passing years had served to hone, rather than to dull, Kawabata's perceptivity and to enrich his creative and expressive capacities.

In *The Old Capital* (*Koto*), published in 1962, Kawabata reverted abruptly to the beauty and sadness he sees in youth and innocence. As in *The Crimson Gang of Asakusa*, the story itself is less important than the traditional beauty of

Kyoto, which is woven into a soft brocade, attractive for its sheer textural elegance.

Thanks to the Nobel Committee, readers of English should soon be given access by our commercial publishers to translations of Kawabata novels which have won praise for their literary quality but have seldom been published in large editions in Japan. The reader might be forewarned, however, of one peculiarity of Kawabata's stories that is distinctly Japanese. Almost all of his stories represent a non-dramatic mode of fiction and remain unresolved. There is no explicit statement of what the tomorrow will bring to Shimamura, Ogata, Gimpei, "old" Eguchi of *Sleeping Beauties*, or the many women in his stories. Most Japanese readers enjoy the pathos born of such vagueness. We too might learn to enjoy pondering the eventual fates of characters in novels. Their lives are no less real than our own. No one, after all, lives quite happily or unhappily ever after.

Source: James T. Araki, "Kawabata: Achievements of the Nobel Laureate (1969)," in *World Literature Today*, Vol. 63, No. 2, Spring 1989, pp. 209–12.

Frederick Smock

In the following review, Smock calls Kawabata's Palm-of-the-Hand Stories *one of "those dozen or so volumes necessary to life."*

Somewhere in my future is a small, simple apartment, maybe a couple of rooms near the sea somewhere, with high windows and a fireplace. On the mantel over the fireplace is a small stack of books, the only books in the place, those dozen or so volumes necessary to life. One of those books is Yasunari Kawabata's *Palm-of-the-Hand Stories*.

These very short stories, which span his writing life, are the distillation of a beautiful talent. Kawabata won the Nobel Prize for Literature in 1968 for his novels, *The Izu Dancer, Thousand Cranes, Snow Country,* and the others, which were so important to Japan's modern literature. But Kawabata believed that the very short story—the story that fits into the palm of one's hand—holds the essence of the writing art. It is to fiction what the haiku is to poetry. (His last work was a miniaturized version of *Snow Country,* shortly before he committed suicide in 1972.)

The grand themes are all here—love, loneliness, our capacity for disillusionment, the tensions between old and new—under the lens of Kawabata's microscope. The short form is suited to his love of detail, his preference for the finite gesture whose meaning reverberates through time.

In "A Sunny Place," the oldest story in the collection, a young man meets a woman at a seaside inn—it is the beginning of love—but the woman is painfully disconcerted by his habit of staring, and turns her head away. Embarrassed, he averts his own gaze, to a sunny spot on the beach, and thus discovers the origin of his bad habit. "After my parents died," he tells us, "I had lived alone with my grandfather for almost ten years in a house in the country. My grandfather was blind. For years he sat in the same room, in the same spot, facing the east with a long charcoal brazier in front of him. Occasionally he would turn his head toward the south, but he never faced the north. . . . Sometimes I would sit for a long time in front of my grandfather staring into his face, wondering if he would turn to the north. . . . I wondered if the south felt ever so slightly lighter even to a blind person." As a happy result, this memory heightens the intimacy the young man feels toward the woman.

A further testament to the power of Kawabata's economical stories: a movie was once made of "Thank You," a four-page story whose dialogue consists chiefly of *thank-yous*. It tells of a bus driver who takes a mother and daughter from their harbor town to the city, where the daughter is to be sold into a wealthy man's harem; but the driver's politeness to the cartmen they pass on the way so touches the daughter that her mother implores him to allow her one night of genuine affection before her enslavement.

I have returned many times to this story, looking for the source of its power—their (ambiguous) night together, the enigmatic figure of the bus driver, the journey's dreaded end? And I cannot be sure that I have located it. But I have felt it.

His better stories work this way. Swiftly. Mysteriously.

Kawabata wrote nearly 150 "palm" stories, of which 70 are published here, including "Gleanings from Snow Country," his last. The translators have rendered the stories in faultlessly simple language, as befits them.

For these stories are like small lanterns whose colored lights can be seen from very far away—little truths, nestled in a valley, the valley of the palm.

Source: Frederick Smock, "Small Lanterns," in *American Book Review*, Vol. 10, No. 6, January/February 1989, p. 15.

SOURCES

Brownstein, Michael C., "Kawabata Yasunari's *Snow Country*," in *Masterworks of Asian Literature in Comparative Perspective: A Guide for Teaching*, edited by Barbara Stoler Miller, M. E. Sharpe, 1994, pp. 482–92.

Cowley, Jason, "The Month of Cherry Blossom," in *New Statesman*, Vol. 135, No. 4806, 1996, p. 47.

Dunlop, Lane, and J. Martin Holman, "Editorial Note" and "Translators' Notes," in *Palm-of-the-Hand Stories*, translated by Lane Dunlop and J. Martin Holman, Farrar, Straus and Giroux, 1988, pp. xi—xiv.

Gessel, Van C., *Three Modern Novelists: Soseki, Tanizaki, Kawabata*, Kodansha International, 1993, pp. 133–94.

Kawabata, Yasunari, "The Jay," in *Palm-of-the-Hand Stories*, translated by Lane Dunlop and J. Martin Holman, Farrar, Straus and Giroux, 1988, pp. 196–201.

Napier, Susan J., "Woman Lost: The Dead, Damaged, or Absent Female in Postwar Fantasy," in *The Fantastic in Modern Japanese Literature: The Subversion of Modernity*, Routledge, 1996, pp. 53–92.

Petersen, Gwenn Boardman, "Kawabata Yasunari," in *The Moon in the Water: Understanding Tanizaki, Kawabata, and Mishima*, University of Hawaii Press, 1979, pp. 121–200.

Varley, H. Paul, "Culture in the Present Age," in *Japanese Aesthetics and Culture: A Reader*, edited by Nancy G. Hume, State University of New York Press, 1995, pp. 295–340.

FURTHER READING

Addiss, Stephen, *The Art of Haiku: Its History through Poems and Paintings by Japanese Masters*, Shambhala, 2012.
Students interested in the haiku style of composition that Kawabata adapted for his palm-of-the-hand stories will benefit from this collection of haiku poems and paintings by revered practitioners of the elegant art.

Jansen, Marius B., *The Making of Modern Japan*, Harvard University Press, 2002.
The Making of Modern Japan traces the path of change in Japanese society in the nineteenth and twentieth centuries, as old traditions fell away to be replaced by a new, modern society.

Kawabata, Yasunari, "Japan, the Beautiful and Myself," Kodansha Amer, 1981.
"Japan, the Beautiful and Myself" is Kawabata's 1968 Nobel Prize acceptance speech. The first Japanese author to be honored with the award, Kawabata used traditional Japanese imagery to define his work and himself while standing for the first time in the international spotlight.

Shirane, Haruo, *Japan and the Culture of the Four Seasons: Nature, Literature, and the Arts*, Columbia University Press, 2012.
Shirane explains the common natural imagery of Japanese art and literature as well as its traditional origins in Japanese history in this informative work on the Japanese aesthetic. *Japan and the Culture of the Four Seasons* is an indispensable guide for those reading Japanese works in translation to aid in a deeper understanding of imagery whose meanings often go unexplained in the subtle fiction of Kawabata.

SUGGESTED SEARCH TERMS

Yasunari Kawabata

The Jay AND Kawabata

Japanese fiction AND modernism

Kawabata AND Kakesu

Kawabata AND haiku

Palm-of-the-Hand Stories

arranged marriage AND Japan

World War II AND Japanese literature

The Long Exile

LEO TOLSTOY

1872

Leo Tolstoy's "The Long Exile" is a work of short fiction about injustice and forgiveness. It is the story of a man, Aksenof, who embarks on a journey to a fair in another village and is subsequently arrested for a murder he did not commit. He is exiled to Siberia for his punishment, where he lives for twenty-six years working in the mines there. When the man who actually committed the murder is also sent to the same prison on other charges, Aksenof soon suspects that the man is the true killer. The man threatens to kill Aksenof at one point but is soon overcome with remorse and asks for Aksenof's forgiveness. Aksenof dies peacefully shortly after this exchange, passing away before the order for his release that has resulted from the murderer's confession has been handed down.

"The Long Exile" was originally published in Russian in 1872 under the title "Bog pravdu vidit, da ne skoro skazhet," or "God Sees the Truth, but Bides His Time," alternately rendered as "God Sees the Truth, but Waits." The short story was published first in the journal *Beseda* and later in 1872 in the *Primer*, which Tolstoy published for children. "The Long Exile" was published in English in 1888 in *The Long Exile, and Other Stories for Children* and is also available in other collections, including *Leo Tolstoy's Twenty Greatest Short Stories Annotated*, published in 2009.

Leo Tolstoy *(Library of Congress)*

AUTHOR BIOGRAPHY

Tolstoy, whose name is also rendered in English as Tolstoi, was born Leo Nicolaivich Tolstoy, on September 9, 1828, in Russia's Tula Province. Tolstoy's first name is also commonly transliterated as Lev or Lyof. (Tolstoy's birthday is sometimes listed as August 28, in accordance with the Julian calendar. The discrepancy derives from the differences in the two calendars that were used during this time period, the Gregorian and Julian. The Julian calendar was established during the reign of Julius Caesar, in 45 BCE. In 1582, Pope Gregory XIII ordered the Julian calendar to be altered to adjust for the slight misalignment of the Julian calendar with the solar calendar. Russia, however, did not adopt the Gregorian calendar until 1918). Tolstoy was one of five children born to Nikolai Tolstoy and Maria Tolstoya. They belonged to an order of Russian nobility, making Tolstoy a count. When Tolstoy was two, his mother died. His father died several years later, in 1837, when Tolstoy was nine. Tolstoy and his siblings were subsequently raised by a distant relative.

Tolstoy entered the University of Kazan in 1844. He left in 1847 without earning a degree and moved back to his family's estate, which was his inheritance from his father. Over the next several years he lived in Moscow intermittently, and in 1852 he entered the army. He published his first short story, "Nabeg" ("The Raid"), in 1853. The following year he received his officer's commission and continued to write. He participated in the siege of Sevastopol during the Crimean War and wrote a series of sketches about his wartime experiences. In 1855, Tolstoy moved to St. Petersburg and developed friendships with a number of prominent literary figures. He retired from the military in 1856 and embarked on a voyage to Europe in 1857. Over the course of the next ten years, Tolstoy traveled often and focused intently on writing. He published short fiction, sketches, and essays, and by 1863 he had begun work on his famous novel *Voina i mir* (*War and Peace*). He maintained several romantic relationships, including one that produced an illegitimate son. In 1862, he married Sofya Andreyevna Bers.

The next period in his career is considered to be his greatest. Following the 1864 birth of his daughter, Tolstoy published the first part of *War and Peace*, in 1865. Over the course of his lifetime, Tolstoy would father thirteen children. In 1869, Tolstoy published *War and Peace* in its entirety. The short story "God Sees the Truth, but Bides His Time," later published as "The Long Exile," was published in 1872. In 1875, Tolstoy published the first installment of another of his most highly respected works, the novel *Anna Karenina*. Over the next two years, the remaining installments of *Anna Karenina* were published.

Having suffered the deaths of a son, a daughter, and an aunt, Tolstoy went through a period of doubt and despair, in which he became focused on death, and in 1878, he abandoned the Russian Orthodox faith, believing it to be a corruption of true Christian faith. He turned toward theological studies and learned the Hebrew language. In 1885, Tolstoy became a vegetarian and gave up alcohol; he also gave up hunting and smoking. Also in 1885, he published *Where Love Is, God Is*. This shift in focus marks the final stage in Tolstoy's career. He penned a number of volumes exploring religion and art. He did not abandon fiction, however, and published such acclaimed works as the 1886 *Smert' Ivana Il'icha* (published as *The Death of Ivan Ilyich* in 1887) and the 1899 *Voskresenie*

(*Resurrection*). His desire to live according to his principles, to give away his property, and to try and help the poor led to conflict with his wife, who sought to maintain an income to help raise the Tolstoy children. In 1910, Tolstoy resolved to escape an atmosphere he found increasingly toxic and fled the marriage. However, he made it only as far as the town of Astapovo, where he grew gravely ill with what was later identified as pneumonia and fell into a coma. He died on November 20, 1910 (or November 7, 1910, on the Julian calendar).

PLOT SUMMARY

"The Long Exile" opens with the introduction of a tradesman named Aksenof. The reader is informed that Aksenof is successful in his business, as the owner of two shops and his own home. After his marriage, he settled down and mostly gave up alcohol. Aksenof informs his wife of his plan to attend a fair in a town some distance away. His wife asks him to remain home, as she has dreamed that something horrible will happen to her husband if he leaves. Aksenof brushes off his wife's concerns, bids his family farewell, and departs.

On his journey, Aksenof meets a fellow tradesman, an acquaintance of his. They travel together and rest at the same tavern, where they share tea and spend the night in adjoining rooms. Not wishing to be delayed in the morning, Aksenof sleeps for only a short time. He wakes his driver, pays his bill, and leaves before sunrise. Growing hungry, Aksenof stops after some time on the road at an inn. He eats and rests, and then around noon he orders tea and begins to play his guitar.

At this time, a team of horses, bearing soldiers and a police inspector, arrives. The soldiers dismount, and the inspector immediately begins to question Aksenof about his identity and his travels. When Aksenof protests, the inspector informs him that his traveling companion from the previous day was murdered at the inn last night. Upon searching Aksenof's belongings, the soldiers discover a bloodied knife in his bag. Aksenof is surprised and confused but manages to protest that the knife is not his. The police inspector insists that as the tavern was locked from the inside and only Aksenof and the other tradesman were in the building, no one else

MEDIA ADAPTATIONS

- Tolstoy's "The Long Exile," published under the title "God Sees the Truth, but Waits: A Leo Tolstoy Short Story," is available as an MP3 download by Audible Audio. This unabridged version, read by Deaver Brown, was released in 2011.

- An unabridged audio recording of William Coon's reading of "The Long Exile," published as "God Sees the Truth, but Waits," was published in 2007 as an MP3 download by the Greatest Tales.

could have committed the crime. Aksenof is sentenced and imprisoned. When his wife comes to see him in prison, Aksenof asks her to petition the Tsar (the ruler) for his release. He maintains his innocence. The wife recalls the dream she had and tells Aksenof he should not have gone on the trip; she then asks her husband if he committed the crime. Aksenof weeps in despair, distressed that she would doubt his innocence or truthfulness. After his wife leaves, Aksenof realizes that only God knows the truth about the crime; only God knows he is innocent. Aksenof is flogged and then sent to Siberia.

Twenty-six years pass, and Aksenof has adopted the role of a compliant, prayerful prisoner. Sentenced to work in the mines, he spends the little time he has left to himself after his labors reading the Bible, singing in the choir at church, and making boots. His submissiveness is praised by the authorities. When a new prisoner, Makar Semyonof, is brought in, Aksenof, along with the other prisoners, listens to his stories. Makar boasts that although he is innocent of the crime for which he has just been sentenced, he has done things in the past that should have resulted in his exile. Upon learning the hometown of the new prisoner, Aksenof, who does not reveal his own name, asks Makar if he knows of the Aksenof family. Makar remarks that he has heard of them, and they are rich, although the father of the family is in Siberia. Although Akse-nof refuses to answer Makar's questions about why he was sent to Siberia, the other prisoners tell his story for him. Makar's comments suggest that he knows who Aksenof is. He notes that Aksenof is growing old, and he states, "How wonderful that we should meet again here!" Aksenof then asks Makar whether he had heard of the crime for which Aksenof was convicted before and whether he knows who killed the tradesman. Makar insists that Aksenof must have been the killer, as the knife was found in his bag. Makar goes on, "For how could the knife have been put into your bag? Was it not standing close by your head? And you would have heard it, wouldn't you?"

Upon hearing this, Aksenof becomes convinced that Makar himself is the real killer. He thinks of all he has lost—his family, his freedom—because of Makar's actions. Aksenof grows angry. Two weeks later, he discovers that Makar has been digging an escape tunnel, and Makar threatens to kill Aksenof if Aksenof reveals his plan. The tunnel is in fact discovered, but Aksenof, who is trusted by the guards, does not implicate Makar. Overcome with gratitude toward Aksenof and by remorse for his own actions, Makar begs Aksenof to forgive him. He confesses that it was he who put the knife in Aksenof's bag, and that he had planned to kill Aksenof as well, but he escaped through the window when he heard a noise. Makar then promises to confess his crimes so that Aksenof can be freed.

Aksenof's reply surprises Makar. Aksenof tells the murderer that he has nothing to go home to and has no wish to leave any longer. Realizing what he has taken away from Aksenof, Makar begins to weep, and Aksenof is then moved to tears as well. He tells Makar that God will forgive him, and that perhaps he himself is "a hundred times worse" than Makar. Aksenof then grows peaceful, and he no longer mourns his losses. Makar still confesses his crime, but when the orders are handed down to release Aksenof, he is found dead.

CHARACTERS

Ivan Dmitrievitch Aksenof

Aksenof is the protagonist of "The Long Exile." As the story opens, he is described as a successful merchant and a pleasant person who could sing

well and once had a propensity to drink too much. Those days are now in his past, however. After marrying his wife, he mostly gave up drinking, although the narrator of the story observes that Aksenof does enjoy the occasional drinking "spree." Tolstoy includes such details to emphasize key points about Aksenof's character. He is both likable and responsible; he works hard and occasionally overindulges. In short, Aksenof is essentially like most people of his time.

As the story proceeds and Aksenof is arrested for a crime in which he had no role, the narrator traces the arc of his emotions. He experiences despair when no one believes him, when even his wife questions whether or not he committed the crime. After twenty-six years have passed in prison, Aksenof has lost his youth and his joyful nature. At the same time, he has found a faith in God that strengthens him. Yet his faith does not make him immune to the anger he feels toward Makar when he learns that Makar committed the crime for which Aksenof was imprisoned. Aksenof relives the despair of being sent to prison, and he recalls the life he lost. When Aksenof is given the opportunity to reveal to the prison authorities that Makar has dug an escape tunnel, he remains silent, even though his thoughts reveal a desire to see Makar pay for his crimes in some way. Aksenof's silence buys Makar's loyalty and repentance. Moved to tears by Makar's grief, Aksenof feels freed from his rage and despair. Overcome with a sense of peace, he dies before the prison officials come to release him.

Aksenof's Children

Aksenof and his wife have two small children, one still an infant, when the story begins. They appear in "The Long Exile" only briefly, when they accompany their mother to prison to visit Aksenof. Aksenof's wife worries about how she will care for her children after Aksenof has been imprisoned. Makar later reveals that he is familiar with the family and that the children have become successful merchants.

Aksenof's Wife

Although Aksenof's wife does not play a major role in the story, her interactions with Aksenof and his memories of her while he is in prison all serve to underscore their love for one another. Her moment of doubt about her husband's innocence is highlighted as a source of deep pain for Aksenof when contrasted with the couple's otherwise loving relationship. At the beginning of the story, Aksenof's wife pleads with him not to go on his journey; her dream has left her with the feeling that something horrible is about to happen to her husband. In her own grief after Aksenof is arrested, Aksenof's wife reminds him of her dream. She feels compelled to ask him if he did in fact commit the crime of which he has been accused, and her doubt both startles and saddens her husband. In prison, Aksenof remembers being a young father and husband, and he recalls his wife's face, eyes, voice, and laughter. His sense of loss regarding the future he could have had with her is conveyed in a few brief but poignant details. In prison, Aksenof, who has had no contact with the outside world since he was sent to Siberia, learns that his family has done well for itself in his absence, but Aksenof wonders whether his wife is even still alive.

Police Inspector

The police inspector questions Aksenof about his involvement in the murder of the tradesman. His investigation is somewhat limited; when the knife is found in Aksenof's bag, Aksenof's fate is sealed and the investigation does not proceed further.

Makar Semyonof

Makar first appears in the story as just another prisoner sent to Siberia. As he discusses his activities prior to his arrest, he reveals enough details to make Aksenof suspect that Makar knows something about the murder that has sent him to Siberia. When Aksenof questions Makar more closely, Makar's comments convince Aksenof that Makar is the true killer. Initially, Makar's recognition of Aksenof amuses him. He comments on how much Aksenof has aged and seems to have little concern for the consequences of his own actions. When Aksenof shows Makar mercy, however, by not reporting him to the prison authorities for digging an escape tunnel, Makar begins to feel remorse. He eventually confesses to Aksenof, begs for forgiveness, and attempts to secure Aksenof's release by confessing to the prison authorities. Aksenof's kindness results in Makar's emotional transformation.

Soldiers

Soldiers accompany the police inspector and do his bidding. They search Aksenof's bag, arrest him, and transport him to prison.

THEMES

Injustice

The prevailing theme of "The Long Exile" is injustice, specifically the injustice endured by Aksenof. He has committed no crime, yet he is sentenced to life in a prison camp in Siberia. Aksenof has been framed—the murderer placed the murder weapon in Aksenof's bag and then escaped, leaving Aksenof to take the blame. All of Aksenof's neighbors testify to the fact that although Aksenof used to drink heavily when he was younger, he has been a respected, sober man for many years. Yet their testimony does not sway the authorities. It does not appear that Aksenof receives a trial before his sentencing. His wife petitions the tsar (or czar) to try and secure Aksenof's release, but to no avail. Before the reader can even begin to understand the full weight of Aksenof's sentence and comprehend the fact that this innocent man is beaten with a knotted whip prior to his exile, the narrator abruptly states, "Aksenof lived twenty-six years in the salt mines." In the paragraph that follows, the narrator describes the changes Aksenof has experienced in the intervening years, from the whitening of his hair and the growth of his beard to the disappearance of his former joyfulness. His losses continue to be enumerated as the story progresses. The reader learns that Aksenof does not receive letters from anyone and has no knowledge of what may have happened to his wife and children.

Tolstoy's exploration of injustice continues when he introduces another character who claims that, like Aksenof, he was sentenced to Siberia for a crime that he did not commit. Unlike Aksenof, however, this man admits to having committed a number of crimes, any one of which could have landed him in prison. He states, "I have done things which long ago would have sent me here, but I was not found out; and now they have sent me here without any justice in it." One of those things, the reader later learns, was the murder of which Aksenof was accused. Aksenof becomes enraged at this injustice, yet he refuses to let these emotions spur him to turn Makar over to the authorities when Makar's escape tunnel is discovered. There is no justice for Aksenof; he dies before Makar's confession has brought about his release. In Tolstoy's story, the innocent are punished while the guilty walk free, and men guilty of heinous crimes such as murder are convicted for minor offenses, such as

TOPICS FOR FURTHER STUDY

- Although young-adult literature did not exist as a genre in nineteenth-century Russia, Tolstoy's *Childhood; Boyhood; Youth* is a collection of three volumes written by Tolstoy in the 1850s. In these works, he depicts the experiences of a young boy, Nikolenka, and the child's emotions, fears, and confusion related to youth and adolescence. With a small group, read the three volumes, published together in a 1964 volume translated by Rosemary Edmonds, and discuss the perceptions of Tolstoy (who was only twenty-three when he began writing *Childhood*) regarding what it is like to grow up. Consider the themes that are universal and transcend time and place. Do young people today experience the same types of feelings and fears that Tolstoy has written about? How do the time and place in which Nikolenka grows up alter the experience of adolescence? Discuss such issues with your class in a blog you create as a forum for the exploration of these works.

- In "The Long Exile," Aksenof spends twenty-six years serving a prison sentence in Siberia. Research the Russian government's use of Siberian prison camps during the late nineteenth century. Was this form of imprisonment reserved for particular offenses? What were living conditions like? What proportion of prisoners were actually freed and allowed to return to their homes? Compile your findings into a research paper that you share with your class either in print format or as a web page you have created. Be sure to cite all of your print and online sources.

- Cynthia Kadohata's young-adult novel *Weedflower*, published in 2008, is centered on a Japanese American girl during World War II. Along with her family, she is forced to live in an internment camp for Americans of Japanese descent. The protagonist soon learns that the camp is situated on a Native American reservation. The young girl's position as a political prisoner living in exile in her own country is set against that of the Mohave boy who befriends her. Read *Weedflower* and consider the way the protagonist's life changes after she has been exiled. How does she feel about the fact that she and her family are innocent of any crime yet are essentially prisoners? What are the conditions like at the camp? How are the protagonist's experiences similar to those of her new friend? Consider these questions as you read and create a report for your class about the book. You may present an oral or written report on the book's plot, themes, and characters, or you may incorporate this information into a web-based time line in which you highlight major historical dates and significant plot points.

- Aksenof's faith and religious feelings are key features of "The Long Exile." Tolstoy himself began to pull away from and ultimately rejected the state religion of Russian Orthodox Christianity. Using print and online sources, research Russian Orthodox beliefs as they currently exist and as they were practiced in the nineteenth century. Write a report in which you summarize these beliefs and highlight the similarities and the differences between the way the religion was practiced in the nineteenth century and the way it is practiced today.

thievery. The government is depicted as being ineffective at dispensing justice, while God's own justice, as Aksenof suggests, is delayed until one's death.

Forgiveness

Makar threatens to kill Aksenof when Aksenof discovers the escape tunnel Makar is digging. Near the story's conclusion, Makar tells Aksenof

"The Long Exile" is set in Vladimir, Russia. *(© Iakov Filimonov | ShutterStock.com)*

that it was he who killed the merchant and put the murder weapon into Aksenof's bag. Makar even tells Aksenof that he was going to kill him as well. When Makar finally grows remorseful and pleads for Aksenof's forgiveness, Makar tells Aksenof that he will confess and that Aksenof will be able to go home. Yet Aksenof cannot accept Makar's assurance that Makar will obtain freedom for Aksenof; he says, "It is easy for you to say that, but how could I endure it?" Pointing out that he has no home to return to, that his wife is probably dead, and that his children would not even remember him, Aksenof concludes, "I have nowhere to go." Makar is moved to greater depths of pity and remorse, and he begins to cry. The sound of Makar sobbing moves Aksenof to grief as well. Aksenof replies, "God will forgive you; maybe I am a hundred times worse than you are." Aksenof's religious studies have taught him that repentance will be rewarded by God's forgiveness. Yet his words may be taken as slightly ambiguous; he does not appear to offer his personal forgiveness to Makar. Possibly, this is implicit in his comment. At the same time, Aksenof seems to be stressing the point that Makar should be seeking God's forgiveness, not his own.

After this conversation with Makar, Aksenof feels a sense of peace settle over him, and he dies in prison having overcome any longing to be free. Aksenof's assurances to Makar of God's forgiveness nurture in Makar a desire to right the wrong he committed so many years before. Aksenof dies peacefully, yet the narrative does not clearly convey the source of Aksenof's peace. Tolstoy perhaps implies that Aksenof's implicit forgiveness of Makar gives him this freedom. At the same time, the exchange with Makar perhaps reminds Aksenof that only God has the power to absolve others of their sins, and that his own forgiveness and fate, like Makar's, are in God's hands. His sense of peace may be rooted in his own faith that God will forgive him.

STYLE

Moral Tale

"The Long Exile" was included in Tolstoy's *Primer*, a collection of instructional, moral tales for children. Therefore, critics such as Hugh McLean in his book *In Quest of Tolstoy* observe that this story is related in straightforward terms. There are only a few key characters, and the plot proceeds quickly, as the innocent Aksenof is implicated in the murder of a fellow tradesman. Aksenof feels the sting of this injustice, and he despairs when everyone, even his wife, doubts him. As he begins to realize that only God knows the truth of what happened, Aksenof turns increasingly to prayer. In prison, he seeks out opportunities to study scriptures, to attend church, to sing in the choir, and to pray. Other prisoners begin to regard Aksenof as a man of God. In portraying Aksenof in this manner, Tolstoy seeks to demonstrate the value of turning to God, as Aksenof has, in order to cope with challenging or painful circumstances.

When Aksenof is confronted by the true murderer, whose actions resulted in Aksenof's suffering, he shows the man mercy, despite his own rage. He feels empathy when Makar expresses remorse and grief, and he attests to the fact that everyone, himself included, is a sinner in need of God's forgiveness. Throughout the story, Aksenof is presented as a man guided by his morals. He steadfastly proclaims his innocence. When despair overcomes him, he turns to prayer. In prison, he is quiet, submissive, and devout. Consumed by rage when he learns the truth about Makar's role in the murder that sent him to prison, Aksenof continues to pray and finds mercy and compassion. Despite the cruelty life has shown him, Aksenof has put his faith in God and dies peacefully. His faithful behavior may be regarded as the model to which Tolstoy drew the attention of his young readers when he opted to include this story among the collection of works for children.

Third-Person Omniscient Narration in Stories for Children

In relating the story of Aksenof and his fate, Tolstoy employs the use of an omniscient (all-knowing) third-person narrator. An omniscient third-person narrator possesses the knowledge of all the characters in the story and what will happen to them, and relates this information to the reader by referring to the characters as "he" or "she." The point of view of this type of narrator is not limited to any one of the characters. Rather, the omniscient third-person narrator has access to the viewpoint and thoughts of any of the characters in the story. (This is in contrast to a first-person narrator, who relates the events in the story from his or her own point of view and refers to himself or herself as "I.")

Tolstoy's narrator opens "The Long Exile" in the once-upon-a-time fashion typical of stories written for young audiences. By combining this opening with omniscient third-person narration, Tolstoy creates a tone of immediacy, as if the narrator is directly telling the story to an audience of young listeners. Further, Tolstoy is able to convey the innermost thoughts of Aksenof as he experiences his range of emotions, from despair to grief to anger to peace. Using an omniscient third-person narrator, Tolstoy can also depict the wife's doubts and her frustration that her husband did not listen to her warnings, and he can further relate the inner turmoil experienced by Makar. Moral tales and fables are often related in this manner, as their didacticism is complimented by the omniscience of the narrator.

HISTORICAL CONTEXT

Russia under Tsar Alexander II

Tsar Alexander II was the son of Tsar Nicholas I. Alexander became tsar upon the death of his father in 1855. Russia had just suffered defeat in the Crimean War, a war of aggression against Turkey. Alexander sought to bring reforms to Russia in order to prevent a revolution. In 1861, he abolished serfdom, a form of slavery in which peasant farmers were legally bound to work the land of their lord's estate. He also established local councils, or *zemstvos*, which had local authority to improve roads, schools, and medical services. Only the wealthy, however, could elect representative members to the councils. Alexander also relaxed some censorship measures and reduced the duration of the compulsory military service. Despite such reforms, many intellectuals still clamored for freedom from state censors and greater representation in the government. Additionally, Alexander remained relatively intolerant of criticism of his government and made full use of the prison system and the tsarist tradition of exiling dissidents, criminals, and political prisoners to a life of hard labor in Siberian prison and labor camps. Under his authority, revolutionaries such as Mikhail Bakunin, along with Polish insurrectionists involved in an uprising, were sentenced to Siberian exile. Andre A. Gentes, writing for

COMPARE
&
CONTRAST

- **1870s:** Russia is an autocracy, a system of government in which absolute power resides with one person. Tsar Alexander II institutes a series of reforms but begins to return to more oppressive measures of government and censorship after an assassination attempt. The military enforces Tsar Alexander's decrees, arresting and imprisoning those who speak out against him.

  Today: Russia is a federation, a group of states governed by a central body but possessing independence in some internal affairs. The Russian Federation is governed by President Vladimir Putin and Prime Minister Dmitriy Medvedev, both elected to their current offices in 2012. Notably, Putin previously served as prime minister from 1999 to 2000, and again from 2008 to 2012, and as president from 2000 to 2008. Medvedev also previously served as president, from 2008 to 2012.

- **1870s:** Russian literature is characterized by an emphasis on the realistic depiction of society, culture, and the lives of individual figures. Tolstoy, Ivan Turgenev, and Fyodor Dostoyevsky are among the most critically acclaimed writers of their time for providing detailed and accurate depictions

of their world and for rejecting an idealism that masks the troubles of society.

  Today: Writers of Russian literature in the twenty-first century explore a variety of genres, from experimental novels set in Tolstoy's time, such as Boris Akunin's *He Lover of Death* (2011), realist works concerned with modern day civil war in Russia, such as Dmitry Bykov's *Living Souls* (2010), historical fiction, such as Ludmila Ulitskaya's *Daniel Stein, Interpreter* (2011), and futuristic works, such as Olga Slavnikova's *2017* (2010).

- **1870s:** Since 1754, the Russian government has sent criminals to live out life sentences in the frozen lands of Siberia. Prisoners are typically sentenced to a life of hard labor, often working in silver, gold, and lead mines.

  Today: Siberia continued to be known as the place to which prisoners and dissidents were exiled during the Soviet era, but the region is no longer associated exclusively with its penal history. Modern Siberia has in some ways become a tourist destination because of its history, but it is also an area rich in oil and minerals, and the people of Siberia's mining communities continue to endure the harsh conditions of this remote region.

---

the journal *Jahrbucher fur Geschichte Osteuropas*, points out that between 1863 and 1868, between 18,000 and 24,000 insurrectionists from Poland, Lithuania, Belorussia, and Ukraine were sentenced to Siberian exile. Censorship of printed works became increasingly rigorous after an assassination attempt on Alexander was made in 1879. No criticism of the government was tolerated, radical publications were banned, and activists were arrested and imprisoned. Alexander was nonetheless assassinated in 1881 by revolutionaries seeking government reform. In the wake of this assassination, Alexander's son, Alexander III, reversed

many of his father's reforms, increasing censorship and reducing the powers of the zemstvos.

Russian Literature in the 1870s
During the 1860s and 1870s, realism characterized the works of Russian writers. Novelists such as Dostoyevsky, Tolstoy, and Turgenev, among others, sought to capture their society in such a way that the details of ordinary life were revealed, fleshed out in detailed prose that refused to give way to the idealism of the past. Social reality was depicted in a manner almost scientific in its objectivity. Tolstoy was admired as a realist who was able to remove himself as the

Russian soldiers and police officers suddenly appear to search Ivan's bags. (© IgorGolovniov/ ShutterStock.com)

author from the scenes he described, whereas Dostoyevsky was noted for his depiction of unusual but authentic characters whose thoughts and motivations were explored in great detail. Dostoyevsky, who had spent years in exile in a Siberian prison camp, offered unique perspectives on the lives of characters who had endured unspeakable hardships. Turgenev, while not entirely rejecting the romanticism of the past, nevertheless conveyed the society and culture of the time in a balanced fashion. A number of realist authors also turned their attention toward examinations of God, faith, and religion. For writers such as Dostoyevsky and Tolstoy, for example, intellectual explorations of faith led to internal spiritual and philosophical struggles. The political reforms of the time period were also an underlying focus for many realist authors. As Richard Freeborn observes in *The Cambridge History of Russian Literature*, "The 'national' issue was of course paramount.

Russian literature of the time period was a self-examining, self-defining literature, concerned to explore the roots of national experience." Freeborn goes on to assert, "Freedom, equality and brotherhood may not have existed in the reality of Russian life, but in the 'realism' of Russian literature they were the motive forces which determined the veracity of the realism."

CRITICAL OVERVIEW

By the time "The Long Exile" was published in Russian in 1872 and in English in 1888, Tolstoy had established himself as an author who had achieved both popular success and critical acclaim. Nathan Haskell Dole, the translator of the 1888 English edition *The Long Exile, and Other Stories for Children*, states in his preface that the collection "is meant for children" and that it is filled with "simple, vivid, delicate, pathetic, often slyly humorous" stories that do not contain "a false note." Dole also observes that "the primary object of the book is to give American children an idea of what Russian children love to read." In discussing *The Long Exile, and Other Stories for Children* in 1894, an anonymous reviewer for the *Scottish Leader* states,

> One may say that it is precisely in such brief and simple tales as 'Long Exile' that some of the best qualities of Count Tolstoi appear. His almost infantile *naïveté*, and his keen and quick sympathy with the half-instinctive life of childhood, make him an ideal fabulist and raconteur for the nursery.

Other critics have commented on the themes Tolstoy explores in the story. Inessa Medzhibovskaya, in *Tolstoy and the Religious Culture of His Time*, describes the work in terms of its depiction of "the theme of resignation and guilt." Observing that "The Long Exile" is a retelling of a parable that appears in *War and Peace*, the critic asserts that "Aksenov feels no bitterness or wrong after forgiving his enemy." Yet A. N. Wilson, in *Tolstoy: A Biography*, finds that this story "strikes a new note in Tolstoy's feelings of anger and alienation with his own country." Wilson goes on to contend,

> If one tried to date this story just in terms of what we know about Tolstoy's biography, one would almost certainly think it was very late: a product of years in which he hated the Government, expressed disillusionment with the penal

system, fallen in and out of love with Christianity and bred his own new breed of religion.

As Wilson goes on to point out, "In fact, *God Sees the Truth but Waits* anticipates all that."

Taking another approach to the story, Hugh McLean centers his analysis, in *In Quest of Tolstoy*, on the ways in which Tolstoy alters the tale of the wrongfully accused merchant, appearing first in parable form in *War and Peace*, then as transformed into a story infused with the qualities characteristic of "Tolstoyan realistic fiction." Working from the original skeleton of the tale, Tolstoy added psychological tension by forcing his protagonist to confront, in prison, the murderer Makar.

CRITICISM

Catherine Dominic

Dominic is a novelist and a freelance writer and editor. In the following essay, she maintains that "The Long Exile," written during a time of transition by Tolstoy, explores the protagonist's struggles with injustice, faith, despair, and forgiveness.

"The Long Exile" was written during a period of transition in Leo Tolstoy's life. He had completed *War and Peace* and would later endure a crisis of faith and confront his disillusionment with the Russian government and the Russian Orthodox religion. In 1872, these issues were already sources of concern for Tolstoy, as "The Long Exile" shows. While some critics regard the work as a simple morality tale that Tolstoy included in his *Primer* for children, others have found evidence in the work of Tolstoy's evolving views on Christianity. Gary Saul Morson regards the story as Tolstoy's exploration of Christian forgiveness, and he states in *Anniversary Essays on Tolstoy* that Aksenof's prolonged suffering in "The Long Exile" provides him with "something much more valuable than justice: the opportunity to forgive." A. N. Wilson, in *Tolstoy: A Biography*, insists that the short story foreshadows Tolstoy's later development "of his own new breed of religion based on Oriental detachment." Wilson in fact characterizes Aksenof's state at the end of the story as one not of "Christian blessedness" but "of almost Buddhist detachment." Positioned as the story is in Tolstoy's life, the story resonates neither with childlike simplicity nor with absolute

pronouncements on faith and forgiveness. Rather, "The Long Exile" is rife with ambiguity and emotional and spiritual conflict. Certainly Aksenof journeys from despair to peace over the course of the story. Yet as he fluctuates from fervent faith and prayer to desperation and rage and back, it becomes clear that Aksenof's conflicted state is more a central feature of the story than his abruptly achieved peacefulness at the story's conclusion.

When Aksenof is accused of the murder of the merchant, he claims to be innocent, but when the police find the knife in his bag, he grows frightened. He obviously does not know how it got there, and his fear causes his voice to tremble and the blood to drain from his face. The narrator describes his appearance by noting that these signs of fear are read differently by the police: Aksenof is "all quivering with fright, like a guilty person." When he is bound and taken to the police wagon, Aksenof makes the sign of the cross. (The sign of the cross is a Christian ritual in which a person touches his or her forehead, upper chest, right shoulder [in the Russian Orthodox tradition], and then left shoulder. In other Christian traditions, the left shoulder is touched first. The movement suggests the cross upon which Jesus Christ was crucified and is a reminder to the faithful of God's love and mercy and Jesus' sacrifice.) Aksenof then weeps. Upon seeing his wife later, Aksenof instructs her to petition to the tsar to grant his release. His wife has already done so, and the request was denied. Aksenof's wife then asks her husband if he did in fact commit the crime. Aksenof's subsequent anguish is clear: "So you, too, have no faith in me!" he cries out.

Following the denial of his petition and the revelation of his wife's doubt, Aksenof turns to his religious faith, thinking, "It is evident that no one but God can know the truth of the matter, and He is the only one to ask for mercy, and He is the only one from whom to expect it." This becomes Aksenof's guiding principle for the next twenty-six years. In prison, he grows old and bent and cheerless. He prays often, and he uses the money he earns making boots to buy holy books. Aksenof reads the scriptures, attends church on holidays, and sings in the church choir. His fellow prisoners refer to him as "the 'man of God.'" Aksenof has chosen a specific path. Seeing that any chance of his release is futile, he adopts a nonconfrontational,

WHAT DO I READ NEXT?

- Tolstoy's highly acclaimed short stories, some of which are collected in *The Death of Ivan Ilyich and Other Stories*, published in 2009 as translated by Richard Pevear and Larissa Volokhonsky, were often used by the author as means of experimenting with various themes, styles, or ideas that he would explore in greater depth in his longer works. They remain emblematic of Tolstoy's dedication to realism and to the richness of his prose.

- Fyodor Dostoyevsky's *Memoirs from the House of the Dead*, originally published in 1862, is a novel based on his own experiences living in Siberia, exiled to a prison camp.

- Ivan Turgenev's *Sketches from a Hunter's Album*, originally appearing in 1852, was published in 1990 in a translation by Richard Freeborn. The work is a collection of twenty-five short prose pieces. While the sketches are rooted in the author's travels as a hunter, they explore the tensions between the ruling classes and the peasants and delineate the suffering of the serfs prior to Alexander II's abolition of serfdom.

- Set in the Russia that Tolstoy experienced at the end of his life, Shelly Sander's young-adult novel *Rachel's Secret*, published in 2012, examines the political and religious tensions of prerevolutionary Russia. The protagonist experiences the events that lead to the violent riots that occurred in 1903.

- In Ji-li Jiang's 1997 young-adult memoir *Red Scarf Girl: A Memoir of the Cultural Revolution*, the author opens her story in 1966, just before the Communist leader of China, Mao Zedong, begins his Cultural Revolution, a series of drastic reforms designed to punish anyone who speaks out against the nation's Communist leadership and policies. Ji-li Jiang recounts her family's great fear that they would become political prisoners, sent away to prison, a labor camp, or rural exile, like so many others.

- Rosamund Bartlett's *Tolstoy: A Russian Life*, published in 2011, incorporates new material regarding Tolstoy's life, only recently available since the demise of the Soviet Union.

submissive attitude and attempts, with the aid of his faith, to plod through his days.

Upon Makar's arrival, Aksenof is transformed, his peacefulness shattered. Although he refuses to tell Makar what crime he was accused of, Aksenof does state that he "was condemned to hard labor on account of my sins." He further insists that he "must have deserved this." Elsewhere in the text, however, the only indication of Aksenof's misdeeds is the reference to his heavy drinking. Although as a Christian Aksenof likely subscribed to the notion that all of humanity is stained by sin, he did not murder, and the reader and Aksenof know this. The punishment of a lifetime in a Siberian mine can only be regarded as an unwarranted punishment for a person who periodically

drank to excess, so Aksenof amplifies the magnitude of his sins when he comments that he must have deserved his fate. As the conversation with Makar continues, however, it becomes clear that it was Makar who murdered the merchant, Makar who framed Aksenof to take the blame and the punishment for the crime. Makar and Aksenof both come to this realization, and Aksenof subsequently becomes plagued by an overwhelming sense of melancholy. He remembers his wife when she was young, and imagines he can hear her voice and laughter. He recalls his two little boys, and he remembers his sense of joyfulness as he played the guitar before his arrest. Aksenof also recalls his humiliation and pain when he was flogged and the suffering he endured during the twenty-six long years that he

POSITIONED AS THE STORY IS IN TOLSTOY'S LIFE, THE STORY RESONATES NEITHER WITH CHILDLIKE SIMPLICITY NOR WITH ABSOLUTE PRONOUNCEMENTS ON FAITH AND FORGIVENESS. RATHER, 'THE LONG EXILE' IS RIFE WITH AMBIGUITY AND EMOTIONAL AND SPIRITUAL CONFLICT."

has spent in prison. Overcome with despair, Aksenof is "tempted to put an end to himself."

Until this point, Aksenof has demonstrated that faith and religion have provided him comfort and peace. His faith is emphasized in the way he reminds himself of God's wisdom and mercy. His religious belief is evidenced in his performance of the sign of the cross, and in his subsequent devotion to scripture. The reader is told that Aksenof reads the "Book of Martyrs" and the Gospels, religious texts that, respectively, describe the lives of Christian martyrs and saints and present the teachings of Jesus Christ. Yet Aksenof has now been driven to the point of considering suicide. This is not an action any man would contemplate lightly, but a religious man like Aksenof would also be faced with the knowledge that suicide is considered a serious sin, punishable by damnation in the afterlife. His anger increases, displacing his despair, and Aksenof is then moved almost to the point of murder, as he becomes "crazy with desire to pay off the load of vengeance." He tries to uses prayer to become calm, but he is unable to find his former peace. Unable to sleep at night, he becomes overwhelmed with sadness and does not know what to do. Confronted by Makar, Aksenof "trembled all over with rage." Aksenof has discovered Makar's escape tunnel, and although Makar threatens to kill him, Aksenof does not reveal whether or not he will tell the guards about the tunnel. Aksenof tells Makar, "To kill me would do no harm; you killed me long ago."

When Aksenof is questioned about the tunnel, his thoughts reveal turmoil. He considers protecting Makar, then asks himself, "But why should I forgive him when he has been my ruin? Let him pay for my sufferings." Thinking he might tell, he observes, "They will surely flog him. But what difference does it make what I think of him? Will it be any the easier for me?" Although he responds to the guards that "God does not bid" him to tell, Aksenof's earlier train of thought is significant. His question "Will it be any the easier for me?" is key to understanding his actions. He realizes in this moment that no matter what happens to Makar, his own fate will still be the same. The twenty-six years he has lost cannot be returned to him, even if Makar is beaten or killed. Makar's fate is independent of his own. Aksenof's losses are his own to bear, and the punishment of another man cannot soothe his despair. Aksenof does not turn Makar in, but his decision does not seem to have come from a sense of religious duty. Although he states, "God does not bid me to tell," his deliberations regarding Makar's fate did not include God, religion, fate, or morality in any way. Aksenof simply began to understand that Makar's suffering would be meaningless. Having endured so much, he feels powerless to feel any joy at all; he would derive little emotional response of any kind from Makar's punishment. Furthermore, and most significantly, Makar's punishment would not make things any easier for Aksenof. With nothing to gain, Aksenof simply pulls away. He does not pray to God and ask what he should do, nor does he scour his memory for lessons from scripture about how one should show mercy to one's enemies.

Makar, grateful, begs Aksenof for forgiveness and assures him he will be released from prison once Makar confesses. Again, Aksenof can see nothing in this course of action that will benefit him. "I have nowhere to go," Aksenof tells Makar. But Makar is tormented with guilt. "Forgive me for Christ's sake!" Makar pleads. He sobs, and in doing so brings Aksenof to tears. The source of Aksenof's grief at this point in the story is unclear. Possibly, he is moved to pity by Makar. Alternatively, as Makar weeps for everything he has caused Aksenof to lose, Aksenof grieves openly for his own loss and suffering. Never before has anyone shared both the knowledge of his innocence and a sense of injustice at what he has endured. For the first time since he was accused of killing the merchant, Aksenof has found true sympathy. He does not state explicitly that he forgives Makar, because he knows that this is as futile as any other action he takes now. Just as revealing Makar as the

Ivan Dmitrich Aksionov is caught with a bloody knife in his suitcase. (© Fotokon / ShutterStock.com)

prisoner who was digging the escape tunnel would have been pointless in Aksenof's view, so is forgiving him. "God will forgive you," he assures Makar, and goes on to say, "Maybe I am a hundred times worse than you are." Maybe. Yet more likely, Aksenof is not, for the reader knows that he has not murdered anyone. Aksenof, however, returns to the one idea that he has clung to for so long, that God knows the truth. He knows the truth about Aksenof, and he knows the truth about Makar.

This belief that God knows the truth has been Aksenof's familiar source of comfort. Nevertheless, it is not a conviction that seems to have guided his actions. The pivotal choice he is faced with in the story is whether or not he should tell the authorities about Makar and the tunnel. Aksenof does not tell, but his silence was not inspired by an understanding that God knows the truth but rather by the pointlessness of the action and the realization that speaking out against Makar would not benefit him, Aksenof, in any way. In the last moments of the story, Aksenof seems to experience the same conflict he has undergone throughout. He does not forgive

Makar personally when Makar begs for absolution, because he perceives that it does not matter.

As the story ends, the narrator tells the reader that at this point, Aksenof "suddenly . . . felt a wonderful peace in his soul. And he ceased to mourn for his home, and had no desire to leave the prison, but thought only of his last hour." One must remember that moments before, Aksenof had already expressed his lack of *ability* to go anywhere should he be released from prison. "I have nowhere to go," he stated flatly. His subsequent lack of *desire* seems really to be a repetition of what he has already stated. Aksenof, in the aftermath of sharing tears with Makar, seems to simultaneously embrace his own futility and to reconnect with the spirituality that has brought him to this point, that is, his faith that God knows the truth, and that God will forgive.

Aksenof's motivations and beliefs at the story's conclusion seem muddled and not entirely accounted for by the events as the narrator relates them. Often the conclusion of the story is explained through the argument that

Aksenof's forgiveness of Makar frees Aksenof from his grief and is the source of his sense of peacefulness. Yet it seems unclear that Aksenof has actually bothered to forgive Makar himself, and further it seems that his peacefulness stems from his ability to weep for his losses with someone, the only person on earth who knows he is innocent of the crime of which he was accused so long ago. His conversation with Makar has released him by lending a sense of connection to the world. Aksenof is consoled that Makar is sorry, and comforted by the notion that Makar knows he is innocent. Aksenof has attempted to recall his faith by telling Makar that God will forgive him. He has also attempted to act out of self-interest, but he finds that he cannot benefit either from exposing Makar or by forgiving him. Aksenof dies peacefully simply because he has nothing left to live for.

Source: Catherine Dominic, Critical Essay on "The Long Exile," in *Short Stories for Students*, Gale, Cengage Learning, 2013.

Radoslav A. Tsanoff

In the following excerpt, Tsanoff considers the relationship of religion to life in Tolstoy's view.

. . . Tolstoy's beliefs were not beliefs about things but beliefs in principles, commitments, and loyalties. Thus believing in the Gospel of Jesus, he was resolved to follow it in directing every part of human life. It became for him the program of all reform—political, social, economic, artistic, intellectual—and not only as a general principle, but as applied to himself, to Leo Tolstoy.

He considered the teachings of Jesus as they should apply to his career as a literary artist, and more generally as a member of the intelligentsia. People speak loftily of the "division of labor"— but what is right division of labor? Do the scientist, the novelist or dramatist, the poet, the musician, the artist serve directly the spiritual needs of the workers who by their labor satisfy directly his physical needs? When a scientist compiles a catalogue of a million beetles, when an artist paints opulence, when a poet indulges in sophisticated fancies, and all help themselves to the products of the peasant's toil, is there any fair division or exchange of labor?

Tolstoy pursued this problem in his essay entitled *What is Art?* Great art is to be judged by its capacity to communicate itself to universal humanity: not only to some aesthetic coterie but

"WHO IS TO JUDGE TOLSTOY'S FAITH AND HIS LIFE?"

to all men and women however simple and humble. A work of art which fails or refuses to perform this chief function for a part, and that by far the greater part of humanity, is bad art, no matter how highly it might be praised by those who, in lauding it, aristocratically isolate themselves from the common people. "The destiny of art in our time is to transmit from the realm of reason to the realm of feeling the truth that well-being for men consists in being united together, and to set up, in place of the existing reign of force, that Kingdom of God, *i.e.*, of love, which we all recognize as the highest aim of human life." "Art is only one and consists in this: to increase the sinless general joys accessible to all—the good of man." Tolstoy applied this principle in a radical and negative rejudgment of traditionally proclaimed literary and artistic masterpieces, and of his own works also; discarding *War and Peace* and *Anna Karenina* and saving only stories like "The Prisoner of Caucasus" as an example of universal art communicating the very slightest feelings common to all men, and "God Sees the Truth" ("The Long Exile") as belonging to religious art, transmitting feelings of love of God and our fellowmen.

Tolstoy applied his understanding of the Gospel of Jesus in dealing with the problems of social-economic reform. He offered his services as a worker to the Russian census bureau, choosing for his district the slums of Moscow, to see directly the homes and lives of the submerged masses. There he learned that those people cannot be saved from squalor and degradation merely by almsgiving. Organized charity cannot cure the ills of poverty, for the idle and wasteful affluence of the upper classes not only impoverishes the multitudes but also corrupts them by rousing in their souls greed and envy and distorted ideas of happiness through mere possession.

The pursuit of pleasure and sensual enjoyment and idle luxury is not repellent to us aristocrats only because we are all morally dull and do not realize the daily enormity of our lives. Consider, my titled friends, Tolstoy exclaimed, bethink yourselves: what are you about? Here are a hundred women at a festive ball. "Each woman at this ball whose dress costs a hundred and fifty rubles was not born at the ball, but she has lived also in the country, has seen peasants, knows her own nurse and maid, whose fathers and brothers are poor, for whom earning one hundred and fifty rubles to build a cottage with is the end and aim of a long, laborious life; she knows this; how can she, then, enjoy herself, knowing that on her half-naked body she is wearing the cottage which is the dream of her housemaid's brother?"

But what is to be done? For this is the title of the book from which we are quoting—*What Is to be Done?* Stop thinking all the time of yourselves, of your desires and pleasures and so-called cultural demands, and think a while of your fellowmen. But you may insist: what difference would it make in the end? My philanthropic drop in the ocean would make no real change; things will go on as they are just the same. "If I came among savages," Tolstoy replied, "who gave me chops which I thought delicious, but the next day I learned (perhaps saw myself) that these delicious chops were made of a human prisoner who had been slain in order to make them; and if I think it bad to eat men, however delicious the cutlets may be, and however general the custom to eat men among the persons with whom I live, and however small the utility to the prisoners who have been prepared for food my refusal to eat them may be, I shall not and will not eat them."

An Oriental proverb has the truth in a nutshell: If there is one man idle there is another dying of hunger. This problem is quite simple; it needs only willingness and resolution to solve it. "If a horseman sees that his horse is tired out, he must not remain on its back and hold up its head, but first of all get off." Feed the horse, Tolstoy said, but first of all get off the horse's back! Make sure, first of all, that by your own personal way of life you are not enslaving the lives of others. The more you spend on yourself, the more you oblige others to labor for you; the less you spend and consume, the more yourself work, the better member of society you are. Give to the poor, yes, but first, stop the spread of poverty by your own excessive drain of the social resources. The realization of this truth was compared by Tolstoy to the experience of a man who, having started on a certain errand, finds out that it is futile and wrong, and turns back home. What had been on his right hand would now be on his left, and what had been to the left would be to the right. This is the meaning of our conversion to the social gospel of Jesus in brief: a gospel to the weary and heavy-laden, but also to a certain rich man.

This teaching could not remain mere preachment; it was initially and finally a self-probing and self-judgment. Tolstoy asked himself: How can I, Lyof Tolstoy, how can I stop exploiting others and using them as my servitors? Well, I can take care of my own room; I can clean my own boots; indeed I can make my own boots; I can go out in the fields and by my own work produce the equivalent of the food which I consume. And only after I have done this, only then shall I have a right to offer my help to my fellowmen without feeling like a robber who returns part of the booty. Nor am I, in so doing, rejecting the true dignity of mental work. The maximum time that I can spend in really productive mental activity is five hours a day. I sleep eight hours. What do I do with the remaining eleven hours? Let me, during this time, relieve the peasant of some manual labor; let me allow him some little rest, a chance to have a cup of tea and think may be for half an hour.

Still, what was Tolstoy to do with his large property, with his thousands of acres of land, with the copyrights of his writings? The rich young man of the Gospel, whom Jesus asked to give his wealth to the poor, was presumably a bachelor; Tolstoy's case was quite different. Would he be justified in giving away all his estate to the poor, to the peasants? That would have compelled his wife and his five sons and three daughters to give up their rich life and follow him, maybe contrary to their personal convictions—and compulsion is wrong, according to the Gospel. Besides, Countess Sonya had helped to increase his wealth: he could not give away her and her children's shares. On the other hand, he could no longer keep it up and remain honest in his convictions. Tolstoy's solution was to renounce all rights to his estate; he turned it over to the Countess to manage as she saw fit. In his own house he remained as a guest. Each day he spent several hours in manual labor, earning his own bread directly. He wrote steadily but declared all his work, from then on, free of copyright, free for anyone to publish and circulate. Only when the Dukhobors faced punishment for their refusal to serve in the army, Tolstoy copyrighted his novel *Resurrection* to raise funds for their planned emigration to Canada where freedom and respect for their religious convictions were promised them. In his stories and essays he advocated the gospel teaching of universal love and fellowship, in opposition to all violence and selfishness.

But still he felt that he was not able to live as unselfishly as he ought, even though only a guest at Yasnaya Polyana. In the year 1897, he wrote the following letter to his wife and put it among his papers, asking that it be delivered to her after his death—only the beginning of it is cited here:

My dear Sonya:

Already for a long time I have been tortured by the contradiction existing between my life and my religious convictions. I could not oblige you to change your life—the habits to which I myself accustomed you ... but I cannot continue living as I have lived here sixteen years; ... and now I have decided to carry out that which for a long time I have wished to do— to go away. ...

More than thirteen years elapsed before Tolstoy carried out this decision, and on November 10, 1910, fled from his house at Yasnaya Polyana to seek his peace in seclusion with God. He was eighty-two years old and, as it turned out, very seriously ill. He was unable to continue on his road in the cold weather and had to stop over at the railway station of Astapovo, where his condition worsened; inflammation of the lungs set in, and his life slowly ebbed away. His last words as he was losing consciousness were: "All is well, ... all is simple and well ... well ... yes, yes."

Who is to judge Tolstoy's faith and his life? His own parable of "The Two Old Men" is addressed as much to himself as to the rest of us. Two peasants, Yefim and Yelisei, set out on a pilgrimage to Jerusalem. But Yelisei is delayed on his journey by the call of mercy and, having spent on a poor family most of the money which he had saved up for his pilgrimage, he is obliged to return to his village. Yefim proceeds on his way alone, wary of strangers and prudently calculating from beginning to end. But when he finally reaches his goal, arriving just in time to elbow his way inside the Church of the Holy Sepulchre, behold! he catches sight of Yelisei, there ahead of him, clear up towards the altar. It is only Yefim's vision, of course, and it is Tolstoy's parable; but its message is unmistakable.

Source: Radoslav A. Tsanoff, "Count Leo Tolstoy," in *Autobiographies of Ten Religious Leaders: Alternatives in Christian Experience*, Trinity University Press, 1968, pp. 201–29.

William Dean Howells

In the following essay, Howells discusses the influence of Tolstoy's religious and philosophical writings on his own works and thoughts.

I come now, though not quite in the order of time, to the noblest of all these enthusiasms, namely, my devotion for the writings of Lyof Tolstoy. I should wish to speak of him with his own incomparable truth, yet I do not know how to give a notion of his influence without the effect of exaggeration. As much as one merely human being can help another I believe that he has helped me; he has not influenced me in aesthetics only, but in ethics, too, so that I can never again see life in the way I saw it before I knew him. Tolstoy awakens in his reader the will to be a man; not effectively, not spectacularly, but simply, really. He leads you back to the only true ideal, away from that false standard of the gentleman, to the Man who sought not to be distinguished from other men, but identified with them, to that Presence in which the finest gentleman shows his alloy of vanity, and the greatest genius shrinks to the measure of his miserable egotism. I learned from Tolstoy to try character and motive by no other test, and though I am perpetually false to that sublime ideal myself, still the ideal remains with me, to make me ashamed that I am not true to it. Tolstoy gave me heart to hope that the world may yet be made over in the image of Him who died for it, when all Caesar's things shall be finally rendered unto Caesar, and men shall come into their own, into the right to labor and the right to enjoy the fruits of their labor, each one master of himself and servant to every other. He taught me to see life not as a chase of a forever impossible personal happiness, but as a field for endeavor toward the happiness of the whole human family; and I can never lose this vision, however I close my eyes, and strive to see my own interest as the highest good. He gave me new criterions, new principles, which, after all, were those that are taught us in our earliest childhood, before we have come to the evil wisdom of the world. As I read his different ethical books, *What to Do, My Confession*, and *My Religion*, I recognized their truth with a rapture such as I have known in no other reading, and I rendered them my allegiance,

" WHAT I FEEL SURE IS THAT I CAN NEVER LOOK AT LIFE IN THE MEAN AND SORDID WAY THAT I DID BEFORE I READ TOLSTOY."

heart and soul, with whatever sickness of the one and despair of the other. They have it yet, and I believe they will have it while I live. It is with inexpressible astonishment that I hear them attainted of pessimism, as if the teaching of a man whose ideal was simple goodness must mean the prevalence of evil. The way he showed me seemed indeed impossible to my will, but to my conscience it was and is the only possible way. If there is any point on which he has not convinced my reason it is that of our ability to walk this narrow way alone. Even there he is logical, but as Zola subtly distinguishes in speaking of Tolstoy's essay on "Money," he is not reasonable. Solitude enfeebles and palsies, and it is as comrades and brothers that men must save the world from itself rather than themselves from the world. It was so the earliest Christians, who had all things common, understood the life of Christ, and I believe that the latest will understand it so.

I have spoken first of the ethical works of Tolstoy, because they are of the first importance to me, but I think that his aesthetical works are as perfect. To my thinking they transcend in truth, which is the highest beauty, all other works of fiction that have been written, and I believe that they do this because they obey the law of the author's own life. His conscience is one ethically and one aesthetically; with his will to be true to himself he cannot be false to his knowledge of others. I thought the last word in literary art had been said to me by the novels of Tourguenief, but it seemed like the first, merely, when I began to acquaint myself with the simpler method of Tolstoy. I came to it by accident, and without any manner of preoccupation in *The Cossacks*, one of his early books, which had been on my shelves unread for five or six years. I did not know even Tolstoy's name when I opened it, and it was with a kind of amaze that I read it, and felt word by word, and line by line, the truth of a new art in it.

I do not know how it is that the great Russians have the secret of simplicity. Some say it is because they have not a long literary past and are

not conventionalized by the usage of many generations of other writers, but this will hardly account for the brotherly directness of their dealing with human nature; the absence of experience elsewhere characterizes the artist with crudeness, and simplicity is the last effect of knowledge. Tolstoy is, of course, the first of them in this supreme grace. He has not only Tourguenief's transparency of style, unclouded by any mist of the personality which we mistakenly value in style, and which ought no more to be there than the artist's personality should be in a portrait; but he has a method which not only seems without artifice, but is so. I can get at the manner of most writers, and tell what it is, but I should be baffled to tell what Tolstoy's manner is; perhaps he has no manner. This appears to me true of his novels, which, with their vast variety of character and incident, are alike in their single endeavor to get the persons living before you, both in their action and in the peculiarly dramatic interpretation of their emotion and cogitation. There are plenty of novelists to tell you that their characters felt and thought so and so, but you have to take it on trust; Tolstoy alone makes you know how and why it was so with them and not otherwise. If there is anything in him which can be copied or burlesqued it is this ability of his to show men inwardly as well as outwardly; it is the only trait of his which I can put my hand on.

After the *Cossacks* I read *Anna Karenina* with a deepening sense of the author's unrivaled greatness. I thought that I saw through his eyes a human affair of that most sorrowful sort as it must appear to the Infinite Compassion; the book is a sort of revelation of human nature in circumstances that have been so perpetually lied about that we have almost lost the faculty of perceiving the truth concerning an illicit love. When you have once read *Anna Karenina* you know how fatally miserable and essentially unhappy such a love must be. But the character of Karenin himself is quite as important as the intrigue of Anna and Vronsky. It is wonderful how such a man, cold, Philistine and even mean in certain ways, towers into a sublimity unknown (to me, at least,) in fiction when he forgives, and yet knows that he cannot forgive with dignity. There is something crucial, and something triumphant, not beyond the power, but hitherto beyond the imagination of men in this effect, which is not solicited, not forced, not in the least romantic, but comes naturally, almost inevitably from the make of man.

The vast prospects, the far-reaching perspectives of *War and Peace* made it as great a surprise for me in the historical novel as *Anna Karenina* had been in the study of contemporary life; and its people and interests did not seem more remote, since they are of a civilization always as strange and of a humanity always as known.

I read some shorter stories of Tolstoy's before I came to this greatest work of his: I read *Scenes of the Siege of Sebastopol*, which is so much of the same quality as *War and Peace*; and I read "Policoushka" and most of his short stories with a sense of my unity with their people such as I had never felt with the people of other fiction.

His didactic stories, like all stories of the sort, dwindle into allegories; perhaps they do their work the better for this, with the simple intelligences they address; but I think that where Tolstoy becomes impatient of his office of artist, and prefers to be directly a teacher, he robs himself of more than half his strength with those he can move only through the realization of themselves in others. The simple pathos, and the apparent indirectness of such a tale as that of "Policoushka," the peasant conscript, is of vastly more value to the world at large than all his parables; and *The Death of Ivan Ilyitch*, the Philistine worlding, will turn the hearts of many more from the love of the world than such pale fables of the early Christian life as Work while ye have the Light. A man's gifts are not given him for nothing, and the man who has the great gift of dramatic fiction has no right to cast it away or to let it rust out in disuse.

Terrible as the *Kreutzer Sonata* was, it had a moral effect dramatically which it lost altogether when the author descended to exegesis, and applied to marriage the lesson of one evil marriage. In fine, Tolstoy is certainly not to be held up as infallible. He is very distinctly fallible, but I think his life is not less instructive because in certain things it seems a failure. There was but one life ever lived upon the earth which was without failure, and that was Christ's, whose erring and stumbling follower Tolstoy is. There is no other example, no other ideal, and the chief use of Tolstoy is to enforce this fact in our age, after nineteen centuries of hopeless endeavor to substitute ceremony for character, and the creed for the life. I recognize the truth of this without pretending to have been changed in anything but my point of view of it. What I feel sure is that I can never look at life in the mean and sordid way that I did before I read Tolstoy.

Artistically, he has shown me a greatness that he can never teach me. I am long past the age when I could wish to form myself upon another writer, and I do not think I could now insensibly take on the likeness of another; but his work has been a revelation and a delight to me, such as I am sure I can never know again. I do not believe that in the whole course of my reading, and not even in the early moment of my literary enthusiasms, I have known such utter satisfaction in any writer, and this supreme joy has come to me at a time of life when new friendships, not to say new passions, are rare and reluctant. It is as if the best wine at this high feast where I have sat so long had been kept for the last, and I need not deny a miracle in it in order to attest my skill in judging vintages. In fact, I prefer to believe that my life has been full of miracles, and that the good has always come to me at the right time, so that I could profit most by it. I believe if I had not turned the corner of my fiftieth year, when I first knew Tolstoy, I should not have been able to know him as fully as I did. He has been to me that final consciousness, which he speaks of so wisely in his essay on "Life." I came in it to the knowledge of myself in ways I had not dreamt of before, and began at least to discern my relations to the race, without which we are each nothing. The supreme art in literature had its highest effect in making me set art forever below humanity, and it is with the wish to offer the greatest homage to his heart and mind, which any man can pay another, that I close this record with the name of Lyof Tolstoy.

Source: William Dean Howells, "Tolstoy," in *My Literary Passions*, Harper & Brothers, 1895, pp. 250–58.

SOURCES

"Alexander II," Spartacus Educational website, http://www.spartacus.schoolnet.co.uk/RUSalexander2.htm (accessed August 1, 2012).

Borrero, Mauricio, "Calendar," in *Russia: A Reference Guide from the Renaissance to the Present*, Facts on File, 2004, p. 105.

Dole, Nathan Haskell, "Translator's Preface," in *The Long Exile, and Other Stories for Children*, by Lyof N. Tolstoi, Thomas Y. Crowell, 1888, pp. iii–vi.

Freeborn, Richard, "The Nineteenth Century: The Age of Realism, 1855–80," in *The Cambridge History of Russian Literature*, edited by Charles A. Moser, Cambridge University Press, 1992, pp. 248–332.

Gentes, Andre A., "Siberian Exile and the 1863 Polish Insurrectionists according to Russian Sources," in *Jahrbucher für Geschichte Osteuropas*, Vol. 51, No. 2, 2003, pp. 197–217.

"Introduction to the Orthodox Catechism," in *The Longer Catechism of the Orthodox, Catholic, Eastern Church*, Pravoslavieto, http://www.pravoslavieto.com/docs/eng/Orthodox_Catechism_of_Philaret.htm (accessed August 1, 2012).

Jahn, Gary J., "Tolstoy as a Writer of Popular Literature," in *The Cambridge Companion to Tolstoy*, edited by Donna Tussing Orwin, Cambridge University Press, 2002, pp. 113–26.

Kendall, Bridget, "Life in the Oil-Rich Siberian Town of Strezhevoy," BBC website, March 2, 2012, http://news.bbc.co.uk/today/hi/today/newsid_9701000/9701618.stm (accessed August 1, 2012).

Laver, John, "Tsarist Russia, 1856–1914," in *The Modernisation of Russia, 1856–1985*, Heinemann Educational Publishers, 2002, pp. 1–21.

McLean, Hugh, *In Quest of Tolstoy*, Academic Studies Press, 2008, pp. 87–94.

Medzhibovskaya, Inessa, *Tolstoy and the Religious Culture of His Time*, Lexington Books, 2008, pp. 131–60.

Morson, Gary Saul, "What Men Quote By: Tolstoy, Wise Sayings, and Moral Tales," in *Anniversary Essays on Tolstoy*, edited by Donna Tussing Orwin, Cambridge University Press, 2010, pp. 199–218.

"Prison Camps in Siberia," Spartacus Educational website, http://www.spartacus.schoolnet.co.uk/RUSsiberia.htm (accessed August 1, 2012).

"Profile: Vladimir Putin," BBC website, May 2, 2012, http://www.bbc.co.uk/news/world-europe-15047823 (accessed August 1, 2012).

Review of *The Long Exile, and Other Stories for Children*, in *Catalogue of Publications of the Salvation Army*, 1894, p. 60; originally published in *Scottish Leader*.

Tolstoy, Leo, "The Long Exile," in *Leo Tolstoy's Twenty Greatest Short Stories Annotated*, edited by Andrew Barger, Bottletree Books, 2009, pp. 263–72.

Wasiolek, Edward, "Leo Tolstoy," in *Dictionary of Literary Biography*, Vol. 238, *Russian Novelists in the Age of Tolstoy and Dostoevsky*, edited by J. Alexander Ogden and Judith E. Kalb, Gale Group, 2001, pp. 315–38.

Wilson, A. N., *Tolstoy: A Biography*, W. W. Norton, 1988, pp. 247–62.

FURTHER READING

Haywood, A. J., *Siberia: A Cultural History*, Oxford University Press, 2010.

Haywood surveys the history of the vast region of Siberia, focusing in some chapters on the Russian appropriation of land and villages for use as penal labor camps. The author also describes the way the region has been transformed in the post-Soviet era.

McGuckin, John Anthony, *The Orthodox Church: An Introduction to Its History, Doctrine, and Spiritual Culture*, Wiley-Blackwell, 2008.

McGuckin, a leading historian of the Orthodox faith, provides a comprehensive history of the church and explores the tenets of the faith.

Moss, Walter G., *Russia in the Age of Alexander II, Tolstoy and Dostoevsky*, Anthem Press, 2002.

Moss provides a detailed exploration of Alexander's reign and the social and political culture in which writers such as Tolstoy, Dostoyevsky, and Turgenev created their major works.

Nabokov, Vladimir, *Lectures on Russian Literature*, Harcourt, 1981.

Acclaimed Russian novelist Vladimir Nabokov presents his lectures on the work of a number of Russian authors, including Dostoyevsky, Tolstoy, Turgenev, Anton Chekhov, Maksim Gorky, and Nikolay Gogol, exploring the authors' styles and themes.

Troyat, Henri, *Tolstoy*, translated by Nancy Armphoux, Doubleday, 1967.

In this biography, Troyat offers a portrait of Tolstoy that analyzes the impact of the author's life on his major works of literature.

SUGGESTED SEARCH TERMS

Tolstoy AND The Long Exile

Tolstoy AND God Sees the Truth, but Bides His Time OR God Sees the Truth, but Waits

Tolstoy AND Russian Orthodoxy

Tolstoy AND faith

Tolstoy AND realism

Tolstoy AND Siberia

Tolstoy AND Alexander II

Tolstoy AND nineteenth-century Russian fiction

Tolstoy AND religious conversion

Tolstoy AND children's fiction

New African

ANDREA LEE

1983

"New African" is a short story by Andrea Lee about a ten-year-old African American girl confronting the ritual of baptism in her family's Philadelphia church in the early 1960s. First published in the *New Yorker* in 1983, "New African" became the foundation for a series of vignettes in the same young woman's life, which together were published as the novel *Sarah Phillips* in 1984. The novel as a whole met with uncertain responses among reviewers and in scholarly circles. Academics have noted that many of their students feel uncomfortable with the text, largely because the narrator fails to live up to conventional expectations for an African American protagonist. Rather than solidifying her black identity in the face of discrimination or oppression in the course of the novel, the light-skinned Sarah distances herself from her black identity, and she seems complicit with discriminatory attitudes.

Appearing as the second chapter of *Sarah Phillips*, "New African" comes first chronologically and thus delves deepest into the origins of Sarah's ambivalent attitude toward her blackness. However, this story is as much about religion as about race. Sarah's father is the pastor at Philadelphia's New African Baptist Church, and her aunts and other church ladies have begun pressuring her to get baptized. The story details a defining episode in Sarah's process of maturing into a freethinking individual. "New African" first appeared in the *New Yorker* issue of April 25, 1983, under the author's

Sarah is the protagonist of "New African." *(© Studio 1One | ShutterStock.com)*

married name at the time, Andrea Lee Fallows. In that version, the protagonist's name is Sarah Ashley. Presenting a nuanced reflection on the role of religion in an adolescent's life, "New African" is especially appropriate for young adults. *Sarah Phillips* was republished in 1993 with an insightful foreword by Valerie Smith as part of the "Northeastern Library of Black Literature" series.

AUTHOR BIOGRAPHY

Lee was born in 1953 in Philadelphia, Pennsylvania, where her mother was an elementary-school teacher and her father was a Baptist minister. She had one brother. When Lee was still young, the family moved to the city's suburbs. Her parents were very active in the civil rights movement; they marched in Washington, DC, and Birmingham, Alabama; participated in boycotts in Philadelphia; and through the church operated fellowship weekends, youth clubs, and work camps to support the African American community.

Lee was the only black girl at a summer camp she attended, where the white girls ostracized her with racist rhymes, and she was one of the first two African American students to attend her suburban preparatory school. There, even when fellow students did not treat her with outright prejudice, they generally excluded her, and she was regarded dismissively, as if she did not belong there, even by the white faculty. In spite of the trying environment, Lee succeeded academically, and she went on to attend Harvard University, earning a bachelor's degree and then a master's in English literature in 1973 and 1974, respectively.

Around this time Lee married Tom Fallows, a doctoral candidate in Russian history. When he gained a fellowship to study in Moscow and Leningrad, Lee went along, and her observations there would constitute her first published volume, *Russian Journal* (1981). Critically praised, *Russian Journal* earned a nomination for the American Book Award for general nonfiction that year. By this time Lee was living in Manhattan and working as a staff writer for the *New Yorker*, where two parts of *Russian Journal*

MEDIA
ADAPTATIONS

- *Sarah Phillips* was recorded as an audio-book on cassette in 1986 by the Royal Blind Society of Australia, as read by Jill McKay.

---

first appeared, and in the ensuing years she would publish in the magazine a number of stories about a maturing young African American woman much like herself. "New African" was the first to appear, in April 1983, and the stories would be collected to form the novel *Sarah Phillips* in 1984. Also around 1983, Lee began writing under her given name, as her marriage ended in the course of the decade. She had a daughter in the mid-1980s.

Through the 1990s, Lee continued to publish stories, essays, and reviews in the *New Yorker* and was also published in periodicals like the *New York Times Magazine*, *Vogue*, and *Time*. Meanwhile, she found new love with an Italian count; they married, and she bore a son around 1995. Her next book was *Interesting Women* (2002), which focuses on expatriate women living in places like Honduras, Milan and Turin in Italy—which by then she called home—and Madagascar, where she and her husband own another residence. She published the novel *Lost Hearts in Italy* in 2006, with a love-triangle plot that spans Turin, Rome, and a number of other luxurious European settings, and she has spoken of being at work on a new novel set in Madagascar.

PLOT SUMMARY

"New African" opens on a Sunday morning in the summer of 1963. The narrator, an adolescent girl, is sitting in a pew in the New African Baptist Church with her older brother, mother, and three aunts while her father, Reverend Phillips, preaches to the congregation. The reader approaching the story in the context of the

novel *Sarah Phillips* will recognize that the narrator is the title character. Sarah is restless; she glumly realizes that the baptismal service may yet last a couple of hours. She would much rather be reading or just sitting in the bushel basket she and her brother installed in a tree in their front yard, a place she finds much more agreeable. Her aunt slips her a butterscotch treat. People cool themselves with fans bearing a picture of a white Jesus.

In the narration, Sarah points out the irony of the church's name, because it was established back in 1813—and so is hardly new anymore—and now supports an African American congregation of "prosperous, conservative, generally light-skinned parishioners" who but faintly reflect their African origins. The church is in urban South Philadelphia, but most of the churchgoers, including the Phillips family, drive in from the suburbs. Sarah finds the city off-putting. She tries to joke with her brother, Matthew, but he, recently baptized and acting the part of the good son, is paying close attention to the service.

Sarah is opposed to getting baptized. She reveals that she has a secular mind-set, partly because her father's status as the pastor has made the mysteries of the church not so mysterious. She does recognize the power of the ritual of baptism, but she has not personally felt a spiritual call to undergo it, despite pressures from certain church ladies and her aunts—but not from her parents. Her aunt Lily, a teacher and surefire life-long spinster, as Sarah sees it, speaks of God like the object of a crush Sarah ought to have. As her father recites verses from Luke 3, Sarah notices him directing his voice toward the bearded white men and long-haired white women in the front row, who admire the pastor's civil rights agenda. Sarah is ambivalent toward her father's status as a down-home African American activist. His speaking style calls to Sarah's mind his clear fanaticism for demonstrating his oratorical skills, which he wields with delight over dinner at home.

The Reverend Phillips urges the congregation to listen for Jesus's advice, which they will hear if they listen closely, and to call on him in times of need. Miss Middleton occasionally exclaims "Amen!" although the congregation at large finds such outbursts of devotion distasteful. The pastor slips offstage, and the choir sings a classical selection before the lights are dimmed and the baptismal service begins. Now the choir sings "We're marching to Zion," while curtains are parted to reveal Sarah's father standing waist-deep in the baptismal pool awaiting the incoming procession of eight robed youths. Urged by her mother and church tradition, Sarah runs to the front for a better view of the ceremony, sitting on the lap of an elderly nanny of theirs, "Aunt" Bessie Gray. When her father recites the story of Jesus and John the Baptist, Sarah cannot help but feel like his disappointing child, compared to Matthew.

The choir sings "Wade in the water," swaying like a gospel chorus, as the first youth, Billy Price, descends into the pool, and Sarah thinks of the river baptisms of African Americans of yore. Billy is laid out in the water by the pastor, comes up sputtering, and is led out to change his clothes, and the other children follow suit. At the end, Sarah's father invites members of the congregation to commit to getting baptized the following month, and Bessie implores Sarah to speak up. Sarah resists, but Bessie scolds her and even tries to drag Sarah forward to volunteer (so to speak). In the darkness, they tussle in the aisle, and Sarah at last breaks free and runs back to rejoin her family, her teeth chattering from this novel victory over an adult.

Sarah's parents later say almost nothing about the incident. Sarah is obliged to apologize to Bessie, but at home she is permitted to climb up to her outpost in the maple tree and read the afternoon away. Yet she remains uneasy; she is not quite sure of the meaning of what has happened, but she avoids thinking critically about it. Still, she cannot forget the confused, uncertain look on her father's face when he found out about it. Afterward, her identity in the church shifts somehow; adults no longer pressure her to get baptized, and her parents never mention the matter again. Although she would continue attending the church even longer than Matthew would, she would remain unbaptized. In this place of religious ambiguity, she suppressed and even denied a vague sense of loss that was there nonetheless. In retrospect, Sarah realizes that her father gave her quite a gift, one of great freedom, through his silence.

CHARACTERS

Aunt Emma
Like the other two aunts in this story, Emma is Sarah's mother's sister. Aunt Emma gives Sarah the butterscotch candy.

Mrs. Gordon
In the sweltering church, Mrs. Gordon imagines that the church may not get air conditioning until the following century.

Bessie Gray
An elderly woman who sometimes sits for the Phillips children, "Aunt" Bessie is entrenched in her idealization of the ways of white people, and so she tends to grate on Sarah, who refuses to idealize anyone's ways. (Bessie's last name can be seen to signal her position in between the black and white worlds.) Especially upsetting was Bessie's insistence, one time, that Sarah wear an oversized straw hat to play in the sun, just like the white children Bessie was paid to care for did. On this day, Sarah ends up planted in Bessie's lap during the baptism ceremony, and the woman takes advantage of the situation to try to press Sarah to volunteer herself for the next baptism. When Sarah resists, Bessie makes a battle of it, trying to drag the girl up the aisle, but Sarah wriggles free and escapes. Afterward, Bessie can only glare vengefully at the girl who succeeded in defying her.

Jordan Grimes
Jordan Grimes, the choirmaster, favors classical selections like works by the German-born composer George Handel (whose *Messiah* is renowned). This sets him in opposition to the choir members, who prefer to sing folksy gospel spirituals.

Aunt Lily
A kindergarten teacher, Aunt Lily has such a "fatally overdeveloped air of quaintness" that even the young Sarah can sense that she will never find a husband. The comment about Lily's quaintness appears to speak to her absorption in the niceties and cutenesses of life, suggesting a disconnect from reality that could render genuine interaction with a man difficult. That Lily speaks about God with "an anxious, flirtatious air" further suggests the unbridgeable gap—like the gap between the human and the divine—that would mark her relations with a romantic interest.

Aunt May
Sarah's aunt May is also in the church on the day described in the story.

Miss Middleton

Although some Baptist churches might encourage outbursts of devotion during the service, the congregants at New African frown upon such religious aggression. Miss Middleton is aware of this but nonetheless defiantly shouts "Amen!" from time to time.

Matthew Phillips

Matthew, Sarah's thirteen-year-old brother, is, in the context of this story, the good son: he has already been baptized and pays respectful attention during the service, and Sarah envies how easily he goes along with the established order of things. Otherwise, the two siblings are like two of a kind, with Sarah often reporting about how "Matthew and I" do this or have experienced that together.

Mrs. Phillips

Sarah's mother is but a secondary character in this story. She is the central figure in sitting among her children and sisters in the pew, but her one and only comment comes when she directs Sarah to go sit closer to the pool. Otherwise, she neither speaks nor acts in the course of the story; only her husband is given a voice in the recalled interactions with their daughter.

Reverend Phillips

The figure of Sarah's father fairly dominates the scene portrayed—naturally, because he presides over the church's baptismal service. With her father being the figurehead of the family's religious identity, Sarah's relationship with her religion/spirituality is in a certain sense an extension of her relationship with her father, and vice versa. Interestingly, although he so loves to speak that he is described as selfishly and gleefully wielding his oratorical skills to humble his children at the dinner table, he does not impose himself on his daughter's spiritual life; he never pressures her to get baptized, neither before nor after the incident with Bessie. For this reason, the independent-minded Sarah holds her father in great esteem—although she is ultimately aware of the loss she has incurred in forgoing baptism and thus forgoing initiation into her father's and her racial kin's religious community.

Sarah Phillips

In that Sarah is both the title character and the narrator of Lee's novel, there can be little question that the focal point throughout is the process of her maturation, the development of

her sensibilities—in sum, her identity. And one of the most fundamental aspects of any person's identity is his or her spiritual/religious orientation. The story "New African" reveals various facets of Sarah's personality but centers on her spirituality—or more accurately, her religiosity, since whether or not she believes in God or any manifestation of the divine is not quite addressed. Her attitude toward baptism, colored by her failure to hear any spiritual call to undergo it, suggests that she may be agnostic (not knowing whether God exists).

In narrating this tale, Sarah makes clear that the central event—her victory over Bessie in refusing to be forced to be baptized—had great significance in her life. It was as if she were on the fence with regard to the matter, and when Bessie tried to pull her over, she fell back to the other side; Bessie's actions necessitated a definitive reaction, one that helped her determine for herself who she is. Sarah does not reject the church, but she would not feel honest submitting to a baptism that she does not feel moved to seek. Sarah also recognizes that, in declining to fully join the church, she is missing out on something. Here her thought process grinds to a halt, as she goes no further than to leave that missed-out-on something as a vague, unnamed emptiness. The reader is left to imagine what the ultimate effects of this episode on Sarah's identity will be.

Billy Price

Billy is the first youth to get baptized on this particular summer day. His staring eyes and trembling lips signify an awestruck countenance, and he aptly demonstrates the submissive role played by a person undergoing baptism.

Deacon West

A very elderly veteran of the Spanish-American War, Deacon West approves of Grimes's selection of a classical setting of Agnus Dei ("Lamb of God"). The deacon is the one to part the curtains and reveal the pastor wading/waiting in the baptismal pool.

THEMES

Adolescence

The pivotal moment depicted in this story—Sarah's battle with Bessie over committing herself to the rite of baptism—is on the one hand not an

TOPICS FOR FURTHER STUDY

- Write a short story about an event from your life that, whether recognized as significant at the time or not, proved to be a pivotal moment in your personal development or emblematic of the person you have become. Include at least a few lines of narration that consider the event retrospectively—that identify things about the event that you failed to notice or realize at first, how your understanding of the event has changed, and so forth.

- While "New African" highlights Sarah's relationship with her father, the ensuing chapter in *Sarah Phillips*, "Mother," delves into her relationship with her other parent. Read this story, which is also set during Sarah's adolescence, and write a paper comparing and contrasting what the two stories reveal about the narrator. How do her relationships with each parent and with the settings they preside over—the church and the home—reflect her engagement with the African American community, her perspective on life, her innermost desires, and other aspects of her character?

- Create a questionnaire that gauges the role of religion in your peers' lives, through at least twenty statements that can be answered quantitatively—that is, not with explanations but with *true* or *false* or choices along a range such as 1 = strongly disagree, 2 = disagree, 3 = neutral, 4 = agree, 5 = strongly agree. (Examples would be "I have been baptized," or "My family has influenced my religious orientation," or "I remember my religious coming-of-age ceremony fondly.") Be sure the questions can apply to people of various religions. Then use an online survey tool such as SurveyMonkey to conduct an anonymous survey over a broad sample and tabulate results. Create a multimedia presentation or give an oral report with visuals to communicate to your classmates the quantified results along with your own in-depth analysis of what the responses signify about the role of religion in your peer community.

- Write a research paper on the roles played by churches, religious organizations, and their leaders in the civil rights movement. Be sure to address the relevance of church doctrine; that is, in what ways did churches function primarily as community organizations, and in what ways did the precepts and ideologies of churches influence the course of the movement?

---

extraordinary event. Thanks to the darkness, few people notice the struggle, and Sarah's family members are not even aware of it until afterward. Because Sarah is the victor, the event itself is actually a nonevent: she succeeds in declining to take any action. For the adolescent Sarah, however, the event is nonetheless one of extraordinary significance. As she mentions, she had never won a victory over an adult before.

The situation was primed for this first victory. While she was sitting on Bessie's lap, Bessie was not officially taking care of Sarah at the time, diminishing her authority. Moreover, Sarah's parents had established a precedent: they were evidently committed to not pressuring their children about getting baptized, a ritual of prime significance in the Baptist Church. Thus, while Bessie tries to insist that Sarah's father wants her to get baptized, she can legitimately reply, "No, he doesn't"—he apparently does not want her to get baptized until she is moved to do so, and she is still unmoved to do so.

At the end of the story, Sarah makes clear how highly she esteems her father for giving her the freedom of choice with regard to this matter; indeed, he gave her not only freedom of choice but full freedom of thought—he never even tried to persuade her to get baptized, to use his argumentative skills to bring that conclusion about. Whether he imagined she would surely be moved eventually or was fully aware that her future baptism was no foregone conclusion, he signaled a key recognition of his daughter's maturity in leaving the decision entirely up to her.

Although Sarah admires her father's parenting approach here as a matter of ethics, she also reveals that she understands she has missed out on something by not becoming a full adult member of the church. Therefore a key question raised by the story is whether or not the father's approach to his daughter's adolescent development was ideal. Adolescents, even more than people of other ages, crave the assertion of their independence, because they are in the midst of the drawn-out process of establishing an identity distinct from their parents. The parents may yet be central role models, as Reverend Phillips evidently is for his son, Matthew. While Matthew can sit still throughout the service, Sarah's fidgeting and desire to be outside signal her own response to confinement: she wants out.

Like a stiff church pew, parental expectations, too, can instill a sense of dire confinement. Perhaps, then, Reverend Phillips's decision not to speak with his daughter about baptism preordained her response: given the freedom in this one matter to stray from what her father's hopes, if not his expectations, surely are, it is no surprise that she chooses to stray. Perhaps had he counseled her toward committing to baptism, the ritual itself would have brought about a spiritual awakening and ensured her full participation in the historic African American community represented by the New African Baptist Church.

Religion

Whereas Sarah's earlier battles with adults were all presumably about rules, demands, parental expectations, and so forth, she discovers through her victory over Bessie a realm in which even her parents cannot truly make a decision for her: the realm of religion, of spirituality. Her parents might, indeed, have tried to coax her into getting baptized, and if they had, she might have relented. However, her father, as a pastor, evidently believes that the ritual will only have the meaning it is intended to have if the person's participation is truly voluntary. Indeed, this would seem to be a key aspect of the doctrine of the Baptist Church.

The Roman Catholic Church, to the contrary, traditionally encourages the baptism of children at an early age—as early as possible, in accord with the view that if a person who has not been baptized dies, that person will not be sent to heaven. This does not really leave the child any choice in the matter, and also, the child may lack the consciousness for the baptism itself to hold personal or spiritual significance. To become a full adult member of the Catholic Church, one is yet expected to undergo "confirmation," but this staid ritual lacks the experiential significance of the act of baptism as depicted in "New African"—of total submersion in sanctified water in submission to a pastor whose words mark the occasion. The Catholic child can remember little of a baptism before the age of four; the Baptist child will likely carry the experience of the ritual, sharply etched in the adolescent's acutely aware mind, for the rest of one's life.

Sarah, as narrator, acknowledges the undeniable significance of the ritual of baptism, even if she is not moved to undergo it herself. Her comments suggest that, thanks to her parents' open-mindedness, she was enabled to realize that religion without a foundation of spirituality is a hollow religion. However, in lamenting the sense of loss that her lack of religion has left her, Sarah suggests that it is unfortunate that, in excluding herself from religion, as a side effect she has also excluded herself from the community that the church provides.

African American Culture

As narrator, Sarah does not make a point of analyzing how her perceptions of African American culture and the black community have affected her personal development. However, she makes a number of minor comments that hint at her perspective and suggest to the reader a complex dynamic between African American culture at large and her identity as an African American woman. For example, early in the story, she reveals her ambivalent feelings toward the church, which is aesthetically pleasing and where the Phillips children are treated like royalty, but which is also "like a dreadful old relative" who necessitates "tedious visits" and who speaks to "a past that came to seem embarrassingly primitive as we grew older."

Primitive, of course, is a very strong characterization, especially as the reader may be surprised to find an African American using a word that white people have historically used to disparage

Sarah's father is the pastor of the New African Baptist Church. *(© bikeriderlondon | ShutterStock.com)*

indigenous origins. Although Sarah does not directly state as much in this chapter of *Sarah Phillips*, she reveals in the first chapter that she, like much of the rest of the New African congregation, is African American but "light-skinned." This fact perhaps allows her to willingly distance herself from the aspects of African American history that she finds distasteful—or "primitive," a word that may actually indicate she perceives all religion, not just African American religion, as such.

When Sarah later suggests that her mother and aunts perceive Miss Middleton's outbursts of devotion as "incomprehensibly barbarous," the reader is left to wonder the extent to which the child has adopted the mother's perspective; the word *barbarous* accurately echoes Sarah's own description of the church as *primitive*. Still later, Sarah does express accord with her mother's characterization of Bessie Gray as "archaic"—as reflecting a shameful phase in African American history when the admiration of white culture was acceptable. Although similar in tone to the words *primitive* and *barbarous*, the word *archaic* as used here actually suggests that Sarah has positive associations with her identity as African American and resents Bessie's orientation toward white culture.

However, Sarah's dismissal of Bessie's pro-white posturing does not prefigure a pro-black stance in any other regard; it is simply one more instance where she is distancing herself from a portion of the African American past. For the reader of the entirety of the novel, the reasons for this distancing are made more clear; for the reader of "New African" alone, Lee provides a delicately balanced portrait of a black adolescent whose ambivalent acceptance of her own blackness both precipitates and is signified by her refusal to be baptized in the New African Baptist Church.

STYLE

Vignette

The chapters/stories contained in Lee's novel *Sarah Phillips* are often referred to as *vignettes*, a word that signals the unique relationship they have to each other and to the novel as a whole. Most of these vignettes, including "New African," were originally published as individual pieces in the *New Yorker*, and they indeed function well as independent stories. The reader of "New African" is given ample information about Sarah's life to appreciate the significance of the episode it treats, and one might even argue that the story functions best this way, alone, because the reader is able to consider the story's themes as uncluttered by the concerns of the broader plot of the novel. That is, the reader can appreciate the significance of this precise moment in Sarah's life without being obliged to draw conclusions about precisely how it affects or reflects her personal development, as evidenced in other chapters. Many short stories are effective in such a manner: they portray an intense, significant episode without defining the precise direction that it gives to the person's life. This open-endedness leaves the reader more room to imagine what the repercussions of the episode might be; instead of being defined by author-imposed facts, the story is defined by possibilities.

Nevertheless, "New African" remains a constituent part of the novel *Sarah Phillips*, and to fully appreciate Lee's literary intentions with regard to this one story, the entire novel ought to be read. "New African" appears as the book's second chapter but chronologically speaking comes first, while the opening chapter, "In France," is chronologically the last. Sarah relates in "In France" how in 1974, after graduating from Harvard, she ended up in Paris living with a young man named Henri and a couple of his friends (in sexually liberated circumstances). The story reveals that Sarah is compromising her identity in associating with Henri, whose true attitude toward her is indicated by the crude racist caricature he employs in a whimsical fictionalization of her mixed-race origins. Both as an African American and as a woman, Sarah is submitting to subjugation and even humiliation in remaining with Henri. By the end of the story, she is determined to enact a "complicated return" to her origins in Philadelphia.

Thus, put simply, "In France" frames the entire remainder of *Sarah Phillips* as the story of how Sarah turned her back on her family's community and her African American identity, only to be made aware of her folly and turn back toward home. As such, where "New African," read alone, is ambivalent about Sarah's acceptance of her African American identity, in the context of *Sarah Phillips*, the reader already knows that Sarah not only strays from her origins but strays too far. She remarks herself in "In France" that her life there was marked by "the experimental naughtiness of children reacting against their training." A dream of Sarah's reveals that subconsciously she is still engaged in a

> monotonous struggle with an old woman with a dreadful spidery strength in her arms; her skin was dark and leathery, and she smelled like one of the old Philadelphia churchwomen who used to babysit with me.

The reader of the novel soon discovers, of course, that this is the spitting image of Bessie Gray. While the struggle in "New African" suggests that Sarah is enabled to put the idea of baptism and the specter of Bessie Gray behind her, "In France" reveals that she has done nothing of the sort; that struggle is still weighing on her mind over a decade later. By virtue of the revelations in the first chapter of *Sarah Phillips*, implicit in the later chapters is a careful critique of the thought processes that led her to where she ended up. In this context, the events of "New African" are all the more poignant.

Postmodernism

The story "New African" and more especially the novel *Sarah Phillips* as a whole are structured in such a way that a postmodern reading is not only fruitful but perhaps necessary for the fiction to be fully appreciated. From the perspective of modernism, the novel can be seen as something of a disappointment, as W. Lawrence Hogue argues in "The Limits of Modernity: Andrea Lee's *Sarah Phillips*." Hogue notes that a central facet of literary modernism is a protagonist's rejection of historical precedent in the interest of fashioning a unique self. In his words, "An individual infused with the modernist impulse wants emancipation from all traditional social roles and traditional modes of servitude because they keep the self stifled and imprisoned." This is indeed an accurate description of the character of Sarah Phillips, as witnessed in the story "New African": at any sign of African American tradition, she seems intent to turn in the opposite direction—but not toward anything else in particular.

If "New African" is considered as a short story, the open-endedness of Sarah's lack of direction can be seen as part of the short-story territory; the reader does not expect full closure or resolution with regard to Sarah's identity. However, if the novel as a whole is considered—and from a modernist perspective, as Hogue views it—the fact that Sarah never achieves an original and sustainable sense of direction is a sign of failure. As revealed in

"In France," Sarah figuratively meanders out into the middle of an ideological nowhere, and then, when she realizes the meaninglessness of that nowhere, simply heads back home. Hogue interprets Sarah's seeming failure as also being the author's failure—as indicating that "Andrea Lee lacks the vision to develop Sarah's own style, to refashion her consciousness, and to have her live an existential, authentic existence."

Adrienne McCormick offers a rebuttal to Hogue's position in her essay "Is This Resistance? African-American Postmodernism in *Sarah Phillips*." McCormick argues that, rather than expecting Sarah to gain a definitive understanding of her identity within the bounds of the novel, the reader should recognize that her flaws, which themselves are made evident, are what prevent her from doing so. That a protagonist's experiences should fail to culminate in the achievement of an improved self-identity may be a disappointment from a modernist perspective, but it fits well with a postmodern perspective. As McCormick notes, "Literary postmodernism resists definitions, but can be identified through such characteristics as disjunction, open-endedness, misinterpretation, dispersal, and indeterminacy."

Such characteristics are evident throughout *Sarah Phillips*, including in "New African." Disjunction is seen in Sarah's decision to separate herself from the church by refusing baptism. Open-endedness is precisely the result of this disjunction, because instead of a predetermined existence as a dutiful Christian, Sarah is free to let her impulses direct her experiences. There are hints of misinterpretation in Sarah's comments about the "primitive" and "barbarous" nature of the church and the devotional practices of the likes of Miss Middleton; the reader can see that her opinions are colored not by a true understanding of the roots of spirituality but by her status as an upper-class, secular-minded, light-skinned African American.

Ultimately, the novel leaves Sarah in the very state of disjunction, misinterpretation, and indeterminacy that she inhabits at the end of "New African." Even if Sarah's inability to achieve a resolution of identity is seen as a failure, "her failure is not necessarily the novel's failure as well," as McCormick asserts. Rather, in the critic's view, the novel as a whole and "New African" as a part should be seen as "exemplifying a postmodern tension between the old and the new—the old, black

bourgeoisie and the new, black escapee (if you will) typified by Sarah." The success of Lee's fiction should not be seen to depend upon the resolution of this tension.

HISTORICAL CONTEXT

Post-integration America

"New African" is set in 1963, when the civil rights movement was reaching its peak, although the story makes only glancing mention of, and bears only a glancing relation to, that movement. The broader historical period in question here may be said to have begun in 1954, when the Supreme Court delivered its historic decision in *Brown v. Board of Education of Topeka*, declaring that "separate but equal" was no longer a legitimate doctrine in public schools; for educational institutions to truly be equal, segregation had to end. The process of integration was a prolonged one, with many southern political figures defiantly refusing to comply. The National Association for the Advancement of Colored People (NAACP), which had initiated the *Brown* suit, was besieged by political attacks and manipulations and suffered the closure of some 246 branches in the South. Subsequently, black churches increased their roles in the ongoing movement, supplying meeting spaces, fund raising, and organizational support. The central religious organization in the movement was Martin Luther King Jr.'s Southern Christian Leadership Conference.

In "New African," Sarah mentions her reverend father's participation in the civil rights movement, but she reveals her own profound emotional dissociation from the movement when she admits that she is "privately embarrassed" to have a father who was jailed in Alabama. Because a majority of African Americans took great pride in the bravery, sacrifices, and accomplishments of civil rights leaders and fighters, Sarah's comment must strike many readers as surprising, but it reflects the facts of her family's circumstances: living in a well-to-do suburb in a northern city far from the flashpoints in the South, this adolescent girl, as with most adolescents, is primarily concerned with her immediate surroundings, and racial turmoil is not part of them. In eloquent wording that seems to reveal an absence of sympathy for those who lived—

COMPARE & CONTRAST

- **1960s:** As of 1960, 23.3 percent of Philadelphia's population is African American, clustered in ghettos in the districts of North Philadelphia, Germantown–Mount Airy, West Philadelphia, and South Philadelphia. The overall population, now at 2 million, is shrinking, as higher-earning residents—especially whites after a riot in 1964—leave for the suburbs.

- **1980s:** As of 1980, around 35 percent of Philadelphians are African American, including proportions ranging from 53 to 70 percent in the most concentrated districts. The total population continues to decline, passing below 1.7 million.

  Today: As of 2000, the demographics of Philadelphia continue to represent the tendency of people of similar race to cluster together and also the differences in income between those in urban and suburban areas. Regarding income, 12 percent of households in urban centers have income over $75,000, whereas 50 percent of suburban households earn as much. African Americans account for some 44 percent of the city's population of just over 1.5 million—a figure whose decline has finally stopped.

- **1960s:** Following the death of Zora Neale Hurston in 1960, few female African American authors, other than Pulitzer Prize–winner Gwendolyn Brooks, reach wide literary audiences. As the decade closes, Maya Angelou (future presidential-inauguration poet), Toni Morrison (future Nobel Prize winner), and Nikki Giovanni (future poet laureate) are all actively writing.

- **1980s:** Alice Walker wins the 1983 Pulitzer Prize for *The Color Purple*. Andrea Lee surfaces as a potentially significant black voice, but *Sarah Phillips* proves her last extensive fictional foray into life in a black community.

  Today: While the likes of Angelou and Morrison still carry the most literary prestige among African Americans, many significant new black voices are emerging from elsewhere, including Edwidge Danticat of Haiti, Zadie Smith of Great Britain, and Chimamanda Adichie of Nigeria.

- **1960s:** The primary goal of the civil rights movement is achieved with the passage of the Civil Rights Act of 1964, and subsequent legislation bolsters African American rights. With Malcolm X and Martin Luther King Jr. assassinated in the course of the decade, no leader of equivalent charisma appears to direct efforts for black advancement.

- **1980s:** While Ronald Reagan's trickle-down economics policies infamously start a decades-long trend where the wealthiest will gain ever-greater shares of the nation's wealth—to the particular disadvantage of impoverished urban populations—black figures make political inroads to greater social equality, with Jesse Jackson running for president and L. Douglas Wilder of Virginia becoming the first elected black governor.

  Today: Although George W. Bush's policies exacerbated the widening gap between rich and poor, African Americans are continuing a trickle-down process of societal advancement, with unequaled power held by such figures as media mogul Oprah Winfrey and President Barack Obama, to the increasing advantage of the black population.

and sometimes died—for the betterment of the African American race, Sarah refers to the famed southern civil rights battlegrounds of Selma, Birmingham, Macon, and Biloxi as "towns I imagined as being swathed in a mist of darkness visible." Indeed, that "darkness" seems

"New African," the second chapter in Sarah Phillips, *involves the New African Baptist Church in Philadelphia.* *(© Jason Tench / ShutterStock.com)*

to signify Sarah's failure to visualize those places and empathize with the black people there.

In distancing herself as early as 1963 from the greater African American community in large part because of her family's upper-middle-class status, Sarah was a bit ahead of her time. The notion of black uplift, or black class advancement, was hailed in the early twentieth century by figures such as W. E. B. Du Bois and Booker T. Washington, who recognized that a black upper class would be in a prime position to help raise the living standards of lower-class blacks as well. Throughout the civil rights movement, class differences among African Americans were generally overlooked for the sake of full racial solidarity. However, as the movement achieved closure with the passage of the Civil Rights Act of 1964 and the Voting Rights Act of 1965, upper-class blacks became more willing to distinguish themselves from their poorer brethren by focusing less on racial equality and more on their own upper-class interests.

In the opening story of *Sarah Phillips*, "In France," Sarah's narration cuttingly characterizes

such upper-class blacks, dubbed "the old-fashioned black bourgeoisie," as a group

which has carried on with cautious pomp for years in eastern cities and suburbs, using its considerable funds to attempt poignant imitations of high society, acting with genuine gallantry in the struggle for civil rights, and finally producing a generation of children educated in newly integrated schools and impatient to escape the outworn rituals of their parents.

The reader likely recognizes Sarah as precisely one of these "impatient" children with the social leeway to consider their parents' essential civil rights activism as no more than played-out "rituals," a word that here suggests something done not out of internal motivation but merely for the sake of doing it. Such dismissive attitudes among higher-class blacks toward the interests and activities of mainstream African Americans would not go unnoticed within the national community. Part of the Black Power ideology of the late 1960s was the notion that upwardly mobile blacks were traitorously abandoning the race in seeking to "become white" by succeeding in a capitalist system still dominated by white interests.

Such accusations were intended not simply as attacks on upper-class blacks but as motivations to reestablish class-blind African American solidarity. The militant aspects of the Black Power movement—as represented by such controversial groups as the Black Panthers, who were violently suppressed by the police and FBI—contributed to a decline in support for black nationalist sentiment. By the 1980s, the era when Lee was writing "New African" and the other stories of *Sarah Phillips*, the broader culture of the United States had shifted toward materialism and consumerism, and upper-class African Americans were not exempt from the era's prevailing mores. In an elite publication like the *New Yorker*, Lee's class-conscious, racially indifferent young Sarah could be welcomed by a primarily white readership with aplomb.

CRITICAL OVERVIEW

Initial reviews of *Sarah Phillips* sounded various notes in considering the literary value of the work. In the *New York Times*, Christopher Lehmann-Haupt declares that Lee's novel is marked by "eloquence and brilliant clarity of detail," but he is disappointed that the novel does not relate Sarah's return from Europe to Philadelphia—where the action finishes in "In France"—because it seems to suggest that Lee told an autobiographical story, based on memory, but could not use her imagination to bring the action to a satisfying resolution. In Lehmann-Haupt's opinion, the novel suggests that for Lee, "straightforward autobiography is more useful to her than fiction."

Susan Richards Shreve, in the *New York Times Book Review*, takes this perspective a step further, asserting that "the stories read like an unsentimental autobiography," in which the reader "is struck by the sometimes chilling objectivity Sarah has toward her life." The reviewer adds that because of "Sarah's intellectual distance, . . . we don't know her well enough to be moved deeply by her insights." Still, Shreve notes that Lee aptly demonstrates "an unstinting honesty and a style at once simple and yet luminous."

More critical was Laura Obolensky in the *New Republic*. She remarks, "*Sarah Phillips* makes for a disconcerting read. . . . What remain deeply troublesome sociological issues are treated tangentially, or with a tone of detachment often bordering on the sardonic." Obolensky concludes that Lee's novel reveals little more than

> that affluence is a powerful equalizer—that no matter how adept the irony, and no matter what her ethnicity, a young lady who behaves like an elitist snob and thinks like an elitist snob is an elitist snob.

In her 1989 essay "Black Feminist Theory," Valerie Smith likewise zeros in on the novel's classist implications. She notes that the mere fact that the stories originally appeared in the *New Yorker* reflects that "in at least one way this is a text of privilege." She cites two initial reviewers who saw this privilege reflected in the contents as well: Mary Helen Washington, in the *Women's Review of Books*, stated that after reading a few stories, she "felt that the privileged kid had become the privileged narrator, no longer willing to struggle over issues of race and class, unable to bear the 'alarming knowledge' that these issues must reveal." And Sherley Anne Williams, in *Ms.*, lamented that Lee's narration mocks "the 'outworn rituals' of black community" instead of a more suitable target, "the pretensions of her upper middle class heroine."

Providing the foreword for the 1993 reissue of the novel, Smith had to acknowledge that it is not "an especially popular work. . . . Moreover, when I have taught *Sarah Phillips* in undergraduate classes, I have found that it disconcerts my students." She defends the writing, however, noting that "Lee's characters are complexly drawn, her descriptions evocative and nuanced, her sensibility both haunting and ironic." What causes her students' "discomfiture," it seems, is the fact that the novel "exposes and undermines many of the expectations that readers typically bring to a work written by a U.S. black writer."

Donald B. Gibson echoed these sentiments in responding to the book's reissue in the *African American Review*. He notes that his own students, in fact, "were openly hostile and angry—to the extent that I was barely able to conduct a rational discussion." (The first chapter, especially, provoked such reactions.) Gibson sees these responses as evidence that "there must be something very worthwhile talking about in *Sarah Phillips*." Gibson focuses on "New African," which he considers "the center of the novel," as the greater plot hinges on the fact that the battle with Bessie Gray that Sarah supposedly wins is in reality no victory at all, because Sarah is still grappling in her dreams with the specter of Bessie Gray more than a decade later, as dramatized in "In France." In considering the juxtaposition of the first two chapters, Gibson notes how "in some profound ways the novel shows the price to be paid for rejecting the racial past, the resulting disrespect of self and the crushing diminishment of self-esteem." Gibson proceeds to assert,

> The book is far more complicated than it at first appears. . . . The author is firmly aware of the tensions produced by the intersections of race, class, and color. The novel is something of a confessional enterprise, in which the author acknowledges the stress and guilt resulting . . . from her failure to embrace her African past.

Gibson concludes that *Sarah Phillips* is "a novel to be reckoned with."

CRITICISM

Michael Allen Holmes

Holmes is a writer with existential interests. In the following essay, he considers how the incidental details of "New African" suggest that beneath Sarah's indifference toward African American culture is a subconscious yearning to connect with the African past.

Andrea Lee's *Sarah Phillips* is a curious book, and therein "New African" is a curious story. Lee presents in the novel's first chapter, "In France," the eponymous narrator, who finds that she has strayed too far from her African American, Baptist, Philadelphia-based roots and must enact a "complicated return" home. Even as this story concludes, the reader is left unsure of the extent to which the author truly feels a profound internal connection with her family and home community. In fact, the author proves so uncritical of the past actions that led her to this seeming existential dead-end that the reader of the second story alone, "New African," can be forgiven for thinking that the narrator is not critiquing but celebrating the victory she achieved in resolving not to get baptized by her pastor father in the New African Baptist Church.

In a couple of passages of narration, Sarah does seem to lament her victory. Afterward, she remarks, "I felt a vague uneasiness floating in the back of my mind—a sense of having misplaced something, of being myself misplaced." And in retrospect she is aware of "a feeling of loss that I was too proud ever to acknowledge." She avoids

> ❝ ALTHOUGH THE STORY MAKES CLEAR THAT SARAH IS AMBIVALENT TOWARD THE AFRICAN AMERICAN CULTURE SHE HAILS FROM, WHAT IS IMPOSSIBLE TO DETERMINE IS WHETHER SHE IS RESPONDING DIRECTLY TO THE CULTURE AS SHE UNDERSTANDS IT OR INDIRECTLY TO THE WHITE CULTURE THAT LIES BEHIND IT. ❞

scrutinizing these feelings, stating, "I was holding myself quite aloof from considering what had happened, as I did with most serious events." Indeed, the reader may feel that not just in those moments but also as a narrator more than ten years later, Sarah fails to adequately consider her own experiences.

This is seen as a failing by some critics, but others recognize a postmodern open-endedness that in a sense obligates the reader to fill in the blanks—to do the psychological footwork, so to speak, on the narrator's behalf. Such a perspective suggests that a nuanced reading of "New African," chronologically the novel's foundational story (in terms of both the plot and the course of publication), could shed light on why Sarah is so frustratingly ambivalent toward her African American identity. Is she simply indifferent by virtue of her class privilege? Or might some more nuanced process be at work?

If one is looking to build a psychological profile of Sarah, certain details in "New African" stand out. The opening paragraph, in setting the scene, reveals little more than that Sarah is restless—hardly a unique quality in a ten-year-old stuck in church. Interestingly, though she spends the bulk of the paragraph describing how hot the building is, she does so only through other people's reactions to it: the elderly Mrs. Gordon laments the lack of air conditioning, while her pastor father "mopped his brow with a handkerchief and drank several glasses of ice water." Sarah herself, however, appears to be completely unfazed by the heat.

As she snaps the elastic strap of her straw hat against her chin, it becomes clear that what this girl needs is some ordinary juvenile stimulation.

WHAT DO I READ NEXT?

- The reader of *Sarah Phillips* might turn next to Lee's collection *Interesting Women* (2002), containing stories—also drawn from Lee's own experiences—mainly about African American women traveling in Europe and beyond, with a consistent focus on their relationships with the men in their lives.

- A nineteenth-century treatment of the intersection between class and race can be found in Frances E. W. Harper's *Iola Leroy* (1892), about a light-skinned African American who is raised as white but later sold into slavery. In response, Iola becomes a public voice for African Americans and also takes a position on the mixing of the races.

- Harlem Renaissance–era author Nella Larsen wrote a semiautobiographical novel titled *Quicksand* (1928) that portrays the experiences of a woman of mixed race, with a Danish mother and West Indian father, as she alternately gravitates toward and distances herself from both white and black communities.

- Larsen also wrote the highly regarded novel *Passing* (1929), which presents two childhood friends with both European and African lineage who grow up to lead opposite lives, with one passing as white and marrying a white racist, the other marrying a black doctor. They reunite as adults with dramatic consequences.

- In his autobiography *The Big Sea* (1940), seminal black author Langston Hughes relates the early years of his life, including a pivotal moment when he feigned religious salvation and in that moment definitively lost faith.

- Toni Morrison's *Song of Solomon* (1977) tells of a character called Milkman who, like Sarah, rejects the community signified by his parents, but who consciously looks further back in history in crafting a new identity for himself.

- Sharon G. Flake's debut novel for middle graders, *The Skin I'm In* (2007), juxtaposes the concerns of an intelligent and especially dark-skinned African American girl who has difficulty responding to teasing with the self-assurance of a black teacher with a glaring white birthmark on her face.

- A story that provides a nuanced treatment of the interplay between African culture and white religion is "Dead Men's Path," by famed Nigerian author Chinua Achebe, found in his collection *Girls at War and Other Stories* (1972).

She states, "What I would really like to do, I decided, would be to go home, put on my shorts, and climb up into the tree house I had set up the day before." In other words, she wants to be dressed in comfortable clothes that allow ease of movement, to be outside close to nature, and to get the visceral thrill of elevating herself off the ground. A tree house need not be especially high to invoke the sense that a fall would cause serious injury; that Sarah wishes to just sit and gaze around the neighborhood or perhaps read up in her tree house suggests that she craves a constant sense of visceral engagement with reality, even while remaining sedentary. Along these lines, her offhand comment that in the tree house one can "sit comfortably, except for a few splinters," suggests an indifference to mild physical pain—as if the prick of a splinter may even be welcome as a reminder of her visceral engagement with reality. Her ensuing comments support the notion that she craves activity in the natural world:

> There was shade and wind and a feeling of high adventure up in the treetop, where the air seemed to vibrate with the dry rhythms of the cicadas; it was as different as possible from the church, where the packed congregation sat in a

near-visible miasma of emotion and cologne, and trolleys passing in the city street outside set the stained-glass windows rattling.

In this understated description, what Sarah singles out as objectionable inside the church are the lack of freedom of movement; the enforced state of simply listening and feeling, rather than doing or sensing; the artificial scents worn by the parishioners; the urban mechanical vehicles causing disruptive vibrations; and the windows that allow no view to the outside world. As "civilized" as this girl is by virtue of her class standing, she seems to have antipathy toward the very trappings of civilization that surround her. This church, of course, where Sarah's father is the pastor, is recognized as signifying the greater African American community, so when Sarah turns her back on the church, this is often read as Sarah's turning her back on the African American community. Thus far, however, the fact that this church is a place of African American community seems less relevant than the fact that it is a restrictive facet of the broader civilization.

Indeed, however quintessentially African American the New African Baptist Church may be, one can hardly say that it is quintessentially African. When Africans were first brought to the Americas as slaves, few had already been persuaded by missionaries to abandon their traditional religious practices. But with many tribes already believing in a single uppermost or creation god, both Islam and Christianity ultimately gained substantial followings in West Africa. Among the earliest generations of African Americans, meanwhile, most were converted, at least nominally, to Christianity. (Elsewhere in the Americas, religions like Cuba's Santeria were formed when African descendants combined traditional and Western religious practices; Santeria recognizes Roman Catholic saints as embodiments of Yoruba deities.)

In sum, as Sarah herself remarks, "There was little that was . . . very African about the New African Baptist Church." Rather, the church represents a community that has drifted and drawn ever closer to the white culture within which it is subsumed. Adopting Anglo-American materialist values, Sarah's mother and aunts have "a weakness for elegant footwear and French perfume." Everyone waves fans bearing a picture of "a hollow-eyed blond Christ holding three fat pink-cheeked children"; as for the church's "few dozen fans bearing the picture of a black child praying," Sarah "rarely

saw those in use." Sarah's aunt Lily's face is visibly covered with "powder, which was, in accordance with the custom of fashionable colored ladies, several shades lighter than her olive skin." The woman who proves Sarah's nemesis in this episode, Bessie Gray, more than any other character signifies the emulation of white culture, in that she takes excessive pride in the rich children she is paid to care for—"her 'white children,' to whom she often unflatteringly compared" Sarah and her brother.

Although the story makes clear that Sarah is ambivalent toward the African American culture she hails from, what is impossible to determine is whether she is responding directly to the culture as she understands it or indirectly to the white culture that lies behind it. Sarah does seem to make a point of noting the colors—or lack thereof—in which the church participants enshroud themselves. Invoking positive flower imagery, she notes that her father "wore white robes, and . . . the heavy material fell in curving folds like the ridged petals of an Easter lily." Meanwhile, Sarah reports a slightly negative impression of the "somber crescent of dark-suited deacons." Emulating the pastor, the children getting baptized "wore white robes, the girls with white ribbons in their hair," but Sarah cannot help but note how "stiff and self-conscious" they look. When she envisions the river baptisms of the southern slaves of the past, the qualities of the colors are telling:

> They walked silently in lines, their faces very black against their white clothes, leading their children. The whole scene was bathed in the heavy golden light that meant age and solemnity, the same light that seemed to weigh down the Israelites in illustrated volumes of Bible stories, and that shone now from the baptismal pool.

Sarah repeatedly notes the juxtaposition of black and white in the religious imagery; this, together with her conception of divine light as "heavy," suggests that she perceives the black emulation of white culture, as seen foremost in the black adoption of white religious practices, as not beneficial but burdensome. She has no interest in shrouding her own self in the (white) stiffness and self-consciousness that Christianity and the ritual of baptism appear to impart.

What does Sarah want, then? She does not wish to get baptized, yet she recognizes that she is missing out on something in declining that rite. What she is missing is most readily identified as full participation in African American culture, as signified by full membership in the church. However, her narration suggests that she does not regret the distance she places between herself and the white-inflected culture of her light-skinned black forebears. Perhaps what she regrets missing out on, then, is not the set of cultural implications that baptism represents but simply the ritual itself. The narration takes on its most reverent tones when Sarah admits that "there was an unassailable magic about an act as public and dramatic as baptism."

Magic, of course, is not a word that Christians typically apply to their own religious rituals. A clergyman would surely prefer to refer to baptism as, for example, "spiritual," "miraculous," "redemptive," "holy," or "divine." Magic, rather, is the realm of certain traditional African religions, which gave rise to such New World practices as voodoo—also termed *vodou, vodun,* or *vodoun*—in Haiti. One might expect a character like Sarah Phillips, who dismisses the African American religious past as "embarrassingly primitive," to have no belief in magic, but she consciously realizes that in rituals like baptism, however much one rationally understands the components of the rite, "there is still something indefinable in the power that makes it a cohesive whole." The ritual as a whole is one that "fascinated and disturbed" her.

The reader learns little more regarding Sarah's sense of the magical within this story, but the author, at least, has revealed her own inclination toward the wondrous side of life. In an interview with *People* magazine about her nonfiction volume *Russian Journal* in 1981, she responded to the question "How did the country first strike you?" by remarking,

> There is an utterly undramatic landscape where we were in Russia, but there's some powerful magic in the forests. All the Russian fairy tales came flooding back to me. The skies are also stunning, with gorgeous sunsets, capricious thunderstorms and towering billows of clouds.

Her initial impressions of this foreign land, then, revolved around the veritably magical essence of the land itself, which is embodied in the nation's fairy tales and which goes hand in hand with the grandest features of the natural world. In a 2006 interview with Milena Vercellino for the *American*, she similarly noted, "What I like to investigate when I write is what people dream about.... What fascinates me is fantasy, the dream of being away, the state of being foreign, of being apart." Being an African American from Philadelphia, Lee proved her

The irony in Lee's stories are that the struggle for racial identity and equality take place in the "city of brotherly love" and the home of the symbols of American freedom and equality. *(© Racheal Grazias / ShutterStock.com)*

need for the foreign in becoming an expatriate who calls Italy home. Yet she did not stop there; as she told Vercellino, "My husband and I built a house on an island off Madagascar and spend a lot of time there, especially in the summer.... It's a remote place, where people go to get lost." All these thoughts idealizing natural, adventurous, dreamlike, fantastic places call to mind Sarah's remarks in "New African" when her wish to be up in her tree house is finally fulfilled:

> In those days, more than now, I fell away into a remote dimension whenever I opened a book; that afternoon, as I sat with rings of sunlight and shadow moving over my arms and legs, and winged yellow seeds plopping down on the pages of *The Story of the Treasure Seekers*....

The reader cannot help but conclude that Sarah Phillips truly does represent Andrea Lee. Sarah relates that her "legs were skinny and wiry, the legs of a ten-year-old amazon, scarred from violent adventures with bicycles and skates"; what a young woman like this wants is a return to a viscerally engaged style of life, one that she happens to associate with mythological

Greek warrior women rather than with any warrior women from Africa (presumably in light of what she has studied in school).

Sarah Phillips as a whole suggests that Sarah needs to enact a "complicated return" to her African American origins, yet critics have lamented that this return goes undramatized. Perhaps the reason why Lee did not dramatize this return is because a successful return to her origins is not, after all, what she envisioned the character to be destined for. The reader can easily imagine that, like Lee herself, the character of Sarah Phillips, if imagined far ahead into her future, ends up not back home entrenched in the culture she drifted away from, but further back in her racial past, and farther away from home, united with an indigenous African milieu in all its natural, magical glory.

Source: Michael Allen Holmes, Critical Essay on "New African," in *Short Stories for Students*, Gale, Cengage Learning, 2013.

Donald B. Gibson

In the following review, Gibson notes how the novel Sarah Phillips *incites feelings of consternation, discomfort, and tension, which make it "a novel to be reckoned with."*

Andrea Lee's 1984 book *Sarah Phillips*, brilliantly introduced in its new incarnation by Valerie Smith, is one of several out-of-print titles to appear in the Northeastern Library of Black Literature. The general editor of the series, Richard Yarborough, has chosen to bring back, for reasons that will be apparent in this review, a work out of print for less than ten years. The "novel," best called that in my view—though its sections, as Smith points out, were initially published as vignettes in the *New Yorker*—centers around a single life and moves from one point in time, 1963, to another, 1974, in the autobiographical narrator's life from age ten to twenty-one.

The reactions of my students to Lee's novel have not been unlike those of Smith's, who were "disconcerted" and "discomfited" by it. In fact, my students were openly hostile and angry—to the extent that I was barely able to conduct a rational discussion. Their aversion led me to conclude that, while the text does not lend itself to the classroom, there must be something very worthwhile talking about in *Sarah Phillips* if the text could trigger responses so utterly different from those generated by works of Gloria Naylor,

> THE FIRST CHAPTER, 'IN FRANCE,' SHOWS US THE HORRIBLE RESULTS STEMMING FROM HER REJECTION OF HER RACIAL PAST. THE SECOND, 'NEW AFRICAN,' REVEALS THE PRIMAL SOURCE OF HER INTOLERABLE AND UNBEARABLE SITUATION IN THE WORLD."

Paule Marshall, Ann Petry, and Toni Morrison. For this reason alone I am most grateful to see the novel back in print.

One of the complaints of long standing among many African American readers of African American literature has been that the general reading population has not been interested in reading about black people, other than characters whose lives are totally consumed by race, and thus distorted—characters who are somehow stunted or less than whole individuals. Where in the literature, it has frequently been asked, is the voice of the well-fed, non-abused, physically healthy African American individual who grows up in a house with neither rats nor roaches, with both a father and mother to love her and a reasonably supportive community? Yet contrary to Mary Helen Washington's prediction that "a novel by a black writer which exalts class privilege and ignores racism is bound to find wide acceptance," Andrea Lee's novel, insofar as it does those things, has been clutched with fond regard to few bosoms. I would argue, along with Val Smith, that we need to explore this text because of what it reveals about the intersection of class values with those of color and race. If, as has been so frequently asserted, the black middle class, in achieving its socioeconomic goals, has traditionally abandoned the working and non-working (frequently unemployed these days) classes, then we should not shun a book that shows us something about that relationship. We should read it, study it, discuss it—not act as though it and whatever phenomena it represents do not exist. Whereas I believe there to be something in what Washington says about the novel, her words need tempering for, as Smith concludes in her foreword, "*Sarah Phillips* promises to shed light upon middle-class African American life in the second half of the twentieth century."

The center of the novel, and the section I will concentrate my brief comments on, is the second chapter—chronologically earliest in time—titled "New African," for there the primary focus of the book, the relation of Sarah Phillips to African American history and culture, is addressed. Everything else in the novel surrounds this point in time, even the first chapter, which takes place long afterward, at the furthest reach of the novel's duration. The tension between the perspective of the retrospective narrator and the character is signaled by the bold and daring effrontery of the challenging, defying, and extraordinarily self-deprecating assertions of the narrator as she declares her existence to the reader:

> The previous June I had graduated from Harvard, having just turned twenty-one. I was tall and lanky and light-skinned, quite pretty in a nervous sort of way; I came out of college equipped with an unfocused snobbery, vague literary aspirations, and a lively appetite for white boys.

The "lively appetite for white boys" sets her at odds with her history only if she sees herself as African American, for knowledge and understanding of the African American past—the casual wholesale rape by white males of African American females—does not allow space for women who conceive of themselves as black yet have a "lively appetite for white boys"—except as, at best, self-confessed traitors to the race.

The basis of her appetite is her apparently (but only "apparently") successful struggle, as depicted in "New African," against the African American past as rendered in her firm resistance to the baptismal rite as administered by her father, a baptism which if undergone would signal her capitulation to the values of the African American past. The nightmare she has in the first chapter, "In France," about a struggle with an old black woman "with a dreadful spidery strength in her arms," emerges from the central episode of the novel, in "New African," where at the age of ten she literally engages in a physical struggle with the figure of her nightmare, an old black Philadelphia churchwoman, Aunt Bessie, who is her nursemaid. On a baptismal Sunday, Aunt Bessie, having decided that Sarah should "go on up and accept Jesus," proceeds to drag her down the aisle toward the baptismal pool. Sarah resists:

> The two of us began a brief struggle that could not have lasted for more than a few seconds but that seemed an endless mortal conflict—my slippery patent-leather shoes braced against the floor, my straw hat sliding cockeyed and lodging against one ear, my right arm twisting and twisting in the iron circle of the old woman's grip, my nostrils full of the dead-leaf smell of her powder and black skirts.

Then Sarah escapes and interprets it as a victory: "It was the first time I had won a battle with a grownup." If Sarah had indeed won the battle, then there would be no *Sarah Phillips*, for the whole novel is about the tensions arising from the problematics of her situation, not the least aspect of which involves her being the child of parents who, despite their commitment to the struggle for civil rights, nonetheless flee from the neighborhood of her father's church to the suburbs. The class differences between her family and the members of her father's congregation are glaringly apparent.

The first chapter, "In France," shows us the horrible results stemming from her rejection of her racial past. The second, "New African," reveals the primal source of her intolerable and unbearable situation in the world. The surrounding chapters show her discomfort, her dis-ease in her non-African world, a world she seems willingly to have chosen and to relish. Her position is marginal, though, and she is forever haunted by the shadows of a past rejected and despised, but not wholly: "The ambiguousness of my rejection of the old church gave me at times an inflated sense of privilege (I saw myself as a romantically isolated religious heroine, a sort of self-made Baptist martyr [in the Western tradition of Joan of Arc]) and at other times a feeling of loss that I was too proud ever to acknowledge."

Sarah Phillips tells of the narrator's attempt to acknowledge that past to the extent that she is able, to explain, perhaps to herself, why she is in the peculiar, psychologically distressing and deeply humiliating position she describes in "In France." In some profound ways the novel shows the price to be paid for rejecting the racial past, the resulting disrespect of self and the crushing diminishment of self-esteem. All these are painfully revealed in the first chapter when her "white boys" gratuitously insult her, signifying mercilessly about her parentage and birth, putting her in the dozens, a variety of cultural discourse she has presumably escaped but ironically has not.

The book is far more complicated than it at first appears. If *Sarah Phillips* were simply a celebration of the lightness of Sarah's color and the privilege of her class, then the book might be as politically contemptible as some readers have seen it as being. But there is more to it than that. The author is firmly aware of the tensions produced by the intersections of race, class, and color. The novel is something of a confessional enterprise, in which the author acknowledges the stress and guilt resulting not only from her failure to embrace her African past but also—and just as painfully—from her simultaneous denial of her father and mother, her personal, direct connections to the African American community and its past. Andrea Lee's *Sarah Phillips* is, as Smith's introduction makes abundantly clear, a novel to be reckoned with.

Source: Donald B. Gibson, Review of *Sarah Phillips*, in *African American Review*, Vol. 29, No. 1, Spring 1995, pp. 164–66.

W. Lawrence Hogue

In the following excerpt, Hogue presents a criticism of the novel's theme of division, using the second chapter, "New African," as an example.

Two of the most common features of literary modernism are the radical rejection of history and the hostility between high art and mass culture. First, for a modern individual to experience the raw, unmediated present, he is required to reject the frozen structures of understanding inherited from the past. The rejection of history constitutes a revelation of time itself, for there is an epochal shift in the very meaning and modality of temporality, a qualitative break in our ideological style of living history (Eagleton 129). In the modern project, there is, what Irving Howe calls, a "bitter impatience with the whole apparatus of cognition and the limiting assumption of rationality" (17). A writer embued with the modernist spirit will be predisposed toward experiment, if only because he or she needs to make visibly dramatic the break from tradition. His or her theme will tend to emphasize temporality, the process of becoming, rather than being in space and time. An individual infused with the modern impulse wants emancipation from all traditional social roles and traditional modes of servitude because they keep the self stifled and imprisoned.

Second, literary modernism or modern art aspires to save the dignity and autonomy of art

> SARAH'S MISPLACEMENT AND ALIENATION IN NEW AFRICAN BAPTIST CHURCH FORCE HER TO SEEK SOCIAL IDENTIFICATION AND HISTORICAL CONTINUITY AND TRADITIONS ELSEWHERE."

and life from the culture of everyday life, from the vulgarities and contaminations of mass culture, and from the constraints of traditional culture that denies individuality. This means that modernism has been obliged to withdraw from what an ever-expanding commercial taste has managed to appropriate and then market as "high art." Literary modernism promises a new life, and the "new" becomes the chief emblem of positive value.

Andrea Lee's *Sarah Phillips* (1984) is a modernist text that breaks with the prevalent styles of perception with the hope of creating a new style. Unlike Toni Morrison's *Song of Solomon* or Paule Marshall's *Praisesong for the Widow*, which break with the prevalent styles of modernists and retreat to the values and conventions of the premodern, pre-urban historical past, Lee's *Sarah Phillips* rejects the values and conventions of the historical past and promises new life. It embraces modernity because it "had to pass through it [modernity] before the lost unity of life and art could be reconstructed on a higher plane" (Huyssen 172). The heroine in this text, Sarah Phillips, wants to achieve some historically unmediated encounter with the real that will compliment her own subjective experiences.

The heroine in *Sarah Phillips* has an existential crisis moment. It is a moment when Sarah can assume ultimate responsibility for her acts of free will without external, moral principles of authority to tell her what is right or wrong. This moment occurs when, according to Paul de Man, a radical rejection of history becomes necessary to the fulfillment not only of her freedom, her "human destiny," but also as the "condition for action." Her break with country, community, family, or the racial past is the radical impulse that stands behind her "genuine humanity" (de Man 147). But, although she represses the past, Sarah Phillips is never able to arrive at a new style, to have a successful unmediated encounter with the real. Unlike Charles Wright in *The Messenger* (1963) who presents an existential protagonist who achieves an authentic, existential life as a way of coping with modernity, Lee's Sarah loses her modernist impulse, reaches an impasse, and becomes a symbol of alienation. Finally, Sarah Phillips atrophies and becomes entrapped in upper middle class conventions and values, or imitations of them, thereby repressing her racial self and her subjective individuality.

In *Sarah Phillips*, Andrea Lee revolts against the prevalent style of the old-fashioned black bourgeoisie—a style in which she was born and raised, which attempts "poignant imitations of high society, acting with genuine gallantry in the struggle for Civil Rights" (Lee 4). Lee in *Sarah Phillips* assaults the old-fashioned black bourgeoisie by incorporating themes such as interracial dating, interracial sex, easy nudity, communal living, the disdain for career, or any combination of these possibilities that are antithetical to its ruling code, norms, values, and sensibilities. *Sarah Phillips* opens in Paris with a detailed description of its young heroine involved in a romantic relationship with a Frenchman, Henri. They clutch "a private exotic vision in the various beds where [they] made love." Although Sarah is Henri's girl, she, "in the spirit of Bruderschaft," spent nights with Alain and Roger, friends who have "grown up with Henri in the city of Nancy."

The novel's heroine, Sarah, revolts against the old-fashioned black bourgeoisie because it excludes her lived, subjective experiences. Therefore, to ferret out a new mode of perception, Sarah attempts to reject the past and to escape from historical imperatives. But, Andrea Lee lacks the vision to develop Sarah's own style, to refashion her consciousness, and to have her live an existential, authentic existence. Therefore, by the end of the novel, Sarah returns precariously, knowledgeably and more wisely to the values and conventions of the old-fashioned black bourgeoisie.

To show how Sarah Phillips comes to reject her past and to seek out in Paris an authentic existence, Lee presents Sarah's life as a series of moments, rather than as a planned progression of events or incidents moving toward a defined terminus. In dealing with the chaos of modern life, Lee's *Sarah Phillips* structurally takes on the appearance, and sometimes the substance, of that chaos. The text focuses on a series of moments that contribute to Sarah's expatriation to Paris.

Although Sarah grows up in the "hermetic world of the old-fashioned black bourgeoisie," she belongs to the first generation of African Americans who are "educated in newly integrated [or predominantly white] schools." The experience in the newly integrated schools alienates and cuts her off from the experience of her parents. Sarah is caught between two worlds, living physically in one and cognitively in the other. Thus, she becomes alienated from both worlds. As a modern subject who needs a temporal unification between the past and the future in the present, she finds herself without social identification and outside any historical tradition. This alienation and fragmentation, this lack of historical continuity and social identification, constitute Sarah's subjective, mod-em experience. It is this modern experience that the text seeks to resolve.

Unlike her parents who grow up in middle class black neighborhoods in South Philadelphia, Sarah grows up on Franklin Place in an insulated, black suburban community that has the appearance of being ahistorical. It is a neighborhood that "lay in a Philadelphia suburb. The town was green and pretty, but had the constrained, slightly unreal atmosphere of a colony or a foreign enclave; that was because the people who owned the rambling houses behind the shrubbery were black. For them—doctors, ministers, teachers who had grown up in Philadelphia row houses—the lawns and tree-lined streets represented the fulfillment of a fantasy long deferred, and acted as a barrier against the predictable cruelty of the world." She attends a predominantly white Quaker elementary school, preps at the prestigious Prescott school for girls where she is the only black student, and attends Ivy League Harvard University. Through education, other social institutions, and her daily social contact with white members of the upper middle class, Sarah internalizes the norms and values, the cognitive style, of this race and class. This newly acquired cognitive style, along with her enlightenment education, which embraces the ideas of progress and activity and seeks to break with history and tradition, alienates Sarah from the world of her parents.

The world of Sarah's parents consists of "prosperous, conservative, generally light skinned" blacks who spend much of their time and energy attempting "poignant imitations of [white] high society." Unlike Sarah, her parents attended all-black private schools and considered New African Baptist Church, where her father is the minister, their "spiritual home." They grew up in segregated black middle class communities in Philadelphia and are very active in the Civil Rights movement—mostly because they see their present and future destiny as being inseparable from that of the rest of the African American community.

In addition, Sarah's parents and the old-fashioned black bourgeoisie are materialistic and socially rigid. They are very conscious of class, with special concerns for such material possessions as houses, perfumes, clothes, food, and so forth. Because the old-fashioned black bourgeoisie is preoccupied with attaining or imitating the decorum of high society, it allows nothing creative or innovative or different (from high society) to enter its lifestyle. For example, New African Baptist Church is not the kind of traditional Baptist church where "shouting was a normal part of the service." New African, like any other high society church, considers shouting an "incomprehensibly barbarous behavior." Lastly, the old-fashioned black bourgeoisie is exclusionary in its opposition to interracial dating and interracial marriage. When Matthew brings his white Jewish girlfriend, Martha, home for dinner, his mother wants to know why they cannot date their own kind.

In addition, Sarah's insulated and almost ahistorical life in the suburb marginalizes her to her parents's historical tradition. She knows very little about the Civil Rights movement and African American history and life. Although her father is integrally involved in the 1963 March on Washington, Sarah has only vague ideas about the march. For her, it was something "happening at a distance." At Prescott, she is "embarrassed to have a parent [her father] who freely admitted to going to jail in Alabama." Sarah also finds it difficult to picture the slaves as her ancestors. When her parents tell her about "the perilous region below the Mason-Dixon Line," Sarah has—"beyond a self-conscious excitement"—"little idea of what they meant."

Sarah's suburban upbringing particularly insulates her from the darker realities of black life. It insulates her from what Cornel West calls "the ragged edges of the Real, of Necessity, not being able to eat, not having shelter, not having health care." She has no sense "of what it means

to be impinged upon by structures of oppression" (Stephanson 277). She is living in what Barbara Ehrenreich calls the "final stage of material affluence—defined by cars, television, and backyard barbecue pits." Looking from the perspective of Franklin Place, Sarah sees "only an endless suburb, with no horizon, no frontier, in sight." She believes "that America had stepped outside of history" (Ehrenreich 17).

But Sarah is not able to escape completely from history, or the ragged edges of the real. Sarah encounters intermittently characters and experiences that serve to historicize her; that is, that force her to, at least, make a symbolic acknowledgment of her place in a broader historical reality (Smith 50–51), that invoke her cultural past or that remind her of the harsher realities of life. For example, she is completely overwhelmed when Mrs. Jeller, one of her father's parishioners, tells Sarah and her mother about how by the time she was fourteen years old, she had been raped, pregnant, married, and separated. Mrs. Jeller's story forces Sarah to deal with "the complicated possibilities of [her] own flesh—possibilities of corruption, confused pleasure, even death." Sarah's encounter with the Gypsies again forces her to acknowledge her connection with a larger, complicated world. "It was not that I had really feared being stolen: it was more, in fact, that [the Gypsies] seemed to have stolen something from me. Nothing looked different, yet everything was, and for the first time Franklin Place seemed genuinely connected to a world that was neither insulated nor serene."

And just as the Gypsies and Mrs. Jeller expose Sarah to a life and a world beyond her "insulated and serene" world, her trip to Camp Grayfeather also exposes her to the harsh realities of inner city life. At camp, Sarah's norm is the "other black kids" who "are overprotected or horribly spoiled products of comfortable suburban childhoods." Sarah sees the arrival of the Thunderbirds, a black teenage gang from Wilmington, Delaware, at the camp as a thrill. "For a day and a half, the Thunderbirds, like a small natural disaster, had given an edge of crazy danger to life at Grayfeather." But these encounters with the harsher realities of life remain "thrills" because Sarah is not able to integrate them into her vision of existence, into her insulated and serene world.

Furthermore, Sarah is equally misplaced in her parents' "spiritual home," New African Baptist Church. Sarah's enlightened education, which is a part of a secular progressive movement that sought the demystification and desacralization of knowledge and social organization in order to liberate individuals, causes her to view New African Baptist Church as belonging to a "past that came to seem embarrassingly primitive" as she grows older. Because her education puts her on the margin, inside yet outside, she has a perspective that allows her to deconstruct the church's rituals as contrivance, as something that is functional. Therefore, she dispels "the mysteries of worship with a gleeful secular eye." She believes that "the decision to make a frightening and embarrassing backward plunge into a pool of sanctified water [means] that one [has] received a summons to Christianity as unmistakable as the blare of an automobile horn," but it is not a call she hears.

Sarah's misplacement and alienation in New African Baptist Church force her to seek social identification and historical continuity and traditions elsewhere. She identifies with marginal heroines in the Bible—seeing herself as "a romantically isolated religious heroine, a sort of self-made Baptist martyr." She also seeks social identification through reading. "I would read with the kind of ferocious appetite that belongs only to garden shrews, bookish children... I plunged into fairy tales, adult novels, murder mysteries, poetry, and magazines."

Sarah's final break with New African Baptist Church, and the first step she takes in rejecting the values and conventions of the old-fashioned black bourgeoisie, comes with her refusal to accept baptism which "fascinated and disturbed [her] more than anything else at church." Despite Aunt Bessie's physical attempts to take her body and "soul to the Lord," Sarah wins in her first battle with a grown-up. When her father learns of her refusal, he recognizes her as different, as an individual for the first time. "I kept remembering the way my father had looked when he'd heard what had happened. He hadn't looked severe or angry, but merely puzzled, and he had regarded me with the same puzzled expression, as if he'd just discovered that I existed and didn't know what to do with me." Later in life, Sarah reflects and acknowledges the "peculiar gift of freedom" her father had given her "through his silence" on the issue of baptism. . . .

Source: W. Lawrence Hogue, "The Limits of Modernity: Andrea Lee's *Sarah Phillips*," in *MELUS*, Vol. 19, No. 4, Winter 1994, pp. 75–90.

Laura Obolensky

In the following excerpt, Obolensky complains that Lee's Sarah Phillips *"is not the novel it is touted to be."*

"What matters is that something—at last—has happened to me!" remarks a young traveling companion to Sarah Phillips, the eponymous narrator of [*Sarah Phillips*]. . . . It's hardly a startling outburst coming from a recent college graduate long numbed by the tedious business of growing up. And the opening chapter makes it clear that Sarah, taking that remark as her cue, has made something happen to her life. Late out of Harvard, black "but light-skinned . . . with a lively appetite for white boys," she is five months into a European romp which has her bouncing between Paris, the French countryside, and London. She also "plays the queen" in a loose menage-a-quatre whose other participants are her full-time lover Henri, "an illegitimate child raised outside Paris by his mother and adopted only recently by his rich uncle," and Henri's two childhood cronies—Alain, who comes "from a large and happy petit-bourgeois family," and Roger, a student sprung "From the pettiest of petty nobility" (Sarah isn't coy about her class consciousness)—both of whom she sleeps with occasionally "in a spirit of Bruderschaft." . . .

Indeed, something has happened to Sarah—something light-years removed from her middle-class Philadelphia upbringing, something which would surely raise the eyebrows of her recently deceased, civil rights activist, Baptist minister father, and of her prim, once schoolmarm mother. Which presumably was the whole point of the escapade. But youthful rebellions can be a punishing business, and by the end of the first chapter Sarah clearly senses that her own binge is turning into a bore. When at the end of a bibulous lunch Henri teases that she is the offspring of a mongrel Irish-woman raped "by a jazz musician as big and black as King Kong, with sexual equipment to match," Sarah expediently concludes her Parisian spree has been "nothing more than a slight hysteria," and calls it quits. (Never mind that until then she has delighted in coaxing poor wisecracking Henri into telling her "nigger jokes.")

The balance of the narrative consists of successive flashbacks to Sarah's growing years which, though intended to justify her subsequent Parisian "hysteria," fall a bit short of the mark. By her own admission, Sarah and her peers are "the overprotected or horribly spoiled products of a comfortable suburban childhood."... In keeping with their middle-class circumstances, the Phillipses seem to have a penchant for conspicuous consumption. Though said to "worship thrift," mother vacations in Europe and shops at Saks, Aunt Emma exudes whiffs of Arpege, and Sunday dinners are invariably "massive" or "extravagant." Brother Matthew goes to summer camp in the Poconos while Sarah heads for Camp Grayfeather in "Wyeth Territory," Delaware; and after the obligatory stints at exclusive private schools, it's Swarthmore for Matthew and Harvard for Sarah. Nothing out of character for any self-respecting affluent suburban family here. Or is there? Well, yes, sort of.

After all, the Phillipses are black, and it's the turbulent early 1960's; though close to being won, the fight for civil rights goes on as does discrimination. Through Reverend Phillips—Lee's strongest characterization apart from that of the narrator herself—we catch glimpses of the Struggle, for this spellbinding preacher, who can throw an occasional member of his mostly female flock "into fits of rapturous shrieks," is also a passionate civil rights activist. When not hectoring from his pulpit, he turns to hectoring the conscience of a refractory America from the airwaves; predictably, he also organizes boycotts and multitudinous marches.

Though she clearly idolizes him, Sarah doesn't quite know what to make of this crusading father. When he lands in an Alabama jail after a more exalted act of civil disobedience, she admits to being "privately embarrassed."... And the tokenism that she experiences firsthand when she becomes the first black student to be enrolled at the exclusive Prescott School for Girls leaves her more thrilled than wretched: "It's a little like being in a play," she tells her mother "looking for a laugh"; "everyone's watching me all the time." To her credit, Lee doesn't shy from daubing the Phillipses with the brush of the very racism against which the good Reverend is constantly inveighing. When sitting with her mother in the evenings, Sarah remarks, "Daddy...would talk unflatteringly about negroes," and rail against their propensity "for spoiling a community." And when later in the book Matthew brings home his Jewish

girlfriend for the parental once-over, it's a reverse case of *Guess Who's Coming to Dinner.*

For all its insight into the little-known world of upper-class blacks, however, *Sarah Phillips* is not the novel it is touted to be, and Lee's forte lies more in the hundred-yard dash of the short story...than in the intricately plotted long-distance narrative....

Sarah Phillips makes for a disconcerting read. Despite its talk about rebelling against a childhood during which "civil rights and concern for the under-privileged (were) served up...at breakfast, lunch, and dinner," Andrea Lee never really dramatizes the dilemma. And what remain deeply troublesome sociological issues are treated tangentially, or with a tone of detachment often bordering on the sardonic. The moral and emotional conflict that should rend her narrator as she struggles between two worlds, neither of which really claims her allegiance, is never demonstrated. Instead, what Lee proves once more is that affluence is a powerful equalizer—that no matter how adept the irony, and no matter what her ethnicity, a young lady who behaves like an elitist snob and thinks like an elitist snob is an elitist snob.

Source: Laura Obolensky, "Scenes from a Girlhood," in *New Republic*, Vol. 191, No. 21, November 19, 1984, pp. 41–42.

SOURCES

Adams, Carolyn, David Bartelt, David Elesh, Ira Goldstein, Joshua Freely, and Michelle Schmitt, *Restructuring the Philadelphia Region: Metropolitan Divisions and Inequality*, Temple University Press, 2008, pp. 29–30.

Adams, Carolyn, David Bartelt, David Elesh, Ira Goldstein, Nancy Kleniewski, and William Yancey, *Philadelphia: Neighborhoods, Division, and Conflict in a Postindustrial City*, Temple University Press, 1991, pp. 76–84.

Dierenfield, Bruce J., *The Civil Rights Movement*, rev. ed., Pearson Longman, 2008, pp. xix–xxi, 22–24, 130–35.

Gibson, Donald B., Review of *Sarah Phillips*, in *African American Review*, Vol. 29, No. 1, Spring 1995, pp. 164–66.

Hogue, W. Lawrence, "The Limits of Modernity: Andrea Lee's *Sarah Phillips*," in *MELUS*, Vol. 19, No. 4, Winter 1994, pp. 75–90.

King, Nicole, "'You Think Like You White': Questioning Race and Racial Community through the Lens of Middle-Class Desire(s)," in *Novel: A Forum on Fiction*, Vol. 35, Nos. 2–3, Spring–Summer 2002, pp. 211–30.

Lee, Andrea, "Altered State," in *New Yorker*, June 30, 2008, p. 36.

————, "Back to School," in *New Yorker*, April 29, 1996, p. 168.

————, "In France" and "New African," in *Sarah Phillips*, Northeastern University Press, 1993, pp. 3–29.

Lee, Jenny, "Andrea Lee," in *Boldtype*, Vol. 6, No. 4, September 2002, http://www.randomhouse.com/boldtype/0902/lee/index.html (accessed August 17, 2012).

Lehmann-Haupt, Christopher, Review of *Sarah Phillips*, in *New York Times*, December 6, 1984, p. C22.

McCormick, Adrienne, "Is This Resistance? African-American Postmodernism in *Sarah Phillips*," in *Callaloo*, Vol. 27, No. 3, Summer 2004, pp. 808–28.

Muller, Peter O., Kenneth C. Meyer, and Roman A. Cybriwsky, *Metropolitan Philadelphia: A Study of Conflicts and Social Cleavages*, Ballinger Publishing, 1976, pp. 12–14.

Murray, Rolland, "The Time of Breach: Class Division and the Contemporary African American Novel," in *Novel: A Forum on Fiction*, Vol. 43, No. 1, Spring 2010, pp. 11–17.

Obolensky, Laura, Review of *Sarah Phillips*, in *New Republic*, Vol. 191, No. 21, November 19, 1984, pp. 41–42.

Rein, Richard K., "An American Student Comes Home from Russia with Love and a Bittersweet Memoir," in *People*, November 23, 1981, http://www.people.com/people/archive/article/0,,20080755,00.html (accessed August 17, 2012).

Shreve, Susan Richards, Review of *Sarah Phillips*, in *New York Times Book Review*, November 18, 1984, p. 13.

Smith, Valerie, Foreword to *Sarah Phillips*, Northeastern University Press, 1993, pp. ix–xxiv.

————, "Black Feminist Theory and the Representation of the 'Other,'" in *Changing Our Own Words: Essays on Criticism, Theory, and Writing by Black Women*, edited by Cheryl A. Wall, Rutgers University Press, 1989, pp. 38–57.

Vercellino, Milena, "Andrea Lee," in *American*, November 1, 2006, http://www.theamericanmag.com/article.php?article=556&p=full (accessed August 17, 2012).

FURTHER READING

Marty, Martin E., *Baptism: A User's Guide*, Augsburg Books, 2008.

This accessible book surveys the approaches to baptism in various Christian denominations and addresses the experiential and symbolic significance of the ritual.

McLennan, Scotty, *Finding Your Religion: When the Faith You Grew Up with Has Lost Its Meaning*, HarperOne, 2000.

A Unitarian minister and chaplain at Tufts University, McLennan provides a guidebook for those looking to reinvigorate their spirituality after having strayed from their childhood faith.

Napier, Winston, *African American Literary Theory: A Reader*, New York University Press, 2000.

This volume is a wide-ranging collection of essays on the thematic and stylistic development demonstrated in the history of African American literature; the reader can gain a greater understanding of what critics have come to expect from black American authors.

Otter, Samuel, *Philadelphia Stories: America's Literature of Race and Freedom*, Oxford University Press, 2010.

Otter delves into the foundations of Philadelphia's literary history in examining the antebellum writings produced in the home to one of the country's most substantial free African American populations.

SUGGESTED SEARCH TERMS

Andrea Lee AND New African

Andrea Lee AND Sarah Phillips

Andrea Lee AND African American literature

Andrea Lee AND New Yorker

Andrea Lee AND interview

Sarah Phillips AND criticism

Philadelphia AND African American history

Philadelphia AND civil rights movement

Baptist Church AND civil rights movement

African Baptist Church

Night Talkers

EDWIDGE DANTICAT

2002

Haitian American author Edwidge Danticat published the short story "Night Talkers" in her 2004 collection *The Dew Breaker*. The stories in this collection each stand alone but are intertwined, with characters from one story often appearing briefly, in person or memory, in other tales. In an interview with Robert Birnbaum in the *Morning News*, Danticat explains the meaning of her title: "It comes from the Creole. It's an expression *choukèt laroze*; it really means somebody who breaks or shakes the dew." The dew breakers would often come in the morning, disrupting the dew on the grass. The true meaning of the term defies its seemingly poetic origins, however; the dew breakers were the minions of dictator François "Papa Doc" Duvalier, who maintained control of Haiti by intimidating and murdering his political opponents. "Night Talkers" is the story of a young Haitian man who lost his parents to one of these thugs. He believes he sees the guilty man years later in New York and returns to Haiti to tell the aunt who raised him. The story touches on many challenging themes, including guilt and forgiveness, loss and healing, and family and cultural traditions. "Night Talkers" first appeared in the journal *Callaloo* in the fall of 2002 and was included in *Best American Short Stories 2003*.

Edwidge Danticat (© *Getty Images*)

AUTHOR BIOGRAPHY

Danticat was born on January 19, 1969, in Port-au-Prince, Haiti, to parents André and Rose. The family lived in Bel Air, a poor section of the city. When Danticat was only four years old, she and her little brother went to live with their uncle and aunt while their parents left for New York. They worked hard, earning money to send back to Haiti and saving what they could in hopes of bringing the children to join them.

They were not able to secure visas for Danticat and her brother until she was twelve. By then, there were two more sons in the family, whom Danticat had met only briefly when her parents brought them on a visit in 1976. In an article in the London *Guardian*, Maya Jaggi reports that Danticat said it was a "big challenge for us to become a family again; I felt like we'd been discarded." However, she later came to understand the sacrifices her parents made and why they made them.

In New York, Danticat was teased at school because of her accent and heritage. As Kevin Meehan and Bernadette Davis explain in the *Dictionary of Literary Biography*, Danticat "faced immersion in a US social milieu full of hostile North American students who stereotyped her and other Haitians as 'Frenchies,' 'boat people,' and HIV-infected health threats." (The US Centers for Disease Control had recently identified Haitians as an at-risk group.) Danticat believes that writing helped her through her difficult childhood. Her first writing as a girl was adapting Ludwig Bemelmans's *Madeline* stories into similar stories about herself, set in Haiti. She also kept a journal and was first published at age fourteen in a publication called *New Youth Connections*, by and for New York teens.

After graduating from Clara Barton High School in Brooklyn, Danticat earned her bachelor's degree in French literature from Barnard College, graduating magna cum laude. Her parents urged her to choose a career with financial security, but she entered the creative-writing program at Brown University, receiving her master of fine arts degree in 1993. Her master's thesis became her first novel, *Breath, Eyes, Memory*, which was published the following year.

Danticat's other books include *Krik? Krak!* (1995), *The Farming of Bones* (1998), *Behind the Mountains* (2002), and the short-story collection *The Dew Breaker* (2004), which includes "Night Talkers." She is also the author of several nonfiction works, many essays, and articles of cultural criticism. Her fiction has earned many awards, including the Pushcart Short Story Prize and the American Book Award. She was also a finalist for such prestigious awards as the National Book Award, the National Book Critics Circle Award, and the PEN/Faulkner Award.

Danticat taught creative writing as a graduate teaching assistant at Brown and then at New York University, the University of Miami, and Texas A&M University. She also worked at director Jonathan Demme's Clínica Estético as a production assistant and researcher. She was the producer for two films, one about Haitian cinema and one about political torture under the regime of Raoul Cédras, a military officer who led the Haitian government when the president was exiled. It was while working with Demme on the film *Beloved* that she met Oprah Winfrey, who selected *Breath, Eyes, Memory* for her book club, making it a best seller.

Danticat was married in 2002 to Faidherbe Boyer, a translator. They have one daughter, Mira.

PLOT SUMMARY

"Night Talkers" starts with a man walking up a mountain in the Haitian countryside. His name is Dany, although that is not revealed until later. Hot, tired, and lost, he gets a stitch in his side and thinks of his roommate back in New York, who had acute appendicitis. He fears that he too may have appendicitis, far from the nearest town. He finds some shade and lies down.

The narrator explains that the man is going to visit his aunt, Estina, who raised him after his parents died when he was a boy. Although no details are given here, the reader learns that Dany "lost his parents to the dictatorship," which refers to the repressive regime of Papa Doc Duvalier, who kept control of Haiti with his army of thugs, the "dew breakers" of the collection's title.

The aunt raised Dany in Port-au-Prince, Haiti's capital, but when he left for New York ten years before, she moved back to the mountain village that was her home, where she used to take him during school holidays. This is the first time he has undertaken the journey to the village without her, and he thinks about how much better his aunt would have planned for the trip: starting earlier, bringing a hat and more water, and arranging for a guide. However, he did not tell her he was coming, wanting to surprise her.

Once Dany has rested, he continues on his way until he comes to a small town, where he finds a young woman using a mortar and pestle, surrounded by children. The girl stops her chore and answers Dany's greeting. He asks for water, and she brings him some. An old man, the young woman's father, appears and asks Dany where he is going. Dany explains that he was going to visit his aunt. The old man knows Estina. He also knows what happened to Dany's parents: Dany states his father's name, and the old man asks, "The one killed with his wife in that fire?" He also remembers that Estina nearly died in the fire as well. The old man says that he is still sad

MEDIA ADAPTATIONS

- An unabridged audiobook of *The Dew Breaker* was released in 2004 by Recorded Books. It is narrated by Robin Miles, and the running time is almost seven hours.

for Dany after all of these years, and he offers to lead him to his aunt.

As they walk through the town, the old man tells all the neighbors who Dany is, and many follow them, curious to see the reunion between nephew and aunt. Aunt Estina's home is surrounded by the bounty of nature. It is in a valley between two mountains where there is a huge waterfall. She has banana, orange, and avocado trees, as well as a flock of chickens. Inside, the house is very simple, with her cot, a chamber pot, and baskets to hold her few possessions.

Dany's aunt is not at home, but the neighbors have sent for her. He spends time catching up with these neighbors he barely remembers. When Dany's aunt arrives, she kisses him but has to ask whether it is really him—she has not seen him for ten years. She teases the old man, whom she calls "Old Zo," about having to be "mixed up in everything."

Dany and his aunt go into the house, and they talk. The narration describes how Dany arranged for a childhood friend, Popo, to check on his aunt and phone with reports about how she has been doing. Aunt Estina is very glad to see Dany, but she worries that he might have been sent back. She explains that some young men have been sent back from America to their relatives in Haiti, presumably because they have gotten into some kind of trouble. She tells Dany that she will introduce him to one of these boys so that they can talk, "one American to another."

Dany tells his aunt why he has come: he believes he has found the man who killed his parents; but before they can discuss this, Old Zo, his daughter, and other neighbors interrupt them, bringing food and lingering for conversation. When the visitors all finally leave, Dany and Estina go to bed, and Dany learns that his aunt talks in her sleep, as he does.

The next morning Estina sends for Claude, the young man she mentioned who has been sent home from America. Dany and Claude talk, and Estina listens, although she does not understand English. Claude explains that he had been in prison but that his family in Haiti have taken him in, putting him back together like a puzzle. Dany quickly tires of Claude's tattoos, vulgar language, and "apparent lack of remorse for whatever it was he'd done." After Claude leaves, Estina tells Dany that he had been in prison for killing his father.

Dany has a dream in which he recalls what happened when his parents were killed. His memories are unclear, but there was an explosion, gunshots, and a fire, and his aunt tried to pin him down to keep him safe, but Dany broke free and saw his parents on the ground. He also saw the dew breaker—whom he later recognized in New York, now a barber with a family. Dany watched the barber, renting a room in his house and going to him regularly for haircuts. He has imagined killing the man or asking him why he did such terrible things in Haiti, but he has done nothing because he is afraid of making a mistake. He does not want to exact revenge on the wrong man.

When Dany awakens from his dream, his aunt is also awake, and they talk about his parents' death. Dany wants to understand why it happened, asking his aunt if they were involved in politics. Estina says his father might have been mistaken for someone else, but she cannot explain. She admits she does not understand it herself and says that she is tired. Dany lets her go back to sleep. When he wakes up in the morning, she has died during the night.

Old Zo's daughter arrives and takes charge, making Dany tea and calling in the neighbors to help. Dany hears people calling her Ti Fanm, which is Creole for "Little Woman." Dany cannot speak, and his stomach hurts. The neighbors arrange for Estina's funeral, the men opening and cleaning the family mausoleum for her burial and the women washing and dressing her body. Claude comes to pay his respects, but Dany cringes away from the hug he offers.

Dany has trouble sleeping that night because of the women keeping watch over his aunt's body. Ti Fanm brings over tea often, and

during one such visit Dany asks her true name: it is Denise Auguste. In the morning, Dany begins to clean the mausoleum, and Claude offers to help. Dany apologizes for rejecting his comfort earlier.

Claude explains how he killed his father: when he was fourteen, he was using and selling drugs, and his father took his supply. When his father refused to give the drugs back, Claude, who was high at the time, shot him with a gun he used to protect himself on the streets. Dany says he is sorry for what happened to Claude, but Claude claims that he is lucky. If he had been an adult instead of a minor, he would have gone to jail for life or perhaps gotten the death penalty. He feels that someone was looking out for him and now wants to live like an "angel."

The story ends with the realization that Claude is also a night talker like Dany and his aunt, that is, "one of those who spoke their nightmares." Dany thinks that Claude is "even luckier than he realized" because he is able to face his nightmares, speaking of them with full awareness in the light of day rather than just in the dark of night when he is asleep.

CHARACTERS

Denise Auguste
See Ti Fanm

Claude
Claude is a young man who was living in the United States but was sent back because he committed a crime. When he returned to Haiti, he spent time in jail and then went to live in a small mountain village with his relatives. Aunt Estina takes Claude under her wing, and when her nephew, Dany, comes to visit, she gets the two young men together so that they can talk, "one American to another." Claude explains to Dany how he got into trouble: he was using drugs, and his father took away his stash, which he had intended to sell. When his father would not return the drugs, Claude shot him. Dany is somewhat disgusted by the way Claude tells his story and by the fact that he seems to feel little remorse for murdering his father. However, Claude does seem to be genuinely trying to live better. He has respect for Estina and is grateful to his family for taking him in and sharing their history with him.

Dew Breaker

Although the dew breaker does not appear in "Night Talkers" (and is not called a "dew breaker" within the story), his importance to Dany makes him essential to the plot. He is the man who killed Dany's parents, and once Dany spots him, he can think of nothing else. The dew breaker is now a barber in New York with a wife and daughter. Dany rents a room in the barber's house and goes to his shop regularly for haircuts. Because he is so obsessed, Dany cannot sleep. He decides to travel back to Haiti and speak to his aunt about the man he thinks is his parents' murderer. Therefore the dew breaker sets the plot of the story in motion.

Dany Dorméus

Dany is the central character in "Night Talkers." The story is told from his point of view. He is a young man who "lost his parents to the dictatorship twenty-five years before." They were killed by a dew breaker, one of the thugs who kept Papa Doc Duvalier in power by arresting and murdering anyone who dared to oppose him. Dany has been living in New York for ten years, but he returns to Haiti to tell his aunt that he thinks he has found the man who killed his parents and started the fire that blinded and scarred her.

Dany seems to be a good person. Although he has not returned before this to visit his aunt, he has arranged for his friend Popo to check on her and has sent money for Popo to buy anything she might need. Although Dany feels a lot of anger and confusion about his parents' death, he does not rush out to take revenge for them when he finds the dew breaker. He has a "dread of being wrong, of harming the wrong man, of making the wrong woman a widow and the wrong child an orphan." He is kind and thoughtful enough to consider the consequences of his actions.

Dany's interaction with Claude also shows that he is basically a good person. There is a stark contrast between the two young men: Dany moved to America to try to improve his life, still making an effort to take care of his aunt, and is only sidetracked by spying the dew breaker, but Claude lived selfishly, using drugs and then shooting his father. Dany is disgusted by the matter-of-fact way Claude describes his crime, but because Estina has taken Claude under her wing, Dany still makes an effort to be polite and get acquainted.

Dany is a night talker, meaning that he talks in his sleep. He sometimes wakes himself up with his own words, with the "lingering sensation that he had been talking, laughing, and at times crying all night long." During his first night sleeping beside his aunt's cot, Dany realizes that she too is a night talker.

Estina Estème

Estina is Dany's aunt. He returns to Haiti to tell her that he has found the man he believes to be the dew breaker who killed his parents years ago. On the night of their death, Estina tried to protect Dany, pinning him down to keep him away from the killer. She was burned in the fire the dew breaker set, and she lost her sight from her injuries. However, she is still very involved in the life of the village, with many friends among her neighbors. Even with her blindness, she helps the village midwife deliver babies (having been a midwife herself). She also has taken Claude under her wing.

Estina loves her nephew dearly and devoted much of her life to raising him. When Dany returns to visit, she tells him, "You have made your old aunt a young woman again." As they talk, she kisses him "for what seemed like the hundredth time." However, she cannot seem to bring herself to talk about his parents' death, although he clearly needs to understand more about what happened. When Dany first tells her that he believes he has found the man who killed his parents, Old Zo and his daughter put a stop to the conversation by bringing in food. Dany is annoyed, but Estina "seemed neither distressed nor irritated by the interruption." Dany dreams "that he was having the conversation he'd come to have with his aunt," but when they both wake in the middle of the night, she is still hesitant to discuss it. Like Dany, Estina is a night talker, saying aloud in her sleep what she perhaps cannot bring herself to say during the day.

Popo

Popo is Dany's childhood friend. Dany has been sending him money to buy whatever his aunt needs, and Popo has been checking on her and reporting to Dany by phone. Popo does not appear in the story, but he is important in that he shows Dany's concern for and care of his aunt, even though he has not been able to visit her for such a long time.

Ti Fanm

Ti Fanm's real name is Denise Auguste. Her nickname is Creole for "Little Woman" (from the French "petite femme"). It is a fitting nickname: Dany thinks "maybe she was twenty, twenty-five, but she looked twelve." In spite of her relative youth and childlike appearance, she takes care of everyone around her, especially Dany. When he first arrives in the village, she brings him water. Then she is among the first of the neighbors to bring food while Dany and Estina talk. After Dany's aunt dies. Ti Fanm brings him countless cups of tea and calls in the neighbors to help with the arrangements for the funeral. They "badgered her with questions," and she answers them "in a firm and mature voice." Ti Fanm is unassuming and shy; she avoids Dany's gaze and talks very little. She tells him her name only when he asks for it directly and is "baffled" that he would ask.

Old Zo

Old Zo is Ti Fanm's father and the first person to really talk to Dany when he comes into the village. The first conversation they have tells the reader a lot about life there. Even though Dany has been gone for ten years, Old Zo quickly understands who he is and remembers exactly what happened to his family. This is Dany's first reminder that unlike in New York, in his aunt's small village he cannot be anonymous.

When Old Zo leads Dany to his aunt's house, she teases him, "Old Zo, why is it that you're always mixed up in everything?" He gets involved in all parts of village life. When Dany first arrives, Old Zo is fetched by a boy to come greet the newcomer. He tells the village children what to do, and they seem to listen to and respect him. Old Zo is one of the men who helps to clean the mausoleum for Estina's burial, and he does not hesitate to put in his two cents about the funeral details, wanting "to transport the body to a church in the next village for a full service." He is a kind of father figure to the entire village, much in the same way Estina cares for her neighbors with motherly affection.

THEMES

Memory

Memory is an important theme in "Night Talkers." The entire plot of the story revolves around Dany's memory of the terrible night when his parents were killed. He cannot forget what happened, but he was so young at the time that he is not able to completely trust what he remembers. He thinks that the barber from whom he rents a room in New York is the dew breaker, but he is afraid of making a mistake. He has a "dread of being wrong."

Aunt Estina, on the other hand, seems to trust her memory. She is blind because of her injuries from the night Dany's parents died, but she still helps the village midwife. She tells Dany that a "baby's still born the same way it was when I had sight" and that she still is familiar with "every corner of these mountains."

However, where Dany wants to learn more and refine his memory of his parents' murder, Estina does not willingly confront that memory or speak of it. Both Dany and his aunt are night talkers, speaking in their sleep what they can or do not say in daylight. Estina uses a metaphor to explain how she feels about bringing memories of that night to mind:

> It's like walking up these mountains and losing something precious halfway. For you, it would be no problem walking back to find it because you're still young and strong, but for me it would take a lot more time and effort.

Dany comes to Haiti hoping that his aunt will help him by filling in the gaps in his memory and explaining their family tragedy. When Dany tries to discuss it with her, however, her "voice was just an echo of things he could no longer enjoy—his mother's voice, his father's laugh." After her death, the neighbors show Dany how to remember the things that really matter; at her wake, they tell stories about her, "which could make one either chuckle or weep." By relating these memories of Estina, the villagers help Dany mourn and begin to heal.

Family

Dany, the main character in "Night Talkers," is a young man born in Haiti who has lived in New York for ten years. When Dany returns to Haiti to visit his aunt, he gets lost climbing the mountain on the way to her village. He no longer knows his way around. When he finally finds the town, Ti Fanm pours him a glass of water from a jar that was "obviously reserved for strangers." Once the neighbors realize who he is, however, he is treated like an old friend or a member of the family. He is welcomed home after his long absence.

TOPICS FOR FURTHER STUDY

- Read "The Book of the Dead," the first story in *The Dew Breaker*, which portrays the dew breaker's guilt and remorse and his fear of telling his daughter. This story allows the readers to see the situation in "Night Talkers" from the other side. Write a scene in which Dany confronts the dew breaker. How do you think he would react? With a partner, perform the scene for your class.

- Research Haiti's turbulent history, using both online and print sources. Using a computer program of your choice, create a time line of major events. Include photos or drawings of key people and episodes to make your time line more interesting and informative.

- Danticat describes Aunt Estina's house and the valley where the village is situated with interesting details: the "lime-green mountains," the plants and animals in her yard, and the laundry drying on the railing. Read these descriptive passages carefully, and paint or draw what you imagine the story's setting looks like. Share your project with your class, explaining what parts of the text inspired various details in the picture.

- In the young-adult novel *Miracle's Boys*, by Jacqueline Woodson, thirteen-year-old Lafayette becomes an orphan and must learn to cope with the loss of his mother. Read *Miracle's Boys* and write an essay comparing Lafayette and Dany. How does each character deal with his grief? Dany is taken care of by his aunt after his parents' death, and Lafayette has two brothers. What role does family play in each character's ability to heal and move on with his life?

The importance of family is also highlighted in this story by the fact that Dany has lost his parents. He feels that loss constantly, and he is driven to try to understand the reasons for his parents' murder. When Dany is trying to figure out what to do after he finds the dew breaker, one of the reasons he does not try to kill the man in revenge is "the realization that he would never know why—why one single person had been given the power to destroy his entire life." Dany has been hugely influenced by the tragic loss of his family.

The story illustrates how the bonds of family are lasting, even after separation and tragedy. When the town is making arrangements for Estina's funeral, the reader learns that her "body would be placed in one of the higher slots, one of two not yet taken." That there is one slot still open in the family mausoleum suggests that there is a space for Dany. It might seem a bit grim to think of where his body might be laid to rest when he is still healthy and young, but it indicates that there is always a place for him with his family.

Assimilation

"Night Talkers" portrays two different young men who went to America and have now returned to Haiti: Dany and Claude. Like most immigrants, both young men were formed by their upbringing and family traditions but have also taken on some of the cultural influence of their adopted country. Dany and Claude have absorbed American culture and behavior to different degrees, however, and studying the two men can reveal Danticat's views regarding tradition and assimilation.

Claude seems to have sunk himself completely into life in the United States and did not make the best choices. Estina first mentions him in the context of other boys like him, "boys here in the village who have been sent back. Many don't even speak Creole anymore." These boys go back to Haiti because "this is the only place they have any family." These families take these boys in despite whatever crimes they have committed to get themselves deported from the United States. Claude was a drug user and, while high, shot his father for trying to take his drugs away.

Dany, on the other hand, has not completely lost his ties to home. He has arranged for a friend to check on his aunt and take care of her, and he understands when the villagers speak Creole in his presence. He has better reason than Claude to be tempted to murder: Claude's father was trying to help him, while Dany feels his life has been ruined by the dew breaker. However, Dany

In "Night Talkers," characters move between Haiti and New York City. (© *Donald R. Swartz | ShutterStock.com*)

does not commit any violence, hinting that Danticat believes that retaining one's ties to tradition, community, and family is necessary for keeping a person stable and helping one do the right thing. Without these supportive ties, Claude was adrift, got himself into serious trouble, and did something he will likely regret for the rest of his life. It was only when Claude returned to Haiti and began to reconnect with his family that his life turned around.

STYLE

Simplicity of Language

Danticat's writing is often praised for what Annabel Lyon of the Toronto *Globe & Mail* calls her "typically relaxed, deceptively simple prose." Throughout Danticat's work, readers find basic vocabulary and straightforward sentences. The characters speak in realistic, uncomplicated dialogue. This is not to suggest that

Danticat's stories themselves are simple—she introduces themes and issues that are challenging and sometimes upsetting. The simplicity of her writing style makes the difficult subjects she tackles both easier to understand, because there is no complicated language to wade through, and more stark and disturbing. These events do not need embellishment to give them impact because the mere facts are enough. When one reads of what happened to Dany when he was a boy, one feels shocked and angry on his behalf. One is able to sympathize with Dany's desire for understanding, closure, and even revenge.

This straightforward language also allows Danticat to portray her characters very subtly. With a few words she conjures a wealth of emotion and history. For example, on Dany's first morning in the village, when he goes to wash in the stream, he wonders, "Had his father ever bathed in this stream?" From this simple sentence, the reader can gather much information about Dany: he thinks often about his parents, even while performing the most basic tasks. He regrets knowing so little about them and wants to imagine what they were like.

Novel versus Short Story

Danticat could have told her story as a novel, but she specifically chose to use the short-story form. In doing so, she reduced her tale to its most important elements. Also, by including "Night Talkers" as one in a collection, she was able to add to the story by placing it in context. As Kyle Minor explains in *Antioch Review*, *The Dew Breaker* is "a work of fiction that so carefully blurs the line between novel and short-story collection that one is hard pressed to identify which it might be." Marjorie Valbrun, in *Black Issues Book Review*, expresses a similar view: "This book could easily be mistaken for a novel because the Dew Breaker is present in every story, either in person or in the memories of the other characters."

Minor asserts that although the "stories are compelling on their own merits," the relationships between the individual stories add significantly to their meaning and impact. Lorna Gibb agrees: "Each story is like a picture in a photograph album and only the complete collection will reveal the complexity of the interrelated lives and the reverberations of the past." Therefore, while "Night Talkers" is an interesting story and tackles important issues all on its own, its place in the collection gives it further depth. By using short stories to gradually reveal the whole story, telling fragments from different points of view, Danticat can relate her tale with great subtlety and grace.

HISTORICAL CONTEXT

Political Conflict in Haiti

In an interview with Robert Birnbaum in the *Morning News*, Danticat declared that "Haiti is a place that suffers so much from neglect that people only want to hear about it when it's at its extreme. And that's what they end up knowing about it." For example, many Americans now associate Haiti with the massive earthquake in January 2010 that killed anywhere from 200,000 to 316,000 people and caused up to $14 million of damage. It is a country that has experienced many extremes over its two-hundred-year

history, but it had a promising and unique beginning.

Haiti had its origins in the French colony of Saint-Domingue, which had become a very wealthy French colony, mostly by producing sugar using slave labor. In August 1791, the slaves in Saint-Domingue revolted. Over the course of almost thirteen years, they faced several foes, all much more powerful and better supplied than they were. Once the slaves defeated the French colonial soldiers, Spain and Britain both invaded but were repelled. The French then returned under Napoleon, but Haitian independence was finally declared on January 1, 1804, marking the only successful Caribbean slave revolt and the establishment of the first black republic.

Unfortunately, the Haitian unity created during the fight for independence was soon torn apart by racial, economic, and political disagreement. Gerald Zarr, in *History* magazine, describes how "fighting broke out between the black majority and the mulatto minority," and the Haitian government became a "succession of coups, assassinations and political turmoil." The constant and often violent political strife continued for over one hundred years, until World War I, when the United States, fearing that Germany might intervene, sent two Marine Corps companies to the island.

The US occupation lasted from 1915 until 1934 and in some ways was helpful to Haiti. The presence of the marines quieted the political disorder, and US money built new roads, schools, and modern medical facilities. However, not all American influence was benevolent aid: the United States installed what Zarr calls "puppet presidents" and imposed a new constitution.

In 1957, Haiti's most notorious leader, François "Papa Doc" Duvalier was elected president. Duvalier established an army of thugs called the *tonton macoutes*, like the dew breaker in "Night Talkers," who assassinated or arrested any who opposed the regime. Many were taken to Fort Dimanche and tortured. When Duvalier ran again in 1961, he was the only candidate. A *New York Times* article, quoted by Zarr, states that "Latin America has witnessed many sham elections... but this was absolutely the worst." President Kennedy cut off all diplomatic relations with Haiti because of this illegal election, and later Duvalier celebrated and even claimed responsibility for Kennedy's assassination.

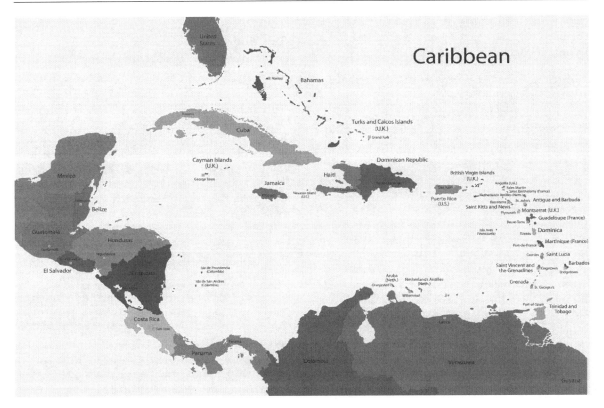

Danticat uses her native Haiti as background in many of her works. (© Volina / ShutterStock.com)

Although little changed in Haiti, US attitudes toward Duvalier relaxed a bit under the influence of anti-Communist fears in the 1960s as Fidel Castro gained power in nearby Cuba.

Papa Doc died in 1971, but not before designating his nineteen-year-old son, Jean-Claude, as his successor. He was dubbed "Baby Doc," and under his control the "regime took on a more humane, even fun-loving appearance," according to Zarr. However, in 1980, not long before Danticat's parents brought her to New York to join them, dozens of liberals and journalists were arrested in Port-au-Prince. The London *Times* explains that these arrests were "seen by political observers here as signalling that the ultra-conservative faction had regained the upper hand." The US State Department said that "if the reports were true they were a cause for grave concern."

The intimidation tactics and questionable legal practices of the father's regime were still used by the son. The London *Times* describes the case of Robert-Jacques Thelusma, who was arrested early in 1979, was not given a trial until well over a year later, and subsequently "declared that he had been tortured with electric shocks while in detention." When he was finally given a trial on a charge of plotting to overthrow the government with three others, it was with only one judge instead of the three required by law. Amnesty International stated that "Thelusma and the three other defendants were sentenced not for involvement in an alleged plot, but for their critical political beliefs."

Although the *tonton macoutes* still existed, the people's fear abated somewhat. The economy improved, with both industry and tourism bringing money into the country. Baby Doc remained in power for fifteen years.

Several factors contributed to Baby Doc's downfall. The first was personal: he married a woman many considered inappropriate. Race and class were still sensitive issues in Haiti, and his wife was from a wealthy mulatto family. They had an extravagant wedding and lived a lavish lifestyle while many Haitians struggled to feed their families. Another factor in Baby Doc's loss of power was economic; a highly infectious and incurable virus destroyed Haiti's pigs, a vital part of the peasant economy. Zarr explains that "the loss of Haiti's pigs destabilized the rural society on whom 'Papa Doc' had built his revolution." Also, the US Centers for Disease Control listed Haitians as a group at high risk for contracting HIV, which hugely damaged Haiti's tourism. Finally, Pope John Paul II visited Haiti, dined with priests instead of the president, and criticized the poverty and fear that he had witnessed. Riots broke out in early 1986, and Jean-Claude Duvalier and his wife fled the country.

After the Duvaliers, Haiti was controlled largely by military regimes until Jean-Bertrand Aristide was elected in December 1990. It was a "vote that seemed to promise a new era for Haiti," according to Zarr, but Aristide was not an effective ruler and was ousted by a military coup after nine months as president. He was restored to office very late in his five-year term and was succeeded by René Préval. It was the first peaceful transition between two legally, democratically elected leaders in Haitian history.

CRITICAL OVERVIEW

Danticat's harshest critics come from a surprising quarter: Haitian readers. As Maya Jaggi of the London *Guardian* explains, some Haitians "have objected to her alleged betrayal of community 'secrets,' or portrayed her as yet another outsider on the trail of Victor Hugo and Graham Greene, who both wrote novels set in Haiti." Danticat's work, however, has received mostly favorable attention from critics.

A review in *Ebony* magazine describes how Danticat "fuses the beauty and tragedy of her native land, a land her characters want to forget and remember all at once." The *Christian Century* calls *The Dew Breaker* "a poignant and haunting work," and in the *Times Literary Supplement*, Lorna Gibb praises Danticat's "beautifully written vignettes," in which "what is unsaid is as important as what is made explicit."

Several critics commend Danticat's skill in writing about painful subjects, as does Marjorie Valbrun in the *Black Issues Book Review*: "Her spare, lyrical prose is ever present in the gentle telling of stories that are soft to the ear even when pain and violence seem to scream from the pages." Junot Díaz, a fellow Caribbean-born author, is quoted by Jaggi describing

Danticat as the "quintessential American writer, tackling the new world's hidden history of apocalypse and how one survives it."

The reviews of *The Dew Breaker* are not entirely positive, however. There is some criticism of the collection because of the constantly shifting points of view. A *Publishers Weekly* review points out that "Danticat does not always stay in one character's mind long enough to fully convey the complexities she seeks." Gibb agrees, describing how the interrelatedness of the stories "can mean that the reader concentrates on looking for the sometimes slender threads that weave the stories together, rather than enjoying the book." However, Gibb concludes that "this is a small flaw in what is an eloquent, atmospheric work." *Publishers Weekly* also concedes that "the slow accumulation of details...makes for powerful reading,...and Danticat is a crafter of subtle, gorgeous sentences and scenes." Annabel Lyon of the Toronto *Globe & Mail* describes the collection as "strong material, shakily told." She believes that "Danticat relies on some heavy symbols...that are too pointed to ring true" but states that "once Danticat shaves off the literary affectation, the stories feel tauter and more compelling."

CRITICISM

Kristen Sarlin Greenberg
Greenberg is a freelance writer and editor with a background in literature and philosophy. In the following essay, she examines how the Haitian tradition of storytelling is highlighted by communication problems in Danticat's "Night Talkers."

In an article published in the London *Guardian*, Maya Jaggi writes that Edwidge Danticat told her that "her happiest memories are of summers in the mountains of Léogne. After sundown, her aunt's mother would tell stories in Creole." Danticat said, "I loved the vibrant interaction between teller and listener." She heard about her family history. "These things are not written anywhere," she told Jaggi; "sitting with an older person tells you another side." Storytelling is very important in Haitian culture, and Neda Atanasoski, in the Voices from the Gaps website by the University of Minnesota, sees that Danticat has been heavily "influenced by the Haitian practice of story-telling which developed because much of the population was not literate at the time."

WHAT DO I READ NEXT?

- Author Junot Díaz was born in the Dominican Republic, which shares the Caribbean island of Hispaniola with Haiti. Like Danticat, Díaz immigrated to the United States as a child. His collection *Drown* (1996) contains short stories about Dominican immigrants living in New York and New Jersey.

- Julia Alvarez, another Caribbean American author, wrote *In the Time of the Butterflies* (1994), an account of the three Mirabal sisters in 1960. Alvarez mixes fiction with history in this tale, describing how the Mirabals became involved in politics and were eventually killed for participating in the revolution against the Trujillo dictatorship in the Dominican Republic.

- In *Behind the Mountains* (2002), Danticat writes about thirteen-year-old Celiane, who lives in Haiti until she, her brother, and her mother move to Brooklyn, where her father has been working. Although the book is fiction rather than autobiography, Danticat has admitted that some of the story's elements came from her own experiences and those of her friends and family.

- *Sammy and Juliana in Hollywood* (2004), by Benjamin Alire Sáenz, shares many themes with "Night Talkers." Juliana is killed, and Sammy is haunted by her death, much as Dany cannot forget his parents' murder. Sammy must learn to cope and move on with his life in spite of his loss.

- Danticat's memoir *Brother, I'm Dying* (2007) is a tribute to her uncle, who cared for her while her parents worked in New York to make a better life for the family. Danticat's uncle was a second father to her, though he kept some emotional distance between them. Danticat moved to the United States with her parents when she was twelve, and much later, once she was an adult and pregnant with her own child, continued political upheaval in Haiti forced her uncle to flee the country. Complications with US customs meant that he was detained for days, and he died before he was released.

- Madison Smartt Bell sheds light on the life of an important figure in Haitian history in *Toussaint Louverture: A Biography* (2007). Louverture was a former slave who turned out to be a brilliant military strategist. His leadership was key in Haiti's fight for independence in the late eighteenth and early nineteenth centuries.

Evidence of Danticat's being inspired by storytelling appears throughout her works. The title of her second novel, *Krik? Krak!* (1995), comes from the Haitian tradition of a storyteller asking, "Krik?" and his audience answering, "Krak!" as an affirmation that they are listening. In a review of *The Dew Breaker* in *Black Issues Book Review*, Marjorie Valbrun points out that "many of Danticat's characters are storytellers themselves. They quote proverbs when they speak of joy and aspirations or when they share their grief and regrets." The oral tradition is echoed in *The Dew Breaker* by the different point of view for each tale, like a group of people telling each other their stories.

Contrasted with the importance of storytelling is a negative thread running throughout the collection: Danticat displays many situations where communication breaks down, showing how modern life, assimilation into American culture, and the inability to discuss the past disconnect people from the traditions and history that give them stability. In the story "Water Child," for example, the central character, Nadine, is a nurse, and she describes a common problem in the hospital where she works:

> Many post-op patients wake up bewildered to discover that their total laryngectomies mean they would no longer be able to talk. No matter how the doctor, nurses, and counselors prepared them, it was still a shock.

" CONTRASTED WITH THE IMPORTANCE OF STORYTELLING IS A NEGATIVE THREAD RUNNING THROUGHOUT THE COLLECTION: DANTICAT DISPLAYS MANY SITUATIONS WHERE COMMUNICATION BREAKS DOWN, SHOWING HOW MODERN LIFE, ASSIMILATION INTO AMERICAN CULTURE, AND THE INABILITY TO DISCUSS THE PAST DISCONNECT PEOPLE FROM THE TRADITIONS AND HISTORY THAT GIVE THEM STABILITY."

Here the lack of ability to talk is associated with an illness. In other stories, there are instances of phone calls that drop out, answering machine messages that are never played, and students in an English language class misunderstanding each other. Perhaps most relevant to a discussion of "Night Talkers" is the fact that in the collection's first story, "The Book of the Dead," the dew breaker himself suffers from an inability to talk; he cannot bring himself to tell his daughter the truth about his past for a very long time. The title of "Night Talkers" points directly to this inability to speak. Dany and his aunt are both "palannits, night talkers, people who wet their beds, not with urine but with words." They speak while sleeping of the things they cannot face or do not understand when they are awake.

From the very beginning of the story, there is a lack of communication. The narration explains that Aunt Estina does not come to meet Dany because she has no idea that he is coming. Dany "wanted to surprise her," but likely he also did not want to explain why he was coming. However, as soon as Dany makes contact with his aunt's neighbors in the village, things begin to improve. He says, "Bonjou, cousins," to the young woman and the children that he first meets, "remembering the childhood greeting his aunt had taught him." This exchange is more significant than the simple act of saying hello because Dany is reminded of his belief, when he was young, that greeting the neighbors as relations meant that he was "part of a massive family, every child his cousin and every adult his aunt or uncle." Indeed, as Dany

meets more of the villagers, he is greeted like a member of the community, even though he has been gone for ten years.

When Dany meets Old Zo, his hesitancy about talking returns. Old Zo quickly recognizes who Dany is, and when he mentions how his parents died, he feels unprepared, with "an egg-sized lump growing in his throat. He hadn't expected to be talking about these things so soon." Danticat contrasts Dany's resistance to discuss his family's tragedy with Old Zo's almost reflexive need to share stories and make a familial connection. He tells Dany, "My grandfather Nozial and [Estina's] grandfather Dorméus were cousins." Old Zo even briefly recounts the story of Dany's parents' death, although he must be aware that Dany knows what happened. There is a group of eavesdropping children, "their eyes beaming as though they were being treated to a frightening folktale in the middle of the day."

When Dany meets Claude, who was deported from the United States because he shot and killed his father, the reader learns that Claude, like Dany, has problems with communication. Aunt Estina tells Dany that "Claude understands Creole and is learning to speak bit by bit." Claude was very much assimilated into a negative part of American culture, using and selling drugs. It is taking a lot of effort for him to get back to his Haitian roots, but his family is helping him. "It's like a puzzle," he tells Dany. "I'm the puzzle and these people are putting me back together, telling me things about myself and my family that I never knew." The storytelling of his family is starting to change him for the better, bringing him back to himself.

Dany tries to discuss finding the dew breaker with his aunt, but she is very resistant. The most extensive conversation he has with her occurs in a dream. When he wakes, she answers a few questions but then tells Dany, "I don't know. . . . All I know is I'm very tired now. Let me sleep." The night Dany's parents died is the defining moment of his life, and finding the man he believes killed them is hugely significant for him. However, his aunt is never able to tell him everything she knows. It is almost as if she dies rather than face discussing the tragedy. Dany has to accept that he will never truly understand.

After Estina dies, Dany is again unable to communicate. As the neighbors take over and make preparations for Estina's burial, the men discuss his silence: "He's in shock," they say.

Danticat's works often feature characters who live between the American and Haitian worlds.

(© Styve Reineck / ShutterStock.com)

"Can't you see he's not able to speak?" Dany notices that they are "speaking about him as though he couldn't understand, as if he were solely an English speaker." Dany mourns his aunt, wanting "to close his eyes until he could wake up from this unusual dream where everyone was able to speak except the two of them."

At Estina's wake, Dany thinks about his aunt: the sacrifices she made for him and how she sent him to New York to give him a new life. He wants to share these things with the neighbors, but he still cannot make himself speak. He does, however, take comfort from the stories the other villagers tell; he enjoys "the time carved out for the mourners to tell stories about the deceased, singular tales of first or last encounters, which could make one either chuckle or weep." Dany begins to understand why these traditions are important—as everyone tires and the conversation lags, "the reason for the all-night gathering had become all too clear, when the purple shroud," hung to mark a house in mourning, "could no longer be ignored."

In the "Night Talkers," there is a constant undercurrent expressing the interest and respect that Haitian culture has for storytelling. Danticat shows how telling stories and sharing history give people the stability of established tradition, teaching them about their past and giving them strength for the future. As Dany learns to mourn and cope with the loss of his aunt, and as Claude learns to live a life without drugs and violence, Danticat shows the healing power of storytelling. In *The Dew Breaker*, Danticat continues the tradition of storytelling, weaving the stories of various Haitian Americans into a narrative that is moving and at times unsettling.

Source: Kristen Sarlin Greenberg, Critical Essay on "Night Talkers," in *Short Stories for Students*, Gale, Cengage Learning, 2013.

Robert McCormick

In the following review, McCormick critiques the structure of The Dew Breaker.

"Ka, your father was the hunter, he was not the prey." With those words, Ka's father reveals the truth to his daughter in "The Book of the Dead," the first section of Edwidge Danticat's recent work, *The Dew Breaker*. One vaguely intuits then why he threw Ka's wooden sculpture of him, called "The Prisoner," into one of Florida's innumerable artificial lakes. We don't understand completely, however, the significance of his prominent facial scar, although we sense, as was the case in Danticat's 1998 novel, *The Farming of Bones* (see *WLT* 73:2, p. 377), that it is the scar of Haiti, the badge Haitians wear as a visible sign of their collective suffering.

Danticat's latest fictional work starts slowly. One suspects the author may have made too many concessions to reality in her photographic representation of the flatness of American life with its newly enriched Haitian American television stars; its motel culture; its police officers from Lakeland, Florida, who don't know the geography of the New World; the social pressure in East Flatbush to put up Christmas decorations, et cetera. There is, too, a bit of the sociologist in her detailing the folklore of Haiti: the ritual "branding" of the clothes of those soon to be buried, her presentation of the "palannits," or the "night talkers, people who wet their beds, not with urine but with words." By the end, however, we understand why Ka's Haitian American parents choose to remain on life's surface.

I wish I could say this text was well constructed. Its powerful final chapter explains certain mysteries, such as the origin of Mr.

Bienaimé's scar. It also illuminates certain ironies of the lives of Ka's parents, such as Anne's patrolling the aisle at midnight mass on Christmas Eve to inform her daughter that a stranger they see there is not the Haitian assassin whom his daughter thinks she recognizes from posters. Or the fact that the son, whose parents were victims of the former "dew breaker," rents a basement apartment from the unobtrusive Mr. Bienaimé, who, in Brooklyn, has become a barber. Some of the nine segments don't seem to belong, though. In fact, almost all the chapters were published previously as short stories.

Unlike *The Farming of Bones*, which focused on Haiti and the Dominican Republic in the late 1930s, this text is grounded in the 1960s but also relates the last few minutes in Haiti of "Baby Doc" Duvalier in 1986 and the subsequent vigilantism directed against the henchmen he left behind. It also vaguely evokes Aristide, because Ka's father, in his last official act, abducts from his church in Bel-Air and then kills a converted Baptist clergyman (Aristide is Catholic), the same clergyman who, in the Casernes Dessalines military barracks, will scar his interrogator's face with the splintered wood of a broken chair in his last defiant act. Running away, bleeding, the torturer encounters the pastor's stepsister outside the barracks, ignorant of his role as her stepbrother's murderer, even of the clergyman's death, she nurses the facial wounds of the Tonton Macoute. The National Palace, however, wanted the preacher alive, so the next day Ka's future parents obtain seats on a plane for New York.

Ultimately, one understands why the father always covers his face and never wants it photographed. We understand why Anne goes to mass regularly and why she must view the "transformation" of her husband as a quasireligious miracle in which she plays the primary role. We understand their unobtrusive lifestyle, why they don't put up Christmas decorations. What we don't know, though, is just as important, for, although Anne ultimately learns her stepbrother was killed, it is not clear whether she ever learns that her husband was the preacher's murderer.

The text presents two levels of truth. One is the father's admission to Ka at the beginning that he was the "hunter." After having read the final chapter, though, we wonder how much he really told his daughter. Did he tell her he killed the preacher? Danticat doesn't tell us how Ka will react to what she has learned after she hangs up on her mother.

Source: Robert McCormick, Review of *The Dew Breaker*, in *World Literature Today*, Vol. 79, No. 1, January–April 2005, pp. 83–84.

Kyle Minor

In the following review, Minor examines the structure of The Dew Breaker, *arguing that it blurs the line between novel and story collection.*

The Dew Breaker is a book without a hero; it is also a work of fiction that so carefully blurs the line between novel and short-story collection that one is hard pressed to identify which it might be. Danticat opens with a tale concerning a father-daughter journey to Florida. The daughter, a sculptor, plans to deliver a bust of her father to a famous Haitian actress. The father disappears with the bust, and when he returns he claims to have thrown it into a lake. Furious, the daughter demands to know why her father destroyed her work on the day of the sale, the day of her coming out as a real artist. Her father explains that he is not the man she thinks he is, that before moving to America he tortured and killed many Haitians, that this was his work. And then, abruptly, Danticat shifts the narrative to seemingly unrelated stories. The stories are compelling on their own merits, but it is their small details—passing references to the other stories—that are telling. These lives have intersected, and the thread that connects them is the father from the first story, the torturer once known as a dew breaker. Rick Moody masterfully pulled off a similar trick in his novella *Ring of Brightest Angels Around Heaven*, a story about unrelated characters cohering because of shared space, shared history, shared pain. But Danticat ups the ante with a novella-sized denouement of her own. The reader is thrown backwards through decades to the defining moment of the dew breaker himself. His horrors—which have appeared throughout the book as muted, awful history—now take center stage. He accosts, tortures, and murders a preacher who has been problematic for the state. His cruelties are legion. Even his superiors are appalled by his conduct. At the story's end he meets the preacher's sister in the street. They move to New York and marry, and she gives birth to a daughter who grows up to become a sculptor.

Source: Kyle Minor, Review of *The Dew Breaker*, in *Antioch Review*, Vol. 62, No. 4, Fall 2004, p. 774.

Rhonda Cobham

In the following review, Cobham offers a stylistic and thematic analysis of The Dew Breaker.

Aristide's desperate struggle to govern in Haiti is barely mentioned in Edwidge Danticat's new novel. Her focus is mostly on the ways in which events in the 1980s, near the end of the Duvalier regime, continue to haunt Haitians who have since migrated to America. Nevertheless, the nagging uncertainties surrounding Haiti's recent crisis reverberated like the shadow pain of an amputated limb all through my reading of *The Dew Breaker*. The narrator in Danticat's last novel, *The Farming of Bones*, bore witness to the genocide of Haitians at the hands of their Dominican neighbors in the mid-1930s. This time, however, both hunter and prey are the monstrous progeny of Haiti itself.

The narrative line in *The Dew Breaker* is strung across a series of linked short stories that leads to a single question: Can the tales we tell about our past offer us any alternatives in the future other than those of becoming either hunter or prey? The answer, like the answer to the riddle about trees and their shadows with which the book closes, depends on perspective: the angles from which the multiple plots illuminate character; the chronology the entire narrative imposes on events; the quotidian details—a stone in a glass of water, an overflowing ashtray, three snippets of fabric—through which the stories locate or sublimate pain. Danticat's unexpected juxtapositions intensify the quiet tragedies on the periphery of the action. Thus, a casual sexual liaison one story mentions in passing seems merely ornamental in a plot that focuses on the protagonist's reunification with his newly arrived wife. When the same liaison resurfaces at the margins of another story, from the perspective of the woman whose happiness it destroyed, we discover that the small cruelties we easily forgive in fictional heroes and close friends may be susceptible to the same scrutiny as the enormities of which we accuse our most sadistic enemies.

Danticat's use of language raises the stakes in the wider debate over the most effective way to represent the Creole voice on the page. Unlike Patrick Chamoiseau's Martinican Creole in his Prix Goncourt–winning novel *Texaco*, which acquires a patina of innocence in response to the corrupting dominance of colonial French, Danticat's Haitian Creole is used by state officials as

> **LIKE DANTICAT'S PREVIOUS NOVELS, *THE DEW BREAKER* SUCCEEDS IN TRANSFORMING HAITI AND ITS DIASPORA FROM AN ABJECT SPECTACLE TO A SYMBOL OF THE PERSISTENCE OF HUMAN DIGNITY IN THE FACE OF TERROR."**

well as ordinary Haitian people. Consequently, her narrators cannot claim to speak a language that has no alliances with institutional authority. Moreover, Danticat sees Caribbean Creoles as vital, increasingly metropolitan, phenomena that change continuously in response to new political and linguistic challenges. The title *The Dew Breaker,* for example, is one translation of *shoukèt laroze,* an expression that refers to the silent, magical way in which dew "falls," or "breaks," as they say in Haitian Creole, on the early morning leaves. As Danticat explains, Haitians under Duvalier's regime often used the term ironically to name the state-sponsored torturers who typically descended upon their victims in the silence before dawn. But Danticat's title also signifies on Jaques Roumain's 1946 novel, *Les Gouverneurs de la rosée,* translated into English by Langston Hughes as *Masters of the Dew.* Roumain co-opts the picturesque, rural imagery of *shoukèl laroze* into his novel's rewriting of *Romeo and Juliet* as Haitian pastoral. His translation of the Creole phrase allows him to connect Haiti's feudal past to his utopian vision for a triumphant proletariat future in a modern nation state, where men will be masters of the elements, capable of transcending narrow allegiances to family and clan. At the time Roumain was writing, nationalism in Europe already had demonstrated a sinister proclivity for co-opting "authentic" folk customs and language to support the agendas of totalitarian regimes. However, Roumain's translation of *shoukèt laroze* elides that possibility in the Creole context. Danticat's alternative translation suggests violence as well as mastery. It makes visible the excesses of the nationalist, socialist, and capitalist ideologies that have stunted Haiti's growth during the six decades that separate *The Dew Breaker* from *Masters of the Dew.*

Freed from the myth of a morally untainted Creole, as well as from the assumption that Creole-speaking subjects never think or speak on their own behalf within the discourse of modernity, Danticat can use any language register she chooses to carry her message. All the registers available to her characters make their appearance in the stories. The text indicates their presence by meticulously documenting the media through which these multiple languages are filtered. There are New York AM talk radio broadcasts in French and Creole; answering machine cassettes containing messages in stilted English that start off with "*Alo!*"; notebooks crammed with English sentences in barely decipherable script; tables bearing food or drinks over which American English is peppered with Haitian expressions like *sezi*—the Creole word for crazy—or *Kennedy*—Creole slang for secondhand American clothes. Much of this linguistic variety is transcribed onto the page in English, but Danticat alerts the reader each time the language shifts. In one tense exchange between the protagonist, Ka, and her father, for example, the three language registers represented are crucial to the emotional nuance of the passage. Ka's continued identification with the father she can no longer trust; his need, after years of silence, to explain himself to her; the necessity and impossibility of their communication—all are indicated in their awkward shifts between Haitian English, Haitian Creole, and American English:

> "I say rest in Creole," he prefaces, "because my tongue too heavy in English to say things like this, especially older things."
> "Fine," I reply defiantly in English.
> "Ka," he continues in Creole, "when I first saw your statue, I wanted to be buried with it, to take it with me into the other world."
> "Like the Ancient Egyptians," I continue in English.
> He smiles, grateful, I think, that in spite of everything, I can still appreciate his passions.

And then there are the endless, empty silences that leave their bearers scarred and bloated: A reflection in a shiny metal elevator door grotesquely inflates the body of a woman who can speak to no one about the pregnancy she has aborted. The bruised, calloused hands of a child bear silent witness to the daily torture of the classroom. Like the novice journalist who interviews a wedding seamstress in one story, the reader is challenged to imagine "men and women whose tremendous agonies filled every

blank space in their lives. Maybe there were hundreds, even thousands, of people like this, men and women chasing fragments of themselves long lost to others." For these silent characters, the issue is not one of authenticity—which choice of language is most politically correct for describing their pain—but of ontology—how does one begin to describe a pain that exists beyond language?

The answer, for Danticat, seems to be that stories must be told with whatever words we have—even the stories about their victims that torturers revisit in their dreams. One crucial moment of storytelling occurs deep in the Haitian countryside. The scene is reminiscent of Joseph Zobel's 1955 novel *Rue Cases-Nègres*, better known to American audiences in its 1983 adaptation for the screen by Euzhan Palcy as *Sugar Cane Alley*. The film follows the conventions of the Caribbean narrative of childhood, in which Creole communities figure as sites of rural innocence that the boy protagonist celebrates, even as he moves away from femininity, orality, and pastoral freedoms towards masculinity, text, and the disciplines of modernity. Danticat's story inverts this paradigm. Instead of sitting with the child protagonist at the feet of a wise old griot who instructs us in the myths of his people's origins, we lounge with the teenager Claude, as he imports the hip-hop idiom of Flatbush Avenue into a new myth of origins about a son who destroys his father in order to feed his drug habit. Claude cannot speak Creole, yet he is one of the few protagonists in the novel who comes close to achieving absolution through narrative. Another man writes down his story in a formal letter addressed to his unborn child. A woman learns how to "parcel out [her] sorrows" in stories and songs among her friends, "each walking out with fewer than we'd carried in."

Like Danticat's previous novels, *The Dew Breaker* succeeds in transforming Haiti and its diaspora from an abject spectacle to a symbol of the persistence of human dignity in the face of terror. Even the hunters in this grim passion play seem to struggle for redemption through the penance of speech. Like their prey, they carry on their bodies the scars left by the indignities they have suffered and inflicted. And yet those same bodies continue to yearn for beauty and order and the possibility of love. There is nothing sentimental about Danticat's novel. It has etched into my imagination images I would prefer to think have no basis in reality. But, like the mouth that contains both speech and silence in the *Egyptian Book of the Dead*, from which Ka gets her name, this novel's unlikely combination of shadows, rhythms, and silences captures the aspirations all immigrants bring with them, the nightmares we are trying to escape, and the fantasies of joy, loss, and longing that tie us inextricably to imagined homelands in the Caribbean, in Brooklyn, and beyond.

Source: Rhonda Cobham, "The Penance of Speech," in *Women's Review of Books*, Vol. 21, No. 8, May 2004, pp. 2–3.

SOURCES

Atanasoski, Neda, "Edwidge Danticat: Biography/Criticism," Voices from the Gaps, University of Minnesota website, February 23, 1998, http://voices.cla.umn.edu/artistpages/danticatEdwidge.php (accessed July 9, 2012).

Birnbaum, Robert, "Edwidge Danticat," in *Morning News*, April 20, 2004, http://www.themorningnews.org/article/birnbaum-v.-edwidge-danticat (accessed July 9, 2012).

Danticat, Edwidge, "Water Child" and "Night Talkers," in *The Dew Breaker*, Alfred A. Knopf, 2004, pp. 55, 87–120.

Gibb, Lorna, "The Torturer's Wife," in *Times Literary Supplement*, No. 5275, May 7, 2004, p. 22.

"Haiti," in *New York Times*, http://topics.nytimes.com/top/news/international/countriesandterritories/haiti/index.html (accessed August 2, 2012).

"HerStory: Fiction," in *Ebony*, Vol. 59, No. 5, March 2004, p. 28.

Jaggi, Maya, "Island Memories," in *Guardian(London, England)*, November 19, 2004, http://www.guardian.co.uk/books/2004/nov/20/featuresreviews.guardianreview9 (accessed July 9, 2012).

"Liberals in Haiti Rounded Up," in *Times(London, England)*, December 1, 1980, No. 60790, Column D, p. 5.

Lyon, Annabel, "A Torturer in Full," in *Globe & Mail* (Toronto, Canada), March 27, 2004, p. D20.

Meehan, Kevin, and Bernadette A. Davis, "Edwidge Danticat," in *Dictionary of Literary Biography*, Vol. 350, *Twenty-First-Century American Novelists, Second Series*, edited by Wanda H. Giles, Gale, Cengage Learning, 2009, pp. 69–79.

Minor, Kyle, Review of *The Dew Breaker*, in *Antioch Review*, Vol. 62, No. 4, Fall 2004, p. 774.

Moorehead, Caroline, "Prisoners of Conscience," in *Times* (London, England), No. 60754, October 20, 1980, p. 5.

Review of *The Dew Breaker*, in *Christian Century*, Vol. 121, No. 25, December 14, 2004, p. 22.

Review of *The Dew Breaker*, in *Publishers Weekly*, Vol. 251, No. 8, February 23, 2004, p. 49.

Valbrun, Marjorie, Review of *The Dew Breaker*, in *Black Issues Book Review*, Vol. 6, No. 4, July–August 2004, p. 43.

Zarr, Gerald, "The Tumultuous History of Haiti," in *History*, February–March 2011, pp. 32–35.

FURTHER READING

Blashfield, Jean F., *Haiti: Enchantment of the World*, Children's Press, 2008.

This introduction to Haiti's history, culture, and geography, though written for younger teens, has a wealth of information for any reader, including maps, time lines, and photographs.

Danticat, Edwidge, *Krik? Krak!*, Soho, 1995.

This collection was a finalist for the National Book Award. In its nine stories, Danticat explores the effects of Haiti's political oppression on its people. The overall tone of the book reflects a sadness for the author's home country, but, as in *The Dew Breaker*, Danticat also shows her characters' strength and resourcefulness.

Morrison, Toni, *Beloved*, Alfred A. Knopf, 1987.

Danticat claims Morrison's writing as an influence on her own. *Beloved*, like "Night Talkers" and *The Dew Breaker* as a whole, is also a story about someone who has done something terrible. The books explore similar themes of loss, guilt, redemption, and forgiveness.

Sandaire, Johnny, *Haiti: A Photographic Documentation*, Lulu Enterprises, 2008.

In this volume, Sandaire shows readers images of Haiti before the devastating 2010 earthquakes. The photographs depict Haitians from all walks of life and display the physical beauty of the island in its cities, beaches, and mountains, as well as its poverty and political tension.

SUGGESTED SEARCH TERMS

Edwidge Danticat

Edwidge Danticat AND The Dew Breaker

Edwidge Danticat AND Night Talkers

Edwidge Danticat AND Haiti

Edwidge Danticat AND short story

Edwidge Danticat AND politics

Haitian immigration to United States

Papa Doc AND tonton macoutes

Oliver's Evolution

JOHN UPDIKE

1998

"Oliver's Evolution" is a short story written by the American author John Updike. First published in *Esquire*'s April 1998 issue, the story was the last of many that Updike published in that magazine. It is an example of a subgenre of fiction variously called snap fiction, flash fiction, micro fiction, or sudden fiction, referring to short stories that are very short. The term *flash fiction* was coined by James Thomas, Denise Thomas, and Tom Hazuka, who were inspired by Ernest Hemingway's 750-word "A Very Short Story" in compiling an anthology of very short stories. Later, James Thomas, along with Robert Shapard, compiled a collection of eighty short stories that are no more than two thousand words in length. Among the stories in their 2006 collection *Flash Fiction Forward* is "Oliver's Evolution," a brief (647-word) tale about a boy with neglectful parents who evolves into a solid, if flawed, man. "Oliver's Evolution" is also included in Updike's *Licks of Love: Short Stories and a Sequel*, published in 2000. It is available online on the *Esquire* website at http://www. esquire.com/fiction/fiction/john-updike-final-story -0498.

AUTHOR BIOGRAPHY

Updike was one of America's preeminent men of letters for the half century and more

John Updike *(© Jeff Morgan 14 / Alamy)*

preceding his death. He appeared twice on the cover of *Time* magazine, and his work was a fixture in the pages of the *New Yorker*, *Esquire*, and other prominent magazines. He published thirty novels, fourteen collections of short stories, ten collections of poetry, thirteen collections of nonfiction essays and criticism, and numerous book reviews and pieces of art criticism for such publications as the *New York Review of Books*. He also won virtually every prestigious award writers can win: the O. Henry Award, the National Book Critics Circle Award for Fiction (twice), the National Book Award for Fiction, the PEN/Faulkner Award for Fiction, and (twice) the Pulitzer Prize for Fiction.

An only child, John Hoyer Updike was born on March 18, 1932, in Reading, Pennsylvania, though he grew up in the nearby town of Shillington, where his father was a high-school science teacher. In Updike's fiction, Reading and Shillington are often represented by the fictional towns of Brewer and Olinger, respectively. Updike would later say that his inspiration to become a writer came from his mother, who was an aspiring writer. When Updike

was thirteen, the family moved to his mother's birthplace, a farmhouse on eighty acres of land near Plowville, just eleven miles away from Shillington.

Updike was a good student, graduating as co-valedictorian and president of his high school class. After high school, he spent his summers working as a copy boy for a Reading newspaper and even wrote several feature stories for the newspaper. He went on to attend Harvard University, where he majored in English and was a frequent contributor to the *Harvard Lampoon*, serving as its president his senior year. While he was still a student, he married Mary E. Pennington. In 1954, he graduated summa cum laude, and that year he sold a short story and a poem to the *New Yorker* magazine, beginning a long and fruitful association with that publication. After a year studying art at Oxford University in England, Updike returned to Manhattan, where he found a job as a staff writer at the *New Yorker*. Nearly two years later, after the birth of his second child, he decided to become a full-time writer and moved to Ipswich, Massachusetts. He would live in Massachusetts for the remainder of his life.

Updike's first novel, *The Poorhouse Fair*, was published in 1959. With the help of a Guggenheim Fellowship, he wrote the first of the "Rabbit" novels, *Rabbit, Run* (1960), which introduced his most recognizable character, a small-town former high-school basketball player named Harry "Rabbit" Angstrom. The book and its sequels would establish Updike as one of the leading authors of his generation. In 1963, he received the National Book Award for his novel *The Centaur*, which was inspired by his childhood. At age thirty-two, he became the youngest person ever elected to the National Institute of Arts and Letters. His best-selling novel *Couples* prompted *Time* magazine to feature him on its cover in 1968. In 1970, he launched a new series with *Bech: A Book*, featuring a fictional novelist named Henry Bech, and in 1971, he published *Rabbit Redux*. In the 1970s, Updike served as a US cultural ambassador and joined with other writers in condemning the Soviet Union's persecution of dissident author Alexander Solzhenitsyn. In 1976, he and his wife were divorced; the next year he married Martha Ruggles and settled with her in Georgetown, Massachusetts.

Updike continued the Rabbit series with *Rabbit Is Rich* in 1981, which won the Pulitzer Prize for Fiction in 1982. Through the 1980s and 1990s, Updike published a trilogy of novels retelling Nathaniel Hawthorne's *The Scarlet Letter*, and in 1991, he published *Rabbit at Rest*, for which he won a second Pulitzer Prize. In 1989, President George H. W. Bush presented him with the National Medal of Art, and in 2003, President George W. Bush presented him with the National Medal for the Humanities. Updike spent his last years in Beverly Farms, Massachusetts, where he wrote his last book, *The Widows of Eastwick*, a sequel to his 1984 novel *The Witches of Eastwick*. He died of lung cancer in Danvers, Massachusetts, on January 27, 2009.

PLOT SUMMARY

"Oliver's Evolution" is a brief short story that contains no dialogue, nor does it contain any of the usual descriptive passages characteristic of fiction. It begins abruptly with the announcement that Oliver's parents did not intend to abuse him. They intended to love him, but he was near the end of a "pack" of children, so the challenge of bringing up a child was "wearing thin" for them. Oliver, too, was prone to mishaps. His feet were turned inward, so for a time he wore casts to straighten them. When the casts were finally removed, Oliver was terrified, for he thought that the casts were a part of his body. When he was a small child, his parents found him in a dressing room with a box of mothballs; some of the mothballs were wet with saliva, suggesting that Oliver had put them in his mouth. His parents took him to the hospital to have his stomach pumped, although later they were not sure that doing so was necessary. On another occasion, he was at the beach with his parents, who swam off together, having spent the previous night drinking at a party and then quarreling. They became aware that Oliver had toddled off into the water only after he was saved from drowning by an alert lifeguard who found him floating on his face.

Oliver, the reader is told, complained the least of any of his parents' children. He cast no blame on his parents or on the authorities at his school for their failure to detect his "sleepy" eye when the eye might have responded to therapy. The result was that the world looked fuzzy when he closed that eye. The reader is told that Oliver's father wept when his son had to hold a schoolbook at an odd angle to the light.

Oliver was the wrong age, thirteen, when his parents separated and divorced. His older brothers, off at boarding school and college, were free of the family; his younger sister was actually excited by eating in restaurants with her father and meeting her mother's friendly dates. But Oliver felt weighed down by the household and shared his mother's sense of abandonment. His father blamed himself when Oliver's grades, first in school, then in college, started to slip. Oliver broke an arm falling down the stairs at a fraternity house, although another account of the incident had it that he leaped from a girl's dormitory window. Oliver also managed to crash several family automobiles, although he escaped these accidents with only bruised knees and loose teeth. The teeth became firm again, preserving one of Oliver's best features: an innocent smile that would slowly spread across his face.

In the story's final paragraph, the reader learns that Oliver married, a marriage characterized as "yet another mishap" that went along with the failed opportunities and abandoned jobs of his young adulthood. His wife, Alicia, was as accident-prone as her husband. She was also given to substance abuse, unwanted pregnancies, and emotional turmoil. However, she looked up to Oliver because he, in comparison, was solid and "surefooted." The narrative then notes that "what we expect of others, they endeavor to provide." In response to Alicia's expectations, Oliver held on to a job. Alicia then "held on to her pregnancies." Oliver is now the father of two children, a fair-haired daughter and a dark-haired son. Oliver can hold the two of them at the same time; he is compared to a tree and to a boulder, with his children as birds in a nest. In the story's final sentence, the reader is told: "He is a protector of the weak."

CHARACTERS

Alicia

Alicia becomes Oliver's young wife. She tends to have unwanted pregnancies and, like her husband, is accident-prone. She also is a substance abuser, although the nature of the substance—alcohol, drugs, or both—is never specified, and she is subject to emotional disturbances. However, she looks up to Oliver, allowing him to evolve into a good husband and father, which in turn allows her to become a more responsible wife and mother.

Oliver

Oliver is the protagonist of "Oliver's Evolution." The story spans his life, from the time that he is an infant, through his childhood, up until the time he is married and the father of two young children. As a child, Oliver was in a sense abused, although the abuse took the form more of neglect than of physical or emotional violence. The reader is told that he was prone to mishaps. As a small child he had to wear casts on his legs because his legs were turned inward. Later, he had to be rushed to the hospital because he put mothballs in his mouth. On another occasion, he nearly drowned when his parents left him alone on a beach. When he was thirteen, his parents separated and divorced, causing Oliver to feel responsible for the household and to share in his mother's sense of abandonment. His grades in school started to decline after his parents' divorce. At college he was injured in a mishap, although the details of the mishap are disputed. The reader is finally told something positive about Oliver when it is noted

that he had an innocent smile that was among his best features. During his young adulthood, he abandoned jobs and missed opportunities. He married Alicia, who in many respects was a mirror of himself. In time, though, Oliver evolved into a firmer, more surefooted person who held on to a job and fathered two children. At the end, he is characterized as a "tree," a "sheltering boulder" and a "protector of the weak."

Oliver's Parents

The reader is told little about Oliver's parents. They remain unnamed, and they are not described in any detail. They had several children, and by the time they had Oliver, they were no longer fully up to the challenges of being parents. Accordingly, they tended to neglect their son, failing to show the care and concern that one would normally expect from parents. Virtually nothing is said about the mother as an individual. The father is said to have wanted to "weep impotently" because of Oliver's eye problem, and he is said to have "impotently grieved" as a consequence of the parents' divorce and Oliver's reaction to it. The repetition of the word *impotently* suggests a person who has no force of character and stands in contrast to the images of potency when Oliver is later compared to a tree and a boulder.

THEMES

Parent-Child Relationships

"Oliver's Evolution" is in large part a story about a child's relationship with his parents. The story opens with the startling statement that Oliver's parents "had not meant to abuse him." They even intended to love him, but after having raised at least two other boys (the "older brothers" referred to in the story's fourth paragraph), they lacked the energy needed to give Oliver the attention and care to which he was entitled. The story goes on to characterize the nature of the parents' neglect. When Oliver was thirteen years old, his parents separated and divorced, changing the nature of his relationship with his parents. Afterward he felt that he had to share his mother's sense of abandonment. Mention is made that Oliver did not blame his parents for their neglect, suggesting that he has a forgiving disposition. At the end of the story, Oliver has established a very different, more positive relationship with his own children.

TOPICS FOR FURTHER STUDY

- Write your own piece of "flash fiction," a brief short story that concentrates on a single character, either in a moment of time or over a span of time. Set yourself a word-count limit, perhaps a thousand words. Post your story on your blog and invite your classmates to comment.

- Locate a copy of Ernest Hemingway's "A Very Short Story"; the story is included in *Sudden Fiction: American Short-Short Stories* (1983), edited by Robert Shapard and James Thomas. Prepare a chart that traces the similarities and differences between Hemingway's story and Updike's. Share your chart with your class. You might focus on theme, point of view, characterization, use of figurative language, and any other elements you identify.

- Imagine that you are Oliver and that you are now a young adult, married, with two children. Further imagine that you have broken off contact with your parents (as they are depicted in the story) but that you want to reestablish contact. Write to them a letter that would attempt to give them some insight into your early life with them and how it shaped you. As a point of departure, you might read *Letters to My Mother* (2007), by Teresa Cárdenas, a young-adult novel about an Afro-Cuban girl living in Cuba whose mother has died. She lives with an aunt and grandmother who mistreat her, and in her letters the girl discusses her feelings about the way she is treated.

- Updike's writing career spanned much of the Cold War, between the United States and its allies on the one hand and the Soviet Union and its satellite states on the other. Write a brief essay in which you speculate on how the Cold War, including the threat of nuclear war and the massive destruction and loss of life it would contribute to, might have affected authors during the second half of the twentieth century.

- Oliver has at least three siblings: older brothers and a younger sister. Rewrite "Oliver's Evolution" from the point of view of one of the siblings. How do you think they would have viewed their brother? Their parents? Post your version of the story on a blog and allow your classmates to comment.

Neglect

Closely related to the theme of parent-child relationships is the theme of neglect. Throughout the opening paragraphs of the story, it is clear that Oliver's parents are guilty of a kind of benign neglect of their son. For example, on one occasion, they found him in a dressing room with a box of mothballs. Some of the mothballs were wet with saliva, suggesting that Oliver had eaten some or perhaps had sucked on them. The parents rushed him to the hospital to have his stomach pumped, but they later wondered whether that had been necessary, a thought suggesting that they did not want to go to any more trouble than they had to for their son. Later, when the family took a beach vacation, the parents attended a party at which they became drunk and quarrelsome. The next day, "striving for romantic harmony," they swam away, leaving Oliver alone. Oliver followed them into the water and was rescued from drowning only by the actions of an alert lifeguard. The neglect on the part of the parents is not active neglect; they do not starve him or otherwise mistreat him. The neglect is more in the nature of passive neglect, a kind of indifference or unwillingness to exert the effort needed to care for a child.

Responsibility

A third theme has to do with the "evolution" of Oliver. In the face of his upbringing, Oliver is prone to mishaps, and in his early adulthood, he

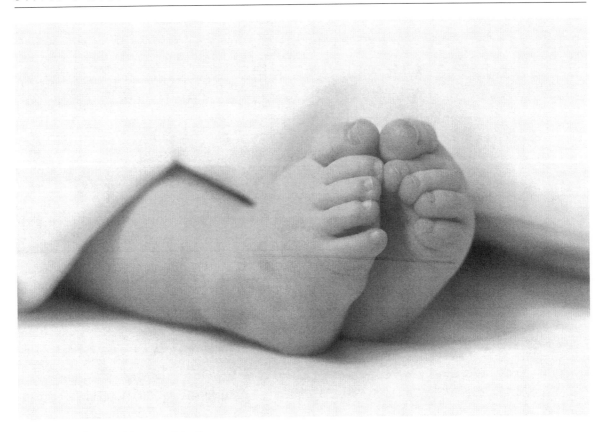

Oliver was born with turned-in feet. (© Jozsef Szasz-Fabian / ShutterStock.com)

is not a very responsible man. He marries a woman who in many respects is as irresponsible as he is; she is a substance abuser, she has unwanted pregnancies, and she leaves others bruised through her emotional turmoil. Oliver is said to have abandoned jobs and to have missed opportunities, although the nature of those opportunities is never specified. Yet despite the rocky start of his life, Oliver manages to grow into a more responsible adult, one who is "surefooted" and "solid."

Self-Realization

Along with achieving a sense of responsibility, Oliver seems to achieve a kind of self-realization. Humanists, psychoanalysts, and others have defined *self-realization* in numerous ways. Gerard Doyle, in his book *Being You: How to Live Authentically*, quotes famed psychologist Abraham Maslow, who defined self-realization as "the impulse to convert oneself into what one is capable of being." This definition could be applied to Oliver. After all the false starts and mishaps of

his earlier life, he evolves into a solid husband and father, one who can provide for his son and daughter and serve for them as a tree and a boulder—that is, as a presence that is solid and stable. At the end of the story, the reader is told that Oliver "is a protector of the weak." This evolution on his part suggests that he has achieved a state of self-realization—that he has converted himself into all that he is capable of being.

STYLE

Third-Person Point of View

The term *point of view* refers to two elements in a work of fiction. One answers the question, who is narrating the story? The other answers the question, from whose perspective is the story being narrated? Point of view is a key feature that distinguishes fiction from other literary genres. Sometimes the answer to the two questions is the same; in Mark Twain's *Huckleberry Finn*, the title character is the narrator, and he is narrating the story from his own perspective, in the first person. In other works of fiction, the answer is different, particularly when the narrator is a third-person "authorial" narrator, as it is in "Oliver's Evolution." Clearly, Oliver is not narrating his own tale, nor is anyone else in his life doing so. The story is being told to the reader by an omniscient narrator who knows everything about Oliver and his life and can outline it in summary fashion. The narrator, however, in places is telling the story less from Oliver's point of view than from his or her own. This becomes particularly apparent in the final paragraph, when the narrator, in his or her own voice, says, "This was the key. What we expect of others, they endeavor to provide." This is the narrator speaking, shifting perspective in order to provide the reader with a moral for the story.

Exposition

Fiction usually comprises a number of elements or modes, including dialogue, description, and exposition. It is noteworthy that "Oliver's Evolution" contains no dialogue and very little in the way of description. The reader has no sense of a time or place (although the modern phrase *substance abuse* used in reference to Alicia suggests a relatively recent time period). The reader is not told anything about where the story takes place; virtually all the reader learns is that Oliver's home is probably somewhere near a beach, but even this is uncertain. Further, characters are not described other than in terms of their behavior. The reader gets to know Oliver, his parents, Alicia, and to a lesser extent his siblings by what they do; otherwise, they are never described for the reader. The only snippet of description is the observation that Oliver has an "innocent smile" that can slowly spread across his face. The result is that the story consists almost entirely of exposition. This choice on Updike's part enables him to present the story as a piece of snap fiction, for he is able to distill the core of what he wants to say about Oliver and his relationships without having to flesh out or describe elements that are of less interest to him.

Metaphor

"Oliver's Evolution" concludes with three distinctive metaphors, that is, figures of speech that create an implied equivalency between two otherwise unlike objects. After Oliver has become the father of two children, it is said that "they are birds in a nest." The next sentence contains two metaphors: "He is a tree, a sheltering boulder." These metaphors, coming at the tail end of a story that overall does not rely on metaphor, symbolism, or other common figures of speech, stand out in stark contrast to the rest of the narration. The children now clearly occupy a position in Oliver's esteem that is unlike the one he occupied with his parents. The comparison of him to a tree suggests that he has put down roots and that his "branches" protect the children in a way that he was never protected as a child. The comparison to a sheltering boulder again emphasizes that Oliver provides his children with shelter and remains a solid presence in their lives, in a way that his parents did not.

Figure of Speech

In addition to metaphor, Updike uses a figure of speech that in formal rhetoric is called meiosis but in everyday speech is called understatement. *Meiosis* is a euphemistic figure of speech that implies that something is less important or smaller than it really is. It is often employed for humorous effect. After the American Civil War, people sometimes euphemistically referred to the conflict as the "recent unpleasantness," a phrase that vastly understates the bloodiness and bitterness of the war. In "Oliver's Evolution," Updike achieves a kind of tongue-in-cheek humorous effect early on when the narration says that "Oliver had come late in their little pack of offspring." The effect is humorous in a way that "Oliver had been born late" would not be. Similarly, the narration goes on to say that Oliver was born "at a time when the challenge of child-rearing was wearing thin, and he proved susceptible to mishaps." As the story goes on, the reader realizes that "wearing thin" understates the degree of his parents' neglect and that "susceptible to mishaps" understates the extent of Oliver's proneness to misfortune and accidents. Again, the understatement has a slightly humorous, tongue-in-cheek effect. A final example might be: "Not one but several family automobiles met a ruinous end with him at the wheel." Again, something like "Oliver wrecked several family cars" would be prosaic, but the understatement lends an air of humor to the observation.

HISTORICAL CONTEXT

"Oliver's Evolution" makes no reference to historical events. Many critics, however, argue that

COMPARE
&
CONTRAST

- **1990s:** The number of reported cases of neglected children in the United States is estimated at about 879,000 per year.

  Today: The number of reported cases of neglected children in the United States is estimated at about 2.4 million per year.

- **1990s:** Of married mothers with children under the age of one, 61.8 percent are in the paid workforce.

  Today: Of married mothers with children under the age of one, 55.8 percent are in the paid workforce.

- **1990s:** The Cold War with the Soviet Union, which Updike did what he could to oppose, is replaced by the growing threat of terrorism, particularly with the first World Trade Center bombing in 1993, the Khobar Towers bombing in Saudi Arabia in 1996, and the bombings of US embassies in Kenya and Tanzania in 1998, the year Updike wrote "Oliver's Evolution."

  Today: In response to the terrorist attacks of September 11, 2001, and the attack on the US embassy in Libya on September 11, 2012, the United States fights the ongoing threat of terrorism in such places as Afghanistan.

Updike's views about society, culture, and politics were shaped by the Cold War, which corresponded with a large portion of his career as a writer, and that he often used the Cold War as a figure of speech in his depiction of personal relationships and cultural realities. Updike also was a member of a group of writers who publicly protested the persecution of dissident Soviet author Alexander Solzhenitsyn. One could make the argument that the frozen, thwarted relationship between Oliver and his parents is a reflection of a kind of "cold war" that affects Oliver's life but also provides Oliver with an opportunity to change and grow, to achieve a kind of self-actualization through his personal freedom, just as the United States changed and grew as it, in Updike's view, sheltered the West from the threat of Communism.

The Cold War was an extraordinarily complex state of tension between the Western allies, led by the United States, and the Communist bloc, led by the Soviet Union and buttressed by the Soviets' satellite states, primarily in Eastern Europe but also in Africa and such places as Cuba. By all rights, the United States and the Soviet Union should have remained allies after World War II, for the two powers fought and defeated a common enemy, Nazi Germany. The wartime marriage, though, was one entirely of convenience. Prior to the war, the two nations had been ideological enemies, and the only reason they formed an alliance during the war was that both fervently wanted to crush Germany under dictator Adolf Hitler. Some observers actually believed that the United States and its allies would have been best served by rearming Germany, turning its army around, and joining it in driving the Soviets out of Eastern Europe.

After the war, the United States formed the North Atlantic Treaty Organization (NATO), a military alliance whose professed goal was the containment of Communism; among NATO's signatory nations were Belgium, the Netherlands, Luxembourg, France, and the United Kingdom, which were then joined by the United States, Canada, Portugal, Italy, Norway, Denmark, and Iceland. Indeed, the Truman Doctrine, promulgated in 1947, stated that the United States would support free people in their quest to remain free of outside pressure and subjugation; the doctrine was issued in the midst of civil war in Greece, which threatened to drive that nation into the Soviet sphere. For its part, the Soviet bloc formed the Warsaw Pact (officially, the Warsaw Treaty Organization of Friendship, Cooperation, and Mutual Assistance) in 1955; this was a military alliance of eight Communist states, including the Soviet Union as well as much of Eastern Europe, including Romania, Hungary, Poland, East Germany, Albania, Czechoslovakia, and Bulgaria.

The term *cold war* was first used in an essay written by George Orwell, "You and the Atomic Bomb," published in 1945; it was first applied to US-Soviet tensions by Bernard Baruch, a financier and presidential adviser, in a speech to the South Carolina House of Representatives in 1947:

> Let us not be deceived; we are today in the midst of a Cold War. Our enemies are to be found abroad and at home. Let us never forget this: Our unrest is the heart of their success.

The war was described as "cold" because it never led to any direct military conflict. Both sides possessed sophisticated military technology, including large and growing arsenals of nuclear weapons, so any eruption of the war into a "hot" war could have led to a nuclear exchange that would destroy the nations involved. In an odd way, peace was maintained through the principle of mutual assured destruction (or, appropriately, MAD).

At times, the Cold War warmed up. In 1948–49, the Soviets blockaded West Berlin, requiring the Western allies to mount a massive airlift of supplies to West Berliners. (Berlin was divided at the end of World War II; in order to get to democratic West Berlin, one had to cross through the territory of Communist East Germany.) The war became warmer still during the Korean War of 1950 to 1953, a proxy war between democratic South Korea (aided by UN troops) and Communist North Korea (aided by Communist China). In 1956 Soviet tanks invaded Hungary when that nation threatened to withdraw from the Warsaw Pact. In 1961, another crisis erupted in Berlin: after NATO refused Soviet demands for withdrawal of all military forces from West Berlin, the Soviets erected the Berlin Wall, partitioning the two parts of the city. That wall stood for decades as a stark symbol of the Cold War. Another frightening episode in the Cold War was the Cuban missile crisis of October 1962. The United States discovered that the Soviets were deploying nuclear missiles in Cuba that were capable of hitting American cities. For thirteen days, the world held its breath as the two superpowers seemed on the brink of going to war. Another proxy war was the conflict in Vietnam, which pitted democratic South Vietnam against Communist North Vietnam. This conflict extended from 1955 to 1975, although the first US ground troops did not see combat action until 1965. Other armed conflicts broke out in Latin America and elsewhere, with the Soviets helping to foment Communist revolutions.

During the 1970s, the United States and the Soviet Union entered a period of "détente," or a lessening of tensions. In the meantime, various nuclear test ban treaties had been signed, and efforts were under way to begin reducing both nations' stockpiles of nuclear weapons. But relations deteriorated after the Soviet invasion of Afghanistan in 1979. Then, in 1983, the United States and its European allies conducted Able Archer 83, a ten-day series of military war games and exercises designed to simulate an outbreak of armed conflict, including a nuclear exchange, in Europe. Those exercises, along with the anticipated arrival of US Pershing II nuclear missiles in Europe, unnerved the Soviets, who believed that NATO was preparing for war and that the United States was about to launch a preemptive first strike against the Soviets. Historians believe that during these days the world came closer to nuclear war than at any time since the Cuban missile crisis.

Meanwhile, President Ronald Reagan, backed by the British prime minister Margaret Thatcher (and with the help of Pope John Paul II, who spoke out against the evils of Communism), began a massive military buildup whose purpose was to spend the Soviets into defeat. By the late 1980s, the Soviet Union was suffering from economic stagnation, and its president, Mikhail Gorbachev, knowing that the Soviets could not win an arms race, urged liberal reforms that reduced tensions dramatically and raised hopes that the Russian states would cast off the yoke of Communism. In the late 1980s, the Soviet bloc disintegrated as various nations overthrew their Communist governments and declared their freedom. On December 25, 1991, the Soviet Union formally dissolved into its constituent states, leaving the United States the world's dominant economic and military power. The Cold War may have ended, but in the ensuing years the relationship between the United States and Russia remained thorny, with the two nations disagreeing on a range of issues.

Although the Cold War remained largely cold, it was marked by the formation of military coalitions, subversion, troop and ship deployments, spying, propaganda campaigns, arms races, efforts to win the allegiance of neutral nations, sports competition, and competition in the areas of science and technology, particularly the space race. The plight

Oliver was saved by a lifeguard from drowning when he was a toddler. *(© Gennady Kudelya | ShutterStock.com)*

of dissident Nobel Prize–winning Soviet writer Alexander Solzhenitsyn came to the world's attention through such books as *The Gulag Archipelago* and *One Day in the Life of Ivan Denisovich*, and it was books such as these that would eventually undermine the moral authority of Communism and the Soviet Union. It would be little exaggeration to say that the Cold War dominated American thinking about virtually every geopolitical issue during the 1950s, 1960s, and beyond, when Updike was establishing himself as a preeminent writer who examined the state of culture and morality in the post–World War II world.

CRITICAL OVERVIEW

For some decades, Updike was one of the nation's most popular authors, but toward the end of his career, his popularity seemed to wane. This phenomenon is observed by Mark Oppenheimer in a review in *Books & Culture* titled "Why Everyone Used to Read Updike . . . and Why His Best Stories Are Still Worth Reading." In his review, Oppenheimer notes, "Those

frequent short stories that grab *New Yorker* space from younger, fresher voices, and those novels appearing at regular intervals, are not read by anyone I know." Oppenheimer then concludes, "Younger writers and book lovers do not read John Updike." Oppenheimer explains this relative decline in popularity in this way: "Updike began writing when his generation of white Christian males, having fought in the Korean War, was returning home to the outwardly staid domesticity of Eisenhower's America." He goes on: "[Updike's] specific vantage point remained the same: men born around 1930, plus their wives, all wistfully wishing they were teenagers again." Further, "Updike's fiction—dense with detail, so lovingly crafted and perfectly described—is difficult to abstract from its time and place," suggesting that later readers would be unable to appreciate it. Nevertheless, Oppenheimer expresses the reaction of many readers to the author's work when he states that "these stories retain the power to remind us of ourselves."

"Oliver's Evolution" was first published in *Esquire* magazine, but it appeared in a collection of short stories (along with a novella, *Rabbit*

Remembered, a sequel to the "Rabbit" series) titled *Licks of Love*. Most reviewers looked on the collection favorably. Ronald Curran, in a review in *World Literature Today*, refers to the "galaxy" of characters in the collection and writes that Updike gives the reader "portraits of despair, aliens from the land of maturity, hopelessness gathering together to substitute proximity for intimacy, sex for love, irritability and defensive redneck conservatism for ego integrity." The collection "ends on a fragile note of optimism," an optimism reflected in "Oliver's Evolution." Writing in *Spectator*, Francis Henry King is less enthusiastic about the short stories in the collection, calling them "largely unremarkable." King grants that "Updike's writing never relaxes its taut, nervy pace," and he refers to Updike's "elegant, well-mannered reasonableness."

Still other reviewers of *Licks of Love* are highly complimentary. In *Newsweek*, Jeff Giles calls the book "a touching, elegiac collection of stories . . . about the weight of family, about the dwindling of years, about the heart." He calls Updike a "resolutely old-fashioned writer," one who "works so slowly and carefully that you rarely see the emotional punches coming." Edward B. St. John, reviewing *Licks of Love* for *Library Journal*, concludes, "All of the stories are written in Updike's typically luscious prose, packed with exquisite descriptions and startling perceptions." Finally, a *Publishers Weekly* contributor writes that in all of the stories, "nostalgia is pierced with insight and regret." The contributor ends with the judgment that most readers would render, that Updike exercises "mastery of the short story form."

CRITICISM

Michael J. O'Neal

O'Neal holds a PhD in English. In the following essay, he examines the tone of "Oliver's Evolution."

One of the most maddeningly difficult features of a work of literature to define and describe is its tone. In everyday use, *tone* refers to an indefinable characteristic of a person's voice that suggests an attitude. Virtually every child at some point is on the receiving end of the parental command "Don't you take that tone with me!" suggesting that the child has been hostile, disrespectful, or snide. Indeed, one

> **TWICE IN THE STORY'S SECOND-TO-LAST PARAGRAPH, THE PHRASE 'IT HAPPENED' IS USED, BOTH TIMES SUGGESTING THAT MATTERS ARE OUT OF OLIVER'S CONTROL AND THAT HE IS A VICTIM OF A PERVERSE UNIVERSE THAT IS LAUGHING AT HIM."**

could argue that a key component of language acquisition is the ability to modulate tone depending on the audience and circumstances, enabling one to be formal or informal, playful or serious, thoughtful or spontaneous, fearful or confident, and so on.

In literature, tone is the reader's often indefinable sense of the author's attitude toward the words on the page, the characters the author has created, and the set of events being recreated. The author deploys language in such a way as to induce the reader to share that attitude. But the tone of a work of literature is not something that can be specified in the same way that, for example, a poem's rhyme scheme or a short story's setting can be. Tone, rather, is more elusive, more difficult to pin down. Usually, the reader has to find adjectives that describe the tone of a work of literature. A writer, for example, can adopt a tone that a reader finds wistful, or indignant. The tone in another piece might convey exhilaration, or perhaps sorrow, regret, anticipation, foreboding—the list could go on and on. Thus, tone is not something that has objective existence. It is something that emerges from the perceptions and responses of a reader, presumably guided by the author's language choices.

Sometimes tone is discussed in terms of formality. Some works of literature adopt a highly formal tone that distances the reader, or that perhaps gives the work an intellectual, thoughtful, almost academic tone. Others might feature a more colloquial, intimate, even playful tone as a way of connecting with the reader in a more direct way. In fiction, tone becomes an important component of the narrative voice, influencing the reader's response to the narrative. In any case, assessment of a short story's tone is a function of the reader's interaction with the story's specific language, the imagined circumstances in

WHAT DO I READ NEXT?

- Another example of a very short story by Updike is "Pygmalion," which can be found in the 1983 collection *Sudden Fiction: American Short-Short Stories*, edited by Robert Shapard and James Thomas.

- One of Updike's most popular and frequently anthologized short stories is "A&P," included in Updike's *The Early Stories: 1953–1975*. The story is about Sammy, a clerk at an A&P grocery store, who stands on principle and quits his job after his store manager embarrasses three girls because they entered the store dressed in beachwear.

- Another story by a contemporary author that features a protagonist who is neglected by her parents is Joyce Carol Oates's "Stalking," available in her 1972 collection *Marriage and Infidelities*. It tells the story of a thirteen-year-old girl whose mother neglects her and whose father is away on frequent business trips.

- A classic novel about alienated teenagers is J. D. Salinger's *The Catcher in the Rye*, published in 1951. For nearly three generations, young-adult readers have found the novel's protagonist and narrator, Holden Caulfield, a mouthpiece for a sense of isolation and loneliness.

- *Celine* (1989), a young-adult novel by Brooke Cole, tells the story of a teenage girl and her relationship with her divorced, self-absorbed parents. She also struggles with writing an essay on Holden Caulfield (the protagonist in *The Catcher in the Rye*) and with trying to define her own identity.

- *The Inner Circle*, a young-adult novel by Australian author Gary Crew, was first published in 1986. It tells the parallel stories of two boys: Tony, who is white and comes from an affluent family but whose divorced parents neglect him, and Joe, an aboriginal boy from a poor but loving family. Joe migrates to the city for a job opportunity but loses it to racism and exclusion.

- Updike, particularly early in his career, faced the issue of censorship because of the content of some of his fiction. Readers interested in a classic treatment of censorship might start with Ray Bradbury's *Fahrenheit 451* (originally published in 1953 but available in a 2011 edition). The novel, whose title refers to the temperature at which paper ignites, is about a future world where the government censors thought and bans books.

- D. Quentin Miller's *John Updike and the Cold War: Drawing the Iron Curtain* (2001) traces how the author's views were an outgrowth of the Cold War, which was taking shape in the 1950s. Critics have noted that Updike often uses the tensions of the Cold War as a metaphor for domestic life and cultural matters in his fictional world as his characters try to achieve spiritual meaning in their lives.

---

which that language is produced, and the emotional and intellectual "space" the story occupies.

Each reader coming to "Oliver's Evolution" will describe the tone in his or her individual way. But one possible way to describe the story's tone is that it is one of bemusement, which in turn can be defined as a kind of wry or tolerant amusement, an attitude of curious dissection and examination from a position of superior awareness. Updike achieves this tone largely through a flow of facetious language and understatement. The latter is a rhetorical figure of speech formally referred to as meiosis. *Meiosis*, or understatement, typically implies that something is less important or smaller than it really is. It diminishes its subject, but not necessarily in a vicious way. The result is a comic presentation of Oliver's life, although the comedy is not of the knee-slapping variety, nor does it approach slapstick. Rather, the comedy derives from a quiet sense of seeing Oliver's circumstances not as tragic but rather as ultimately able to redeem him and allow him to evolve into a responsible, solid adult.

Virtually every line of the story, at least through the first four paragraphs, conveys this tone of bemused observation, beginning with the announcement that Oliver was a "big fetus" (a detail not included in the original *Esquire* publication but added when the story was included in *Licks of Love.*) Take, for example, the end of the first paragraph. After the reader is told that Oliver had to wear corrective casts on his feet, the narrative says, "When they were at last removed, he cried in terror because he thought those heavy plaster boots scraping and bumping along the floor had been part of himself." Oliver is in "terror," yet the reader cannot help but smile at the observation and at the image of Oliver dragging the casts on his feet, converting his disability—in-turned feet—into a comic setback that he will overcome. A similar tone is adopted in the narration of the incident involving the mothballs. Oliver could have poisoned himself to death. But instead, he is taken to the hospital to "have his poor little stomach pumped." Again, potential tragedy is averted, and the author's tone converts the incident into wry comedy: he did not simply receive emergency care, he had his *poor little* stomach pumped." (Imagine responding to a frightened puppy by saying "Poor little thing!") The comedy is emphasized when the reader is told that his face was gray-green afterward; but then, after the incident at the beach, when Oliver almost drowned, the reader is told: "This time, his face was blue." The tone once again converts Oliver's distress into comedy. The pattern continues when the problem Oliver has with his eye becomes comic. The eye is described with the word "sleepy" rather than by a clinical term. Everything became "fuzzy" when he closed the eye. The narration about this issue concludes with a comic reflection on the father's reaction: "Just the sight of the boy holding a schoolbook at a curious angle to the light made his father want to weep impotently." The reader can imagine the scene: Oliver is holding a schoolbook up to the light at an odd angle; he is trying to see what he is reading; the father observes this and wants to weep, but his sorrow is impotent.

Yet another incident adopts a similar tone: Oliver's accident at the fraternity house in college. The narrative says that he "broke his arm falling down the frat stairs," but then it goes on to say "or leaping, by another account of the confused incident, from a girl's window." The reader senses that the first of these explanations is the one given out to save Oliver embarrassment and that the second, perhaps presupposing that he was illicitly in a girl's dorm room, is the true explanation. Tragedy is again averted when "several family automobiles met a ruinous end with him at the wheel." The phrasing almost suggests that Oliver was not responsible, that he happened to be sitting in the driver's seat when the cars were damaged but that he was not the cause of apparently multiple accidents: the cars simply met their end, itself a good example of pure understatement for comic effect. Again, the tone is one of wry amusement. Twice in the story's second-to-last paragraph, the phrase "it happened" is used, both times suggesting that matters are out of Oliver's control and that he is a victim of a perverse universe that is laughing at him.

The tone of "Oliver's Evolution" takes an abrupt turn in the final paragraph. Gone are the facetious language and the comic understatement characteristic of the preceding paragraphs (with the exception of the use of the word "mishap" to describe his marriage to Alicia). Here, Updike avoids the indirection of the preceding paragraphs, making clear, unambiguous, straightforward statements about Oliver and Alicia and their behaviors. Then, in the story's final sentences, the narrative voice passes judgment on the characters. Oliver is called "solid and surefooted." Alicia is said to look up to him. The narrator draws a conclusion: "This was the key. What we expect of others, they endeavor to provide." The narrator intrudes by saying, "You should see him now." Then in the final sentences, the extent of Oliver's evolution into a responsible adult is made clear. The tone in this final paragraph is no longer one of wry amusement. The tone now could be characterized as one of triumph. It is designed to honor a life that has surmounted difficulties and disappointments and that recognizes the possibility of change.

Source: Michael J. O'Neal, Critical Essay on "Oliver's Evolution," in *Short Stories for Students*, Gale, Cengage Learning, 2013.

Oliver grew into a fine man and father with two children. (© *Monkey Business Images | ShutterStock.com*)

Ronald Curran

In the following review, Curran explores the dysfunctional nature of the relationships in Licks of Love.

Licks of Love is the title of the novella that dominates John Updike's new short-story collection [*Licks of Love*]. This final narrative picks up the Angstrom clan nine years after their flawed patriarch breathed his last. Joseph Street in Brewer now houses sixty-three-year-old Janice, Rabbit's widow; Nelson, Rabbit's son; and cuckold Ronnie Harrison, Janice's second husband, he whose former wife became the long-term apple of Rabbit's eye. Ruth Leonard, the local nymphomaniac, is dead, and the illegitimate daughter she had with Rabbit has just been told that the rodent is her father. Naturally, Annabelle comes calling on Janice in order to manage a family connection and to attach herself to this branch of the magnetic chain of humanity. Strawberry marks on backs or shoulders are scarce, but acrimony is plentiful as Annabelle, sans gypsy ancestress, snags a friendship with Nelson and ultimately a relationship with one of his friends.

Continuing in the Puritan vein of the American Renaissance, Hawthorne in particular, they all at times smart, rage, or otherwise marinate in decades of misdeeds and gloomy wrong. So Rabbit's death cannot be without its postscript. But Updike suffers as much as Hawthorne did from the same problems of creating "romance" in such a young country and with such thin background in historical time. Unfortunately, without mystery, the Stuarts, or the French Revolution, Updike turns out stereotypical characters reminiscent of case studies in a social worker's files. They come across as anecdotal figures drawn from letters to Dear Abby. Perhaps this is why Nelson, also cuckolded by his father, has become a "mental health counselor" who wears "a kind of social worker's uniform."

As I read *Licks of Love*, other books and chapters in American literature and sociology came to mind. I thought of Anderson's *Winesburg, Ohio* and David Riesman's *Lonely Crowd.* From the opening group of short stories to the novella that usurps the collection, I felt Winesburg's gravity pulling *Licks of Love* into a familiar American solar system moving around a black sun. Intertextuality at its best. Olinger and the Dutch farm country of eastern Pennsylvania began to feel like it was littered with the "knurled apples" in Anderson's vignettes. I also recalled Roth's Neil Klugman in *Goodbye, Columbus* struggling with the three-headed monster of Capitalism, Social Stratification, and Sexuality. Caught up in the gaze of this American Cyclops, Neil was transfixed by the biggest head of them all, the one-eyed Jack.

Rabbit's surviving son and literary allusionist, Nelson, wants members of his clan to see *American Beauty* (1999). After viewing the film, Pru, Nelson's ex-wife, says, "I think that [the sex scene between Kevin Spacey and Mena Suvari] was unrealistic, too. Most men would have just screwed her anyway." Even in death Rabbit haunts his surviving family members and friends. His substantial presence inflated by his absence made me feel that rabbits should be treated like coyotes were in Brautigan's *Trout Fishing in America*. Aging has not been kind to these characters. Getting and staying interested in them tends to exhaust the lingering curiosity that motivates readers of the earlier novels to find out how these contemporary velveteen rabbits are moving through time. In many ways, Updike's fourth in the series, *Rabbit at Rest* (1990), brought his masterwork to a satisfying close.

This latest sequel to Updike's spate of burrowing-mammal books tends to decelerate in terms of impact like the third sequel of an initially popular film. It often feels like yet another episode of "Hares of Our Lives." The combination of interest and respect that *Licks of Love* generates feels like a Yankee version of the regard felt by the townspeople who went to look into Emily Grierson's home at the end of Faulkner's "A Rose for Emily." Death and aging run like a leitmotiv throughout the collection. The generational picture of Updike's sex-besotted or sex-wounded "grotesques" has led to a predictable early old age for them all. They are as emotionally bereft and relationally baffled as the generation Gertrude Stein labeled "lost."

Updike's characters stumble at the starting gate and never recover. They haven't moved through the cycle of life growing and developing. They are all stuck in time, bugs in amber, artifacts of anxiety, stress, and depression. Their lives are as meaningless as they have found themselves to be. They exist and provide the "hell" that Sartre declared was other people in his play *No Exit*. The only Eros they know is sexual, and they are never more animated and eloquent than when they are in heat. No wonder Nelson wants them to see *American Beauty* and Updike portrays them as misunderstanding it.

They trust no one, even themselves. Alienated from others and without any genuine autonomy, they wallow in doubt and shame. Guilt so galvanizes them with inanition that new initiatives become second editions of the defenses that failed them in the past. Inferiority replaces industry as energy drained by depression turns against them in the form of self-devaluation. Their failure as companions is replaced by their failure as spouses, which itself is followed by their failure as parents as they reproduce replicas of their dysfunctional selves. Their social roles are striated with confusion, as they cannot embody or integrate any identity offered to them. Incapable of intimacy, they stay sealed in their permanent isolation, deprived of the dynamic necessary for the growth that intimacy provides. They are stagnant. Their experience of generativity which came accidentally in the form of pregnancy and birth confirmed the magic in the wand and provided yet another challenge to their capacity for separation, abandonment, and loss.

Thus we have this galaxy of predictable characters in *Licks of Love*: portraits of despair, aliens from the land of maturity, hopelessness gathering together to substitute proximity for intimacy, sex for love, irritability and defensive redneck conservatism for ego integrity. They face their fear of the grim reaper with disingenuous forms of denial. Nonetheless, *Licks of Love* ends on a fragile note of optimism that someone in the splintering barrel would survive the worm and not be so grotesquely unhappy. Thus, when Annabelle tells Nelson that she is seeing Billy, he balks at her faith in his old friend's thinking she is wonderful merely because she was able to admit her sexual abuse in front of him and Nelson. "Well, is that a good reason—?" Nelson questions. "Nelson," Annabelle responds, "*no reason is perfect. But then neither are we.*" Mrs. Hopewell in Flannery O'Connor's "Good Country People" could not have said it better.

Source: Ronald Curran, Review of *Licks of Love*, in *World Literature Today*, Vol. 76, No. 1, Winter 2002, pp. 149–50.

Francis Henry King

In the following review, King pans the stories in the collection, concluding that they failed to surprise, amaze, disconcert, or enrage him.

Most of this volume consists of a novella-length sequel to the quartet of novels, featuring Harry 'Rabbit' Angstrom, for which John Updike is likely to be chiefly celebrated by posterity. Since 'Rabbit Remembered' is strong enough and, at 183 pages, long enough to stand on its own, it is a pity that he or his publishers decided that it needed to be buttressed by twelve short stories, the majority of which are too frail to offer anything but token support.

At the start of the novella, Harry is dead and his widow, Janice, has remarried. Living with the couple in an overlarge house inherited by Janice from her parents, is her son by Harry, Nelson, now separated from his wife and working as a mental health counsellor. Suddenly, unannounced, a 39-year-old, unmarried, strangely innocent hospital nurse called Annabel turns up on the doorstep. She announces that she is Harry's illegitimate daughter by a now dead hooker, with whom Janice's second husband, Ronnie, also once had a brief affair. From this emissary from the grave, 'a whiff of Harry, a pale glow, an unsettling drift' emanates. She becomes the butt of the feelings of envy, resentment and even hatred that, despite his narcissistic charm, her father so often inspired in those closest to him.

Annabel and Nelson, reluctant and clumsy, step by step, grow closer and closer to each other, in the course of a series of encounters that show Updike at his most psychologically acute. There is the same fluent mastery in the scenes that exhibit Nelson at work with his patients, one of whom, a young Jewish boy, eventually kills himself in a desperate bid to silence the hallucinatory voices prompting him to murder his parents. Scarcely less impressive, in a more frivolous way, is the description of a women's bridge session, at which cat's paws of malice intermittently rake the lacquered surface of conventional good manners that the four participants are struggling to maintain.

Unfortunately Updike bungles the climax of his novella with some crude melodrama. On Thanksgiving Day, Janice and Ronnie invite Annabel to join the celebration along with other members of the clan. After a fractious argument about the morality of the Clintons, Ronnie's suppressed rage against the dead Harry suddenly boils over, to scald Annabel, whose mere existence is now intolerable to him. As the climax of a number of insults, he tells her that 'it must feel funny being the illegitimate

daughter of a hooker and a bum.' That a middle-class, provincial, church-going American explodes publicly in so brutal a fashion makes for good theatre, but not for conviction. Despite this defect, and despite Updike's wearisome obsession with both the topography of his small Pennsylvania town and, in the manner of John Braine, with brand names, this novella shows him near, if not at, his formidable best.

One of the stories, a flimsy sketch entitled 'New York Girl,' begins 'In those days....' It is with 'those days,' 40 or more years ago, that most of the narratives concern themselves, with elderly folk looking back, often from second marriages or from loveless first ones, at bygone sexual adventures and misadventures. Adultery and divorce have been constants in all Updike's fiction, and so it is here. But as the old pro once again goes through the well-worn routines, there is something embarrassingly flaccid and nerveless about the performance. Exceptional is 'How Was It Really?,' a brilliant little illustration of the fallibility of memory in old age, as a man struggles to gather together elusive shards of recollection in an attempt to reconstruct the crumbling edifice of his life. Almost as good is the title story 'Licks of Love,' in which the State Department ludicrously despatches a banjo virtuoso to the then Soviet Union as cultural emissary.

Throughout, whether in the fine novella or in the largely unremarkable short stories, Updike's writing never relaxes its taut, nervy pace. But, as with the paintings of Joshua Reynolds or the music of Saint-Saens, the very consistency of the accomplishment threatens, paradoxically, to become an irritation. Ungratefully, I ended by wishing that, having dropped his elegant, well-mannered reasonableness, this admirable novelist had just for one moment surprised, amazed, disconcerted or even enraged me.

Source: Francis Henry King, Review of *Licks of Love*, in *Spectator*, Vol. 286, No. 9008, March 31, 2001, p. 42.

Ron Charles

In the following review of Licks of Love, *Charles finds the novella "Rabbit Remembered" inferior to the "Rabbit" tetralogy but, as far as the collection goes, finds "emotional depth and grace" in a few of the stories.*

Rabbit may be dead, but that's no rest for his creator, John Updike, Pulitzer Prize winner redux. Even after four rich novels about Harry "Rabbit" Angstrom, he still writes. Ah, writes. Writes.

Coming at the end of a collection of 12 short stories [*Licks of Love*], this sequel, "Rabbit Remembered," isn't in the same league as that quartet which dissected middle-class America with such devastating precision. But for the millions of readers who followed Rabbit's disturbing life, this novella is an engaging look at the wake he left behind.

It turns out Rabbit had a daughter by the woman he lived with during the three months he abandoned his wife and children in *Rabbit, Run* (1960). Now 39 years old, Annabelle appears at his widow's door and announces her existence.

Janice, Rabbit's long-suffering wife, isn't thrilled. She's moved on since her husband's lonely death in *Rabbit at Rest* (1990). She's married to Ronnie Harrison now, Rabbit's old high-school rival. He's boorish but predictable, reliable in a way her first husband never was. With her divorced son still living at home, she has no interest in revisiting another of Rabbit's offenses.

But for her son, Nelson, this new half sister means something entirely different. Estranged from his own wife and children, he sees Annabelle as someone to help and take care of.

What a long way this famously dysfunctional family has come! Rabbit was "narcissistically impaired." Janice accidentally drowned their infant daughter in a fit of drunken depression.

But now, a generation later, Rabbit's children are cautious, hard-working people, determined not to hurt anyone. Nelson has none of his father's hotshot charm, nor the shallow spirituality that Rabbit used to maintain his own sense of innocence and entitlement.

Nelson and Annabelle are amused to discover they both work as caregivers for society's most helpless members, people their father would have found frightening or depressing.

All the usual Updike qualities are here: the contemporary references that make his Rabbit novels historical markers to the 20th century; the sexual detail that seems more pathological than erotic; the witty narrative voice that skewers modern life perfectly.

And yet there's something more minor about this sequel than just its length (182 pages). Nelson's loneliness is tenderly explored, particularly his stilted efforts to be a good dad, but the other characters remain rather flat.

And too soon after a brutal Thanksgiving dinner that derails Nelson's plans to integrate Annabelle into the family, the story wraps up like a Shakespearean comedy—happy new marriages all around. This seems a bit forced from the master of regret, but perhaps after running through so much heartache, the Angstroms deserve a little gladness.

The 12 stories that precede "Rabbit Remembered" are a mixed bag. Some, like the two-page "Oliver's Evolution," are cute experiments. Others, like "The Woman Who Got Away," cover ground Updike has traversed so much before about the emptiness of sexual promiscuity. He does this well, but it's starting to sound repetitious. Similarly, another story about Henry Bech, his literary alter ego, is dull.

The best stories involve a man looking back at his parents. In "My Father on the Verge of Disgrace," the narrator recalls his overgenerous dad, a school teacher who played fast and loose with the ticket money from high school football games. It's a story that captures a son's mixture of pride and embarrassment.

In "The Cats," the narrator must dispose of a farm his mother left, along with dozens of feral felines. He struggles between the desire to return home and the urge to be rid of its entanglements.

The emotional depth and grace in these witty stories make them among Updike's best.

Source: Ron Charles, "Harry's Troubles Are Still Multiplying Like Rabbits," in *Christian Science Monitor*, Vol. 93, No. 5, November 30, 2000, p. 19.

SOURCES

"Child Maltreatment 2010: Summary of Key Findings," Child Welfare Information Gateway, http://www.child welfare.gov/pubs/factsheets/canstats.pdf (accessed on September 29, 2012).

Curran, Ronald, Review of *Licks of Love*, in *World Literature Today*, Vol. 76, No. 1, Winter 2002, pp. 149–50.

Divine, Robert A., T. H. Breen, George M. Fredrickson, and R. Hal Williams, *America: Past and Present*, 2nd ed., Scott, Foresman, 1987, pp. 808–976.

"Dow Jones Industrial Average (DJIA) History," FedPrimeRate.com, http://www.nyse.tv/dow-jones-industrial-average-history-djia.htm (accessed July 2, 2012).

Doyle, Gerard, *Being You: How to Live Authentically*, Balboa Press, 2012, p. 28.

English, Diane L., "The Extent and Consequences of Child Maltreatment," in *Future of Children*, Vol. 8, No. 1, pp. 39–53.

Giles, Jeff, "Picks and Licks: Updike's Still Steady Hand," Review of *Licks of Love*, in *Newsweek*, Vol. 136, November 13, 2000, p. 84.

Glass, Andrew, "Bernard Baruch Coins Term 'Cold War,' April 16, 1947," Politico, April 16, 2010, http://www.politico.com/news/stories/0410/35862.html (accessed July 2, 2012).

Haddock, Shelley A., Toni Schindler Zimmerman, Scott J. Ziemba, and Kevin P. Lyness, "Practices of Dual Earner Couples Successfully Balancing Work and Family," in *Journal of Family and Economic Issues*, Vol. 27, No. 2, Summer 2006, pp. 207–34.

"John Updike," Academy of Achievement website, http://www.achievement.org/autodoc/page/upd0bio-1 (accessed July 1, 2012).

King, Francis Henry, Review of *Licks of Love*, in *Spectator*, Vol. 286, No. 9008, March 31, 2001, p. 42.

Miller, D. Quentin, *John Updike and the Cold War: Drawing the Iron Curtain*, University of Missouri Press, 2001.

Moyer, Steve, "John Updike Biography," National Endowment for the Humanities website, http://www.neh.gov/about/awards/jefferson-lecture/john-updike-biography (accessed July 1, 2012).

Oppenheimer, Mark, "Why Everyone Used to Read Updike...and Why His Best Stories Are Still Worth Reading," Review of *The Early Stories, 1953–1975*, in *Books & Culture*, Vol. 10, No. 1, February 2004, p. 32.

Orwell, George, "You and the Atomic Bomb," http://orwell.ru/library/articles/ABomb/english/e_abomb (accessed July 2, 2012); originally published in *Tribune* (London, England), October 19, 1945.

Review of *Flash Fiction Forward: 80 Very Short Stories*, edited by James Thomas and Robert Shapard, Free Library, http://www.thefreelibrary.com/Flash + Fiction + Forward %3A + 80 + Very + Short + Stories.-a0166189556 (accessed July 1, 2012).

Review of *Licks of Love*, in *Publishers Weekly*, Vol. 247, No. 44, October 30, 2000, p. 47.

St. John, Edward B., Review of *Licks of Love*, in *Library Journal*, Vol. 125, No. 18, November 1, 2000, p. 140.

Updike, John, "Oliver's Evolution," in *Licks of Love: Short Stories and a Sequel*, Knopf, 2000, pp. 85–87.

"Women Leaving and Re-entering the Work Force," Catalyst website, http://www.catalyst.org/publication/249/women-leaving-re-entering-the-work-force (accessed September 29, 2012).

FURTHER READING

Bendixen, Alfred, and James Nagel, eds., *A Companion to the American Short Story*, Wiley-Blackwell, 2010.

For readers interested in examining Updike's short stories in the context of the history of the American short story, this volume, part of the "Blackwell Companions to Literature and Culture" series, will be useful. The volume examines the American short story from its beginnings up to the early twenty-first century. A section of the book examines individual authors, including Updike.

De Bellis, Jack, ed., *The John Updike Encyclopedia*, Greenwood Press, 2000.

As the title suggests, this volume is an alphabetically arranged encyclopedia with entries that extend from "Abortion," a common topic in Updike's fiction, to "Zimmerman, Louis," a character in a short story titled "C." De Bellis surveys Updike's works and examines such themes as art, science, religion, and history. The volume also includes information about plots, characters, themes, references, key ideas, and influences.

Olster, Stacy, ed., *The Cambridge Companion to John Updike*, Cambridge University Press, 2006.

This volume was written by an international team of contributors who examine the major themes in Updike's writing. They also look at the sources of controversy that have sometimes surrounded his work, and they consider how historical and cultural changes in the last decades of the twentieth century shaped Updike's fiction.

Plath, James, ed., *Conversations with John Updike*, University Press of Mississippi, 1994.

This volume collects thirty-two interviews Updike gave from 1959 to the early 1990s. The volume is part of a celebrated series of collected interviews with major writers published by the University Press of Mississippi. Readers can gain firsthand accounts of Updike's preoccupations in his fiction.

Schiff, James A., *John Updike Revisited*, Twayne, 1998.

This volume is part of the "Twayne's United States Authors Series." It presents a concise introduction to Updike and his major works with an emphasis on new ways of examining the work under consideration. The book, like all those in the series, is written with high-school readers in mind.

SUGGESTED SEARCH TERMS

flash fiction

John Updike AND censorship

John Updike AND Cold War

John Updike AND biography

John Updike AND Oliver's Evolution

John Updike AND Rabbit series

John Updike AND short stories

micro fiction

Pulitzer Prize for Fiction

snap fiction

The Possibility of Evil

SHIRLEY JACKSON

1965

Shirley Jackson's story "The Possibility of Evil" was first published on December 18, 1965, in the *Saturday Evening Post*, a few months after her death in August of that year. The manuscript of the story is dated 1958, but it is classified as one of Jackson's later works. Jackson's stories typically fall into two categories: those that can be classified as horror and those that contain more subtle gothic elements. "The Possibility of Evil" belongs to the latter category. Like many of Jackson's short stories, it deals with the actions of a woman who is psychologically troubled or disunified in some way. Through this character, Jackson explores the concept of evil, exactly what it is and how it should be dealt with. The story has a quaint and mostly pleasant small-town veneer, but again, like many of Jackson's other works, it has clear gothic influences and explores dark themes and subjects. "The Possibility of Evil" can be found in the Jackson collection *Just an Ordinary Day* (1995) as well as in *Shirley Jackson: Novels and Stories*, published by the Library of America in 2010.

AUTHOR BIOGRAPHY

Jackson was born on December 14, 1916, in San Francisco, California, to Leslie and Geraldine Jackson, but she spent most of her childhood in Burlingame, California, where her family moved

Adela accidentally drops a letter containing hurtful gossip on the way to the post office.
(© Ratikova / ShutterStock.com)

when she was young. Jackson became interested in writing early on, and she produced her first written works when she was a teenager. In 1933, Jackson's family moved to Rochester, New York, where she would later attend the University of Rochester. After about a year, she left the university and moved home to focus on her writing. In 1937, she enrolled at Syracuse University, majoring in English. There, she published her first short story, "Janice," and served as fiction editor of the university's humor magazine. It was also at Syracuse that she met her future husband, Stanley Edgar Hyman, who would go on to be an acclaimed literary critic. Together, Jackson and Hyman founded the college's literary magazine, *Spectre.*

After Jackson and Hyman graduated in 1940, they moved to Greenwich Village in New York City and worked a variety of day jobs to support their literary aspirations. They were married that year. Jackson worked on her writing every day and soon began to gain recognition for her efforts, as her stories were selected for publication in the *New Republic* and the *New Yorker.* Her story "Come Dance with Me in Ireland" was selected for publication in the *Best American Short Stories* collection in 1944.

The couple moved to North Bennington, Vermont, in 1945, when Hyman was offered a teaching position at Bennington College. It was here that Jackson gave birth to and raised her

four children: Laurence, Joanne, Sarah, and Barry. Her days were spent raising her children, taking care of the house, and working on her writing. Jackson has stated that she loved to write for many reasons, not the least of which was that it was the only time she got to sit down.

In 1948, Jackson published her first novel, *The Road through the Wall,* and the short story for which she is best known, "The Lottery." Like much of Jackson's work, "The Lottery" contains dark and chilling elements. It is the story of a cold-blooded ritualistic stoning of a woman in a small town. The *New Yorker* received what was at the time the highest volume of mail it had ever received in the wake of the story's publication, most of which was from shocked, offended, and confused readers. To this day, it is one of the most famous short stories in American literature.

The family moved to Westport, Connecticut, in 1949, when Hyman landed a job on the *New Yorker* staff. As both Hyman and Jackson had by this time earned a significant amount of acclaim, their house became something of a literary hub, drawing visitors as famous as National Book Award–winning author Ralph Ellison. However, in 1951, the family moved back to North Bennington.

Jackson produced a plethora of work during the 1950s, including her novels *Hangsaman, Life among the Savages, The Bird's Nest, Witchcraft of Salem Village, Raising Demons,* and *The Sundial.* Her short stories "The Summer People" and "One Ordinary Day with Peanuts" were chosen for the *Best American Short Stories* series. Her best-known novel, *The Haunting of Hill House,* which has been adapted for feature films twice, was published in 1959.

In the 1960s Jackson received several awards, including an Edgar Allan Poe Award for "The Possibility of Evil," and *Time* magazine included *We Have Always Lived in the Castle* in its list of ten best novels of the year. She was invited to teach at the Bread Loaf Writers' Conference in 1963, and in 1965 she was awarded the Arents Pioneer Medal for Outstanding Achievement from Syracuse University.

On August 8, 1965, Jackson died unexpectedly in her sleep of heart failure. She was forty-eight years old. A great deal of her work was published after her death, including "The Possibility of Evil," which first appeared on December 18, 1965, in the *Saturday Evening Post.*

PLOT SUMMARY

As "The Possibility of Evil" opens, Miss Adela Strangeworth, a seventy-one-year-old woman, makes her way down Main Street in the small town where she lives, heading toward the grocery store. As she walks, she enjoys the fresh summer weather and the clean look of the town. Miss Strangeworth feels a sense of ownership of the town because she and her family have lived there for so long and played an integral role in its formation. Her grandfather built one of the first houses in the town, the house on Pleasant Street where Miss Strangeworth lives, and her grandmother planted the rose bushes around the house. From early on in the story it is clear that Miss Strangeworth feels a strong and almost bizarre connection to the town. She likes to brag that she has never been away from it for more than a day; she will never allow tourists to take a rose from her bushes as she cannot bear the idea of the roses leaving the town. In fact, she never lets anyone else have her roses, always placing them around her house when she picks them.

As Miss Strangeworth makes her way toward the grocery store, she periodically stops to exchange pleasantries with people she knows. When she enters the store, several people call out greetings. These details highlight the fact that Miss Strangeworth is well known and respected around town. Miss Strangeworth greets Mr. Lewis, the grocer, noticing that he seems worried and preoccupied. She gives her order and he begins to assemble it, quietly. Miss Strangeworth comments that he has forgotten to remind her to buy her weekly supply of tea, which, she points out, is unusual. While she is waiting to check out, Miss Strangeworth notices that another customer, Mrs. Harper, seems nervous and uneasy, much as Mr. Lewis does.

Miss Strangeworth leaves the grocery store and continues making her way through the town. She stops to make friendly small talk with several people along the way, one of whom is Helen Crane. Helen and her husband just had their first baby recently, and Miss Strangeworth stops to admire the baby. Helen confides that she is worried her baby is not developing fast enough, but Miss Strangeworth reassures her that her worries are unfounded. It seems that Miss Strangeworth makes a point of keeping in touch with the town's residents and what is going on their lives. She stops to talk for a while with Miss Chandler, the town librarian, noticing that she too seems preoccupied and that her hair seems messier than usual. As Miss Strangeworth walks away, she reflects that many townspeople seem to have been upset recently. She remembers that just the day before she saw Linda Stewart, a fifteen-year-old girl, running through the street crying. It is clear that Miss Strangeworth is puzzled by this collection of odd behavior.

As Miss Strangeworth gets closer to her house, she catches the scent of her roses and hastens her step. Roses are obviously deeply comforting and significant to her. As she approaches her house, she admires it and then enters. The narrator notes that the townspeople always wonder how she keeps it so perfectly pristine. She considers having tea but decides that it is too late in the afternoon. Instead, she decides to go sit down in her living room, which is heavily fragranced with the scent of roses. She goes over to her desk in the corner and sits down to compose a letter. Rather than using her personalized stationery, she pulls out a notebook of multicolored paper that is popular around town for writing notes and shopping lists, and rather than using her nice fountain pen she uses a stubby pencil. On a sheet of pink paper, she quickly writes in childish print, *"Didn't you ever see an idiot child before? Some people just shouldn't have children, should they?"* After writing the note, she feels very self-satisfied. At this point, the reader might infer that this letter will be sent to Helen Crane, the new mother who was feeling insecure about her daughter's late development; in fact, Miss Strangeworth soon addresses a matching envelope to Don Crane. It is important to remember that earlier in the story Miss Strangeworth assured Helen that her daughter would be fine, but now, with this letter, she seems to be preying on the new parents' insecurities. Next, she decides to write a letter to Mrs. Harper, apparently the latest of several such letters. This letter implies that Mrs. Harper's husband has been having an affair and that the entire town knows about it and is making fun of her for not knowing.

The narrator explains that Miss Strangeworth's letters are based never on actual facts but rather on her own suspicions. She believes that since there is so much evil in the world, it is her responsibility, as a Strangeworth, to point out the potential for it. Her letters are meant to arouse the suspicions of the recipients and, supposedly, put them on guard. She writes them with a sense of urgency, as if she is protecting the purity of the town by doing so. Days earlier, she had written a letter to Mr. Lewis, the grocer, suggesting that his grandson was stealing money from the register. Miss Chandler and the parents of Linda Stewart have also been the recipients of Miss Strangeworth's letters. (To the Stewarts, she likely claimed that their daughter had become intimate with one of the boys in the town, Dave Harris.)

Miss Strangeworth composes a third letter, this time to Mrs. Foster, a woman who is scheduled to have an operation soon. The letter insinuates that the doctor might kill her and make it look like a mistake to earn extra money through one of her heirs. At this point, the reader understands that all of the odd, nervous behavior in the town is a result of Miss Strangeworth's anonymous, accusatory letters that are always full of troubling suspicions, often presented as if they are factual statements.

Miss Strangeworth has been writing these letters sporadically for the past year, but of course never receives an answer because she sends them anonymously. She reminds herself that she is doing it because her town needs to be kept clean and innocent. Interestingly, she does not seem to connect the townspeople's bouts of nervousness and unease to the letters she is sending.

After finishing her three letters, she eats her lunch and then walks through her perfectly arranged and tidy house to her bedroom to take her afternoon nap. After working in her garden and eating supper, she heads out for her evening walk with the letters in her pocketbook. Miss Strangeworth has arranged her days so as to take her evening walks when the post office is closed, so that no one will see her drop off her letters. Several young people, including Linda Stewart and Dave Harris, are hanging out around the post office. Miss Strangeworth eavesdrops on them having a tearful discussion. Linda tells Dave that her father has banned him from coming to the Stewart house, but she claims that she cannot tell him why; the reason is too "nasty."

Miss Strangeworth drops her letters in the mail slot, not noticing that one of them catches in the slot and falls on the ground outside. Dave Harris picks up the letter and calls after her, but she does not hear him. Dave and Linda see that the letter is addressed to Don Crane, and they decide to do Miss Strangeworth a favor and drop it off at the Crane house on their way home.

The next morning, Miss Strangeworth awakes feeling very happy; she is unsure why until she remembers the letters she sent the day before. After getting up and getting dressed, she walks downstairs, contemplating what she will eat for breakfast. She sees the daily mail on the floor in the hallway and picks it up, noticing a letter that looks very similar to one of her own. When she opens it, she is devastated to read, "*Look out at what used to be your roses,*" and she mourns all of the wickedness in the world.

It is left unstated who sent the letter, but the reader can infer that when Dave and Linda delivered her letter, the Cranes, and perhaps the teens as well, were able to figure out that Miss Strangeworth was responsible for the hateful mail they had been receiving. The letter implies that they took their revenge on Miss Strangeworth's prized rose bushes.

CHARACTERS

Miss Chandler

Miss Chandler is the town librarian and the recipient of at least one of Miss Strangeworth's letters. A passage near the middle of the story implies that Miss Strangeworth has sent her a letter suggesting that the man Miss Chandler is currently seeing may have killed his first wife. Miss Strangeworth encounters Miss Chandler outside the library while she is one her way home from the grocery store, and they make small talk. Miss Strangeworth notices that the librarian seems absentminded and that her hair is in disarray.

Don and Helen Crane

Don and Helen Crane are a young couple in town who dote on their six-month-old daughter. Miss Strangeworth encounters Helen Crane on her way home from the grocery store and compliments her on her baby. She assures Helen, who is worried that the baby's development might be slow, that the baby is perfectly normal. Miss Strangeworth later writes the couple one of her anonymous letters, claiming that the child is an idiot. This letter falls out of the mail slot when Miss Strangeworth attempts to mail it, and it is delivered to the Cranes by Dave Harris and

Linda Stewart. It is this letter that exposes Miss Strangeworth as the author of the hateful mail that many townspeople have received.

Mrs. Foster

Mrs. Foster is an elderly woman who is the recipient of the third letter that Miss Strangeworth writes on the day that the story takes place. She is scheduled to have an operation shortly. The letter Mrs. Strangeworth sends her implies that the surgeon may kill her and make it look like an accident to earn extra money by sharing the spoils of her inheritance.

Mrs. Martha Harper

Mrs. Harper is a town resident whom Miss Strangeworth encounters at the grocery store; she has been the recipient of several letters. The first ones were sent before the story opens, and their messages are never revealed. When Miss Strangeworth sees Mrs. Harper at the grocery store, she notices that she does not look well and that her hands are shaking, but does not realize that her being upset is a direct result of receiving the letters. During the course of the story, Miss Strangeworth sends another letter to Mrs. Harper, which implies that her husband is having an affair and everyone in the town knows about it.

Dave Harris

Dave Harris is a teenage boy who is either good friends with or has been dating Linda Stewart. Prior to the beginning of the story, he was a welcome fixture in the Stewart household; however, that changed when the Stewarts received one of Miss Strangeworth's letters, which must have implied (perhaps crudely) that he and Linda were having intimate relations. Miss Strangeworth herself admits that most likely nothing of the sort ever happened. Dave and Linda are present at the post office when Miss Strangeworth goes to drop off her mail, and she eavesdrops on their conversation. Dave notices that one of Miss Strangeworth's letters did not make it into the mailbox, and he decides to personally deliver it to Don Crane.

Mr. Lewis

Mr. Lewis is the town grocer and the recipient of one of Miss Strangeworth's letters. He and Miss Strangeworth are about the same age and had attended high school together. Miss Strangeworth's letter to him hinted that his grandson

may be stealing money out of the register at the grocery store.

Linda Stewart

Linda Stewart is a fifteen-year-old girl who is either good friends with or has been dating Dave Harris. Linda's parents ban Dave from the house after receiving one of Miss Strangeworth's anonymous letters, which insinuates that Linda and Dave have been intimately involved. Linda is very upset by these claims, which are false, and is seen running through town crying one morning. She later tells Dave that he cannot come to her house anymore, but won't tell him the reason, claiming that it is too "nasty." During this conversation, she and Dave see Miss Strangeworth drop one of her letters outside of the post office. When Dave suggests that they kindly deliver it for her, Linda protests, put Dave insists.

Miss Adela Strangeworth

Miss Adela Strangeworth is a prim and proper seventy-one-year-old who is the protagonist of the story. Her actions may lead the reader to believe she is a sociopath or otherwise mentally disturbed. Though it is not specified in the story, it seems that she has never married or had any children. Miss Strangeworth's family has lived in the unnamed town where the story is set for three generations, and her grandfather played a significant role in the founding and development of the town. Miss Strangeworth's family history is very important to her, and she prides herself on being a Strangeworth. She still lives in the house that her grandfather built on Pleasant Street, and she still tends the rose bushes that her grandmother planted outside. The rose bushes are an important part of Miss Strangeworth's life; she feels highly protective of them and refuses to let strangers take even one. Instead, she fills her house with their blossoms in vases and bowls. Miss Strangeworth is obsessive about keeping her house in perfect shape. Inside, everything is arranged the same way her mother and grandmother had left it, and outside, the house is always perfectly white and clean.

Miss Strangeworth is also highly preoccupied with the appearances and actions of other townspeople. For instance, it bothers her very much to see Miss Chandler's hair sloppily arranged. Though Miss Strangeworth makes it a point to maintain friendly relationships with all of her fellow townspeople, she is constantly judging them silently. For some reason, she views it as her personal responsibility to maintain a level of high moral order in the town. She sees evil lurking around every corner and believes that she should prevent it before it occurs. At the slightest rumor or suspicion of evil, Miss Strangeworth sends an anonymous letter to interfere. For instance, if she believes a husband is having an affair, she will send an anonymous letter to his wife suggesting that he is. Even though the things she writes are not factual, she believes it is better to put people on their guard than risk evil going unchecked. However, Miss Strangeworth does not have the self-awareness to realize that it is her letters that are upsetting everyone in the town. She seems to have a psychological block that prevents her from recognizing the evil within herself.

THEMES

Evil

Evil is the most obvious and prominent theme addressed in "The Possibility of Evil." Here, Jackson seems to be exploring what evil is and how it is created. Though Miss Strangeworth thinks she is doing the town and its people a favor by beating back the possibility of evil, she is actually acting in an evil manner herself and creating evil with her letters. She does not view the letters as evil, even though they cause harm to their recipients, because she believes that they are exposing or preventing actions that she sees as wicked, such as theft, adultery, and premarital sex. In fact, all she is doing is emotionally disturbing her recipients and filling their heads with ideas of evil that may not have been there in the first place. She is completely oblivious to the fact that her obsession with evil is unhealthy and perhaps signifies some sort of repression. Everything that happens around town seems, to Miss Strangeworth, nothing but a platform from which evil might spring. In reality, perhaps none of the things she suspects ever actually happen. They are pure fantasy on her part, and the possibilities seem to excite her. She takes everyday occurrences and perverts them under the guise of moral superiority.

It seems that Jackson may be suggesting that evil can come in innocent-seeming packages. No one would suspect that Miss Strangeworth, a prim and proper, well-respected, elderly lady, who is friendly with everyone in the town, would be responsible for such ugly, hateful letters. Miss Strangeworth herself does not even seem to understand the harm she is causing. In the end, her harmful actions breed further evil when at the end of the story, someone destroys her bushes in revenge. Sadly, Miss Strangeworth does not understand the meaning of this and still refuses to see the error of her ways.

Delusions

Jackson also explores the idea of having delusions, that is, holding beliefs about the world in spite of contradictory evidence. Miss Strangeworth is clearly delusional in a deep and pathological way. She views herself as the moral judge of the town, though there is no evidence to suggest that it needs one and no evidence to suggest that she is any more morally righteous than her neighbors. She seems to believe that as a Strangeworth she was born with infallible morality. This deep-seated but incorrect belief prevents her from understanding that writing her letters, which are not only based on falsities but are also written in an indelicate, petty, and cruel manner, constitutes an act of evil. In presenting readers with Miss Strangeworth's character in a story called "The Possibility of Evil," Jackson seems to be begging the question of whether her misguided, harmful actions are truly evil, as they are based on delusions.

Justice

Another theme addressed in "The Possibility of Evil" is the notion of justice. The clearest example occurs at the very end of the story, when Miss Strangeworth discovers that her beloved rose bushes have been destroyed. This is the punishment that the townspeople have exacted on her for terrorizing them with her hateful letters. However, the fact that Miss Strangeworth is delusional complicates the ending, which otherwise could be read as the story's villain finally being punished for her crimes. The fact that Miss Strangeworth does not seem to understand that what she did was wrong may cause the reader to question whether the destruction of her most prized possession was really just.

STYLE

Gothic Influences

Although "The Possibility of Evil" was written in the modern era, it exhibits elements of gothic

TOPICS FOR FURTHER STUDY

- Jackson's stories, including "The Possibility of Evil," were heavily influenced by the gothic tradition. The influence of gothic concepts is not exclusive to literature and can be seen in many modern horror films, artworks, and musicians' styles. Using the Internet, research the most common elements of gothic literature. Then, choose a current work of art that you enjoy and that you think exhibits gothic influences, and write an essay explaining those influences. The work of art can be a film, a visual artwork, or a song.

- Read the young-adult short-story collection *Being Dead*, by Vivian Vande Velde. Like Jackson's work, this collection features many troubled female protagonists. Which character in the collection do you think is the most similar to Miss Strangeworth? Why? Be sure to consider how the respective social and cultural environments of the two characters may have affected or contributed to their problems. Discuss your thoughts with a classmate, and together create a Venn diagram that documents the ways in which they are similar and different.

- Working with several classmates, adapt "The Possibility of Evil" as a film script. Then, using a digital camera and video-editing software, act out the script and make it into a short film. Feel free to take artistic license in adapting the work, so long as you do not affect its overall meaning. For instance, this story is set around the time when Jackson wrote it, the late 1950s, but the setting could be reworked for the present day. In a contemporary adaptation, Miss Strangeworth might send her letters via anonymous email, perhaps from the public library, instead of sending them in the mail.

- Several of Jackson's critics have described her as underappreciated, arguing that she has never received the attention she deserves. Read one of Jackson's novels—other than the renowned volume *The Haunting of Hill House*—and write an essay about why it may have been critically overlooked, citing reviews if possible, and why it nonetheless deserves critical attention, providing your own close analysis.

---

literature, as do many of Jackson's stories. Jackson wrote predominantly in the horror genre, which sprang out of the gothic tradition. Gothic literature dates from the late eighteenth century and is associated with old, gloomy, or mysterious settings; secrets and prophecies; the possible presence of the supernatural; and hidden threats, especially threats to women. One gothic element that is present in "The Possibility of Evil" is a pervasive sense of doom and heightened sense of anxiety. As Miss Strangeworth walks around town, she notices that many of the townspeople seem agitated and distracted, but she does not realize why. Because the reader is also unaware of the reason at first, the mood of the town is mysterious, and the reader is filled with a sense of anticipation or unease. The fact that Miss Strangeworth is bright and cheery and going about business as usual while everyone else seems to be having a mental breakdown only adds to the sense of eeriness.

Another gothic element of the story is the setting. Though Miss Strangeworth's house is not an ancient castle or crumbling manor, as it might have been in traditional gothic literature, it certainly has mythical or fantastical elements. Near the beginning of the story, the narrator mentions that the townspeople constantly wonder how Miss Strangeworth manages to keep it sparkling clean, inside and out; the task seems impossible for her to manage. Also, bizarrely, Miss Strangeworth has kept everything in the house exactly as it had been when her

Adela Strangeworth's most prized possessions were the beautiful rose gardens started by her grandfather. (© Joshua Haviv / ShutterStock.com)

grandmother and mother ran the house, as if their presence lingers there, ghostlike.

Parable

Critics have noted that many of Jackson's stories, including "The Possibility of Evil," contain qualities of parables, simple stories intended to teach a particular lesson, often a moral lesson, or make a point. Jackson's writing style in the story, which is simple, to the point, and almost journalistic, is reminiscent of the style of most parables. The story is also written in the realistic style typical of parables. Most importantly, "The Possibility of Evil" seems designed to teach a moral lesson. While Miss Strangeworth is constantly preoccupied with the evil in those around her, she is incapable of seeing the evil within herself. This blindness to her own corruption is what allows her to write vicious letters to her fellow townspeople without realizing the harm they are inflicting. In short, her obsession with the evil around her, and not within her, allows her to create evil. At the end of the story, justice is served when the townspeople discover who is responsible for the letters and destroy Miss Strangeworth's rose bushes. The ending seems to teach the lesson that one should examine one's own character before placing judgment on others. An alternative lesson is that justice always prevails. Either way, the story is structured as a parable, with the final scene serving as a lesson-learning moment.

HISTORICAL CONTEXT

Second-Wave Feminism and The Feminine Mystique

Around the time that "The Possibility of Evil" was published, the second wave of the feminist movement was gaining steam. This second wave began in the early 1960s and was spurred on by the 1963 publication of Betty Friedan's classic work *The Feminine Mystique*, which concerns the then-widespread unhappiness of American housewives. Jackson herself was a suburban housewife during this era, and much of her life was typical of the housewives Friedan discusses

COMPARE
&
CONTRAST

- **1960s:** Betty Friedan's 1963 book *The Feminine Mystique* becomes the first widely read work to highlight the unbalanced situation of American housewives such as Jackson. Limited by social expectations to a life of homemaking, many women have found themselves depressed and unfulfilled.

  Today: American women have many options besides being a housewife. Many choose not to have children or to pursue their careers before starting a family or concurrently with it. According to a 2012 Gallup poll, only 14 percent of American women are stay-at-home mothers.

- **1960s:** In 1960, the birth control pill is approved by the Food and Drug Administration. By 1963, more than one million American women are using it, much to the chagrin of social conservatives.

  Today: More than five decades later, the birth control pill is still a source of contention among social conservatives. In 2012, President Barack Obama's plan to require free insurance coverage of contraceptives for women is met with many objections.

- **1960s:** More than 90 percent of Americans identify themselves as Christian. This is the religion that has clearly influenced Miss Strangeworth's notions of morality.

  Today: The percentage of Americans who identify as Christian has been steadily dropping, and according to a 2009 Gallup poll, it stands at 77 percent.

---

in her book. Jackson's critics have noted that she often expressed frustration at being classified by many people as simply a housewife, instead of a writer. Even though she defied the stereotypical roles for a woman of her era and enjoyed a reasonable amount of success as a writer, she was still largely viewed as a wife and mother first and foremost.

In *The Feminine Mystique*, Freidan claims that confining women strictly to the roles of wife, mother, and homemaker causes widespread discontent. Again, typical of the women described in the work, Jackson's critics and biographers have documented her bouts of emotional instability and her complicated relationship with her own children. The reason that the publication of *The Feminine Mystique* was so profoundly significant in the context of the women's movement was that it was the first widely read document addressing the prevalence of discontentment among housewives, what Freidan called "the problem that has no name." It was also published at an opportune moment in history, which its predecessors, such as Elizabeth Hawes's *Why Women Cry* (1943) and Simone de Beauvoir's *The Second Sex* (published in English in 1953), were not.

The Sexual Revolution of the 1960s and the Birth Control Pill

"The Possibility of Evil" was published in 1965, in the midst of the sexual revolution in the United States. This movement challenged traditional moral codes and customs relating to many aspects of sexual behavior and gender roles. A major part of the sexual revolution, at least socially, was women's new ability to gain access to birth control with the pill. The pill was first released as a treatment for gynecological disorders in 1957, and it was approved by the U.S. Food and Drug Administration in 1960. By 1963, one and a half million women were using it. As it became increasingly popular, social conservatives became increasingly anxious about the pill, blaming it for the sexual revolution and women's sexual freedom. While feminists and progressives viewed the sexual revolution, the pill, and women's sexual liberation as positive and healthy, conservatives viewed these things as major threats to traditional family values.

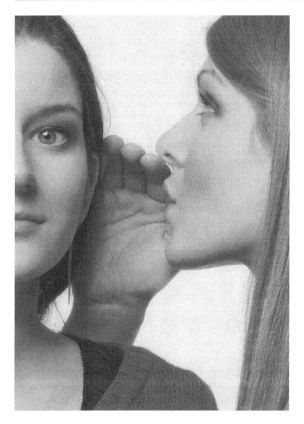

Adela has hurt many people by being the town gossip. (© Muriel / ShutterStock.com)

In "The Possibility of Evil," the elderly Miss Strangeworth is one such social conservative. She certainly classifies anything outside of marital sex as sinister, but she seems to be somewhat fixated on it herself. At least two of the letters she has written are accusations of extramarital sex. The first, addressed to Linda Stewart's parents, accused Linda of having premarital sex. The second, her letter to Mrs. Harper, suggests that Mr. Harper is having an affair. It is clear that Miss Strangeworth has some anxiety about sex, perhaps as a result of the evolving social norms of her community.

CRITICAL OVERVIEW

Though Jackson did enjoy some recognition during her lifetime, according to Angela Hague in her 2005 essay "'A Faithful Anatomy of Our Times': Reassessing Shirley Jackson," her work

is largely forgotten today. Thus, many of her short stories, including "The Possibility of Evil," which received an Edgar Allan Poe Award the year after its publication, have not received much critical attention. Hague argues that this neglect is tragic, as Jackson's work is far more culturally relevant than she is given credit for. Hague writes:

> History has not been kind to Shirley Jackson. Today she is remembered almost entirely for her much-anthologized short story "The Lottery" (1948) and her 1959 novel *The Haunting of Hill House*, a fact that does not do justice to the number and complexity of the novels and short stories she produced.

In this essay, in which she seeks to correct this oversight, Hague further comments: "I want to position Jackson as a quintessential writer of the 1950s whose work dramatizes the concerns and fears of that decade in ways that are not always immediately obvious."

Jackson's name and work were not always as obscure as they are today. In her 1988 review of the book *Private Demons: The Life of Shirley Jackson*, published in the *Women's Review of Books*, Julie Zuckman notes,

> What *is* rare about Jackson, who died in 1965 at the age of 48 and is best known today for her short story "The Lottery," is that her work still reigns supreme as among the most elegant, uniquely disturbing and scary stories ever published in the male-dominated horror genre.

Zuckman also comments that Jackson is known for "works which explore the clinically disturbed mind from within," of which "The Possibility of Evil" is an excellent example.

In one of the rare assessments of "The Possibility of Evil," the 1978 essay "'The Possibility of Evil': A Key to Shirley Jackson's Fiction," published in *Studies in Short Fiction*, John G. Parks claims that the story is typical of her work. He asserts that this "superb" story

> provides a key to much of her fiction. It contains many of the elements basic to her work, including a sensitive but narrow female protagonist, a gothic house, economy of language, intimations of something "other" or "more," a free-floating sense of depravity, experiences of dissociation, and a final turn about in events or a judgment.

Although her work has been largely overlooked, some critics express regret and surprise that it has not been more widely read, and in recent years it has been widely anthologized, so it is possible that it will enjoy greater popularity in the future. The first comprehensive overview of her work, Darryl Hattenhauer's *Shirley Jackson's American Gothic*, was published in 2003.

CRITICISM

Rachel Porter

Porter is a freelance writer and editor who holds a bachelor of arts in English literature. In the following essay, she argues that in "The Possibility of Evil," Miss Strangeworth is psychologically dysfunctional and her house on Pleasant Street is symbolic of her dysfunction.

In the introduction to his study of Shirley Jackson's work, *Shirley Jackson's American Gothic*, Darryl Hattenhauer writes, "Her characters are usually disunified. Their psychological boundaries are usually violated by Others.... Most of her protagonists are decentered, estranged from Others.... They are reproductions of conflicting identities, traces of identifications with contradictory representations." The protagonist of "The Possibility of Evil," Miss Strangeworth, is a perfect example of Jackson's disunified characters. In Hattenhauer's view, she has an extreme and puritanical understanding of what is right and wrong. Her subconscious anxiety about the potential for evil within herself has caused her to create a psychological split between what she views as her own purity and the rampant degradation of others around her. It is this split that causes her to project her own evil thoughts onto others and attack them for it with her vicious letters. Though her actions may seem, on the surface, to be purely evil, they are in fact the result of psychological dysfunction—a disturbed mental state. The source of Miss Strangeworth's dysfunction is never discussed explicitly in the story; however, Jackson's descriptions of the Strangeworth House on Pleasant Street offer it up as a symbolic key to the strange behavior of her otherwise pleasant protagonist.

To fully understand how the Strangeworth house functions as a symbol, it is necessary to understand the profound split between Miss Strangeworth's public and private lives. In her essay "The Uncollected Stories: Seeking the Self," published in *Shirley Jackson: A Study of the Short Fiction*, Joan Wylie Hall states that in "The Possibility of Evil" Jackson "so exaggerated

> THE SOURCE OF MISS STRANGEWORTH'S DYSFUNCTION IS NEVER DISCUSSED EXPLICITLY IN THE STORY; HOWEVER, JACKSON'S DESCRIPTIONS OF THE STRANGEWORTH HOUSE ON PLEASANT STREET OFFER IT UP AS A SYMBOLIC KEY TO THE STRANGE BEHAVIOR OF HER OTHERWISE PLEASANT PROTAGONIST."

conflicting aspects of the main character's personality that a Jekyll-Hyde effect, far beyond simple hypocrisy, results." As Hall makes clear, Miss Strangeworth is not merely a hypocrite, she is a woman with a pathological division in her mind. She is incapable of fully realizing how her actions affect other people, specifically, how the letters she writes within her house affect those outside it. This is evidenced at several points throughout the story. For example, when she sees Mrs. Harper, the woman to whom she has written letters claiming that her husband is having an affair and has made her a public laughingstock, she cannot comprehend that her cruel and likely unfounded allegations are the direct cause of Mrs. Harper's look of agitation. Later in the story, the reader learns about the latest such letter. Most people would of course be profoundly affected by the knowledge or even the accusation of spousal infidelity. Moreover, most people who would falsely accuse someone and thus torture that person's spouse, as Miss Strangeworth does, would be fully aware that their actions were cruel and morally wrong. There is nothing morally ambiguous about falsely besmirching someone's character—knowing the accusations to be false—and then taunting one of that person's loved ones about it. It is clearly wrong. Yet Miss Strangeworth, seeing Mrs. Harper upset, merely wonders if she has been taking care of herself. She cannot fathom the fact that her own actions are deliberately harmful and, by extension, evil.

One of the best examples of her duality is the difference between her public and private treatment of Helen Crane, the new mother she encounters on her way home from the grocery store. Helen confides to Miss Strangeworth that she has been feeling anxious about her baby: she

WHAT DO I READ NEXT?

- *The Lottery and Other Stories*, edited by A. M. Homes and published in 2005, contains most of Jackson's best-known short stories, including the one that made her famous, "The Lottery." As this book contains works from the beginning of her career to the end, it provides a comprehensive look at Jackson's body of work.

- *The Gothic Tradition*, by David Stevens, published in 2000, examines the influence that the gothic tradition has had on modern writers. Some of the writers included in this work were either contemporaries of Jackson or were influenced by her.

- Jack Gantos's young-adult novel *The Love Curse of the Rumbaughs*, published in 2006, is about a young girl named Ivy who becomes acquainted with a bizarre set of elderly twins, Abner and Adolph Rumbaugh, who live across the street from her. Like Jackson's work, this novel includes dysfunctional characters and dark, gothic themes.

- *Japanese Gothic Tales*, published in 1996, is a collection of sort stories by Japanese author Izumi Kyoka. Kyoka is one of the most prominent authors of the Japanese gothic tradition, and the setting, atmosphere, and themes of his tales are very much in line with those of classic gothic authors such as Edgar Allan Poe.

- "A Rose for Emily," published in 1930, is one of William Faulkner's most famous Southern gothic short stories. Several critics have compared aspects of Jackson's fiction to Faulkner's work. The protagonist of "The Possibility of Evil," Miss Strangeworth, has many similarities to the elderly, shut-in protagonist of "A Rose for Emily."

- The 1987 work *The Dark Descent* was edited by David G. Hartwell. The book is a collection of some of the greatest works of American horror fiction; it includes contributions from Jackson, Edgar Allan Poe, D. H. Lawrence, Edith Wharton, and many others.

is worried that the baby is not moving around enough. Miss Strangeworth kindly comforts her and assures her that everything will be fine. Yet within the confines of her own home Miss Strangeworth composes a letter to the Cranes saying, "*Didn't you ever see an idiot child before? Some people just shouldn't have children, should they?*" This letter is not only at odds with Miss Strangeworth's previous behavior, it is unnecessarily cruel. Miss Strangeworth has no concrete evidence to prove that the baby is an "idiot," she is simply preying on the insecurities of the two new parents. Even if the child truly were developmentally disabled, Miss Strangeworth's letter would only increase the parents' insecurities about it. It is the opposite of kind, understanding, and helpful. Yet Miss Strangeworth believes her letters are beneficial, not harmful. Even when Miss Strangeworth overhears Linda Stewart describing one of her letters as "nasty" and saying, "You've

got to have a dirty, dirty mind for things like that," Miss Strangeworth simply projects that nastiness onto the young people. As she walks away, she mournfully reflects that "there was so much evil in people," unable to realize that the only evil present in this particular situation is her own creation. The only point in the story when she exhibits a slight glimmer of self-awareness occurs in the second to last paragraph, when she acknowledges that her letters may seem "harsh, perhaps, at first," but even here her inner monologue is still an idealized version of the truth. Her entire conception of herself is so wrapped up in the belief that she, as a Strangeworth, is morally pure, that she cannot even consider the possibility that her letters contain evil.

The delusional belief that she is morally infallible may have originated in and is represented by the Strangeworth house. This house, which was built by her grandfather and was one of the first in the town, has been home to three generations of Strangeworths. It is the place where her identity was formed, and to a large degree it mirrors her mind-set. On the outside the house is pristine. It always appears to be newly whitewashed, and the windows are always sparkling clean. It is surrounded by beautiful rose bushes that have been tended by three generations of Strangeworths. It is so perfect, in fact, that the townspeople often wonder how Miss Strangeworth manages to keep it up. Inside, too, "all the furniture was spare and shining." Bowls and vases of rose bushes fill the house with a pleasant scent. This obsession with keeping the interior and exterior of the house perfectly white, clean, and orderly did not originate with Miss Strangeworth but seems to be a quality that she inherited from her mother and grandmother. Jackson writes that the house "still glowed from the hands of her mother and grandmother." Everything is exactly the way that they left it, almost as if their ghostly presence lingers in the house. Miss Strangeworth clearly idolizes the Strangeworths who have come before her. She credits her grandfather with the development of the town, so much so that she feels they should build a statue to immortalize him. She does not decorate her house to suit her own taste but leaves it exactly the way her mother and grandmother arranged it. She even wears their hats around town, instead of her own. These details signify that Miss Strangeworth does not have an identity of her own but has inherited her identity from her mother and grandmother, trying to make herself match her conceptions of these women as closely as possible. First and foremost, she views herself as a Strangeworth, and like the building that has housed them for three generations, Strangeworths are unmarred by blemishes on their character.

Miss Strangeworth feels the same sense of satisfaction when she observes her lovely, perfect house as she does when she reflects on her own morality in contrast with the evilness of others. Yet tucked away in a corner of this perfect house is the desk that is locked by a key where Miss Strangeworth allows her evil thoughts to leave her mind and be transferred onto paper. It is in this corner of her house, and this sick corner of her mind, that she adopts her separate and evil identity. Jackson writes, "Although Miss Strangeworth had never given the matter any particular

thought, she had always made a point of mailing her letters very secretly." This indicates that on some subconscious level Miss Strangeworth knows that what she is doing is wrong, or at the very least upsetting to others, but she does not think about that. Her conscious mind ignores the bad part of what she is doing and instead chooses to create the alternative narrative that she is mailing her letters for the good of the town. The paper and pencil she uses to create them are locked away, hidden from sight in her obsessively perfect house, just as the evil part of Miss Strangeworth is locked away in her mind, hidden from her own consciousness.

Thus, Jackson's descriptions of Miss Strangeworth's compulsively perfect house, steeped in family tradition and legacy, help readers to understand the immense pressure Miss Strangeworth feels to keep every part of her life, including her mind, up to what she feels are the very high standards the Strangeworth name demands. Every imperfection, both physical and mental, must be scoured clean in order for her sense of self to remain intact. Perhaps Jackson is suggesting that Miss Strangeworth is not an evil woman, just one who has never been challenged to alter her rigid notions of herself and her family and who has become psychologically repressed as a result of those notions. Though Miss Strangeworth never seems to reform, even at the end of the story, the destruction of the rose bushes that form a barrier between Miss Strangeworth's house and the outside world may be symbolic of the potential for the dissolution of the barrier between Miss Strangeworth's inner and outer selves.

Source: Rachel Porter, Critical Essay on "The Possibility of Evil," in *Short Stories for Students*, Gale, Cengage Learning, 2013.

Publishers Weekly

In the following review, a contributor calls Just an Ordinary Day *a Jackson classic.*

From the hilarious first story in this treat of a collection, in which a college girl tricks the devil (horns, hoofs and all) into selling her his soul, we know we are in Jackson territory—the Jackson of the classic short story "The Lottery" and the novel *The Haunting of Hill House.* For Jackson devotees, as well as first-time readers, this is a feast: more than half of the 54 short stories collected here have never been published before. The circumstances that inspired the volume are appropriately bizarre. According to Jackson's children, "a carton of cobwebbed files discovered in a Vermont barn" arrived in the mail one day without notice; along with the original manuscript of her novel, the box contained six unpublished stories. Other pieces, culled from family collections, and from archives and papers at the San Francisco Public Library and the Library of Congress, appeared in print only once, in various magazines. The stories are diverse: there are tales that pillory smug, self-satisfied, small-town ladies; chilling and murderous chronicles of marriage; witty romantic comedies; and tales that reveal an eerie juxtaposition of good and evil. The devil, who can't seem to get an even break, makes several appearances. Each of Jackson's ghost stories—often centered around a child, missing or dead—is beautifully anchored in and thoroughly shaped by a particular point of view. A few pieces that qualify as humorous takes on the predicaments of modern life add a relaxed, biographical element to a virtuoso collection. . . .

Source: Review of *Just an Ordinary Day*, in *Publishers Weekly*, Vol. 243, No. 42, October 14, 1996, p. 63.

Brad Hopper

In the following review, Hopper notes the variety in Just an Ordinary Day.

The late author of "The Lottery," a short story found in nearly every anthology and never to be forgotten once read, left behind several published novels and story collections. She also left many unpublished story manuscripts as well as several stories that were published in magazines but never gathered in book form; now her children have selected 54 of these stories for inclusion in this posthumous collection, all of which they believe are "up to Shirley Jackson's finely tuned standards." Artistic development is obvious as we read through her career's worth of writing, from her salad days in college (when she was already demonstrating considerable talent) to the flowering of her mastery of the short story form in the 1960s, the last decade of her life. Not all of them are dark in the fashion of "The Lottery," some are light and funny. One of the most delightful is one of the unpublished pieces, "Maybe It Was the Car," about a woman—writer, wife, and mother—who one day walks out on frying the supper hamburgers in a moment of self-assertion. An important addition to fiction collections.

Source: Brad Hopper, Review of *Just an Ordinary Day*, in *Booklist*, Vol. 93, No. 3, October 1, 1996, p. 291.

John G. Parks

In the following essay, Parks focuses on the economy of language, the female protagonist, and the sense of depravity in "The Possibility of Evil."

"The Possibility of Evil," one of Shirley Jackson's superb stories, provides a key to much of her fiction. It contains many of the elements basic to her work, including a sensitive but narrow female protagonist, a gothic house, economy of language, intimations of something "other" or "more," a free-floating sense of depravity, experiences of dissociation, and a final turn about in events or a judgment.

At seventy-one, Miss Adela Strangeworth, the protagonist of "The Possibility of Evil," lives alone in the house on Pleasant Street built two generations earlier by her family. She is proud of her house—"with its slimness and its washed white look"—and especially proud and protective of the beautiful roses that lined the front of the house. She knows everyone in town, and she loves her town so much that she has never spent more than a day away from it her entire life. In fact, "she sometimes found herself thinking that the town belonged to her." As she goes about her life she wonders about the behavior of her fellow townsmen, and sometimes comments, if not to them, then to herself.

For a year now Miss Strangeworth has been sending little notes to various townspeople, using common colored writing paper and writing with a dull stub pencil in a childish block print. She did not sign her name. "She was fond of doing things exactly right." The notes were cruel, gossipy, and vicious, based on half-truths or on none at all. "Miss Strangeworth never concerned herself with facts, her letters dealt with the more negotiable stuff of suspicion." She was always after the "possible evil lurking nearby," because "as long as evil existed unchecked in the world, it was Miss Strangeworth's duty to keep her town alert to it. . . . There were so many wicked people in the world and only one Strangeworth left in the town. Besides, Miss Strangeworth liked writing her letters." This is her secret contribution to keeping her town sweet and clean, her private war with the forces of evil. After her nap and dinner she takes her evening walk in order to mail the notes she had written that day. She thinks: "There was so much evil in people. Even in a charming little town like this one, there was still so much evil in people." Preoccupied, she did not notice when one of her letters fell onto the ground. But two teenagers saw it and picked it up; since Miss Strangeworth did not hear them when they called her, they decided to deliver the letter to the address; they thought: "Maybe it's good news for them." Miss Strangeworth awakes the next morning happy that three more people will receive her notes: "Harsh, perhaps, at first, but wickedness was never easily banished, and a clean heart was a scoured heart." But when she opens her own mail that morning she finds a little letter very much like the ones she sends. "She began to cry silently for the wickedness of the world when she read the words: Look Out at What Used to Be Your Roses."

Like many Jackson stories this one has a parable-like quality about it—we do not know where or when the story takes place; we are given just enough information to see the universality of the human problem involved. Even with the undercurrent of comic irony the story is reminiscent of many of Hawthorne's tales, his characters haunted by the idea of a knowledge beyond knowledge and so utterly committed to achieving it that they become perverted in the process, such as Goodman Brown and Ethan Brand. Here, Shirley Jackson summons up one more fierce Puritan who personally takes on the forces of evil, and who thus demonstrates, in William Van O'Connor's phrase, "the evil lurking in the righteous mind." Miss Strangeworth is not aware that her own humanity is corroded by making the struggle against evil her sole reason for living. She is corrupted by her own narcissism. As Lionel Rubinoff observes: ". . . by pretending to be angels we shall surely become devils. . . . [Because] the possibility of real virtue exists only for a man who has the freedom to choose evil." This freedom Miss Strangeworth cannot and will not give, because she herself holds an evil belief: "a belief that one *cannot do wrong*," to use D. H. Lawrence's remarks about one of Hawthorne's characters. Lawrence concludes: "No men are so evil to-day as the idealists, and no women half so evil as your earnest woman, who feels herself a power for good." Paradoxically, Miss Strangeworth is doing evil in order to further good. Miss Strangeworth reveals the unscrupulosity of the devout, and the only people more unscrupulous than the devout are the frightened, and they are often the same people.

Shirley Jackson reveals a fundamental problem here, one especially crucial in American culture: the revelation of the imagination that sees evil only *out there*, and which thus must be smashed at any cost. Miss Strangeworth does not see that evil is a component within us all that can be transcended only through its recognition and acceptance. Heinrich Zimmer, writing of the meaning of an ancient tale, says:

> The function of evil is to keep in operation the dynamics of change. Cooperating with the beneficient forces, though antagonistically, those of evil thus assist in the weaving of the tapestry of life; hence the experience of evil, and to some extent this experience alone, produces maturity, real life, real command of the powers and tasks of life. The forbidden fruit—the fruit of guilt through experience, knowledge through experience—had to be swallowed in the Garden of Innocence before human history could begin. Evil had to be accepted and assimilated, not avoided.

Accordingly, Lionel Rubinoff observes: "It is the excessive rationalistic and abstract apocalyptic imagination that defines evil as an object of scorn, or as an incurable disease. The apocalyptic imagination is sober, passive, and detached. It seeks to reduce mystery to rational order. It sits in judgment, protected by certainty, and condemns." This is Miss Strangeworth before she opens her own letter of judgment which may have torn the veil of innocence from her imagination and open her to a reconsideration of "the possibility of evil."

Though she is northern and urban Shirley Jackson is here reminiscent of Flannery O'Connor, who frequently brought a "moment of truth" to her characters, though it usually arrived too late, as in her story "Greenleaf." Writing about her own work Flannery O'Connor said: "St. Cyril of Jerusalem . . . wrote: 'The dragon sits by the side of the road, watching those who pass. Beware lest he devour you. We go to the Father of Souls, but it is necessary to pass by the dragon.' No matter what form the dragon may take, it is of this mysterious passage past him, or into his jaws, that stories of any depth will always be concerned to tell." This aptly describes what Shirley Jackson is doing in her fiction. She brings many of her characters by or into the dragon, or, to change the image, she brings them to the edge of the abyss: some fall, some cling desperately to the edge, and only a few find their way to safety, but such are evil's possibilities.

Source: John G. Parks, "'The Possibility of Evil': A Key to Shirley Jackson's Fiction," in *Studies in Short Fiction*, Vol. 15, No. 3, Summer 1978, pp. 320–23.

SOURCES

"The Birth of the Pill," University of Southern California website, http://www-scf.usc.edu/~nicoleg/history.htm (accessed August 10, 2012).

Hague, Angela, "'A Faithful Anatomy of Our Times': Reassessing Shirley Jackson," in *Frontiers: A Journal of Women Studies*, Vol. 26, No. 2, 2005, pp. 73–96.

Hall, Joan Wylie, "The Uncollected Stories: Seeking the Self," in *Shirley Jackson: A Study of the Short Fiction*, edited by Gordon Weaver, Twayne Publishers, 1993, pp. 75–90.

Hattenhauer, Darryl, *Shirley Jackson's American Gothic*, State University of New York Press, 2003, pp. 1–15.

Hubbard, Kristen, "The Works of Shirley Jackson," Virginia Commonwealth University website, http://www.courses.vcu.edu/ENG-jkh/ (accessed August 5, 2012).

Jackson, Shirley, "The Possibility of Evil," in *Shirley Jackson: Novels and Stories*, edited by Joyce Carol Oates, Library of America, 2010, pp. 714–24.

Menand, Louis, "Books as Bombs: Why the Women's Movement Needed *The Feminine Mystique*," in *New Yorker*, January 23, 2011, http://www.newyorker.com/arts/critics/books/2011/01/24/110124crbo_books_menand (accessed August 10, 2012).

Newport, Frank, "This Easter, Smaller Percentage of Americans Are Christian," Gallup website, April 10, 2009, http://www.gallup.com/poll/117409/easter-smaller-percentage-americans-christian.aspx/ (accessed August 15, 2012).

Oates, Joyce Carol, "Distress Signals: Shirley Jackson's Fiction—Including Some Previously Unpublished Work—Explores Psychic Turmoil," Review of *Just an Ordinary Day*, in *New York Times*, December 29, 1995, p. BR10.

Parks, John G., "'The Possibility of Evil': A Key to Shirley Jackson's Fiction," in *Studies in Short Fiction*, Vol. 15, No. 3, Summer 1978, pp. 320–23.

Pear, Robert, "Passions Flare as House Debates Birth Control Rule," in *New York Times*, February 16, 2012, http://www.nytimes.com/2012/02/17/us/politics/birth-control-coverage-rule-debated-at-house-hearing.html?_r=1 (accessed August 15, 2012).

"People and Events: The Pill and the Sexual Revolution," PBS website, http://www.pbs.org/wgbh/amex/pill/peopleevents/e_revolution.html (accessed August 10, 2012).

Saad, Lydia, "Stay-at-Home Moms in U.S. Lean Independent, Lower-Income," Gallup website, April 19, 2012, http://www.gallup.com/poll/153995/stay-home-moms-lean-independent-lower-income.aspx (August 10, 2012).

"Shirley Jackson," Shirley Jackson website, http://shirleyjackson.org/ (accessed August 5, 2012).

"Shirley Jackson, Author of Horror Classic, Dies," in *New York Times*, August 10, 1965, http://www.nytimes.com/learning/general/onthisday/bday/1214.html/ (accessed August 5, 2012).

Zuckman, Julie, "Bleak Housewife," Review of *Private Demons: The Life of Shirley Jackson*, in *Women's Review of Books*, Vol. 6, No. 3, December 1988, pp. 7–8.

FURTHER READING

Jackson, Shirley, *We Have Always Lived in the Castle*, illustrated by Thomas Ott, Penguin Classics, 2006.
We Have Always Lived in the Castle is one of Jackson's better-known horror novels. Since the inexplicable deaths of four family members, the remaining inhabitants of Blackwood House have had a difficult time attracting guests—that is, until cousin Charles arrives seeking the family fortune.

James, Henry, *The Turn of the Screw*, Akasha, 2008.
This work of horror is one of James's best-known stories. Joyce Carol Oates has stated that of all the influences on Jackson's work, Henry James had the most noticeable impact. Elements of Jackson's horror can be seen in *The Turn of the Screw*.

Oates, Joyce Carol, ed., *American Gothic Tales*, Plume, 1996.
Oates, who has written extensively about Jackson's work, has included her in this anthology of American gothic fiction. The forty stories included in this work span a two-hundred-year time period.

Oppenheimer, Judy, *Private Demons: The Life of Shirley Jackson*, Ballantine Books, 1989.
Oppenheimer's work is the first and to date the only comprehensive biography of Jackson. The author focuses on the mental and emotional hardships that plagued Jackson throughout her life. Oppenheimer also examines the less than positive relationship between Jackson and her mother.

SUGGESTED SEARCH TERMS

Shirley Jackson

Shirley Jackson AND writer

Shirley Jackson AND gothic

Shirley Jackson AND horror

Shirley Jackson AND short stories

Shirley Jackson AND The Possibility of Evil

The Possibility of Evil AND gothic

gothic literature AND 1960s

Shirley Jackson AND parable

Shirley Jackson AND The Lottery

The Princess and the Tin Box

JAMES THURBER

1945

James Thurber gained fame as the author of humorous essays and sketches penned for the *New Yorker* and for short fiction such as "The Secret Life of Walter Mitty." Yet Thurber also authored numerous fantasy stories, fables, and fairy tales for children. "The Princess and the Tin Box" is framed as a fairy tale but also serves as subtle, satirical commentary on contemporary society.

In the story, the king, who has showered his daughter with wealth since her birth, tells her she must select a husband from the suitors who will soon be bringing her gifts. Four are wealthy and bring expensive gifts, while a poor but handsome prince brings pretty but worthless stones he has collected along his journey. The princess's eager response to the handsome prince's gift suggests initially that she will select his gift as her favorite and consequently select him for her mate, but she chooses one of the wealthy princes. A moral at the end of the story scolds any reader who thought the princess would do otherwise. Thurber's tale both embraces and mocks the conventions of the fairy story and at the same time satirizes the materialism inherent in his society. "The Princess and the Tin Box" was originally published in the *New Yorker* on September 29, 1945, and appeared later in Thurber's short-story collection *The Beast in Me and Other Animals: A New Collection of Pieces and Drawings about Human Beings and Less Alarming Creatures*, published in 1948.

James Thurber *(The Library of Congress)*

AUTHOR BIOGRAPHY

Thurber was born on December 8, 1894, to Charles Leander and Mary Agnes Fisher Thurber. He grew up in Columbus, Ohio, with his parents and two brothers. A childhood accident left him blind in one eye, and he later underwent a series of operations in the remaining eye. Thurber studied at Ohio State University but left in 1918 without having earned a degree. He then traveled to France, working in Paris until 1920 as a clerk for the U.S. State Department. Thurber returned to Ohio and secured a position at the local newspaper, the *Columbus Evening Dispatch*. He married Althea Adams in 1922, and the couple moved to France, where they lived from May 1925 to June 1926.

Thurber lived the life of an expatriate in Paris alongside other Americans writers, including Ernest Hemingway, Gertrude Stein, and F. Scott Fitzgerald, although the social circles of these authors did not overlap with Thurber's. Thurber worked as a staff writer for the Paris *Tribune* during this time. Upon his return to the United States, Thurber landed in New York and worked as a staff member for the *New Yorker*.

He coauthored a nonfiction work with E. B. White and then published his first solo work in 1931, a collection of essays and stories called *The Owl in the Attic and Other Perplexities*. Thurber's 1933 memoir, *My Life and Hard Times*, was a critical success and would later be counted among his best works.

In 1935, Thurber divorced his first wife and married Helen Wismer. He left the *New Yorker* and returned to France in 1937 with his new wife. Thurber published his first children's book, *The Last Flower: A Parable in Pictures*, in 1939. Left nearly blind after a number of eye surgeries, Thurber also suffered from depression during the war years, yet he continued to write and published a number of works, including children's fiction. He published the story "The Princess and the Tin Box" in 1945 in the *New Yorker* and another longer worker for children, *The Thirteen Clocks*, in 1950. He continued writing for children and adults for the next decade and died on November 2, 1961, of pneumonia.

PLOT SUMMARY

"The Princess and the Tin Box" is a short, satirical fairy tale that opens with the traditional "Once upon a time." The narrator introduces a wealthy king who is the father of "the prettiest princess in the world." The reader is told how the princess has been deluged all her life with toys encrusted with jewels, with the most lavish playthings money could by. She threw pearls at her brother's wedding instead of rice. She is serenaded by nightingales, wears jeweled slippers, and bathes in a jewel-encrusted bathroom. The princess has just turned eighteen. Her father informs her she must marry. The king has sent ambassadors to the five neighboring kingdoms, promising that he will bestow his daughter's hand in marriage to whichever prince brings her the gift she prefers above all others.

The narrator next recounts the arrival of each prince, describing the horse each prince rides and the type of gift each prince brings. The first prince rides in a white stallion and brings a solid gold apple, stolen from a dragon horde. The apple and all the subsequent gifts are laid out on an ebony table before the princess. The second prince, riding a gray charger, offers the princess a nightingale figurine made of "a thousand diamonds." Next, a prince arrives astride a black horse. He brings with him a large jewelry box, made from platinum and sapphires. The fourth prince, who rides a yellow horse, arrives next and presents the princess with a heart made out of rubies and pierced with an arrow of emeralds.

When the narrator begins to describe the arrival of the fifth prince, the tone of the story shifts. The fifth prince and his gift are not listed in the catalog-like manner in which the other princes are introduced. The fifth prince, rather, is described as strong and handsome, stronger and handsomer in fact than any of the other princes. However, he is the son of a poor king, "whose realm had been overrun by mice and locusts and wizards and mining engineers so that there was nothing much of value left in it." This prince rides a plow horse to the princess's palace. His gift is a small box made of tin. Inside it are stones, such as mica and feldspar, which the prince has gathered along the way to the palace. The other princes mock the fifth prince, laughing at him and his worthless gift. The princess, however, is delighted. The simple stones are uncommon in her bejeweled world, and she is pleased by the gift.

The king informs his daughter that she must now select the gift she likes the most and marry the prince who brought that gift. Without hesitation the princess selects the jewelry box, the gift of the third prince. She explains that the box, as enormous and expensive as it is, will be able to be filled with all the gems she expects to receive from admirers who will visit her in the future. The couple is married that day. Thurber includes a moral at the end of the story in which he scolds any reader who thought the princess would select the poor but handsome prince who brought her stones, stating that those readers must "stay after class and write one hundred times on the blackboard, 'I would rather have a hunk of aluminum silicate than a diamond necklace.'"

CHARACTERS

King

The king is a standard fairy-tale king who has showered his daughter with jewels and wealth throughout her life and seeks to marry her off to a wealthy suitor once she has come of age. Rather than asking suitors to joust or perform

various feats of courage, as is often the case in fairy tales, the king asks the princes from the neighboring kingdoms to bring gifts for his daughter.

The Princes

The first prince rides a white horse and brings a large golden apple for the princess. The second prince arrives on a gray horse and brings a nightingale made of diamonds. The third prince rides a black horse and brings a large jewelry box. The fourth prince arrives on a yellow horse and brings a heart made out of rubies, pierced by an arrow made from emeralds. The fifth prince is poor but handsome and strong. His gift is meager but so different from the other expensive gifts that it delights the princess. Her pleased response to the fifth prince's gift leads the reader to expect she will select his gift as her favorite, but the fifth prince's gift is rejected. The princess selects the third prince's gift as her favorite, because it seems the most useful to her. The third prince and the princess are married immediately following her selection of the gift.

Princess

The princess, like most fairy-tale princesses, is beautiful beyond belief. Her father has kept her from anything he deemed unworthy of their family's wealth. Subsequently, simple things like the tin box and the stones brought by the fifth prince are fascinating to her. Thurber defies fairy tale conventions, however, when his princess does not select the gift of the poor but handsome prince. She instead selects a very practical yet lavish gift as her favorite. The princess is wealthy and beautiful and expects to remain that way; she believes admirers will visit and bring her jewels, and the gift of the third prince provides her with a place to put them.

THEMES

Materialism

In "The Princess and the Tin Box," Thurber uses the characters in the story as a means of commenting on the materialism inherent in the post-war society of America. References to wealth and riches occupy much of the text of the story, from descriptions of the princess's childhood nursery and bathroom to the gifts brought by the princes. As the narrator observes, the

TOPICS FOR FURTHER STUDY

- Thurber experimented with the conventions of the fairy tale in some of his writings, including "The Princess and the Tin Box." With a small group, write your own fairy tale in which you incorporate references to today's society or values through tone, details, characters, or plot. To present your story to the class, have your group act out the tale. Either present a live performance or film your presentation and have a screening for your class. Be prepared to discuss the ways you incorporated standard fairy-tale elements and also used the format as a means of commenting on today's society.

- In the aftermath of World War II, the American economy experienced a decisive expansion. American industry flourished, and a society that had experienced wartime deprivations now enjoyed spending disposable income on goods and services once considered luxuries. Explore this time period in American history and write a research paper in which you discuss the relationship between economic growth and American materialism. Be sure to cite all of your sources. Present your paper to the class in print, as an oral report, or on a web page you have created.

- In the 2002 collection *Japanese Fairy Tales*, Japanese author Yei Theodora Ozaki offers a retelling of fairy tales from Japan. Read these tales and consider the ways in which Japanese fairy tales are similar to or different from standard Western fairy tales. Who are the heroes and who are the villains? What supernatural creatures or elements do the stories contain? Do the tales convey obvious morals about human behavior or society? Prepare an essay in which you present your observations about these issues. Alternatively, create a poster or a PowerPoint presentation in which you isolate and discuss the key components of the fairy tales.

- *The Lion, the Witch, and the Wardrobe* is the first novel C. S. Lewis published in the series collectively known as "The Chronicles of Narnia." The novel was first published in 1950, and it opens with a reference to World War II. Read the novel and consider its war references and its postwar publication date. In what ways may the book be regarded as escapist fiction, created by Lewis in part as a way for young readers to escape the harsh realities of their war experiences? Write an essay in which you describe the plot and characters and in which you discuss the book as postwar young-adult escapist fiction. Post your essay on your blog and allow your classmates to comment.

---

princess "was not permitted to have wooden blocks or china dolls or rubber dogs or linen books, because such materials were considered cheap for the daughter of a king." The king withholds from his daughter's experience anything considered common. Even blackbirds are banished from the palace grounds, and only the nightingale sings for the princess. She has been so isolated from reality that simple stones and tin delight her, because she has never seen or handled such ordinary objects before.

Because the princess has been schooled her entire life to believe that she will always be beautiful and admired and that as a beautiful princess she will always be showered with expensive jewels, her choice of the jewel-encrusted jewelry box as her favorite gift is not surprising. It is, as she explains, the perfect place to put the gems her admirers will continue to bring her. Meeting the poor, handsome prince with his fascinating stones was an enjoyable diversion for the princess, but he does not have a place within her worldview.

At the end of the story, Thurber chastens his readers who thought the fairy-tale version of romance would prevail. His "moral" at the end

This is a fairy tale about a beautiful princess choosing her prince. (© Pushkin / ShutterStock.com)

Because the princess is deprived of any contact with the real, ordinary world, her first contact with simple, natural objects (the mica, feldspar, and hornblende) and with ordinary craftsmanship (the tin box) results in the princess becoming extremely interested and incredibly delighted. The reader now expects the princess to fall in love with the man who has shown her something new. (He also happens to be the "strongest and handsomest of all the five suitors," which the reader expects will come into play in swaying the princess as well.) Nevertheless, the princess's expectation and desire for ever more riches triumphs over her delight at the gift of the fifth prince, and she selects the prince who has brought her a jewelry box.

If there is a villain in this fairy tale, it is the materialism that squelches the reader's (and perhaps the poor fifth prince's) desire for a "happily ever after" ending that includes a budding romance between the handsome prince and the beautiful princess. In fact, the "moral" at the end of the story makes the reader feel a little silly for even expecting the princess to make a choice other than the one she makes. Romantic love is the object of derision in this tale. It does not exist, and readers who wished for its presence in the story are scolded.

of the story questions those who hoped the princess would select the tin box and the poor, handsome prince, and he forces those readers to consider whether they would truly prefer "a hunk of aluminum silicate" over a necklace encrusted with diamonds.

Romantic Love

The love and romance one expects in a fairy tale do not exist within the boundaries of Thurber's tale. Nevertheless, their absence is thematically significant. Upon its publication in the *New Yorker* in 1945, "The Princess and the Tin Box" appeared under the heading "Fairy Tales for Our Time." The work then proceeds as a standard fairy tale, opening with "Once upon a time" and quickly introducing a king, his beautiful daughter, and her five suitors. The structure establishes within the reader an expectation that romantic love will be the outcome of this tale, as it is with most such stories.

STYLE

Fairy Tale

"The Princess and the Tin Box" appeared under the heading "Fairy Tales for Our Time" in its debut in the *New Yorker*. In the story, Thurber both incorporates and thwarts typical fairy-tale conventions and at the same time includes references to the modern world. The story immediately places itself within the fairy-tale framework by opening with the familiar phrase "Once upon a time" and continues by locating the setting "in a far country."

Once the king and princess are introduced, the king's wealth and the princess's beauty become the focus of the narrator's attention. The king believes his daughter should only be surrounded by the finest things in life, and he refuses to let her play with anything made from materials he believes to be substandard, such as wood or china or linen. Her surroundings are so jewel encrusted, the narrator observes, "her nursery looked like Cartier's window." Thurber here references the exclusive French jeweler, Cartier.

Returning to the fairy-tale format, Thurber presents a common fairy-tale problem: a princess comes of marriageable age, and her father must devise a method by which an appropriate suitor may be selected. Although most fairy stories incorporate some sort of adventure into this selection process, the king decides that a prince from each of the five neighboring kingdoms will bring gifts. The princes are informed that the princess will select which gift she likes best and, in doing so, select her prince.

One of the five princes is poor but handsome. Although she is not dazzled by his lackluster gift, she is delighted; the common stones the prince brings are anything but ordinary to the princess. In paying special attention to the poor prince, in describing him as the handsomest and strongest of the princes, and in depicting the princess's eager response to his gift, Thurber builds an expectation in the reader that the poor prince will be the one the princess selects. He is not. The story's moral emphasizes the foolishness of the reader who expected the princess to act differently than she does. The true love that finds its way into so many fairy tales is absent here, and Thurber's mocking of the reader's expectation of this element underscores the fact that this is a satirical take on the traditional fairy tale.

Humor

Well known as a humorist, Thurber infused his fairy tale "The Princess and the Tin Box" with his characteristic wit. The reference to the Cartier window is one instance of his incorporating the modern world—he evokes the swanky Fifth Avenue store in New York—into what is on the surface a children's story about a king, his daughter, and her suitors. In describing the princess's unparalleled beauty, Thurber compares her eyes to the cornflower, the smell of her hair to hyacinth, and then adds this detail: "her throat made the swan look dusty." Although Thurber here draws attention to her neck being longer and whiter than a swan's, by using *dusty* and *throat* to make this comparison, he amuses the reader through his irreverence for the more formal language often associated with fairy tales.

Later in the story, Thurber combines the use of a modern reference with a list of details that can only be described as silly in their juxtaposition with one another. He states that the prince hailed from a realm that "had been overrun by mice and locusts and wizards and mining engineers so that there was nothing much of value left in it." Vermin and pests are cataloged alongside traditional fantasy characters (wizards) before mining engineers—a detail with a distinctly modern tone—are thrown into the mix.

As the story goes on, the princess selects her favorite gift and hence her prince. She then describes her choice, using a casual tone. She begins, with "The way I figure it" and then explains that the jewelry box will serve as a storage unit for all the other gems she will receive from admirers once she is married. At her wedding, "more than a hundred thousand pearls were thrown at her and she loved it." The princess's being pelted with pearls and her enjoyment of this projectile shower are the story's conclusion and stand in for the more traditional "happily ever after" ending.

Thurber then mocks his readers with the story's moral, insisting that readers who thought the princess would select the tin box must "stay after class" and write on the blackboard that they would prefer "a hunk of aluminum silicate to a diamond necklace." He points out with sarcasm the ridiculousness of the idea of the princess choosing the poor prince instead of her wealthy one.

HISTORICAL CONTEXT

Materialism in Post–World War II America

Thurber first published "The Princess and the Tin Box" in September 1945, just months after the ending of World War II. From the close of the war and for the next two decades, America experienced a tremendous economic boom, spurred in part by its industrial wartime production of military goods. Johannes Malkmes explains, in *American Consumer Culture and Its Society: From F. Scott Fitzgerald's 1920s Modernism to Bret Easton Ellis' 1980s Blank Fiction*,

> As soon as the United States was involved in World War, machinery, artillery, weapons, aircrafts, or ships had to be quickly produced in enormous numbers. Men became soldiers and women were trained to be nurses or worked in domestic factories.

Unlike other countries involved in World War II, the United States did not experience combat on its own land, except for the attack

COMPARE
&
CONTRAST

- **Mid-1940s:** Popular fiction in postwar America is in many ways regarded as a reaction to the recently ended World War II. Some authors attempt to use realism to depict the harsh realities of warfare, while others experiment with narrative techniques and surrealist images as a means of addressing a reality that has lost meaning. Still others turn to fantasy and older models of storytelling, such as fables and fairy tales.

  Today: Popular fiction in the twenty-first century is equally as varied as the fiction that emerged in the late 1940s in the aftermath of World War II. Literary realist novels remain popular, yet there is a surge in the popularity of postapocalyptic fiction and supernatural fiction—works featuring such otherworldly creatures as vampires and zombies.

- **Mid-1940s:** In postwar America, women who had, during the war, become a significant part of the workforce are largely expected to return to the domestic sphere and their roles as homemakers and mothers. This leads to tensions between the sexes and fuels the "second wave" of feminism, in which women fight for greater access to education and employment opportunities.

  Today: Activists continue to fight for equal rights for women. The Equal Rights Amendment (ERA), introduced by advocates for women's rights in the 1920s, was approved by the Senate in 1972 but has failed to become law, because it has never garnered enough votes by the states to ratify the amendment. The amendment has been reintroduced to Congress at every congressional session. In 2011, Senator Robert Mendoza of New Jersey and Representative Carolyn Maloney of New York introduce ERA ratification bills into Congress.

- **Mid-1940s:** The booming economy of the years immediately following World War II fuels America's consumerist tendencies. America becomes a nation with a burgeoning middle class with significant disposable income. Job growth leads to an unemployment rate of less than 4 percent by 1948.

  Today: Following a worldwide financial crisis in 2008–2009, the United States has begun to see some improvements in the economy, but growth remains sluggish. The economy is expanding, but at a rate that cannot yet boost job growth; the unemployment rate still hovers around 8 percent.

---

on Pearl Harbor. There was little rebuilding to do on the home front. Additionally, as Peter Schwartz, Peter Leyden, and Joel Hyatt observe in *The Long Boom: A Vision for the Coming Age of Prosperity*, "Many of the technologies that had been invented in the 1930s and during the war in the 1940s moved into the mainstream, including television, atomic energy, and mainframe computers." This boom fueled a growing sense of materialism in American society. Malkmes further asserts, "When the war came to an end in 1945, Americans were able to dedicate their consumptions towards consumerism, again." The insatiable American appetite for consumer goods continued to expand.

Randall Bennett Woods notes in *Quest for Identity: America since 1945* that Americans became obsessed with consumption. Woods states,

> Everyone rushed to purchase the newest novelty—for the working class, televisions, hoola-hoops, disposable lipsticks, and electric carving knifes; for the wealthy, Corvettes, Christian Dior gowns, and larger houses. European tours, previously considered the domain of the very rich, became commonplace for millions of middle-class Americans.

The princess's Cartier-inspired nursery and unquenchable thirst for jewels in Thurber's "The Princess and the Tin Box" is reflective of this ever-growing obsession with consumerism, a thirst for material goods that occupied Americans in the period between the wars and that resurfaced at the close of World War II.

Adult and Children's Literature in the Aftermath of World War II

The literature written during the immediate aftermath of the war incorporated a variety of genres and approaches. Some American fiction writers, such as Irwin Shaw in 1948's *The Young Lions*, composed realist novels about World War II, exposing the horrific details of modern warfare. This followed a tradition established in the aftermath of World War I, which shocked writers into exploring new ways to convey the human experience in a world that had so violently changed. Some opted for unvarnished realism, while others experimented with new narrative forms.

Similarly, after World War II, as the essay "Novels and Short Stories from 1945" in *American Literature from 1945 through Today* observes, some novelists were "profoundly shaken by the bombing of Hiroshima and the real threat of human annihilation" and subsequently "found the conventions of realism inadequate for treating the war's nightmarish implications." Authors such as Joseph Heller applied dark humor and elements of both satire and horror to their depictions of the military experience. John Barth and William S. Burroughs turned toward innovative narrative techniques that deliberately displaced the reader through, for example, nonlinear and erratic narrative shifts, although such developments occurred in the 1950s and beyond. Authors writing in the immediate aftermath of the war, such as Saul Bellow, remained dedicated to depicting social realities, as Bellow does in works such as 1947's *The Victim*, in which he also incorporates elements of dark humor.

Some authors, however, turned toward writing fantasy and fairy stories for children. The escapism provided by such works was a welcome distraction both for the authors who understood the horrors of war and for young audiences who had also experienced the trauma and anxiety produced by the war. Fantasy fiction for children was not a new genre—American children had enjoyed the *The Wonderful Wizard of Oz* since 1900. However, writers such as Ray Bradbury and James Thurber, who were primarily

One of the prince suitors presents a shiny golden apple. (© Ninell | ShutterStock.com)

writing fiction for adults, also explored the world of fantasy fiction in the postwar years.

Brian Attebery, in *The Fantasy Tradition in American Literature from Irving to LeGuin*, observes that Bradbury transforms his youth to something that "borders on the fantastic" in *Dandelion Wine*, which he began writing in 1946, though it was not published until 1957. A darker, more fantastic exploration of childhood is depicted in his later novel *Something Wicked This Way Comes* (1962). Attebery also studies the way Thurber's work moves from the "far-fetched" to works "*about* fantasy" to full-fledged fable, fairy, and fantasy stories, as in the 1945 novel *The White Deer* and the 1950 novel *The Thirteen Clocks*. These stories incorporate princes, princesses, quests, and magic, but they also include "philosophical inquiry" and serve as "the natural vehicles for Thurber's qualified reaffirmation of faith in his craft and in mankind."

CRITICAL OVERVIEW

"The Princess and the Tin Box" is one of Thurber's minor works and as such has received little individual critical attention, although his fairy tales and fables in general have generated much critical debate and discussion. In assessing Thurber's fables, W. M. Hagen, in an essay for the *Journal of American Culture*, describes the way Thurber incorporates humor into his works and in doing so becomes "a moral satirist." Attebery, in *The Fantasy Tradition in American Literature*, finds that Thurber's works display a certain level of self-consciousness, as he injects details pertinent to the twentieth century into tales otherwise timeless. In studying "The Princess and the Tin Box" for *Marvelous Geometry: Narrative and Metafiction in Modern Fairy Tale*, Jessica Tiffin notes that "the classic pattern of choice between valuable and worthless gifts is resolved with the Princess's practical choice of wealth." Tiffin goes on to contend that the fact that the princess makes this particular choice emphasizes that "in the context of the fables the obvious and well-worn paths of fairy-tale structure are somewhat inadequate in the real world."

CRITICISM

Catherine Dominic

Dominic is a novelist and a freelance writer and editor. In the following essay, she explores Thurber's negative portrait of society in general and the princess in particular in "The Princess and the Tin Box."

James Thurber was known for his humorous approaches to human relationships, and he famously paired with writer E. B. White to write the 1929 volume *Is Sex Necessary?*, a parody of the contemporary studies of sexual relationships that were emerging at the time. John Updike, in a foreword to the volume, describes the "sexual perplexity" both White and Thurber felt in 1929, as both authors were entangled in troubled romantic relationships.

In "The Secret Life of Walter Mitty," published in the *New Yorker* in 1939, Thurber explores the way a mercilessly henpecked husband can only survive his marriage by escaping into a fantasy world. The depictions of Walter Mitty's wife and of other, similar female characters have inspired some modern critics to label Thurber a misogynist (a man who hates women). Sarah Gordon, in *Flannery O'Connor: The Obedient Imagination*, observes, "Stereotypical portraits of the selfish, shrewish wife combine with images of woman as dominating, suffocating, and shrill throughout Thurber's fiction and cartoons to indicate the author's deep misogyny." By the time Thurber published "The Princess

WHAT DO I READ NEXT?

- Thurber's *My Life and Hard Times*, first published in 1933, is his memoir of his childhood and one of his best-known works.

- *The Thirteen Clocks*, originally published in 1950, is a book-length fairy tale Thurber wrote for young readers. As in most of his fables and fairy tales, the story employs traditional conventions while incorporating unexpected derivations and satirical twists.

- Barbara G. Walker's 1996 young-adult collection *Feminist Fairy Tales* offers retellings of classic tales in which she revises characters and plot lines to create works featuring empowered heroines who do not simply wait for marriage or rescuing by princes.

- Dorothy Parker, a contemporary of Thurber's and a fellow humorist and satirist, wrote numerous short stories and sketches focused on her society, collected in the 2002 volume *Complete Stories*.

- In *Okinawa: Two Postwar Novellas*, Oshiro Tatushiro and Higashi Mineo provide first-person narrative accounts of life and culture in Japan in the years immediately following World War II. In both novellas, as characters struggle to return to normalcy after the war, the presence of US occupying forces figures prominently. This book was published in English in 1989 as translated by Steve Rabson.

- *Technology in Postwar America*, written by Carroll Pursell and published in 2007, examines the ways in which technological innovations—including television, contraception, automobiles, and Tupperware—shaped American culture and society and fueled the American postwar economy.

and the Tin Box" in 1945, the dynamics of gender in the United States had shifted dramatically. World War II had changed the role of women in America, because many women had

GIVEN THURBER'S PREVIOUS WORKS IN WHICH GENDER ROLES AND RELATIONSHIPS BETWEEN THE SEXES ARE THE FOCUS, IT IS DIFFICULT TO IGNORE THE WAY THE FEMALE AND MALE CHARACTERS IN 'THE PRINCESS AND THE TIN BOX' ARE PORTRAYED; THE PRINCESS IS DEPICTED IN A DECIDEDLY UNFLATTERING WAY."

entered the workforce during the war to become factory workers and to fill the positions of men who had been drafted. As Randall Bennett Woods asserts in *Quest for Identity: America since 1945*, following the war, working women "were told to go back to the home, make room in the workforce, and prepare to be the perfect helpmate to their returning veteran-husbands."

Many women did just this, and what followed was a surge in the birthrate. In the late 1940s and 1950s, women were encouraged to embrace their roles as homemakers and mothers. This phenomenon became known as the "cult of feminine domesticity." However, other women were not content with these roles, having enjoyed the personal and financial independence their wartime jobs had given them. This led to a movement that became known as the second wave of feminism. The first wave was the fight for women's suffrage, or the right to vote, achieved in 1920 with the passage of the Nineteenth Amendment. With the second wave, women fought for greater access to birth control, education, and employment opportunities.

Thurber published his story "The Princess and the Tin Box" in 1945 in the *New Yorker*. The story appeared under the heading "Fairy Tales for Our Time." Although the work appears to be a simple story about a princess, the work, like so many of Thurber's pieces, reveals and satirizes contemporary society. It further highlights society's, and possibly Thurber's, feelings about women. Given Thurber's previous works in which gender roles and relationships between the sexes are the focus, it is difficult to ignore the way the female and male characters in "The Princess and the Tin Box" are portrayed; the princess is

depicted in a decidedly unflattering way. Although the male characters are not characterized in glowing terms either, the moral of the story, in its focus on the princess and her choice, draws the reader's attention to the princess's character—and the princess's shortcomings in particular.

The story opens with the narrator revealing the sheltered, spoiled manner in which the princess is raised by her father, the king. She touches nothing that is not coated in gems or gold. The king has extremely high standards about what may be considered good enough for his daughter, and toys such as blocks and dolls are not counted among the worthy objects. Thurber presents the father and daughter as wealthy and snobbish beyond belief.

Upon the princess's eighteenth birthday, the king decides that his daughter must be married immediately. The method he devises for selecting a son-in-law emphasizes a commercial view of marriage and underscores the materialism that drives the characters in the story. The princes from the neighboring kingdoms are to bring gifts to the princess. All the princes and the princess are given the same instructions: the princess is to choose which *gift* she likes the best, and the prince who has brought it will become her groom. The princes have nothing to prove but their wealth. The king does not ask the young men to compete in a joust, or slay a dragon, or carry out some other quest. They only have to bring the princess a present.

The princess, for her part, accepts her father's parameters and does not object to the fact that she is not allowed to consider the *men* themselves. Rather, only their *gifts* may inform her choice. Additionally, this game the king has devised is actually nothing more than an economic exchange—the prince's wealth for the daughter herself. Although this exchange is described in such formal terms as the king giving his daughter's hand in marriage to the prince, the king is, in essence, exchanging his daughter like a commodity. The princess does not object to these terms.

One might argue that these are the conventions of the fairy story and reflect the mentality of earlier times. However, Thurber has no issue with drawing his reader's attention to the contemporary world that exists outside the parameters of the story, as when he makes a reference to the real-life jeweler Cartier. The story is meant, as the heading "Fairy Tales for Our Times" indicates, to be representative of contemporary life in some way. The notion of marriage as a commercial venture is depicted as consistent with the materialism of the society in which Thurber lived.

The princess witnesses the arrival of all the princes and is presented with each gift. Significantly, there is no communication between the princess and the princes—they simply hand her a gift, which is then placed on a table. However, when the poor but handsome and strong prince arrives, the princess reacts favorably. Although the other princes laugh at the poor prince, his gift elicits squeals of delight. The reader is led to believe, largely because of this response and because this prince is also the most handsome and strong, that the princess will select this gift, and therefore this prince.

Next, the king instructs his daughter to "select the gift you like best and marry the prince that brought it." Again, she has implicitly been asked to ignore the men themselves and consider *only* their gift. In her compliance with this request, the princess demonstrates her loyalty and obedience to her father. She smiles after the king has spoken and picks up the jewelry box off of the table. She admires its size and its monetary worth. She imagines putting gems from admirers inside it. The princess describes the box as "the most valuable of all the gifts my suitors have brought me," and therefore she likes it "the best."

Thurber depicts a king who is ruled by his wealth and his desire to stay rich and powerful and who has raised his daughter to have the same desires. The princes—the four rich ones and the poor one alike—are mute automatons who function like pawns in the story. They express no love for the princess but simply do as they are bade. None of them utters a word throughout the story. The poor prince is at least provided with a backstory: an explanation of how his father's kingdom became so poor. Despite these descriptions of the males as either greedy or essentially empty characters, the princess is depicted in an even harsher light. Content to be sold in marriage to a stranger, the princess happily selects a gift that will allow her a place to put more wealth—a jewelry box for the many gems she is sure she will receive. Today's reader must recognize, however, that the princess has been raised to view herself and her world in relation to wealth alone.

In this story, society as a whole is regarded as rather vapid, guided only by the desire for riches. Thurber scolds his readers at the end of the story and in doing so emphasizes the extreme shallowness of the princess by drawing the reader's attention to her choice. He states,

> All those who thought the princess was going to select the tin box filled with worthless stones instead of one of the other gifts will kindly stay after class and write one hundred times on the blackboard, "I would rather have a hunk of aluminum silicate than a diamond necklace."

The reader is either implicated as just as shallow and greedy as the princess—if one expected the princess to chose one of the lavish gifts—or condemned as a foolish romantic, if one expected her to choose the tin box.

In contrast to her father, who as a king has a realm to rule and its future to consider, the princess is shown to be frivolous, more interested in the party and pearl throwing that comes with getting married than with the man she is to marry. In contrast to the princes, who are devoid of personality, the princess asserts her personality, and strongly. Without hesitation she makes a claim for her shallow desires and ignores the only person she has been exposed to who was able to show her something new. The fact that Thurber's moral admonishes the reader who wanted the princess to chose the tin box demonstrates his bleak view of society in general and women in particular. In Thurber's story and in his moral, the princess is simultaneously lauded for her practicality and decisiveness but is sarcastically mocked at the same time.

Thurber also seems to express throughout the whole of the story that the princess made a choice consistent with her upbringing and her father's values. Despite the humor Thurber injects into the work, the story is a little sad and rather dark, when one considers that the society Thurber scoffs at is his own, a world in which women were expected to obey the men in their lives and were chastised or ridiculed for wanting something of their own. The things many women sought in the late 1940s—such as personal and financial independence—were often deemed to be inappropriate desires. Other women, like the wives in some of Thurber's other fiction, became the butt of jokes when their efforts to assert themselves, at least within the confines of their own marriage, caused them to be regarded as shrews or shrill hens, forever pecking at their husbands.

The very handsome but poor fifth prince presents a tin box filled with ordinary minerals and stones.
(© Dr. Margorius / ShutterStock.com)

The princess in "The Princess and the Tin Box" knows what she wants, but what she wants is what she has been *told* to want all of her life. She is depicted as a materialistic young woman behaving exactly as her materialistic society dictates. Because her story is related as a fairy tale, her failure to step out of her role is disappointing. The reader is chastised for being disappointed in the princess and at first chuckles at Thurber's success in thwarting one's expectations. Ultimately, Thurber's message is muddled—his princess refuses to make a choice satisfying to readers, and his wealthy society is flat and static. The princess's choice defies the conventions of the fairy tale, but she acts in accordance with what her (and Thurber's) society depressingly expects of her as a woman.

Source: Catherine Dominic, Critical Essay on "The Princess and the Tin Box," in *Short Stories for Students*, Gale, Cengage Learning, 2013.

Paul Johnson

In the following essay, Johnson discusses the genius of Thurber's works.

People who are infuriated by the huge sums paid for stuffed animals in tanks and the adulation heaped on Francis Bacon's squiggly horrors should grasp that there is no reason or logic in aesthetics. Andy Warhol, no mean exponent of effrontery, if not of skill, summed up the game for all time: 'Art is what you can get away with.' This is certainly true of modern fashion art. Was it always true? In studying the history of the subject, I am often struck by the bizarre careers of artists. For instance, that obscure figure Grunewald was better known in his day as a hydraulic engineer than as the painter of the Isenheim Altarpiece. The monks saw him as more useful in getting water from the nearby mineral springs to their hospital than in directing thoughts heavenwards by his images. The leprosy and other skin diseases which figure so strikingly on his panels required treatment as well as prayers.

One has to admit that luck or accident is a prominent player in the game. The hair of Christ which covers up the right side of his face in

Velazquez's 'Crucifixion' was his way of dealing with a mess left when his hand slipped. Turner likewise claimed that the miracles of beauty Ruskin read into a square inch of a certain landscape of his were nonsense—it was just a mistake. An even more striking instance was the entire career as a comic draughtsman of James Thurber.

No one doubts that Thurber was a genius of a kind. He left to posterity four masterpieces of prose: 'The Night the Bed Fell,' 'The Day the Dam Broke,' 'The Night the Ghost Got In,' and 'The Secret Life of Walter Mitty.' They are just as funny, for reasons which go right to the dark heart of the soul, as when they were written three quarters of a century ago. Thurber worked like an inspired maniac on such pieces, writing them over countless times. He sweated over every word, and words were jewels to him. His approach to art was quite different. When aged six, in 1901, his left eye was destroyed by a toy arrow shot by his brother. His mother, a Christian scientist, refused to let his condition be properly treated, and as a result 'sympathetic ophthalmia' developed in his right eye, and eventually led to virtual sightlessness. By the time I met him, in 1958 I think, he was effectively blind.

But he always did drawings, with a pen or pencil, very fast, recklessly. He sometimes did them on walls and tablecloths. He thought nothing of them and threw them away, though sometimes, when drunk at parties, he would give them to girls in return for a fumble. In 1929, while sharing an office with E.B. White at the *New Yorker*, he drew a seal sitting on a rock, with two dots in the distance. It took him five seconds. Without thinking, he put a caption beneath: 'Hm, explorers.' He was about to throw it on the floor when White said, 'Hey, give me that. It's funny.' He insisted on taking the drawing, done on yellow lined copy paper, to the weekly art conference. Rea Irvin, the art editor, just pushed it away. Later, he sent Thurber a drawing: 'This is the way a seal's whiskers go.' Nevertheless, White insisted on showing it to Harold Ross, the editor. Ross was annoyed, and said to Thurber: 'How the hell did you get the idea you could draw?' Later, White found Thurber trying to improve the drawing with shade and hatching. He said: 'Don't do that. If you ever get good, you'd be mediocre.'

White subsequently got Thurber to illustrate a little collection of his pieces, *Is Sex Necessary?* It sold 50,000 copies in 1930 and was much talked about. Ross was puzzled by its success, largely attributed by critics to Thurber's drawings, and said (as he often did when baffled by the editing game): 'How I pity me!' He sent for Thurber. 'Where is that drawing of a seal? I want it.' 'But I threw it away, Mr Ross.' Mr Ross, angrily: 'Don't throw things away just because I reject them. Do it again.'

Thurber tried, but failed. He could not get the rock right. Unlike his prose, his drawing could not be improved. After various fresh starts, he found the seal was resting on what looked like a bed-head. So he drew a bed underneath, and a man and a woman lying on it. The woman looked cross and the man bewildered. So he thought of a line for the woman to say: 'All right, have it your way—you heard a seal bark!' By then it was December 1931. He took it into Ross, who had forgotten about the original drawing, but half-liked this one. Anyway, he ran it in the paper on 30 January 1932. It was an immediate success with readers, and was eventually reprinted more often than any other 20th-century cartoon. Tireless, placeless, classless, colourless, it made people laugh in China, India, Brazil, South Africa and Russia, as well as throughout the West.

The gestation of this famous cartoon, over three years, and by a series of accidents, gives a curious slant on Thurber's genius, for though he cannot exactly be credited with the thing, in strict truth, there is an element of genius in it, and if it is not his, whose is it? There was another curious case, of an animal with horns, which Thurber did for a query series, 'Our Pet Department.' The reader thought it was a moose with loose antlers. Thurber's reply: 'The animal is obviously a horse with a pair of antlers strapped to his head.' What he intended to do when he started is unclear. The drawing was a mistake which he rationalised. Moreover, possibly when drunk, he allowed one of his floozies to draw in teeth, which gives the animal a suggestive leer of derision. Another 'accidental' cartoon has the caption: 'That's my first wife up there, and this is the present Mrs Harris.' The original scheme was quite different, but the drawing failed, and Thurber turned it into a bookcase and put the first Mrs Harris on top of it. Dorothy Parker claimed she was stuffed, but she is obviously still alive.

It is a curious fact that Thurber, who could draw very few things, had a knack of turning failures into bookcases, which occurs in two other masterpieces, the Rabbit Doctor joke and the English Butler joke ('It's Parkins, Sir, we're 'aving a bit of a time below stairs.') Thurber drew hundreds of drawings, and 'gave them away like smiles'—especially to 'drunken ladies at drunken parties,' sometimes as many as 30 in an evening, he said. A score of his published cartoons are masterly, and five in the highest class in history. When I contemplate them, I sometimes feel that after a lifetime of studying and practising art, I know nothing about it.

Thurber's drawings were compared to Matisse's. In fact Matisse was a much better draughtsman: that is, he could usually draw what he wanted to, whereas Thurber could not. It was claimed Thurber was Matisse's favourite artist, though he did not say so. In 1937, Matisse's secretary haughtily denied the claim: 'Le Maitre knows nothing of Thurber.' But in 1947 when Matisse was asked to name his favourite American artist, he replied: 'Monsieur Toobay.' Asked to spell it out, he eventually wrote down 'Thurber.'

Personally, I would rather own a good Thurber joke than anything in Le Maitre's entire oeuvre. The experts may consider Matisse a better artist than Thurber. But he never made anyone laugh. Except, possibly, his bank manager.

Source: Paul Johnson, "The Cartoonist Who Could Make Even God the Father Laugh," in *Spectator*, Vol. 308, No. 9398, October 11, 2008, p. 26.

Pack Carnes

In the following excerpt, Carnes examines the motifs and characters in some of Thurber's traditional fables.

James Thurber's place in the literary history of the United States is a secure and happy one. The satirical, incisive humor of the Columbus, Ohio writer and the internationally famous drawings have ranked him among the very finest of America's humorists. Among his most effective works are his fables. These fables stand four-square in the tradition of fable writing that goes back in an unbroken, though often changing line from earliest times. Yet Thurber's fables are markedly different, and are clearly literary forms of that peculiarly interesting genre with a foot in both literary and folklore camps. These literary forms are very much dependent upon traditional materials; indeed a great deal of their effectiveness is due directly to the use of those materials. The essential interest of this study is the specific use of those materials and the humor involved. The surface humor will be

> THE PARODIED PROVERB OF THE MORAL IS MORE THAN A MORAL. IT IS A FORM PARODYING ITSELF."

seen to be in part an artifact of the irony produced by the use of traditional fabular and other folklore motifs in modern contexts, and stands in strong contrast to the underlying pessimism of the fables.

The fabular motifs are part of a complicated set of transferred raw materials and forms. The form of the fable is for Thurber a constant in these collections, but Thurber has used much more. He has borrowed *Märchen* or "fairy tales," individual characters, character features, motifs and even formulae. Fabular motifs, from both the Aesopic tradition and from the literary repliques they have engendered as well as new motifs are found everywhere. But Thurber does not rely upon these alone. Anything, any short narrative structure that Thurber can tag with a "moral" enters the collection with the title: "fable." True to his idea of the form, Thurber uses proverbs in the same sort of intimate relationship found all through the tradition of Aesopic fables, both in the oral and in the literary reflexes of the form.

Thurber's fables are found in two volumes: *Fables for Our Time* and *Further Fables for Our Time*. The fables are at first glance remarkably homogeneous, but closer examination reveals some important differences. The first volume contains twenty-eight fables and more traditional fabular motifs than the second volume, which contains a total of forty-seven. Together there are seventy-five fables, which is a significant corpus for a fabulist today. The two collections are actually quite different from each other in tone, a subject which is too far afield to pursue here, but the second collection is very much a continuation of a very successful form. It is the form of the traditional fable, and, very importantly, Thurber's reliance upon his reader's responses to the inherited idea of a fable that are our concerns here. In many ways the only real genre determinant used by Thurber in these collections is the surface structure the fable had inherited from the Middle Ages, that of a specific story line, usually quite short, followed by a copulative line introducing an epimythic moral, often expressed by a proverb or proverbial saying. Thurber uses the simplest form of the fable: narrative and epimythium. The latter is always introduced by Thurber's version of the "fabula docet" copulative line, invariably the word "moral" followed by a colon. The Thurber epimythium is treated in much the same way as the narrative itself often is. It is a proverb or saying, but given the same sort of Thurber twist as the other elements of the fable, into what Wolfgang Mieder has called "Anti-Proverb" (*Antisprichwort*).

The Aesopic fable has had a long history of adjustments or mutations in its long lifetime as a genre. Most of these have been literary replications of the same story-lines. A simple retelling of the old narratives would no longer do nowadays. A few millennia of doing that had fairly well exhausted the possibilities there, although this is still a successful strategy for the nursery, where a very few traditional motifs are still told. Indeed this is very likely the essential key in insuring the viability of the primary motifs; one can count on the general reader recognizing a few central motifs from his experience with them as a child. Thurber's use of traditional materials is very different from a literary reworking *à la* La Fontaine, for example, but depends upon that form of narration to a very great extent. This is one of the hallmarks of the modern fable. The modern forms often go their own way completely, but nevertheless depend upon the Aesopic fables for form and building materials. The new fable, perhaps more importantly, depends upon the reader's reception of the idea and shape of a fable for a response in keeping with the author's intent.

Thurber is thus building upon a series of changes as he brings "The Country Mouse and the City Mouse" into the world of modern transportation. His world of trains and buses is no accident, for it is precisely this aspect of modern times that Thurber wants to focus upon. The city mouse tries to visit the country mouse in Thurber's version, but gets nowhere with the maze of connections, and finally walks home not having visited his country cousin after all. The story is not much of a narrative, nor is it supposed to be, for Thurber wants to get to his moral: "Stay where you are, you're sitting pretty." Several points can be made here. First of all, Thurber depends upon his reader to know the fable of the country mouse and the city mouse. But he is acutely aware of the expectations of his implied readers, that is, that they expect a twist, a parody or a refashioning of the tale, and would not stand for a simple re-telling. Secondly, traditional characterization is used for the actors in the fable. We expect the mice to behave in certain ways, just as we expect the lion to be the king of beasts and the fox to be sly. And just as we expect the mice to respond in specific ways, so too do we respond to form, which explains Thurber's insistence upon a separate epimythic "moral," in effect a punchline, often a proverb or popular saying which stands in the same relationship to its antecedent as the Thurber fable does to its Aesopic original if any. Much of the humor in these short pieces is the result of the parodies of these traditional forms, on both a microstructural as well as the macrostructural level of the motif as a whole. All through the two collections on every page are found single phrases parodied in the same manner as the larger structures.

Thurber uses a great deal of traditional materials in his fables. Not only fables, of course, but a number of types of building materials from a variety of traditional narrative forms. Two of these are the fable and the *Märchen*. Thurber refashions these forms into his fables, so as to use the most effective aspects of both forms. In "The Little Girl and the Wolf" (*FOT* [*Fables for Our Time*]), for example, he takes the *Märchen* motif of *Rotkäppchen* or "Little Red Riding Hood" and molds it into a Thurber fable, with the form of a Thurber fable, complete with a moral. Thurber depends upon the reader to recognize the tale:

> One afternoon a big wolf waited in the dark forest for a little girl to come along carrying a basket of food to her grandmother.

There could hardly be anyone who is not set for the tale of "Little Red Riding Hood." But we also know Thurber and are at least a little gunshy. We do not expect the nursery tale; we would be disappointed if that were all there were to read. We are naturally not disappointed:

> When the little girl opened the door of her grandmother's house she saw that there was somebody in bed with a nightcap and nightgown on. She had approached no nearer than twenty-five feet from the bed when she saw that it was not her grandmother but the wolf, for even in a nightcap a wolf does not look any more like your grandmother than the Metro-Goldwyn lion looks like Calvin Coolidge. So

the little Girl took an automatic out of her basket and shot the wolf dead.

Moral: It is not as easy to fool little girls nowadays as it used to be.

Note that Thurber is very clear about his relationship to his material. Of course the girl recognizes the wolf. A wolf does not look like a grandmother and never did. You cannot trust the old clichés any more, and you cannot rely upon the timely arrival of the woodcutter either. There is much more here than the simple moral implying that young girls today have to do it by themselves nowadays. The underlying bass note is far more pervasive. The old standby simplistic logic and "things to live by" system of the traditional materials do not count for much, if anything, nowadays.

Another particularly apt example is the familiar story of the "Tortoise and the Hare." In Thurber's version a wise young tortoise read "in an ancient book" about a tortoise who had beaten a hare in a race. He read all the other books but in none of them was there any record of a hare who had beaten a tortoise. The tortoise naturally assumes, trusting the wisdom of the ancient book, that he could beat any rabbit and sets off looking for an opponent. He finally comes to a hare and shows him the story in the ancient book, complete with the moral about the swift not always being so terribly fast. The animals set off, after a series of choice Thurber insults:

When the hare crossed the finish line, the tortoise had gone approximately eight and three-quarter inches.

Moral: A new broom may sweep clean, but never trust an old saw. (*FOT*)

The parodied proverb of the moral is more than a moral. It is a form parodying itself. Here the story is told again, to make the point that the story is not to be trusted. The ancient book is obviously Aesop, and the tortoise blindly follows the collected wisdom of the ages, only to see that the hare wins. Of course the hare wins and how could we have thought otherwise. The Thurber fable refers to itself throughout the narrative: "read in an ancient book," a technique that Thurber uses in other fables, to drive home the point that the fable itself is being called into question. He does this again in the moral: "never trust an old saw," i.e., the maxim-like wisdom found in these materials. Thurber is suggesting these clichés are no longer operative in our society. And in this way his fables, no matter how humorous they may seem, betray a certain

underlying pessimism, indeed even occasionally gloom. The humor is a surface feature, born in part in the discrepancy between the inherited motif and Thurber's treatment of it. It is funny to see the tortoise lose after winning for these thousands of years, and Thurber presents the new narrative in a startlingly witty manner, but it is none the less disturbing when the consequences are examined. Something is gone when these standby nuggets of wisdom and moral dicta are paraded out only to be discounted.

Some of the moral attitudes or lessons are still valid today, of course, but they are generally the negative ones. Note the persistence of the traditional motif in the following fable:

A crow, perched in a tree with a piece of cheese in his beak attracted the eye and the nose of a fox.

"If you can sing as pretty as you sit," said the fox, "then you are the prettiest singer within my scent and sight." The fox had read somewhere, and somewhere, and somewhere else, that praising the voice of a crow with cheese in his beak would make him drop the cheese and sing. But this is not what happened to this particular crow in this particular case.

Again Thurber has the fable refer to itself as the fox had "read somewhere, and somewhere, and somewhere else," a prescription for getting a crow to drop cheese from his mouth. But not this time. Not necessarily because it does not work, but because the tactics are different. The crow knows about the fox.

"They say you are sly and they say you are crazy," said the crow, having carefully removed the cheese from his beak with the claws of one foot, "but you must be nearsighted as well. Warblers wear gay hats and colored jackets and bright vests and they are a dollar a hundred. I wear black and I am unique."

"I am sure you are," said the fox, who was neither crazy nor nearsighted, but sly. "I recognize you, now that I look more closely, as the most famed and talented of all birds, and I fain would hear you tell about yourself, but I am hungry and must go."

"Tarry awhile," said the crow quickly, "and share my lunch with me." Whereupon he tossed the cunning fox the lion's share of the cheese and began to tell about himself.

The crow knows about the fox only to the extent of the traditional materials about the fox. "Clever as a fox," "sly like a fox" are traditional sayings, but are of little help in dealing with actual foxes. The crow then spoke at great length about himself, concluding:

"Last, but never least, my flight is known to scientists and engineers, geometrists and scholars, as the shortest distance between two points. Any two points."

"Oh, every two points, I am sure," said the fox. "And thank you for the lion's share of what I know you could not spare." And with that he trotted away into the woods. . . .

Moral: 'Twas true in Aesop's time and La Fontaine's and now, no one else can praise thee quite so well as thou. (*FF* [*Further Fables for Our Time*])

This is a new fable, yet it is based upon a story known so well, that the reader might have passed over the change in emphasis from the traditional praising of the crow and gaining the cheese, to having the crow praise *himself* and gaining the cheese, and thus the new moral. "The ancient book" returns in lines such as "the fox had read somewhere," and helps to make this a different tale. Hearing the fox refer to the fable that he had "read somewhere," we tend to expect something other than the Aesopic Fox and Crow story we have known since childhood. Thurber then tricks us again by giving us fundamentally the same motif, with something close to the same generalized moral of vanity (if not the specialized one of succumbing to the flattery of another). Thurber shows us that human weaknesses have not changed ("'Twas true in Aesop's time and La Fontaine's and now"), but the means by which they are made obvious have been altered.

Thurber depends upon traditional materials in the fabric of the narrative as well. In addition to noting that the fox is crazy and sly, the crow tosses the fox "the lion's share" of the cheese, referring to the famous Lion's Share fable complex, which Thurber will also refashion into his own form. These techniques are highly visible in his next version of the Fox and Crow fable, the second of five in total.

A Fox, attracted by the scent of something, followed his nose to a tree in which sat a crow with a piece of cheese in his beak. "Oh, cheese," said the fox scornfully. "That's for mice."

The crow removed the cheese with his talons and said, "You always hate the things you cannot have, as, for instance, grapes."

"Grapes are for the birds," said the fox haughtily. "I am an epicure, a gourmet, and a gastronome."

The embarrassed crow, ashamed to be seen eating mouse food by a great specialist in the art of dining, hastily dropped the cheese. The fox caught it deftly, swallowed it with relish, said "Merci," politely, and trotted away. (*FF*)

The crow here not only recognizes the fox from his "own" fable, but also recognizes him as the actor in the "Fox and Grapes" fable. The "sour grapes" response from the fox here rings true: "Grapes are for the birds," speaks more to the actual state of affairs than the original. Foxes do not of course eat grapes and birds naturally do. Here the fox tricks the crow again, and with a new and more clever con, one with at least the veneer of sophistication.

In the last three variations of this fable, the crow is shown to have stolen the cheese in the first place and introduces the farmer who comes on the scene with his rifle looking for his cheese. In number three, the crow betrays the fox with: "there goes the son of a vixen himself." In number four the fox is determined not to be "outfoxed by a crow," and did not run, but said to the farmer:

"The teeth marks in this cheese are mine, but the beak marks were made by the true culprit up there in the tree. I submit this cheese in evidence as Exhibit A, and bid you and the criminal a very good day." Whereupon he lit a cigarette and strolled away. (*FF*)

The last of these variations actually reminds us of the original fable again as it begins:

In the great and ancient tradition, the crow in the tree with the cheese in his beak began singing, and the cheese fell into the fox's lap. (*FF*)

Here the traditional fable is over at the beginning. We begin at the point at which the Aesopic form ends, with the fox in possession of the cheese. Here the fox, now with no need to either flatter the bird or to have him flatter himself, insults the bird. "You sing like a shovel," he says, but Thurber doubles back on us and the crow gets the cheese back by frightening the fox with the information that the farmer is on his way with a gun. The crow is now the deceiver and finally enjoys his cheese. The crow ends with

"Dearie me, my eyes are playing tricks on me— or am I playing tricks on you? Which do you think?" But there was no reply, for the fox had slunk away into the woods. (*FF*)

The traditional fable is assumed in Thurber's Lion's Share Fable. It is the fabular characterization of the lion that is needed here. We are no longer dealing with the fabular motif, although Thurber again, just as in the case of the Tortoise and the Hare, reminds us of the Aesopic form. The traditional lion was King of all and the Lion's

Share fable with its "Might Makes Right" moral, was typical among the lion fables. Once again, the "traditional" fable is in effect over when the Thurber fable begins:

> The Lion had just explained to the cow, the goat, and the sheep that the stag that they had just killed belonged to him, when three little foxes appeared on the scene.
>
> "I will take a third of the stag as a penalty," said one, "for you have no hunter's license."
>
> "I will take a third of the stag for your widow," said another, "for that is the law."
>
> "I have no widow," said the lion.
>
> "Let us not split hairs," said the third fox, and he took his share of the stag as a withholding tax. "Against a year of famine," he explained.
>
> "But I am King of Beasts," roared the lion.
>
> "Ah, then you will not need the antlers, for you have a crown," said the foxes, and they took the antlers, too.
>
> Moral: It is not as easy to get the lion's share nowadays as it used to be. (*FF*)

This lion has been thrust into the twentieth century. Everything here is new, but built upon the old. The hunting party in the beginning is only stage scenery. The foxes are representatives of the modern age, and the lion, the King of Beasts, simply does not fit. The foxes get the stag, and the system gets the lion. . . .

Source: Pack Carnes, "The American Face of Aesop: Thurber's Fables and Tradition," in *Moderna Språk*, Vol. 80, No. 1, 1986, pp. 3–17.

Robert M. Coates

In the following excerpt, Coates reviews My Life and Hard Times, *Thurber's 1933 autobiography.*

Isn't it about time, people have been demanding lately—with, it must be confessed, occasionally a hint of grimness in their tones—that we discovered just what this man Thurber is up to? Those stories of ladies who supervise their own axe-murders, and of men looking for little boxes to hide in: what do they mean? Those drawings, of crowds running as if the wind harried them, of people collapsing in slow involutions over obscure problems of their own: what do they signify?

Whither is he leading us? Or, to put it another way, is he leading us anywhere? We have only to open [*My Life and Hard Times*] to come upon a clue. There we find him, in one of its opening pages, describing as if inadvertently a curious hallucination that often overcomes him—a fear that he is being followed ". . . by little men padding along in single file, about a foot and a half high, large-eyed, and whiskered." In the next breath, of course, he is speaking of Ford Madox Ford and Walter Lippmann, in the next of his (Thurber's) digestion, and in the next after that (though by then he's getting a little bit breathless himself) of the shrinkage of the earth's crust. But the reader will not be misled by such tergiversations. We have seen generals who were at times hard put to it to determine whether they were leading an army or being pursued by a mob, and to the serious student of psychoanalysis (there must still be some serious students of psychoanalysis left, mustn't there?) it will be obvious that Mr. Thurber is in something of the same predicament. He isn't really trying to lead anybody anywhere. Mostly, he is trying to escape.

But then, one may find many clues to an understanding of this strange personality, in a reading of this chronicle of the author's younger, more settled years. For, unlike most of us, it wasn't till he was nearing middle age that he took to wandering—with what results his epilogue sets forth. His youth he spent in Columbus, Ohio (in itself a feat to tax the strongest), and had nobody but his grandfather to worry about. To be sure, his grandfather was the victim of a slight obsession: namely, that the Civil War was still being fought, usually just outside the front door—and to the sensitive artist, particularly in the formative period of his life, this would be upsetting. But when you have added to this an uncle who suffered from chestnut blight and an aunt who whanged shoes up and down the hall at night to scare away burglars; a succession of hired girls, some of whom saw ghosts and others who did their dusting at three in the morning—well, you get some idea of what the boy Thurber was up against. . . . Mr. Thurber came through it all, unscathed or nearly so—through the night the bed fell on father, and the night the ghost got in, through wild escapades with electric runabouts and still wilder ones with roller coasters, through even that historic day when the whole town of Columbus went momentarily cuckoo, and ran madly en masse from a dam that hadn't burst—came through it to write about these youthful adventures, in the pleasantest possible mixture of fantasy and understanding, one of the funniest books of recent times.

. . . Oh, what the hell! Let's say *the* funniest.
. . .

Source: Robert M. Coates, "James G. Thurber, the Man," in *New Republic*, Vol. 77, No. 993, December 13, 1933, pp. 137–38.

1900–1960, edited by John Cech, Gale Research, 1983, pp. 315–20.

Woods, Randall Bennett, "Capitalism and Conformity: American Society, 1945–1960," in *Quest for Identity: America since 1945*, Cambridge University Press, 2005, pp. 121–54.

SOURCES

Attebery, Brian, "The Baum Tradition," in *The Fantasy Tradition in American Literature: From Irving to LeGuin*, Indiana University Press, 1980, pp. 134–53.

"Chronology of the Equal Rights Amendment, 1923–1996," National Organization for Women website, http://www.now.org/issues/economic/cea/history.html (accessed August 5, 2012).

D'Innocenzio, Anne, and Martin Crutsinger, "US Economy Appears Weaker as Retail Sales Slump," in *Bloomberg Businessweek*, July 16, 2012, http://www.businessweek.com/ap/2012-07-16/us-retail-sales-fell-0-dot-5-percent-in-june (accessed September 28, 2012).

"The ERA in Congress, 112th Session," Equal Rights Amendment website, http://www.equalrightsamendment.org/congress.htm (accessed August 5, 2012).

Gordon, Sarah, "The Case of the Fierce Narrator," in *Flannery O'Connor: The Obedient Imagination*, University of Georgia Press, 2000, pp. 32–82.

Hagen, W. M., Review of *Writings and Drawings*, by James Thurber, in *Journal of American Culture*, Vol. 20, No. 4, Winter 1997, pp. 113–24.

"Labor Force Statistics from the Current Population Survey," Bureau of Labor Statistics website, http://www.bls.gov/cps/prev_yrs.htm/ (accessed August 5, 2012).

Malkmes, Johannes, "The Rise of Consumerism," in *American Consumer Culture and Its Society: From F. Scott Fitzgerald's 1920s Modernism to Bret Easton Ellis' 1980s Blank Fiction*, Diplomica Verlag, 2011, pp. 22–37.

"Novels and Short Stories from 1945," in *American Literature from 1945 through Today*, edited by Adam Augustyn, Britannica Educational Publishing, 2011, pp. 21–78.

Schwartz, Peter, Peter Leyden, and Joel Hyatt, "Introduction: The Historic Moment," in *The Long Boom: A Vision for the Coming Age of Prosperity*, Basic Books, 2000, pp. 1–18.

Thurber, James, "The Princess and the Tin Box," in *New Yorker*, September 29, 1945, p. 29.

Tiffin, Jessica, "Nice and Neat and Formal: James Thurber," in *Marvelous Geometry: Narrative and Metafiction in Modern Fairy Tale*, Wayne State University Press, 2009, pp. 31–65.

Updike, John, Foreword to *Is Sex Necessary? or, Why You Feel the Way You Do*, by James Thurber and E. B. White, Perennial, 2004, pp. xiii–xxii.

Vousden, E. Charles, "James Thurber," in *Dictionary of Literary Biography*, Vol. 22, *American Writers for Children,*

FURTHER READING

Bernstein, Burton, *Thurber: A Biography*, William Morrow, 1996.

> Bernstein provides a detailed study of Thurber's life and works, examining Thurber's youth in Ohio and the path that led him toward becoming a famous writer and *New Yorker* columnist.

Cohen, Lizabeth, *A Consumer's Republic: The Politics of Mass Consumption in Postwar America*, Knopf, 2003.

> In tracing the history of consumerism in postwar America, Cohen examines the wartime and postwar economic conditions that led to the heightened sense of materialism in the American consumer.

Meyerowitz, Joanne, ed., *Not June Cleaver: Women and Gender in Postwar America, 1945–1960*, Temple University Press, 1994.

> Meyerowitz's collection of essays explores the gender stereotypes present in postwar America. The essays describe the ways in which women were expected to leave their wartime jobs and return to the domestic sphere and function exclusively as homemakers and mothers.

Zipes, Jack, *The Irresistible Fairy Tale: The Cultural and Social History of a Genre*, Princeton University Press, 2012.

> Zipes details the history of fairy tales as a literary genre, exploring the conventions of the genre, the elements that have contributed to the popularity of the fairy tale as a literary form, and the way the genre has evolved over time.

SUGGESTED SEARCH TERMS

Thurber AND The Princess and the Tin Box

Thurber AND New Yorker

Thurber AND fairy tales

Thurber AND fables

Thurber AND misogyny

Thurber AND social commentary

Thurber AND satire

Thurber AND postwar America

Thurber AND The Beast in Me

Thurber AND consumerism

The Shawl

LOUISE ERDRICH

2001

Louise Erdrich's short story "The Shawl" first appeared in the *New Yorker* issue of March 5, 2001. The story then appeared in *Sister Nations: Native American Women Writers on Community* (2002), edited by Heid E. Erdrich and Laura Tohe. It was later anthologized in Erdrich's *The Red Convertible: Selected and New Stories* (2009). An often-overlooked story, "The Shawl" tells the heartbreaking tale of a family's generational pain and sacrifice. The narrator is a man recalling a chapter of his childhood, and the story encompasses his experience and insight, along with that of the Anishinaabe tribe, of which he is a member. Like so many of Erdrich's stories, this one features Native American characters and settings but offers universal themes such as family, heartbreak, sacrifice, and healing.

The story begins with a story shared among the local Anishinaabeg (plural form of Anishinaabe) about a broken family, a deserted husband, and the death of a child. Then Erdrich's narrative picks up with the words of a young boy, telling of his own childhood made difficult by his mother's death and an alcoholic, abusive father. Readers should be cautioned that there is an unsettling scene in which the boy faces his father in a physical fight and even feels like killing him. A profane word in the thoughts of such a young narrator demonstrates the intensity of the experience for the boy. Ultimately, Erdrich brings the story to a touching conclusion that is both wrenching and healing.

Louise Erdrich (© *ZUMA Wire Service | Alamy*)

AUTHOR BIOGRAPHY

Karen Louise Erdrich was born on June 7, 1954, in Little Falls, Minnesota. She was the first of seven children born to Ralph and Rita Joanne Gourneau Erdrich, both of whom taught for Bureau of Indian Affairs schools. Erdrich is three-eighths Chippewa (also called Ojibwe or Ojibwa); her father has German lineage, and her mother is French and Chippewa. Erdrich was reared in Wahpeton, North Dakota, near the Turtle Mountain Chippewa Reservation, where her mother's parents lived. Although they did not live there, the family visited the reservation often, giving Erdrich a strong sense of her Native American heritage. Both parents encouraged their eldest daughter's early interest in writing.

In 1972, Erdrich enrolled at Dartmouth College, participating in history by being in the first group of women admitted to the school. She graduated with a degree in English in 1976 and then taught for the Poetry in the Schools Program sponsored by the North Dakota Arts Council. In 1978, she entered Johns Hopkins University, where she completed a master's degree in creative writing a year later.

While at Dartmouth, Erdrich studied with Michael Dorris, a writer who also claimed Native American heritage. Nine years her senior, Dorris was an anthropologist who chaired the then-new Native American Studies Program. After Erdrich graduated, she and Dorris stayed in touch and became literary companions. In 1980, Erdrich returned to Dartmouth as a writer in residence, and a year later she married Dorris. In addition to the three Native American children Dorris had already adopted, he and Erdrich eventually had three children of their own. Dorris eventually left his career in academia to oversee Erdrich's literary career and pursue his own creative writing. The couple enjoyed a great deal of success as literary collaborators until their separation in 1995. Two years later, Dorris committed suicide.

Erdrich's first novel was *Love Medicine* (1984), in which the fourteen chapters tell independent stories, tied together by the same characters and setting. The setting of a Chippewa reservation in North Dakota would become familiar to Erdrich's readers. "The Shawl" also takes place on a Chippewa reservation, but this one is in Minnesota. The story first appeared in the *New Yorker* on March 5, 2001, and was later anthologized in 2009's *The Red Convertible*. To date, Erdrich's prolific career has produced novels, stories, poetry, and children's fiction.

Although it would be easy to categorize Erdrich as a women's author, or as a Native American or Western author, critics caution against it. Her fiction demonstrates her ability to write to and about men as well as women, and her themes are played out in Native American contexts but are not necessarily unique to Native culture.

PLOT SUMMARY

"The Shawl" begins with a first-person narrator relating a story known among the local Anishinaabe people (a Native American people in the northern United States and Canada, especially concentrated in the Great Lakes areas). In the story, a married woman named Aanakwad gives birth to another man's baby. She already has a five-year-old boy and a nine-year-old daughter. Although she is a good mother, she is moody and deeply in love with the other man. The daughter is very attentive to the new baby, sometimes even more so than Aanakwad. Aanakwad is torn by her intense love for the other man, but she cannot stop loving him. This drives her into a depression that keeps her from caring for her family. The daughter is exhausted from covering so many of her mother's tasks, and from being awakened from sleeping under her plaid shawl by her father, who is afraid to wake his wife himself. Instead, the daughter has to wake her mother.

Eventually, the husband has to face the reality that the wife he loves will never love him again. He sends for the other man's uncle to come get Aanakwad to take her to the other man. While they wait for the uncle to arrive, they argue about where the children will go. Finally, the husband gives in and allows the daughter to go with his wife. Pained by what is happening, the husband turns his face away and closes his ears. When the son realizes he is about to be separated from his mother and sister, he cries. He runs after the wagon and grabs it, but Aanakwad pulls his fingers loose. He falls but starts chasing the wagon, unwilling to give up on being with them. It is icy and very cold, and the boy is only wearing light clothes, but this does not deter him.

The boy runs, despite the pain of the cold air in his lungs and the fact that the wagon is going faster than he can. Finally, his body gives out and he falls to the ground. When he looks up and sees the wagon disappearing with his mother and sister, something inside him breaks. He no longer cares if he lives or dies, even when he sees gray shapes and shadows moving among the trees on both sides of the trail.

When the boy regains consciousness, he is in his father's arms, wrapped up and being carried home. When the boy tells his father about the shapes, the father initially thinks his son has been visited by spirits. After hearing more details about the shapes, however, the father understands that they were wolves. Once the boy is safe beside the fire in the cabin, the father takes his gun back out to the trail to scare away the wolves. Because people had killed so many animals for food and furs, the wolves had too little to hunt, so they had become a threat to humans. The narrator goes so far as to say that the wolves hunted the people. To correct this, the people allowed the wild animals to increase their numbers for a while in order to give the wolves adequate prey.

On the trail, looking for wolves, the father discovers something that will haunt him for the rest of his life. He sees where the pack of wolves attacked the horses' legs and started jumping at the wagon. He follows the trail to where it dead-ends at a crossing at a frozen lake. That is where he sees, as the reader soon learns, his daughter's tattered shawl among what is left of her remains, being picked by ravens since the wolves were finished.

The father does not tell his son what he saw for a while. The boy asks about the shawl, but his father will not tell him anything. Later, as the father is dying of tuberculosis, he tells his son the story many times. He tells him that the wolves attacked the wagon and that Aanakwad threw her daughter to them. The boy is horrified and wonders how his sister felt, imagining that something inside her broke as it had in him when he collapsed on the trail. He imagines his mother setting the baby down, picking his sister up by the waist, and swinging her out over the side of the wagon. He pictures her red and brown plaid shawl in the air as the wagon with its sled runners disappeared forever.

The story then switches to the narrator telling his own story. He describes how after his mother died, his father no longer drank only on weekends or celebrations. He began drinking all the time, even leaving his children alone at home for days. The narrator says that he was the oldest at ten, and his twin siblings, Doris and Raymond, were six. When their father returned home, they would escape out a window into the woods until he fell asleep.

Because of their situation, the narrator learned to take good care of his siblings. He says that they have always been close and that now that they are adults, they sometimes talk about those difficult childhood times. The narrator also says that most other people understand because their story was not unusual. Still, talking about it helps the three siblings compare memories and perspectives.

The older brother used to hide their father's belt because he used it to hit them. After a while, however, he just started using other things to hit the children. For them, with experience came the ability to avoid being hit, presumably because the father was so drunk he was weak and wobbly. The three kids had a place in the woods where they built a campfire, and they used the money they snuck from their father's shoes to buy what they needed. The narrator explains that they had stopped seeing him as a father—or even a person—and instead saw him as something to be avoided and exploited.

At thirteen, the narrator has grown more than other boys his age. One night, as he and his brother and sister are examining what little food they have, they hear their father making his way home. Doris and Raymond take off for the window and try to get their older brother to come with them, but he insists he is staying this time.

When his father comes in the door after being drunk for five days, he looks terrible. He stops, sees that his son is there, and smiles in a mean way. The son has been practicing punching on a hay bag and a padded board to toughen and quicken his fists. The father is surprised when his son punches him. The son knows his father is still bigger and stronger, but he wants to teach him not to mess with him anymore. Once he starts fighting his father, there is something about the experience that takes hold of him. He feels it with the second punch; it is a mix of fear, despair, and joy, and it makes him giddy. It also makes him want to destroy or even kill his father. He thinks of his younger brother and sister as he alternates between silence and screaming.

As the fight rages, and he and his father hit each other with furniture and pieces of broken furniture, he almost feels like a bystander watching the entire scene play out before him. The son realizes that he has gotten the better of his father. That is when he sees him again as a father, not as the inhuman thing he and his siblings have been accustomed to seeing. The boy kneels down, feeling like a son, and reaches for something to wipe the blood off his father's face. It is a piece of old, faded red and brown plaid blanket or shawl. As the son cleans off his father's face, he regrets having gone too far.

His father reaches up and stops his wrist and takes the shawl. He holds it in his hands and puts it to his forehead in a posture of prayer. They stay that way for a while, until his father breaks the silence by asking (in a sober voice that would become familiar after this event) if the boy knew that he (the father) once had a sister.

The story shifts again, and the narrator describes a time when the government moved his people from the farthest parts of the reservation into areas with towns and housing. Although it seemed like a good arrangement at first, it was not. Eventually, too many people

were alcoholics, dead, or depressed. He remarks that the old kind of good people who would do anything for anyone were all gone. He adds that it was during this time his mother died and his father became abusive. Now that time has passed, things seem less desperate, but past events and family history are still a burden. The narrator's siblings both got married and live down the street; their father has a new woman; and the narrator prefers to live alone.

Once, when the father is telling his sister's story again (the story at the beginning of "The Shawl"), the son has the chance to share a few things with his father. He tells him that he should burn the shawl and send it to his sister's spirit because it is wrong to hang onto clothing that belonged to the dead. The father agrees. The son also shares a new perspective on the story of his sister. He describes his father's sister as being like the old, good kind of people and being brave and caring. He suggests that she saw the grim reality of the situation—her brother was back lying helpless in the snow, the baby would not survive without the mother, only the uncle knew the way to drive the wagon, and the wolves' need was not malicious, it was just a need. Perhaps she offered herself to the wolves so everyone would not have to die. He imagines that she thought of the good of others, raised up her shawl, and jumped.

CHARACTERS

Aanakwad

In a story told among the Anishinaabeg of the area, Aanakwad is a wife and mother who falls in love with another man and has his baby. Her love for the other man grows, creating a deep depression in her that brings anger toward her husband. She gladly leaves her husband, taking with her the daughter they share and the baby she had by the other man. When her son (by her husband) tries to follow, she forces him to let her go. Erdrich describes Aanakwad with imagery of stormy weather. Although the narrator talks about her with some degree of compassion, her husband sees only the worst in her and blames her for their daughter's death.

Aanakwad's Daughter

The daughter in the story told among the Anishinaabeg is nine years old. She is mature, selfless, and responsible, and she makes sure that the new baby receives proper care. She has a red and brown plaid shawl that she wears to keep warm and that she uses as a blanket when she sleeps at night. When she is killed by the wolves, the shawl is torn in the attack, letting her father know who was killed. Toward the end of the story, the reader learns that the narrator's father was the girl's brother.

Aanakwad's Husband

Aanakwad's husband is loving and patient, and he cares for his children. When it becomes clear that he will never again have his wife's love and that his home situation will only worsen, he arranges for her to be reunited with her lover. He does not want to lose his children but agrees to allow their nine-year-old daughter to go with his wife, while their five-year-old son stays with him. The death of his daughter and the circumstances surrounding it haunt him for the rest of his life. He discovers what is left of his daughter after the wolf attack, and he keeps her shawl. In his mind, his wayward, selfish wife threw the daughter to the wolves.

Aanakwad's Son

The son in the story told among the Anishinaabeg is five years old. He is still attached to his mother, longing for connection, and is devastated when his mother leaves without him in the wagon. Little is said about the son until the part of the story where the mother leaves, and then he becomes central. He is so desperate not to be left by his mother that he runs in the cold night after her until he collapses, his heart broken and his will to live gone.

Later, when his father tells him that his sister died when his mother threw her to the wolves, the son shows remarkable empathy in his concern for how his sister felt at that moment. Toward the end of the story, the reader learns that that little boy is the narrator's father. His years of destructive behavior were the result of his brokenness over his sister.

Doris

Doris is the narrator's younger sister and Raymond's twin. They are four years younger than their elder brother. Before the narrator stays to fight their father, Doris and Raymond go out the window and try to pull their older brother with them so he will be safe, but he is determined to stay. As an adult, Doris and Raymond marry a

brother and a sister. Doris lives on the same road as her siblings.

Narrator

The narrator is an adult who tells about his difficult childhood with an alcoholic, abusive father. The narrator's mother died, and he had younger twin siblings he took care of as his father was unfit. At the time his mother died and his father started drinking heavily, the narrator was ten. He was resourceful, smart, brave, and caring as a child.

At thirteen, he determines not to live in fear of his father anymore, so after training himself for a fight, he faces off with his father. The fight releases feelings in him he did not expect, but at the end, he feels compassion and a little bit of regret. At that moment, the father tells his son about his sister (Aanakwad's daughter). The narrator gains insight into the father's deep emotional scars.

As an adult, the narrator maintains relationships with both siblings and his father, although he prefers to live alone. He is concerned about the despair among his people but does not see a solution.

At the end of the tale, the narrator offers a new perspective on the story of the sister and her shawl. Erdrich does not reveal whether or not the father accepts his son's perspective, leaving the reader to decide whether the narrator's interpretation should be seen as true.

Raymond

Raymond is the narrator's younger brother and Doris's twin. They are four years younger than their brother. Before the narrator stays to fight their father, Doris and Raymond go out the window and try to pull their older brother with them so he will be safe, but he is determined to stay. As an adult, Doris and Raymond marry a brother and a sister. Raymond lives on the same road as his siblings.

Uncle

Aanakwad's husband sends for his wife's lover's uncle to come get her and take her back with him so she can live with her lover. The uncle arrives in a wagon equipped with sled runners, prepared for the snowy terrain. There is no real description of the uncle aside from his role as the driver, but the fact that he went out in icy weather to pick up Aanakwad demonstrates family loyalty.

TOPICS FOR FURTHER STUDY

- Research the realities, opportunities, and strategies in the economy on a Native American reservation. Create one to three different illustrations, charts, or diagrams to communicate your findings. Then consider the topic globally by doing the same thing for another indigenous population somewhere else in the world. They do not necessarily need to be living on a reservation, but look at whether they have been separated from mainstream society and how they live and support themselves. Again, create one to three illustrations, charts, or diagrams to compare with the others. Prepare an introduction and a conclusion to complete your report.

- How are modern Native American arts different from early Native American arts? Put together an "art gallery" by using Power-Point or another computer software program to show viewers at a glance what has changed and what has not. Be sure to include examples of techniques, purpose, subject matter, ceremony, and other important aspects of Native American art.

- The husband in "The Shawl" eventually gives his wife over to the other man, loving her despite her unfaithfulness. How are adultery and unfaithfulness handled in cultures around the world? Research various cultural views on this topic and write for each country or culture how Aanakwad would have been treated in each. For example, "In Italy, Aanakwad would have . . . ," or, "Among the Amish, Aanakwad would have . . . ." Choose a creative way to present your findings, such as a slideshow or a drama. Include at least eight different cultures or countries.

- How dangerous can a pack of wolves be to humans? Read about wolves and their hunting needs, and find out how they adapt when food supplies are low. Also, see what you can find out about what causes low food supplies. Are there populous areas that are affected by wolf issues today? Write your findings in an essay, or write a script for a news show, then film it. You may want to include photos, maps, or video to bring your news story to life.

- Alan M. Gratz's *Samurai Shortstop* (2008) takes place in 1890s Tokyo and features a generational story about a son whose father teaches him the traditional ways of the samurai. The son is initially resistant because he is more interested in the modern sport of baseball. Read the novel, paying special attention to the father-son relationship, the sources of tension, the role of tradition in their home, and the meaning of growing into a man. Compare and contrast *Samurai Shortstop* with "The Shawl" and gather your observations as a list of similarities and differences. Using quotes from the stories and visual arts (drawings, collage, etc.), create a digital presentation (such as with Prezi) to present your material. Wrap it up with personal insight into the general nature of father-son relationships and how culture mediates them, if at all.

THEMES

Loyalty

The theme of family loyalty runs throughout "The Shawl." In the story told among the people, the daughter demonstrates a deep loyalty to her family as she tends to the new baby when her mother does not. The daughter makes sure her mother nurses the baby, and she gets up at night to change diapers and keep the baby clean. She never complains when her father gets her up to go wake her mother, and she does not complain when she is separated from her father and brother. She accepts her responsibilities in the family and carries them out lovingly. If the narrator's interpretation of the original story is accurate, the daughter is so loyal that she actually sacrifices her life so everyone else can live.

In contrast, Aanakwad demonstrates a lack of loyalty. She is unfaithful to her husband and allows herself to hate him for the mere fact that he is not the other man. She sometimes ignores her baby because, according to the story, she loves it too much, just as she loves the other man too much. When her husband arranges for her to go be with her lover, she insists on taking the daughter with her instead of at least leaving her husband with his own children. Aanakwad does not sacrifice for her family; she seems loyal only to herself.

When the narrator tells the reader his own story, it is apparent that he (also the oldest child) demonstrates deep family loyalty. When he loses his mother and his father becomes an abusive alcoholic, he, at the age of ten, readily assumes the role of caretaker of his two six-year-old siblings. He tries to protect them all from being hit, and he makes sure they all have something to eat when it is apparent that their father will not take care of that. When the narrator stands up to his father, he does so in an effort to take back some power in the house, so he can protect all the innocents against the ravages of the alcoholic adult. Even after the fight, he realizes he is loyal to his father, and he shows compassion. At the end, the reader sees the narrator redeeming his family's history by suggesting the alternate interpretation of his father's memory.

Again in contrast, a parent offers a counterpoint to the oldest child's loyalty. The narrator's father tries to escape from the pain of his past and present by drinking too much. At the very time when his children most need a stable and loving parent, he abandons them by drinking and being abusive. To his credit, he turns around after his son challenges him, and he chooses healing and sobriety.

Sacrifice

Erdrich develops the theme of sacrifice in "The Shawl" in the characters of Aanakwad's daughter and the narrator. There are many parallels between the two, as Erdrich shows a family history of generational struggle. In both cases, the eldest child is willing to sacrifice for the good of the family. The daughter sacrifices her own time, energy, and desires for the good of her family as

she sees to the baby's care. She willingly gives up her own path so that she can serve her family, even when it means separating from her father and brother. Ultimately, the reader is led to believe that she may very well have made the ultimate sacrifice in giving up her life for the others. It is no coincidence that the one who suggests this about her is the other character who makes many sacrifices for his family, the narrator.

The narrator began at the age of ten giving up his own desires and self-preservation for the sake of his younger siblings. He makes sure they are safe by leading them to a safe place in the woods where they can build a fire and wait for their father to fall asleep. He also makes sure that his siblings have food. He could look out only for himself, but he does not. In fact, when he is older and stronger, he offers himself as a sacrifice to his father in an effort to teach his father not to mess with him anymore. He does not expect to win the fight; he knows that his father is bigger and stronger, but he wants to make a point with his father so that he might at least think twice before trying to hit him again. As the protector of his brother and sister, the narrator hopes this "lesson" will ensure the safety of the younger kids, so he is willing to take injuries to make it happen.

Because the narrator was himself a kid who had to grow up quickly and take on adult-sized responsibilities, including sacrificing himself for the others, he has particular insight into Aanakwad's daughter's life and thoughts. They have similar characters. Because of this, the reader should take seriously the way Erdrich has the narrator explain Aanakwad's daughter's dilemma and choice. His interpretation of the story is likely accurate because he is the only character in the story who would be able to correctly interpret her point of view.

STYLE

Motif

In describing Aanakwad, Erdrich utilizes a motif of cloudy weather. Her name means "cloud," and the narrator says that she could change like one. Her mood could go from gloomy to silly from moment to moment. During her sullen times, her eyes are described as being stormy. When she becomes depressed at being separated from the man she loves, she is compared to an

"The Shawl" begins with the birth of a baby in the bushes. (© Tom McNemar | ShutterStock.com)

overcast sky. This kind of consistent imagery attached to her character gives a strong indication as to what kind of person she was and how she affected those around her.

Symbolism

The shawl's significance is evident in that Erdrich titles the story after it. The reader knows from the start to be watchful for the shawl and to take note of its place in the story. The shawl becomes a symbol for Aanakwad's daughter's courage and sacrifice. When she was alive, it was what she wore during the day to keep warm and what she wrapped around herself at night. It reflects her self-sufficiency as she takes care of other members of her family. As the girl gets in the wagon with her mother, the narrator describes how the father looked away so as not to have to watch her, wrapped in her shawl, preparing to leave. The shawl's connection to the girl's identity is strong.

When the girl's father discovers the torn shawl amidst the remains of the wolves' attack, he knows it was she who was killed. That he cannot let it go is further evidence of how much it represents the girl's strong character and bravery. He keeps the tattered shawl, even when his young son asks about it and worries that his sister is cold without it. Years later, that same little brother now has the shawl in his adulthood. It is a cathartic object that he holds to his head after the vicious fight with his thirteen-year-old son. The narrator (the son) recalls how the man held it to his head as if in prayer. After that, he gives up drinking, so he was likely praying to his sister for her strength so he could be the man his family needed.

At the end of the story, the son advises the father to let the shawl go and burn it. He says it is not good to keep clothing that belonged to someone who has died. When the father agrees to burn it, the shawl represents the strength and sacrifice of the father. Finally able to cope with the pain in his life, he gives up drinking and allows himself to heal.

Storytelling

Erdrich uses an interesting story structure in "The Shawl" that connects it to the tradition of oral storytelling so important in Native

American culture. Just as generations before have kept tribal stories, legends, and heroes alive by telling them to one another, she starts this story with a story told among the local Anishinaabeg. It is a sort of a legend, although not from long ago. Still, the story has the feel of a legend, and it is being preserved by an oral tradition.

Erdrich then brings the reader into the story of the narrator's childhood, which reads more like a modern story than a legend. When the two stories are merged in the father's telling his son about his sister, the legend becomes personal. Erdrich effectively fuses the lore of oral tradition with the real lives of the narrator's family.

HISTORICAL CONTEXT

The Anishinaabeg

The Anishinaabeg (which is the plural form of Anishinaabe) are also known as the Ojibwe or Chippewa. *Anishinaabe* is considered the most traditional of the names, and its use is becoming preferred and more common. The Anishinaabeg settled in the general areas surrounding the Great Lakes, including Michigan, Wisconsin, and Minnesota, as well as up into Canada.

The Anishinaabeg believe in the presence of spirits all around, including in the water, earth, and sky. In "The Shawl," when the boy's father believes the boy saw *manidoog*, these are the kinds of spirits he meant. A *manidoo* is a kind of master spirit that directs the members of its species on earth. Every species has one. It should be noted, however, that the *manidoo* does not dictate movements. It motivates by offering blessings, but individuals make their own choices. The Anishinaabeg also have a deep respect for maintaining good relationships with nature and animals. Although they do not worship nature, they take seriously the importance of having a respectful relationship. For example, it is common to leave part of a hunted deer's liver and its entrails for wolves, who are particularly special to the Anishinaabeg. In this light, it is easy to see how Aanakwad's daughter would have seen the wolves' hunger as a need they could not help and that needed to be met.

Reservation Life

Erdrich mentions how life changed when the government moved the Anishinaabe people from the outreaches of the reservation into more populated areas that looked like towns. The narrator describes how bad things got among his people and how it was at this time that he lost his mother and his father became a violent alcoholic. The narrator says that things are not as bad as they once were, but reservation life is described as difficult and desperate. These comments are consistent with the experiences of many Native Americans living on reservations in the United States.

Because their ways of life were significantly altered, tribes have had to adapt over time to relying on government assistance. Reservations are plagued by minimal opportunity and thus high unemployment, poor education, disease and alcoholism, and generation gaps widening because of Americanized schools. Life on the reservation is regarded by many who live there as hopeless. Rates of depression, suicide, and sexual abuse are the highest in the country. The problem of alcohol explored in "The Shawl" is a serious one among Native American populations. Originally used by some colonial Europeans to weaken the indigenous people, alcohol remains an ongoing problem today.

Shirley M. Frisbee explains in *Indian Life*, "As American Indians, we have used alcohol as a means of coping with low self-esteem, anxiety, feelings of frustration, powerlessness, hopelessness, and despair resulting from oppression." Between 1985 and 2000, the death rate from alcohol among Native Americans was seven times that of the total American population. Fetal alcohol syndrome occurs at higher rates among American Indians than other groups. Worse, there is a growing drug problem on reservations that threatens the next generation. Crystal meth has become a close second to marijuana as the most common illegal drug used on reservations.

Although change has been slow, improvement has come in some areas. Unemployment and poverty rates are decreasing, and more people have moved back to reservations since 2000 than lived there in the 1980s. One factor has been the success of casinos for many tribes. Casinos have provided income and jobs for Native American groups in twenty-eight states. This is by no means a perfect solution; some casinos have lost money or closed, and some are subject to state regulations.

Native American culture is still preserved by numerous families committed to teaching their

The boy saw the wolves coming out of the shadows. (© Michael Ninger | ShutterStock.com)

children the history, customs, language, and morality of their people. Faced with a strong American cultural reach in schools and the media, many Native American parents on reservations are giving their children knowledge, respect, and pride in their heritage.

CRITICAL OVERVIEW

Erdrich's work as a whole has received significant critical attention, but "The Shawl" as an individual piece has gone largely unnoticed. Erdrich included it in her first short-story collection, *The Red Convertible: Selected and New Stories* (2009). Critics for the most part praised the collection, finding so much of Erdrich's longer fiction and work as a whole encapsulated in the stories. Even Bruce Allen of the *Washington Times*, who declares the collection "inevitably uneven," also concludes that it is an "overall invaluable collection of the short stories that accompany... Erdrich's 11 published novels,

that portray cultural and familial collisions." Similarly, John Freeman states in the *St. Petersburg Times,*

> The tales revolve around the folly and fever of desire, the complicated ties of family, the gravitational tug of human weakness. You can count on thing goings awry in an Erdrich story, often as a combination of the above.

New York Times Book Review contributor Liesl Schillinger calls Erdrich "a wondrous short story writer," later adding, "With great delicacy, Erdrich handles the emotions of indelicate people, as they're tripped up by the uneven terrain of their lives." A reviewer for *Bookmarks* echoes these sentiments, deeming Erdrich "one of the most significant Native American writers of our time" and later praising *The Red Convertible* for interweaving "history, myth, tragedy, comedy, earthiness, spirituality, sensitivity, and violence."

The wide range of characters, anecdotes, and emotions represented in Erdrich's short stories is also noted by Joanne Wilkinson of *Booklist*, who states, "Erdrich effortlessly conveys her characters' earthy humor, drunken despair, and ever-present spirituality, making their struggles at once particular and universal." "The Shawl" is written in first person in the voice of a male narrator. Leann Restaino of *Library Journal* observes that Erdrich "writes equally well in both male and female voices. First-person narration makes this collection more intimate."

CRITICISM

Jennifer Bussey

Bussey is a freelance writer specializing in literature. In the following essay, she examines the parallels between Aanakwad's daughter and the narrator in "The Shawl."

Louise Erdrich opens her short story "The Shawl" with a story that has the ring of a local legend. The way the narrator tells the story and the fact that it is well known among his Anishinaabe people (Native Americans also known as Chippewa or Ojibwe) make the story part of the local lore. Of course, Native Americans have a cultural affinity with the oral tradition, passing ancient stories and history from generation to generation by telling the stories aloud.

Once the narrator finishes telling the reader the story, he switches perspective to tell the reader about his own life, beginning with his

WHAT DO I READ NEXT?

- Recognized as a leading Native American author for young people, Joseph Bruchac adds his comments and insights to traditional stories in 2003's *Our Stories Remember: American Indian History, Culture, and Values through Storytelling*. Bruchac includes stories from various tribes to give the reader a broad scope of reading.

- Erdrich's *Love Medicine* (1984; most recently revised in 2009) is the author's first novel, one that remains a favorite of critics and authors. Told from multiple points of view and skipping from the past to the present, the book is a collection of eighteen short stories that are connected into a larger narrative. Readers of Faulkner will begin to see why Erdrich is so often compared to him.

- Jeffrey Lent's *In the Fall* (2001) is set against the backdrop of the American Civil War and its aftermath. When a teenage boy returns from war with an escaped slave as his wife, the family and community eventually come to terms with this unexpected turn of events. Years later as the Great Depression looms, their son explores his family history to discover destructive secrets and racial hardships.

- In *Children of Alcoholism: A Survivor's Manual* (1986), Judith S. Seixas and Geraldine Youcha have compiled interviews with more than two hundred people who lived through living with an alcoholic parent. Intended to encourage children and teens who often feel alone in their struggles, the authors include discussions of abuse, holidays and family gatherings, chaos at home, and more.

- Ron Terpening's 2001 novel *The Turning* is set in 1964 and tells the story of sixteen-year-old Artie, who comes to a turning point in which he is ready to face his abusive father. Although the story unfolds over the course of just one night, the circumstances and experiences of Artie's whole life are in play.

- Novelist David Treuer grew up on an Ojibwe reservation in Minnesota, very similar to where "The Shawl" takes place. In his nonfiction book *Rez Life* (2012), he describes public policy and legislation, as well as the realities of issues like poverty and the ways the Ojibwe preserve and pass on their culture from generation to generation.

---

mother's death when he was only ten. What follows is a heartbreaking story that ultimately brings healing. To bring the two stories together and deepen the meanings of both, Erdrich creates parallels between the daughter in the legend and the narrator in his childhood. In the legend, a woman named Aanakwad and her husband have two children—a nine-year-old daughter and a five-year-old son. However, Aanakwad falls deeply in love with another man and has his baby. After that, she can no longer live happily with her family, and she falls into a depression while her daughter makes sure the new baby is fed and clean. Eventually, the husband arranges for his wife to leave to go be with the

other man, but wolves attack the wagon carrying her, the baby, and the daughter, and the daughter is killed.

In the narrator's story, the reader learns that the situation on the reservation got bad right around the time his mother died and his father became an abusive alcoholic. At ten, the narrator takes on the responsibility of looking after his six-year-old siblings. Three years later, he has gotten physically strong enough to be ready to face off with his father. Even though he knows he will be hurt and probably cannot win the fight, he is determined to teach his father to stop hitting him. Knowing what we now know about the narrator, who has been like a father to

> **BOTH THE DAUGHTER AND THE NARRATOR ARE FORCED TO SUSPEND CHILDHOOD BECAUSE OF CHAOTIC PARENTS; WHERE THE ADULTS GIVE THEMSELVES OVER TO THEIR PAIN, THE CHILDREN MAKE MATURE CHOICES AND SACRIFICES FOR THEIR FAMILIES."**

his brother and sister for three years, it is easy to see that this move is not just for his own protection, but also for theirs.

Erdrich subtly but intentionally draws parallels between Aanakwad's daughter and the narrator, and the importance of these parallels becomes clear at the end of the story. In the legend, the daughter is nine; she is described as responsible and competent, and her actions show her to be caring, maternal, loyal, humble, and proactive. She seems to give no thought to her own interests or desires, instead dedicating herself to doing everything she can for her crumbling family. She does not complain and is not resentful as she wakes up at night to care for the baby, and she works so hard all day that she sleeps an exhausted sleep under the red and brown plaid shawl she always wears.

The strength and nobility of her character is mirrored in the narrator, first introduced at ten years old. At approximately the same age as the daughter, he willingly takes on the role of caretaker for those who are otherwise helpless. Like the daughter, he seems to understand that the innocence of the younger ones needs protection, even if it means self-sacrifice. Both characters demonstrate maturity beyond their preteen years. They also both have a deep commitment to their families, looking after the younger children without disrespecting the chaotic adults in their lives.

Neither the daughter nor the narrator has friends their own age, nor do they have hobbies or interests they pursue. As important as these things are to nine- and ten-year-olds today, these characters do not think twice about it. They willingly set aside the things that would express their individuality and allow them to have fun with

peers. Why? Because priorities are not negotiable. They do what needs to be done because it needs to be done, and there is no place for complaining or resentment. The daughter is fully committed to the baby and to being a go-between for her parents. She sees what the adults are missing. The family is falling apart, and someone needs to step up to hold it together as much as possible for as long as possible.

Even when her mother leaves her father, she accepts that she has no vote in where she goes. From the way the son empathizes with his sister later and from what we know of her character, she obviously loved her five-year-old brother very much. However, when it is time to go, she accepts the decision of her fighting parents and goes with her mother and the baby, off to live on another part of the reservation with people she does not know. At this moment, she is not thinking about leaving her friends behind or making new friends. None of this is part of her world, because her family is all that matters. She shows tremendous strength in peacefully agreeing to leave half of her family, perhaps never to see them again.

Similarly, the narrator spends his time with his six-year-old siblings. Erdrich cleverly sets the ages of the older and younger siblings almost identical in her parallel. The narrator could very easily have escaped the house to hang out with friends or pursue his own interests. Instead, he never leaves his siblings to fend for themselves against their father. Once he grows accustomed to his father's drinking and the new habits and lifestyle it brings, he runs interference. He hides his father's belt when he can, and he takes his siblings with him when he escapes out the window. Once safely out of the house, he brings them with him to the woods, where they build a fire and wait for their father to fall asleep. At no point does he leave the younger, weaker siblings so he can go do something else. He is just like Aanakwad's daughter in this way.

Both the daughter and the narrator are forced to suspend childhood because of chaotic parents; where the adults give themselves over to their pain, the children make mature choices and sacrifices for their families. Aanakwad is consumed by her love for the other man to the point that she hates her own husband more and more just because he is not the man she loves. She pines for her lover all day, ignoring her baby. She claims that she loves the baby too much. just as she loves its father, and that nurturing the child is painful. According to the legend, Aanakwad does not try to set aside her own feelings for the sake of her family but drops deeper and deeper into a depression, frightening her own husband with her temper and withdrawing from the lives of her three children. Once her husband arranges for her to go live with her lover, she fights fiercely for what she wants as far as the children are concerned.

When we get to the narrator's childhood story, we see a father dealing with grief and loneliness by abusing alcohol. The alcohol takes over his life, and he is absent from the home for days, only to be abusive to his children when he returns. It is a terrifying and unpredictable way to live. The narrator, like the daughter, must have felt an abiding sense of uncertainty about the future. His father disregards the fact that his children are also grieving their mother (as he is grieving his wife) and completely ignores his responsibility to fulfill their basic needs, let alone their emotional needs. Like the daughter, the narrator sees a hole in the family and steps in to fill it.

Ultimately, both the daughter and narrator make incredibly courageous decisions to sacrifice themselves for the good of the family. The daughter is killed and eaten by a pack of hungry wolves. Her father discovers the scene, keeps the torn shawl, and tells his son that the mother threw the daughter to the wolves. In his mind, the daughter was sacrificed, but at the mother's hands.

The narrator also is willing to sacrifice himself. He waits three years until he is physically (and emotionally) strong enough to stand up to his father. He even plans for it by training his fists and practicing punches. As the day comes for him to fight his father, he does not really know how it will end. He is not deterred by the knowledge that his father is still stronger and bigger. He wants to send his father a message that there will no longer be child abuse in the home, and he is willing to take whatever physical injuries come with it. He fights his father, experiences an unexpected psychological catharsis, and ultimately finds compassion for his father. When his father asks his son if he knew he (the father) used to have a sister, the breakthrough is complete. The father is ready to talk about the pain of losing his sister and his wife. As it turns out, the narrator's father was Aanakwad's son.

The daughter in the legend is the narrator's aunt, whom he never met because of the tragedy.

Watching how carefully Erdrich parallels the lives and characters of the daughter and the narrator, the reader comes to the end of the story. Erdrich has brought us here, and the narrator offers his father an alternate interpretation of the story of his sister. It is not the way Aanakwad's husband interpreted the story of his daughter's death but an entirely new way to understand it. The narrator gets into the daughter's heart and mind and suggests that, because her brother was helpless in the snow from collapsing after chasing the wagon with his mother, because the baby needed its mother and the man driving the wagon was the only one who knew the way, the daughter saw that the only way to save everyone from the hungry wolves was to give herself to them. The mother did not grab her daughter and toss her over the side of the wagon, but instead the daughter saw a need, so she met it with full sacrifice.

Is the narrator's interpretation of the legend accurate? It is. We know this because the narrator is so like the daughter, and Erdrich makes sure we know this. She has brought the reader to this moment by paralleling the two characters and showing that only the narrator could really see into the daughter's decision. He knows because he would have done the same thing.

Source: Jennifer Bussey, Critical Essay on "The Shawl," in *Short Stories for Students*, Gale, Cengage Learning, 2013.

Yvonne Zipp

In the following review, Zipp examines the range of writing in The Red Convertible*'s new and republished stories.*

When reading for pleasure, I don't usually choose short stories. I've got exceptions, such as Flannery O'Connor, Jhumpa Lahiri, Angela Carter, and, of course, Alice Munro. But often, it doesn't seem like there are enough pages for me to fully sink inside a tale.

That's not a problem with Louise Erdrich's gloriously fat new collection of short stories, *The Red Convertible*. At a hair under 500 pages, it's stuffed with 30 years' worth of Erdrich's gorgeous prose. And her fictional town of Argus, N.D., and its environs is so detailed, you could walk for days without finding the backs of the sets.

Presented in chronological order (you can tell how much real time has passed by noting

The mother sacrifices herself by jumping off the wagon. *(© Michaela Stejskalova / ShutterStock.com)*

when "Chippewa" changes to "Ojibwe"), most of the stories will be familiar to fans. More than half are excerpted from Erdrich's novels, and the names are old friends.

The Nanapush, Kashpaw, and Pillager families jostle and squabble, but there's enough room in the anthology for everyone to get their say. By my count, her earliest novels, *Love Medicine* and *The Beet Queen*, get the most representation, with five stories culled from each.

Last year's *A Plague of Doves* gets only one, but it's a particularly good one. Shamengwa was one of my favorite characters, and rereading the story of how he acquired his violin was no hardship.

There are six stories that have never before been published, but they make up less than 80 pages of the total. Now, this could strike some as cheating (probably the purists who sniff scornfully when a band puts out a greatest hits album).

But here's the thing: A lot of us plebeians liked listening to those albums (before MP3 players rendered them quaint). And when

you're dealing with a writer like Erdrich, you're talking about a lot of hits.

The stories range from athletic feats—a former trapeze artist rescuing her daughter from a fire in "The Leap"—to acts of grace that get a little boost from magic, such as the US soldier who rescues a baby from a massacre in "Father's Milk."

Erdrich is perhaps best known as a creator and chronicler of native American fables, and "Father's Milk" is an excellent example of her talents in magic realism. She also excels at the haunting first sentence: "The first time she drowned in the cold and glassy waters of Lake Turcot, Fleur Pillager was only a girl."

But Erdrich never lets the air get too thin. *The Red Convertible* is also populated with tall tales such as "Le Mooz," in which a hunt turns into a summertime sleigh ride, thanks to laziness and some unfortunately placed fishhooks; and "The Gravitron," which made me laugh so hard, I woke my family. And while male characters are occasionally swallowed up by the ground, sometimes the supernatural has a pragmatic side, such as the ugly reality behind a teenage girl's "stigmata" in "Saint Marie."

Whether Ojibwe or white, Erdrich's women have broad shoulders and impressive stomach muscles. And most of them need this strength, since, as one character remarks, "Life is just bad timing to begin with."

These women can turn even the most domestic task into an act of war. Take an expectant mother in "Scales": "She knit viciously, jerking the yarn around her thumb until the tip whitened, pulling each stitch so tightly that the little garments she finished stood up by themselves like miniature suits of mail."

The men—unless they're predators—tend to be bemused fast-talkers who can't quite figure out either life or women.

"Time was rushing around me like water around a big wet rock," explains Nector Kashpaw in "The Plunge of the Brave." "The only difference is, I was not as durable as stones. Very quickly I would be smoothed away."

Money evaporates before it can be spent, new cars inevitably get wrecked, and land is swiped out from under those tending it. Faith offers some promise, but religion's role is more suspect. (The Roman Catholic church and its long missionary history plays a role in several stories.) Romantic love offers temporary respite, if at all.

Despite the fact that I'd read many of the stories before, they all still compelled attention—no mean feat for a 500-page book. If you've never encountered Erdrich before, the anthology offers readers an insider's tour of Argus.

For those who have read her novels, *The Red Convertible* will hold few surprises, but many pleasures.

Source: Yvonne Zipp, "A Louise Erdrich Sampler," in *Christian Science Monitor*, Vol. 101, No. 42, January 27, 2009, p. 14.

Leann Restaino

In the following review, Restaino notes the use of several literary devices in the stories of The Red Convertible.

Erdrich, the author of 12 novels (e.g., *A Plague of Doves*) as well as volumes of poetry and children's books, presents her first collection of short stories—30 years' worth of both previously published and new tales. Most of the protagonists are Native American, and Erdrich

writes equally well in both male and female voices. First-person narration makes this collection more intimate. And although some situations may be far removed from readers, it is easy to find relatable aspects. Erdrich uses both comedy and poignant realities throughout—sometimes within the same story—to create realistic plots that move the stories along briskly. Although organized chronologically, the stories can be read alone in any order. An enjoyable collection best suited to libraries where short story collections are popular.

Source: Leann Restaino, Review of *The Red Convertible: Selected and New Stories, 1978–2008*, in *Library Journal*, Vol. 134, No. 2, February 1, 2009, p. 68.

Joanne Wilkinson

In the following review, Wilkinson comments on the exploration and expression of emotions in Erdrich's story collection.

This collection spanning 30 years brings together for the first time the inventive Erdrich's short stories, many of which provided the groundwork for her dozen novels. Of the 36 stories included, most have been previously published, but there are also 6 new tales. The stories are laid out in chronological order and give readers the full breadth of Erdrich's meticulously drawn world, one on a par with Faulkner's fictional Yoknapatawpha County, although for Erdrich, the theme of endurance takes on a special significance, placed as it is within the context of an Ojibwa reservation in North Dakota, where Native Americans struggle mightily to prevent the decimation of their culture. Like Faulkner, Erdrich combines a supple, poetic style with a vividly realized setting and unforgettable characters, often setting up complex, interlocking narratives. Readers familiar with her novels will be stunned once again by the sheer virtuosity of her storytelling. Here, on rich display, are characters from the principal families in Erdrich's world as well as those who haunt them: sadistic Sister Leopolda, the pie-making Kashpaw sisters and their alcoholic men, enigmatic Fleur Pillager, the bingo-playing Lipsha Morrissey, and aged and comical wise man Nanapush and his stubborn wife, Margaret. Erdrich effortlessly conveys her characters' earthy humor, drunken despair, and ever-present spirituality, making their struggles at once particular and universal. What makes Erdrich such a mesmerizing storyteller, though, is the way she so fearlessly explores and expresses human emotion. A must-have for serious fiction collections.

Source: Joanne Wilkinson, Review of *The Red Convertible: Selected and New Stories, 1978–2008*, in *Booklist*, Vol. 105, No. 6, November 15, 2008, p. 5.

SOURCES

Allen, Bruce, "The Many Worlds of Louise Erdrich," in *Washington Times*, March 15, 2009, p. M26.

Erdrich, Louise, "The Shawl," in *The Red Convertible: Selected and New Stories, 1978–2008*, Harper, 2009, pp. 391–98.

Freeman, John, "Collection Sees Life with the Top Down: Thirty Years' Worth of Stories Race through Farce and Tragedy," in *St. Petersburg Times*, January 11, 2009, p. 9L.

Frisbee, Shirley M., "Effects of Alcohol Abuse on American Indians," in *Indian Life*, Vol. 26, No. 3, November–December 2005, p. 14.

Long, Lyle, and Cynthia Thomas, "On Eagles' Wings," in *Today's Christian*, Vol. 45, No. 3, May–June 2007, p. 42.

Murr, Andrew, "A New Menace on the Rez: As if Alcoholism and Unemployment Weren't Enough, Crystal Meth Is the Latest Scourge Bedeviling Native Americans," in *Newsweek*, September 27, 2004, p. 30.

"Native Americans," in *International Encyclopedia of the Social Sciences*, edited by William A. Darity Jr., Macmillan Reference USA, 2008, pp. 423–28.

Restaino, Leann, Review of *The Red Convertible: Selected and New Stories, 1978–2008*, in *Library Journal*, Vol. 134, No. 2, February 1, 2009, p. 68.

Review of *The Red Convertible: Selected and New Stories, 1978–2008*, in *Bookmarks*, March–April 2009, p. 38.

Schillinger, Liesl, "All American," in *New York Times Book Review*, January 4, 2009, p. 11.

"Substance Abuse," in *Encyclopedia of Race and Racism*, edited by John Hartwell Moore, Macmillan Reference USA, 2008, pp. 103–107.

Wilkinson, Joanne, Review of *The Red Convertible: Selected and New Stories, 1978–2008*, in *Booklist*, Vol. 105, No. 6, November 15, 2008, p. 5.

FURTHER READING

Diamond, Michael J., *My Father before Me: How Fathers and Sons Influence Each Other throughout Their Lives*, W. W. Norton, 2007.

Diamond, a respected psychologist, explains the profound connection between fathers and sons at every stage of life. He explains how both influence each other, how fathers learn to be fathers, and how masculinity is defined.

Niatum, Duane, ed., *Harper's Anthology of Twentieth Century Native American Poetry*, HarperOne, 1988.

Although many books have been written to preserve the legends of lore of the Native American people, Niatum's volume preserves a century of Native American poetry. Thirty-six poets are represented here, including Erdrich, reflecting diverse experiences, perspectives, and ways of joining the past with the present.

Prussing, Erica, *White Man's Water: The Politics of Sobriety in a Native American Culture*, University of Arizona Press, 2011.

Prussing offers a thorough look at the historic and modern ramifications of alcohol among the Northern Cheyenne. By researching history, culture, age, gender, causes, and treatments, Prussing's treatment of this topic has been regarded as insightful and academically significant.

Werlin, Nancy, *Rules of Survival*, Dial, 2006.

In this work of fiction, in a series of letters to one of his sisters, seventeen-year-old Matt chronicles life with their unpredictable, abusive mother. In addition to writing about the adults in their lives, Matt writes about the sibling bonds and protection that grew out of such a difficult home life.

SUGGESTED SEARCH TERMS

Louise Erdrich

Erdrich AND The Shawl

Native American literature

alcoholism AND Native Americans

Anishinaabe

Chippewa

Ojibwe

reservation life

sibling protection

self-sacrifice

family lore

Tuesday Siesta

GABRIEL GARCÍA MÁRQUEZ
1962

"Tuesday Siesta" is a short story by Colombian author Gabriel García Márquez, first published in Spanish as part of the short-story collection *Los funerales de la Mam̀ Grande* (*Big Mama's Funeral*) in 1962. It was first published in English in 1968. In an interview with Plinio Apuleyo Mendoza, García Márquez referred to "Tuesday Siesta" as "my best short story." He was inspired to write the tale after seeing a woman and her daughter dressed in black, walking in the burning desert sun, carrying a black umbrella.

The story describes the journey by train of a woman and her twelve-year-old daughter, dressed in poor mourning clothes, to a small town, where the mother asks the town's priest for keys to the cemetery where her son is buried. The reader learns that the son was a thief who was shot while attempting to break into a woman's home. As the woman tries to persuade the priest to help her, a crowd gathers outside, having figured out that the mother of the thief has come to town.

The story showcases the dignity and pride of the poor woman in the face of the priest's authority and the disdain of the townspeople. She perseveres in her quest despite the heat, the priest's objections, and the gathering (possibly hostile) crowd of curious onlookers, who have arisen from their midday siesta to gawk at the thief's mother. The story can be found in the volume *No One Writes to the Colonel and Other*

Gabriel García Márquez *(© Everett Collection Inc / Alamy)*

Stories (1968) as well as in *Collected Stories: Gabriel García Márquez* (1999).

AUTHOR BIOGRAPHY

García Márquez was born on March 6, 1927, in Aracataca, a town in northern Colombia. Luisa Santiaga Márquez Iguarán, his mother, had left her parents' home to marry Eligio García because her parents disapproved of him. Luisa returned home briefly for the birth of her son. For the first six years of his life, García Márquez was raised by his grandparents, and then his parents moved back in as well. Therefore García Márquez's grandparents were the most influential figures of his childhood. He attributes his storytelling abilities to his grandmother's influence, and he was deeply affected by the death of his grandfather in 1936, after which the family moved to Sincé, another northern Colombian town.

García Márquez was sent to a boarding school just outside of Colombia's capital city of Bogotá when he was thirteen. During his years at high school, he became interested in writing as

well as Marxism. He returned to Sincé after his graduation in 1946.

In 1948, García Márquez attended the Universidad de Cartagena and also began working as a journalist. In 1950, he wrote his first novella, titled *La hojarasca* (*Leaf Storm*). He returned to Bogotá in 1952. There he continued working as a journalist and wrote a series of stories that angered the Colombian government, so he went abroad. While in Paris, France, he began work on *El coronel ne tiene quien le escriba* (*No One Writes to the Colonel*) and *La mala hora* (*In Evil Hour*). In 1957, García Márquez returned to South America, working for a magazine in Caracas, Venezuela. He briefly returned to Colombia in March 1958 to marry Mercedes Raquel Barcha Pardo.

García Márquez was a supporter of Fidel Castro's Cuban revolution; his friendship with Castro brought him criticism but endured throughout his life. In 1959, García Márquez founded the Colombian branch of Castro's news agency. That year also saw the birth of the author's first child, Rodrigo.

In 1961, *El coronel ne tiene quien le escriba* and *La mala hora* were first published. "Tuesday Siesta" was first published as part of the short story collection *Los funerales de la Mama Grande* (*Big Mama's Funeral*) in 1962, the same year that the author welcomed his second son, Gonzalo, into the world. In 1965, García Márquez began work on the novel that would bring him international acclaim and establish him as the premier practitioner of magical realism. *Cien años de soledad* (*One Hundred Years of Solitude*) was published in 1967. The novel is considered by many to be García Márquez's greatest work.

During the early 1970s, García Márquez published no new fiction, but his fame grew as translations of *One Hundred Years of Solitude* were published around the world. He also founded the left-wing political magazine *Alternativa* in Colombia in 1974; throughout his life, he has been committed to giving a voice to the common man in Colombia and to the cause of peace in Latin America. Other novels were published in the late 1970s and the 1980s, including *El amor en los tiempos del cólera* (*Love in the Time of Cholera*), which was later made into a motion picture. But the most significant event in his career at that time was receiving the Nobel Prize for Literature in 1982.

In 1999, García Márquez was diagnosed with lymphatic cancer; while recovering, he wrote his memoir, *Vivir para contarla* (*Living to Tell the Tale*). In 2004, *Memorias de mis putas tristes* (*Memories of My Melancholy Whores*), his first novel in a decade, was released. As of 2012, García Márquez, in his eighties, was living in Mexico City with his wife, although he was suffering from dementia and no longer able to write.

PLOT SUMMARY

As the story opens, a mother and daughter are traveling on a train; they are the only passengers in the car. The train is traveling past mile after mile of banana plantations. Smoke and soot from the train blow in through the open window, and the heat and humidity are oppressive. The mother and daughter are poor and are dressed in mourning clothes. The girl holds a bouquet of flowers wrapped in newspaper and a bag containing a meager lunch. The two share the lunch on the train, and the mother naps briefly.

After a few hours, the mother tells the girl to put on her shoes and comb her hair, for they will soon arrive at their destination. The mother warns her daughter, "If you feel like doing anything, do it now.... Later, don't take a drink anywhere even if you're dying of thirst. Above all, no crying." The girl nods her agreement.

When they arrive, no one greets them at the station. They enter a small town that is nearly deserted, because everyone is taking their afternoon siesta. The mother and her daughter walk to the parish house of the town and ask to see the priest. The housekeeper says he is sleeping, but the mother insists upon seeing him. The housekeeper leaves to talk to the priest and returns to tell the woman to come back later, as the priest is just lying down to sleep. The woman insists again that she must see him, because she must catch the afternoon train back home. The housekeeper relents and lets them inside.

The sleepy priest finally appears, and the woman asks him for the keys to the cemetery. When the priest asks whose grave she wishes to visit, the woman replies that she wants to see the grave of her son, Carlos—the thief who was killed in the town a week earlier. He had attempted to break into the house of a widow, who shot him through the door. He was found dead on the doorstep the next day. He was a stranger in town, so no one could identify him.

After the woman tells her story, the priest asks her to sign a form and then he gives her the keys. He asks why she never tried to straighten out her son, to guide him. The mother proudly asserts that her son was a good man, that he had tried to earn money as a boxer, that she had instructed him "never to steal anything that anyone needed to eat," and that he had followed her advice. She does not apologize for her son or succumb to tears.

The priest, rather stunned by the mother's pride and composure, gives her directions to her son's grave. However, when he goes to the door to let her out, he sees that a crowd of townspeople has gathered outside to see the mother of the infamous thief. Seeing the crowd, the priest suggests that the woman should wait until dark to make her visit. Refusing to be intimidated, the woman takes her daughter's hand and walks boldly out into the street.

CHARACTERS

Carlos Centeno Ayala

Carlos, the deceased son of the main character, is portrayed as a casualty of the extreme poverty the family endures. Although he died a thief, details revealed by his mother and sister paint a more complex portrait; his mother insists without apology that Carlos was "a very good man." The reader learns that Carlos had attempted to support the family by boxing, but the bouts were so brutal that "all his teeth had to be pulled out," and his mother could not bear the thought that her son had to suffer so much to put food on the table. As a result, she endorsed, or at least implicitly condoned, his thievery, but she warned him never to steal anything that people needed to eat, and he obeyed. The reader is left with the image of Carlos as a good son forced to compromise his integrity for his family's survival. His devotion to his mother is revealed in his last words before dying: "Ah, Mother."

Daughter

The mother's twelve-year-old daughter barely speaks throughout the story but quietly and obediently follows the directions given to her. Confident in her mother's ability to handle any situation, she seems more relaxed in the parish house than her mother does. When the house-keeper indicates that they may sit, the mother remains standing, but her daughter sits down and later removes her shoes to get more comfortable. Throughout the story, the daughter speaks just once, to support her mother's claim that Carlos was nearly killing himself as a boxer in his attempt to support the family. When the mother heads toward the door despite the crowd that has gathered outside, the daughter follows her without hesitation. The reader gets the impression that the daughter is learning this same dignity, pride, and composure from her mother's example.

Housekeeper

The housekeeper, who is the priest's sister, is a spinster who lives in the parish house. She quietly follows the dictates of her brother. The smile she gives the mother when she insists on seeing the priest and her concerned offer of a parasol to protect them from the heat (and the prying eyes of the townspeople) indicate kindness, but she says very little throughout the mother's visit to the priest. Her meekness is a stark contrast to the strong woman who insists on visiting her son's grave.

Mother

The mother of Carlos Centeno is the central character of the story. Her distinguishing characteristics are her pride and dignity and her refusal to be cowed by the authority of the priest or the intimidation of the crowd outside the parish house. García Márquez's description of her early in the story hints at this trait; when she sits on the train, she is not slumped or defeated but sits with "her spinal column braced firmly against the back of the seat."

Poverty has aged her prematurely, and she looks too old to be the mother of the twelve-year-old girl who travels with her. Her words to her daughter are mostly brief commands: "Put on your shoes," "Comb your hair," and "Above all, no crying." From these commands, the reader can see that the mother is attempting to pass on her pride and composure to her daughter; she will not allow her daughter, despite their poverty, to be seen barefoot or with messy hair (she also instructs her to stay away from the window so she will not get soot in her hair). According to the narrator, the mother has "the conscientious serenity of someone accustomed to poverty." When she tells the priest the story

of her son's death, without embarrassment of any kind, it is the priest who blushes and begins to sweat. In a scenario where one might expect humility and shame—the woman is poor and her son has died a thief—she exhibits instead an indomitable pride and declares that her son was a good man.

However, García Márquez provides some clues that the mother's composure belies the deep emotion she feels at the death of her son. When the housekeeper goes to get the priest, the mother remains standing, "with both hands clutching the handbag." The intensity of the verb *clutching* and the fact that she does not sit down even after the housekeeper has invited her to do so reveal the tension and stress the woman is under, despite her outward composure. Later, when she tells the priest her son's name, she adds poignantly, "He was my only boy."

Priest

The mother must receive the permission of the parish priest to visit her son's grave; the priest is about to retire for his afternoon siesta and is reluctant to see her. García Márquez portrays the priest as a man caught up in routine, who has been doing his job for so many years that he has ceased to question why he does what he does. After the mother tells the sad tale of her son's life, the priest responds with "God's will is inscrutable," but the narrator adds that he says it "without much conviction." Throughout the interview with the mother, the priest is lethargic from the heat and his delayed or missed nap. Although he has a greater standing in the community and more official authority than the poor woman, he lacks her purpose and conviction. According to the narrator, "experience had made him a little skeptical"; the priest realizes his clichés about God's will are inadequate comfort for a woman who has lost her only son to the ravages of poverty, yet he has little else to offer her.

THEMES

Poverty
García Márquez describes in this story a family living in extreme poverty. Rather than just tell that the family is poor, he shows through descriptive details such as their clothing, their behavior, and their modes of transportation. For instance, the mother and daughter are dressed in "severe

TOPICS FOR FURTHER STUDY

- "Tuesday Siesta" is written in a very objective style; for the most part, García Márquez does not state what the mother is thinking but instead implies it through her actions. Try writing a version of the scene between the mother and the priest, in first person, from the mother's point of view. How does this alter the reader's perception of the mother? Post your scene on a blog and ask your friends to comment on it.

- Use the Internet to research the role of the United States in Colombia's drug war. How effective has the war on drugs been? What are the negative consequences of America's involvement? Write a report, including graphs detailing spending by the United States. Conclude the report with your opinion on whether or not the drug war has been successful.

- Read *The Boxer* (2004), by Kathleen Karr, a historical young-adult novel about a fifteen-year-old boy who seeks to get his family out of poverty through boxing. How is Johnny's experience as a boxer different from that of Carlos Centeno in "Tuesday Siesta"? How is

it similar? Write a brief essay comparing the two stories.

- The extreme heat is an important factor in "Tuesday Siesta." Do some research on the climate in Colombia. What is the average temperature in each month of the year? Now compare this with the climate where you live. Plot the monthly temperatures of both regions on a graph, and provide commentary on whether you think a story like this one could have been written in your region. How might the setting and circumstances be altered?

- Go to the Gabriel García Márquez author page on the Modern Word website and read his poignant report titled "Shipwrecked" (http://www.themodernword.com/gabo/gabo _shipwrecked.html), which tells the story of young Elian Gonzalez. Although this is a true story, García Márquez's distinct style comes through. Go through the report and highlight the phrases that make this story read more like fiction and less like a news report, and write a commentary on what you highlighted.

---

and poor mourning clothes," and when Carlos's story is told, García Márquez writes that his body was found barefoot, wearing "everyday pants with a rope for a belt." The daughter frequently removes her shoes, first on the train and later in the parish house, indicating that she, too, is more accustomed to going barefoot. Poverty has aged the mother beyond her years; she "seemed too old" to be the girl's mother. Other details such as their meager lunch on the train (they share a corn pancake, each eating half) and the fact that they are traveling in a third-class car on the train illustrate their lack of means.

García Márquez demonstrates the dire effects of poverty by challenging the reader's notions of right and wrong. When the mother unashamedly describes her son as "the thief who

was killed here last week," the reader (much like the priest in the tale) assumes that her son was a wayward youth who had strayed off the path of honest living. However, as the story progresses, this assumption is gradually destabilized. First the mother proclaims without apology that her son "was a very good man." Then the reader learns that Carlos attempted to earn money for the family by boxing but was regularly beaten so severely that he would be laid up in bed for days afterward. When Carlos died, his last words were "Ah, Mother." The portrait of a devoted son driven to desperation to provide for himself and his family is at odds with the reader's first reaction to the word *thief*. In this way, García Márquez shows the crippling effects of poverty and how want and desperation can force even the best of men into lives of crime and violence.

"Tuesday Siesta" begins with a young girl looking out the window of a train. (© gabczi | ShutterStock.com)

Pride

García Márquez portrays the mother in the story as a woman of great pride, a woman who, despite her station in life, believes in her innate worth as a human being. She does not cower in the face of authority or beg forgiveness for her son's actions, and she insists upon her right to visit her son's grave even though she is first turned away by the priest's housekeeper.

The theme of "pride" in literature is often used negatively (such as in Jane Austen's *Pride and Prejudice*). However, the pride that García Márquez describes here is not a feeling that one is better than others but rather a refusal to admit that one is less. Through her actions and her attitude, the mother conveys the belief that even though she is poorer or of a lower station than others (such as the priest), she is equal in her basic rights and her worth as a person. She asserts her son's worth as well, when she insists that he was a good man.

The reader sees her passing this pride on to her daughter, by instructing her, "Above all, no crying." The mother is clearly aware that as the poor mother and sister of a thief who has been killed while committing a crime, they will be the objects of both pity and scorn, and she is determined to give the people of the town no additional reason to pity them.

When the priest sees the curious (and possibly hostile) crowd gathering outside, he suggests that the mother should wait until after dark to leave. Through this suggestion he implies that the mother has reason to be ashamed and that her visit to her son's grave would be better carried out under cover of darkness. His sister offers them a parasol—another "shield" from the eyes of the crowd—saying that they'll "melt" in the heat of the day. The heat thus becomes a metaphor for the scrutiny and disapproval of others. When the mother refuses these suggestions and strides confidently out with her daughter, she affirms that she can take the "heat" and refuses to "melt" under the glare of the crowd.

Religious Criticism

The Catholic Church and its doctrines exert a great deal of influence over the people of many countries, and nowhere more so than in Latin

American countries such as Colombia, where this story takes place. This was even more the case in the early 1960s, when this story was written. The Catholic priest was an important authority figure who was both revered and feared by his parishioners. Many priests were not above using this power to intimidate their parishioners.

In this tale, however, García Márquez portrays the priest as a weak, tired man who lacks conviction in his own calling. Rather than intimidate the mother, he finds himself intimidated by her; although he scrutinizes her, she simply stares back at him, unfazed. The priest blushes and sweats throughout the rest of the interview. The only words of comfort he offers are "God's will is inscrutable," which he says "without much conviction." He seems to realize that he has little help to offer a woman in such a difficult position.

STYLE

Magical Realism

Although "Tuesday Siesta" is not written in the style of magical realism, it is worth mentioning here because García Márquez is considered the seminal writer of the style. *Magical realism* is a stylistic approach in which magical, bizarre, and illogical events happen in an otherwise realistic setting. These bizarre events are related in a straightforward, realistic manner. For example, in García Márquez's story "A Very Old Man with Enormous Wings," the lives of an ordinary couple are thrown into chaos when an old man with wings crash lands in their yard. In García Márquez's most famous novel, *One Hundred Years of Solitude*, some characters live for impossibly long periods of time, over several generations. "Tuesday Siesta" does not have most of the elements of magical realism, but the odd manner of Carlos Centeno's death leans in that direction. Centeno is shot through a door, with a pistol that has not been shot in many years, and is only found the next day with "his nose blown to bits."

Metaphor

Throughout the story, the heat becomes a metaphor for the scrutiny and disapproval of others and for hardship in general. On the train trip to the parish house, the heat gradually increases as the mother and daughter get closer to the town

where they must confront the priest and visit Carlos's grave. Over and over, the mother proves that she can withstand the "heat" without breaking down. In contrast, the rest of the town avoids the heat by taking a midday siesta, and the priest sweats and tires; by the end of the story he is "almost completely asleep."

García Márquez frequently mentions bananas, banana plantations, and "the banana company" throughout the brief tale. Plantation workers in Colombia were exploited for years by large corporations, most notably the United Fruit Company. Thus, bananas and banana plantations become a metaphor in the story for oppression and exploitation. For instance, García Márquez makes a point of mentioning that most of the houses in the town are "built on the banana company's model"; just as the terms of the mother's visit to her son's grave are dictated by the priest and the church, the design of the people's homes are dictated to them by the banana company. Their poverty puts them at the mercy of others who control their lives. The mother's refusal to be cowed by the priest and the church is an act of defiance. While the others sleep through the heat (bow to oppression and hardship), she chooses to fight through it.

Minimalism

Although García Márquez is usually associated with magical realism, "Tuesday Siesta" is written in a more minimalist manner. Minimalism has been a movement in many different art forms—architecture, fine art, music, and literature. In literature, the term refers to a spare, observational style, in which flowery and elaborate language is avoided in favor of simpler, straightforward prose. Perhaps the most well-known practitioner of the minimalist literary style is Ernest Hemingway, who wrote in direct, simple sentences with few adverbs. Other well known minimalists include Raymond Carver and Frederick Balthelme.

Many of the sentences in "Tuesday Siesta" have simple subject-verb construction. For instance, these four consecutive, simple sentences describe part of the mother and daughter's journey on the train:

> The train did not pick up speed. It stopped at two identical towns with wooden houses painted bright colors. The woman's head nodded and she sank into sleep. The girl took off her shoes.

Another feature of the minimalist style is that emotions are more often implied by the character's actions rather than stated directly. For example, the narrator does not directly state that the priest is uncomfortable during his interview with the mother, but the reader knows this because the priest cannot hold her gaze, and he blushes and sweats while he writes down the information she gives him.

HISTORICAL CONTEXT

La Violencia

Colombia was torn by a violent political conflict that began in 1946 with the arrival of a new Conservative government with newly elected president Mariano Ospina Pérez at the helm. The new president formed a coalition government, including members of the Liberal party at all levels. However, the leader of the Liberal party at this time, Jorge Eliécer Gaitán, disliked compromising with the Conservatives and eventually withdrew the party from the coalition.

Conflict between the two parties often led to violent incidents, but it was not until April 9, 1948, that the worst violence occurred. It was on this day that Gaitán was shot and killed on the street in Bogotá. In response to the killing, rioting occurred in Bogotá and throughout Colombia. Although there was no evidence that the Conservatives were responsible for Gaitán's death, most Liberals believed this was the case, a belief that led to continued violent conflict between members of the two parties. The violence temporarily abated when the Liberals rejoined the coalition shortly after Gaitán's death, but the compromise was short lived.

The era of La Violencia, as it came to be known, continued until the early 1960s. "Tuesday Siesta" was first published in 1962 and illustrates a life disrupted by both poverty and violence. Although the violence in the story is not politically motivated, it is arguably the result of living in a society permeated by conflict. In fact, the gun used by the widow to shoot Carlos is described as "an ancient revolver that no one had fired since the days of Colonel Aureliano Buendía," reminding the reader of the long history of political and military conflict in the country.

The Banana Industry

García Márquez mentions the banana plantations and the banana company in "Tuesday Siesta." The United Fruit Company (which later became Chiquita) was the biggest corporation controlling the banana industry in Colombia (and many other Latin American countries). Perhaps the most famous incident involving United Fruit in Colombia was the strike of 1928. Local workers, upset that they were being paid less than foreign workers who were brought to Colombia to supplement the local workforce, went on strike. While they were demonstrating in the city of Ciénaga, United Fruit called upon the Colombian military to open fire upon the unarmed workers, killing many. This incident is described in *One Hundred Years of Solitude*; in the novel, thousands are killed. The exact number killed is not known, however, and García Márquez has admitted that he exaggerated the number killed for dramatic effect in his novel. The massacre occurred in the Magdalena region of Colombia, where García Márquez grew up.

By the time "Tuesday Siesta" was published in 1962, the banana industry had changed in Colombia. United Fruit had reduced its direct involvement in banana production and instead was subcontracting with local growers. Although this encouraged some local entrepreneurship, it also eliminated some jobs and the benefits that went with them. In addition, the contracts that the local growers signed with United Fruit did not always give the farmers the most favorable terms. Conflicts between United Fruit and the banana workers' union in Magdalena encouraged the company to concentrate its business in Urabá, where there were fewer conflicts. By 1965, the company had ceased doing business in Magdalena.

United Fruit, during its history, gained a reputation for ruthlessness, oppression, and exploitation that it has spent many years trying to erase. Given the history of the massacre in Magdalena and the company's later abandonment of the area, it is unlikely that García Márquez would look kindly upon the corporation. Thus, the mentions of "the banana company" and the banana industry throughout the story serve as reminders of the oppression and hardship the characters (and the region in which they live) encounter.

COMPARE & CONTRAST

- **1960s:** The United Fruit Company gradually reduces its involvement in banana production, making marketing its main focus and subcontracting through local banana growers. The company does not enjoy a very positive reputation because of some questionable business practices throughout Latin America.

  Today: Chiquita (formerly United Fruit) faces trouble again: In 2007, company leaders confessed to paying off right-wing death squads that threatened their operations and also allowing them to use Chiquita facilities to ship and store their weapons; the corporation paid a $25 million fine. In 2012, Chiquita faces a lawsuit from over four thousand Colombians seeking compensation for the violence done to them by these death squads.

- **1960s:** After the overthrow of leader Rojas Pinilla in 1957, a bipartisan coalition government called the National Front is established that gradually reduces the violent feuding between the Liberal and Conservative parties.

  Today: Violence continues in Colombia but no longer stems from the Liberal-Conservative political feud. Now violence occurs between a group called the Fuerzas Armadas Revolucionarias de Colombia, which claims to defend the rights of poor Colombians, and a collection of paramilitary groups known as the Autodefensas Unidas de Colombia, which is heavily involved in drug trafficking. Also involved in the violence are drug traffickers and the Colombian army. Colombia supplies 80 percent of the cocaine that comes into the United States.

- **1960s:** After briefly living in New York City in 1961, García Márquez moves to Mexico City, unwilling to return to Colombia because of continued political violence that began in 1948 (La Violencia). While in New York, he writes for *Prensa Latina*, a publication dedicated to communicating the truth of what is happening in Fidel Castro's Cuba.

  Today: Because of his declining health, Fidel Castro stepped down as leader of Cuba in 2008, and his brother Raúl took over. As of 2012, he is rarely seen in public. García Márquez, suffering from dementia, resides in Mexico.

CRITICAL OVERVIEW

Although "Tuesday Siesta" was originally published in Spanish in 1962, critics in the United States did not get a look at it until 1968, when it was released as part of a collection titled *No One Writes to the Colonel and Other Stories*. The excitement over García Márquez's novel *One Hundred Years of Solitude*, which was published in Spanish the year before and was to be released in English in 1969, encouraged the English release of *No One Writes to the Colonel*, to give English readers a preview of García Márquez's unique style.

For the most part, critics enjoyed the collection. In a very positive review in the *New York Times Book Review*, James R. Frakes describes García Márquez as "an absolute master" and calls "Tuesday Siesta" and "Artificial Roses" (another tale in the collection) "gems of obliquity." In the *Saturday Review*, Robert G. Mead agrees: "This book . . . and the publication next year of his novel *100 Years of Solitude*, will secure a place for García Márquez among the growing constellation of Latin American authors who are familiar to U.S. readers."

Even some critics with mixed reactions to the collection still had positive comments regarding García Márquez's skill as a writer. In a review in the *Nation*, Oliver T. Myers praises the character of the Colonel (from *No One Writes to the Colonel*), calling him "one of the most memorable in Spanish-American fiction." However, concerning the collection as a whole, he writes that it "whets the appetite but does not fully satisfy."

The train stops in a hot, dry, dusty town during siesta time. *(© Fotomicar / ShutterStock.com)*

Some critics felt the stories are too negative, dwelling too heavily on the characters' poverty and despair. E. A. Dooley, in *Best Sellers*, sums up the collection as "a wordy photograph of life in a very depressing town." Mildred K. Badger, in a more positive review in *Library Journal*, admits that the stories are "not for the reader looking for escape."

Overall, even most of the less enthusiastic critics had something positive to say, and the next year when *One Hundred Years of Solitude* was released, the praise was far more effusive. Robert Kiely of the *New York Times Book Review*, describes that novel as one "so filled with humor, rich detail, and startling distortion that it brings to mind the best of Faulkner." For García Márquez, a longtime admirer of Faulkner, this must have been high praise indeed.

CRITICISM

Laura B. Pryor

Pryor has a master's degree in English and over twenty-five years experience as a professional writer. In the following essay, she examines the *themes of power, control, and violence in "Tuesday Siesta."*

A villain from J. K. Rowling's "Harry Potter" series says to the boy wizard, "There is no good and evil, there is only power, and those too weak to seek it." In the history of Colombia's violent struggles, it is certainly difficult to pinpoint good guys and bad guys—only the desire for power and control and can be identified. For example, the Revolutionary Armed Forces of Colombia was ostensibly formed to protect the Colombian rural poor, but over time they have used morally reprehensible methods for funding their activities, such as the drug trade and kidnapping for ransom. An opposing group, the United Self-Defense Forces of Colombia, comprising several paramilitary groups, regularly uses violence to achieve its aims and is heavily involved in drug trafficking. Good guys? Bad guys? Or just power seekers and victims?

When author Gabriel García Márquez was just a baby, the Colombian military massacred hundreds of unarmed striking banana workers who had the audacity to try and gain control over their wages and working conditions. García

WHAT DO I READ NEXT?

- Some minor characters mentioned in "Tuesday Siesta" also appear in García Márquez's novel *One Hundred Years of Solitude* (1969). It is considered by many to be his greatest work.

- Franz Kafka's tale *The Metamorphosis* (1915), in which the main character wakes up one morning to discover he has been transformed into a giant insect, had an enormous impact on García Márquez in his youth. The short novel has many of the qualities associated with magical realism, a literary style García Márquez mastered later in his career (though "Tuesday Siesta" is not written in this style).

- Another popular Latin American practitioner of magical realism is the Chilean novelist Isabel Allende. Her critically acclaimed novel *House of the Spirits* (first published in Spanish in 1982) was her breakthrough work.

- A simplified biography of García Márquez can be found in the charming children's picture book, *My Name Is Gabito/Mi llamo Gabito: The Life of Gabriel García Márquez/La vida de Gabriel García Márquez* (2007). Author Monica Brown uses imagery from García Márquez's novels to tell his life story in both English and Spanish.

- In Lyn Miller-Lachmann's young-adult novel *Gringolandia* (2009), the main character's father is arrested and imprisoned for publishing an underground newspaper exposing Chile's military regime. García Márquez published a similar newspaper in Colombia and often provoked the ire of the Colombian government with his work as a journalist. The family in the novel moves to the United States; when the father joins them there after his incarceration, he is haunted by his experience of torture and imprisonment.

- García Márquez was strongly influenced by the writing of William Faulkner. *The Collected Stories of William Faulkner* (2010) contains forty-two of Faulkner's short stories, including classics such as "Barn Burning" and "A Rose for Emily."

- In *Autobiography of My Dead Brother* (2006), award-winning young-adult author Walter Dean Myers tells the story of Jesse and Rise, two close friends living in Harlem. As in "Tuesday Siesta," poverty, hopelessness, and violence result in death. Jesse, an aspiring artist and cartoonist, tries to make sense of Rise's death by telling his story, in both words and art. The book is illustrated by Christopher Myers, the author's son.

- *Living to Tell the Tale* (2003) is García Márquez's memoir of his life as a young man and his beginnings as a writer. He describes the influence of his grandparents, who raised him as a child, and his early (and often penniless) years as a journalist. Though not written in any strict chronological fashion, the book covers the author's life from his childhood through the mid-1950s.

Márquez grew up in this climate of oppression and violence, as did millions of other Colombians. It is no surprise, then, to see themes of power, control, violence and powerlessness permeate his work. These themes arise in García Márquez's short story "Tuesday Siesta."

From the moment the story begins, the main characters—a poor mother and her daughter—

are at the mercy of forces beyond their control. They travel to their destination in the worst heat of the day, at the mercy of the train schedule. According to Harley D. Oberhelman, the title of the story is based on a Spanish proverb stating that Tuesday is an ill-fated day to get married, take a trip, or leave one's family. However, the timing of the son's death, and the train schedule,

" THE WOMAN CONFIDENTLY DICTATES HER INFORMATION TO THE PRIEST, JUST AS SHE DICTATES THE TONE OF THEIR EXCHANGE THROUGH HER PROUD, DIGNIFIED DEMEANOR."

dictate the time and conditions of the mother's travel. Once on the train, the mother advises her daughter to close the window so that the train's soot and smoke will not get in her hair, but this simple precaution is also beyond her control, because the window shade of the third-class car is rusted in place.

The train passes through a monotonous chain of banana plantations, of identical towns and identical houses; in one town a band plays for a crowd in the plaza, but it must play under the glare of "the oppressive sun." When they arrive at their destination, there are more identical homes, "built on the banana company's model." Like the poor woman, these people's lives and homes are controlled by someone with more power: the banana company. We learn that the mother has come to this town to visit the grave of her son, who was shot and killed while attempting to break into the house of a widow. Even for this sad errand, however, the mother must seek someone else's permission. She must ask the parish priest for the key to the cemetery.

The pattern of "open" and "closed" rules the mother and daughter's journey. The train window is open and cannot be closed. When they arrive in town, everything is closed for the midday siesta except for the hotel and the telegraph office. The door to the parish house is not only closed but covered by a metal grating through which the priest's housekeeper scrutinizes the mother. And of course, they must petition the priest for the cemetery key, because that too is closed to them. Ironically, the son that is buried there was killed *through* a closed door; even his last attempt to break beyond barriers was a failure. The closed door barred his entry but did not prevent violence from destroying him.

In the scene between the priest and the mother, however, the idea of control shifts from external, physical control (doors, windows, gates, boundaries) to internal, psychological

control. When the housekeeper tells her, "He says you should come back after three," the mother replies that her train leaves at three-thirty. Here, the mother uses the very restriction that dictated her own actions to get what she wants, to exert her own control. When she announces that she is the mother of the thief who was killed the week before, the priest scrutinizes her, attempting to intimidate her. However, García Márquez writes, "She stared at him with quiet self-control, and the Father blushed." Afterward, the priest "lowered his head"—conceding defeat—"and began to write." The woman confidently dictates her information to the priest, just as she dictates the tone of their exchange through her proud, dignified demeanor.

Throughout the entire episode at the parish house, the mother never *asks* for anything. When she first arrives and the housekeeper asks what she wants, she states, "I need the priest." When the priest asks what she wants, she replies, "The keys to the cemetery." She does not say, "May I have the keys to the cemetery?" Nothing the mother says, throughout the story, ends with a question mark. Early in the story, García Márquez subtly introduces the notion that the mother represents an equal and worthy adversary to the priest. In his short physical description of her, he writes that she is wearing a dress "cut like a cassock." A *cassock* is a traditional garment worn by priests in the Roman Catholic Church. Here, before the mother ever meets the priest, García Márquez presents her as an authority figure in her own right.

When the priest goes to the cabinet to get the keys to the cemetery, the daughter imagines that they are St. Peter's keys, the keys to the gates of heaven. Her musing reminds the reader that the priest himself represents a barrier of sorts; in the Catholic Church it is the priest's blessings, in the form of baptism and last rites, that allow one's spirit to pass through the gates of heaven. It is also the intercession of the priest, on the behalf of confessing parishioners, that grants them God's forgiveness. The priest attempts to use this authority to shame the mother, asking, "Didn't you ever try to get him on the right track?" (In contrast to the mother's declarative style, the priest asks five questions of the mother during their interaction.) The mother bypasses the question entirely by stating, "He was a very good man," denying the priest's assumption that her son was on "the wrong track."

The woman asks the priest for the keys to the cemetery. (© *Anastasija Popova | ShutterStock.com*)

After the mother and daughter tell the priest of Carlos's harrowing experiences as a boxer, the priest comments feebly, "God's will is inscrutable." With this remark the priest makes one last attempt to reclaim control of the encounter in the name of the church (and himself, by association). He implies that it was God's will, not the family's poverty or the exploitation of others, that allowed Carlos to be beaten in the boxing ring. Even the priest recognizes how inadequate the platitude sounds, under the circumstances, and he says it "without much conviction."

The threat of violence lingers throughout the story, especially for the reader familiar with the area's history. The ubiquitous banana company (the train travels through "interminable banana plantations") with its violent history, the death of Carlos (effected by a gun that had not been used "since the days of Colonel Aureliano Buendia," reminding the reader of Colombia's long history of military violence), and the story of his brutal boxing bouts all combine to keep the specter of violence hovering near the family from beginning to end.

Finally, near the end of the tale the priest discovers that a crowd has gathered outside the parish house, having realized that the thief's mother is inside. The reader is left unsure as to the crowd's intent: Are they merely curious? Angry? Armed? Regardless, the mother is undaunted; she takes her daughter's hand and walks outside. She is accustomed to circumstances beyond her control, but she possesses an enviable control over her own mind and emotions. Through this strong, dignified character, García Márquez demonstrates that self-mastery is the ultimate victory. It is a power that stems from within, not from the domination of others, and the one power that cannot be taken away.

Source: Laura B. Pryor, Critical Essay on "Tuesday Siesta," in *Short Stories for Students*, Gale, Cengage Learning, 2013.

Rubén Pelayo

In the following excerpt, Pelayo offers a narrative structure summary of "Tuesday Siesta."

"TUESDAY SIESTA"

. . . The opening of the short story sparks no particular interest in a reader of García Márquez, who generally uses more startling beginnings. Instead, as if in slow motion, "Tuesday Siesta" starts with a train coming out of a tunnel and passing by towns surrounded by banana plantations. Nevertheless, as if it were a still photo, it immediately awakens in the reader a quest for understanding that remains unsatisfied even after the story ends. The sudden dialogue in reported speech (someone else is quoting what the characters say) makes the reader wonder who is talking. Who is this old woman dressed in black, and to whom is she talking when she says: "'you'd better close the window.'...The girl tried to, but the shade wouldn't move because of the rust"?

The reader soon feels the solitude expressed by the description: there are only two people traveling in this third-class car, and they are going to a destination that is never disclosed. The narrator's ambiguity in speaking contributes to the reader's sense of intrigue. The twelve-year-old girl is the woman's daughter, but the woman, readers are told, "seemed too old to be her mother, because of the blue veins on her eyelids." An hour later, at twelve noon, on a "bright August Tuesday," the two women are approaching "a town larger but sadder than the earlier ones." Although, on the one hand, a specific time frame is insistently confirmed, on the other, neither the town nor the main characters are completely identified. The characters are known by their roles: the traveling mother, her daughter, and the priest. A recurring symbol used to mark time in *Leaf Storm* and "Isabel's Monologue," the train whistle is important once again in "Tuesday Siesta." The train, in fact, works as a narrative thread to help the reader understand the otherwise confusing plot. When the travelers get off the train, around two o'clock (three hours since the story has begun), the townspeople are taking a siesta. The old woman and her daughter "went directly to the parish house." Here the reader finally starts putting the puzzle together, and the story starts to make sense. The mother and her daughter are making a trip to bring flowers to her son's tomb. The town's priest has the keys to the cemetery, and the old woman wants them. Nowhere is the woman's pride and dignity more obvious than at the priest's home. Examples of her pride and dignified bearing are noted previously, as, for example, in the way she sits in the train, although nobody but her daughter is watching. At the parish house she never loses her composure, and she succeeds in getting what she needs: the

keys to the cemetery. The priest, who happens to be taking a siesta, wants her "to come back after three"; the woman responds that she is taking the train back at three-thirty. So determined is she that the priest gives in. When he asks whom she is coming to see, she gives the name Carlos Centeno: "he's the thief who was killed here last week...I am his mother."

The omniscient narrator relates that a lonely widow named Rebeca, an old woman living alone for the past twenty-eight years, killed the thief at three in the morning. Rebeca, readers are told, killed the thief with an old revolver "that no one had fired since the days of Colonel Aureliano Buendía."

The reference to Colonel Aureliano Buendía might pass unnoticed by someone who has not read *Leaf Storm*, "Big Mama's Funeral," or *One Hundred Years of Solitude*. However, although only fleetingly mentioned in several of the stories, his name seems to connect all the short stories. Each story, then, although able to stand alone, appears as a part of a layered world.

The end of the story, as is typical of Gabriel García Márquez's writing, is open to multiple interpretations. Although the townspeople were supposed to be taking a siesta, everybody, instead, was at their windows or on the streets, while the old woman, with the keys to the cemetery in her hand, "took the girl by the hand and went into the street." That is how the story ends. Any climax or further conclusion is left to the reader's imagination....

Source: Rubén Pelayo, "The Short Stories," in *Gabriel García Márquez: A Critical Companion*, Greenwood Press, 2001, pp. 63–87.

John Simon

In the following essay, Simon offers a negative critique of García Márquez's work as a whole.

Frequently the history of literature (or the history of human gullibility) spews up a novel that becomes an "intellectual bestseller"—a book that all persons with literary or intellectual pretensions feel obliged to acquire, and some even to read. It may be the worst work by an established artist whose "bestseller time" has come.... Or it may simply be the book of a mediocre but newly emerged writer of strange origin or bent that strikes even some usually judicious people as unusual, original, unique (never mind that it is factitious, trivial, and, to be honest about it, boring). Such a book is—was—Gabriel García

" WE KNOW SOMETHING ABOUT THE MOTHER, VERY LITTLE ABOUT THE DAUGHTER, AND NOTHING AT ALL ABOUT THE TOWNSPEOPLE EXCEPT THAT THEY LOVE THEIR SIESTA."

Márquez's *One Hundred Years of Solitude*, which earned its author the Nobel Prize, won by such other prodigious Latin American writers as Miguel Angel Asturias (at least unpretentious) and the unspeakable Gabriela Mistral, but never by Jorge Luis Borges, the one who most deserves it.

To read *One Hundred Years of Solitude* is to dive into a mountain of cotton candy head first and brain last, and endlessly, suffocatingly, sickeningly try to eat one's way out of it. This book that, without false modesty, could call itself *One Thousand Years of Solitude* is repetitious beyond anything but an old-time movie serial, with characters that even a genealogical chart cannot individuate (why should it? since when is the writer's job done by a chart?); the same sticky-sweet mixture of fantasy and social satire stretches on and on. Its mischievousness loses whatever edge it might have through iteration, lip-smacking enjoyment of its own cleverness, and flights into a fancy that seems to me the evasion rather than the extension of truth.

I had no better luck with two short novels by this writer, *The Autumn of the Patriarch* and *Chronicle of a Death Foretold*. Still, it seemed possible that he could achieve more with less—in the short story, which might curb his passion for prolixity. And indeed there are in the *Collected Stories* a few relatively unassuming, predominantly realistic tales that qualify García Márquez as a potential Hispanic Somerset Maugham. There is even one concluding novella in the author's dubious surrealist manner that works well enough, aside from some straining for effect and misfired jokes. For the rest, despite the odd powerful image and some passages of acerb mockery, these stories are mostly exercises in epigonous surrealism, with fantasy squeezed as desperately and self-destructively as when a novice milkmaid mistakes a bull's scrotum for a cow's udder.

The earliest stories, from the collection *Eyes of a Blue Dog*, are the poorest, though here the author has the excuse of his early twenties. In several of them, the protagonist is either a corpse somehow still alive or a living person relentlessly verbose in death. Death-in-life, life-in-death—these parvenu archetypes are pounded in with elaborately contrived, carefully self-contradictory detail. "Madam," says the doctor in "The Third Resignation," the opening story,

> your child has a grave illness: he is dead. Nevertheless . . . we will succeed in making his organic functions continue through a complex system of autonutrition. Only the motor functions will be different. . . . We shall watch his life through growth, which, too, shall continue on [sic] in a normal fashion. It is simply 'a living death.' A real and true death. . . .

Here the preposterous conceit—it has no satirical thrust—has at least a kind of fairy-tale diaphaneity. Presently, pseudopsychological obfuscation sets in. The living corpse hears terrible noises inside his head: "The noise had slippery fur, almost untouchable," yet our cadaver-hero will "catch it" and "not permit it to enter through his ear again, to come out through his mouth, through each of his pores . . ." etc. But forthwith this "furry" noise "[breaks] its cutglass crystals, its ice stars, against the interior walls of his cranium." Nevertheless, our hero proposes to "Grab it. Squeeze it. . . . Throw it onto the pavement and step on it [until it is] stretched out on the ground like any ordinary thing, transformed into an integral death." Notice that the noise goes from soft and furry to hard and crystalline and back again to something squeezable, thence to something animate that can be stomped on and stamped out with an "integral death." A pious hope, that; in García Márquez no death is integral enough.

Surrealism is all very well if it has some fidelity to its own bizarre self. A Max Ernst must remain an Ernst; it cannot, must not, transform itself into a Tanguy, a Matta, a Wilfredo Lam, at the whim of its undisciplined creator. Let the image be as crazy and hellish as it wants to be, but let it stay in focus. Out of focus, hell itself is not hell any more. It is only an amorphous blur. Yet from García Márquez's paragraphs of chaos a fine image, at times, surfaces—such as that "silence, as if all the lungs of the earth had ceased breathing so as not to break the soft silence of the air."

In the second story, "The Other Side of Death," a similarly living corpse is haunted by a smell instead of a sound. If, in the previous story, the author played around with tenses, here he fools with pronouns:

> They were traveling in a train—I remember it now [this 'I' comes out of nowhere]—through a country-side—I've had this dream frequently—like a still life, sown with false, artificial trees bearing fruit of razors, scissors, and other diverse items.... He'd had that dream a lot of times but it had never produced this scare in him. There behind a tree was his brother, the other one, his twin, signaling—this happened to me somewhere in real life—for him to stop the train.

Note the confusion of they, I, and he in what is mostly a third-person-singular story. Note also the sloppiness of "other diverse items." And note the theme of the brother, the twin, the alter ego, that crops up with tiresome frequency in these stories—once it is even a mirror image that bleeds when the shaver does not—and later in the same paragraph another García Márquez favorite, the tumor.

"Bitterness for Three Sleepwalkers" is even less scrutable. It may—just may—be about the death of a mother as perceived by her three sons. In any case, "she," whoever she is, seems to "become dissolved in her solitude" and to have "lost her natural faculty of being present."... In the title story, "Eyes of a Blue Dog," a man and a woman inhabit each other's dreams but cannot find each other when awake, because the sleeper, upon waking, forgets the watchword "Eyes of a blue dog" with which to recognize the other. Kipling did this sort of thing better in "The Brushwood Boy."

There follows a straightforward story about a whore who has killed one of her johns and elicits a fake alibi from an ugly restaurateur who adores her and feeds her free of charge. Entitled "The Woman Who Came at Six O'Clock," it is a neatly managed mood piece, situated in the bar-eatery before the evening's clients arrive, and containing such nice turns of phrase as "the man looked at her with a thick, sad tenderness, like a maternal ox." But in "Nabo: The Black Man Who Made the Angels Wait," we are back in the thick of the old farrago with yet another figure hovering in a state that is neither life nor death, and a plot, if that is the word for it, obscurer than any. We get several more such stories, some with ghosts in them, and

one, "The Night of the Curlews," that is totally impenetrable. But it is the first to offer a favorite García Márquezian theme: the curious behavior of certain animals. In this instance it is curlews, who blind three men for no apparent reason.

In the stories from the next collection, *Big Mama's Funeral*, Macondo, the mythical locale of most of García Márquez's fiction, becomes more important yet. This Macondo can be anything from a pathetic hamlet to a good-sized town running to seed, and is peopled with the author's stock company of characters who pop up throughout his fiction, short or long. Here the writing is more assured, and some of the besetting mannerisms are kept relatively at bay. They are replaced, however, by new tricks no less annoying. Thus "Tuesday Siesta," is a potentially interesting story about a poor woman who travels wretchedly, with her small daughter, to a distant town where her son, caught in the act of robbery, was killed and buried. She carries a cheap bouquet to lay on his grave, and rouses the indolent priest, during the hot hour of the siesta, for the key to the cemetery. But the townsfolk, aroused by her presence, gather ominously around the priest's house as the story abruptly ends.... We know something about the mother, very little about the daughter, and nothing at all about the townspeople except that they love their siesta. There is not enough to make up for missing confrontation. There is not even a denouement, only an anticlimax of the thudding rather than the teasing variety. García Márquez has said that he considers revelations "a bad literary device" and consequently avoids them. The avoidance, I think, is mutual.

Finally, the stories from the *Eréndira* volume, written between 1968 and 1972, are in the author's maturest style and perfectly display its generous flaws and niggardly virtues. Here the surrealism has become formulaic: in "A Very Old Man With Enormous Wings," a senile, moth-eaten angel falls out of the sky and confounds Macondo, which, however, loses interest when the side-shows of an itinerant carnival become more popular. Eventually, the angel just flies away. Conversely, in "The Handsomest Drowned Man in the World," the sea washes up a gorgeous, oversized male corpse, impeccably preserved; as the townswomen all fall in love with him while dressing him in whatever large enough finery they can muster, he has to be tossed back into the waves.

The long and fairly controlled title novella, *The Incredible and Sad Tale of Innocent Eréndira and Her Heartless Grandmother*, is probably all the García Márquez one needs to read for a full sampling of his ideas, strategies, and techniques. A mélange of the surreal, scurrilous, and occasionally poetic, it tells of a monstrous, larger-than-life grandmother who, having always exploited her lovely granddaughter Eréndira, now travels all over with her and prostitutes her to all comers until her alleged debt for supposedly causing their house to burn down is paid back.... Along its way, the novella takes satirical potshots at government, religion, capitalism, family relations, passion, and whatnot, and generally maintains its narrative propulsion despite its curlicues and discontinuities. Though there is wit, horror, and even wistfulness aplenty, the supernatural elements contribute little beyond a superficial exoticism, and one must finally wonder whether the story's eccentricities do not cancel one another out.

[The pieces in *Collected Stories*] sorely lack a philosophical or emotional center. "In García Márquez's world, love is the primordial power that reigns as an obscure, impersonal, and all-powerful presence," wrote Octavio Paz in *Alternating Current*. Obscurity and impersonality, to be sure, abound in these *Collected Stories*, but they contain more obfuscatory deliquescence than concentrated power. And they seem to have precious little to do with love, unless you can love a minor writer's obsession with telling tall tales such as his beloved grandmother told him, a boy of eight, to make him sleep. "Nothing interesting has happened to me since," García Márquez has said, and we are compelled to believe him. But he has certainly learned his grandmother's lessons well: with his fabulating, he can put even grown-ups to sleep.

Source: John Simon, "Incontinent Imagination," in *New Republic*, Vol. 192, No. 5, February 4, 1985, pp. 32–35.

SOURCES

Badger, Mildred K., Review of *No One Writes to the Colonel and Other Stories*, in *Library Journal*, May 15, 1968, p. 2021.

Bucheli, Marcelo, *Bananas and Business: The United Fruit Company in Colombia, 1899–2000*, New York University Press, 2005, pp. 1–23, 118–79.

Bushnell, David, *The Making of Modern Colombia: A Nation in Spite of Itself*, University of California Press, 1993, pp. 201–49.

Chatterjee, Pratap, "Chiquita Banana to Face Colombia Torture Claim," CorpWatch website, March 30, 2012, http://www.corpwatch.org/article.php?id = 15697 (accessed August 21, 2012).

Dooley, E. A., Review of *No One Writes to the Colonel and Other Stories*, in *Best Sellers*, October 15, 1968, p. 284.

Frakes, James R., Review of *No One Writes to the Colonel and Other Stories*, in *New York Times Book Review*, September 29, 1968, p. 56.

García Márquez, Gabriel, *One Hundred Years of Solitude*, Harper Perennial Modern Classics, 2006.

———, "Tuesday Siesta," in *Collected Stories: Gabriel García Márquez*, translated by Gregory Rabassa and J. S. Bernstein, Harper Perennial, 1999, pp. 105–13.

Kiely, Robert, Review of *One Hundred Years of Solitude*, in *New York Times Book Review*, March 8, 1970, pp. 5, 24.

Mead, Robert G., Jr., Review of *No One Writes to the Colonel and Other Stories*, in *Saturday Review*, December 21, 1968, p. 26.

Mendoza, Plinio Apuleyo, and Gabriel García Márquez, "Excerpts from *The Fragrance of Guava*," in *Gabriel García Márquez: A Study of the Short Fiction*, edited by Harley D. Oberhelman, Twayne, pp. 64–71.

Moore, William, "Para-business Gone Bananas: Chiquita Brands in Columbia," Truthout website, August 22, 2011, http://truth-out.org/index.php?option = com_k2&view = item&id = 2833:parabusiness-gone-bananas-chiquita-brands-in-columbia (accessed August 21, 2012).

Myers, Oliver T., Review of *No One Writes to the Colonel and Other Stories*, in *Nation*, December 2, 1968, pp. 600–601.

Oberhelman, Harley D., ed., *Gabriel García Márquez: A Study of the Short Fiction*, Twayne, pp. 20–22.

Pelayo, Ruben, *Gabriel García Márquez: A Biography*, Greenwood Press, 2009.

Rowling, J. K., *Harry Potter and the Sorcerer's Stone*, Scholastic, 1997, p. 291.

FURTHER READING

Cohen, Rich, *The Fish That Ate the Whale: The Life and Times of America's Banana King*, Farrar, Straus and Giroux, 2012.

    Cohen tells the fascinating story of Sam Zemurray, a poor Russian immigrant who rose to great wealth and power as the head of the United Fruit Company. The United Fruit Company controlled much of the banana industry in Colombia, as well as in many other countries, and was criticized for its exploitative and sometimes ruthless business practices. Zemurray's rise from obscurity through his own hard work and ingenuity, coupled with his later ruthlessness, make his story inspirational, cautionary, and quintessentially American.

González Echevarría, Roberto, *Modern Latin American Literature: A Very Short Introduction*, Oxford University Press, 2012.

Part of Oxford's "Very Short Introduction" series, this slim volume provides an excellent introduction to Latin American literature and its most influential authors. Echevarria provides a broad look at the history of Latin American literature, beginning in the late eighteenth century, and profiles authors such as García Márquez, Jorge Luis Borges, Mario Vargas Llosa, Carlos Fuentes, Pablo Neruda, and Octavio Paz.

LaRosa, Michael, and Germán Mejía, *Colombia: A Concise Contemporary History*, Rowman and Littlefield, 2012.

This history, covering the nineteenth and twentieth centuries, is unique in its positive emphasis on the life of the Colombian people rather than the country's tragedies and problems. Although the authors do not avoid these issues, they give a closer look at the country's fascinating culture, its art, its literature, and the admirable spirit of its people in the face of adversity.

Martin, Gerald, *Gabriel García Márquez: A Life*, Vintage, 2010.

Martin used information gleaned from interviewing over three hundred friends, relatives, and critics of García Márquez, as well as time spent with the author himself, to craft this exhaustive biography. Although Martin avoids more controversial topics (for instance, he spends little time examining the author's often-criticized friendship with Fidel Castro), the book provides a thorough and in-depth exploration of García Márquez's life and work.

SUGGESTED SEARCH TERMS

Tuesday Siesta

Gabriel García Márquez AND Catholic Church

Gabriel García Márquez AND Fidel Castro

Colombia AND banana industry

Colombia AND boxing

Colombia AND poverty

Colombia AND violence

Colombia AND United Fruit Company

Glossary of Literary Terms

A

Aestheticism: A literary and artistic movement of the nineteenth century. Followers of the movement believed that art should not be mixed with social, political, or moral teaching. The statement "art for art's sake" is a good summary of aestheticism. The movement had its roots in France, but it gained widespread importance in England in the last half of the nineteenth century, where it helped change the Victorian practice of including moral lessons in literature. Oscar Wilde and Edgar Allan Poe are two of the best-known "aesthetes" of the late nineteenth century.

Allegory: A narrative technique in which characters representing things or abstract ideas are used to convey a message or teach a lesson. Allegory is typically used to teach moral, ethical, or religious lessons but is sometimes used for satiric or political purposes. Many fairy tales are allegories.

Allusion: A reference to a familiar literary or historical person or event, used to make an idea more easily understood. Joyce Carol Oates's story "Where Are You Going, Where Have You Been?" exhibits several allusions to popular music.

Analogy: A comparison of two things made to explain something unfamiliar through its similarities to something familiar, or to prove one point based on the acceptance of another. Similes and metaphors are types of analogies.

Antagonist: The major character in a narrative or drama who works against the hero or protagonist. The Misfit in Flannery O'Connor's story "A Good Man Is Hard to Find" serves as the antagonist for the Grandmother.

Anthology: A collection of similar works of literature, art, or music. Zora Neale Hurston's "The Eatonville Anthology" is a collection of stories that take place in the same town.

Anthropomorphism: The presentation of animals or objects in human shape or with human characteristics. The term is derived from the Greek word for "human form." The fur necklet in Katherine Mansfield's story "Miss Brill" has anthropomorphic characteristics.

Anti-hero: A central character in a work of literature who lacks traditional heroic qualities such as courage, physical prowess, and fortitude. Anti-heroes typically distrust conventional values and are unable to commit themselves to any ideals. They generally feel helpless in a world over which they have no control. Anti-heroes usually accept, and often celebrate, their positions as social outcasts. A well-known anti-hero is Walter Mitty in James Thurber's story "The Secret Life of Walter Mitty."

Archetype: The word archetype is commonly used to describe an original pattern or model from which all other things of the same kind are made. Archetypes are the literary images that grow out of the "collective unconscious," a theory proposed by psychologist Carl Jung. They appear in literature as incidents and plots that repeat basic patterns of life. They may also appear as stereotyped characters. The "schlemiel" of Yiddish literature is an archetype.

Autobiography: A narrative in which an individual tells his or her life story. Examples include Benjamin Franklin's *Autobiography* and Amy Hempel's story "In the Cemetery Where Al Jolson Is Buried," which has autobiographical characteristics even though it is a work of fiction.

Avant-garde: A literary term that describes new writing that rejects traditional approaches to literature in favor of innovations in style or content. Twentieth-century examples of the literary avant-garde include the modernists and the minimalists.

B

Belles-lettres: A French term meaning "fine letters" or" beautiful writing." It is often used as a synonym for literature, typically referring to imaginative and artistic rather than scientific or expository writing. Current usage sometimes restricts the meaning to light or humorous writing and appreciative essays about literature. Lewis Carroll's *Alice in Wonderland* epitomizes the realm of belles-lettres.

Bildungsroman: A German word meaning "novel of development." The *bildungsroman* is a study of the maturation of a youthful character, typically brought about through a series of social or sexual encounters that lead to self-awareness. J. D. Salinger's *Catcher in the Rye* is a *bildungsroman*, and Doris Lessing's story "Through the Tunnel" exhibits characteristics of a *bildungsroman* as well.

Black Aesthetic Movement: A period of artistic and literary development among African Americans in the 1960s and early 1970s. This was the first major African-American artistic movement since the Harlem Renaissance and was closely paralleled by the civil rights and black power movements. The black aesthetic writers attempted to produce works of art that would be meaningful to the black masses. Key figures in black aesthetics included one of its founders, poet and playwright Amiri Baraka, formerly known as Le Roi Jones; poet and essayist Haki R. Madhubuti, formerly Don L. Lee; poet and playwright Sonia Sanchez; and dramatist Ed Bullins. Works representative of the Black Aesthetic Movement include Amiri Baraka's play *Dutchman*, a 1964 Obie award-winner.

Black Humor: Writing that places grotesque elements side by side with humorous ones in an attempt to shock the reader, forcing him or her to laugh at the horrifying reality of a disordered world. "Lamb to the Slaughter," by Roald Dahl, in which a placid housewife murders her husband and serves the murder weapon to the investigating policemen, is an example of black humor.

C

Catharsis: The release or purging of unwanted emotions—specifically fear and pity—brought about by exposure to art. The term was first used by the Greek philosopher Aristotle in his *Poetics* to refer to the desired effect of tragedy on spectators.

Character: Broadly speaking, a person in a literary work. The actions of characters are what constitute the plot of a story, novel, or poem. There are numerous types of characters, ranging from simple, stereotypical figures to intricate, multifaceted ones. "Characterization" is the process by which an author creates vivid, believable characters in a work of art. This may be done in a variety of ways, including (1) direct description of the character by the narrator; (2) the direct presentation of the speech, thoughts, or actions of the character; and (3) the responses of other characters to the character. The term "character" also refers to a form originated by the ancient Greek writer Theophrastus that later became popular in the seventeenth and eighteenth centuries. It is a short essay or sketch of a person who prominently displays a specific attribute or quality, such as miserliness or ambition. "Miss Brill," a story by Katherine Mansfield, is an example of a character sketch.

Classical: In its strictest definition in literary criticism, classicism refers to works of ancient Greek or Roman literature. The term may also be used to describe a literary work of recognized importance (a "classic") from any time period or literature that exhibits the traits of classicism. Examples of later works and authors now described as classical include French literature of the seventeenth century, Western novels of the nineteenth century, and American fiction of the mid-nineteenth century such as that written by James Fenimore Cooper and Mark Twain.

Climax: The turning point in a narrative, the moment when the conflict is at its most intense. Typically, the structure of stories, novels, and plays is one of rising action, in which tension builds to the climax, followed by falling action, in which tension lessens as the story moves to its conclusion.

Comedy: One of two major types of drama, the other being tragedy. Its aim is to amuse, and it typically ends happily. Comedy assumes many forms, such as farce and burlesque, and uses a variety of techniques, from parody to satire. In a restricted sense the term comedy refers only to dramatic presentations, but in general usage it is commonly applied to nondramatic works as well.

Comic Relief: The use of humor to lighten the mood of a serious or tragic story, especially in plays. The technique is very common in Elizabethan works, and can be an integral part of the plot or simply a brief event designed to break the tension of the scene.

Conflict: The conflict in a work of fiction is the issue to be resolved in the story. It usually occurs between two characters, the protagonist and the antagonist, or between the protagonist and society or the protagonist and himself or herself. The conflict in Washington Irving's story "The Devil and Tom Walker" is that the Devil wants Tom Walker's soul but Tom does not want to go to hell.

Criticism: The systematic study and evaluation of literary works, usually based on a specific method or set of principles. An important part of literary studies since ancient times, the practice of criticism has given rise to numerous theories, methods, and "schools," sometimes producing conflicting, even contradictory, interpretations of literature in general as well as of individual works. Even such basic issues as what constitutes a poem or a novel have been the subject of much criticism over

the centuries. Seminal texts of literary criticism include Plato's *Republic*, Aristotle's *Poetics*, Sir Philip Sidney's *The Defence of Poesie*, and John Dryden's *Of Dramatic Poesie*. Contemporary schools of criticism include deconstruction, feminist, psychoanalytic, poststructuralist, new historicist, postcolonialist, and reader-response.

D

Deconstruction: A method of literary criticism characterized by multiple conflicting interpretations of a given work. Deconstructionists consider the impact of the language of a work and suggest that the true meaning of the work is not necessarily the meaning that the author intended.

Deduction: The process of reaching a conclusion through reasoning from general premises to a specific premise. Arthur Conan Doyle's character Sherlock Holmes often used deductive reasoning to solve mysteries.

Denotation: The definition of a word, apart from the impressions or feelings it creates in the reader. The word "apartheid" denotes a political and economic policy of segregation by race, but its connotations—oppression, slavery, inequality—are numerous.

Denouement: A French word meaning "the unknotting." In literature, it denotes the resolution of conflict in fiction or drama. The *denouement* follows the climax and provides an outcome to the primary plot situation as well as an explanation of secondary plot complications. A well-known example of *denouement* is the last scene of the play *As You Like It* by William Shakespeare, in which couples are married, an evildoer repents, the identities of two disguised characters are revealed, and a ruler is restored to power. Also known as "falling action."

Detective Story: A narrative about the solution of a mystery or the identification of a criminal. The conventions of the detective story include the detective's scrupulous use of logic in solving the mystery; incompetent or ineffectual police; a suspect who appears guilty at first but is later proved innocent; and the detective's friend or confidant—often the narrator—whose slowness in interpreting clues emphasizes by contrast the detective's brilliance. Edgar Allan Poe's "Murders in the Rue Morgue" is commonly regarded as the earliest example of this type of story. Other practitioners are Arthur Conan Doyle, Dashiell Hammett, and Agatha Christie.

Dialogue: Dialogue is conversation between people in a literary work. In its most restricted sense, it refers specifically to the speech of characters in a drama. As a specific literary genre, a "dialogue" is a composition in which characters debate an issue or idea.

Didactic: A term used to describe works of literature that aim to teach a moral, religious, political, or practical lesson. Although didactic elements are often found inartistically pleasing works, the term "didactic" usually refers to literature in which the message is more important than the form. The term may also be used to criticize a work that the critic finds "overly didactic," that is, heavy-handed in its delivery of a lesson. An example of didactic literature is John Bunyan's *Pilgrim's Progress*.

Dramatic Irony: Occurs when the reader of a work of literature knows something that a character in the work itself does not know. The irony is in the contrast between the intended meaning of the statements or actions of a character and the additional information understood by the audience.

Dystopia: An imaginary place in a work of fiction where the characters lead dehumanized, fearful lives. George Orwell's *Nineteen Eighty-four,* and Margaret Atwood's *Handmaid's Tale* portray versions of dystopia.

E

Edwardian: Describes cultural conventions identified with the period of the reign of Edward VII of England (1901–1910). Writers of the Edwardian Age typically displayed a strong reaction against the propriety and conservatism of the Victorian Age. Their work often exhibits distrust of authority in religion, politics, and art and expresses strong doubts about the soundness of conventional values. Writers of this era include E. M. Forster, H. G. Wells, and Joseph Conrad.

Empathy: A sense of shared experience, including emotional and physical feelings, with someone or something other than oneself. Empathy is often used to describe the response of a reader to a literary character.

Epilogue: A concluding statement or section of a literary work. In dramas, particularly those of the seventeenth and eighteenth centuries, the epilogue is a closing speech, often in verse, delivered by an actor at the end of a play and spoken directly to the audience.

Epiphany: A sudden revelation of truth inspired by a seemingly trivial incident. The term was widely used by James Joyce in his critical writings, and the stories in Joyce's *Dubliners* are commonly called "epiphanies."

Epistolary Novel: A novel in the form of letters. The form was particularly popular in the eighteenth century. The form can also be applied to short stories, as in Edwidge Danticat's "Children of the Sea."

Epithet: A word or phrase, often disparaging or abusive, that expresses a character trait of someone or something. "The Napoleon of crime" is an epithet applied to Professor Moriarty, arch-rival of Sherlock Holmes in Arthur Conan Doyle's series of detective stories.

Existentialism: A predominantly twentieth-century philosophy concerned with the nature and perception of human existence. There are two major strains of existentialist thought: atheistic and Christian. Followers of atheistic existentialism believe that the individual is alone in a godless universe and that the basic human condition is one of suffering and loneliness. Nevertheless, because there are no fixed values, individuals can create their own characters—indeed, they can shape themselves—through the exercise of free will. The atheistic strain culminates in and is popularly associated with the works of Jean-Paul Sartre. The Christian existentialists, on the other hand, believe that only in God may people find freedom from life's anguish. The two strains hold certain beliefs in common: that existence cannot be fully understood or described through empirical effort; that anguish is a universal element of life; that individuals must bear responsibility for their actions; and that there is no common standard of behavior or perception for religious and ethical matters. Existentialist thought figures prominently in the works of such authors as Franz Kafka, Fyodor Dostoyevsky, and Albert Camus.

Expatriatism: The practice of leaving one's country to live for an extended period in another country. Literary expatriates include Irish author James Joyce who moved to Italy and France, American writers James Baldwin, Ernest Hemingway, Gertrude Stein, and F. Scott Fitzgerald who lived and wrote in Paris, and Polish novelist Joseph Conrad in England.

Exposition: Writing intended to explain the nature of an idea, thing, or theme. Expository writing is often combined with description, narration, or argument.

Expressionism: An indistinct literary term, originally used to describe an early twentieth-century school of German painting. The term applies to almost any mode of unconventional, highly subjective writing that distorts reality in some way. Advocates of Expressionism include Federico Garcia Lorca, Eugene O'Neill, Franz Kafka, and James Joyce.

F

Fable: A prose or verse narrative intended to convey a moral. Animals or inanimate objects with human characteristics often serve as characters in fables. A famous fable is Aesop's "The Tortoise and the Hare."

Fantasy: A literary form related to mythology and folklore. Fantasy literature is typically set in non-existent realms and features supernatural beings. Notable examples of literature with elements of fantasy are Gabriel Gárcia Márquez's story "The Handsomest Drowned Man in the World" and Ursula K. Le Guin's "The Ones Who Walk Away from Omelas."

Farce: A type of comedy characterized by broad humor, outlandish incidents, and often vulgar subject matter. Much of the comedy in film and television could more accurately be described as farce.

Fiction: Any story that is the product of imagination rather than a documentation of fact. Characters and events in such narratives may be based in real life but their ultimate form and configuration is a creation of the author.

Figurative Language: A technique in which an author uses figures of speech such as hyperbole, irony, metaphor, or simile for a particular effect. Figurative language is the opposite of literal language, in which every word is

truthful, accurate, and free of exaggeration or embellishment.

Flashback: A device used in literature to present action that occurred before the beginning of the story. Flashbacks are often introduced as the dreams or recollections of one or more characters.

Foil: A character in a work of literature whose physical or psychological qualities contrast strongly with, and therefore highlight, the corresponding qualities of another character. In his Sherlock Holmes stories, Arthur Conan Doyle portrayed Dr. Watson as a man of normal habits and intelligence, making him a foil for the eccentric and unusually perceptive Sherlock Holmes.

Folklore: Traditions and myths preserved in a culture or group of people. Typically, these are passed on by word of mouth in various forms—such as legends, songs, and proverbs—or preserved in customs and ceremonies. Washington Irving, in "The Devil and Tom Walker" and many of his other stories, incorporates many elements of the folklore of New England and Germany.

Folktale: A story originating in oral tradition. Folk tales fall into a variety of categories, including legends, ghost stories, fairy tales, fables, and anecdotes based on historical figures and events.

Foreshadowing: A device used in literature to create expectation or to set up an explanation of later developments. Edgar Allan Poe uses foreshadowing to create suspense in "The Fall of the House of Usher" when the narrator comments on the crumbling state of disrepair in which he finds the house.

G

Genre: A category of literary work. Genre may refer to both the content of a given work—tragedy, comedy, horror, science fiction—and to its form, such as poetry, novel, or drama.

Gilded Age: A period in American history during the 1870s and after characterized by political corruption and materialism. A number of important novels of social and political criticism were written during this time. Henry James and Kate Chopin are two writers who were prominent during the Gilded Age.

Gothicism: In literature, works characterized by a taste for medieval or morbid characters and situations. A gothic novel prominently features elements of horror, the supernatural, gloom, and violence: clanking chains, terror, ghosts, medieval castles, and unexplained phenomena. The term "gothic novel" is also applied to novels that lack elements of the traditional Gothic setting but that create a similar atmosphere of terror or dread. The term can also be applied to stories, plays, and poems. Mary Shelley's *Frankenstein* and Joyce Carol Oates's *Bellefleur* are both gothic novels.

Grotesque: In literature, a work that is characterized by exaggeration, deformity, freakishness, and disorder. The grotesque often includes an element of comic absurdity. Examples of the grotesque can be found in the works of Edgar Allan Poe, Flannery O'Connor, Joseph Heller, and Shirley Jackson.

H

Harlem Renaissance: The Harlem Renaissance of the 1920s is generally considered the first significant movement of black writers and artists in the United States. During this period, new and established black writers, many of whom lived in the region of New York City known as Harlem, published more fiction and poetry than ever before, the first influential black literary journals were established, and black authors and artists received their first widespread recognition and serious critical appraisal. Among the major writers associated with this period are Countee Cullen, Langston Hughes, Arna Bontemps, and Zora Neale Hurston.

Hero/Heroine: The principal sympathetic character in a literary work. Heroes and heroines typically exhibit admirable traits: idealism, courage, and integrity, for example. Famous heroes and heroines of literature include Charles Dickens's Oliver Twist, Margaret Mitchell's Scarlett O'Hara, and the anonymous narrator in Ralph Ellison's *Invisible Man*.

Hyperbole: Deliberate exaggeration used to achieve an effect. In William Shakespeare's *Macbeth,* Lady Macbeth hyperbolizes when she says, "All the perfumes of Arabia could not sweeten this little hand."

I

Image: A concrete representation of an object or sensory experience. Typically, such a representation helps evoke the feelings associated with the object or experience itself. Images are either "literal" or "figurative." Literal images are especially concrete and involve little or no extension of the obvious meaning of the words used to express them. Figurative images do not follow the literal meaning of the words exactly. Images in literature are usually visual, but the term "image" can also refer to the representation of any sensory experience.

Imagery: The array of images in a literary work. Also used to convey the author's overall use of figurative language in a work.

In medias res: A Latin term meaning "in the middle of things." It refers to the technique of beginning a story at its midpoint and then using various flashback devices to reveal previous action. This technique originated in such epics as Virgil's *Aeneid*.

Interior Monologue: A narrative technique in which characters' thoughts are revealed in a way that appears to be uncontrolled by the author. The interior monologue typically aims to reveal the inner self of a character. It portrays emotional experiences as they occur at both a conscious and unconscious level. One of the best-known interior monologues in English is the Molly Bloom section at the close of James Joyce's *Ulysses.* Katherine Anne Porter's "The Jilting of Granny Weatherall" is also told in the form of an interior monologue.

Irony: In literary criticism, the effect of language in which the intended meaning is the opposite of what is stated. The title of Jonathan Swift's "A Modest Proposal" is ironic because what Swift proposes in this essay is cannibalism—hardly "modest."

J

Jargon: Language that is used or understood only by a select group of people. Jargon may refer to terminology used in a certain profession, such as computer jargon, or it may refer to any nonsensical language that is not understood by most people. Anthony Burgess's *A Clockwork Orange* and James Thurber's "The Secret Life of Walter Mitty" both use jargon.

K

Knickerbocker Group: An indistinct group of New York writers of the first half of the nineteenth century. Members of the group were linked only by location and a common theme: New York life. Two famous members of the Knickerbocker Group were Washington Irving and William Cullen Bryant. The group's name derives from Irving's *Knickerbocker's History of New York*.

L

Literal Language: An author uses literal language when he or she writes without exaggerating or embellishing the subject matter and without any tools of figurative language. To say "He ran very quickly down the street" is to use literal language, whereas to say "He ran like a hare down the street" would be using figurative language.

Literature: Literature is broadly defined as any written or spoken material, but the term most often refers to creative works. Literature includes poetry, drama, fiction, and many kinds of nonfiction writing, as well as oral, dramatic, and broadcast compositions not necessarily preserved in a written format, such as films and television programs.

Lost Generation: A term first used by Gertrude Stein to describe the post-World War I generation of American writers: men and women haunted by a sense of betrayal and emptiness brought about by the destructiveness of the war. The term is commonly applied to Hart Crane, Ernest Hemingway, F. Scott Fitzgerald, and others.

M

Magic Realism: A form of literature that incorporates fantasy elements or supernatural occurrences into the narrative and accepts them as truth. Gabriel Gárcia Márquez and Laura Esquivel are two writers known for their works of magic realism.

Metaphor: A figure of speech that expresses an idea through the image of another object. Metaphors suggest the essence of the first object by identifying it with certain qualities of the second object. An example is "But soft, what light through yonder window breaks? / It is the east, and Juliet is the sun" in William Shakespeare's *Romeo and Juliet*. Here, Juliet, the first object, is identified with qualities of the second object, the sun.

Minimalism: A literary style characterized by spare, simple prose with few elaborations. In minimalism, the main theme of the work is often never discussed directly. Amy Hempel and Ernest Hemingway are two writers known for their works of minimalism.

Modernism: Modern literary practices. Also, the principles of a literary school that lasted from roughly the beginning of the twentieth century until the end of World War II. Modernism is defined by its rejection of the literary conventions of the nineteenth century and by its opposition to conventional morality, taste, traditions, and economic values. Many writers are associated with the concepts of modernism, including Albert Camus, D. H. Lawrence, Ernest Hemingway, William Faulkner, Eugene O'Neill, and James Joyce.

Monologue: A composition, written or oral, by a single individual. More specifically, a speech given by a single individual in a drama or other public entertainment. It has no set length, although it is usually several or more lines long. "I Stand Here Ironing" by Tillie Olsen is an example of a story written in the form of a monologue.

Mood: The prevailing emotions of a work or of the author in his or her creation of the work. The mood of a work is not always what might be expected based on its subject matter.

Motif: A theme, character type, image, metaphor, or other verbal element that recurs throughout a single work of literature or occurs in a number of different works over a period of time. For example, the color white in Herman Melville's *Moby Dick* is a "specific" motif, while the trials of star-crossed lovers is a "conventional" motif from the literature of all periods.

N

Narration: The telling of a series of events, real or invented. A narration may be either a simple narrative, in which the events are recounted chronologically, or a narrative with a plot, in which the account is given in a style reflecting the author's artistic concept of the story. Narration is sometimes used as a synonym for "storyline."

Narrative: A verse or prose accounting of an event or sequence of events, real or invented.

The term is also used as an adjective in the sense "method of narration." For example, in literary criticism, the expression "narrative technique" usually refers to the way the author structures and presents his or her story. Different narrative forms include diaries, travelogues, novels, ballads, epics, short stories, and other fictional forms.

Narrator: The teller of a story. The narrator may be the author or a character in the story through whom the author speaks. Huckleberry Finn is the narrator of Mark Twain's *The Adventures of Huckleberry Finn*.

Novella: An Italian term meaning "story." This term has been especially used to describe fourteenth-century Italian tales, but it also refers to modern short novels. Modern novellas include Leo Tolstoy's *The Death of Ivan Ilich*, Fyodor Dostoyevsky's *Notes from the Underground,* and Joseph Conrad's *Heart of Darkness*.

O

Oedipus Complex: A son's romantic obsession with his mother. The phrase is derived from the story of the ancient Theban hero Oedipus, who unknowingly killed his father and married his mother, and was popularized by Sigmund Freud's theory of psychoanalysis. Literary occurrences of the Oedipus complex include Sophocles' *Oedipus Rex* and D. H. Lawrence's "The Rocking-Horse Winner."

Onomatopoeia: The use of words whose sounds express or suggest their meaning. In its simplest sense, onomatopoeia may be represented by words that mimic the sounds they denote such as "hiss" or "meow." At a more subtle level, the pattern and rhythm of sounds and rhymes of a line or poem may be onomatopoeic.

Oral Tradition: A process by which songs, ballads, folklore, and other material are transmitted by word of mouth. The tradition of oral transmission predates the written record systems of literate society. Oral transmission preserves material sometimes over generations, although often with variations. Memory plays a large part in the recitation and preservation of orally transmitted material. Native American myths and legends, and African folktales told by plantation slaves are examples of orally transmitted literature.

P

Parable: A story intended to teach a moral lesson or answer an ethical question. Examples of parables are the stories told by Jesus Christ in the New Testament, notably "The Prodigal Son," but parables also are used in Sufism, rabbinic literature, Hasidism, and Zen Buddhism. Isaac Bashevis Singer's story "Gimpel the Fool" exhibits characteristics of a parable.

Paradox: A statement that appears illogical or contradictory at first, but may actually point to an underlying truth. A literary example of a paradox is George Orwell's statement "All animals are equal, but some animals are more equal than others" in *Animal Farm*.

Parody: In literature, this term refers to an imitation of a serious literary work or the signature style of a particular author in a ridiculous manner. Atypical parody adopts the style of the original and applies it to an inappropriate subject for humorous effect. Parody is a form of satire and could be considered the literary equivalent of a caricature or cartoon. Henry Fielding's *Shamela* is a parody of Samuel Richardson's *Pamela*.

Persona: A Latin term meaning "mask." Personae are the characters in a fictional work of literature. The persona generally functions as a mask through which the author tells a story in a voice other than his or her own. A persona is usually either a character in a story who acts as a narrator or an "implied author," a voice created by the author to act as the narrator for himself or herself. The persona in Charlotte Perkins Gilman's story "The Yellow Wallpaper" is the unnamed young mother experiencing a mental breakdown.

Personification: A figure of speech that gives human qualities to abstract ideas, animals, and inanimate objects. To say that "the sun is smiling" is to personify the sun.

Plot: The pattern of events in a narrative or drama. In its simplest sense, the plot guides the author in composing the work and helps the reader follow the work. Typically, plots exhibit causality and unity and have a beginning, a middle, and an end. Sometimes, however, a plot may consist of a series of disconnected events, in which case it is known as an "episodic plot."

Poetic Justice: An outcome in a literary work, not necessarily a poem, in which the good are rewarded and the evil are punished, especially in ways that particularly fit their virtues or crimes. For example, a murderer may himself be murdered, or a thief will find himself penniless.

Poetic License: Distortions of fact and literary convention made by a writer—not always a poet—for the sake of the effect gained. Poetic license is closely related to the concept of "artistic freedom." An author exercises poetic license by saying that a pile of money "reaches as high as a mountain" when the pile is actually only a foot or two high.

Point of View: The narrative perspective from which a literary work is presented to the reader. There are four traditional points of view. The "third person omniscient" gives the reader a "godlike" perspective, unrestricted by time or place, from which to see actions and look into the minds of characters. This allows the author to comment openly on characters and events in the work. The "third person" point of view presents the events of the story from outside of any single character's perception, much like the omniscient point of view, but the reader must understand the action as it takes place and without any special insight into characters' minds or motivations. The "first person" or "personal" point of view relates events as they are perceived by a single character. The main character "tells" the story and may offer opinions about the action and characters which differ from those of the author. Much less common than omniscient, third person, and first person is the "second person" point of view, wherein the author tells the story as if it is happening to the reader. James Thurber employs the omniscient point of view in his short story "The Secret Life of Walter Mitty." Ernest Hemingway's "A Clean, Well-Lighted Place" is a short story told from the third person point of view. Mark Twain's novel *Huckleberry Finn* is presented from the first person viewpoint. Jay McInerney's *Bright Lights, Big City* is an example of a novel which uses the second person point of view.

Pornography: Writing intended to provoke feelings of lust in the reader. Such works are often condemned by critics and teachers, but those which can be shown to have literary value are viewed less harshly. Literary works that have been described as pornographic include D. H. Lawrence's *Lady Chatterley's Lover* and James Joyce's *Ulysses*.

Post-Aesthetic Movement: An artistic response made by African Americans to the black aesthetic movement of the 1960s and early 1970s. Writers since that time have adopted a somewhat different tone in their work, with less emphasis placed on the disparity between black and white in the United States. In the words of post-aesthetic authors such as Toni Morrison, John Edgar Wideman, and Kristin Hunter, African Americans are portrayed as looking inward for answers to their own questions, rather than always looking to the outside world. Two well-known examples of works produced as part of the post-aesthetic movement are the Pulitzer Prize–winning novels *The Color Purple* by Alice Walker and *Beloved* by Toni Morrison.

Postmodernism: Writing from the 1960s forward characterized by experimentation and application of modernist elements, which include existentialism and alienation. Postmodernists have gone a step further in the rejection of tradition begun with the modernists by also rejecting traditional forms, preferring the anti-novel over the novel and the anti-hero over the hero. Postmodern writers include Thomas Pynchon, Margaret Drabble, and Gabriel García Márquez.

Prologue: An introductory section of a literary work. It often contains information establishing the situation of the characters or presents information about the setting, time period, or action. In drama, the prologue is spoken by a chorus or by one of the principal characters.

Prose: A literary medium that attempts to mirror the language of everyday speech. It is distinguished from poetry by its use of unmetered, unrhymed language consisting of logically related sentences. Prose is usually grouped into paragraphs that form a cohesive whole such as an essay or a novel. The term is sometimes used to mean an author's general writing.

Protagonist: The central character of a story who serves as a focus for its themes and incidents and as the principal rationale for its development. The protagonist is sometimes referred to in discussions of modern literature as the hero or anti-hero. Well-known protagonists are Hamlet in William Shakespeare's *Hamlet* and Jay Gatsby in F. Scott Fitzgerald's *The Great Gatsby*.

R

Realism: A nineteenth-century European literary movement that sought to portray familiar characters, situations, and settings in a realistic manner. This was done primarily by using an objective narrative point of view and through the buildup of accurate detail. The standard for success of any realistic work depends on how faithfully it transfers common experience into fictional forms. The realistic method may be altered or extended, as in stream of consciousness writing, to record highly subjective experience. Contemporary authors who often write in a realistic way include Nadine Gordimer and Grace Paley.

Resolution: The portion of a story following the climax, in which the conflict is resolved. The resolution of Jane Austen's *Northanger Abbey* is neatly summed up in the following sentence: "Henry and Catherine were married, the bells rang and every body smiled."

Rising Action: The part of a drama where the plot becomes increasingly complicated. Rising action leads up to the climax, or turning point, of a drama. The final "chase scene" of an action film is generally the rising action which culminates in the film's climax.

Roman a clef: A French phrase meaning "novel with a key." It refers to a narrative in which real persons are portrayed under fictitious names. Jack Kerouac, for example, portrayed various friends under fictitious names in the novel *On the Road*. D. H. Lawrence based "The Rocking-Horse Winner" on a family he knew.

Romanticism: This term has two widely accepted meanings. In historical criticism, it refers to a European intellectual and artistic movement of the late eighteenth and early nineteenth centuries that sought greater freedom of personal expression than that allowed by the strict rules of literary form and logic of the eighteenth-century neoclassicists. The Romantics preferred emotional and imaginative expression to rational analysis. They considered the individual to be at the center of all experience and so placed him or her at the center of their art. The Romantics believed that the creative imagination reveals nobler truths—unique feelings and attitudes—than those that could be discovered by logic or by scientific examination. "Romanticism" is also used as a general term to refer to a type of sensibility found in all periods of literary history and usually considered to be in opposition to the principles of classicism. In this sense, Romanticism signifies any work or philosophy in which the exotic or dreamlike figure strongly, or that is devoted to individualistic expression, self-analysis, or a pursuit of a higher realm of knowledge than can be discovered by human reason. Prominent Romantics include Jean-Jacques Rousseau, William Wordsworth, John Keats, Lord Byron, and Johann Wolfgang von Goethe.

S

Satire: A work that uses ridicule, humor, and wit to criticize and provoke change in human nature and institutions. Voltaire's novella *Candide* and Jonathan Swift's essay "A Modest Proposal" are both satires. Flannery O'Connor's portrayal of the family in "A Good Man Is Hard to Find" is a satire of a modern, Southern, American family.

Science Fiction: A type of narrative based upon real or imagined scientific theories and technology. Science fiction is often peopled with alien creatures and set on other planets or in different dimensions. Popular writers of science fiction are Isaac Asimov, Karel Capek, Ray Bradbury, and Ursula K. Le Guin.

Setting: The time, place, and culture in which the action of a narrative takes place. The elements of setting may include geographic location, characters's physical and mental environments, prevailing cultural attitudes, or the historical time in which the action takes place.

Short Story: A fictional prose narrative shorter and more focused than a novella. The short story usually deals with a single episode and often a single character. The "tone," the author's attitude toward his or her subject and audience, is uniform throughout. The short story frequently also lacks *denouement*, ending instead at its climax.

Signifying Monkey: A popular trickster figure in black folklore, with hundreds of tales about this character documented since the 19th century. Henry Louis Gates Jr. examines the history of the signifying monkey in *The Signifying Monkey: Towards a Theory of Afro-American Literary Criticism,* published in 1988.

Simile: A comparison, usually using "like" or "as," of two essentially dissimilar things, as in "coffee as cold as ice" or "He sounded like a broken record." The title of Ernest Hemingway's "Hills Like White Elephants" contains a simile.

Socialist Realism: The Socialist Realism school of literary theory was proposed by Maxim Gorky and established as a dogma by the first Soviet Congress of Writers. It demanded adherence to a communist worldview in works of literature. Its doctrines required an objective viewpoint comprehensible to the working classes and themes of social struggle featuring strong proletarian heroes. Gabriel Gárcia Márquez's stories exhibit some characteristics of Socialist Realism.

Stereotype: A stereotype was originally the name for a duplication made during the printing process; this led to its modern definition as a person or thing that is (or is assumed to be) the same as all others of its type. Common stereotypical characters include the absent-minded professor, the nagging wife, the troublemaking teenager, and the kind-hearted grandmother.

Stream of Consciousness: A narrative technique for rendering the inward experience of a character. This technique is designed to give the impression of an ever-changing series of thoughts, emotions, images, and memories in the spontaneous and seemingly illogical order that they occur in life. The textbook example of stream of consciousness is the last section of James Joyce's *Ulysses.*

Structure: The form taken by a piece of literature. The structure may be made obvious for ease of understanding, as in nonfiction works, or may obscured for artistic purposes, as in some poetry or seemingly "unstructured" prose.

Style: A writer's distinctive manner of arranging words to suit his or her ideas and purpose in writing. The unique imprint of the author's personality upon his or her writing, style is the product of an author's way of arranging ideas and his or her use of diction, different sentence structures, rhythm, figures of speech, rhetorical principles, and other elements of composition.

Suspense: A literary device in which the author maintains the audience's attention through the buildup of events, the outcome of which will soon be revealed. Suspense in William Shakespeare's *Hamlet* is sustained throughout by the question of whether or not the Prince will achieve what he has been instructed to do and of what he intends to do.

Symbol: Something that suggests or stands for something else without losing its original identity. In literature, symbols combine their literal meaning with the suggestion of an abstract concept. Literary symbols are of two types: those that carry complex associations of meaning no matter what their contexts, and those that derive their suggestive meaning from their functions in specific literary works. Examples of symbols are sunshine suggesting happiness, rain suggesting sorrow, and storm clouds suggesting despair.

T

Tale: A story told by a narrator with a simple plot and little character development. Tales are usually relatively short and often carry a simple message. Examples of tales can be found in the works of Saki, Anton Chekhov, Guy de Maupassant, and O. Henry.

Tall Tale: A humorous tale told in a straightforward, credible tone but relating absolutely impossible events or feats of the characters. Such tales were commonly told of frontier adventures during the settlement of the west in the United States. Literary use of tall tales can be found in Washington Irving's *History of New York,* Mark Twain's *Life on the Mississippi,* and in the German R. F. Raspe's *Baron Munchausen's Narratives of His Marvellous Travels and Campaigns in Russia.*

Theme: The main point of a work of literature. The term is used interchangeably with thesis. Many works have multiple themes. One of the themes of Nathaniel Hawthorne's "Young Goodman Brown" is loss of faith.

Tone: The author's attitude toward his or her audience maybe deduced from the tone of the work. A formal tone may create distance or convey politeness, while an informal tone may encourage a friendly, intimate, or intrusive feeling in the reader. The author's attitude toward his or her subject matter may also be deduced from the tone of the words he or she uses in discussing it. The tone of John F. Kennedy's speech which included the appeal to "ask not what your country can do for you" was intended to instill feelings of camaraderie and national pride in listeners.

Tragedy: A drama in prose or poetry about a noble, courageous hero of excellent character who, because of some tragic character flaw, brings ruin upon him- or herself. Tragedy treats its subjects in a dignified and serious manner, using poetic language to help evoke pity and fear and bring about catharsis, a purging of these emotions. The tragic form was practiced extensively by the ancient Greeks. The classical form of tragedy was revived in the sixteenth century; it flourished especially on the Elizabethan stage. In modern times, dramatists have attempted to adapt the form to the needs of modern society by drawing their heroes from the ranks of ordinary men and women and defining the nobility of these heroes in terms of spirit rather than exalted social standing. Some contemporary works that are thought of as tragedies include *The Great Gatsby* by F. Scott Fitzgerald, and *The Sound and the Fury* by William Faulkner.

Tragic Flaw: In a tragedy, the quality within the hero or heroine which leads to his or her downfall. Examples of the tragic flaw include Othello's jealousy and Hamlet's indecisiveness, although most great tragedies defy such simple interpretation.

U

Utopia: A fictional perfect place, such as "paradise" or "heaven." An early literary utopia was described in Plato's *Republic,* and in modern literature, Ursula K. Le Guin depicts a utopia in "The Ones Who Walk Away from Omelas."

V

Victorian: Refers broadly to the reign of Queen Victoria of England (1837-1901) and to anything with qualities typical of that era. For example, the qualities of smug narrow-mindedness, bourgeois materialism, faith in social progress, and priggish morality are often considered Victorian. In literature, the Victorian Period was the great age of the English novel, and the latter part of the era saw the rise of movements such as decadence and symbolism.

Cumulative Author/Title Index

Cumulative Nationality/Ethnicity Index

Subject/Theme Index